Advanced iOS 4 Programming: Developing Mobile Applications for Apple iPhone, iPad, and iPod touch

Maher Ali, PhD

Bell Labs, Alcatel-Lucent

A John Wiley and Sons, Ltd., Publication

This edition first published 2010

Registered office
John Wiley & Sons Ltd, The Atrium, Southern Gate, Chichester, West Sussex, PO19 8SQ, United Kingdom

Editorial office
John Wiley & Sons Ltd, The Atrium, Southern Gate, Chichester, West Sussex, PO19 8SQ, United Kingdom

For details of our global editorial offices, for customer services and for information about how to apply for permission to reuse the copyright material in this book please see our website at www.wiley.com/wiley-blackwell.

ISBN 978-0-470-97123-9 (paperback),
ISBN 978-0-470-97144-4 (ebk),
ISBN 978-0-470-97165-9 (ebk),
ISBN 978-0-470-97954-9 (ebk)

A catalogue record for this book is available from the British Library.

Typeset in 10/12 Times by Laserwords Private Limited, Chennai, India
Printed in the United States of America

Contents

Preface

Welcome to *Advanced iOS 4 Programming*, a text that targets the development of mobile applications on devices (such as the iPhone, iPad, and iPod touch) running the iOS 4 operating system.

This text covers a wide variety of essential and advanced topics, including

- The Objective-C programming language and runtime
- Collections
- Cocoa Touch
- Interface Builder
- Building advanced mobile user interfaces
- Core Animation and Quartz 2D
- Model-view-controller (MVC) designs
- Table views
- Core Data
- Developing for the iPad
- Grand Central Dispatch
- File management
- Parsing XML documents using SAX, DOM, and TouchXML
- Working with the Map Kit API
- Remote and local push notification
- Multitasking
- Working with the address book
- Consuming RESTful web services
- Blocks (closures) in Objective-C
- Building advanced location-based applications
- Developing database applications using the SQLite engine
- Cut, copy, and paste

- GameKit framework
- Undo management
- Unit testing
- Advanced networking
- Internationalization
- Building multimedia applications

Is This Book for You?

This book is aimed primarily at application developers with a basic understanding of the C language and object-orientation concepts such as encapsulation and polymorphism. You don't need to be an expert C coder to follow this book. All you need is a basic understanding of structures, pointers, and functions. That said, you will find coverage of general topics such as databases and XML processing. These topics are covered assuming basic knowledge.

What Else Do You Need?

To master iPhone SDK programming, you will need the following:

- An Intel-based Mac running Mac OS X Snow Leopard.
- iOS SDK 4. Download from `http://developer.apple.com/iphone`.
- Optional: membership of the iPhone Developer Program so that you can use the device for development. (You will need to pay a fee for membership.)
- Source code. The source code of the applications illustrated in this book is available online at `http://code.google.com/p/iphone4/`.

Conventions Used in This Book

`Constant width` type is used for

- Code examples and fragments
- Anything that might appear in a program, including operators, method names, function names, class names, and literals

`Constant-width bold` type is used for

- C, Objective-C, SQL, HTML, and XML keywords, whether in text or in a program listing

Italic type is used for

- New terms and concepts when they are introduced
- Specifying emphasis in text

Organization

Chapter 1 This chapter serves as a quick introduction to the tools bundled with the SDK. It also shows you the basic development phases, including coding, UI design, and debugging.

Chapter 2 This chapter presents the main features of the Objective-C language under the Cocoa environment. We introduce the main concepts behind classes in Objective-C. You will learn how to declare a new class, define it, and use it from within other classes. You will also be exposed to important Cocoa classes and data types. You will learn about memory management in iOS4. You will learn how to create new objects as well as how to deallocate them. You will also learn about your responsibility when obtaining objects from Cocoa frameworks or other frameworks. We also introduce the topic of Objective-C protocols. You will learn how to adopt protocols and how to declare new ones as well. This chapter also covers language features such as properties, categories, and posing. Exceptions and error handling techniques are both covered in this chapter, and you will be exposed to the concept of key-value coding (KVC). You will also learn about blocks, how to utilize multithreading (including Grand Central Dispatch), and use notifications, and will be exposed to the Objective-C runtime system.

Chapter 3 This chapter addresses the topic of collections in Cocoa. It discusses arrays, sets, and dictionaries. You will learn about immutable and mutable collections, the different approaches used for copying collections, and several sorting techniques.

Chapter 4 In this chapter, we discuss the basic steps needed to build a simple iPhone application. First, we demonstrate the basic structure of a simple iPhone application and then we show the steps needed to develop the application using XCode.

Chapter 5 This chapter explains the main concepts behind views. You will learn about view geometry, view hierarchy, the multitouch interface, animation, and basic Quartz 2D drawing.

Chapter 6 In this chapter, you will learn about the base class for all controls, `UIControl`, and the important target-action mechanism. This chapter also presents several important graphical controls that can be used in building attractive iPhone applications.

Chapter 7 In this chapter, you will learn about the available view controllers that are provided to you in the iPhone SDK. Although you can build iPhone applications without the use of these view controllers, you shouldn't. As you will see in this chapter, view controllers greatly simplify your applications. This chapter provides a gentle introduction to view controllers. After that, detailed treatment of tab-bar controllers, navigation controllers, and modal view controllers is provided.

Chapter 8 In this chapter, we present several important subclasses of the UIView class. We discuss picker views and show how they can be used for item selection. We investigate progress views and also talk about activity indicator views. After that, we show how to use scroll views in order to display large views. Next, we present text views used in displaying multiline text. After that, we show how to use alert views for the display of alert messages to the user. Similar to alert views are action sheets, which are also discussed. We also deal with several aspects of web views.

Chapter 9 This chapter will take you on a step-by-step journey through the world of table views. We start by presenting an overview of the main concepts behind table views. After that, we present a simple table view application and discuss the mandatory methods you need to implement in order to populate and respond to users' interactions with the table view. We show how easy it is to add images to table rows. We introduce the concept of sections and provide a table view application that has sections, with section headers and footers. We introduce the concept of editing a table view. An application that allows the user to delete rows is presented and the main ideas are clarified. We address the insertion of new rows in a table view. An application is discussed that presents a data entry view to the user and adds that new data to the table's rows. We continue our discussion of editing mode and present an application for reordering table entries. The main concepts of reordering rows are presented. We discuss the mechanism for presenting hierarchical information to the user. An application that uses table views to present three levels of hierarchy is discussed. We deal with grouped table views through an example. After that, we present the main concepts behind indexed table views. Next, we present a dynamic table view controller class that can be used to show cells with varying heights. Finally, we address the issue of turning the text color to white when a custom cell is selected.

Chapter 10 This chapter covers the topic of file management. Here, you will learn how to use both high- and low-level techniques for storing and retrieving file data. First, we talk about the Home directory of the application. Next, we show how to enumerate the contents of a given directory using the high-level methods of NSFileManager. You will learn more about the structure of the Home directory and where you can store files. After that, you will learn how to create and delete directories. Next, we cover the creation of files. We also cover the topic of file and directory attributes. You will learn how to retrieve and set specific file and directory attributes in this chapter. We also demonstrate the use of application bundles and low-level file access.

Chapter 11 In this chapter, we will cover the basics of the SQLite database engine that is available to you in the iPhone SDK. SQLite is an embedded database in the sense that there is no server running, and the database engine is linked to your application. First, we describe basic SQL statements and their implementation using SQLite function calls. Second, we discuss handling of result sets generated by SQL statements. Third, we address the topic of prepared statements. Fourth, we talk about extensions to the SQLite API through the use of user-defined functions. Finally, we present a detailed example for storing and retrieving BLOBs.

Chapter 12 In this chapter, you will learn how to effectively use XML in your iPhone application. The chapter follows the same theme used in other chapters and exposes the main concepts through a working iPhone application: an RSS feed reader. First, we explain the main concepts behind XML and RSS. Next, we present a detailed discussion of DOM and SAX parsing. After that, we present a table-based RSS reader application. Finally, we provide a summary of the main steps you need to take in order to effectively harness the power of XML from within your native iPhone applications.

Chapter 13 In this chapter, we will address the topic of location awareness. First, we will talk about the Core Location framework and how to use it to build location-aware applications. After that, we will discuss a simple location-aware application. Next, we cover the topic of geocoding. You will learn how to translate postal addresses into geographical locations. You will also learn how to sample movement of the device and display that information on maps. Next, we discuss how to relate zip codes to geographical information. Finally, we show you how to utilize the Map Kit API to add an interactive map to your view hierarchy.

Chapter 14 In this chapter, we demonstrate the use of the several devices available on the iPhone. We discuss the use of the accelerometer, show how to play small sound files, and show how to play video files. After that, we discuss how to obtain iPhone and iPod touch device information. Using the built-in camera and the photo library are also discussed in this chapter. After that, we show you how to obtain state information regarding the battery of the device. Finally, we discuss the proximity sensor.

Chapter 15 In this chapter, we start by looking at a step-by-step procedure for localizing strings for a set of supported languages. Next, we look at date formatting. After that, we cover formatting currencies and numbers. Finally, we discuss how to generate a sorted list of countries.

Chapter 16 In this chapter, we show how to marry various UI components and build custom reusable ones. First, we show how to build an alert view with a text field in it. Next, we present a table view inside an alert view. Finally, we show how to build a progress alert view.

Chapter 17 This chapter addresses several advanced networking topics. We start by looking at how we can determine network connectivity of the device. After that, we tackle the issue of uploading multimedia content (e.g., photos) to remote servers. Next, we present a category on NSString that allows you to easily compute the MD5 digest of a string. This is important as some services, such as Flickr, require posting parameters with the appropriate signature. After that, we show you how to present a responsive table view whose data rows are fed from the Internet without sacrificing the user experience. Next, we address the topic of remote and local push notifications. After that, we tackle some aspects of multitasking and use it in downloading a large file after the application is suspended. Finally, we discuss sending email from within an iPhone application.

Chapter 18 In this chapter, we discuss the foundation of the address book API and several UI elements that can be used to modify the contacts database. First, we provide a brief introduction to the subject. Next, we discuss property types. After that, we show how to access single-value and multivalue properties. Next, we go into the details of the person record and the address book. Issues related to multithreading and identifiers are then addressed. After covering the foundation of the address book API, we provide several sample applications.

Chapter 19 In this chapter, you learn how to use the Core Data framework in your application. First, you learn about the main components of the Core Data application. Next, we talk about the major classes in the Core Data framework. After that, you learn how to use the graphical modeling tool to build a data model. Next, we address the basic operations in persistence storage using Core Data. After that, we show how to use relationships in the Core Data model. Finally, we present a search application that utilizes Core Data for storage.

Chapter 20 In this chapter, you learn about undo management support in iOS. First, we discuss the basic steps needed to utilize undo management. After that, we present a detailed example that shows how to use undo management. Finally, we summarize the main rules in using the undo capabilities in an application.

Chapter 21 This chapter examines the copy and paste capabilities of iOS and the supporting APIs. We start by discussing pasteboards. Next, you learn about pasteboard items and the various methods available to you to manipulate them. After that, we address the subject of the editing menu, which allows users to issue editing commands. Finally, we put all the ideas behind copy and paste together and present a simple image editing application.

Chapter 22 This chapter presents several techniques that can help you develop applications that are graceful under bad network connectivity conditions.

Chapter 23 In this chapter, you learn how to use the GameKit framework to build applications that talk to each other over Bluetooth technology. This technology is used to communicate small amounts of data. We show you how to develop a simple chat application for transmitting text and small images between two iPhones.

Chapter 24 In this chapter, we investigate the different view controllers available on the iPad. You learn about popovers, split view controllers, and different presentation styles for modal view controllers.

Appendix A In this appendix, you will learn how to use property lists for saving and restoring the application state. This will give the user the illusion that your application does not quit when he or she hits the Home button.

Appendix B Here, you will learn how to programmatically invoke iPhone applications from within your application. In addition, you will learn how to publish services that other iPhone applications can utilize.

Appendix C This appendix explains the major steps needed to publish your application in the App Store.

Appendix D In this appendix, we cover several topics related to using XCode. First, we show some useful shortcuts. Next, we talk about writing custom templates for your classes, and after that we cover build configuration. Finally, we show you how to add references to other libraries (also known as frameworks).

Appendix E In this appendix, we show you how to add unit tests to your project. By adding unit testing support, you'll be able to write tests for your business logic. These tests will be added as a dependency on the building of your application. This will result in the tests being run before you actually build your application. The appendix walks you through a step-by-step process for adding unit testing for a simple business model.

Appendix F In this appendix, we use Interface Builder to build a couple of iPhone applications. The techniques you learn from building these applications should prove to be useful in building similar iPhone applications.

Publisher's Acknowledgments

Some of the people who helped bring this book to market include the following:

Editorial and Production
VP Consumer and Technology Publishing Director: Michelle Leete
Associate Director — Book Content Management: Martin Tribe
Associate Publisher: Chris Webb
Publishing Assistant: Ellie Scott
Project Editor: Juliet Booker
Development Editor: Kathy Simpson
Copy Editor: Kathy Simpson

Marketing
Senior Marketing Manager: Louise Breinholt
Marketing Executive: Kate Parrett

Composition Services
Compositor: Laserwords Pvt Ltd, Chennai, India
Proof Reader: Gareth Haman
Indexer: Robert Swanson

1
Getting Started

This chapter serves as a quick introduction to the tools bundled with the iOS SDK. It also shows you basic development steps used on the iOS operating system that include coding, user interface (UI) design, and debugging. You do not have to understand everything in this chapter as we will go over these concepts throughout the book. What you need to get from this chapter is a feeling for iOS development using XCode.

We start with some basics of the XCode IDE in Section 1.1. Next, Section 1.2 talks about the UI design tool Interface Builder. After that, we show you how to use the built-in debugger in XCode in Section 1.3. Next, Section 1.4 shows you different sources of information for obtaining additional help. Finally, we summarize the chapter in Section 1.5.

1.1 iOS SDK and IDE Basics

In this section, we walk you through the process of creating your first iPhone application. But first, you need to obtain the iOS SDK and install it on your Intel-based Mac.

1.1.1 Obtaining and installing the SDK

Obtaining and installing the iOS SDK is easy. Just follow these steps:

1. Get your iPhone developer Apple ID and password from:
   `http://developer.apple.com/iphone/`
2. Download the latest iOS SDK from the site mentioned above.
3. Install the iOS SDK on your Mac.

Now, you're ready to create your first project — read on!

1.1.2 Creating a project

Let's use XCode to create an iOS project targeting the iPhone device. First, locate XCode and launch it. You can use `Spotlight` to find it or you can navigate to `/Developer/Applications/XCode`.

XCode is the central application for writing, designing, debugging, and deploying your iOS applications. You will use it a lot, so go ahead and add it to the `Dock`.

From XCode, select `File` → `New Project`. You should see a window, similar to the one shown in Figure 1.1, asking you for the type of project you want to create. Choose the default and create a window-based application. This is the most generic type of iPhone project and the one that can be customized for different needs.

Figure 1.1   Choosing a window-based application in the project creation process.

Click `Choose`, enter the name of your project (here, we're using `My Project`), and click `Save`. A new directory is created with the name you entered, and several files are generated for you. You should now see the newly created iPhone project as shown in Figure 1.2.

Figure 1.2   A newly created iPhone project in XCode.

1.1.3   Familiarizing yourself with the IDE

As you can see from Figure 1.2, the main window is divided into several areas. On the top, you will find the toolbar (Figure 1.3). The toolbar provides quick access to common tasks. It is fully configurable; you can add and remove tasks as you want. To customize the toolbar, Control-click it and choose `Customize Toolbar`. A window with a set of items will be shown so you can drag your favorite task on the toolbar. Click `Done` when you're finished. To remove an item, Control-click on it and choose `Remove Item`.

Figure 1.3   The XCode toolbar.

On the left-hand side, you'll see the `Groups & Files` list (Figure 1.4).

This list is used to organize the source code, frameworks, libraries, executables, and other types of files in your project.

The list shows several files and groups. Groups can contain other groups and files. You can delete a group as well as create a new one. The group indicated by the blue icon whose name is the same as the name you've chosen as the project name is a *static group*. Underneath it, you see all your headers, implementations, resources (images, audio files, and so on), and other related files. The folderlike

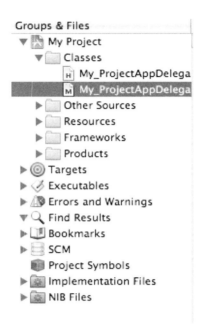

Figure 1.4   The `Groups & Files` list in XCode.

yellow groups act conceptually as containers. You can have containers inside other containers and all files inside these containers live in the same directory on the disk. The hierarchy only helps you organize things. You have full freedom to organize your project's layout as you like. The compiler will pick up the resources, headers, and implementation files when it builds your application.

The other kind of groups that are listed below the project group are called *smart groups*. There are two types of smart groups: (1) built-in smart groups and (2) custom smart groups. The content of the built-in smart groups cannot be customized. Examples of these groups include executables, bookmarks, errors/warnings, and targets. Customized smart groups are shown in purple, and two predefined groups are created for you when you create a new project. The first group is named Implementation Files, and all implementation files are listed underneath it. The other is called Nib Files, underneath which all UI files are listed.

Figure 1.5 shows the `Details` view and the text editor beneath it.

Selecting an item in the `Groups & Files` list will result in its details being shown in the `Details` view. You can go to a full-editor window using `Command-Shift-E`.

1.1.4   *Looking closely at the generated code*

Expand the `Classes` and `Other Sources` groups. You will notice several files that live underneath these two groups. Click on the `main.m` file and expand to a full-editor view.

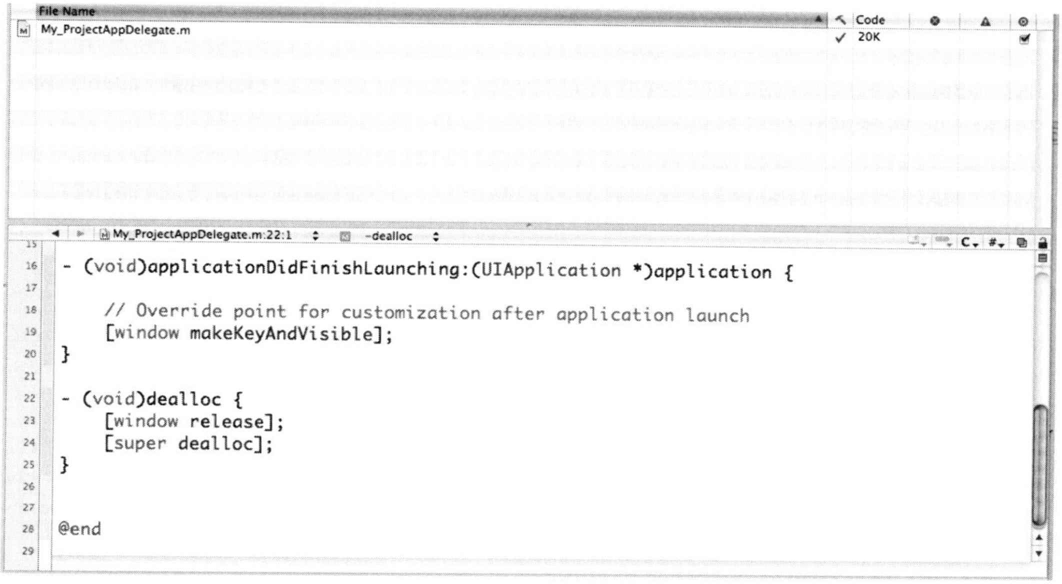

Figure 1.5   The Details view with the text editor view.

The `main.m` file looks very similar to a C file with a `main()` function. As we will see later in this book, all that `main()` does is prepare for memory management and launch the application.

Click on the `My_ProjectAppDelegate.h` file under the `Classes` group. You will notice that the editor changes its content. This file contains the declaration of the application delegate class. Every application that runs on iOS has a delegate object that handles critical phases of its life cycle.

Click on `My_ProjectAppDelegate.m`. This file with the `.m` extension is the counterpart of the previous `.h` file. In it, you see the actual implementation of the application delegate class. Two methods of this class are already implemented for you. The `applicationDid-FinishLaunching:` method is one of those methods; it handles a particular phase of the application life cycle. The other method, `dealloc`, is a method where memory used by this object is released. In iOS, you manage the allocation and freeing of memory as there is no garbage collection. Memory management is crucial in iOS development, and mastering it is very important. The first chapters in this book are dedicated to teaching you exactly that — and much more.

The generated files and resources are adequate for starting the application. To launch the application, click on `Build and Go` in the toolbar or press the `Command-Enter` key combination. You'll notice that the application starts in the simulator and it shows only a white screen with the status bar on top. Not very useful, but it works!

1.2   Creating Interfaces

To be useful, an iPhone application needs to utilize the amazing set of UI elements available from the SDK. Our generated iPhone application contains a single UI element: a window.

All iPhone apps have windows (usually one). A *window* is a specialized view that is used to host other views. A *view* is a rectangle piece of real estate on the 320×480 iPhone screen. You can draw in a view, animate a view by flipping it, and receive multitouch events on it. In iPhone development, most of your work goes towards creating views, managing their content, and animating their appearance and disappearance.

Views are arranged into a hierarchy that takes the shape of a tree. A tree has a root element and zero or more child elements. In iOS, the window is the root element and it contains several child views. These child views can in turn contain other child views and so on and so forth.

To generate views and manage their hierarchy, you can use both Interface Builder (IB) and Objective-C code. IB is an application that comes with the SDK that allows you to graphically build your view and save it to a file. This file is then loaded at runtime and the views stored within it come to life on the iPhone screen.

As we mentioned before, you can also use Objective-C code to build the views and manage their hierarchy. Using code is preferred over using IB for the following reasons. First, as a beginner, you need to understand all aspects of the views and their hierarchy. Using a graphical tool, although it simplifies the process, does hide important aspects of the process. Second, in advanced projects, your views' layouts are not static and change depending on the data. Only code will allow you to manage this situation. Finally, IB does not support every UI element all the time. Therefore, you will sometimes need to go in there and generate the views yourself.

The following section teaches you how to use IB. However, for the most part in this book, Objective-C code is used to illustrate the UI concepts. For extensive coverage of Interface Builder, please see Appendix E.

1.2.1   Interface Builder

The project has a basic window resource file. This file can be found under the `Resources` group. Expand the `Resources` group and locate the file `MainWindow.xib`. This file contains the main window of the application. This file is an `.xib` file that stores the serialized objects in the interface. When the project is built, this file is converted to the more optimized format `.nib` and loaded into memory when one or more of the UI components stored in it are requested.

Double-click on the `MainWindow.xib` file to launch IB. IB starts by opening four windows. The first window shows the main window stored in the file. The second window shows the document window listing the different objects stored in the file. The third window is the Library window containing all the UI objects that you can add to the file. The fourth and final window is the Inspector window with its four panes.

The Inspector window shows the attributes of the currently selected object. If you click on an object, the Inspector window shows you its attributes distributed among four different panes. Each pane has several sections. You can change these attributes (such as color, position, and connections) and the changes will propagate to your project's user interface.

The main window of the application is white; let's change it to yellow. Click on the window object in the document window. In the Inspector window, make sure that the leftmost pane is selected. In the View section of this pane, change the background color to yellow as shown in Figure 1.6.

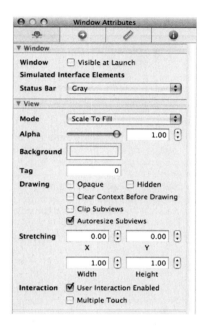

Figure 1.6   The attributes pane in the Inspector window of Interface Builder.

Go to XCode and run the application. Notice how the main window of the application has changed to yellow.

It is important to keep the project open in XCode while working with IB. XCode and IB communicate well when both applications are open.

To build a user interface, you start with a view and add to it subviews of different types. You are encouraged to store separate views in separate .xib files. This is important, as referencing one object in a file will result in loading all objects to main memory. Let's go ahead and add a label view to our window. This label will hold the static text Hello iPhone.

A label is one of the many UI components available for you. These components are listed under several groups in the Library. Select Tools → Library to show the Library window if it's not shown. As shown in Figure 1.7, locate the Inputs & Values section.

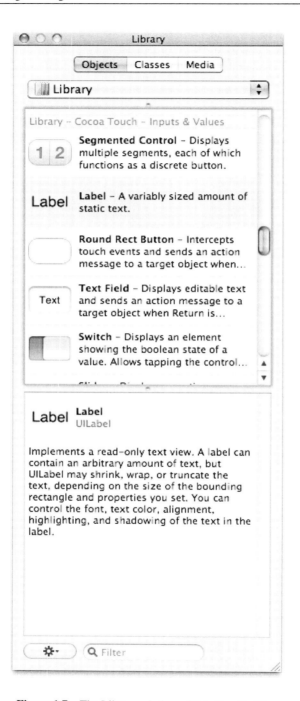

Figure 1.7   The Library window of Interface Builder.

Figure 1.8   Adding a label view to a window in IB.

Click on the `Label` item and drag it onto the middle of the window. Expand the dimensions of the label as shown in Figure 1.8.

When the label is selected, the Inspector window changes to reflect the attributes of the label. Figure 1.9 shows a portion of the attributes of a label in the Inspector window. You can change these attributes and observe the effect they have on the object instantaneously.

The label's text is left-justified; let's make it centered. In the `Layout` item of the attributes, click on the icon indicating center. Notice how the label text becomes centered. The text of the label can be changed in the Text item. Change `Label` to `Hello iPhone`. Go to XCode and hit `Build and Go`. You will notice the window showing `Hello iPhone` in the middle.

The text of the label is small, so let's make it bigger. Click on the `Text` item and choose a text size of 48 points. Go to XCode and hit `Build and Go`. Figure 1.10 shows a screen shot of the completed `Hello iPhone` application.

Congratulations on your first successful iPhone application!

1.2.2   Revising the application

You deliver the product to the client and he is happy. However, he wants the application to have more interaction with the user. He asks you to revise the application by adding a button that the user can tap on to change the text displayed in the label.

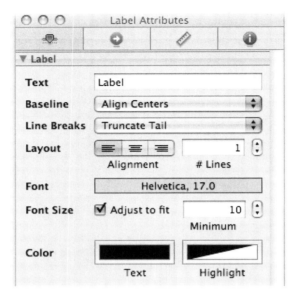

Figure 1.9   Attributes of a label in the Inspector window.

Figure 1.10   A screen shot of the completed `Hello iPhone` application.

Figure 1.11   The main window after adding a new button.

Open the `MainWindow.xib` document (see Figure 1.2), if it is not already open. Locate the `Round Rect Button` item under `Inputs & Values` in the `Library` window. Drag and drop it under the label in the main window.

Change the button's title by entering `Change` in the `Title` field of the attribute window as shown in Figure 1.11.

The main window should look like the one shown in Figure 1.12.

Now that we have a button, we want to have a method (a function) in our code to get executed when the user touches the button. We can achieve that by adding a connection between the button's touch event and our method.

Click on the button so that it becomes selected. Click on the second pane in the Inspector window. This pane shows the connections between an object and our code. The pane should look like the one in Figure 1.13.

Now, we want to add a connection between the `Touch Down` event and a method we call `button-Tapped`. Let's first add this method in `My_ProjectAppDelegate` class.

In the `My_ProjectAppDelegate.h` file, add the following before **@end**:

```
-(IBAction)buttonTapped;
```

In the `My_ProjectAppDelegate.m` file, add the `buttonTapped` method body. The `My_Project-AppDelegate.m` file should look something like the one in Listing 1.1.

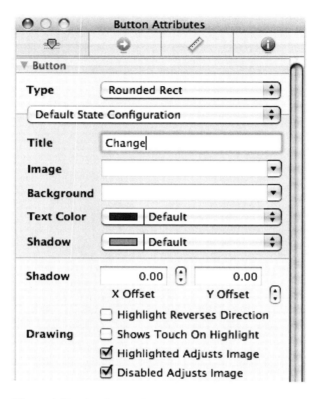

Figure 1.12   Attributes of a button in the Inspector window.

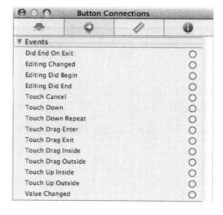

Figure 1.13   The connections pane of our new button.

Listing 1.1   The application delegate class after adding a new method.

```
#import "My_ProjectAppDelegate.h"
@implementation My_ProjectAppDelegate
@synthesize window;
- (void)applicationDidFinishLaunching:(UIApplication *)application {

    // Override point for customization after application launch
    [window makeKeyAndVisible];
}

-(IBAction)buttonTapped{
  UILabel *label = (UILabel*)[window viewWithTag:55];
  if([label.text isEqualToString:@"Hello iPhone"])
    label.text = @"Hello World";
  else
    label.text = @"Hello iPhone";
}

- (void)dealloc {
    [window release];
    [super dealloc];
}
@end
```

The buttonTapped method simply obtains a reference to the label and changes its text to either Hello World or Hello iPhone. You don't need to understand this code at this stage. All you need to understand is that the label on the screen is encapsulated by the UILabel class and is tagged with the number 55.

Now, let's switch to IB and add a tag to the label so that it can be retrieved from the code. Click on the label, and in the Inspector window, choose the first pane. In the second section, enter 55 for the Tag field (fourth item).

We still need to perform one last step: We need to connect the touch event with the method we just created. Click on the button and choose the connections pane (second pane). Control-click or right-click on the circle on the right-hand side of the Touch Down event; drag it on top of the My_Project App Delegate object in the Document window; and let go, as shown in Figure 1.14.

When you release the mouse, IB shows you potential methods (actions) that you can connect this event to. Right now we only have one action and that action is buttonTapped. Select that action and you'll notice that a connection has been made as shown in Figure 1.15.

Now, switch to XCode and hit Build and Go. You'll notice that tapping on the button changes the text value of the label.

Figure 1.14   Making a connection between an event and a method in another object.

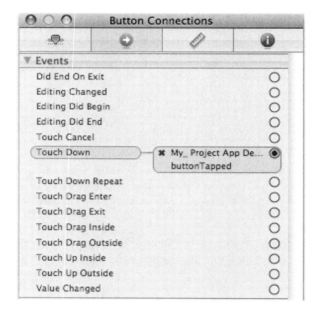

Figure 1.15   A connection between a touch event and an action.

1.3   Using the Debugger

During the development of your applications, things often go wrong and the feature that you've just added does not function properly. At these moments, the built-in debugger becomes invaluable.

Let's introduce a bug into our code. Go to `My_ProjectAppDelegate.m` file, change the tag's value used to obtain the label from 55 to 54, and click `Build and Go`. Now, tapping the button has no effect on the label's text.

First, you want to make sure that the buttonTapped method gets called. In XCode, click in the left margin of the first line in the buttonTapped method as shown in Figure 1.16. After you click there, a breakpoint (shown in blue) is added.

```
22   -(IBAction)buttonTapped{
23     UILabel *label = (UILabel*)[window viewWithTag:54];
24     if([label.text isEqualToString:@"Hello iPhone"])
25       label.text = @"Hello World";
26     else
27       label.text = @"Hello iPhone";
28   }
29
```

Figure 1.16   Adding a breakpoint in the buttonTapped method.

Click Build and Go to debug the application. When the application launches, tap on the button. You'll notice that the execution hits the breakpoint as shown in Figure 1.17. At least we know that we made our connection correctly.

```
22   -(IBAction)buttonTapped{
       UILabel *label = (UILabel*)[window viewWithTag:54];
24     if([label.text isEqualToString:@"Hello iPhone"])
25       label.text = @"Hello World";
26     else
27       label.text = @"Hello iPhone";
       }
```

Figure 1.17   Hitting a breakpoint in the buttonTapped method.

Let's step over the statement that obtains the label from the window. Click on the Step Over button located beneath the toolbar as shown in Figure 1.18.

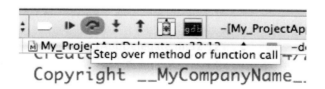

Figure 1.18   Step over a function or method call button.

After stepping over the statement, we need to inspect the value obtained. Hover the mouse over label in the statement just executed as shown in Figure 1.19. A tip appears, showing its value.

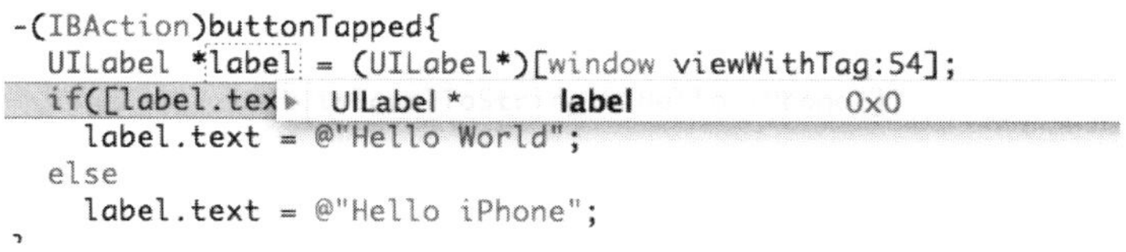

```
-(IBAction)buttonTapped{
  UILabel *label = (UILabel*)[window viewWithTag:54];
  if([label.tex▸  UILabel *      label              0x0
    label.text = @"Hello World";
  else
    label.text = @"Hello iPhone";
⌐
```

Figure 1.19   Inspecting the value of the label after obtaining it from the window.

Notice that the value is $0x0$. In Objective-C, this value is called `nil` and means that no object is stored in this variable. After inspecting the tag value and going back and forth between XCode and IB, we find the problem, fix it, remove the breakpoint by clicking on it to turn it off, and hit `Build and Go`.

1.4   Getting More Information

There are plenty of sources for information on the SDK. These sources include the following:

- **Developer documentation**. The best locally stored source of information is the developer documentation. In XCode, select `Help → Documentation`. The documentation window appears as shown in Figure 1.20. You can search using the search box in the top-right corner for any defined type in the SDK. The documentation is hyperlinked and you can go back and forth between different pieces of information. It's easy to use and it will become your friend.

- **Developer documentation from within XCode**. If you're in XCode and you need more information about something, Option-double-click it, and the developer documentation opens with more information.

- **Other help from within XCode**. If you're in XCode and you need to get the declaration and possible implementation of a given token (e.g., class, tag, variable, etc.), Command-double-click it. If there are multiple pieces of information, or disambiguation is needed, a list of items to choose among will be shown.

- **iPhone Dev Center**. The center is located at `http://developer.apple.com/iphone/`. The iPhone Dev Center has a large collection of technical resources and sample code to help you master the latest iPhone technologies.

- **Apple's forums**. You can start with the site at `https://devforums.apple.com/`.

- **The web**. There is plenty of information on the web. Just enter a relevant query and let Google do its magic!

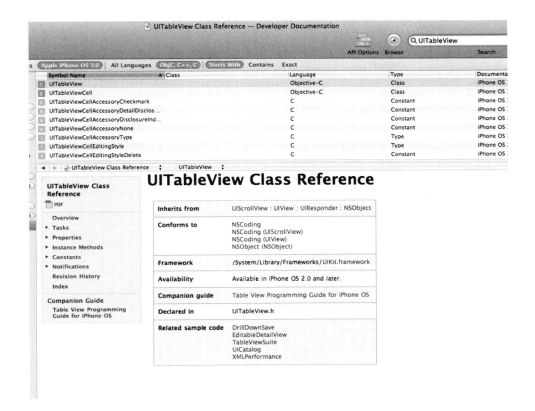

Figure 1.20   The developer documentation in XCode.

1.5   Summary

This chapter provided a gentle introduction to the world of iOS development. We showed you in Section 1.1 how to download and install the iOS SDK. After that, we iterated through the development of an iPhone application and showed you how to use Interface Builder to design user interfaces. Next, Section 1.3 discussed how to debug an iPhone application using the built-in visual debugger in XCode. You were also exposed to different sources for obtaining further help on the tools and the SDK in general in Section 1.4.

The rest of the book will detail all aspects of iOS development. However, from now on, because we want to teach you everything you need, we will stop using Interface Builder and show you how to build your UI using code. This will help you gain a solid understanding of the process. You can, of course, mix and match with Interface Builder as you wish.

The next two chapters cover the Objective-C language and the coding environment that you will be working with: *Cocoa*. We hope you're as excited as we are!

Exercises

(1) Check out the UILabel.h header file and read about the UILabel class in the documentation.

(2) What are IBOutlet and IBAction? Command-double-click to see their definitions in the UINibDeclarations.h header file.

(3) Explore the XCode IDE by reading the XCode Workspace Guide under the Help menu of the XCode application.

(4) Explore Interface Builder by choosing Interface Builder Help from the Help menu of the Interface Builder application.

2

Objective-C and Cocoa

This chapter presents the main features of the Objective-C language under the Cocoa environment. Section 2.1 introduces the main concepts behind classes in Objective-C. In that section, you learn how to declare a new class, define it, and use it from within other classes. You also learn about important Cocoa classes and data types.

After that, in Section 2.2 you learn about memory management in iOS. You learn how to create new objects as well as how to deallocate them, and you also learn your responsibility when obtaining objects from Cocoa frameworks or other frameworks.

Section 2.3 introduces the topic of Objective-C protocols. There, you learn how to adopt protocols and how to declare new ones as well. Section 2.4 covers properties, an Objective-C language feature that allows you to access instance variables using the dot notation. The concept of categories is the subject of Section 2.5. Categories allow you to extend existing classes by adding new methods. Posing is another technique that is slightly different from categories. Posing allows you to replace a given class with one of its descendants. This is discussed in Section 2.6.

Exceptions and error handling are important features in any modern language. Section 2.7 covers both of these techniques and shows you the appropriate use of each feature. After viewing exceptions and errors, you are exposed to the concept of key-value coding (KVC) in Section 2.8. KVC is an important and widely used technique in Cocoa. KVC allows you to indirectly access object properties.

Next, you learn how to use multithreading in your iOS applications (Section 2.9). Cocoa makes it very easy to use multithreading and you will learn, using a step-by-step approach, how to make a task run in the background. After that, we cover the topic of notifications in Section 2.10. In Sections 2.11 and 2.12, we introduce blocks and Grand Central Dispatch. In Section 2.13, we discuss, at great length, the topic of the Objective-C runtime system. Finally, we provide a summary of this chapter in Section 2.14.

We have a lot to cover, so let's get started.

2.1 Classes

In object-oriented languages, an *object* encapsulates attributes and provides methods. These methods can be used by the outside world (i.e., other objects) to change the object's state as well as to interact with the object. All this can be achieved without opening the actual implementation of the object's behavior to the outside world.

In Objective-C, in order to create a new class, you first need to declare it using an *interface* and then define it using an *implementation*. The declaration and the definition are usually written in two separate files. The declaration part (described more fully in the following sections) is customarily done in a .h file having the same name as the class, while the implementation, which also has the same name as the class, is in a .m file. Both the declaration and the definition parts use compiler directives. A *compiler directive* is an instruction to the Objective-C compiler prefixed by the @ sign. The declaration is signaled to the compiler using the **@interface** directive, while the actual definition is signaled using the **@implementation** directive.

2.1.1 Class declaration

To declare a class, MyClassName, as a subclass of class MyParentName, you simply write

```
@interface  MyClassName : MyParentName{
    // attribute declarations
}
    // method declarations
@end
```

Here, we are telling the compiler that a new class type, MyClassName, is being declared. MyClass-Name is a subclass of the MyParentName class. In addition, we list the definition of all instance variables between the curly brackets. The methods are declared between the end of the curly bracket and the **@end** compiler directive.

There are a few important aspects of the **@interface** declaration:

- The attributes declared between the curly brackets are *instance* variables. At runtime, every class has a unique *class* object and zero or more instances of the class. Every instance (object) of MyClassName has its own values for these attributes. The unique class object has no access to these instance variables.

- Methods declared can be either instance methods or class methods. An instance method is called by sending a *message* to an actual instance (i.e., an object) of the class. A class method does not require a class instance. You call a class method by sending a message to the unique class object. In Objective-C, every class has exactly one class object during the runtime of the program. An instance method is declared/defined by a - prefix, while a class method is declared/defined by a + prefix.

  For example:

  ```
  -(Address *) getAddress;
  ```

  is an instance method, while

  ```
  +(id) getANewInstance;
  ```

  is a class method.

- Objective-C does not support class variables. However, you can use the familiar **static** keyword in an implementation file of a given class. This will allow instance methods (i.e., those with a - prefix in their definition) to have access to the single value of this variable shared by all instances of that declared class. If you define a **static** variable inside a method, then that method is the *only* method that has access to that variable. If you put the definition of the **static** variable outside the class implementation, then all methods have access to that variable.

2.1.2 How do I use other declarations?

As a Cocoa developer, you will need to be able to use classes that other developers have written. In addition, if the declaration and the definition of your classes are in separate files, you will need to inform the compiler about the location of the class declaration in the implementation file.

If you use the name of a class without accessing its methods or instance variables, you can just use the **@class** directive. This gives the compiler enough information to successfully compile the code. Usually the **@class** directive is used in class declarations. For example, consider the following declaration:

```
@class Address;
@interface Person{
    Address *address;
}
@end
```

Here, we have a `Person` class declaration that uses the `Address` class. The compiler only needs to know that the `Address` is a class type. No details about the actual methods and attributes are needed because we just use the type.

If, on the other hand, you use the methods and/or the attributes of a given class, then you need to point the compiler to the location of the file that contains the declaration. There are two ways to do that: (1) using **#include** and (2) using **#import**. **#include** and **#import** are almost identical, except that **#import** loads the given file only once during the compilation process. The **#import** directive is much simpler, is fully supported by Apple, and produces potentially fewer problems. Bottom line: Use **#import**.

2.1.3 Class definition

To actually define a class, you need to specify the implementation of the class/instance methods declared in the **@interface** part. To define the class, you write

```
#import "MyClassName.h"
@implementation MyClassName
    // method definitions
@end
```

Notice that we needed to import the declaration file. This import allowed us to skip repeating the parent's class name as well as the instance variables. Both can be deduced by the compiler so there is no need to repeat them.

2.1.4 Method invocation and definition

Method invocation in Objective-C addresses a problem that those of you who have used Java will be familiar with. In Java, a method is invoked using its name followed by a pair of left and right parentheses. If the method requires parameters, the values of these parameters are inserted inside the parentheses and separated by commas. For example, if aPoint is a Java object representing a point in 3D, setLocation (float x, float y, float z) can represent a method for changing the location of this point object. aPoint.setlocation(3, 6, 9) asks the aPoint object to change its location to (3, 6, 9). One problem with this notation is readability. If you come across such a statement written by another programmer, you cannot know for sure what these values represent. You have to look at the method's signature and read about what each position in the parameters list represents.

Because Objective-C is an object-oriented language, it, too, provides *data encapsulation*. With data encapsulation, the outside world interacts with an object by sending *messages* to that object. To send an object (aObject) a message (aMessage) you use square brackets and write [aObject aMessage]. A message is composed of two parts: (1) keywords and (2) parameters. Every message has at least one keyword. A keyword is an identifier followed by a colon.

Let's make these definitions concrete by writing the setlocation method invocation in Objective-C. In Objective-C, you write something like

```
[aPoint setLocationX:3 andY:6 andZ:9];
```

Notice the improved readability of the invocation of the method. Just by looking at it, we know that 6 is used to change the y-coordinate. This message has three keywords: setlocationX:, andY:, andZ:. The method is represented by setLocationX:andY:andZ:. This representation is called a *selector*. A selector is a unique name (within a class) of a method used by the runtime to locate the code implementing that method. The method is declared in the interface as

```
-(void)setLocationX:(float) x andY:(float) y andZ:(float) z;
```

The statement [aPoint setLocationX:3 andY:6 andZ:9] as a whole is called a *message expression*. If this expression evaluates to an object, then it, too, can receive a message. Objective-C allows nested message invocation. For example, you can write:

```
[[addressBook getEntryAtIndex:0] printYourself];
```

First, the message getEntryAtIndex:0 is sent to the addressBook object. The method identified by the selector getEntryAtIndex: returns an object. This object is then sent a printYourself message.

It's worth noting that if a method has zero parameters, you should not use the : when the method is invoked. This notation can be difficult to deal with at first, but after a time it becomes natural.

Methods in Objective-C are always *public*. There is no such thing as a private method. Instance variables default to *protected*, a setting that works well for you most of the time.

2.1.5   Important types

We mentioned before that every class in a Cocoa application has a singleton class object. The type of this class object is Class. A null class pointer is of type Nil. Nil is basically (Class)0. We also mentioned that a class can be instantiated. An instance of a class A is declared as:

```
A      *anObject;
```

There is, however, a defined type in Cocoa that represents an arbitrary object. This type is named **id**. If anObject does not point to any object, its value is nil. A nil is basically (**id**)0.

SEL is a defined type that represents a selector. To obtain the SEL of a method, aMethod:, use the directive @selector as follows:

```
SEL mySelector = @selector(aMethod:);
```

If you want mySelector to point to a null selector, assign it NULL.

You can also obtain the SEL of a method from a string representation of its name. The function to use is NSSelectorFromString(), which is declared as

```
SEL NSSelectorFromString (NSString *aSelectorName);
```

NSSelectorFromString will always return a SEL named by a non-nil aSelectorName even if the selector is not found. If there is no selector with the name aSelectorName, a new selector is registered with this name and returned. If the parameter aSelectorName is nil or the function faces memory problems, it will return NULL — basically (SEL)0.

2.1.6   Important Cocoa classes

There are several important Cocoa classes that you will often use in your iOS applications. This section discusses just the ones needed in this chapter. Other classes will be covered throughout this book.

- NSObject. This is the base class of most Cocoa classes. An object is not considered a Cocoa object if it is not an instance of NSObject or any class that inherits from NSObject. This class defines the runtime methods required for allocating and deallocating objects.

- NSString. This is the main class representing strings in Cocoa. Using this class, you can store an arbitrary text. However, once you store a value in an object of this type, you cannot change it. This kind of class is referred to as *immutable*. To be able to change a string's value (e.g., append text to it, etc.), you need the *mutable* string class NSMutableString. You can create a constant string using the @ sign. For example, @"Plano" represents an NSString instance.

- NSArray. Instances of this class represent Cocoa array objects. The mutable version of this class is NSMutableArray. See Section 3.1 for more information on arrays in Cocoa.

- NSSet. Instances of this class represent Cocoa set objects. The mutable version is NSMutableSet. See Section 3.2 for more information on sets in Cocoa.

2.2   Memory Management

Modern computer languages employ garbage collection. A *garbage collector* is a runtime algorithm that scans the allocated objects in your program and reclaims (deallocates) objects that you have lost contact with. For example, if you created an object and stored its location in a variable pointer named ptr and later you set ptr to nil, the memory block allocated, whose address was stored in ptr, is no longer accessible by your code. The garbage collector, at a time of its choosing, intervenes on your behalf and deallocates this memory so that future allocation requests can use it.

Cocoa under iOS does not employ a garbage collector. Instead, Cocoa applications must use *managed memory*. Applications running on this platform should clean up after themselves. Because iOS applications run in a memory-constrained environment, you, as a developer, should pay extra attention to memory usage.

2.2.1   Creating and deallocating objects

You learned in Section 2.1.6 that NSObject is the root class in the Cocoa programming environment. NSObject defines the methods required for memory management and much more. One of the most important methods of NSObject is the alloc method. When you send an alloc message to a class object, the class object allocates memory for a new object instance of the class and sets its attributes to zero. For a class instance to start receiving messages, the init method usually needs to be invoked. Every class implements at least one init method either explicitly or implicitly through the inheritance chain. If you override init, you should call your parent's init first and then perform your initialization. This can be achieved using the **super** keyword. The keyword **super** makes the search for the method (here, init) start from the parent class rather than the class of the object, while the variable name **self** makes the search start from the class of the object where this statement is being executed. You can change the value of **self** at runtime, but you cannot change **super**. To change **super**, you have to change the parent class in the interface and then build your code.

We have talked about how a new object is born, but how can we know when we can get rid of it? The solution to this problem is simple: Keep a counter per object. This counter tells us how many other objects are interested in this object. When an object wants to put a claim on our object, it increments this counter. When it wants to remove this claim, it decrements the counter.

This counter is maintained by the NSObject and is called the *retain count*. When you allocate the object, the retain count is set to 1. Any time another object wants to put a claim on this object, it sends it a retain message; thus increasing the retain count by 1. If the object wants to remove the claim, it sends it a release message, which in effect decrements the retain count by 1. When the retain count reaches 0, the object is deallocated by the system.

2.2.2 Preventing memory leaks

To keep your program from leaking memory, you need to release any object whose memory you are responsible for after it is no longer needed. You are mainly responsible for an object's memory in the following three scenarios:

- **You allocated the object using** alloc. If you allocated the object, you have to release it at the end.
- **The object is a result of a** copy **made by you**. If you create an object by copying it from another object, you are responsible for releasing it at the end.
- **The object was** retain**ed by you**. If you express your desire to keep a given object alive, you have to express your desire that the object should die when you are no longer in need of it.

We are left with one problem, which can be illustrated by the following code:

```
// In one of your methods
// Ask an object to create a new object for you
NSMutableString *aString = [anObject giveMeANewString];
```

In the above code, you are asking anObject to give you a brand-new object of type NSMutableString. The question is: Who is responsible for releasing this new object when you are no longer in need of it?

One solution to this problem is to delay the release of the object. Basically, the giveMeANewString method creates a brand-new NSMutableString object (e.g., using alloc) and puts that object in a pool for later release. When the time comes and you want to free up some memory, you release this pool and the pool will go over its content and send a release message to each and every object added to it.

Development under iOS involves using shared libraries called frameworks. One of the most important framework defined by Cocoa is the Foundation Framework. This framework is automatically added to your project when you create it for the first time.

The Foundation Framework provides the NSAutoreleasePool class for managing delayed releases. Every thread in your program needs to have at least one instance of this class.

You create an instance of the class as follows:

```
NSAutoreleasePool *pool = [[NSAutoreleasePool alloc] init];
```

This line will make `pool` the active autorelease pool for the code that follows. Any time your code or any of Cocoa's framework functions sends an `autorelease` message to an object, a reference to that object is added to this pool. You can think of an autorelease pool as a list of entries. Each entry consists of a reference to an object (i.e., its address) and an integer counting the number of autorelease messages sent to this object on this pool.

To dispose of a pool, you send a `release` message to it, e.g., `[pool release]`. This will cause the pool to send `release` messages to every object it has a reference to. The number of `release` messages is equal to the number of `autorelease` messages sent to this object on this pool (a variable kept in the object's entry in the pool). Therefore, the retain count of every object will be reduced by the same number of delayed releases (i.e., autoreleases) it has received.

Autorelease pools can be nested. When you create a pool, this pool is pushed onto a stack. Any time an object receives an `autorelease` message, the runtime will send a reference to that object to the pool on top of the stack.

Having nested pools allows the developer to optimize memory usage. Let's assume, as an example, that `giveMeANewString` creates a large number of temporary objects in order to compute the return value. At the end of this method, these temporary objects are not needed. If you have only one autorelease pool in your application, these objects will linger until the end of the current run loop and then get released.

To be able to reclaim the memory used by these temporary objects, you can create a new autorelease pool at the beginning of this method. All autoreleased objects generated by the method code (or calls made by the method) will go to this pool as it is on top of the pool stack. Before you return from this method, you `release` this local pool, thereby causing all these temporary objects to be released as well.

Listing 2.1 shows how the `giveMeANewString` method can be implemented. Here, we assume that producing the string is a rather involved process that requires extensive memory allocation of temporary objects.

Listing 2.1   Demonstration of local autorelease pools.

```
-(NSMutableString*) giveMeANewString{
   NSAutoreleasePool *pool = [[NSAutoreleasePool alloc] init];
   NSMutableString  *returnString = [[NSMutableString alloc] init];
   // code that generates large amount of
   // autoreleased objects.
   .
   .
   .
   // update the returnString with calculated data
   [returnString appendString:computedData];
   [pool release];
   return [returnString autorelease];
}
```

All temporary objects created inside the method will be deallocated. The value returned is autoreleased and will be available to the caller as long as its immediate pool is not released.

If your class retains or allocates other objects, you need to make sure that these objects are released when your instance is released. The `dealloc` method is used for this purpose. It is called before the instance of an object is released. You should release any object that you are responsible for and propagate the deallocation up the inheritance chain by calling [**super** `dealloc`] as the very last statement in this method.

2.3   Protocols

A *protocol* is an important language feature in Objective-C. Protocols provide, among other things, the ability to realize multiple inheritance in a single-inheritance language.

Think of a protocol as an interface in the Java language. Just as classes in Java can implement multiple interfaces, so can classes in Objective-C *adopt* multiple protocols.

A protocol is just a list of methods. Each method in this list can be tagged as either required (**@required**, the default) or optional (**@optional**). If a class adopts a protocol, it must implement at least all required methods in that protocol. For example, to define a `Litigating` protocol, you would write something like this:

```
@protocol Litigating
-(int)sue:(id<Litigating>)someone;
-(int)getSuedBy:(id<Litigating>)someone;
@end
```

Any class can adopt this protocol by listing it, using angle brackets, in its declaration after the superclass name. For example:

```
@interface Citizen: Human <Litigating>
```

A class can adopt multiple protocols. For example, you could write

```
@interface Citizen: Human <Litigating, MilitaryService, TransferFunds>
```

Two classes with different inheritance chains can implement the same protocol. For example:

```
@interface DemocraticCountry: Country<Litigating>
```

A democratic country does adopt the `Litigating` protocol; it can be sued and it can sue others. A dictatorship or a fascist country, on the other hand, does not adopt such a protocol.

It is also worth noting that a protocol can incorporate other protocols. For example:

```
@protocol LegalEntity <Taxable>
```

A class that adopts a protocol must implement all required methods of that protocol as well as the required methods of protocols incorporated by that protocol (and so on recursively). Moreover, protocol methods are inherited by subclasses — that is, a subclass conforms to a given protocol if its superclass also conforms to that protocol.

To work with protocols, you need to understand the concept of protocol conformance. Suppose you want to model a system where citizens travel to different countries and can be potential candidates to be sued or to sue the host country. How can you, elegantly, test to see if a country can be sued? You cannot just send a message to the country instance and hope it will respond favorably.[1]

In Objective-C, protocols provide an elegant solution for this. You can test, at runtime, whether an object is an instance of a class that adopts a given protocol. You do that by sending that object a conformsToProtocol: message. For example, to test that a given country, aCountry, can be sued, you write

```
if([aCountry conformsToProtocol:@protocol(Litigating)]){
    [aCountry getSuedBy:self];
else
    [self letItGo];
}
```

The conformsToProtocol: method is defined in NSObject twice, once as a class method (with a + sign) and another as an instance method (with a - sign). Both are identical and are provided for convenience. For example, the class version is defined as

```
+ (BOOL)conformsToProtocol:(Protocol *)aProtocol
```

It takes one argument: a protocol object. We can use @protocol (protocol-name) to get an instance of the protocol protocol-name. This instance is most of the time a unique instance during the lifetime of your program. However, it is safer to assume that it is not, and not cache the protocol object.

conformsToProtocol: returns YES if the class of the receiving object adopts the protocol-name and NO otherwise. It is important to note that conformance is defined based on the declaration of the receiver's class, not based on whether the methods of the protocols have actually been implemented. For example, if you have

```
@interface DemocraticCountry: Country<Litigating>
@end

@implementation DemocraticCountry
@end
```

and you have

```
DemocraticCountry *aCountry = [[DemocraticCountry alloc] init];
```

the statement

```
[aCountry conformsToProtocol:@protocol(Litigating)]
```

---

[1]In real life, this can be very dangerous!

will return YES (1). However, the statement

```
[aCountry getSuedBy:self];
```

will result in an application crash.

2.4   Properties

A *property* is a neat feature of Objective-C that allows you to generate setter/getter methods for your instance variables. These setter and getter methods can be invoked without you even specifying them. To get/set the value of the instance variable, you use the dot notation. For example, if you have a defined NSString* property, name, in an object, aObject, you can write: aObject.name = @"Plano". This statement is actually translated by the compiler to something like [aObject setName:@"Plano"]. Note that the instance variable, name, is still a non-public variable, but it appears as if we are accessing the variable directly from the outside.

You use the @property directive in the class declaration in order to declare a property. To actually generate the getter and/or setter method(s), you use the @synthesize directive in the class definition (i.e., implementation). This feature of Objective-C allows you to request only getter methods for instance variables that are read-only.

2.4.1   Property declaration

Properties are declared in the methods' section (i.e., after the curly bracket) of the **@interface** part of your class. The format for property declaration is

```
@property(property-attributes) property-type property-name;
```

The property attributes are used to influence how the compiler generates the getter/setter methods. You can use the following attributes:

- nonatomic. By using this attribute, you tell the compiler that it does not need to generate extra code for guaranteeing thread safety. If you do not specify nonatomic, the compiler will generate that extra code. If you know that the property will be accessed from a single thread, then specifying nonatomic can improve performance. Having an atomic accessor means that the setter/getter are thread-safe; it does not necessarily mean, however, that your code, as a whole, is correct. Having a code that is thread-safe involves more work from your side than guaranteeing the atomicity of a single operation such as a getter or a setter method. See Section 2.9 for more information on multithreading.

- readonly. This attribute tells the compiler that the property can be read but it cannot be set. The compiler will generate only a getter method. If you attempt to write code that assigns a value to the property via the dot notation, the compiler will generate a warning.

- readwrite. This is the default. Both a getter and a setter will be generated for you by the compiler when you use the @synthesize directive.

- `assign`. The value you use to set the property is directly assigned to the instance variable. This is the default.

- `copy`. You use this attribute when you want to store a copy of the object being assigned to your instance variable rather than the reference to that object. The value being assigned has to be an object that knows how to copy itself (i.e., implements the `NSCopying` protocol).

- `retain`. This specifies that you are interested in putting an ownership claim on this object. The compiler will invoke a `retain` on this object and assign it to the instance variable. If the caller later `released` this object, it does not get `deallocated` because you `retained` it. You need to `release` it, either when you are finished with it or in the `dealloc` method of your object.

- `getter=getterName, setter=setterName`. By default, the name of the automatically generated setter of a property, `prob`, is `setProb`, and the getter is `prob`. You can change this naming convention for the setter, the getter, or both.

After declaring the property, you have two choices: (1) Ask the compiler to generate the getter/setter methods by using the `@synthesize` directive, or (2) implement the methods yourself by using the `@dynamic` directive.

Let's look at an example demonstrating these concepts. Consider the `Employee` class declared and defined in Listing 2.2.

Listing 2.2   The `Employee` class declaration and definition demonstrating Objective-C properties.

```
@interface Employee : NSObject{
  NSString          *name;
  NSString          *address;
  NSMutableArray    *achievements;
  BOOL              married;
  Employee          *manager;
  NSString          *_disability;
}

@property (nonatomic, copy)    NSString*  name;
@property (nonatomic, retain)  Employee* manager;
@property (nonatomic, assign)  NSString* address;
@property (nonatomic, copy)    NSMutableArray* achievements;
@property (nonatomic, getter=isMarried) BOOL married;
@property (nonatomic, copy) NSString* disability;
@end

@implementation Employee
@synthesize name, address, manager, achievements, married,
            disability=_disability;
@end
```

The first property declaration
```
@property (nonatomic, copy) NSString* name
```
can be realized by the compiler as follows:

```
-(NSString*) name{
  return name;
}
-(void) setName:(NSString*) aName{
  if(name != aName){
    [name release];
    name = [aName copy];
  }
}
```

The getter accessor returns a reference to the name instance variable. The setter accessor first checks to see if the new value for name is not the same as the current name value. If they are different, then the old object is released, and a copy (as instructed by the @property directive) of the aName is made and stored in the name instance variable. Note that in the dealloc method, you need to release name.

The second property declaration
```
@property (nonatomic, retain) Employee* manager
```
can be realized by the compiler as follows:

```
-(Employee*) manager{
  return manager;
}

-(void) setManager:(Employee*) theManager{
  if(manager != theManager){
    [manager release];
    manager = [theManager retain];
  }
}
```

The setter first checks to see if theManager is not the same as the instance variable manager. If they are different objects, the old manager object is released and the manager instance variable is set to a retained theManager. Note that you need to release manager in the dealloc method.

The third property declaration
```
@property (nonatomic, assign) NSString* address
```
can be realized by the compiler as follows:

```
-(NSString*) address{
  return address;
}

-(void) setAddress:(NSString*)anAddress{
  address = anAddress;
}
```

Notice that because the property directive is `assign`, the setter just stores the memory address of `anAddress` in the instance variable.

The fourth property declaration is

`@property (nonatomic, copy) NSMutableArray* achievements`

When dealing with mutable collections such as `NSMutableArray`, the compiler-provided setter/getter might not be appropriate. Let us see a possible synthesis of the `achievements` property:

```
-(NSMutableArray*) achievements{
  return achievements;
}
-(void) setAchievements:(NSMutableArray*) newAchievements{
  if(achievements != newAchievements){
    [achievements release];
    achievements = [newAchievements copy];
  }
}
```

There are two problems with such a synthesis:

1. The caller of the getter will receive a reference to the actual `achievements` array. That means that the caller will be able to modify the state of the `Employee` instance. In some cases, you might not want such a behavior.

   You might try to rewrite the getter yourself as

   ```
   -(NSArray*) achievements{
     return achievements;
   }
   ```

   This, however, will not solve the problem because the returned reference, although made to be an immutable array, is still an `NSMutableArray` and can be changed by the caller. One solution to this problem is to return an autoreleased copy of the collection as follows:

   ```
   -(NSArray*) achievements{
     return [[achievements copy] autorelease];
   }
   ```

   This way, the caller will receive an immutable array. Note that following the memory management convention, the caller is not responsible for deallocating the returned value; thus, we `autorelease`d it before returning it. If it seems confusing to you at present, please return to this discussion after reading Chapter 3.

2. The synthesized setter will assign an immutable copy to the mutable array instance variable. You will not be able to add/remove objects to/from this array. Therefore, you have to write the setter yourself. The following is a possible valid implementation:

   ```
   -(void) setAchievements:(NSMutableArray*)newAchievements{
     if(achievements != newAchievements){
       [achievements release];
   ```

```
      achievements = [newAchievements mutableCopy];
    }
  }
```

Notice the use of the `mutableCopy` instead of the `copy`. Refer to Chapter 3 for further information on arrays and collections in general.

The fifth property
```
@property (nonatomic, getter=isMarried) BOOL married
```
instructs the compiler to change the name of the getter accessor to `isMarried` instead of the conventional name `married`. The following is a possible implementation of the property:

```
-(BOOL) isMarried{
  return married;
}

-(void) setMarried:(BOOL)newMarried{
  married = newMarried;
}
```

The sixth property
```
@property (nonatomic, copy) NSString* disability
```
has a synthesis directive as `@synthesize disability=_disability`. It will be synthesized exactly as we saw the synthesis of the first property, except that we tell the compiler to associate the `disability` property with the `_disability` instance variable.

A possible synthesis of this property is as follows:

```
-(NSString*) disability{
  return _disability;
}

-(void) setDisability:(NSString*)newDisability{
  if(_disability != newDisability){
    [_disability release];
    _disability = [newDisability copy];
  }
}
```

We have seen how we can realize the different types of property declarations. Of course, you will, for most of the time, rely on the compiler to generate the accessor methods and not write them yourself. In some special cases, such as mutable collections, and depending on your application's requirements, you may want to write some of these accessor methods yourself.

2.4.2   Circular references

You need to be extra careful when dealing with properties and retaining objects in general. The way you define properties has a direct impact on memory usage and the health of your application. If you are not careful, the memory footprint of your application can keep growing until iOS terminates your application.

In addition to being careful about releasing unused memory, you need to make sure that your object design does not introduce circular references. *Circular references* occur when two or more objects in a group hold references to other objects in the group such that the dealloc method of any of these objects will never be called.

To illustrate this concept, we present a contrived example based on the design pattern of delegation. Delegation is one of the most widely used patterns in Cocoa. In delegation, an object can act as a helper to another object. It is sometimes used as a substitute to subclassing.

The delegation pattern can be employed in two different cases. In one case, an object may request help from its delegate to execute a specific task. In the other case, an object may be notified by its delegate of the occurrence of important events. In either case, the object and its delegate need to know about each other (hold pointers to each other).

Consider the X class shown below. An X instance holds a reference to its delegate. This reference is a *strong* reference in the sense that an X instance retains it. An instance of this class does the right thing and it releases its delegate in the dealloc method. It achieves that by relying on the behavior of the synthesized setter, which does release an instance variable before retaining the assigned value. Because the assigned value is nil, and all messages sent to nil result in nil, no harm is done and we achieve our goal. This approach of releasing instance variables is found by many to be superior to releasing the instance variable directly and setting its value to nil.

```
@interface X : NSObject{
   id delegate;
}
@property(retain) id delegate;
-(void)hi;
@end

@implementation X
@synthesize delegate;

-(void)hi{
   [delegate hello];
}

-(void)dealloc{
   self.delegate = nil;
   [super dealloc];
}
@end
```

An instance of the class A, shown below, creates an instance of class X and retains it. It then sets the delegate of the X instance to **self**. This is a typical situation that arises frequently if you think of class X as a view and class A as another view that uses it. Or maybe X is a monitor of some external source and A is a controller that uses it.

The `dealloc` method does the right thing. It releases the X instance and propagates the deallocation to **super**.

```objc
@interface A : NSObject{
   X *myX;
}
@property(retain) X *myX;
@end


@implementation A
@synthesize myX;

-(id)init{
   if(self = [super init]){
     self.myX = [[[X alloc] init] autorelease];
     myX.delegate = self;
   }
   return self;
}

-(void)hello{
   NSLog(@"Hello");
}

-(void)dealloc{
   self.myX = nil;
   [super dealloc];
}
@end
```

In the listing below, we create an instance of A, print its retain count, and then release it. You would expect that the A and X objects would be released and their respective `dealloc` methods would get called. But neither of these events occurs!

```objc
int main(int argc, char *argv[]) {
  NSAutoreleasePool * pool = [[NSAutoreleasePool alloc] init];
  A *a = [[A alloc] init];
  NSLog(@"a's retain count is %d", a.retainCount);
  [a release];
  [pool release];
  return 0;
}
```

The X instance and whatever objects it has created and retained, and the A instance and whatever other objects it has created and retained, remain in memory. Of course, in the situation above, this memory will be reclaimed by iOS when the application terminates, but that's just the example. In real life, these will linger for a long time during the lifetime of the application. Worse, they can reoccur, resulting in an ever-expanding memory footprint and eventual crashes of the application.

One solution to this problem is to have x's delegate be a *weak* reference. Just changing

```
@property(retain) id delegate;
```

to

```
@property(assign) id delegate;
```

will do the trick.

2.5 Categories

A *category* is an Objective-C feature that allows you to extend the capabilities of a given class. This feature works even if you do not have access to the source code of the class you are extending.

When you extend a given class through a category, the extension is inherited by all its subclasses. Of course, the additional methods defined by the category are seen only by your program.

To illustrate this powerful feature, let us extend the NSObject class by adding an instance method to it:

```
@interface NSObject(EnhancedObject)
-(NSComparisonResult) rankSelf:(NSObject*)anotherObject;
@end

@implementation NSObject(EnhancedObject)
-(NSComparisonResult) rankSelf:(NSObject*)anotherObject{
  if([self retainCount] > [anotherObject retainCount]){
    return NSOrderedDescending;
  }
  else if ([self retainCount] < [anotherObject retainCount]){
    return NSOrderedAscending;
  }
  else return NSOrderedSame;
}
@end
```

To declare a category on an existing class such as NSObject, you add the name of the category in parentheses after the class name. The actual definition of the category follows a similar form. You define the category methods in the methods' section as you define regular methods.

The following illustrates the usage of this category. Because all objects are descendants of NSObject, all objects in your application will be able to rank themselves.

```
NSMutableString *string =
    [[NSMutableString alloc] initWithString:@"string"];
Employee  *emp1 = [[Employee alloc] init];
[emp1 retain];
NSComparisonResult result = [emp1 rankSelf:string];
```

Here, we ask the `emp1` object of type `Employee` to rank itself with the string object of type `NSMutableString`. Neither the `Employee` class nor the `NSMutableString` class defines the `rankSelf:` method. The category `EnhancedObject` defined on `NSObject`, the ancestor of both, however, does define such a method. When `emp1` receives the message `rankSelf:`, the message is propagated up the inheritance chain to `NSObject`.

This feature is widely used in Cocoa. For example, the `UIStringDrawing.h` file defines a category `UIStringDrawing` (see Listing 2.3) on `NSString`, thus making every `NSString` object capable of drawing itself.

Listing 2.3   An example of a Cocoa category defined on `NSString` for the purpose of drawing.

```
@interface NSString(UIStringDrawing)
- (CGSize)drawAtPoint:(CGPoint)point withFont:(UIFont *)font;
- (CGSize)drawAtPoint:(CGPoint)point forWidth:(CGFloat)width
        withFont:(UIFont *)font
        lineBreakMode:(UILineBreakMode)lineBreakMode;
...
@end
```

2.6   Posing

Posing is part of the Objective-C language. Unfortunately, this feature is not available in iOS. You may want to look at Section 2.13 for metaprogramming techniques that can be used to realize posing. Posing is covered here for completeness.

Posing is an Objective-C programming feature that allows you to swap one class, A, with another class, B. Swapping will result in all active instances that are subclasses of A, as well as all future instances of A or its subclasses, using B instead of A. Therefore, after posing, all messages sent to A will instead be sent to B. This requires that B be a subclass of A. B can override existing methods and add new methods, but it cannot add new instance variables.

Unlike categories, where the same method defined in the category replaces the one defined in the original class, a posing class that overrides one of its parent's methods can still call the overridden method using **super**. Posing is customarily used in testing scenarios.

The posing is achieved by a single call to the `NSObject`'s class method defined as:

```
+ (void)poseAsClass:(Class)aClass
```

For example:

```
[B poseAsClass: [A class]];
```

This should be done at the beginning of the program before any instance of A is created.

2.7   Exceptions and Errors

As a developer, you will find that even the simplest of your applications will someday face an unexpected event resulting in a change in the normal execution of your code. This event could simply be a division-by-zero, sending an undefined message to an object, or adding an element to an immutable collection. Regardless of the type of the error, your application needs to be aware of the possibility of its occurrence so that it can handle it gracefully when it does occur.

Cocoa divides these unexpected events into two categories: (1) those that are the developer's fault and (2) those that are the user's fault. The problems that the developer is responsible for are called *exceptions*, while the problems that are user-specific are called *errors*. In Cocoa, exceptions are dealt with during the development of the application, and errors are used during the lifetime of the application. Cocoa frameworks use exceptions and errors. Therefore, as a Cocoa developer, you are expected to master both techniques.

2.7.1   Exceptions

Modern languages, such as Java and C++, provide language constructs for exception handling. Objective-C is no exception, for it provides the same capabilities. To capture a possible exception, you enclose the problematic code with a `try` block. To process the actual exception, you use a `catch()` block. If you want to execute some statements regardless of whether an exception occurred (e.g., releasing memory, etc.), you enclose these statements in a `finally` block.

But what is an exception and how it is signaled? An exception can be any Cocoa object. However, as a Cocoa developer, you should use NSException or any subclass of it. An exception is signaled by being *thrown* or *raised*. Objective-C provides the @throw directive for throwing an exception and the NSException class defines a `raise` instance method for raising an exception. Using the @throw directive, you can throw any Cocoa object, not just an instance of NSException. However, using the raise method, you can only throw an NSException object. Other than that, both techniques accomplish the same thing.

The structure of exception handling follows the following pattern:

```
@try {
    //statements that may cause an exception
}
@catch (NSException *e) {
    //statements that handle an exception
    @throw; // optionally rethrowing the exception
```

```
}
@finally {
    //statements that should be executed regardless
    //of having an exception or not
}
```

You basically surround the potentially problematic code with a `@try` directive. To actually process the exception, you use a `@catch()` block. The `catch` block takes the exception object as its only parameter. As we mentioned above, the exception object does not have to be an instance of NSException; any Cocoa object can be thrown/caught. For example, you can have code like the following, where an instance of NSString is being caught:

```
@catch(NSString *str){
.
.
.
}
```

However, as we mentioned above, you should stick with NSException or any of its subclasses.

Optionally, you can put in a `finally` block in any code that is required to be executed regardless of the occurrence of an exception. This code usually releases memory and closes opened files.

You can optionally rethrow the exception to the next level on the call stack. You use the `@throw` directive to do that. You do not need to specify the exception object, however, as it is implied. Note that if you rethrow an exception, the `@finally` block gets executed before actually throwing the exception to the lower level.

Exception example

Let's illustrate these concepts with a concrete example as shown below:

```
#import <Foundation/Foundation.h>
int main(int argc, char *argv[]) {
  NSAutoreleasePool * pool = [[NSAutoreleasePool alloc] init];
  NSMutableArray *myArray = [[NSMutableArray alloc] initWithCapacity:0];
  [myArray addObject:@"an object"];
  [myArray replaceObjectAtIndex:1 withObject:@"another object"];
  [myArray release];
  [pool release];
  return 0;
}
```

The code above creates an array and adds an element to it. After that, it attempts to replace that element with another object. If we run this code, an exception will occur and the program will be terminated with an error message similar to the following:

```
Exception Type:  EXC_BREAKPOINT (SIGTRAP)
```

```
Exception Codes: 0x0000000000000002, 0x0000000000000000
Crashed Thread:   0

Application Specific Information:
*** Terminating app due to uncaught exception 'NSRangeException',
reason: '*** -[NSCFArray replaceObjectAtIndex:withObject:]:
index (1) beyond bounds (1)'
```

What has happened here is that we are using an invalid index (1) on an array of size 1. The method replaceObjectAtIndex:withObject: raised an exception upon seeing this invalid index. This method is declared as:

```
- (void)replaceObjectAtIndex:(NSUInteger)index withObject:(id)anObject
```

If you look at the documentation of this method, you will notice that the method can potentially raise two exceptions: (1) It raises an NSRangeException if index is beyond the end of the receiver, and (2) it raises an NSInvalidArgumentException if anObject is nil.

Let's rewrite the main() function, adding an exception handler:

```
int main(int argc, char *argv[]) {
  NSAutoreleasePool * pool = [[NSAutoreleasePool alloc] init];
  NSMutableArray *myArray = nil;
  @try {
    myArray = [[NSMutableArray alloc] initWithCapacity:0];
    [myArray addObject:@"an object"];
    [myArray replaceObjectAtIndex:1 withObject:@"another object"];
  }
  @catch (NSException *e) {
    printf("Exception Name: %s. Reason: %s", [[e name] cString],
           [[e reason] cString] );
  }
  @finally {
    [myArray release];
    [pool release];
  }
  return 0;
}
```

We surrounded the problematic code with a try block. In catching the exception, we just print an error message. The finally block is important as we need to release the allocated memory. Instead of the application being terminated, it outputs the following useful message but, most important, exits gracefully:

```
Exception Name: NSRangeException.
Reason: *** -[NSCFArray replaceObjectAtIndex:withObject:]:
index (1) beyond bounds (1)
```

Creating exceptions

There are three important pieces of information that every instance of `NSException` has:

1. `name`. A string that identifies the exception. This name has to be unique, relatively short, and never `nil`. You should never start the names of your exceptions with `NS`, but start names with something unique to your application and organization.

2. `reason`. This string attribute is also mandatory. It stores a human-readable explanation of the exception.

3. `userInfo`. This attribute is an optional dictionary (see Section 3.3). Using this dictionary, the code that generates the exception can communicate additional information to the exception handler.

If you are writing a method and you would like to communicate with the caller via exceptions, you need to be able to create exceptions and then throw them. To create an exception, you can use `NSException`'s class method `exceptionWithName:reason:userInfo:` declared as

```
+ (NSException *)exceptionWithName:(NSString *)name
                 reason:(NSString *)reason
                 userInfo:(NSDictionary *)userInfo
```

This method returns an autoreleased `NSException` object having the specified attributes. It returns `nil` if no such exception can be created.

In the following, we present an example of creating and throwing an exception:

```
-(void) myMethod:(NSString*) string{
  if(string == nil){
    NSException *anException =
        [NSException exceptionWithName:@"NSInvalidArgument"
                    reason:@"Argument is nil"
                    userInfo:nil];
    @throw anException; // OR [anException raise];
  }
  else{
    // proceed normally
  }
}
```

Nesting exceptions

Because an exception handler can optionally rethrow the exception (or a new one), exceptions can be nested. For example, consider the scenario where you have a method that adds a record to a database. This method calls another low-level method that handles the actual physical insertion of the record in a file. The following two listings show the database `addRecord:` and the `insertRecord:` methods:

```
-(void) addRecord:(Record*) record{
  @try {
    [file insertRecord:record];
  }
  @catch (NSException * e) {
    // create a new exception, db,
    // name=MYDBException
    @throw db;
  }
  @finally {
    // close files, etc.
    // release memory
  }
}

-(void) insertRecord:(Record*) record{
  @try {
    // open the file
    // seek
    // insert record
  }
  @catch (NSException * e) {
    // locally handle exception
    @throw;
  }
  @finally {
    //close file
    // release memory
  }
}
```

Here, we see the nested exceptions. If an exception occurs while accessing the file, that exception is caught in the `insertRecord:` method, dealt with locally, and rethrown. The `addRecord:` method has an exception handler that catches the rethrown exception. It creates a new exception, named `MYDBException`, and throws it. This last exception is communicated to the caller of the `addRecord:` method. In case of a failure, the caller of `addRecord:` sees a meaningful *database* exception rather than the low-level *file* access exception. Note that nesting levels can be arbitrary.

2.7.2   Errors

As a C programmer, you must be used to using error codes as a means of conveying errors to the caller. This approach is limited in that you can convey only a single piece of information (a number) to the caller.

Cocoa uses objects of type NSError (or subclasses of it) as the main mechanism to convey runtime errors to users.

A Cocoa method follows a pattern in conveying errors:

- The return value of a method is used to indicate failure or success. If the return value is of type BOOL, a NO indicates an error. If, on the other hand, the return value is of type **id**, a nil indicates a failure.

- As a secondary mechanism to further elaborate on the error, the user can pass a pointer to an NSError object as the last parameter of the method. If this parameter is not NULL, the method stores a new autoreleased NSError object using that pointer.

An NSError object stores three important attributes:

- domain. A string representing the error domain. Different frameworks, libraries, and even classes have different error domains. Examples of error domains are NSPOSIXErrorDomain and NSCocoaErrorDomain. Applications can, and should, create their own unique error domains. If you are creating an error domain, make sure it is unique by prefixing the domain name with the name of the application and your organization's name.

- code. An integer error code that has meaning within the domain. Two NSError objects with the same error code but different domains are different.

- userInfo. A dictionary (see Section 3.3) containing objects related to the error.

Error example

Let's illustrate error handling in Cocoa. The following example deliberately causes an error. It handles the error by displaying the three attributes of the error described above.

```
NSError *myError = nil;
NSURL *myUrl = [NSURL URLWithString:@"http://fox.gov"];
NSString *str =  [NSString stringWithContentsOfURL:myUrl
                          encoding:NSUTF8StringEncoding
                          error:&myError];
if(str == nil){
    printf("Domain: %s. Code: %d \n", [[myError  domain] cString],
           [myError code]);
    NSDictionary *dic = [myError userInfo];
    printf("Dictionary: %s\n", [[dic description] cString]);
}
```

You do not necessarily need to know URL loading at this stage as we will go over it in detail in Section 17.7. What you need to know is that we make a call to a Cocoa method to obtain an object (here, this object is the page as an NSString object). The method returns nil if there was an error and allows the user to specify a pointer to an NSError object for further information on the error. We pass a pointer to an NSError object and make the call. Because the site http://fox.gov does not exist, the returned value of the method is `nil`, and the `NSError` object is created and autoreleased by the Cocoa method.

The output of this code snippet is the error domain code and the contents of the dictionary:

```
Domain: NSCocoaErrorDomain. Code: 260
Dictionary: {
    NSURL = http://fox.gov;
    NSUnderlyingError = Error Domain=NSURLErrorDomain
     Code=-1003
     UserInfo=0x4183a0 "can\325t find host";
}
```

We notice that the domain is `NSCocoaErrorDomain` with code `260`. The `userInfo` dictionary contains two entries: (1) the `NSURL` with value `http://fox.gov` and (2) the `NSUnderlyingError` with value `Error Domain=NSURLErrorDomain Code=-1003 UserInfo=0x4183a0 "can't find host"`.

Creating an NSError instance

We have seen how we can handle an error object that was created for us, but often, we are required to write methods that return an autoreleased error object to our clients. To create an `NSError` object, you can use one of the several class/instance methods available. For example, the class method `errorWithDomain:code:userInfo:` returns an autoreleased error object. Another way to obtain an error object is to allocate it using `alloc` and initialize it using `initWithDomain:code:userInfo:`. For example, assuming the last argument of your method, `error`, is of type `NSError**`, the following will create a new `NSError` object for the caller:

```
*error = [[[NSError alloc] initWithDomain:CompanyCustomDomain
                        code:12 userInfo:dictionary] autorelease];
```

2.8   Key-Value Coding (KVC)

Up to now, we have seen two ways of accessing the instance variables in an object: using accessor methods or accessing them directly. Cocoa defines a third way that allows you to access the instance variables of a class indirectly. This technique is called *key-value coding* (*KVC*).

KVC is declared in the protocol `NSKeyValueCoding`. This protocol is implemented by `NSObject`, the root of all Cocoa objects. At the heart of this protocol, there are two basic methods that you use: (1) `setValue:forKey:` sets the value of a given key, and (2) `valueForKey:` retrieves the value of a given key.

The `valueForKey:` method is declared in the protocol as

```
- (id)valueForKey:(NSString *)key
```

where `key` is an ASCII-encoded string that starts with a lowercase letter and does not contain white space.

The `setValue:forKey` method is declared in the protocol as

```
- (void)setValue:(id)value forKey:(NSString *)key
```

where `value` is a Cocoa object (i.e., a subclass from `NSObject`), and `key` is an instance of `NSString` with the same restrictions as stated above.

For KVC to work, you need to follow some Cocoa conventions in naming accessor methods. Given a key `xyz`, you should have an accessor named `xyz` or `isXyz` defined in your class in order to use the `valueForKey:` method. Similarly, to use the `setValue:forKey:` method, your class should define a setter named `setXyz:`.

Several keys can be dot-separated to form what is called a *key path*. The key path defines the sequence of object properties to traverse. For example, the key path `key1.key2.key3` says: Obtain the object specified by `key1` from the receiver, then obtain the object specified by `key2` from the object you have just obtained from the receiver, and finally obtain the object specified by `key3` from the last object you have obtained using `key2`.

To retrieve the value of a given key path, use the method `valueForKeyPath:`. To set the value for a key path, use the `setValue:forKeyPath:` method.

2.8.1 An example illustrating KVC

Let's illustrate KVC through an example. Consider the `Person` class declared and defined as follows:

```
@interface Person: NSObject{
    NSString *name;
    NSArray  *allies;
    Person   *lover;
}
@property NSString *name;
@property NSArray  *allies;
@property Person   *lover;
-(id)initWithName:(NSString*) theName;
@end

@implementation Person
@synthesize name, allies, lover;
-(id)initWithName:(NSString*) theName{
  if(self = [super init]){
    name = theName;
  }
  return self;
}
@end
```

In addition, consider the `Community` class declared and defined as follows:

```
@interface Community : NSObject{
    NSArray *population;
}
@property NSArray *population;
@end

@implementation Community
@synthesize population;
@end
```

The first thing you need to notice in this example is how the `initWithName:` method is implemented. First, notice how we invoke the **super**'s init method first and use the result as the value of the variable **self**. Second, notice that we assign the instance variable, `name`, directly. The reason we do that has nothing to do with our KVC example. It just shows that if you want the assignment to use the synthesized setter, you should use

```
self.name = theName
```

The setter is `assign` (default), so we skip it and assign the instance variable directly. Be careful when you set instance variables inside your class. If you do not use **self**, you end up assigning the value rather than invoking the setter. Also, be careful when you implement the setter yourself. If, in your setter, you set the instance variable using **self**, you end up with an infinite loop, which results in a stack overflow and an application crash.

2.8.2 KVC in action

Let's use the above two classes to put KVC into action. Listing 2.4 shows the main function that demonstrates KVC.

Listing 2.4   Demonstration code for key-value coding (KVC).

```
int main(int argc, char *argv[]) {
  NSAutoreleasePool * pool = [[NSAutoreleasePool alloc] init];
  Person   *kate = [[Person alloc] initWithName:@"Kate"];
  Person   *jack = [[Person alloc] initWithName:@"Jack"];
  Person   *hurley = [[Person alloc] initWithName:@"Hurley"];
  Person   *sawyer = [[Person alloc] initWithName:@"Sawyer"];
  Person   *ben = [[Person alloc] initWithName:@"Ben"];
  Person   *desmond = [[Person alloc] initWithName:@"Desmond"];
  Person   *locke = [[Person alloc] initWithName:@"Locke"];
  Community *lost = [[Community  alloc] init];
  [kate   setValue:[NSArray arrayWithObjects:locke, jack, sawyer, nil]
          forKey:@"allies"];
```

```
[hurley setValue:[NSArray arrayWithObjects:locke, nil]
        forKey:@"allies"];
[sawyer setValue:[NSArray arrayWithObjects:locke, nil]
        forKey:@"allies"];
[desmond setValue:[NSArray arrayWithObjects:jack, nil]
        forKey:@"allies"];
[locke  setValue:[NSArray arrayWithObjects:ben, nil]
        forKey:@"allies"];
[jack   setValue:[NSArray arrayWithObjects:ben, nil]
        forKey:@"allies"];
[jack setValue:kate  forKey:@"lover"];
[kate setValue:sawyer forKey:@"lover"];
[sawyer setValue:hurley forKey:@"lover"];
[lost setValue:[NSArray arrayWithObjects: kate, jack, hurley,
                sawyer, ben, desmond,
                locke, nil] forKey:@"population"];
NSArray *theArray = [lost  valueForKeyPath:@"population"];
theArray = [lost  valueForKeyPath:@"population.name"];
theArray = [lost  valueForKeyPath:@"population.allies"];
theArray = [lost  valueForKeyPath:@"population.allies.allies"];
theArray = [lost  valueForKeyPath:@"population.allies.allies.name"];
theArray = [lost  valueForKeyPath:@"population.allies.name"];
NSMutableSet    *uniqueAllies = [NSMutableSet setWithCapacity:5];
for(NSArray *a in theArray){
  if(![a isMemberOfClass:[NSNull class]]){
    for(NSString *n in a){
      printf("%s ", [n  cString]);
      [uniqueAllies addObject:n];
    }
    printf("\n");
  }
}
NSString *luckyPerson  =
        [jack valueForKeyPath:@"lover.lover.lover.name"];
[kate release];
[jack release];
[hurley release];
[sawyer release];
[ben release];
[desmond release];
[locke release];
[pool release];
return 0;
}
```

We first create and initialize seven `Person` instances and one `Community` instance. Next, we use KVC to set the `allies` array. KVC is used after that to set the `lover` attribute. Then we set the `population` of the lost `Community` instance with an array instance containing the seven `Person` instances.

Now, we would like to use KVC to retrieve values using keys and key paths. The line

```
[lost  valueForKeyPath:@"population"];
```

retrieves the `population` array in the `lost` object. The key `population` is applied to the `lost` instance producing the array of `Person` instances returned to the caller. Figure 2.1 shows the result graphically.

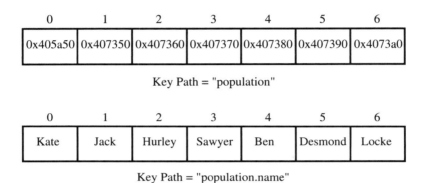

Figure 2.1 Using keys and key paths to retrieve the `population` array and an array of names of `population` from the `lost` instance.

Next, the line

```
[lost  valueForKeyPath:@"population.name"];
```

retrieves an array of names representing the `population` in the `lost` instance. This is a keypath example. First, the key `population` is applied to the receiver, `lost`. This will produce an array of `Person` instances. Next, the key `name` is applied to each and every entry in this array. This will produce an instance of `NSString`. The array of `NSString` instances will be returned as the result. Figure 2.1 shows the result graphically.

The line

```
[lost  valueForKeyPath:@"population.allies"];
```

is an interesting one. Let's follow it to come up with the result. First, the `population` key is applied to the receiver `lost`. This will produce an array of `Person` instances. Next, the key `allies` is applied to each and every `Person` instance in that array. This will produce an array of `Person` instances. So, now we have an array of an array of `Person` instances. This will be the result and will be returned to the caller. Figure 2.2 shows the result graphically.

Key Path = "population.allies"

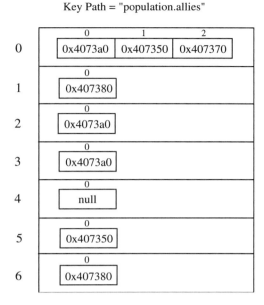

Figure 2.2 Graphical representation of the result obtained from applying the key path `population.allies` to the `lost` instance.

The line

```
[lost  valueForKeyPath:@"population.allies.allies"];
```

goes even further. The subkey path `population.allies` produces the exact result as above, but now we apply another key, `allies`, to the result. This will produce an array of an array of an array of `Person` instances as shown in Figure 2.3.

The line

```
[lost  valueForKeyPath:@"population.allies.allies.name"];
```

does the same as above, except that it further applies the key `name` to every `Person` instance in the array of an array of an array of `Person` instances.

The code

```
theArray = [lost  valueForKeyPath:@"population.allies.name"];
NSMutableSet    *uniqueAllies = [NSMutableSet setWithCapacity:5];
for(NSArray *a in theArray){
  if(![a isMemberOfClass:[NSNull class]]){
    for(NSString *n in a){
      printf("%s ", [n  cString]);
      [uniqueAllies addObject:n];
```

```
        }
      printf("\n");
    }
  }
```

demonstrates the structure of the result from applying the key path `population.allies.name`. It enumerates all names and produces a set of unique names. See Chapter 3 for more information on arrays and sets.

One thing you need to be aware of is the `nil` problem. Because some of the instance variables of objects can be `nil`, and collections in Cocoa cannot have `nil` entries, Cocoa uses the `NSNull` class to represent `nil` entries. In the above code, we just check to see if the entry is an instance of `NSNull`. If so, we skip it.

Some may confuse collections and key paths, thinking that a key path always results in a collection instance. But that is not true as these two concepts are orthogonal. The statement

```
NSString *luckyPerson = [jack valueForKeyPath:@"lover.lover.lover.name"];
```

will result in an instance of `NSString` with the value `@"Hurley"`.

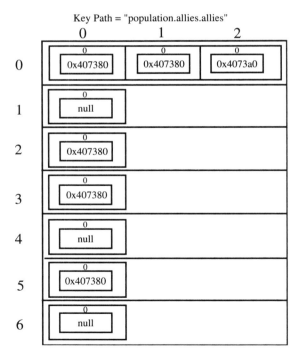

Figure 2.3 Graphical representation of the result from applying the key path `population.allies.allies` to the `lost` instance.

2.9   Multithreading

Multithreading is an important subject in computing. In a single-core system, multithreading gives the user the illusion of concurrent processing. It allows the developer to have an application with a responsive user interface while performing time-consuming tasks in the background. In a multicore system, the importance of multithreading is highlighted even further. Developers want to design applications to utilize the multicore computers more efficiently. Even if the computer system is single-core, they still want to design the application to be usercentric and to have maximum flexibility.

Multithreading in Cocoa is very simple to achieve. All you have to do is to make sure that you design the multithreaded tasks[2] to have minimal interaction with either the main thread or among the other threads. When threads interact with each other by using shared data structures, problems manifest themselves in the form of corrupted data or difficult-to-find bugs.

A simple approach for multithreading is the use of *operation objects*. You can use operation objects by either subclassing the `NSOperation` class or by using a concrete subclass of it called `NSInvocationOperation`. Using the latter approach makes transforming your code into a concurrent application even easier.

Let's assume that you have a method, possibly calling other methods, in a class, and you want to run this method in the background. Without multithreading, the structure of your code will look something like the following.

In one of your objects, you have in one of the methods

```
[myComputationallyIntensiveTaskObject  compute:data];
```

In the class that actually does the job (i.e., the class of `myComputationallyIntensive-TaskObject`) which defines the `compute:` method, you have

```
-(void) compute:(id)data{

// do some computationally intensive calculations on data
// store the either partial or final results
// in some data structure, ds, for others to use
}
```

The `compute:` method operates on `data` and performs computationally intensive calculations. It either stores partial results in an instance variable for other threads to consume or waits until it finishes the computation to present the final results for consumers. It all depends on the application.

Here are the steps you need to take in order to put the `compute:` method in the background, thus making the main thread responsive to the user while performing this task:

---

[2]A *task* is a piece of code that accomplishes a specific goal (e.g., find the square root of a number).

1. Create a launching method. Create a method in the class of `myComputationally-IntensiveTaskObject`. This method will be the one used by other objects if they choose to run the task in the background. Call it something meaningful such as `initiateCompute:` or `computeInBackground:`.

2. In `computeInBackground:`, create an operation queue. An *operation queue* is an object of type `NSOperationQueue` that holds operation objects. You do not necessarily have to create the operation queue here, as long as you have a queue created somewhere in the program.

3. Create an `NSInvocationOperation` object. This will be your operation object. You configure this object with enough information so that the new thread will know where to start executing.

4. Add the newly created operation object to the queue so that it starts running.

5. Because every thread requires its own autorelease pool, in the original `compute:` method, add a new autorelease pool at the beginning and `release` it at the end.

6. If the `compute:` method produces data to be used by other threads, synchronize access to this data using locks. Use locks to access this data in *all* places within your program that use (either read or write) this data.

And that's all! Let's apply these steps to our example and see how easy it is to use multithreading in Cocoa. Listing 2.5 shows the updated code.

Listing 2.5   A multithreaded application using operation objects.

```
// Changes to interface
@interface MyComputationallyIntensiveTask:NSObject{
...
  NSInvocationOperation *computeOp;
  NSOperationQueue      *operationQueue;
}
...
-(void) computeInBackground:(id)data;
-(BOOL) computationFinished;
-(DS*)  computationResult;
@end


@implementation MyComputationallyIntensiveTask
...
// additional methods
-(void) computeInBackground:(id)data{
  operationQueue = [[NSOperationQueue alloc] init];
  computeOp = [[[NSInvocationOperation alloc]
                        initWithTarget:self
                        selector:@selector(compute:)
                        object:data] autorelease];
  [operationQueue addOperation: computeOp];
}
```

```objc
-(BOOL)computationFinished{
  @synchronized(ds){
    // if ds is complete return YES, else return NO
  }
}

-(DS*) computationResult{
  if([self computationFinished] == YES){
    return ds;
  }
  else
    return nil;
}

//changes to original method
-(void) compute:(id)data{
 NSAutoreleasePool * threadPool = [[NSAutoreleasePool alloc] init];

  // do some computationally intensive calculations
  // on data store the (either partial or final) results
  // in  some data structure, ds, for others to you
  @synchronized(ds){
    // store result in ds
  }
  [threadPool release];
}

// Usage from another object
-(void)someOtherMethod{
  ...
  [myComputationallyIntensiveTaskObject computeInBackground:data];
  // be responsive to user GUI
  ...
  //If you need some results or all results
  if(myComputationallyIntensiveTaskObject computationFinished]  == YES){
    result = [myComputationallyIntensiveTaskObject computationResult];
  }
}
@end
```

We added two instance variables in the class, one for the operation and the other for the operation queue. We also added three methods: the `computeInBackground:` for initiating background computation, the `computationFinished` to check if the final result is ready, and `computationResult` for retrieving the final result. This is the simplest interthread communication. Depending on your application requirements, you might opt for more sophisticated protocols. In the method that initiates the background thread, `computeInBackground:`, we start by allocating the operation queue. Next, we allocate the `NSInvocationOperation` and initialize it with the tasks object, main method, and the input data. The initialization method, `initWithTarget:selector:object:` is declared as

```
- (id)initWithTarget:(id)target selector:(SEL)sel object:(id)arg
```

The `target` is the object defining the selector `sel`. The selector `sel` is the method that is invoked when the operation is run. You can pass at most one parameter object to the selector through the `arg` argument. Note that the selector has exactly one parameter. In the cases where you do not have a need to pass an argument, you can pass a `nil`.

After setting up the operation queue and creating and initializing the new operation object, we add the operation object to the queue so that it starts executing. This is done using the `addOperation:` method of the `NSInvocationOperation` object.

As we have mentioned before, autorelease pools are not shared across threads. Because our `compute:` method will be run in its own thread, we create and initialize an `NSAutoreleasePool` object at the beginning and release it at the end of the method. We keep the original `compute:` method intact.

Any time the shared data, ds, is accessed, we use a locking mechanism in order to guarantee data integrity. The shared data can be an instance variable of the object defining the method `compute:` or it can be in another object. Regardless of what shared data you have, if it is accessed from more than one thread, use a lock.

Locking is made easy with the `@synchronized()` directive. The `@synchronized()` directive is used to guarantee exclusive access to a block of code for only one thread. It takes one object as an argument. This object will act as the lock to that piece of code. It is not necessary that the data you are trying to protect be used as a lock. You can use **self**, another object, or even the `Class` object itself as the lock. It is important to note that if the sensitive data structure you are trying to protect is accessed from other parts of your program, the *same* locking object must be used. To enhance the concurrency of your program, delay access to the shared data till the end (i.e., when it needs to be written) and use different locking objects for different unrelated sections of your code.

2.10   Notifications

The delegate pattern allows an object to delegate a task to another object. Sometimes, this pattern is not adequate to the task. For example, suppose that several objects are interested in the result of a given object, O. When O completes its task, it needs to notify interested parties of the result so they can act on it. Object O can maintain an array of these parties and notify them when needed. However, this will require that the other objects know about O (its address), which gives rise to tight-coupling problems. In general, this approach is not adequate.

The iOS runtime provides a centralized object called the *notification center* that acts as a switchboard between objects. The center relays messages from objects that produce events to other objects interested in these events. If an object is interested in a specific event, the object registers with the center for that event. If an object wants to broadcast an event, that object informs the center, and the center, in turn, notifies *all* objects that registered for that event.

The unit of communication between the objects and the center is referred to as a *notification*. NSNotification class encapsulates this concept. Every notification consists of three pieces of data:

- **Name.** A name is some text that identifies this notification. It can be set during initialization and read using the name method.

- **Object.** Each notification can have an object associated with it. This object can be set during initialization and retrieved using the object method.

- **Dictionary.** If additional information needs to be included in a notification, then a dictionary is used. The aUserInfo is used for that purpose. It can be set during initialization and retrieved afterwards using the userInfo method.

To post a notification, an object first obtains the default notification center and then sends it a postNotificationName:object:userInfo: message. To obtain the default notification center, send a defaultCenter class message to NSNotificationCenter.

The postNotificationName:object:userInfo: method is declared as follows:

```
- (void)postNotificationName:(NSString *)aName
        object:(id)anObject userInfo:(NSDictionary *)aUserInfo;
```

If your user info dictionary is not needed, you can use postNotificationName:object:, instead. This method simply calls postNotificationName:object:userInfo: with a nil aUserInfo. You can also post a notification with only a name using the postNotification: method. This method simply passes nil for the second and third arguments.

Objects can express their interest in notifications by adding themselves as *observers*. An object can add as many observations as it needs. To add an object, o, as an observer, send addObserver:selector:name:object: to the default center. You must pass in the reference to o and a selector representing the method to be executed when the notification occurs. The last two parameters (name and object) define four possibilities. If you pass nil for both, object o will receive all notifications that occur in your application. If you specify a specific name and set the object parameter to nil, o will receive all notifications with name regardless of the sender. If you specify values for name and object, o will receive all notifications with name coming from the object. Finally, if you specify nil for name and a value for object, o will receive all notifications from that object. The method for adding an observer is declared as follows:

```
- (void)addObserver:(id)observer selector:(SEL)aSelector
        name:(NSString *)aName object:(id)anObject;
```

The selector aSelector must represent a method that takes exactly one argument: the notification object (i.e., instance of NSNotification).

When an object posts a notification, the notification center goes through its table, determines the objects that need to receive the notification, and invokes their respective selectors passing the notification. The order of notification is undefined. Once the notification is delivered to every object that needs it, control is returned to the object that posted that notification. In other words, posting a notification using this method is *synchronous*.

It's important to note that the notification center does not *retain* the observer. Therefore, you must remove an observer in its `dealloc` method; otherwise, the notification center will send a notification to a `dealloc`ated object and the application will crash. You can use the `removeObserver:` instance method of `NSNotificationCenter` class to remove an observer. The single parameter of this method is a reference to the observer object. This will result in the removal of all entries related to that observer. To remove some observations and keep others, you use the `removeObserver:-name:object:` method. The method is declared as follows:

```
- (void)removeObserver:(id)observer name:(NSString *)aName
        object:(id)anObject;
```

You must pass in a value for `observer`. The `aName` and `anObject` are optional parameters.

For an example application that uses notification, please see Section 17.4.

2.11   Blocks

Blocks are special Objective-C objects that encapsulate a piece of code and a binding to local variables. Blocks (often referred to as `closures`) are very popular in other languages such as Ruby and were introduced to iOS development in iOS 4.

In this section, we will cover the basics of blocks and show you how you can utilize them to make your code more readable.

2.11.1   Declaration and definition

Blocks are declared similarly to function pointers. The following statement declares a block variable that has no return value and takes two parameters:

```
void (^myBlock)(NSString *str1, int val);
```

To declare a type of this block, you can simply write

```
typedef void (^MyBlockType)(NSString *str1, int val);
```

To use this type to declare a variable, you can write

```
MyBlockType myBlock;
```

2.11.2   Block literal

Consider a block type defined as follows:

```
typedef BOOL (^PassBlockType)(NSString*);
```

To declare a variable of this type and specify a literal value for it, you can write something like the following:

```
PassBlockType myBlock = ^(NSString* v){
  if([v isEqualToString:@"v2"]){
    return NO;
  }
  return YES;
};
```

Here, the block literal value starts with the ^ symbol and ends with the } symbol.

2.11.3   Invocation

To invoke a block, you simply follow the same syntax you're used to in invoking functions or function pointers. To invoke myBlock, you write something like the following:

```
myBlock(@"v3");
```

To pass a block to other methods, you follow the same procedure you are used to in passing other objects. For example, consider the following class method declared in the Worker class:

```
+ (NSString*) generate:(NSArray*)data
            withBlock:(BOOL (^)(NSString*))aBlock;
```

This method takes as its last parameter a block. To invoke this method, you write something like the following:

```
NSString *value = [Worker generate:data withBlock:^(NSString* v){
       if([v isEqualToString:@"v2"]){
           return NO;
       }
       return YES;
}];
```

Here, we specify the block value as a literal. Because the return value of the block can be inferred by the compiler, all we have to do is specify the parameter definition and the code.

The method in the Worker class can be implemented as follows:

```
+ (NSString*) generate:(NSArray*)data
            withBlock:(BOOL (^)(NSString*))aBlock{
   NSMutableString *str = [NSMutableString string];
```

```
    for(NSString *v in data){
        if(aBlock(v)){
            [str appendString:v];
        }
    }
    return str;
}
```

Here, notice how the `aBlock` parameter is invoked for each element in the `data` array.

You can also pass a block variable as follows:

```
NSString *value = [Worker generate:data withBlock:myBlock];
```

`myBlock`'s value is already set with a block.

Let's consider another example. Consider a method that does some calculation, and when it's finished it invokes either some code signifying success or different code signifying failure. The success and failure codes are variables passed in as parameters.

Let's make things concrete and look at a possible implementation of such a method:

```
+ (void) calculate:(NSData*) data onSuccess:(Handler) success
        onFailure:(Handler) failure{
    //perform long calculation
    BOOL       fail = NO; // demo purpose, should be result of calc
    NSInteger  code = 5;  // demo purpose, should be result of calc
    fail ? failure(code) : success(code);
}
```

The `Handler` type is declared as follows:

```
typedef  void (^Handler)(NSInteger);
```

To invoke such a method, you can simply write

```
 [Worker      calculate:[NSData data]
            onSuccess:^(NSInteger error){
                NSLog(@"Success with code %d", code);
            }
            onFailure:^(NSInteger code){
              NSLog(@"Failed with error %d", error);
            }];
```

Notice how concise and readable this code is!

2.11.4   Variable binding

In addition to the code, blocks have access to local variables that are available in their context. For example, the following block has access to a local variable (`refVal`) available in its context:

```
NSString refVal = @"v2";
NSString *value = [Worker generate:data withBlock:^(NSString* v){
    if([v isEqualToString:refVal]){
        return NO;
    }
    return YES;
}];
```

By default, the block has read-only access to local variables. To declare local variables as mutable, prefix their declaration with a __block qualifier as follows:

```
__block int counter = 0;
```

Inside a block, you can write something like the following:

```
counter++;
```

2.12   Grand Central Dispatch (GCD)

As of iOS 4.0, you have access to Grand Central Dispatch (GCD). GCD provides a very simple, yet powerful, interface for the execution of concurrent code. You specify the code you want to execute in a block and schedule it to be executed on a queue.

We have covered blocks in the previous section, so let's start by talking about queues.

2.12.1   Queues

There are three kinds of queues available to you:

- **Main.** This queue executes blocks serially and ensures that the blocks run on the main thread.
- **Concurrent.** This queue provides execution of blocks concurrently with first-in-first-out order. It manages the threads for you.
- **Serial.** A queue of this type executes blocks one at a time with first-in-first-out order.

To obtain a concurrent queue, you use the dispatch_get_global_queue(), which is declared as follows:

```
dispatch_queue_t
dispatch_get_global_queue(long priority, unsigned long flags);
```

The first parameter is for the queue priority and the second is for future use. You can specify 0 for default priority, 2 for high priority, and -2 for low priority. The system executes items in a default-priority queue after all high-priority queues have been scheduled for execution. Items in a low-priority queue are executed after high- and default-priority queues have been scheduled. You pass in a 0 value for the flags parameter.

To obtain the `main` queue, you use the function `dispatch_get_main_queue()`.

To create a new queue, you use the function `dispatch_queue_create()`, which is declared as follows:

```
dispatch_queue_t dispatch_queue_create(
    const char *label
    dispatch_queue_attr_t attr);
```

The `label` is usually a reverse-DNS string such as `com.examples.iphone` and the second parameter currently must be `NULL`. Note that you need to release the queue when you're done with it by calling the `dispatch_release()` function.

2.12.2   Scheduling a task

To run a complex task in the background and allow the user interface to be responsive while doing so, you can simply write

```
 dispatch_async(dispatch_get_global_queue(0, 0), ^{
     // perform long running task in background
   });
```

Here, we are using the `dispatch_async()` function passing in a queue (concurrent queue) and a block.

2.12.3   Putting it together

Let's say you want to download a PDF file from the Internet in the background. The following code shows how to do so:

```
- (IBAction) download{
    navigationController.navigationBar.topItem.
        rightBarButtonItem.enabled = NO;
    dispatch_async(dispatch_get_global_queue(0, 0), ^{
        NSData *data = [NSData dataWithContentsOfURL:
          [NSURL
            URLWithString:@"http://www.nwcg.gov/pms/pubs/GSTOP7.pdf"]];
        dispatch_async(dispatch_get_main_queue(), ^{
            RootViewController *root = (RootViewController*)
                navigationController.topViewController;
            [root showPDF:data];
            navigationController.navigationBar.topItem.
              rightBarButtonItem.enabled  = YES;
        });
    });
}
```

Of course, many of the API calls used in this example will be introduced to you throughout this text. What you need to know is that after downloading the PDF file in the background, we schedule the actual showing of the PDF file on the main thread using another call to `dispatch_async()` but passing in the `main` queue instead of a concurrent queue.

The complete application that demonstrate background processing using GCD can be found in the GCD project in the source downloads.

2.13   The Objective-C Runtime

This section can be skipped without loss of continuity. Come back here when you have some time to spare.

At the heart of the object-oriented programming paradigm is the concept of a class. A *class* is a blueprint from which objects can be created. This blueprint specifies what instance variables (state) and what methods (behavior) are available to any object produced by this blueprint. In other words, a class is an object factory: To get a brand-new object whose instance variables are initialized to zeros, you ask its class to produce a new object.

Objects that are created using the same class share the same behavior (methods) but have their own copy of the instance variables. Class-level variables can be declared using the **static** keyword. These variables can be declared outside any method of the class, which makes them accessible from any method in the class, or they can be defined inside a given method, which means they will be accessible only from within that method. In both cases, all instances (objects) of this class share the same static variable, and changes from one object to that variable are seen by all objects of this class.

Given a class, we can define a new class that inherits from this class but optionally adds new state/behavior. The original class is referred to as the *superclass* of the new class. Objective-C is a single-inheritance programming language; which means that a class can have at most one superclass.

The creation of new classes can be done at both compile time and runtime. At compile time, a new class is created using the **@interface** and **@implementation** compiler directives. The compiler generates the C code that is responsible for bringing the class into existence at runtime. As you will see later in this section, you can use the runtime library to create a new class dynamically at runtime.

In iOS, a class is also an object. Because a class is an object, that means it needs a blueprint (a class) to create it. A class that is used to create class objects is referred to as a *metaclass*. The same way that any object is an instance of exactly one class, every class object is an instance of exactly one metaclass. Metaclasses are compiler generated and you rarely interact with them directly.

You access a given behavior (i.e., a method) of an object by sending it a message. A *message* is the name of the method and any arguments to that method. Methods are implemented using C functions. The actual implementation of the method (i.e., the C function) is, however, separate from the actual message. An object can, at runtime, change how it implements a given message. An object can even forward messages to other objects if it does not want to deal with these messages itself.

In iOS, the root class is NSObject. All objects must be instances of this class or sub-classes of it. To have an instance of NSObject is really not that useful; you usually create new (or use existing) classes that inherit from NSObject. NSObject has no superclass.

2.13.1   Required header files

Before getting into the runtime system functions, you need to add the following include statements to any code that accesses these functions:

```
#import <objc/objc.h>
#import <objc/runtime.h>
#import <objc/message.h>
```

Furthermore, you need to target the device, not the simulator, in your build.

2.13.2   The NSObject class

The question is: What is an NSObject? If you examine the NSObject.h header file, you will notice that NSObject is declared as a class with one instance variable and a bunch of class and instance methods. In addition, the class adopts a protocol with the same name.

```
@interface NSObject <NSObject> {
    Class    isa;
}
// a bunch of class and instance methods
@end
```

The sole instance variable is called isa and it is of the type Class. This pointer points to the class used to generate the instance of the object. That means that every object, whether it is an instance object, a class object, or a metaclass object, has a pointer to its class. Through this pointer, the runtime can find out what messages this object can respond to and the implementation of these methods.

The Class type is defined as follows:

```
typedef struct objc_class *Class;
```

It is basically a pointer to a C structure. The C structure is declared as follows:

```
struct objc_class {
    Class isa;

#if !__OBJC2__
    Class super_class                         OBJC2_UNAVAILABLE;
    const char *name                          OBJC2_UNAVAILABLE;
    long version                              OBJC2_UNAVAILABLE;
    long info                                 OBJC2_UNAVAILABLE;
```

```
    long instance_size                    OBJC2_UNAVAILABLE;
    struct objc_ivar_list *ivars          OBJC2_UNAVAILABLE;
    struct objc_method_list **methodLists OBJC2_UNAVAILABLE;
    struct objc_cache *cache              OBJC2_UNAVAILABLE;
    struct objc_protocol_list *protocols  OBJC2_UNAVAILABLE;
#endif

} OBJC2_UNAVAILABLE;
```

The OBJC2_UNAVAILABLE availability macro indicates that the tagged variables are not available in iOS. They, however, provide insights into how the Objective-C class is structured.

As we saw in the NSObject class declaration, the first member variable in an Objective-C class is a pointer to another Objective-C class. The existence of this pointer in every instance, every class object, and every metaclass object provides us with a linked-list data structure that the runtime can traverse.

In addition to the isa pointer, a class object has a super_class pointer to its superclass. Because the NSObject class is the root class, the NSObject class object has this pointer set to nil. The NSObject metaclass object is reached using the isa pointer of any instance, class object, or metaclass object including itself.

All classes, whether regular classes or metaclasses, have NSObject class as their root class. This also includes the NSObject metaclass. That means that if you traverse this super_class link from any instance object, any class object, or any metaclass object, you will reach the NSObject class object and eventually nil.

2.13.3 Objective-C methods

At the time of allocating a new object of a given class, the class object representing that class provides information that guides the runtime in its memory allocation of that object's instance variables. Once the memory space has been reserved for the new object, all its instance variables are initialized to zeros. This excludes, of course, the isa instance variable.

The class object also plays a crucial role in providing the runtime with information on what kind of messages objects generated using it can receive. By the same token, the messages accepted by this class (i.e., class methods) are determined by its metaclass object.

Let's look at what happens when the following Objective-C statements is executed:

```
float value = [market stockValue:@"ALU"];
```

The compiler translates this statement into a C function call similar to the following statement:

```
float value = ((float (*)(id, SEL, NSString*)) objc_msgSend)
            (market, @selector(stockValue:), @"ALU");
```

Here, the objc_msgSend() function is called with three arguments: (1) the receiver object, (2) the selector of the method, and (3) the sole argument to the method.

The `objc_msgSend()` function is declared as follows:

```
id objc_msgSend(id theReceiver, SEL theSelector, ...)
```

This is basically a function that takes at least two arguments and returns an object. Because this function is used by the compiler to translate any messaging statement, the compiler casts the function to the appropriate signature.

The `objc_msgSend()` function starts by obtaining a reference to the class object of `market`. This is, of course, the value of the `isa` pointer and it is located in the first few bytes of the memory pointed to by the pointer `market`. Once the class object has been determined, it is queried for the method corresponding to the selector `stockValue:`.

The class object maintains a table called *dispatch table*. Each entry in this table contains a selector and a pointer to a C function implementing that selector.

If the class does not recognize this message, its superclass is queried, and so on. If the message is not recognized by any of the classes in the inheritance chain, the runtime sends the receiver a `doesNotRecognizeSelector:` message. This method is declared in `NSObject` as follows:

```
- (void)doesNotRecognizeSelector:(SEL)aSelector
```

This method must always result in an exception being thrown. The default behavior is to throw `NS-InvalidArgumentException`. If you override this method, you must either raise this exception yourself or propagate the message to **super**.

The preceding paragraph highlights a powerful feature of Objective-C: dynamic binding. The name of the method (i.e., the message) and its actual implementation are not known until runtime. Not only that, but the receiver itself is also unknown until runtime.

A reference to the C implementation of the method is stored in a variable of type IMP. IMP is declared as follows:

```
typedef  id (*IMP)(id, SEL, ...);
```

The preceding simply declares IMP to be a pointer to a function that takes two arguments and optionally zero or more additional arguments, and returns an object. These two arguments are passed in as **self** and _cmd, respectively.

To access the implementation of a given method, you can use the `NSObject` instance method `methodForSelector:` passing in the selector of the method. This method is declared as follows:

```
- (IMP)methodForSelector:(SEL)aSelector
```

Once you have the pointer to the implementation function, you can invoke the function directly as you do with any C function.

Let's look at an example. Suppose we have the following declaration and definition of a class, RT1:

```
@interface RT1 : NSObject
-(float)valueForStock:(NSString*)stock onDay:(NSDate*)day;
```

@end

@implementation RT1
-(**float**)valueForStock:(NSString*)stock onDay:(NSDate*)day{
    return 33.5;
}
@end

To invoke the C implementation of the method valueForStock:onDay:, you first declare a function prototype as in the following statement:

typedef float(*StockFunc)(**id**, SEL, NSString*, NSDate*);

Notice, again, that the first two arguments are an object of type **id** representing the receiver of the message and the SEL value representing the method.

The following function creates a new instance of the RT1 class, obtains the implementation function, and invokes it directly:

```
void illustration1(){
    RT1 *rt = [[[RT1 alloc] init] autorelease];
    SEL selector = @selector(valueForStock:onDay:);
    StockFunc theFunc = (StockFunc)[rt methodForSelector:selector];
    NSLog(@"Stock value: %.2f",
                        theFunc(rt, selector, @"ALU", [NSDate date]));
}
```

Calling implementations directly should be done with care. You need to have justification for using such a technique and bypassing the message-forwarding mechanism. A good example of using this technique is if you have, say, thousands of objects, all of the same type, and you want to send each the same message. Using this technique will sharply speed up this task.

The Objective-C runtime defines the type Method as a representation of any method in a class. This type is declared as follows:

typedef struct objc_method *Method;

The objc_method structure is declared as follows:

```
struct objc_method {
    SEL      method_name;
    char     *method_types;
    IMP      method_imp;
}
```

As you might have guessed, a method has three components: (1) a name, (2) the types of its parameters and return value, and (3) the actual C function implementing the method.

Here, we see that the name of the method is of type SEL, the parameters/return value types are encoded and stored in a C string, and the actual C implementation of the method is a pointer to a function.

The SEL type is used to represent the name of the Objective-C method. In the Mac environment, it is represented as a C string. You still need to use the @selector directive for managing selectors.

The encodings of the parameters' types are performed by the compiler. The directive @encode can be used to generate encodings of most types (including new classes).

There are specific encodings for the different known and unknown types. For example:

- **Object.** An object type is encoded as @.
- **Selector.** A SEL type is encoded as :.
- **Void.** A **void** type is encoded as v.
- **Class object.** A class object is encoded as #.
- **Integer.** An **int** type is encoded as i.
- **Boolean.** A BOOL type is encoded as B.
- **Character.** A **char** type is encoded as c.

You access the Method data using functions as illustrated, through examples, in the next section.

2.13.4   Examples

In this section, we present examples that are used to illustrate the main concepts behind the Objective-C runtime library.

Obtaining instance and class methods

Consider the following new class declaration and definition:

```
@interface RT2 : RT1
-(void)anInstanceMethod;
+(void)aClassMethod;
@end

@implementation RT2
-(void)anInstanceMethod{}
+(void)aClassMethod{}
@end
```

This class inherits from RT1 and defines additional instance and class methods. It doesn't, however, override any method.

To obtain an instance method, you use the function class_getInstanceMethod(), which is declared as follows:

```
Method class_getInstanceMethod(Class cls, SEL name)
```

The method takes the class object from which to start the search and the name of the method as a SEL argument.

Searching for the method starts from the specified class and goes up the inheritance chain until the method is found.

To retrieve a class method, you use `class_getClassMethod()` function. The following code shows how to retrieve three methods. First it retrieves an instance method defined by the class. Next, it retrieves a class method defined by the class. Finally, it retrieves an instance method defined by the superclass.

```
void illustration2(){
  Method method =
    class_getInstanceMethod([RT2 class], @selector(anInstanceMethod));
  methodLog(method);
  method =
    class_getClassMethod([RT2 class], @selector(aClassMethod));
  methodLog(method);
  method =
    class_getInstanceMethod([RT2 class],@selector(valueForStock:onDay:));
  methodLog(method);
}
```

Logging some of the method information is done using the following function:

```
void methodLog(Method method){
  NSLog(@"Name: %@", NSStringFromSelector(method_getName(method)));
  NSLog(@"IMP at: %p", method_getImplementation(method));
}
```

To obtain a method's name (i.e., a SEL) from a Method variable, we use the function `method_getName()`. This SEL value is then converted into an NSString object using the NSStringFromSelector() function. To obtain the implementation (i.e., a pointer to the C function implementing this method), we use the `method_getImplementation()` function.

In RT2 above, had we overridden the method valueForStock:onDay: defined in its parent, the `class_getInstanceMethod()` would have produced the implementation of RT2, not that of RT1.

Querying response to messages

Sometimes, you have an object and do not know its capabilities, but you would like to send it a message nevertheless. You can test to see if an object responds to a selector by using the respondsToSelector: method.

When this method is invoked on a class object, it return YES if and only if that class (or one of its superclasses) implements a class method with that name. When invoked on an instance of a class, it returns YES if and only if an instance method is defined in the class (or one of its superclasses) representing that object.

The following code fragment shows how to use this method on the RT2 class:

```
void illustration3(){
  NSLog(@"Class method is %@ found in class RT2",
          [RT2 respondsToSelector:@selector(aClassMethod)]?@"":@"NOT");
  NSLog(@"Class method is %@ found in class RT2",
        [RT2 respondsToSelector:@selector(anInstanceMethod)]?@"":@"NOT");
  RT2 *r2 = [[[RT2 alloc] init] autorelease];
  NSLog(@"Instance method is %@ found in class RT2",
          [r2 respondsToSelector:@selector(anInstanceMethod)]?@"":@"NOT");
  NSLog(@"Instance method is %@ found in class RT2",
       [r2 respondsToSelector:@selector(valueForStock:onDay:)]?@"":@"NOT");
}
```

To test whether the superclass implements a specific method, you can use the instancesRespond-ToSelector: class method on the superclass object.

Consider the following new class RT3:

```
@interface RT3 : RT2
-(void) test;
@end

@implementation RT3
-(void) test{
  if([RT2 instancesRespondToSelector:@selector(anInstanceMethod)]){
    [super anInstanceMethod];
  }
  else{
    NSLog(@"Superclass does not implement anInstanceMethod.");
  }
}
@end
```

Here, we have the method checking whether the parent class RT2 implements a specific method. If the answer is yes, a message is sent to **super**. Otherwise, no message is sent to **super** and no exception is thrown.

Replacing existing implementation

Objective-C methods defined in the class implementation are translated into equivalent C functions. For example, consider the following instance method:

```
-(NSString*)addToString:(NSString*)data{
  return [data stringByAppendingString:@"!"];
}
```

The compiler will translate this method into something similar to the following C function:

```
NSString* addToString(id self, SEL _cmd, NSString* data){
  return [data stringByAppendingString:@"!"];
}
```

The function will receive a reference to the object (the receiver) and a selector of the method. The rest of the parameters follow.

If you want to replace the behavior of a message with another behavior, you can, at any time, replace the implementation of the method representing this message with a new implementation with the appropriate C function signature.

Consider class RT2. Right now, the instance method anInstanceMethod does not do anything. Let's replace its implementation with a new, more useful, behavior as shown below:

```
void impNew(id self, SEL _cmd){
  NSLog(@"My new implementation");
}
```

To replace the existing implementation with the above function, first obtain the Method value for this selector from the RT2 class as follows:

```
Method method =
    class_getInstanceMethod([RT2 class], @selector(anInstanceMethod));
```

Here, we use the class_getInstanceMethod() function to obtain the method of the selector anInstanceMethod.

After obtaining the method, we set its implementation with our new function as follows:

```
method_setImplementation(method, (IMP)impNew);
```

The method_setImplementation() function takes as the first argument the Method value and as the second argument a function pointer.

Once the new implementation is set, all subsequent anInstanceMethod messages sent to instances of RT2 will result in the execution of our C function:

```
  RT2 *rt2 = [[[RT2 alloc] init] autorelease];
  [rt2 anInstanceMethod];
```

Patching methods

Sometimes, you face a situation where your application is using a given class in several places and you decide that you need to modify the behavior of some of its methods. Because you do not have access to its source code, you want to patch these methods with your code somehow. You want the flexibility of calling the original method before, after, or between your custom code.

Using the runtime system, achieving this goal is easy. We already know that a message and its implementation are two independent pieces. All we need to do is to simply swap the old and the new implementations and have the new implementation call the old one at the appropriate time(s).

You already know how to set the implementation of a method in a class, so the following code fragment, which swaps two implementations, should be familiar to you:

```
Method m1 = class_getInstanceMethod(aClass, original);
Method m2 = class_getInstanceMethod(aClass, new);
IMP imp1 = method_getImplementation(m1);
IMP imp2 = method_getImplementation(m2);
method_setImplementation(m1, imp2);
method_setImplementation(m2, imp1);
```

In the above code, the implementations of selectors `original` and `new` in class `aClass` are swapped.

Fortunately, there is a convenience function that does the swapping for us, atomically. This function is `method_exchangeImplementations()`, which is declared as follows:

```
void method_exchangeImplementations(Method m1, Method m2)
```

Armed with this knowledge, we are ready to add a category on `NSObject` to equip every class with the ability to swap the implementations of two of its methods:

```
@interface NSObject(Patching)
+(void)swapMethod:(SEL)original withMethod:(SEL)new;
@end

@implementation NSObject(Patching)
+(void)swapMethod:(SEL)original withMethod:(SEL)new{
  method_exchangeImplementations(
                     class_getInstanceMethod(self, original),
                     class_getInstanceMethod(self, new)
                     );
}
@end
```

Because the swapping method is a class method, **self** refers to the class object and it should be passed as the first argument to the `class_getInstanceMethod()` function.

Let's look at an example. Consider the following class:

```
@interface RT4 : NSObject
@end

@implementation RT4
-(void) originalMethod{
  NSLog(@"Inside originalMethod.");
}
@end
```

The RT4 class has a single instance method that logs a message. We want to patch this method with another new method. We define a category on RT4 as follows:

```
@implementation RT4(CategoryOnMyClass)
-(void)anotherMethod{
  NSLog(@"Inside anotherMethod");
  [self anotherMethod];
}
@end
```

The method anotherMethod above looks weird. It's calling itself! However, if we swap its implementation and that of originalMethod, any call to originalMethod will effectively call anotherMethod and any call to anotherMethod will result in a call to originalMethod.

The following code fragment illustrates the concept:

```
RT4 *test = [[[RT4 alloc] init] autorelease];
NSLog(@"Before patching ...");
[test originalMethod];
[RT4 swapMethod:@selector(originalMethod)
     withMethod:@selector(anotherMethod)];
NSLog(@"After patching ...");
[test originalMethod];
```

Obtaining all methods defined by a class

If you want to get an array of all methods defined by a class and not by any of its superclasses, you can use the function class_copyMethodList(). This function returns an array of methods implemented by the class, and it is declared as follows:

```
Method * class_copyMethodList(Class cls, unsigned int *outCount)
```

The first argument is the class object and the second is a reference to an integer. If you want to get the instance methods, you pass in the class object. If, on the other hand, you want a list of all class methods, you need to pass in the metaclass object. This makes sense as the blueprint for the class (needed to obtain its methods) is it smetaclass object. If outCount is not NULL, the number of elements in this array is returned. The returned array consists of pointers to Method type. You need to free the returned array when you are finished with it.

Let's illustrate through an example. Consider the following class:

```
@interface RT5 : NSObject
+(void)simpleS;
+(NSString*)complexS:(NSNumber*)aNumber
              andAString:(NSString*)aString;
-(void)simple;
-(NSString*)complex:(NSNumber*)aNumber
              andAString:(NSString*)aString;
@end
```

```
@implementation RT5
+(void)simpleS{}
+(NSString*)complexS:(NSNumber*)aNumber
              andAString:(NSString*)aString{
  return @"Hi";
}
-(void)simple{}
-(NSString*)complex:(NSNumber*)aNumber
              andAString:(NSString*)aString{
  return @"Hello";
}
@end
```

To list the class methods, we make a call to our `listAllMethods()` function as follows:

```
listAllMethods(object_getClass([RT5 class]));
```

Here, we are passing in the metaclass object of class RT5 as the sole argument. We obtain the metaclass object through the runtime function `object_getClass()` passing in the class object.

To list all instance methods, we pass in the class object as follows:

```
listAllMethods([RT5 class]);
```

The `listAllMethods()` function is shown below:

```
void    listAllMethods(Class class){
  unsigned int methodCount;
  Method *methods = class_copyMethodList(class, &methodCount);
  for(int i=0; i < methodCount; i++){
    char buffer[256];
    SEL     name = method_getName(methods[i]);
    NSLog(@"The method's name is %@", NSStringFromSelector(name));
    //OR
    //NSLog(@"The method's name is %s", name);
    char    *returnType = method_copyReturnType(methods[i]);
    NSLog(@"The return type is %s", returnType);
    free(returnType);
    // self, _cmd + any others
    unsigned int numberOfArguments =
        method_getNumberOfArguments(methods[i]);
    for(int j=0; j<numberOfArguments; j++){
      method_getArgumentType(methods[i], j, buffer, 256);
      NSLog(@"The type of argument %d is %s", j, buffer);
    }
  }
  free(methods);
}
```

The function above starts by obtaining the array of methods for the class object passed in as an argument. After obtaining the array of methods, the function iterates through this array logging specific attributes of each method. The function above logs the name of the method, the return type, and the type of each argument.

To obtain the return type of a method, you can use the `method_copyReturnType()` function declared as follows:

```
char *method_copyReturnType(Method m)
```

To obtain the type of a specific argument, you can use the `method_getArgumentType()` function declared as follows:

```
void method_getArgumentType(Method m, unsigned int index,
                            char *dst, size_t dst_len)
```

You pass in the method object as the first parameter. The index of the argument whose type you are looking for is passed in as the second parameter. A pointer to the buffer used to store the returned type is passed in as the third parameter. Finally, the size of the buffer is passed in as the fourth parameter.

For example, here is output related to one of the class methods:

```
The method's name is complexS:andAString:
The return type is @
The type of argument 0 is @
The type of argument 1 is :
The type of argument 2 is @
The type of argument 3 is @
```

Notice that the first two arguments are the implicit arguments of every method.

Adding a new method

If you want to add a new method to a class, you can use the `class_addMethod()` function declared as follows:

```
BOOL class_addMethod(Class cls, SEL name, IMP imp, const char *types)
```

The first three parameters should be familiar to you. The last parameter is where you provide a C string with the encoded return and argument types. The method `name` must not be implemented by the class `cls`. If it is declared in one of the superclasses of `cls`, it will be overridden.

Let's illustrate through an example. Consider a class `RT6` that defines no methods. Suppose we wanted to add a new instance method with the selector `newOne:withData:` whose signature is as follows:

```
-(NSString*) newOne:(BOOL)flag withData:(NSData*)data;
```

The C function implementing this new method is shown below:

```
NSString* newOneImplementation(id self,SEL _cmd,BOOL flag,NSData* data){
  NSLog(@"self: %@, _cmd: %@", self, NSStringFromSelector(_cmd));
  NSLog(@"The flag is: %@ and the data is: %@", flag?@"YES":@"NO", data);
  return @"Done!";
}
```

To add the new method, we simply call the `class_addMethod()` function as shown below:

```
class_addMethod([RT6 class], @selector(newOne:withData:),
               (IMP)newOneImplementation, "@@:B@");
```

We pass in the class object because it's an instance method we are adding. The name of the method is passed in the second argument. A pointer to our implementation is passed in the third argument. The fourth argument is a C string with several encodings. We know that every method receives as the first two arguments an object encoded as @ and a selector encoded as :. The return type is NSString* and is encoded as @. The first and second arguments of our method are BOOL (encoded as B) and NSData* encoded as @. Notice that the return type is always listed first.

Once we have added the new method, we can call it as any Objective-C method. You will, however, get a compiler warning. The Objective-C compiler is smart, but it's not that smart!

```
RT6 *t = [[[RT6 alloc] init] autorelease];
NSLog(@"%@", [t newOne:YES withData:[NSData data]]);
```

To add a class method, pass in `object_getClass([RT6 class])` as the first argument to the `class_addMethod()` function.

Sending a message to an object

We have already seen our friend `objc_msgSend()` function. If you find a need to use this function, you can utilize it as you please. For example, consider the following class:

```
@interface RT7 : NSObject
+(NSUInteger) lengthS:(NSString*)theString;
-(NSUInteger) length:(NSString*)theString;
@end

@implementation RT7
+(NSUInteger) lengthS:(NSString*)theString{
  return [theString length];
}
-(NSUInteger) length:(NSString*)theString{
  return [theString length];
}
@end
```

To call the instance method `length:`, you can write the following:

```
RT7 *rt = [[[RT7 alloc] init] autorelease];
NSUInteger value;
value =  ((int(*)(id, SEL, NSString*))objc_msgSend)(
         rt, @selector(length:), @"hi");
```

Casting the `objc_msgSend()` function is optional. It only removes the compiler's warning.

To call the class method `lengthS:`, you can write

```
value =  ((int(*)(id, SEL, NSString*))objc_msgSend)(
         [RT7 class], @selector(lengthS:), @"hello");
```

Accessing instance variables

You can directly access instance variables of objects. To access an instance variable, use the function `object_getInstanceVariable()` function, which is declared as follows:

```
Ivar
   object_getInstanceVariable(id obj, const char *name, void **outValue);
```

The return value is of type `Ivar`, the runtime's type for instance variables. This return value represents the instance variable that you are accessing. You pass in the object whose instance you are retrieving in the first argument. The name of the instance variable is passed in as a C string and the third argument is a pointer to `void*`, where the value of the instance variable should be stored.

Consider the following class:

```
@interface RT8 : NSObject{
   NSNumber *val;
}
@property (nonatomic, assign) NSNumber *val;
@end

@implementation RT8
@synthesize val;
@end
```

Let's create a new instance and change the value of the instance variable as follows:

```
RT8 *rt8 = [[[RT8 alloc] init] autorelease];
rt8.val = [NSNumber numberWithInt:99];
```

To access the value of the instance variable, you can write something like the following statements:

```
void *outValue;
object_getInstanceVariable(rt8, "val", &outValue);
NSLog(@"The number is %d", [(NSNumber*) outValue intValue]);
```

Creating new classes dynamically

If your application requires the creation of new classes at runtime, you can use the support that the runtime provides to achieve your goal.

To create a new class, you start by creating it and its metaclass using the function `objc_allocate-ClassPair()`. This function is declared as follows:

```
Class objc_allocateClassPair(Class superclass, const char *name,
                             size_t extraBytes)
```

The first argument is the class object of the superclass. The second argument is the C string name of the new class. The third and final argument specifies extra allocation bytes and should usually be zero.

After creating the new class, you can add instance variables and instance/class methods. After that, you register the class and its metaclass using the function `objc_registerClassPair()` passing in the return value of the call to the `objc_allocateClassPair` function.

Let's illustrate this topic through a concrete example. Consider the following existing class:

```
@interface RT9 : NSObject{
  NSNumber *val;
}
@property(nonatomic, retain) NSNumber *val;
@end

@implementation RT9
@synthesize val;

-(id)init{
  if(self = [super init]){
    self.val = [NSNumber numberWithInt:99];
  }
  return self;
}

-(void)dealloc{
  NSLog(@"dealloc in super");
  self.val = nil;
  [super dealloc];
}
@end
```

`RT9` is a simple class that we want to use as a superclass for a new class called `MyAwesomeClass`. To create the new class, we start with the following statement:

```
Class dynaClass =
    objc_allocateClassPair([RT9 class], "MyAwesomeClass", 0);
```

After that, we add an instance variable using the function `class_addIvar`, which is declared as follows:

```
BOOL class_addIvar(Class cls, const char *name, size_t size,
                   uint8_t alignment, const char *types)
```

The first argument is the class object. This class object cannot refer to a metaclass. The second argument is the C string name of the new variable. The third argument is the size of the new instance variable. The fourth argument is the alignment of the storage. The fifth and final argument is the type encoding of the instance variable. The function returns `YES` if and only if the instance variable was successfully created.

To add an instance variable called `vertices` of type `NSArray*`, we write something like the following:

```
class_addIvar(dynaClass, "vertices", sizeof(id), log2(sizeof(id)), "@");
```

Next, let's add the methods `many` and `dealloc` as follows:

```
class_addMethod(dynaClass, @selector(many),
                (IMP)manyImplementation, "@@:");
class_addMethod(dynaClass, @selector(dealloc),
                (IMP)deallocImplementation, "v@:");
```

Finally, we register the class and its metaclass as follows:

```
objc_registerClassPair(dynaClass);
```

The implementation of the `many` method is shown below:

```
NSNumber* manyImplementation(id self, SEL _cmd){
  void *outValue1;
  void *outValue2;
  object_getInstanceVariable(self, "vertices", &outValue1);
  object_getInstanceVariable(self, "val", &outValue2);
  return [NSNumber numberWithInt:
                ((NSArray*)outValue1).count +
                [(NSNumber*)outValue2 intValue]];
}
```

Notice how we access the instance variable, `val`, inherited from the superclass.

The implementation of `dealloc` method is shown below:

```
void deallocImplementation(id self, SEL _cmd){
  void *outValue;
  object_getInstanceVariable(self, "vertices", &outValue);
  [(id) outValue release];
  object_setInstanceVariable(self, "vertices", nil);
  struct objc_super obS;
  obS.super_class = [self superclass];
```

```
    obS.receiver = self;
    objc_msgSendSuper(&obS, @selector(dealloc));
}
```

Here, we retrieve the `NSArray` object and `release` it. We also propagate the `dealloc` call to **super** by sending a message to **super** using the function `objc_msgSendSuper()`, which is declared as follows:

```
id objc_msgSendSuper(struct objc_super *super, SEL op, ...);
```

The first argument is the `objc_super` structure and the second is the selector. The `objc_super` structure is declared as follows:

```
struct objc_super {
    id receiver;
    Class super_class;
};
```

The following shows how we can use this new class:

```
//create an object of this class
  id dynaObject = [[NSClassFromString(@"MyAwesomeClass") alloc] init];
  // OR [dynaClass alloc]
  //assign a value to an instance variable of this class
  object_setInstanceVariable(dynaObject, "vertices",
    [[NSArray arrayWithObjects:@"Bart", @"lisa", nil] retain]);
  //invoke a method on this class
  NSNumber    *numb = [dynaObject many];
  NSLog(@"The returned number is %@", numb);
  [dynaObject release];
```

Alternatives to executing methods

The `performSelector` method declared in the `NSObject` protocol allows you to send a message to an object. There are three versions of this method taking zero, one, or two arguments. These three methods are declared in the `NSObject` protocol as follows:

```
- (id)performSelector:(SEL)aSelector;
- (id)performSelector:(SEL)aSelector withObject:(id)object;
- (id)performSelector:(SEL)aSelector
        withObject:(id)object1 withObject:(id)object2;
```

Consider the following class:

```
@interface Person : NSObject
-(void)play;
-(void)work;
-(void)eat:(NSString*)food;
-(void)cook:(NSString*)food1 withFood:(NSString*)food2;
```

```
-(float)difficultyForRecipe:(NSString*)recipe
        resources:(float)resources patience:(NSNumber*)patience;
@end


@implementation Person

-(void)play{
    NSLog(@"playing...");
}

-(void)work{
    NSLog(@"working...");
}

-(void)eat:(NSString*)food{
    NSLog(@"eating %@...", food);
}
-(void)cook:(NSString*)food1 withFood:(NSString*)food2{
    NSLog(@"cooking %@ with %@", food1, food2);
}
-(float)difficultyForRecipe:(NSString*)str1 resources:(float)v1
        patience:(NSNumber*)t3{
    return 0.8;
}
@end
```

At runtime, you might vary the message sent to an object of type Person by varying the selector. Consider the following example:

```
Person *person = [[[Person alloc] init] autorelease];
srand([NSDate timeIntervalSinceReferenceDate]);
if(rand() % 2)
  [person performSelector:@selector(play)];
else
  [person performSelector:@selector(work)];
```

In the above code fragment, we create a new instance of Person and use a random number to determine which message to send to the object. This is part of the dynamic binding capabilities of Objective-C. If you find yourself needing to vary the message sent to an object during the runtime of your application, performSelector is your friend.

If you want to pass one or two objects to the method, you can use the other versions as in the following example:

```
[person performSelector:@selector(eat:) withObject:@"Banana"];
[person performSelector:@selector(cook:withFood:)
        withObject:@"Spaghetti" withObject:@"meat"];
```

When the return type is not an **id**, the arguments to the method are not objects, or you need to pass in more than two objects, you can resort to the NSInvocation class.

An NSInvocation object encapsulates an Objective-C message. It stores the selector, receiver, arguments, and return value. To create an instance of this class, you use the invocationWithMethodSignature: method declared as follows:

```
+ (NSInvocation*)invocationWithMethodSignature:(NSMethodSignature *)sig;
```

You pass in a method signature and you obtain an autoreleased NSInvocation object.

An NSMethodSignature instance is an object that stores the types for the return value and arguments for a method. To obtain a method's signature, you can use NSObject's method instanceMethodSignatureForSelector: class method passing in the selector. Alternatively, you can use its class method signatureWithObjCTypes: passing in a C string with encoded types. This method is declared as follows:

```
+ (NSMethodSignature *)signatureWithObjCTypes:(const char *)types;
```

After obtaining the NSInvocation object, you set the selector using its setSelector: method. Next, you set any of the arguments you want using the setArgument:atIndex: method, which is declared as follows:

```
- (void)setArgument:(void *)argumentLocation atIndex:(NSInteger)idx;
```

You start with index 2 as the first two indices are used by **self** and _cmd. You also pass in a reference to the argument location as we shall see shortly.

After that, you can set the target and send the object an invoke message or call invokeWithTarget: passing in the target. Either way, the message is sent, and control is returned to the next statement after the execution of the method representing the message finishes. You can retrieve the return value, if any, using getReturnValue: method passing in a buffer pointer. The buffer should be large enough to accommodate the return value. If you don't know the size of the return value, you can get that size from the signature object by sending it a methodReturnLength message.

The following illustrates how to call the selector difficultyForRecipe:resources:patience:.

```
NSMethodSignature *sig =
[Person    instanceMethodSignatureForSelector:
    @selector(difficultyForRecipe:resources:patience:)];
 NSInvocation *invocation =
    [NSInvocation invocationWithMethodSignature:sig];
 [invocation setSelector:
    @selector(difficultyForRecipe:resources:patience:)];
 NSString *arg1 = @"Hi";
 float     arg2 = 4.5;
 NSNumber *arg3 = [NSNumber numberWithBool:YES];
 [invocation setArgument:&arg1 atIndex:2];
 [invocation setArgument:&arg2 atIndex:3];
```

```
[invocation setArgument:&arg3 atIndex:4];
[invocation invokeWithTarget:person];
float outValue;
[invocation getReturnValue:&outValue];
NSLog(@"return value is %.2f", outValue);
```

Forwarding messages to other objects

We mentioned before that when you send a message to an object and that object does not recognize that message, the runtime sends a doesNotRecognizeSelector: message to that object. This invocation must result in raising an NSInvalidArgumentException exception. The runtime does, however, give the object an opportunity to recover before pursuing this track. The runtime creates an NSInvocation object representing this message and sends the object a forwardInvocation: message with that NSInvocation object as an argument. Objects can forward this invocation object to other objects. In essence, the object delegates the message.

To take advantage of this feature, you need to override the forwardInvocation: method as well as the methodSignatureForSelector: method.

Consider the RT10 class in Listing 2.6. An instance of this class maintains a list of objects that can be used to respond to messages it does not recognize.

Listing 2.6   A class that delegates messages to its friends.

```
@interface RT10 : NSObject{
 NSArray *myFriends;
 }
@end


@implementation RT10


-(id)init{
  if(self = [super init]){
    RT5    *friend1 = [[[RT5 alloc] init] autorelease];
    RT7    *friend2 = [[[RT7 alloc] init] autorelease];
    myFriends = [[NSArray arrayWithObjects:friend1, friend2, nil] retain];
  }
  return self;
}


- (NSMethodSignature *)methodSignatureForSelector:(SEL)aSelector {
  NSMethodSignature *signature = nil;
  for(id friend in myFriends){
    if(signature = [friend methodSignatureForSelector:aSelector]){
      break;
    }
  }
  if(signature){
```

```
      return signature;
   }
   else{
      return [super methodSignatureForSelector:aSelector];
   }
}

- (void)forwardInvocation:(NSInvocation *)anInvocation{
   for(id friend in myFriends){
      if([friend respondsToSelector:[anInvocation selector]]){
         return [anInvocation invokeWithTarget:friend];
      }
   }
   [super forwardInvocation:anInvocation];
}

-(void) dealloc{
   [myFriends release];
   [super dealloc];
}
@end
```

In the `init` method, we create and initialize two other objects and store them in an array. When a message is sent to RT10 instance and the runtime cannot find a corresponding method for it, `methodSignatureForSelector:` gets called. This method simply iterates through the list of friend objects asking if any has a valid signature for that selector. If there is one object that has a valid signature, then that signature is returned. Otherwise, the message is propagated to **super**.

If there is a friend that has a valid signature for the selector, the `forwardInvocation:` method is called. This method iterates through the list, in the same order as above, and forwards the invocation by `invokeWithTarget:` passing in the first friend object that responds to the selector of the invocation object.

The following demonstrates message forwarding to other objects:

```
RT10 *rt10 = [[[RT10 alloc] init] autorelease];
NSLog(@"Values: %@ and %d",
      [rt10 complex:[NSNumber numberWithFloat:33.5] andAString:@""],
      [rt10 length:@"k"]);
```

RT10 instance is sent two messages and can understand neither. However, it successfully produces a result in each case thanks to message delegation.

2.14 Summary

We have certainly covered a lot of ground in this chapter. In Section 2.1, we introduced the mechanism for declaring and defining classes. Then we talked about how an object interacts with other objects by sending messages to them. In Section 2.2, we covered the topic of memory management. We illustrated how to allocate objects and how to initialize these objects. We discussed the concept of retain count and how every object maintains one such counter. We also covered the topic of autorelease pools and outlined the responsibilities that clients have with respect to releasing objects. In Section 2.3, we discussed the protocols feature of Objective-C. Protocols were shown to be a powerful feature that allows, among other things, the ability to realize multiple inheritance in a single-inheritance language. In Section 2.4, we discussed properties. A property is a feature of Objective-C that allows you to declaratively generate setter/getter accessor methods for instance variables. After that, we covered the topic of categories in Section 2.5. We showed how, using the category feature, you can extend the capabilities of existing classes without even having their source code. Posing was covered in Section 2.6. This facilitates the replacement of one class by another class that is a descendant of it, and it is mostly useful as a testing feature. Exceptions and errors were covered in Section 2.7. Exceptions are usually used by the developer for finding bugs, while errors are used in production code for conveying runtime errors due to the user's environment. In Section 2.8, we introduced the concept of key-value coding (KVC). KVC provides the ability to access object properties indirectly. KVC is widely used in Cocoa and we gave a lengthy treatment of the subject. Next, multithreading was discussed in Section 2.9. In particular, we outlined a simple approach for multithreading using operation objects. After that, we covered the topic of notifications in Section 2.10. In Sections 2.11 and 2.12, we introduced blocks and Grand Central Dispatch. Finally, Section 2.13 discussed, at great length, the topic of the Objective-C runtime system.

Exercises

(1) Consider the following class declaration, definition, and usage:

```
@interface A
-(int)doSomething;
@end
@implementation A
-(int)doSomething{
    return 1;
}
@end
int main(int argc, char *argv[]){
  A *a = [[A alloc] init];
  int v = [a doSomething];
  [a release];
}
```

Study the above code and comment on the outcome of the `main()` function.

(2) Consider the following class and its usage in the `main()` function. What is the last statement executed and why?

```
1  @interface B : NSObject{
2      NSString *myString;
```

```
 3  }
 4  @property(nonatomic) NSString * myString;
 5  -(unichar)getFirstCharacter;
 6  @end
 7
 8  @implementation B
 9  @synthesize myString;
10  -(unichar)getFirstCharacter{
11      return [myString characterAtIndex:0];
12  }
13  @end
14
15  int main(int argc, char *argv[]){
16      NSAutoreleasePool * pool1 = [[NSAutoreleasePool alloc] init];
17      NSMutableString *str =
18          [NSMutableString stringWithString:@"Where am I?"];
19      B *b = [[B alloc] init];
20      b.myString = str;
21      [pool1  release];
22      unichar x = [b getFirstCharacter];
23      [b release];
24  }
```

(3) The following code declares and defines a `Person` and a `Dog`, and then uses the two classes

```
@interface Person: NSObject{}
-(void)bark;
@end

@implementation Person
-(void)bark{
  printf("Woof\n");
}
@end

@interface Dog : NSObject{}
-(void)bark;
-(void)bark:(NSString*)a;
@end

@implementation Dog
-(void)bark:(NSString*)a{
  printf("Woof\n");
}
-(void) bark{
  printf("Woof woof\n");}
@end
```

```
int main(int argc, char *argv[]) {
  NSAutoreleasePool * pool = [[NSAutoreleasePool alloc] init];
  SEL sel = @selector(bark);
  SEL sel1 = @selector(bark:);
  Person *aPerson = [[Person alloc] init];
  Dog *aDog = [[Dog alloc] init];
  .
  .
  .
}
```

Answer the following questions:

(a) What is the value of `equal` after the following statement?

```
BOOL equal = sel == sel1;
```

(b) What happens when the following statement is executed?

```
[aPerson performSelector:sel];
```

(c) What happens when the following two statements are executed?

```
[aDog bark];
[aDog bark:@""];
```

(d) What is the result of the following statement?

```
[aPerson performSelector:NSSelectorFromString(@"bark:")];
```

(e) What does the following statement do?

```
[aDog bark:];
```

(4) Consider the following code. Describe the outcome of each line. What is the last line executed?

```
1   NSAutoreleasePool * pool1 = [[NSAutoreleasePool alloc] init];
2   NSMutableArray *arr;
3   arr = [NSMutableArray arrayWithCapacity:0];
4   NSAutoreleasePool * pool2 = [[NSAutoreleasePool alloc] init];
5   NSMutableString *str =
6     [NSMutableString stringWithString:@"Howdy!"];
7   [arr addObject:str];
8   [pool2 release];
9   int n = [arr count];
10  str = [arr objectAtIndex:0];
11  [arr release];
12  n = [str length];
13  [pool1 release];
```

(5) The following function will cause an application crash. Why? (Hint: A large percentage of iPhone application crashes have to do with illegal memory access.)

```
void function(){
  NSAutoreleasePool *pool = [[NSAutoreleasePool alloc] init];
  NSString     *myString =
           [[[NSString alloc] initWithString:@"Hello!"] autorelease];
  @try {
    [myString appendString:@"Hi!"];
  }
  @catch (NSException * e) {
    @throw;
  }
  @finally {
    [pool release];
  }
}
```

3

Collections

As a Cocoa developer, you are provided with many classes that can help you group several of your objects in specific ways. This chapter discusses the main collection classes available to you.

Section 3.1 addresses the topic of arrays. You learn about immutable and mutable arrays, the different approaches used for copying arrays, and several sorting techniques. Section 3.2 covers the topic of sets. *Sets* are collections that do not impose ordering on the objects they contain. You learn about immutable and mutable sets as well as several interesting operations on sets. Section 3.3 discusses dictionaries. *Dictionaries* allow you to store objects and retrieve them using keys. As you saw in Section 2.7, dictionaries are widely used in Cocoa frameworks and understanding them is essential. Finally, we provide a summary in Section 3.4.

3.1 Arrays

You use NSArray and NSMutableArray if you would like to store/access your objects in an ordered way. NSArray is the immutable version of the array, allowing you to store your objects only once (during initialization). NSMutableArray is a subclass of NSArray that allows you to add/remove objects even after initialization of the collection.

To help illustrate the main concepts behind arrays, let us use the simple class Person shown in Listing 3.1.

Listing 3.1   The class Person used in the arrays examples.

```
#import <Foundation/Foundation.h>
@interface Person : NSObject{
  NSString  *name;
  NSString  *address;
}
@property(copy) NSString  *name;
@property(copy) NSString  *address;
-(id)initWithName:(NSString*) theName andAddress:(NSString*) theAddress;
-(id)init;
@end
```

```
@implementation Person
@synthesize name;
@synthesize address;
-(id)initWithName:(NSString*) theName andAddress:(NSString*) theAddress{
  self = [super init];
  if(self){
    self.name     =    theName;
    self.address  =    theAddress;
  }
  return self;
}
-(id)init{
  return [self initWithName:@"" andAddress:@""];
}
-(void)dealloc{
  [name      release];
  [address   release];
  [super     dealloc];
}
@end
```

Now that you have created the `Person` class, Listing 3.2 demonstrates how you can configure a static array using the `NSArray` class. We start by creating five instances of the class `Person`. Figure 3.1 shows the state of these five objects before being added to the array.

Listing 3.2   Creating a simple immutable array.

```
int main(int argc, char *argv[]){
  NSAutoreleasePool * pool = [[NSAutoreleasePool alloc] init];
  Person  *a  = [[Person alloc] init];
  Person  *b  = [[Person alloc] init];
  Person  *c  = [[Person alloc] init];
  Person  *d  = [[Person alloc] init];
  Person  *e  = [[Person alloc] init];
  NSArray *arr1 = [NSArray arrayWithObjects: a,b,c,d,e,nil];
  [pool release];
  [a release];
  [b release];
  [c release];
  [d release];
  [e release];
  return 0;
}
```

There are several ways to create and initialize an `NSArray` instance. Here, we use the class method `arrayWithObjects:` and list the objects that we want to initialize the array with, in a comma-separated form. The final parameter must be `nil`, which means that an `NSArray` instance cannot have a `nil` element. Because the creation method used does not contain `alloc` or `new` in its name,

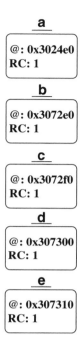

Figure 3.1   Five instances of `Person` before being added to an `NSArray` instance. @ denotes an address, and `RC` denotes retain count.

and we do not use a `copy` method to obtain the new instance, this `NSArray` instance is not owned by us and we are not responsible for releasing it. Once the `NSArray` instance is initialized, you cannot remove/add elements from/to it. It remains static until it is deallocated.

One thing you need to be aware of is that if an object is added to a collection, its retain count is incremented by that collection. In our example, the five objects will each have a retain count of 2, right after the initialization of the `NSArray` instance as shown in Figure 3.2. Notice how the array just holds pointers to its elements.

Once we are finished with a collection, we can release it. When you release an instance of `NSArray`, that instance sends a `release` message to each of its elements (remember that collections retain their objects when the objects are added). Because we do not own `arr1`, just releasing the autorelease pool will release `arr1` and our five `Person` instances. We still have to send a `release` message to these five objects because we own them.

3.1.1   Immutable copy

Now that you know the basics of `NSArray`, let us look at the syntax and the semantics of making a copy of an `NSArray` instance. Listing 3.3 shows sample code demonstrating this behavior.

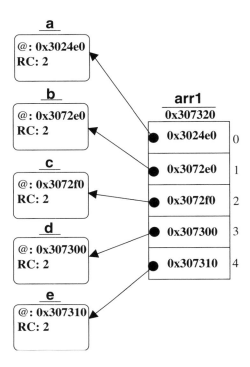

Figure 3.2   State of the five instances of Person after being added to an instance of NSArray. @ denotes an address, and RC denotes retain count.

We create and add our five Person instances as we did before. After that, we ask arr1 to make a copy of itself and we store that new copy in an NSArray* local variable.

Listing 3.3   Immutable copy of an NSArray instance.

```
int main(int argc, char *argv[]){
  NSAutoreleasePool *pool = [[NSAutoreleasePool alloc] init];
  Person  *a  = [[Person alloc] init];
  Person  *b  = [[Person alloc] init];
  Person  *c  = [[Person alloc] init];
  Person  *d  = [[Person alloc] init];
  Person  *e  = [[Person alloc] init];

  NSArray *arr1 = [NSArray  arrayWithObjects: a,b,c,d,e,nil];
  NSArray *arr2 = [arr1 copy];

  Person  *aPerson  = [arr1 objectAtIndex:0];
  aPerson.name  = @"Marge Simpson";
  aPerson.address = @"Springfield";
  // Result of the following line is:
```

```
    // Person at 0 is: Name: Marge Simpson, Addr: Springfield
    printf("Person at %d is: Name: %s, Addr: %s\n",
        0,
        [[[arr2 objectAtIndex:0] name]
                cStringUsingEncoding:NSUTF8StringEncoding],
        [[[arr2 objectAtIndex:0] address]
                cStringUsingEncoding:NSUTF8StringEncoding]);
    // Must release arr2 since we created it using copy.
    [arr2 release];
    // must release all objects
    [a release];
    [b release];
    [c release];
    [d release];
    [e release];
    [pool release];
    return 0;
}
```

After making a copy of the array, we change the first element of the original array, `arr1`. Remember that `NSArray` and `NSMutableArray` are ordered collections. Each stored element has a specific location or index. To retrieve the first element, we use the `objectAtIndex:` method with the index `0`.

After changing the first element in the original array, we inspect the first element in the copy, and we discover that that element was also changed. Why? The documented semantics of how an `NSArray` makes a copy of itself is as follows. First, `NSArray` makes a shallow copy of its elements. This means that only the pointers to these elements are copied. Second, the new instance of the `NSArray` is owned by the caller and is not autoreleased. Figure 3.3 shows the state of our five objects after making a copy of the `NSArray`.

What we notice is that we did not even obtain a new instance of `NSArray`. All that happened is: (1) `arr2` got a copy of the address of `arr1`, which is basically a simple assignment; (2) the `arr1` retain count was incremented by 1; and (3) the retain count of all five objects was incremented by 1. This behavior of the immutable copy makes sense because the original array object is static and does not change.

Finally, even though `arr2` is just `arr1`, we did obtain it using a method that has `copy` in it. Therefore, we have to release it when we are finished with it.

3.1.2   Mutable copy

Until now, we have been working exclusively with `NSArray` and its static behavior. `NSMutableArray` is a mutable version of this class, which means that the number of objects stored in it can grow and shrink during the lifetime of the program. As shown in Listing 3.4, we can obtain a mutable copy of an immutable source. However, instead of using `copy`, we use `mutableCopy`.

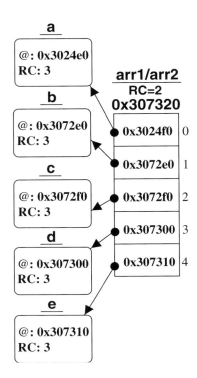

Figure 3.3 State of an NSArray and its immutable copy.

Listing 3.4 Illustration of how you can obtain a mutable copy of an immutable instance of NSArray.

```
int main(int argc, char *argv[]){
  NSAutoreleasePool *pool = [[NSAutoreleasePool alloc] init];
  Person  *a  = [[Person alloc] init];
  Person  *b  = [[Person alloc] init];
  Person  *c  = [[Person alloc] init];
  Person  *d  = [[Person alloc] init];
  Person  *e  = [[Person alloc] init];
  NSArray *arr1 = [NSArray arrayWithObjects: a,b,c,d,e,nil];
  NSMutableArray  *arr2 = [arr1 mutableCopy];
  Person  *f  = [[Person alloc] init];
  [arr2 addObject:f];
  [arr2 removeObject:a];
  [arr2 release];
  [a release];
  [b release];
  [c release];
  [d release];
  [e release];
  [f release];
```

```
    [pool release];
    return 0;
}
```

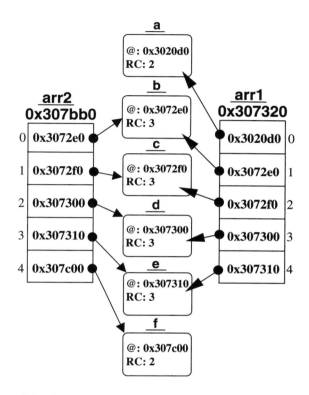

Figure 3.4   Illustration of a mutable copy of an immutable NSArray.

Having an NSMutableArray instance allows you to dynamically remove objects from, and add objects to, that instance. In the code example, we add a new object, f, and remove an existing object, a.[1] Besides the change in the existing elements' positions within the array and their retain count, the retain count of f is incremented by 1 and that of a is decremented by 1. Figure 3.4 illustrates the state of the objects at this stage. Notice that although the two arrays are now distinct, they still share pointers to the same elements.

3.1.3   Deep copy

Until now, we have been dealing with shallow copies. Shallow copying is the default behavior of NSArray and NSMutableArray regardless of the type of copy (i.e., whether the copy is mutable

---

[1] removeObject: removes all occurrences of the object in the collection.

or immutable). However, sometimes you want to have a copy of an object that is independent of the original. Such a copy is referred to as a *deep copy*.

For an object to be able to make a clone of itself, its class has to implement the NSCopying protocol. The NSCopying protocol defines only one method: copyWithZone:. This method must be implemented by the adopting class. It should return an independent, functionally equivalent copy of an object whose instance variables have identical values of the object at the time of copying.

The following summarizes how copying is done:

1. Your class must be a descendant of NSObject and it must adopt the NSCopying protocol.

2. It must implement the copyWithZone: method. Unless the superclass is NSObject, a call to the super's copyWithZone: (with the same zone that you have received) should be the first statement in your implementation of copyWithZone:.

3. Inside copyWithZone:, you create a new instance of your class and initialize it with the same state that your instance is in. Depending on how deep a copy you want to achieve, you may want to propagate the copying to the instance variables themselves. It all depends on the requirements of your code.

4. The copyWithZone: method returns the new copy instance to the caller. The caller owns that copy and is the one responsible for its eventual release.

These are the basic steps you can take in order to generate a new copy of the original object.

One question remains. How does sending a copy message to an instance end up sending it a copyWithZone: message? The answer to this question is simple. The NSObject has a convenience copy method that calls copyWithZone: with a nil zone. Note that NSObject does not adopt the NSCopying protocol itself. Obviously, if none of the classes in the inheritance chain implements a copyWithZone: method, an exception (see Section 2.7.1) is raised. Therefore, it is important to understand that sending a copy message to an array object will always result in a shallow copy regardless of whether the objects it contains adopt the NSCopying protocol.

Listing 3.5 shows the updated Person class with the added NSCopying protocol adoption. You can easily notice that this class follows a deep copying approach. We generate a new instance of the object containing new instance variables and are not just copying pointers. The new instance variables come from the property attribute copy used for both instance variables, name and address.

Listing 3.5   Enhanced Person class adopting the NSCopying protocol.

```
#import <Foundation/Foundation.h>

@interface Person : NSObject<NSCopying>{
  NSString  *name;
  NSString  *address;
}
@property(copy) NSString  *name;
```

```
@property(copy) NSString *address;
-(id)initWithName:(NSString*) theName andAddress:(NSString*) theAddress;
-(id)init;
-(id)copyWithZone:(NSZone *)zone;
@end

@implementation Person
@synthesize name;
@synthesize address;
-(id)initWithName:(NSString*) theName andAddress:(NSString*) theAddress{
  self = [super init];
  if(self){
    self.name    =    theName;
    self.address =    theAddress;
  }
  return self;
}
-(id)init{
  return [self initWithName:@"" andAddress:@""];
}
-(void)dealloc{
  [name    release];
  [address  release];
  [super  dealloc];
}

// Implementing copyWithZone: declared  in NSCopying
-(id)copyWithZone:(NSZone *)zone{
    Person *aPerson =
        [[[self class] allocWithZone: zone]
            initWithName:[self name] andAddress:[self address]];
    return aPerson;
}
@end
```

Listing 3.6 shows the demonstration code for acquiring a deep copy of an NSArray object. We use the same class method arrayWithObjects: that we used before to get a new instance of NSArray. The objects, however, are now copies of the original objects: a, b, c, d, and e.

Listing 3.6 Implementing a deep copy of an array of objects.

```
int main(int argc, char *argv[]){
  NSAutoreleasePool *pool = [[NSAutoreleasePool alloc] init];
  Person *a  = [[Person alloc] init];
  Person *b  = [[Person alloc] init];
  Person *c  = [[Person alloc] init];
  Person *d  = [[Person alloc] init];
  Person *e  = [[Person alloc] init];
```

```
NSArray *arr1 = [NSArray   arrayWithObjects: a,b,c,d,e,nil];
NSArray *arr2 = [NSArray  arrayWithObjects:
    [[a copy] autorelease],
    [[b copy] autorelease],
    [[c copy] autorelease],
    [[d copy] autorelease],
    [[e copy] autorelease],
    nil
  ];
Person *aPerson =   [arr1  objectAtIndex:0];
aPerson.name  = @"Marge Simpson";
aPerson.address = @"Springfield";
// Result of the following line is:
// Person at 0 is: Name: , Addr:
printf("Person at %d is: Name: %s, Addr: %s\n",
    0, [[[arr2 objectAtIndex:0] name]
           cStringUsingEncoding:NSUTF8StringEncoding],
    [[[arr2 objectAtIndex:0] address]
           cStringUsingEncoding:NSUTF8StringEncoding]);
// must release all objects
[a release];
[b release];
[c release];
[d release];
[e release];
[pool release];
return 0;
}
```

Because the copy message returns a new object that we own, we send an autorelease message to the copy object before adding it to the new array. At the end of creating and initializing the new array, the state of the objects is as depicted in Figure 3.5.

As the figure illustrates, the arrays are independent. Every object involved is unique and has its own identity. If we change an element in arr1, no change occurs in arr2, and vice versa. This is illustrated in the code when we change the state of the object at index 0 in arr1 and observe no change in arr2 or in its contained objects.

To clean up, we only need to release the objects a, b, c, d, e, and pool. All other objects are autoreleased and will be released when we release the autorelease pool at the end.

3.1.4   Sorting an array

There are several approaches available to you for sorting an array. The two main options available are (1) write a function that finds the proper order of two objects and (2) add a method to your class that enables an instance to compare itself with another instance of the same class.

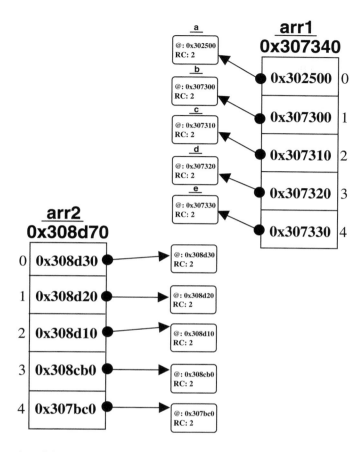

Figure 3.5   Illustration of the state of the objects involved in a deep copy of the contents of an array of objects.

In Listing 3.7, we have updated the Person class as follows. First, we added a new instance variable called personID of type NSInteger (which is basically an **int**), and second, we added a new method nameAscCompare: that enables a Person object to compare itself with another Person instance.

Listing 3.7   The updated Person class with a sorting method.

```
#import <Foundation/Foundation.h>

@interface Person : NSObject{
  NSString    *name;
  NSString    *address;
  NSInteger   personID;
}
@property(copy) NSString  *name;
```

```
@property(copy) NSString  *address;
@property NSInteger personID;

-(id)initWithName:(NSString*) theName andAddress:(NSString*) theAddress
     andID:(NSInteger) theID;
-(id)init;
- (NSComparisonResult)nameAscCompare:(Person *)aPerson;
@end

@implementation Person
@synthesize name;
@synthesize address;
@synthesize personID;

-(id)initWithName:(NSString*) theName andAddress:(NSString*) theAddress
      andID:(NSInteger) theID{
  self = [super init];
  if(self){
    self.name = theName;
    self.address  = theAddress;
    personID = theID;
  }
  return self;
}
-(id)init{
  return [self initWithName:@"" andAddress:@"" andID:0];
}
-(void)dealloc{
  [name    release];
  [address  release];
  [super   dealloc];
}

- (NSComparisonResult)nameAscCompare:(Person *)aPerson{
  return [name caseInsensitiveCompare:[aPerson name]];
}
@end
```

Suppose you want to sort an array containing Person objects in ascending order by personID. NSArray provides an instance method called sortedArrayUsingFunction:context:. This method is declared as follows:

```
- (NSArray *)sortedArrayUsingFunction:
            (NSInteger (*)(id, id, void *))comparator
            context:(void *)context
```

The first parameter is a pointer to a function that takes two arbitrary objects as the first two parameters and (void*) as the third parameter. It returns an NSInteger. The second parameter is a generic C pointer so that your implementation, if it wishes to, can use it as a context. This second pointer is actually the third pointer used in each call made to your implementation of `comparator`.

Your implementation of the `comparator` function should return

- `NSOrderedAscending`, if the first object is less than the second
- `NSOrderedSame`, if the two objects have the same ordering
- `NSOrderedDescending`, if the first object is greater than the second.

In Listing 3.8, we show the function `intSort()` that will be used as the `comparator`. The implementation of this function depends on the requirements of the application. Here, we just compare the `personID` of the two objects and return an appropriate comparison result.

Listing 3.8   Two different schemes for sorting an array.

```
NSInteger intSort(id p1, id p2, void *context){
    int v1 = [(Person*)p1 personID];
    int v2 = [(Person*)p2 personID];
    if (v1 < v2)
        return NSOrderedAscending;
    else if (v1 > v2)
        return NSOrderedDescending;
    else
        return NSOrderedSame;
}


int main(int argc, char *argv[]){
    NSAutoreleasePool *pool = [[NSAutoreleasePool alloc] init];
    Person  *a  = [[Person alloc]
                    initWithName:@"Kate Austen" andAddress:@"" andID:5];
    Person  *b  = [[Person alloc]
                    initWithName:@"Sayid Jarrah" andAddress:@"" andID:4];
    Person  *c  = [[Person alloc]
                    initWithName:@"Sun Kwon" andAddress:@"" andID:1];
    Person  *d  = [[Person alloc]
                    initWithName:@"Hurley Reyes" andAddress:@"" andID:2];
    Person  *e  = [[Person alloc]
                    initWithName:@"Jack Shephard" andAddress:@"" andID:3];
    NSArray *arr1 = [NSArray  arrayWithObjects: a,b,c,d,e,nil];
    NSArray *intSortedArray =
            [arr1 sortedArrayUsingFunction:intSort context:NULL];
    NSArray *strSortedArray =
            [arr1 sortedArrayUsingSelector:@selector(nameAscCompare:)];
    // must release all objects
    [a release];
    [b release];
    [c release];
```

```
    [d release];
    [e release];
    [pool release];
    return 0;
}
```

In Listing 3.8, we send the following message to `arr1`:

```
sortedArrayUsingFunction:intSort context:NULL
```

We store the new array reference in `intSortedArray`. Note that the new array is `autoreleased` and the objects in it are the same as objects in the original array, `arr1`.

The second approach to sorting an array is equipping the object with a way to compare itself with other siblings. Listing 3.7 shows the addition of the new method: `nameAscCompare:`. This method simply compares the value of the instance variable `name` with the other object's `name` instance variable. It uses the `caseInsensitiveCompare:` method to do the actual comparison.

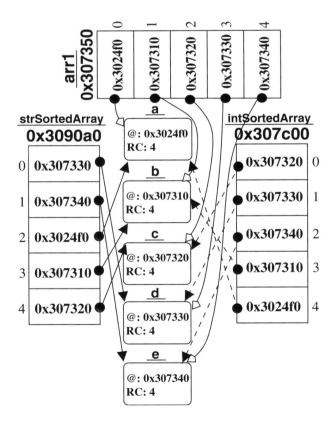

Figure 3.6   State of original array and two copies of it, sorted differently.

In Listing 3.8, we show how we can sort the array using this method. We use the `sortedArrayUsingSelector:` method. Notice that no context is needed as a parameter because you have the **self** and class object pointers.

Figure 3.6 shows the state of the three array objects and their elements. Notice how the retain count of the array elements is now 4 (1 for each array and 1 for the `alloc`).

3.2   Sets

We saw in the previous section how we can store ordered objects in an array. Some scenarios, however, do not require object ordering, but are mostly concerned with maintaining unique objects and providing a fast verification mechanism on object membership.

The set collection provides such a behavior. As in the array case, sets come in two flavors: (1) static sets represented by the `NSSet` class and (2) dynamic or mutable sets represented by the `NSMutableSet` class.

3.2.1   Immutable sets

Listing 3.9 provides a sample code demonstrating the use of immutable sets.

To create an immutable set, you have to specify the members during the initialization phase. The method `initWithObjects:` does just that. This method is similar to the one in the `NSArray` class. The code below creates three sets.

Listing 3.9   Demonstration of immutable sets.

```
NSSet    *favoriteShows = [[NSSet alloc] initWithObjects:
             @"Everybody Loves Raymond",
             @"Lost",
             @"Nova",
             @"Late Show",
             @"Tom and Jerry",
             nil
             ];
NSSet    *reallyFavoriteShows = [[NSSet alloc] initWithObjects:
             @"Everybody Loves Raymond",
             @"Lost",
             nil
             ];
NSSet *hatedShows = [[NSSet alloc] initWithObjects:
             @"Heroes",
             @"60 Minutes",
             @"The Tonight Show",
             @"Deal or No Deal",
             nil
             ];
printf("Number of elements = %d\n", [favoriteShows count]);
```

```
if( [favoriteShows intersectsSet:hatedShows] == YES){
    printf("makes no sense!\n");
}
if( [reallyFavoriteShows isSubsetOfSet:favoriteShows] == YES){
    printf("makes sense!\n");
}

if( [reallyFavoriteShows isEqualToSet:favoriteShows] == YES){
    printf("makes some sense!\n");
}

NSString *anyShow =[favoriteShows anyObject];
if([hatedShows containsObject:anyShow] == YES){
  printf("makes no sense!\n");
}
```

To find the number of elements in a set, use the count instance method.

NSSet also provides methods that implement the mathematical operations defined on a set. For example, the code above demonstrates how you can find whether a set instance intersects (has common elements) with another set. The intersectsSet: method is declared as

```
- (BOOL)intersectsSet:(NSSet *)otherSet
```

It returns YES if at least one element is shared by the receiver and otherSet, and NO otherwise.

You can also test if a set instance is a subset of another set using the isSubsetOfSet:, declared as

```
- (BOOL)isSubsetOfSet:(NSSet *)otherSet
```

For this method to return YES, every element in the receiver must be present in otherSet.

If you want to see if all members of the receiver are present in another set and vice versa, use the method isEqualToSet:. The method returns YES if and only if the number of elements in the receiver and the argument set is the same and every element available in the receiver is also found in the argument set. The method is declared as follows:

```
- (BOOL)isEqualToSet:(NSSet *)otherSet
```

The method anyObject returns an arbitrary (not necessarily random) element in the set. The method containsObject: returns YES if a given element is present in a set and NO otherwise. It is declared as

```
- (BOOL)containsObject:(id)anObject
```

3.2.2 Mutable sets

Listing 3.10 is a continuation of Listing 3.9. Here, we continue our example and demonstrate the dynamic version of the set collection: NSMutableSet.

Listing 3.10   Demonstration of mutable sets.

```
NSMutableSet  *dynamicSet = [[NSMutableSet alloc] initWithCapacity:2];
[dynamicSet addObject:@"Lost"];
[dynamicSet addObject:@"Nova"];
[dynamicSet addObject:@"Heroes"];
[dynamicSet addObject:@"Lost"];
[dynamicSet removeObject:@"Everybody Loves Raymond"];
[dynamicSet removeObject:@"Nova"];
printf("dynamicSet = %s\n", [[dynamicSet description] cString]);
[dynamicSet unionSet:reallyFavoriteShows];
printf("dynamicSet = %s\n", [[dynamicSet description] cString]);
[dynamicSet minusSet:reallyFavoriteShows];
printf("dynamicSet = %s\n", [[dynamicSet description] cString]);
```

To create a mutable set instance, you use `alloc` and set the initial capacity of the set. This initial capacity is not a limitation on the set size because it can grow and shrink dynamically. The statement `[[NSMutableSet alloc] initWithCapacity:2]` creates a new mutable set with an initial capacity of two elements.

To add an element to the set, use `addObject:`. As we saw in the array collection, the set does not copy the object you are adding, but it puts a claim on it by sending a `retain` message to it. If you add an element that is already in the set, the method has no effect on the set or the element. To remove an element from the set, use the `removeObject:` method. No side effect occurs if the element you are trying to remove is not found in the set.

After adding and removing objects from the set, we display the set using the `description:` method. The first `printf` statement produces

```
dynamicSet = {(
    Heroes,
    Lost
)}
```

You can merge (make a union) of two sets using `unionSet:` declared as

```
- (void)unionSet:(NSSet *)otherSet
```

The `unionSet:` adds every object in `otherSet` that is not a member of the receiver to the receiver. After the union operation, the `dynamicSet` is displayed as

```
dynamicSet = {(
    Everybody Loves Raymond,
    Heroes,
    Lost
)}
```

The method `minusSet:` is declared as

```
- (void)minusSet:(NSSet *)otherSet
```

It removes every member in `otherSet` from the receiver set. The content of `dynamicSet` after executing the statement `[dynamicSet minusSet:reallyFavoriteShows]` is

```
dynamicSet = {(
    Heroes
)}
```

3.2.3   Additional important methods for NSSet

To remove all elements of a set, you can use

- (**void**)removeAllObjects

To remove all elements of a set and then add all the elements in another set to it, use

- (**void**)setSet:(NSSet *)otherSet

If you have an array of elements and you would like to add all its elements to a set, use

- (**void**)addObjectsFromArray:(NSArray *)anArray

To send every object in a set a message, use

- (**void**)makeObjectsPerformSelector:(SEL)aSelector

The method specified by the selector `aSelector` must not take any arguments.

If you want to communicate with the members of the set using an object, you can use

- (**void**)makeObjectsPerformSelector:(SEL)aSelector
        withObject:(**id**)anObject

This method will use a selector representing a method that takes exactly one argument of type **id**. In both methods above, the selector must not change the set instance itself.

3.3   Dictionaries

The immutable `NSDictionary` and its mutable subclass `NSMutableDictionary` give you the ability to store your objects and retrieve them using keys. Each entry of the dictionary consists of a key and a value. The key can be any object as long as it adopts the `NSCopying` protocol. Usually, instances of the `NSString` class are used as keys, but any class can be used.

In a dictionary, keys have to be unique. Keys and values cannot be `nil`. The framework, however, provides you with the class `NSNull` for storing null objects. When you add entries to the dictionary, the dictionary class makes a copy of the key and uses this copy as the key to store the value object. The storage follows a hash model, but the classes shield you from the implementation details. The value object is retained rather than copied.

As with the array collection classes, once the immutable dictionary is initialized, you cannot add or remove entries to/from it. You can get a mutable dictionary from an immutable one and vice versa. Listing 3.11 demonstrates working with dictionaries.

Listing 3.11   Working with dictionaries.

```
#import <Foundation/Foundation.h>

int main(int argc, char *argv[]){
  NSAutoreleasePool * pool = [[NSAutoreleasePool alloc] init];
  NSMutableArray *kArr = [NSMutableArray arrayWithObjects:
                    @"1", @"2", @"3", @"4", nil];
  NSMutableArray *aArr = [NSMutableArray arrayWithObjects:@"2", nil];
  NSDictionary *guide =
                [NSDictionary dictionaryWithObjectsAndKeys:
                kArr, @"Kate", aArr, @"Ana-Lucia",  nil];

  NSEnumerator *enumerator = [guide keyEnumerator];
  id key;
  while ((key = [enumerator nextObject])) {
    if([[key  substringToIndex:1] isEqual:@"K"]){
      [[guide objectForKey:key]  addObject:@"5"];
    }
  }

  NSMutableDictionary *dynaGuide = [guide mutableCopy];
  for(key in dynaGuide){
    if([[key  substringToIndex:1] isEqual:@"A"]){
      [[dynaGuide objectForKey:key]  addObject:@"5"];
    }
  }
  NSArray *keys = [dynaGuide allKeys];
  for(key in keys){
    if([[key  substringToIndex:1] isEqual:@"A"]){
      [dynaGuide  removeObjectForKey:key];
    }
  }
  [dynaGuide release];
  [pool release];
  return 0;
}
```

In the code above, we create an immutable dictionary whose keys are strings and whose values are mutable arrays. The creation of the dictionary is achieved using the method `dictionaryWithObjectsAndKeys:`. The method takes a list of alternating values and keys that is null-terminated.

To access the values stored in a dictionary, you can use an enumerator of the keys. The method `keyEnumerator` returns such an enumerator from a dictionary object. The code uses the enumerator to check for all objects whose key starts with A. For each such key, it updates the value stored in that entry. To retrieve the value of a given key, you use the `objectForKey:` method.

To generate a mutable copy of a dictionary, you use the `mutableCopy` method. This will create a new mutable dictionary initialized with the recipient dictionary's element. Because the method used has a `copy` in it, you own that object and you should release it when you're done with it.

Another way to traverse the dictionary is to use fast enumeration. The line **for**(key **in** dynaGuide) enumerates the keys in the dictionary dynaGuide.

You can add/remove entries to/from a mutable dictionary. To remove a given entry, you use the `removeObjectForKey:` method. You should not, however, do that while enumerating a dictionary. You should, instead, make a snapshot of the keys and then update the dictionary. To get an NSArray instance of all the keys, use the `allKeys` method. Once you have that, you can enumerate the keys and update the dictionary as you wish.

The method `isEqualToDictionary:` returns YES if the receiver has the same number of entries, and for every key, the corresponding values in the two dictionaries are equal (i.e., `isEqual:` returns YES). The method is declared as follows:

- (BOOL)isEqualToDictionary:(NSDictionary *)otherDictionary

The method `allValues` creates a new array with the values contained in the dictionary entries. The method is declared as follows:

- (NSArray *)allValues

The method `keysSortedByValueUsingSelector:` generates an array of keys ordered by sorting the values using a comparator. The method is declared as follows:

- (NSArray *)keysSortedByValueUsingSelector:(SEL)comparator

The method `addEntriesFromDictionary:` adds the entries in `otherDictionary` to the receiver of the message. If the receiver already has an entry with the same key, that entry receives a `release` before being replaced. The method is declared as follows:

- (**void**) addEntriesFromDictionary:(NSDictionary *)otherDictionary

3.4   Summary

This chapter covered the topic of collections. Collections are Cocoa objects that act as containers to other Cocoa objects. We introduced three types of collections defined in the Foundation Framework. We first discussed the array collection in Section 3.1. Immutable arrays are instances of the NSArray class. NSArray allows for the creation of a static array that cannot be changed once initialized. The mutable version of NSArray is NSMutableArray. An instance of NSMutableArray can be modified by adding and removing elements during the lifetime of the program. The NSArray is more efficient than the NSMutableArray class. You should use instances of NSArray if the array is not required to change once initialized.

We discussed the concepts of shallow and deep copying. A shallow copy of an object is a new instance that shares the references (pointers) to other objects that the original object has. A deep copy, by contrast, propagates the copying to the referenced objects. Collections implement a shallow copy regardless of what kind of objects they hold. For a class to implement a deep copy, it needs to adopt the NSCopying protocol and implement the copyWithZone: method. To produce a deep copy of a collection, you need to iterate through the objects contained in that collection, sending a copy message to each object, autoreleaseing each object, and adding it to the collection, in that order.

We also discussed sorting and presented two schemes to accomplish that: (1) using a function for comparing two instances or (2) adding a method so that an instance can compare itself with another. The first scheme is employed in the array instance method sortedArrayUsing-Function:context:, while the second scheme is employed in the array instance method sorted-ArrayUsingSelector:.

In Section 3.2, we covered the set collection. Immutable sets are instances of the NSSet class, while mutable sets are instances of NSMutableSet. We also presented several methods that implement mathematically inspired set operations.

In Section 3.3, we covered the dictionary collection. Dictionaries allow for the retrieval of objects using keys. Several examples were presented illustrating immutable and mutable dictionaries.

Exercises

(1) List all the ways you can create an empty NSArray instance.

(2) What's wrong with the following statement? Assume array property is declared as retain.

```
self.array = [[NSArray alloc] initWithArray:[NSArray array]];
```

(3) Write a method that returns a sorted array from an array of dictionaries. Base your sorting on the key name.

(4) Study the header file NSDictionary.h.

4

Anatomy of an iPhone Application

This chapter discusses the basic steps needed to build a simple iPhone application. Section 4.1 demonstrates the basic structure of a simple iPhone application. Next, Section 4.2 shows the steps needed to write the application using XCode. Finally, Section 4.3 summarizes the chapter.

4.1 Hello World Application

This section demonstrates the basic structure of a simple iPhone application that displays the message `Hello World!` to the user. Follow these steps to develop the application.

4.1.1 Create a main.m file

As in any C program, the execution of Objective-C applications starts from `main()`. You need to create the `main()` function in the `main.m` file as follows:

```
#import <UIKit/UIKit.h>

int main(int argc, char *argv[]) {
  NSAutoreleasePool * pool = [[NSAutoreleasePool alloc] init];
  int retVal = UIApplicationMain(argc,argv,nil,@"HelloWorldAppDelegate");
  [pool release];
  return retVal;
}
```

The `main()` function starts by creating an autorelease pool and ends by releasing it. In between, it makes a call to the `UIApplicationMain()` function. `UIApplicationMain()` is declared as follows:

```
int UIApplicationMain(int argc, char *argv[],NSString *principalClassName,
                      NSString *delegateClassName)
```

This function takes four parameters. The first two parameters are the arguments passed in to the `main()` function. These parameters should be familiar to any C programmer. The third parameter is the name of the application class. If a `nil` is specified, the UIApplication class is used to instantiate the unique application object. The fourth and last parameter is the name of the application delegate class.

The `UIApplicationMain()` instantiates the application and the application delegate objects. After that, it sets the delegate property of the application object to the application delegate instance. The main run loop of the application is established. From this moment on, events, such as user touches, are queued by the system, and the application object dequeues these events and delivers them to the appropriate objects in your application (usually the main window.)

The `main.m` file is generated automatically when you create the project as we shall see shortly.

4.1.2   Create the application delegate class

The instance of the application delegate class will receive important messages from the application object during the lifetime of the application. The following is a typical application delegate class:

```
#import <UIKit/UIKit.h>

@class MyView;
@interface HelloWorldAppDelegate : NSObject <UIApplicationDelegate> {
    UIWindow      *window;
    MyView        *view;
}
@end
```

Notice that the application delegate class adopts the UIApplicationDelegate protocol. In addition, references to the user-interface objects that will be created and presented to the user are stored in instance variables. Most of the time, you will have one window object and several views attached to it. In the example above, the variable `window` stores a reference to the main window object and `view` is used to store a reference to a custom view of type `MyView`.

One of the most important methods of the UIApplicationDelegate protocol is the `applicationDidFinishLaunching:` method. This method is invoked by the application object to inform the delegate that the application has finished launching. You usually implement this method to initialize the application and create the user interface. The following is a listing of the implementation of the application delegate class. In the `applicationDidFinishLaunching:` method, we first create the main window of the application.

```
#import "HelloWorldAppDelegate.h"
#import "MyView.h"

@implementation HelloWorldAppDelegate

- (void)applicationDidFinishLaunching:(UIApplication *)application {
  window=[[UIWindow alloc] initWithFrame:[[UIScreen  mainScreen] bounds]];
  CGRect    frame = [UIScreen mainScreen].applicationFrame;
```

```
    view = [[MyView alloc] initWithFrame:frame];
    view.message = @"Hello World!";
    view.backgroundColor =[UIColor whiteColor];
    [window addSubview:view];
    [window makeKeyAndVisible];
}

- (void)dealloc {
    [view   release];
    [window release];
    [super dealloc];
}
@end
```

Windows are instances of the class UIWindow. UIWindow is a subclass of the UIView class. UIView is the base class of user-interface objects. It provides access to handling user gestures as well as drawings. Like any other object, a UIWindow instance is allocated and then initialized. The initializer (as we shall see in Chapter 5) specifies the frame that the window object will occupy. After that, an instance of the MyView class is created and initialized with the frame that it will occupy. After configuring the MyView instance and setting its background color, we add it as a subview to the window and make the window object key and visible.

The application delegate class is generated automatically for you when you create the project. You need, however, to customize it for your own needs.

4.1.3   Create the user interface subclasses

To receive the user events (e.g., the touches) and draw in the view, you need to create a subclass of UIView and override its event-handling and drawing methods. The declaration of the MyView class used in our HelloWorld application is shown below:

```
#import <UIKit/UIKit.h>

@interface MyView : UIView {
    NSString  *message;
}
@property(nonatomic, retain) NSString *message;
@end
```

The implementation of the MyView class is shown below. This class overrides the event-handling method for ending of touches (we will cover the multitouch interface in the next chapter) and the drawRect: for drawing in the view area.

For drawing, we simply draw the contents of the message instance variable with a specific font. Whenever the user's finger is lifted from the screen, that event is stored in the application queue. The application object retrieves the event from the queue and sends it to the main window. The window searches its subviews for the view that should receive this event and delivers that event to it. In our example, because `MyView` instance spans the screen, all touch events will be delivered to it and the `touchesEnded:withEvent:` method will be invoked. You can put your code in this method to update the state of the application, change its appearance, or both.

The `dealloc` method releases memory owned by the view and propagates the deallocation process to **super**. Notice how the instance variable `message` is released by relying on the behavior of the synthesized setter. By assigning a `nil` value to the property, the synthesized setter first releases the memory and then sets the value of the instance variable to `nil`.

```
#import "MyView.h"

@implementation MyView
@synthesize message;

- (void)touchesEnded:(NSSet *)touches withEvent:(UIEvent *)event{
  if( [(UITouch*)[touches anyObject] tapCount] == 2){
    // handle a double-tap
  }
}

- (void)drawRect:(CGRect)rect{
    [message drawAtPoint:CGPointMake(60,180)
            withFont:[UIFont systemFontOfSize:32]];
}

-(void)dealloc{
  self.message = nil;
  [super dealloc];
}
```

4.2   Building the Hello World Application

The following are the steps you need to take to realize the `HelloWorld` application.

1. **Create a new project in XCode.** In XCode, select `File→New Project` and select the `Window-Based Application` template (Figure 4.1). Name the project `HelloWorld` and click `Save` as shown in Figure 4.2.

2. **Update the project for building the user interface programmatically.** You can create the user interface with Interface Builder, programmatically, or both. Interface Builder accelerates the development process, but it also hides important concepts. If you are a beginner, we suggest that you build the user interface programmatically and do not rely on Interface Builder. This will help you understand what is going on. Once you have mastered this subject, you can use Interface Builder in your development.

   The project template assumes that you are using Interface Builder, so you need to make some small changes to fully use the programmatic approach. Select the `Info.plist` file in the

Figure 4.1   Choosing a template for a new project.

Figure 4.2   Naming a new project.

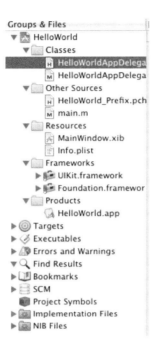

Figure 4.3   The `Groups & Files` window.

`Groups & Files` window (Figure 4.3) so that its content appears in the editor. Right-click on `Main nib file base name` and select `Cut`. Right-click on the file `MainWindow.xib` in the `Groups & Files` window and select `Delete`. Click on `Also Move to Trash`.

Select the `main.m` file and change the `UIApplicationMain()` invocation by adding the name of the application delegate class to it as shown below:

```
int retVal=UIApplicationMain(argc,argv,nil,@"HelloWorldAppDelegate");
```

3. **Write your code.** Select the `HelloWorldAppDelegate.h` file and replace its content with the listing described in the previous section. Do the same for the `HelloWorldAppDelegate.m` file.

4. **Create a subclass of UIView.** Select `File→New File`, select the `UIView` subclass, and hit `Next` (see Figure 4.4). Name the file `MyView.m` and hit `Finish` (see Figure 4.5). A subclass of `UIView` will be created for you. Change the contents of `MyView.h` and `MyView.m` with the listings shown in the previous section.

5. **Build and run the application.** Click on `Build and Go` (see Figure 4.6) to build and launch the application (see Figure 4.7).

The source code for this application can be found in the `HelloWorld` project, available in the source downloads.

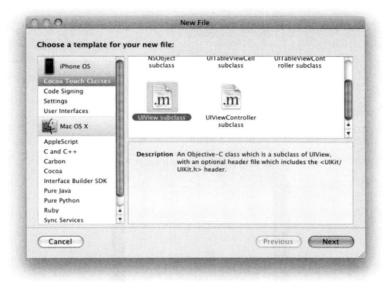

Figure 4.4   Choosing a template for a new file.

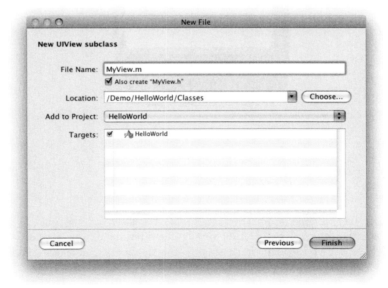

Figure 4.5   Naming the new UIView subclass.

Figure 4.6   The XCode toolbar.

Figure 4.7   The `HelloWorld` application.

4.3   Summary

The execution of any iPhone application starts in the `main()` function. In this function, you create an autorelease pool to be used during the lifetime of the application. After that, the `UIApplicationMain()` is called, passing in the application delegate class name as the last argument.

The application delegate class, a skeleton of which is produced automatically when you create a new project, creates a window, attaches additional views to it, and makes it key and visible. From that point on, the application runs an infinite loop looking for external events such as screen touches, external data, external devices, etc. When an event occurs, your application changes its view hierarchy, the content of the current views, or both.

In the rest of the book, you will learn about views, data representation and manipulation, devices, and much more.

Exercises

(1) Locate the `UIApplication.h` header file and familiarize yourself with it.

(2) Locate the `UIView.h` header file and familiarize yourself with it.

5

The View

This chapter explains the main concepts behind views. You learn about view geometry in Section 5.1. In Section 5.2, we cover the topic of view hierarchy. Next, Section 5.3 discusses, in great detail, the multitouch interface. In this section, you learn how to recognize multitouch gestures. After that, we discuss several animation techniques in Section 5.4. Next, Section 5.5 deals with how to use Quartz 2D functions for drawing inside a view. Finally, we summarize the chapter in Section 5.6.

5.1 View Geometry

This section covers the three geometric properties of the `UIView` class that you need to understand: `frame`, `bounds`, and `center`. Before explaining these properties, let's first look at some of the structures and functions used in specifying their values.

5.1.1 Useful geometric type definitions

The following types are used throughout the text:

- `CGFloat` represents a floating-point number and is defined as

  ```
  typedef float CGFloat;
  ```

- `CGPoint` is a structure that represents a geometric point. It is defined as

  ```
  struct CGPoint {
     CGFloat x;
     CGFloat y;
  };
  typedef struct CGPoint CGPoint;
  ```

  The x value represents the x coordinate of the point and the y value represents its y coordinate.

You will use CGPoint a lot. CGPointMake() is a convenient function defined to make a CGPoint from a pair of x and y values, and is defined as follows:

```
CGPoint CGPointMake (
    CGFloat x,
    CGFloat y
);
```

- CGSize is a structure used to represent width and height values. It is declared as follows:

```
struct CGSize {
    CGFloat width;
    CGFloat height;
};
typedef struct CGSize CGSize;
```

width is the width value and height is the height value.

To make a CGSize structure from a width and a height, use the utility function CGSizeMake(), declared as follows:

```
CGSize CGSizeMake (
    CGFloat width,
    CGFloat height
);
```

- CGRect is used to represent the location and dimensions of a rectangle. It is declared as follows:

```
struct CGRect {
    CGPoint origin;
    CGSize size;
};
typedef struct CGRect CGRect;
```

The origin value represents the upper-left point of the rectangle, and size represents its dimensions (i.e., its width and height).

To make a CGRect structure, you can use the utility function CGRectMake() declared as follows:

```
CGRect CGRectMake (
    CGFloat x,
    CGFloat y,
    CGFloat width,
    CGFloat height
);
```

5.1.2   The UIScreen class

The UIScreen class is provided to you in order to obtain the dimensions of the device's screen. The device's screen is 320×480 abstract points as shown in Figure 5.1.

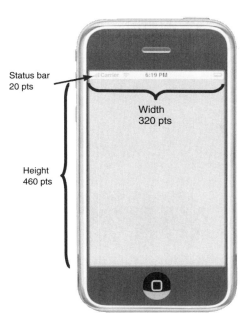

Figure 5.1   The dimensions of the device screen.

The status bar takes 20 points from the total height, leaving 460 points for the application. You can turn off the status bar using the following statement:

```
[UIApplication sharedApplication].statusBarHidden = YES;
```

You can retrieve the size of the device's screen as follows:

```
[[UIScreen  mainScreen] bounds].size
```

In the above statement, we first obtain the singleton UIScreen instance and then obtain the size of its bounding rectangle.

The application window resides just below the status bar. To retrieve the application's frame, use the following statement:

```
CGRect frame =  [[UIScreen  mainScreen] applicationFrame]
```

If there is a status bar, the application's frame is 320×460. Otherwise, it is equal to the screen's bounds.

5.1.3   The frame and center properties

The UIView class declares the frame property, which is used to locate and dimension the UIView instance inside another UIView instance. The property is declared as follows:

```
@property(nonatomic) CGRect frame
```

You usually specify the frame of a view during the initialization phase. For example, the following creates a UIView instance whose origin is located at (50, 100) in its superview's coordinates and whose width and height are 150 and 200, respectively.

```
CGRect  frame = CGRectMake(50, 100, 150, 200);
aView = [[UIView alloc] initWithFrame:frame];
[window addSubview:aView];
```

Figure 5.2 shows the result of adding the above UIView instance to a full-screen window (minus the status bar).

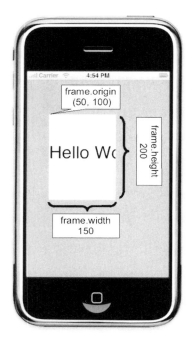

Figure 5.2   The frame geometric property for a subview of a main window.

The origin of this view is (50, 100) and its center is (125, 200), all in the parent view's (window) coordinates.

Changes to the center will result in changes to the origin of the frame. Similarly, changes to the origin or to the size of the frame will result in changes in the center. For the example above, if the x coordinate of the center property is increased by 80 points, the frame's origin will be equal to (130, 100), which would result in the view being shifted as a whole a distance of 80 points to the right as shown in Figure 5.3.

Figure 5.3   Moving the view location by changing its center property.

5.1.4 The bounds property

The bounds property is used to specify the origin and size of the view in the view's own coordinate system. The property is declared as follows:

```
@property(nonatomic) CGRect bounds
```

When you initialize the view, the bound's origin is set to (0, 0) and its size is set to frame.size. Changes to the bounds.origin have no effect on the frame and center properties. Changes to bounds.size, however, will result in a change in the frame and center properties.

As an example, consider Figure 5.2. The bound.origin is equal to (0, 0). The view draws a string's value as shown below:

```
- (void)drawRect:(CGRect)rect {
  int x = 0;
  int y = self.bounds.size.height/3;
  [@"Hello World!"
      drawAtPoint:CGPointMake(x,y)
      withFont:[UIFont systemFontOfSize:40]];
}
```

The x axis of the point at which the string `"Hello World!"` is drawn is equal to 0. If we change the value of `bounds.origin.x` from 0 to 50, the string drawn will move 50 to the left as shown in Figure 5.4.

Figure 5.4 Changes to the `bounds` property's `origin` affect the content of the view, not its dimension/location.

5.2 The View Hierarchy

Most of the time, you will have one main window for the application and several views and controls with different sizes and locations. The main window (an instance of `UIWindow`, which is a subclass of `UIView`) will act as a root of a tree. When you want to add a view to the application, you add that view to the window or to an existing view. Eventually, you end up with a tree structure rooted at that window. Every view will have exactly one parent view called the *superview* and zero or more child views called *subviews*. To access the superview instance, use the property `superview`, which is declared as follows:

```
@property(nonatomic, readonly) UIView *superview
```

To retrieve the children of a given view, use the property `subviews`, which is declared as follows:

```
@property(nonatomic, readonly, copy) NSArray *subviews
```

To add a view to an existing view, you allocate it, initialize it, configure it, and then add it as a subview. The following two statements create a view that occupies the full screen (minus the status bar):

```
CGRect  frame = [UIScreen mainScreen].applicationFrame;
view1 = [[UIView alloc] initWithFrame:frame];
```

The initializer that is usually used is the `initWithFrame:` initializer.

To add a view as a subview, use the `addSubview:` method, which is declared as follows:

- (**void**)addSubview:(UIView *)view

After invoking this method, the superview will `retain` the instance `view`.

To remove a view from the view hierarchy, you use the method `removeFromSuperview`. In addition to removing the view from the tree, this method will `release` the view.

5.3   The Multitouch Interface

When the user touches the screen, he or she is requesting feedback from the application. Given that the application presents multiple views, subviews, and controls to the user at the same time, there is a need for the system to figure out which object is the intended recipient of the user's touches.

Every application has a single `UIApplication` object for handling users' touches. When the user touches the screen, the system packages the touches in an event object and puts that event object in the application's event queue. This event object is an instance of the class `UIEvent`.

The event object contains all the touches that are currently on the screen. Each finger on the screen has its own touch object, an instance of the class `UITouch`. As you will see later, each touch object can be in different phases, such as has just touched the screen, moving, stationary, etc. Each time the user touches the screen, the event object and the touches objects get mutated to reflect the change.

The `UIApplication` unique instance picks up the event object from the queue and sends it to the key window object (an instance of `UIWindow` class). The window object, through a mechanism called *hit testing*, figures out which subview should receive that event and dispatches the event to it. This object is referred to as the *first responder*. If that object is interested in handling the event, it does so and the event is considered as delivered. If, on the other hand, that object is not interested in handling the event, it passes it through a linked list of objects called the *responder chain*.

The responder chain of a given object starts from that object and ends in the application object. If any object on this chain accepts the event, then the event's propagation towards the application instance stops. If the application instance receives the event and does not know of a valid recipient of it, it throws that event away.

5.3.1   The UITouch class

Each finger touching the screen is encapsulated by an object of the `UITouch` class. Following are some of the important properties and methods of this class:

- `phase`. This property is used to retrieve the current phase of the touch. The property is declared as follows:

  ```
  @property(nonatomic,readonly) UITouchPhase    phase
  ```

  There are several `UITouchPhase` values, including:

  > `UITouchPhaseBegan`, which indicates that the finger touched the screen.
  > `UITouchPhaseMoved`, which indicates that the finger moved on the screen.
  > `UITouchPhaseStationary`, which indicates that the finger has not moved on the screen since the last event.
  > `UITouchPhaseEnded`, which indicates that the finger has left the screen.
  > `UITouchPhaseCancelled`, which indicates that the touch is being canceled by the system.

- `timestamp`. This property is the time when the touch changed its phase. The `UITouch` object keeps mutating during an event. This value refers to the last mutation.

- `tapCount`. This property is the number of taps that the user made when he or she touched the screen. Successive tapping on the same place will result in a tap count greater than `1`. The property is declared as follows:

  ```
  @property(nonatomic,readonly) NSUInteger    tapCount
  ```

- `locationInView:`. This method returns the location of the touch in a given view. The method is declared as follows:

  ```
  - (CGPoint)locationInView:(UIView *)view
  ```

  The returned value is in the coordinate system of `view`. If you pass `nil`, the returned value is in the window's coordinate system.

- `previousLocationInView:`. The previous location of the touch in a given view can be retrieved using this method. The method is declared as follows:

  ```
  - (CGPoint)previousLocationInView:(UIView *)view
  ```

5.3.2   The UIEvent class

A multitouch sequence is captured by an object of the class `UIEvent`. The application will receive the same `UIEvent` object throughout its lifetime. This object will be mutated during the execution of the application. You can retrieve the time stamp of this event using the `timestamp` property. To retrieve the touches that this event represents, use the `allTouches` method, which is declared as follows:

```
- (NSSet *) allTouches
```

5.3.3 The UIResponder class

User interface objects, such as instances of `UIView`, receiving touches are subclasses of the `UIResponder` class. To understand the multitouch interface, we need to understand the `UIResponder` class and its four main multitouch-handling methods.

The following are the main methods that subclasses of `UIResponder` class (such as `UIView` subclasses) need to override in order to handle gestures:

- `touchesBegan:withEvent:`. This method is invoked to tell the responder object that one or more fingers just touched the screen. The method is declared as follows:

    - (**void**)touchesBegan:(NSSet *)touches withEvent:(UIEvent *)event

    The first parameter is a set of `UITouch` objects that have just touched the screen. The second parameter is the event these touches are associated with.

- `touchesMoved:withEvent:`. This method is invoked to tell the responder object that one or more fingers just moved on the screen. The method is declared as follows:

    - (**void**)touchesMoved:(NSSet *)touches withEvent:(UIEvent *)event

    The first parameter is a set of `UITouch` objects that just moved on the screen. The second parameter is the event these touches are associated with.

- `touchesEnded:withEvent:`. This method is invoked to tell the responder object that one or more fingers just lifted from the screen. The method is declared as follows:

    - (**void**)touchesEnded:(NSSet *)touches withEvent:(UIEvent *)event

    The first parameter is a set of `UITouch` objects that just lifted from the screen. The second parameter is the event these touches are associated with.

- `touchesCancelled:withEvent:`. This method is invoked by the system to tell the responder object that the event has been canceled. The method is declared as follows:

    - (**void**)touchesCancelled:(NSSet *)touches withEvent:(UIEvent *)event

    The first parameter is a set containing a single `UITouch` object whose phase is `UITouchPhaseCancel`. The second parameter is the event that has been canceled.

It is best to understand the multitouch mechanism through a detailed example. Let's imagine three fingers — `F1`, `F2`, and `F3` — touching the screen, moving on the screen, and ending at various times. We will show the invocation of the responder's methods as a result of these fingers. For each invocation, we show the content of the `touches` set as well as the `allTouches` set of the `event` object.

The following assumes a starting condition just prior to step 1 where no fingers are touching the screen:

1. Two fingers, F1 and F2, touched the screen.
   touchesBegan:withEvent: is called.
   touches: a set of two elements:

   ```
   Touch T1 representing F1:  <UITouch: 0x14a360>  phase: Began
   Touch T2 representing F2:  <UITouch: 0x14a0f0>  phase: Began
   ```

   event: <UIEvent: 0x143ae0>. The allTouches set:

   ```
   T1:  <UITouch: 0x14a360>  phase: Began
   T2:  <UITouch: 0x14a0f0>  phase: Began
   ```

2. Fingers F1 and F2 moved.
   touchesMoved:withEvent: is called.
   touches: a set of two elements:

   ```
   T1:  <UITouch: 0x14a360>  phase: Moved
   T2:  <UITouch: 0x14a0f0>  phase: Moved
   ```

   event: <UIEvent: 0x143ae0>. The allTouches set:

   ```
   T1:  <UITouch: 0x14a360>  phase: Moved
   T2:  <UITouch: 0x14a0f0>  phase: Moved
   ```

3. Finger F1 moved.
   touchesMoved:withEvent: is called.
   touches: a set of one element:

   ```
   T1:  <UITouch: 0x14a360>  phase: Moved
   ```

   event: <UIEvent: 0x143ae0>. The allTouches set:

   ```
   T1:  <UITouch: 0x14a360>  phase: Moved
   T2:  <UITouch: 0x14a0f0>  phase: Stationary
   ```

4. Finger F2 moved.
   touchesMoved:withEvent: is called.
   touches: a set of one element:

   ```
   T2:  <UITouch: 0x14a0f0>  phase: Moved
   ```

   event: <UIEvent: 0x143ae0>. The allTouches set:

   ```
   T1:  <UITouch: 0x14a360>  phase: Stationary
   T2:  <UITouch: 0x14a0f0>  phase: Moved
   ```

5. Finger F3 touched the screen, Finger F2 moved.
   touchesBegan:withEvent: is called.
   touches: a set of one element:

```
T3:   <UITouch: 0x145a10> phase: Began
```

event: <UIEvent: 0x143ae0>. The allTouches set:

```
T1:   <UITouch: 0x14a360> phase: Stationary
T2:   <UITouch: 0x14a0f0> phase: Moved
T3:   <UITouch: 0x145a10> phase: Began
```

touchesMoved:withEvent: is called.
touches: a set of one element:

```
T2:   <UITouch: 0x14a0f0> phase: Moved
```

event: <UIEvent: 0x143ae0>. The allTouches set:

```
T1:   <UITouch: 0x14a360> phase: Stationary
T2:   <UITouch: 0x14a0f0> phase: Moved
T3:   <UITouch: 0x145a10> phase: Began
```

6. Fingers F2 and F3 moved.
   touchesMoved:withEvent: is called.
   touches: a set of two elements:

```
T2:   <UITouch: 0x14a0f0> phase: Moved
T3:   <UITouch: 0x145a10> phase: Moved
```

event: <UIEvent: 0x143ae0>. The allTouches set:

```
T1:   <UITouch: 0x14a360> phase: Stationary
T2:   <UITouch: 0x14a0f0> phase: Moved
T3:   <UITouch: 0x145a10> phase: Moved
```

7. Finger F2 moved, Finger F3 lifted.
   touchesMoved:withEvent: is called.
   touches: a set of one element:

```
T2:   <UITouch: 0x14a0f0> phase: Moved
```

event: <UIEvent: 0x143ae0>. The allTouches set:

```
T1:   <UITouch: 0x14a360> phase: Stationary
T2:   <UITouch: 0x14a0f0> phase: Moved
T3:   <UITouch: 0x145a10> phase: Ended
```

touchesEnded:withEvent: is called.
touches: a set of one element:

```
T3: <UITouch: 0x145a10> phase: Ended
```

event: <UIEvent: 0x143ae0>. The allTouches set:

```
T1:   <UITouch: 0x14a360> phase: Stationary
T2:   <UITouch: 0x14a0f0> phase: Moved
T3:   <UITouch: 0x145a10> phase: Ended
```

8. Finger F2 moved.

   `touchesMoved:withEvent:` is called.

   `touches`: a set of one element:

   ```
   T2:   <UITouch: 0x14a0f0> phase: Moved
   ```

   event: `<UIEvent: 0x143ae0>`. The `allTouches` set:

   ```
   T1:   <UITouch: 0x14a360> phase: Stationary
   T2:   <UITouch: 0x14a0f0> phase: Moved
   ```

9. Finger F2 moved, Finger F1 lifted.

   `touchesMoved:withEvent:` is called.

   `touches`: a set of one element:

   ```
   T2:   <UITouch: 0x14a0f0> phase: Moved
   ```

   event: `<UIEvent: 0x143ae0>`. The `allTouches` set:

   ```
   T1:   <UITouch: 0x14a360> phase: Ended
   T2:   <UITouch: 0x14a0f0> phase: Moved
   ```

   `touchesEnded:withEvent:` is called.

   `touches`: a set of one element:

   ```
   T1:   <UITouch: 0x14a360> phase: Ended
   ```

   event: `<UIEvent: 0x143ae0>`. The `allTouches` set:

   ```
   T1:   <UITouch: 0x14a360> phase: Ended
   T2:   <UITouch: 0x14a0f0> phase: Moved
   ```

10. Finger F2 moved.

    `touchesMoved:withEvent:` is called.

    `touches`: a set of one element:

    ```
    T2:   <UITouch: 0x14a0f0> phase: Moved
    ```

    event: `<UIEvent: 0x143ae0>`. The `allTouches` set:

    ```
    T2:   <UITouch: 0x14a0f0> phase: Moved
    ```

11. Finger F2 lifted.

    `touchesEnded:withEvent:` is called.

    `touches`: a set of one element:

    ```
    T2:   <UITouch: 0x14a0f0> phase: Ended
    ```

    event: `<UIEvent: 0x143ae0>`. The `allTouches` set:

    ```
    T2:   <UITouch: 0x14a0f0> phase: Ended
    ```

Listing 5.1 shows a `UIView` subclass that overrides three responder methods and logs the touches and events for all three phases. Use this in an application to test your understanding of the multitouch interface.

Listing 5.1   A `UIView` subclass that overrides three responder methods and logs the touches and events for all three phases.

```
@interface ViewOne : UIView {}
@end

@implementation ViewOne

- (void)touchesBegan:(NSSet *)touches withEvent:(UIEvent *)event{
  for(UITouch *t in touches)
    NSLog(@"B: touch: %@", t);
  NSLog(@"B: event:  %@", event);
}

- (void)touchesMoved:(NSSet *)touches withEvent:(UIEvent *)event{
  for(UITouch *t in touches)
    NSLog(@"M: touch: %@", t);
  NSLog(@"M: event:  %@", event);
}

- (void)touchesEnded:(NSSet *)touches withEvent:(UIEvent *)event{
  for(UITouch *t in touches)
    NSLog(@"E: touch: %@", t);
  NSLog(@"E: event:  %@", event);
}
@end
```

The complete application can be found in the `TheView1` project in the source downloads.

5.3.4   Handling a swipe

In this section, we demonstrate how you can intercept the phases of the user's touches in order to recognize a swipe gesture. The application that we are about to build will recognize a right/left swipe and present its speed (in points per second) in a view.

Listing 5.2 shows the declaration of the application delegate class. The `SwipeAppDelegate` application delegate uses the `SwipeDemoView` view as the main view for the application.

Listing 5.2   The declaration of the application delegate class `SwipeAppDelegate`.

```
#import <UIKit/UIKit.h>
#import "SwipeDemoView.h"

@interface SwipeAppDelegate : NSObject <UIApplicationDelegate> {
```

```
   UIWindow              *window;
   SwipeDemoView         *viewOne;
}
@property (nonatomic, retain) UIWindow *window;
@end
```

Listing 5.3 shows the implementation of the application delegate class. The `applicationDid-`
`FinishLaunching:` method creates an instance of the `SwipeDemoView` view class and enables it
for multitouch by setting its `multipleTouchEnabled` property to YES. If you do not do that, the
`touches` set in the four responder methods will always have a size of 1.

Listing 5.3   The implementation of the application delegate class `SwipeAppDelegate`.

```
#import "SwipeAppDelegate.h"

@implementation SwipeAppDelegate
@synthesize window;

- (void)applicationDidFinishLaunching:(UIApplication *)application {
  window =
      [[UIWindow alloc] initWithFrame:[[UIScreen  mainScreen] bounds]];
  CGRect  frame = [UIScreen mainScreen].applicationFrame;
  viewOne = [[SwipeDemoView alloc] initWithFrame:frame];
  viewOne.multipleTouchEnabled = YES;
  viewOne.backgroundColor = [UIColor whiteColor];
  [window addSubview:viewOne];
  [window makeKeyAndVisible];
}

- (void)dealloc {
  [viewOne release];
  [window release];
  [super dealloc];
}
@end
```

The view will keep track of the two touches' time and location. In addition, it uses a `state` variable
to help in recognizing a swipe. If the view is in state `S0`, that means we haven't received any touch. If,
however, it is in state `S1`, then that means that we have received exactly one touch and we are waiting
for it to be lifted. Listing 5.4 shows the declaration of the `SwipeDemoView` view class. Notice that
we have two instance variables for the location and two instance variables for the time. The time is
specified in `NSTimeInterval` (**double**), which is measured in seconds.

Listing 5.4   The declaration of the `SwipeDemoView` view class.

```
#import <UIKit/UIKit.h>
typedef enum  {
  S0,
```

```
    S1
} STATE;

@interface SwipeDemoView : UIView {
    CGPoint              startLocation, endLocation;
    NSTimeInterval       startTime, endTime;
    STATE                state;
}
@end
```

Let's start analyzing the logic behind the recognition of a swipe gesture and displaying its speed. Listing 5.5 shows the `touchesBegan:withEvent:` method of the `UIResponder` class overridden by the `SwipeDemoView` class. What we would like to do in this method is to first make sure that we haven't received any touches before (i.e., we are in state `S0`). In addition, we would like to make sure that the number of touches in the `event` object and the number of elements in the `touches` object is the same and is equal to 1. After making sure that this condition holds, we record the start time and start location of the touch, and enter state `S1`.

Listing 5.5   The `touchesBegan:withEvent:` method used in the swipe-determination application.

```
- (void)touchesBegan:(NSSet *)touches withEvent:(UIEvent *)event{
    int noTouchesInEvent  = ((NSSet*)[event allTouches]).count;
    int noTouchesBegan  = touches.count;
    NSLog(@"began %i, total %i", noTouchesBegan, noTouchesInEvent);
    if((state == S0) && (noTouchesBegan== 1) && (noTouchesInEvent==1)){
        startLocation  = [(UITouch*)[touches anyObject] locationInView:self];
        startTime = [(UITouch*)[touches anyObject] timestamp];
        state = S1;
    }
    else{
        state = S0;
        [self setNeedsDisplay];
    }
}
```

Listing 5.6 shows the `touchesEnded:withEvent:` method. In this method, we make sure that we are in state `S1` (i.e., we started with one touch and it is being lifted). We also make sure that the touch is the last one leaving the screen. We achieve that by ensuring that the number of touches in the `event` is equal to that in `touches` and is equal to 1. Once we have these conditions met, we record the location and time of the touch, and display the result to the user.

Listing 5.6   The `touchesEnded:withEvent:` method used in the swipe-determination.

```
- (void)touchesEnded:(NSSet *)touches withEvent:(UIEvent *)event{
    int noTouchesInEvent  = ((NSSet*)[event allTouches]).count;
    int noTouchesEnded  = touches.count;
    NSLog(@"ended %i %i",touches.count,((NSSet*)[event allTouches]).count);
    if( (state==S1) && (noTouchesEnded == 1) && (noTouchesInEvent==1)){
```

```
      endLocation = [(UITouch*)[touches anyObject] locationInView:self];
      endTime     = [(UITouch*)[touches anyObject] timestamp];
      [self setNeedsDisplay];
  }
}
```

Listing 5.7 shows the remainder of the SwipeDemoView class definition.

Listing 5.7   The remainder of the SwipeDemoView class definition.

```
- (id)initWithFrame:(CGRect)frame {
  if (self = [super initWithFrame:frame]) {
    state = S0;
  }
  return self;
}


- (void)drawRect:(CGRect)rect {
  NSString  *message;
  if(state==S0){
    [@"\t\t\t\t\t\t\t\t\t\t" drawAtPoint:CGPointMake(10,100)
        withFont:[UIFont systemFontOfSize:16]];
    [@"\t\t\t\t\t\t\t\t\t\t" drawAtPoint:CGPointMake(10,150)
        withFont:[UIFont systemFontOfSize:16]];
    [@"\t\t\t\t\t\t\t\t\t\t" drawAtPoint:CGPointMake(10,200)
        withFont:[UIFont systemFontOfSize:16]];
  }
  if(state == S1){
    message =
    [NSString
          stringWithFormat:@"Started (%.0f, %.0f), ended (%.0f, %.0f)",
                         startLocation.x, startLocation.y,
                         endLocation.x, endLocation.y];
    [message drawAtPoint:CGPointMake(10,100)
          withFont:[UIFont systemFontOfSize:16]];

    message =
    [NSString stringWithFormat:@"Took %4.3f seconds",endTime-startTime];
    [message drawAtPoint:CGPointMake(10,150)
          withFont:[UIFont systemFontOfSize:16]];

    if( (fabs(startLocation.y - endLocation.y) <= Y_TOLERANCE) &&
        (fabs(startLocation.x - endLocation.x) >= X_TOLERANCE)){
      char *direction;
      direction = (endLocation.x > startLocation.x) ? "right" : "left";
      message =
      [NSString
```

```
        stringWithFormat:
         @"Perfect %s swipe, speed: %4.3f pts/s", direction,
        (endTime-startTime) > 0 ?
            fabs(endLocation.x - startLocation.x) /(endTime-startTime) : 0
        ];
     [message drawAtPoint:CGPointMake(10,200)
            withFont:[UIFont systemFontOfSize:16]];
  }
  else{
    [@"\t\t\t\t\t\t\t\t\t\t" drawAtPoint:CGPointMake(10,200)
                              withFont:[UIFont systemFontOfSize:16]];
  }
  state = S0;
 }
}
```

The `drawRect:` method presents to the user information about the swipe. If the state is `S0`, we clear the statistics from the previous swipe. If the state is `S1`, we check to see if the gesture was a swipe. The following statement checks to see whether: (1) The absolute difference in the y coordinates of the beginning and ending touch is below or equal to the value `Y_TOLERANCE` and (2) the absolute difference in the x coordinates of the beginning and ending touch is above or equal to the value `X_TOLERANCE`:

```
if( (fabs(startLocation.y - endLocation.y) <= Y_TOLERANCE)  &&
    (fabs(startLocation.x - endLocation.x) >= X_TOLERANCE))
```

The tolerance values are defined as follows:

```
#define Y_TOLERANCE 20
#define X_TOLERANCE 100
```

You can specify the values that best fit your application.

Once we have determined that it is a swipe, we determine the direction of the swipe using the following statement:

```
direction = (endLocation.x > startLocation.x) ? "right" : "left";
```

Finally, we determine the speed of the swipe using the following statement:

```
fabs(endLocation.x - startLocation.x) /(endTime-startTime)
```

The result is displayed to the user as shown in Figure 5.5.

It is worth noting that this gesture-recognition algorithm does not take into account the intermediate movements of the touch. For that, you need to override the `touchesMoved:withEvent:` method and make sure that the `Y_TOLERANCE` value is not violated.

The complete application can be found in the `Swipe` project in the source downloads.

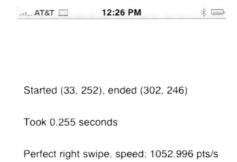

Started (33, 252), ended (302, 246)

Took 0.255 seconds

Perfect right swipe, speed: 1052.996 pts/s

Figure 5.5   A screen shot of the swipe-determination application showing a perfect right swipe.

5.3.5   *More advanced gesture recognition*

In this section, we provide yet another application that deals with multitouch gestures. This application recognizes the following gesture: Two fingers touch the screen together or at most within 2 seconds. The fingers move either together or separately. At the end, the two fingers are lifted from the screen together at the same time. The application will display the following statistics: (1) the percentage of the time that the two fingers moved together and (2) the average distance (in points) between the two fingers.

The application delegate is identical to the one you saw in the previous section. The only difference is the custom view class `ResponderDemoView`. Listing 5.8 shows the declaration of the view class. We define three states: (1) `S0`, the initial state, (2) `S1`, the state where we have received two touches within a reasonable time and statistics can be collected, and (3) `S2`, where we have received only one touch and we are waiting for the second. We keep track of the current state in the instance variable `state`. The variables `movedTogether` and `movedSeperate` record the number of movements of the two fingers together and separately, respectively. The total distance between the two fingers is accumulated in the `accDistance` variable. In addition, the first touch's information (in the case of a delayed second touch) is cached in the two variables `firstTouchLocInView` and `firstTouchTimeStamp`.

Listing 5.8   The declaration of the view class `ResponderDemoView`.

```
#import <UIKit/UIKit.h>

typedef enum   {
  S0,
  S1,
  S2
} STATE;

@interface ResponderDemoView : UIView {
  STATE                   state;
  float                   movedTogether, movedSeperate;
```

```
  float                 accDistance;
  CGPoint               firstTouchLocInView;
  NSTimeInterval        firstTouchTimeStamp;
}
@end
```

Listing 5.9 shows the `touchesBegan:withEvent:` method for the advanced gesture-tracking application.

Listing 5.9   The `touchesBegan:withEvent:` method for the advanced gesture-tracking application.

```
- (void)touchesBegan:(NSSet *)touches withEvent:(UIEvent *)event{
  int noTouchesInEvent  = ((NSSet*)[event allTouches]).count;
  int noTouchesBegan     = touches.count;
  NSLog(@"began %i, total %i", noTouchesBegan, noTouchesInEvent);
  if((noTouchesBegan== 2) && (noTouchesInEvent==2)){
    NSArray *touchArray = [touches allObjects];
    state = S1;
    movedTogether = 1;
    movedSeperate = 0;
    accDistance =
        distance([[touchArray objectAtIndex:0] locationInView:self],
                 [[touchArray objectAtIndex:1] locationInView:self]);
  }
  else if((state!= S2)&&((noTouchesBegan== 1)&&(noTouchesInEvent==1))){
    state = S2; // S2 means we got the first touch
    UITouch *aTouch = (UITouch*)[touches anyObject];
    firstTouchTimeStamp = aTouch.timestamp;
    firstTouchLocInView = [aTouch locationInView:self];
  }
  else if((state == S2) && (noTouchesInEvent==2) ){
    UITouch *aTouch = (UITouch*)[touches anyObject];
    if((aTouch.timestamp - firstTouchTimeStamp) <= MAX_ELAPSED_TIME){
      // S1 means we got the second  touch within reasonable time
      state = S1;
      movedTogether = 1;
      movedSeperate = 0;
      accDistance = distance([aTouch    locationInView:self],
                                        firstTouchLocInView);
    }
    else {
      firstTouchTimeStamp = aTouch.timestamp;
      firstTouchLocInView = [aTouch locationInView:self];
    }
  }
  else state = S0;
}
```

There are three major sections of this method. The first checks to see if two simultaneous fingers have touched the screen. If that is the case, the method changes the state to S1 and initializes the variables for collecting the statistics. The initial distance is also calculated and used to initialize the accumulated distance variable. The distance, in points, is calculated using the distance() function shown below:

```
float distance(CGPoint a, CGPoint b){
  return sqrt( pow((a.x - b.x), 2) + pow((a.y - b.y), 2));
}
```

If the user did not use two fingers together at the same time, we check to see if this is a single touch and the first touch that is received. If that is the case, we enter state S2 (meaning that we have one touch and we are waiting for the second) and cache in the vital information about the touch.

If, on the other hand, we are in state S2 and the event object has two touches, we check to see if the second touch is received within an acceptable time. The following statement checks to see if the difference in arrival time of the two touches is below a threshold:

```
if((aTouch.timestamp - firstTouchTimeStamp) <= MAX_ELAPSED_TIME)
```

If that is the case, we enter state S1; otherwise, the touch is considered the first touch and we wait for the next. The value for MAX_ELAPSED_TIME is defined to be equal to 2 seconds:

```
#define MAX_ELAPSED_TIME   2
```

Listing 5.10 shows the touchesMoved:withEvent: method. If the number of touches is two and we are in the state S1 (collecting statistics), we increment the movedTogether counter and update the distance in accDistance. If, on the other hand, we receive just one movement, we increment the movedSeperate counter.

Listing 5.10   The touchesMoved:withEvent: method for the advanced gesture-tracking application.

```
- (void)touchesMoved:(NSSet *)touches withEvent:(UIEvent *)event{
  NSLog(@"moved %i %i", touches.count,
      ((NSSet*)[event allTouches]).count);
  NSArray *allTouches = [touches allObjects];
  if((state == S1) && ([touches count] == 2) ){
    movedTogether++;
    accDistance +=
      distance([[allTouches objectAtIndex:0] locationInView:self],
               [[allTouches objectAtIndex:1]  locationInView:self]);
  }
  else if((state == S1) && ([touches count] == 1) ){
    movedSeperate++;
  }
}
```

Listing 5.11 shows the touchesEnded:withEvent: method. The method makes sure that the two fingers have been lifted at the same time and requests the display of the statistics by sending the view instance a `setNeedsDisplay` message. This will eventually trigger the invocation of the `drawRect:` method in Listing 5.13.

Listing 5.11   The `touchesEnded:withEvent:` method for the advanced gesture-tracking application.

```
- (void)touchesEnded:(NSSet *)touches withEvent:(UIEvent *)event{
  NSLog(@"ended %i %i",touches.count,((NSSet*)[event allTouches]).count);
  if((state == S1) && ([touches count] == 2) ){
    NSLog(@"started together and ended together,"
         "moved together %.0f%% "
         "of the time. AVG distance:%4.2f",
         (movedSeperate+movedTogether) ?
         100*(movedTogether/(movedTogether+movedSeperate)) : 100.0,
         movedTogether ? accDistance/movedTogether : 0.0);
    [self setNeedsDisplay];
  }
  state = S0;
}
```

If the system is canceling the event, we reset the variables as shown in Listing 5.12.

Listing 5.12   The overridden method `touchesCancelled:withEvent:` for the advanced gesture-tracking application.

```
- (void)touchesCancelled:(NSSet *)touches withEvent:(UIEvent *)event{
  state = S0;
  movedTogether = movedSeperate = 0;
  accDistance =0;
}
```

Listing 5.13 shows the remainder of the definition of the view class. The `initWithFrame:` initializer sets the statistics and state variables to their initial values. The `drawRect:` method, invoked when the view receives a `setNeedsDisplay` message, displays the percentage of the time that the two touches moved together and the average distance between them when they did move together.

Listing 5.13   The remainder of the implementation of the view class used in the advanced gesture-tracking application.

```
- (id)initWithFrame:(CGRect)frame {
  if (self = [super initWithFrame:frame]) {
    state = S0;
    movedTogether = movedSeperate = 0;
    accDistance =0;
  }
  return self;
}

- (void)drawRect:(CGRect)rect {
```

```
NSString   *message =
[NSString stringWithFormat:@"Moved together %.0f%% of the time.",
                (movedSeperate+movedTogether) ?
    100*(movedTogether/(movedTogether+movedSeperate)) : 100.0];
[message drawAtPoint:CGPointMake(10,100)
        withFont:[UIFont systemFontOfSize:16]];
message =
    [NSString stringWithFormat:@"Average distance:%4.2f.",
          movedTogether ? accDistance/movedTogether : 0.0];
[message drawAtPoint:CGPointMake(10,150)
        withFont:[UIFont systemFontOfSize:16]];
}
```

Figure 5.6 shows a screen shot of the application.

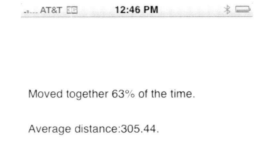

Figure 5.6   A screen shot of the advanced gesture-tracking application.

The complete application can be found in the `ResponderDemo` project in the source downloads.

5.4 Animation

Animation is a major feature of the iOS. In this section, we discuss basic examples that achieve animation. These examples do not require knowledge of image processing. We start by discussing how you can use the `UIView` class to animate properties of views. Next, we show how to animate a sliding view. After that, we discuss how you can animate the flipping of a view. Finally, we give an example that performs view transitioning.

5.4.1   Using the UIView class animation support

The geometric properties of a view can actually be animated with ease. The `UIView` class provides several class methods that can be used to perform simple animations such as moving a view instance to a new position or enlarging it.

To animate views' properties, you must do that between two UIView class calls: beginAnimations:context: and commitAnimations. Inside this animation block, you specify the characteristics of the animation (e.g., its length, timing function, etc.) and change the view's properties (e.g., its center) to the final value. When you commit the animation, the view's properties are animated to the new values.

Building an animated application

Let's start by building an application that enables the user to move a view around the screen by double-tapping on the new position. The move of the view is animated by changing its center. We will create a new subclass of UIView named AnimView. AnimView adds as a subview another child view and waits for the user's tapping. When the user double-taps a location in an AnimView instance, the child view's center property is animated and changed to the location where the user double-tapped.

Listing 5.14 shows the application delegate class for the application. The applicationDidFinishLaunching: method creates a main window and adds to it an instance of the AnimView class. The AnimView instance occupies the full screen that is available to the user and has a gray background color.

Listing 5.14   The application delegate class for animating a view's center property.

```objc
#import <UIKit/UIKit.h>
#import "AnimView.h"

@interface AnimationApp1AppDelegate : NSObject <UIApplicationDelegate> {
    UIWindow *window;
}
@end

@implementation AnimationApp1AppDelegate
- (void)applicationDidFinishLaunching:(UIApplication *)application {
    window = [[UIWindow alloc]
                        initWithFrame:[[UIScreen mainScreen] bounds]];
    CGRect  frame = [UIScreen mainScreen].applicationFrame;
    AnimView *view = [[AnimView alloc] initWithFrame:frame];
    view.backgroundColor = [UIColor grayColor];
    [window addSubview:view];
    [view release];
    [window makeKeyAndVisible];
}

- (void)dealloc {
    [window release];
    [super dealloc];
}
@end
```

Listing 5.15 shows the `AnimView` class.

Listing 5.15   The `AnimView` class used in animating the `center` property of a child view.

```objc
#import <UIKit/UIKit.h>
#import <QuartzCore/QuartzCore.h>

@interface AnimView : UIView {
  UIView *childView;
}
@end


@implementation AnimView

- (id)initWithFrame:(CGRect)frame {
  if (self = [super initWithFrame:frame]) {
    childView = [[UIView alloc]
                          initWithFrame:CGRectMake(100, 150, 100, 150)];
    childView.backgroundColor = [UIColor whiteColor];
    [self addSubview:childView];
  }
  return self;
}

- (void)touchesEnded:(NSSet *)touches withEvent:(UIEvent *)event{
  if( [(UITouch*)[touches anyObject] tapCount] == 2){
    UITouch *touch = [touches anyObject];
    [UIView beginAnimations:nil context:NULL];
    [UIView setAnimationCurve:UIViewAnimationCurveEaseOut];
    [UIView setAnimationDuration:1];
    childView.center = [touch locationInView:self];
    [UIView commitAnimations];
  }
}

- (void)dealloc {
  [childView release];
  [super dealloc];
}
@end
```

The class maintains a reference to a child view in the instance variable `childView`. The `initWithFrame:` initializer creates the `childView` instance, configures it with a white background color, and adds it as a subview.

The logic behind moving the child view to a new location is found in the `touchesEnded:with-Event:` method. The method first checks that we have a double-tap from the user. If that is the case, it starts the animation block with the following statement:

```objc
[UIView beginAnimations:nil context:NULL];
```

The class method is declared as follows:

```
+ (void)beginAnimations:(NSString *)animationID context:(void *)context
```

The two parameters of this method can be NULL. The animationID and context parameters can be used to communicate with animation delegates. Our example does not use an animation delegate, so we pass NULL values.

After starting the animation block, the method sets the optional animation curve. The following statement overrides the default animation curve and sets it to UIViewAnimationCurveEaseOut:

```
[UIView setAnimationCurve:UIViewAnimationCurveEaseOut];
```

The setAnimationCurve: method is declared as follows:

```
+ (void)setAnimationCurve:(UIViewAnimationCurve)curve
```

The following are some of the curves available:

- UIViewAnimationCurveEaseInOut. This curve specifies that the animation should be slow at the beginning and at the end. This curve is the default.
- UIViewAnimationCurveEaseIn. This curve specifies that the animation should be slow at the beginning only.
- UIViewAnimationCurveEaseOut. This curve specifies that the animation should be slow at the end only.
- UIViewAnimationCurveLinear. This curve specifies that the animation should be constant throughout.

The duration of the animation is set using the method setAnimationDuration:, which is declared as follows:

```
+ (void)setAnimationDuration:(NSTimeInterval)duration
```

The duration parameter is specified in seconds. The default is 0.2 seconds.

After the animation is set up, the method changes the properties of the views, which in our case is one property (center) and one view (childView), and commits the animation. The center property is changed in the following statement:

```
childView.center = [touch locationInView:self]
```

Using an animation delegate

Sometimes you want to receive a message when the animation ends. You can set a delegate to the animation using the method setAnimationDelegate:. Calls are made to two methods in this delegate: animationDidStart: and animationDidStop:finished:. These methods are defined by the category CAAnimationDelegate on NSObject in CAAnimation.h.

Let's update our animation application to change the color of the child view and animate its size. When the animation is finished, we revert to the original size and color. The following is the updated touchesEnded:withEvent:.

```
- (void)touchesEnded:(NSSet *)touches withEvent:(UIEvent *)event{
  if( [(UITouch*)[touches anyObject] tapCount] == 2){
    childView.backgroundColor = [UIColor blueColor];
    [UIView beginAnimations:nil context:NULL];
    [UIView setAnimationCurve:UIViewAnimationCurveEaseOut];
    [UIView setAnimationDuration:0.5];
    [UIView setAnimationDelegate:self];
    childView.transform = CGAffineTransformMakeScale(1.5, 1.5);
    [UIView commitAnimations];
  }
}
```

In the code fragment above, on a double-tap, we change the color of the child view outside the animation block. This will result in an instantaneous color change rather than an animated change if it has been done inside the animation block. After that, the animation block is started, and the curve, duration, and delegate are set. To change the scale of the child view by increasing it by 50 percent, the method updates the transform property of the view. The property is declared as follows:

```
@property(nonatomic) CGAffineTransform transform
```

The transform is done using a 3×3 matrix that is used to rotate, scale, or translate the view. CGAffineTransform stores the first two columns of this matrix. The third column is always [0, 0, 1]. To scale the child view up by 50 percent, we use the following statement:

```
childView.transform =   CGAffineTransformMakeScale(1.5, 1.5)
```

In the above statement, we obtain an affine transform for scaling 50 percent using the CGAffine-TransformMakeScale() function and set the value to the transform property.

After the animation ends, and the child view is enlarged 50 percent, a call is made to the method animationDidStop:finished:, defined in the AnimView class as follows:

```
- (void)animationDidStop:(CAAnimation *)theAnimation finished:(BOOL)flag{
  childView.transform = CGAffineTransformIdentity;
  childView.backgroundColor = [UIColor whiteColor];
}
```

The method above changes the child view's background color to white and transforms (instantaneously) the dimensions to no scaling.

The complete application can be found in the AnimationApp1 project in the source downloads.

5.4.2   Sliding view

Writing a sliding view is a simple task using the basic `UIView` animation functionality. The project `SlidingUpDownView`, available in the source downloads, shows a complete application demonstrating this idea.

Initially, you set the frame of the view that you want to slide down to something like the following:

```
self.slidingView  =
[[[MyView alloc]
           initWithFrame:CGRectMake(0, -SLIDING_VIEW_HEIGHT, 320,
                                    SLIDING_VIEW_HEIGHT)] autorelease];
```

In essence, the view is outside its parent's bounds, making it hidden from the user.

To animate sliding the view down, you change the frame (inside an animation block) to have a y origin equal to `0`. To slide it up, set the y origin to a negative value of its height. The following shows a method that does just that. Refer to the project for further information.

```
-(void)slideView:(Direction)_direction{
  [UIView beginAnimations:nil context:nil];
  [UIView setAnimationDuration:0.75f];
  slidingView.frame =
  CGRectMake(0, _direction==DOWN?0:-SLIDING_VIEW_HEIGHT,
               320, SLIDING_VIEW_HEIGHT);
  [UIView commitAnimations];
}
```

5.4.3   Flip animation

Sometimes, you want the same view to flip from right to left or from left to right. This can be easily achieved using basic animation. The following method flips a view to the right. It sets the animation transition to flip from right for a given view. Caching is set to YES to improve performance; otherwise, a NO will result in the view being rendered for each frame — each animation frame, that is.

```
-(void)right{
  [UIView beginAnimations:nil context:nil];
  [UIView setAnimationDuration:1.0];
  [UIView setAnimationTransition:UIViewAnimationTransitionFlipFromRight
         forView:self.view cache:YES];
  [UIView commitAnimations];
}
```

To flip to the left, use `UIViewAnimationTransitionFlipFromLeft` instead. Consult the `Flip-Animation` project, available in468 the source downloads, for a complete application demonstrating this feature.

5.4.4   *Transition animation*

The UIView class is actually a wrapper class that takes its event-handling capabilities from the UIResponder class through the inheritance chain and its animation capabilities from its unique CALayer instance variable. layer, an instance of CALayer, is the Core Animation object that encapsulates information about the animation that should be rendered to the display.

When you make changes to a UIView instance by, for example, adding and removing subviews, the changes happen instantaneously. To animate these changes, you create an animation object, configure it, and add it to the layer property. In this section, we show how you can animate the substitution of one view with another through transition animation. The application demonstrating this will create two subviews of the main window and add one of them to the window. When the user double-taps on the active view, the application will replace the view with the other inactive view and animate the change by moving the new view from right to left.

The animation is performed in the application delegate class. Listing 5.16 shows the declaration of the application delegate class. The class maintains two references to AnimView instances representing the two views. The showOtherView: method is used to animate the replacement of one view with the other.

Listing 5.16   The declaration of the application delegate class used in animating the transition of views.

```
#import <UIKit/UIKit.h>
@class AnimView;
@interface AnimationApp2AppDelegate : NSObject <UIApplicationDelegate> {
    UIWindow    *window;
    AnimView    *view1, *view2;
}
-(void)showOtherView:(UIView*) oldView;
@end
```

Listing 5.17 shows the implementation of the application delegate class. The applicationDid-FinishLaunching: method creates the main window as well as two subviews. It adds one view to the window and makes the window key and visible.

Listing 5.17   The implementation of the application delegate class used in animating the transition of views.

```
#import <QuartzCore/QuartzCore.h>
#import "AnimationApp2AppDelegate.h"
#import "AnimView.h"

@implementation AnimationApp2AppDelegate
- (void)applicationDidFinishLaunching:(UIApplication *)application {
  window = [[UIWindow alloc]
                        initWithFrame:[[UIScreen  mainScreen] bounds]];
  CGRect  frame = [UIScreen mainScreen].applicationFrame;
  view1 = [[AnimView alloc] initWithFrame:frame];
  view1.message = @"View 1";
```

```
   view1.backgroundColor =[UIColor whiteColor];
   [window addSubview:view1];
   view2 = [[AnimView alloc] initWithFrame:frame];
   view2.message = @"View 2";
   view2.backgroundColor =[UIColor yellowColor];
   [window makeKeyAndVisible];
}
-(void)showOtherView:(UIView*) oldView{
   if(oldView == view1){
      [view1   removeFromSuperview];
      [window addSubview:view2];
   }
   else{
      [view2   removeFromSuperview];
      [window addSubview:view1];
   }
   CATransition *animation = [CATransition animation];
   [animation setType:kCATransitionMoveIn];
   [animation setSubtype:kCATransitionFromRight];
   [animation setDuration:0.5];
   [animation setTimingFunction:[CAMediaTimingFunction
            functionWithName:kCAMediaTimingFunctionEaseInEaseOut]];
   [[window layer] addAnimation:animation forKey:@"mykey"];
}
-  (void)dealloc {
   [view1   release];
   [view2   release];
   [window release];
   [super dealloc];
}
@end
```

When the current view asks the application delegate to switch to the other view, the showOtherView: is called with the reference to the active subview. The current view is removed from the window and the other view is added. To animate this change, we create an animation object and add it to the window's layer property.

Animation objects are instances of the class CAAnimation. The CATransition is a subclass of CAAnimation that makes it easy to animate transitions. We first obtain a new animation object by using the class method animation. Next, the type, duration, and timing of the animation are configured. The type of animation is moved in from the right, and the duration chosen is 0.5 seconds. Also, an ease-in-ease-out timing function is used. To add the animation, we use the method addAnimation:forKey:, which is declared as follows:

```
-  (void)addAnimation:(CAAnimation *)anim forKey:(NSString *)key
```

The anim parameter is an instance of CAAnimation that represents the animation, and the key (can be nil) is to distinguish different animations on a given layer. Because the anim parameter is copied by the method, you need to invoke this method after you have configured the animation object.

Listing 5.18 shows the AnimView class. The class maintains a message instance variable whose content is drawn to the screen. This will serve as a distinguishing mark between the two transitioning views.

Listing 5.18   The AnimView class used in the view-transition application.

```
#import <UIKit/UIKit.h>
#import <QuartzCore/QuartzCore.h>


@interface AnimView : UIView {
  NSString  *message;
}
@property(nonatomic, copy) NSString *message;
@end


@implementation AnimView
@synthesize message;

- (void)touchesEnded:(NSSet *)touches withEvent:(UIEvent *)event{
  if( [(UITouch*)[touches anyObject] tapCount] == 2){
    [[UIApplication sharedApplication].delegate showOtherView:self];
  }
}

- (void)drawRect:(CGRect)rect{
  [message drawAtPoint:CGPointMake(100,100)
          withFont:[UIFont systemFontOfSize:32]];
}
@end
```

The complete application can be found in the AnimationApp2 project in the source downloads.

5.5   Drawing

In this section, we cover some of the basic ideas behind Quartz 2D, a C framework for two-dimensional graphics. First, we casually illustrate some of the fundamental concepts and then we present a complete application that utilizes Quartz 2D to build a custom component.

5.5.1   Fundamentals

The drawRect: method is an ideal place for drawing in a view. The view will set up the environment for you, making it easy to draw. You use Quartz 2D functions for drawing both simple and complex shapes. These functions require a graphics context as the first parameter. A *graphics context* defines basic drawing attributes such as color, font, line width, etc. A drawing command uses the context to accomplish its intended functionality. You can obtain a graphics context using the function UIGraphicsGetCurrentContext().

Once you have a graphics context, you can use it to draw paths. A *path* is a collection of one or more shapes. Once you construct the path, you can stroke it, fill it, or both.

Listing 5.19 shows a drawRect: that draws several shapes. The result of this drawing is shown in Figure 5.7. After obtaining the graphics context, we set the line width of the path to 5 pixels (the default is 1). Then we signal a new path location using the function CGContextMoveToPoint(). The function CGContextAddLineToPoint() is used to add a line to the path starting from (50, 100) and ending at (200, 100). At this stage, we have only one shape (a straight line) in this path. To draw it, we use the CGContextStrokePath() function. This function will draw the path and clear the current path.

Listing 5.19   A drawRect: that draws several shapes.

```
- (void)drawRect:(CGRect)rect {
  CGContextRef  context = UIGraphicsGetCurrentContext();
  CGContextSetLineWidth(context, 5.0);
  CGContextMoveToPoint(context, 50, 100);
  CGContextAddLineToPoint(context, 200, 100);
  CGContextStrokePath(context);
  CGContextAddEllipseInRect(context,CGRectMake(70.0, 170.0, 50.0, 50.0));
  CGContextStrokePath(context);
  CGContextAddEllipseInRect(context,CGRectMake(150.0, 170.0, 50.0, 50.0));
  CGContextFillPath(context);
  CGContextSetRGBStrokeColor(context, 0.0, 1.0, 0.0, 1.0);
  CGContextSetRGBFillColor(context, 0.0, 0.0, 1.0, 1.0);
  CGContextAddRect(context,CGRectMake(30.0, 30.0, 60.0, 60.0));
  CGContextFillPath(context);
  CGContextAddArc(context,260, 90, 40, 0.0*M_PI/180, 270*M_PI/180, 1);
  CGContextAddLineToPoint(context, 280, 350);
  CGContextStrokePath(context);
  CGContextMoveToPoint(context, 130, 300);
  CGContextAddLineToPoint(context, 80, 400);
  CGContextAddLineToPoint(context, 190, 400);
  CGContextAddLineToPoint(context, 130, 300);
  CGContextStrokePath(context);
}
```

To draw an ellipse, use the function CGContextAddEllipseInRect(). When you follow it up with the function call to CGContextStrokePath(), the ellipse is drawn. If you want to fill the ellipse, use the function CGContextFillPath().

You can set the stroke color using the function CGContextSetRGBStrokeColor(). In this function, you specify the red, green, and blue (RGB) components and the alpha (opacity level).

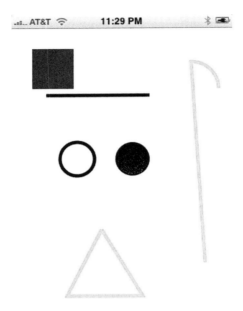

Figure 5.7   Drawing several shapes using Quartz 2D.

Similarly, the fill color can be set using the function CGContextSetRGBFillColor(). Similar to the way you draw lines and ellipses, you can draw rectangles, curves, arcs, etc.

The complete application can be found in the QuartzDemo project in the source downloads.

5.5.2   The Summary View application

In Chapter 9, you will be using table views to present information to the user. Tables on the iPhone are one-column. Each column is referred to as a *cell*. A cell has a content view, which is a view like any other view.

Often, you are faced with the requirement of showing summary information in the cell. For example, you may want to show how many replies a blog post has received or how many other users actually liked it.

One way of presenting this summary information is to use a summary view such as the ones shown in Figures 5.8, 5.9, and 5.10.

💬 **52 comments**

Figure 5.8   An example of a summary view with one entry.

Figure 5.9   An example of a summary view with three entries.

Figure 5.10   A summary view in selection state.

In this section, we will develop this `SummaryView` class as well as any other related classes. First, we will develop the `MiniItem` class, which represents an entry in a summary view. After that, we will develop the `SummaryView` class, which has a rounded rectangle and tip, and can host a variable number of `MiniItem` objects. Quartz 2D will be used to realize the rounded rectangle and for the display of the text and images inside the summary view.

The MiniItem class

The `MiniItem` class represents an item that is shown in the summary view. An *item* consists of a text and an image. The `MiniItem` is declared in Listing 5.20.

Listing 5.20   The declaration of the `MiniItem` class.

```
@interface MiniItem : NSObject {
    NSString     *itemText;
    UIImage      *itemImage;
}

@property (nonatomic, retain)    NSString    *itemText;
@property (nonatomic, retain)    UIImage     *itemImage;

+ (MiniItem*) itemWithText:(NSString*)text;
+ (MiniItem*) itemWithText:(NSString*)text andImage:(UIImage*)image;

@end
```

The implementation of the `MiniItem` class is shown in Listing 5.21.

Listing 5.21   The implementation of the `MiniItem` class.

```
#import "MiniItem.h"

@implementation MiniItem
```

```
@synthesize itemText, itemImage;

+ (MiniItem*) itemWithText:(NSString*)text andImage:(UIImage*)image{
    MiniItem *v = [[[MiniItem alloc] init] autorelease];
    v.itemText  = text;
    v.itemImage = image;
    return v;
}

+ (MiniItem*) itemWithText:(NSString*)text{
    MiniItem *v = [[[MiniItem alloc] init] autorelease];
    v.itemText  = text;
    return v;
}

- (void) dealloc{
    self.itemText  = nil;
    self.itemImage = nil;
    [super dealloc];
}
@end
```

The class uses two Objective-C properties, one for the text and the other for the image. Two class factory methods are implemented to generate MiniItem instances depending on whether the item has an image or not.

The SummaryView class

The SummaryView class is the view that the client uses to configure as a container for one or more MiniItems it wants to present. This class is declared in Listing 5.22.

Listing 5.22   The declaration of the SummaryView class.

```
#import <QuartzCore/QuartzCore.h>
#import "MiniItem.h"

@protocol SummaryViewDelegate

- (void) viewTapped:(UIView*)view;

@end

@interface SummaryView : UIView {
    BOOL                         selected;
    id<SummaryViewDelegate>      delegate;
}
```

```
@property (nonatomic, assign) id<SummaryViewDelegate>      delegate;

- (id)    initWithFrame:(CGRect)frame xOffset:(CGFloat)offset
          andContent:(NSArray*) content;
- (void)  setContent:(NSArray*)cont;
@end
```

This class is a subclass of `UIView`. It keeps track of its selected state using the `selected` instance variable. A `delegate` property can be used to notify the client of this class when the user taps on it. The `SummaryViewDelegate` protocol defines one method, `viewTapped:`. The `content`, composed of an array of `MiniItems`, can be assigned either during the initialization phase, using the custom initializer `initWithFrame:xOffset:andContent:`, or at any point thereafter. The summary view will reconfigure itself whenever that happens.

The custom initializer is declared as follows:

```
- (id) initWithFrame:(CGRect)frame xOffset:(CGFloat)offset
       andContent:(NSArray*) content{
    if (self = [super initWithFrame:frame]) {
      self.clipsToBounds = YES;
      self.backgroundColor = [UIColor clearColor];
      InnerView *v = [[[InnerView alloc]
          initWithFrame:CGRectMake(0, 5, frame.size.width,
                                frame.size.height-10)
    xOffset:offset andContent:content] autorelease];
      v.tag = 120;
      v.userInteractionEnabled = NO;
      [self addSubview:v];
    }
    return self;
}
```

The main point to take from the above method is that it creates a subview of type `InnerView` (to be discussed later) and adds it to its view hierarchy. This view has its user interaction disabled, which means that it does not receive the user's touches. The view is tagged so that it can be retrieved later and asked to update itself as we shall see.

The `SummaryView` object needs to inform the client when the user taps on it. In order to achieve that, we override three `NSResponder` methods as shown in Listing 5.23.

Listing 5.23   Overriding the `NSResponder` touch events handling.

```
- (void) touchesBegan:(NSSet *)touches withEvent:(UIEvent *)event {
    UITouch *touch = [touches anyObject];
    CGPoint point = [touch locationInView:self];
    CGRect childsFrame = [self viewWithTag:120].frame;
    if(CGRectContainsPoint(childsFrame, point)){
        selected = YES;
```

```
          [self setNeedsDisplay];
          [self tellChild];
     }
}

- (void) touchesEnded:(NSSet *)touches withEvent:(UIEvent *)event{
     selected = NO;
     [self setNeedsDisplay];
     [self tellChild];
     [self.delegate viewTapped:self];
}

- (void) touchesCancelled:(NSSet *)touches withEvent:(UIEvent *)event{
     selected = NO;
     [self setNeedsDisplay];
     [self tellChild];
}
```

When the view is first touched and the touch lies inside the InnerView child, it sets its selected state to **true** and updates itself by calling the setNeedsDisplay method, which in turn will require the drawRect: method to be executed and tells its InnerView instance (its child) to update itself.

If the touches are canceled, the selected state is set to **false** and the view and its child are updated. In the case that the touches ended with the user lifting his or her finger, the two views are updated and the delegate is informed by calling viewTapped: passing in the SummaryView reference.

The tellChild method is shown below:

```
- (void) tellChild{
     InnerView *v = (InnerView*)[self viewWithTag:120];
     v.selected = selected;
}
```

It simply retrieves the InnerView reference and sets its selected property to the current selected property of the SummaryView instance. The selected property of InnerView is declared as **@dynamic** as we shall see shortly.

The drawRect: method of the SummaryView class is shown in Listing 5.24.

Listing 5.24   The drawRect: method of the SummaryView class.

```
- (void) drawRect:(CGRect)rect {
     [super drawRect:rect];
     CGContextRef context = UIGraphicsGetCurrentContext();
     CGContextSaveGState(context);
     if(!selected){
          CGContextSetFillColor(context, BKG_COLOR);
     }else{
          CGContextSetFillColor(context,
```

```
                CGColorGetComponents( [[UIColor blueColor] CGColor]));
    }
    UIView *c = [self viewWithTag:120];
    CGFloat width = c.bounds.size.width;
    CGContextBeginPath(context);
    CGContextSetLineWidth(context, 0.00001);
    CGContextMoveToPoint(context,c.frame.origin.x+width/4.0,13);
    CGContextAddLineToPoint(context,c.frame.origin.x+width/4.0+10,4);
    CGContextAddLineToPoint(context,c.frame.origin.x+width/4.0+20,13);
    CGContextClosePath(context);
    CGContextFillPath(context);

    CGContextRestoreGState(context);
}
```

The drawing functions take a context as the first parameter. We first obtain the current context and save it. At the end, we restore that context using the `CGContextRestoreGState()` function. Between these two calls, the method sets the fill color according to the selection state. The child view will take care of setting its background. The `SummaryView`, however, needs to set the background color of its tip. We draw a filled rectangle by concatenating simple lines and filling it using the `CGContextFillPath()` method. Keep in mind that the `(0, 0)` coordinates of the view start in the bottom-left corner.

The InnerView class

The declaration of the `InnerView` class is shown in Listing 5.25.

Listing 5.25   The declaration of the `InnerView` class.

```
@interface InnerView : UIView {
    NSArray        *content;
    BOOL           selected;
    CGFloat        offset;
    CGRect         originalFrame;
}

@property (assign)              BOOL       selected;
@property (nonatomic, retain) NSArray    *content;
@property (assign)              CGFloat    offset;
@property (assign)              CGRect     originalFrame;

- (id)    initWithFrame:(CGRect)frame xOffset:(CGFloat)offset
          andContent:(NSArray*)ct;
- (void) layout;

@end
```

The `InnerView` instance maintains an array of `MiniItem` instances using the `content` instance variable. In addition, the selected state is saved in the `selected` instance variable.

The custom initializer for this class is shown below:

```
- (id) initWithFrame:(CGRect)frame
        xOffset:(CGFloat)xOffset andContent:(NSArray*)ct{
    if (self = [super initWithFrame:frame]) {
        content = [ct retain];
        self.offset = xOffset;
        self.originalFrame = frame;
        self.backgroundColor = [UIColor clearColor];
        [self layout];
    }
    return self;
}
```

The initializer keeps tracks of the content, offset, and the original frame given to it. In addition, it invokes the `layout` method on itself. The `layout` method determines the actual bounds of the view as a function of the items in its `content` array. This method is shown below:

```
- (void) layout{
    CGFloat totalMw = 0.0;
    for (MiniItem *e in content){
        totalMw +=  [InnerView minWidthForText:[e itemText]
                        withMaxHeight:self.originalFrame.size.height];
        totalMw += [e itemImage].size.width;
    }
    self.bounds = CGRectMake(0, 0, totalMw + SPACING*(content.count+1),
            self.originalFrame.size.height - SPACING);
    self.center = CGPointMake(self.bounds.size.width/2.0 + self.offset,
            self.bounds.size.height);
}
```

The method goes through the `MiniItems` in `content`, accumulating the width needed for each `MiniItem`. A `MiniItem` instance contributes to the width via its text and/or its image. The image's width is easily retrieved from the `size` property of the `UIImage` instance. The width of the text is computed by the class method `minWidthForText:withMaxHeight:`, which is implemented as follows:

```
+ (CGFloat) minWidthForText:(NSString*)_text
            withMaxHeight:(CGFloat) height{
    if(!textFont){
        textFont = [UIFont boldSystemFontOfSize:12];
    }
    return [_text
            sizeWithFont:textFont
            constrainedToSize:CGSizeMake(99999, height)
            lineBreakMode:UILineBreakModeClip
            ].width;
}
```

The method uses the `sizeWithFont:constrainedToSize:lineBreakMode:` declared in a category on `NSString`. This method is declared as follows:

```
- (CGSize)sizeWithFont:(UIFont *)font
        constrainedToSize:(CGSize)size
        lineBreakMode:(UILineBreakMode)lineBreakMode;
```

The `lineBreakMode` parameter can be any value from the `UILineBreakMode` enumeration type. Here, we use `UILineBreakModeClip`. Because we want the minimum width, we give the method a size whose width is very high. The `width` value of the size is the value returned from this method. Notice the use of the **static** `textFont` variable, which is shared among all instances of the `InnerView` class.

Now, we cover the actual `drawRect:` method that lays out all `MiniItems` inside the view. This method is shown in Listing 5.26.

Listing 5.26   The `drawRect:` of the `InnerView` class.

```
- (void)drawRect:(CGRect)rect {
    CGFloat radius = 15.0;
    CGContextRef context = UIGraphicsGetCurrentContext();
    CGContextSaveGState(context);

    CGContextBeginPath(context);
    if(!selected){
        CGContextSetFillColor(context, BKG_COLOR);
    }else{
        CGContextSetFillColor(
                context,
                CGColorGetComponents([[UIColor blueColor] CGColor]));
    }
    CGContextMoveToPoint(context, CGRectGetMinX(rect) + radius,
                    CGRectGetMinY(rect));
    CGContextAddArc(context, CGRectGetMaxX(rect) - radius,
                CGRectGetMinY(rect)+radius, radius,3*M_PI/2,0,0);
    CGContextAddArc(context, CGRectGetMaxX(rect) - radius,
                CGRectGetMaxY(rect)-radius,radius,0,M_PI/2,0);
    CGContextAddArc(context,CGRectGetMinX(rect)+radius,
                CGRectGetMaxY(rect)-radius,radius,M_PI/2,M_PI,0);
    CGContextAddArc(context,CGRectGetMinX(rect)+radius,
                CGRectGetMinY(rect)+radius,radius,M_PI,3*M_PI/2,0);
    CGContextFillPath(context);

    if(!selected){
        [[UIColor colorWithRed:0.1 green:0.5 blue:0.9 alpha:0.9] set];
    }else{
        [[UIColor whiteColor] set];
    }
    CGContextMoveToPoint(context, 10, 5);
    CGFloat drawingAreaHeight = self.bounds.size.height;
```

```
    for (MiniItem *e in content){
        [[e itemImage] drawInRect:
            CGRectMake(CGContextGetPathCurrentPoint(context).x + 5,
                    (drawingAreaHeight-[e itemImage].size.height)/2.0,
                    [e itemImage].size.width,[e itemImage].size.height)];

        [[e itemText] drawAtPoint:
            CGPointMake(CGContextGetPathCurrentPoint(context).x +
                        [e itemImage].size.width + 8,
                    CGContextGetPathCurrentPoint(context).y)
                    withFont:textFont];
        CGFloat width =
                [InnerView minWidthForText:[e itemText]
                        withMaxHeight:self.bounds.size.height];
        CGContextMoveToPoint(
                        context,
                        CGContextGetPathCurrentPoint(context).x + width +
                            [e itemImage].size.width + SPACING,
                        CGContextGetPathCurrentPoint(context).y);
    }
    CGContextRestoreGState(context);
}
```

The method draws a rounded rectangle whose arcs have a radius of 15 pixels. The text's color is determined by the selection state. If the view is selected, the color is white; otherwise, the color is arbitrarily determined by supplying the RGB and alpha components as shown below:

```
static  float  BKG_COLOR[] = {0xee/255.0, 0xee/255.0, 0xf5/255.0, 1.0};
```

You can pick your own color if you like.

The items are drawn one by one by going through the content array. An image is drawn using the drawInRect: method of UIImage. The text is drawn using the drawAtPoint:withFont: method of NSString.

Wrapping up

Using the SummaryView is quite easy. For example, to add a SummaryView with three items to a window, use the following:

```
SummaryView    *summaryView =
    [[[SummaryView alloc]
        initWithFrame:CGRectMake(10, 220, 300, 50)
        xOffset:0.0 andContent:nil] autorelease];

UIImage  *i1 = [UIImage imageNamed:@"flag.png"];
NSString *s1 = [NSString stringWithFormat:@"%d flags", 4];
```

```
MiniItem *o1 = [MiniItem itemWithText:s1 andImage:i1];

UIImage  *i2 = [UIImage imageNamed:@"alert.png"];
NSString *s2 = [NSString stringWithFormat:@"%d alert", 1];
MiniItem *o2 = [MiniItem itemWithText:s2 andImage:i2];

UIImage  *i3 = [UIImage imageNamed:@"favourites.png"];
NSString *s3 = [NSString stringWithFormat:@"%d bookmarks", 23];
MiniItem *o3 = [MiniItem itemWithText:s3 andImage:i3];

NSArray *all = [NSArray arrayWithObjects:o1,o2,o3,nil];
[summaryView setContent:all];

[window  addSubview:summaryView];
```

A complete application demonstrating the use of the summary view can be found in the Summary project in the source downloads.

5.6   Summary

This chapter explained the main concepts behind views. We covered the topic of view geometry in Section 5.1. In Section 5.2, we addressed the topic of view hierarchy. Next, Section 5.3 discussed, in great detail, the multitouch interface. In that section, you learned how to recognize multitouch gestures. After that, we discussed several animation techniques in Section 5.4. Finally, Section 5.5 dealt with how to use Quartz 2D functions for drawing inside a view.

Exercises

(1) What are the differences between the frame and the bounds of a view?

(2) Study the UIView class by reading the documentation and the UIView.h header file.

(3) Develop a subclass of UIView that recognizes a heart shape that is drawn with only two fingers.

6

Controls

Controls are graphical objects used by the user of the application to express an objective. For example, a slider control can be used by the user as a way to fine-tune a specific value. A switch control, on the other hand, can be used to turn an option on and off. In this chapter, we present several important graphical controls that can be used in building attractive iOS applications.

This chapter starts in Section 6.1 by covering the base class of all controls, UIControl, and the important target-action mechanism. After that, you learn about several important UI components such as text fields (Section 6.2), sliders (Section 6.3), switches (Section 6.4), buttons (Section 6.5), segmented controls (Section 6.6), page controls (Section 6.7), and date pickers (Section 6.8). We summarize the chapter in Section 6.9.

6.1 The Foundation of All Controls

Controls are subclasses of the UIControl class. The position of the UIControl class in the class hierarchy is shown in Figure 6.1. The common behavior of controls is captured by this class. Therefore, understanding this class is essential to using its concrete subclasses such as UITextField, UISlider, UIDatePicker, etc.

6.1.1 UIControl attributes

As a superclass of controls, the UIControl class has several shared attributes that can be configured using accessor methods. These attributes include

- enabled. This is a Boolean attribute that represents whether the control is enabled or not. The property is defined as

  ```
  @property(nonatomic, getter=isEnabled) BOOL enabled
  ```

  If the value for enabled is NO, the user's touch events are ignored.

- highlighted. This Boolean value controls whether the control is highlighted or not. By default, the value is NO. When the user touches the control, the value of this attribute is YES,

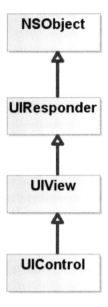

Figure 6.1   `UIControl` inheritance hierarchy.

and the control is highlighted. When the user's touch leaves the control, the value is NO, and the control is not highlighted. The property declaration of this attribute is

```
@property(nonatomic, getter=isHighlighted) BOOL highlighted
```

- `selected`. This Boolean attribute indicates whether the control is selected or not. Most subclasses of `UIControl` do not use this. However, the `UISwitch` subclass might use it. The declaration of this property is as follows:

```
@property(nonatomic, getter=isSelected) BOOL selected
```

- `state`. This is a read-only attribute of type `UIControlState`. `UIControlState` is defined as an unsigned integer (`NSUInteger`). `state` is a bit mask representing more than one state. Examples of defined states are `UIControlStateHighlighted`, `UIControlStateDisabled`, and `UIControlStateNormal`.

The property is defined as follows, but note that this attribute is read-only:

```
@property(nonatomic, readonly) UIControlState state
```

6.1.2   Target-action mechanism

`UIControl` and its subclasses use the target-action mechanism to inform interested parties when changes to the control object occur. Basically, an object, which is usually a controller, sends a message to the control informing it that it is interested in monitoring some event related to the control. When such an event occurs, the control will inform the object (e.g., the controller).

An object registering itself using the target-action mechanism is required to include three pieces of information:

- A pointer to the object (target) that should receive the message (usually itself)
- The selector (action) representing the action method
- The control event it is interested in

When the control receives the registration message, it stores this information in an internal dispatch table. Note that the same target can register for different events with different selectors. Moreover, different targets can register for the same event.

When the event (such as a change in the value of the control) occurs, the control sends itself the `sendActionsForControlEvents:` message. This method will then consult the internal dispatch table (the same table built incrementally as a result of the registration messages) to find all target-action entries for this event. The control then sends the singleton `UIApplication` instance a `sendAction:to:from:forEvent:` message for each such entry. The `UIApplication` instance is the one responsible for actually sending the action messages to the targets.

An object registers with a control using the following `UIControl` declared instance method:

```
- (void)addTarget:(id)target action:(SEL)action
        forControlEvents:(UIControlEvents)controlEvents
```

The `target` is usually the instance registering for this event (e.g., a controller). The `action` is a selector that identifies the action message of the `target` (i.e., the method that gets called by the `UIApplication` instance when the event occurs). The selector takes any of the following three forms:

```
- (void)action
- (void)action:(id)sender
- (void)action:(id)sender forEvent:(UIEvent *)event
```

The `controlEvents` is a bit mask specifying the control events that trigger the sending of an action message to the `target`. There are several of these control events defined in `UIControl.h`. Some examples include

- `UIControlEventValueChanged`. The value of the control has changed — for example, the slider moved.
- `UIControlEventEditingDidBegin`. The control (e.g., `UITextfield`) started editing.
- `UIControlEventEditingDidEnd`. A touch ended the editing of a field by leaving its bounds.
- `UIControlEventTouchDown`. A single touch occurred inside the control's bounds.

Figure 6.2 shows a sequence diagram for a target-action scenario. Here, we have two controllers, `ctrl1` and `ctrl2`, interested in the control event `UIControlEventValueChanged`. The diagram shows the role that the `UIApplication` singleton instance plays in delivering the action messages.

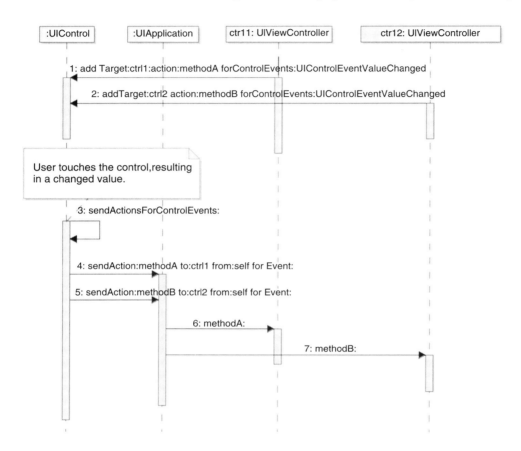

Figure 6.2   Sequence diagram illustrating the target-action mechanism. Two controllers, `ctrl1` and `ctrl2`, add themselves as `targets` for the control event `UIControlEventValueChanged`.

There are several other important methods available in the `UIControl` class that are related to the target-action mechanism:

- `removeTarget:action:forControlEvents:`. This method is used to remove a specific target and action entry from the dispatch table for particular control events. The method is declared as

  - (**void**) removeTarget: (**id**) target action: (SEL) action
      forControlEvents: (UIControlEvents) controlEvents

- `allTargets`. This method returns all target objects related to a control object. The method is declared as

  - `(NSSet *)allTargets`

- `allControlEvents`. This method returns all control events related to a control object. The method is declared as

  - `(UIControlEvents)allControlEvents`

- `actionsForTarget:forControlEvent:`. This method return the actions associated with a specific target and a particular control event:

  - `(NSArray *)actionsForTarget:(`**`id`**`)target`
            `forControlEvent:(UIControlEvents)controlEvent`

  The return value is an `NSArray` of `NSString` objects of selector names. If there are no actions associated with the control events, the returned value is `nil`.

Now that we understand the `UIControl` class, let's look at some of its concrete implementations.

6.2   The Text Field

The `UITextField` class (see Figure 6.3) encapsulates a text-editing control that allows the user to enter a small amount of information. This control provides an optional Clear button on the right for clearing the text. `UITextField` uses the `UITextFieldDelegate` protocol for communicating with the delegate class (usually a controller). The `UITextField` itself adopts the `UITextInputTraits` protocol. This protocol must be implemented by any control that uses the keyboard. You create an instance of `UITextField` and add it to a view as a subview.

UIText Field

Figure 6.3   A `UITextField` control.

There are several important properties of this control:

- `text`. Using this property, you can obtain and set the text displayed by the control. The property is declared as

  `@property(nonatomic, copy) NSString *text`

- `textAlignment`. This property is used to control the technique used to align the text inside the control. The property is declared as

```
@property(nonatomic) UITextAlignment textAlignment
```

The `textAlignment` can be set to one of the following values: `UITextAlignmentLeft` (the default), `UITextAlignmentCenter`, and `UITextAlignmentRight`.

- `textColor`. This property sets the color of the text inside the control. The property is declared as

```
@property(nonatomic, retain) UIColor *textColor
```

Having a value of `nil` (the default) results in opaque black text.

- `background`. This property sets an image that represents the background of the control. The property is declared as

```
@property(nonatomic, retain) UIImage *background
```

The default value is `nil`.

- `clearButtonMode`. This property manages the appearance of the Clear button. The property is declared as

```
@property(nonatomic) UITextFieldViewMode clearButtonMode
```

You can set its value to one of the following: `UITextFieldViewModeNever` (Clear button never appears), `UITextFieldViewModeWhileEditing` (appears only when the user is editing text), `UITextFieldViewModeUnlessEditing` (appears only when the user is not editing text), and `UITextFieldViewModeAlways` (always appears).

- `borderStyle`. This property is used to set the border style of the control. It is declared as

```
@property(nonatomic) UITextBorderStyle borderStyle
```

The value can be one of the following border-style values: `UITextBorderStyleNone` (default), `UITextBorderStyleLine`, `UITextBorderStyleBezel`, and `UITextBorderStyleRoundedRect`.

- `delegate`. Use this property to assign the delegate of the control. The property declaration is as follows:

```
@property(nonatomic, assign) id<UITextFieldDelegate> delegate
```

If the value of this property is not `nil`, the control will send special messages to the delegate informing it of important editing changes, such as the user's tapping the Return key on the keyboard. We will go over the `UITextFieldDelegate` protocol shortly.

- `disabledBackground`. If the value of this attribute is not `nil`, the `disabledBackground` value will be used as a background for the control when it is disabled. The property is declared as

```
@property(nonatomic, retain) UIImage *disabledBackground
```

- `editing`. This is a read-only attribute indicating whether the control is in edit mode. The property is declared as

  `@property(nonatomic, readonly, getter=isEditing) BOOL editing`

- `font`. The value represents the font of the text. The property declaration is as follows:

  `@property(nonatomic, retain) UIFont *font`

  If this value is `nil` (the default), the font used is 12-point Helvetica plain.

- `placeholder`. The value entered here appears in the text control if there is no text in the field. The declaration of the property is as follows:

  `@property(nonatomic, copy) NSString *placeholder`

  The default value is `nil` (i.e., no placeholder string). If the value is not `nil`, the string is drawn in 70 percent grey.

6.2.1   Interacting with the keyboard

We mentioned above that the `UITextField` control conforms to the `UITextInputTraits` protocol. This protocol must be implemented by any control that wishes to interact with the user using the keyboard. The protocol defines several properties:

- `keyboardType`. This property controls the style of the keyboard associated with the text field. The property is declared as

  `@property(nonatomic) UIKeyboardType keyboardType`

  There are several types of keyboard. Examples include

  `UIKeyboardTypeDefault`. The default keyboard.
  `UIKeyboardTypeAlphabet`. The standard alphanumeric (qwerty) keyboard.
  `UIKeyboardTypeNumbersAndPunctuation`. A keyboard with numbers and punctuation.
  `UIKeyboardTypeURL`. A keyboard style that makes it easy to enter a URL.
  `UIKeyboardTypeNumberPad`. A numeric keyboard suitable for PIN entry.
  `UIKeyboardTypePhonePad`. A keyboard designed for entering phone numbers.
  `UIKeyboardTypeNamePhonePad`. A keyboard designed for entering a person's name or phone number.
  `UIKeyboardTypeEmailAddress`. A keyboard style for entering email addresses.

  Figures 6.4 and 6.5 show some of the available keyboard styles.

- `secureTextEntry`. This property is used to signal that the text entered should be hidden (e.g., each character replaced by an asterisk). The property is declared as

  `@property(nonatomic, getter=isSecureTextEntry) BOOL secureTextEntry`

UIKeyboardTypeDefault

UIKeyboardTypePhonePad

Figure 6.4   Two keyboard types: `UIKeyboardTypeDefault` and `UIKeyboardTypePhonePad`.

- `returnKeyType`. This property is used to define the title for the Return key. The property is declared as

```
@property(nonatomic) UIReturnKeyType returnKeyType
```

The attribute `returnKeyType` can hold any of the following values:
`UIReturnKeyDefault`, `UIReturnKeyGo`, `UIReturnKeyGoogle`,
`UIReturnKeyJoin`, `UIReturnKeyNext`, `UIReturnKeyRoute`,
`UIReturnKeySearch`, `UIReturnKeySend`, `UIReturnKeyYahoo`,
`UIReturnKeyDone`, and `UIReturnKeyEmergencyCall`.

- `keyboardAppearance`. This attribute is used to distinguish between text entry inside the application and text entry inside an alert panel. The property is declared as

```
@property(nonatomic) UIKeyboardAppearance keyboardAppearance
```

The value can be either `UIKeyboardAppearanceDefault` (default) or `UIKeyboard-AppearanceAlert`.

- `enablesReturnKeyAutomatically`. If the value is `YES`, the keyboard's Return key is disabled until the user enters some text. The default is `NO`. The property is declared as follows:

UI KeyboardTypeEmailAddress

UI KeyboardTypeNumbersAndPunctuation

Figure 6.5 Two keyboard types: `UIKeyboardTypeEmailAddress` and `UIKeyboardType-NumbersAndPunctuation`.

```
@property(nonatomic) BOOL enablesReturnKeyAutomatically
```

- `autocorrectionType`. This property is used to manage the autocorrection of the user's input. The property is declared as

```
@property(nonatomic) UITextAutocorrectionType autocorrectionType
```

The property can take one of the following values:
`UITextAutocorrectionTypeDefault` (chooses the appropriate autocorrection)
`UITextAutocorrectionTypeNo` (no autocorrection)
`UITextAutocorrectionTypeYes` (autocorrection is enabled)

- `autocapitalizationType`. Determines when the Shift key is automatically pressed to produce capital letters. The property is declared as

```
@property(nonatomic)
            UITextAutocapitalizationType autocapitalizationType
```

The property can take one of the following values:
`UITextAutocapitalizationTypeNone` (do not automatically capitalize)
`UITextAutocapitalizationTypeWords` (capitalize the first character of every word)

`UITextAutocapitalizationTypeSentences` (capitalize the first character of each sentence)

`UITextAutocapitalizationTypeAllCharacters` (capitalize all characters automatically)

6.2.2   The delegate

We mentioned above that the control uses a delegate to communicate important editing events. The delegate protocol used is `UITextFieldDelegate`. It declares several optional methods:

- `textFieldShouldReturn:`. This delegate method is declared as follows:

  `- (BOOL)textFieldShouldReturn:(UITextField *)textField`

  It is called when the user presses the Return key. Because this is a single-line text field, you can use this event as a signal to end editing of the text field and hide the keyboard. The appearance of the keyboard and the first-responder status of the text field are linked. If you want to show the keyboard so that the user starts editing a text field, just send the text field a `becomeFirstResponder` message. If you want to end editing and hide the keyboard, you need to remove the first-responder status of the text field, which will result in hiding the keyboard. To resign the text field as a first responder, just send it a `resignFirstResponder` message.

- `textFieldShouldClear:`. This method is called when the Clear button is pressed. The method is declared as

  `- (BOOL)textFieldShouldClear:(UITextField *)textField`

  If you return `YES`, the text field content is cleared; otherwise, it is not.

- `textFieldDidBeginEditing:`. This method is called when the text field begins as the first responder ready for user input. The method is declared as

  `- (**void**)textFieldDidBeginEditing:(UITextField *)textField`

- `textField:shouldChangeCharactersInRange:replacementString:`. This method is called asking the delegate's permission to change the specified text. The method is declared as

  `-(BOOL)textField:(UITextField *)textField`
  `       shouldChangeCharactersInRange:(NSRange)range`
  `       replacementString:(NSString *)string`

  `range` is the range of characters to be replaced, and `string` is the replacement string.

- `textFieldDidEndEditing:`. This method is called after the text field ends editing. The method is declared as

  `- (**void**)textFieldDidEndEditing:(UITextField *)textField`

- `textFieldShouldBeginEditing:`. This method is called asking permission from the delegate so that the text field can start editing. The method declaration is as follows:

  - `(BOOL)textFieldShouldBeginEditing:(UITextField *)textField`

  Returns YES to start editing and NO otherwise.

- `textFieldDidBeginEditing:`. This method is called when the text field starts editing. The method declaration is as follows:

  - (**void**)`textFieldDidBeginEditing:(UITextField *)textField`

6.2.3   *Creating and working with a UITextField*

This section demonstrates how you can create a `UITextField` instance and add it to a view. Listing 6.1 shows how to create a text-field instance, configure it, and attach it to the view.

Listing 6.1   Creating and configuring a `UITextField` instance as a subview.

```
CGRect rect = CGRectMake(10,10, 150, 30);
myTextField = [[UITextField alloc] initWithFrame:rect];
myTextField.textColor = [UIColor blackColor];
myTextField.font = [UIFont systemFontOfSize:17.0];
myTextField.placeholder = @"<enter text>";
myTextField.backgroundColor = [UIColor whiteColor];
myTextField.borderStyle = UITextBorderStyleBezel;
myTextField.keyboardType = UIKeyboardTypeDefault;
myTextField.returnKeyType = UIReturnKeyDone;
myTextField.clearButtonMode = UITextFieldViewModeAlways;
myTextField.delegate = self;
[theView addSubview:myTextField];
```

You usually create these controls in the `loadView` method of the view controller. Here, we make **self** (i.e., the view controller) the delegate. You have a choice of which of the optional delegate methods you want to implement. Here, we implement the `textFieldShouldReturn:` method shown in Listing 6.2.

Listing 6.2   Implementation of the `textFieldShouldReturn:` method for a `UITextField` instance.

```
- (BOOL)textFieldShouldReturn:(UITextField *)textField{
  if(myTextField == textField){
    if ((([[myTextField text] isEqualToString:@"Hillary"]) == NO){
      [myTextField resignFirstResponder]; // hide KB
      return NO; // It's a text field, no need for new line
    }
    else return NO; // It's a text field, no need for new line
  }
  return NO; // It's a text field, no need for new line
}
```

In the code above, we first test to see if the `textField` is the instance `myTextField`. If yes, we check the text entered. If it is `Hillary`, we do not resign the first responder and return `NO`. Otherwise, we send the text-field control a `resignFirstResponder` message asking it to stop being the first responder. This will result in the disappearance of the keyboard. After that, we return `NO`. As we have mentioned above, the return value has no effect in a single-line text field.

6.3 Sliders

A `UISlider` control (see Figure 6.6) is that familiar horizontal control used to select a single value from a continuous range of values.

UISlider

Figure 6.6   A `UISlider` control.

The following are the essential properties needed to set up a slider:

- `value`. This attribute contains the current value indicated by the slider. The property is declared as

  `@property(nontatomic) float value`

  You can read and write this value. If you set this value, the slider will redraw itself.
- `minimumValue`. This attribute contains the minimum value of the slider control. The property is declared as

  `@property(nontatomic) float minimumValue`
- `maximumValue`. This attribute contains the maximum value of the slider control. The property is declared as

  `@property(nontatomic) float maximumValue`
- `continuous`. This Boolean attribute controls how frequently the slider sends updates with its current value to the associated target-action. If the value is `YES` (the default), the slider continuously sends updates of its current value as the user drags the slider's thumb. If the value is `NO`, it sends it only once: when the user releases the slider's thumb. The property is declared as follows:

  `@property(nonatomic, getter=isContinuous) BOOL continuous`

Listing 6.3 shows how you can configure a slider instance and add it to a view as a subview.

Listing 6.3   Creating and configuring a `UISlider` instance.

```
CGRect rect = CGRectMake(10,60, 200, 30);
mySlider = [[UISlider alloc] initWithFrame:rect];
[mySlider addTarget:self
          action:@selector(sliderValueChanged:)
          forControlEvents:UIControlEventValueChanged];
mySlider.backgroundColor = [UIColor clearColor];
mySlider.minimumValue = 0.0;
mySlider.maximumValue = 10.0;
mySlider.continuous = YES;
mySlider.value = 5.0;
[theView addSubview: mySlider];
```

The slider's range is from `0.0` to `10.0`. It continuously sends updates to the action method `sliderValueChanged:` as the user changes its value.

To receive updates of the current value of the slider, we use the target-action mechanism. We add the action method `sliderValueChanged:` (shown in Listing 6.4) for the control event `UIControlEventValueChanged`.

Listing 6.4   The `sliderValueChanged:` action method.

```
- (void)sliderValueChanged:(id)sender{
  UISlider *slider = sender;
  if(mySlider == slider){
    printf("Value of slider is %f\n", [mySlider value]);
  }
}
```

6.4   Switches

A `UISwitch` (see Figure 6.7) is a control that allows you to present an on/off switch to the user. The `UISwitch` class defines a property `on` for retrieving and setting the current state of the switch. The property is declared as

```
@property(nonatomic, getter=isOn) BOOL on
```

UISwitch

Figure 6.7   A `UISwitch` control.

You can also use the method `setOn:animated:`, which allows you to set the switch's state, optionally animating the change. The method is declared as

```
- (void)setOn:(BOOL)on animated:(BOOL)animated
```

If `animated` is `YES`, the change in the state is animated.

As you can for any control, you can set up a target-action and associate it with an event. As a developer, you are mostly interested in the event when the user flips the switch. You can use the `UIControlEventValueChanged` event for this purpose. Listing 6.5 shows the creation and configuration of a `UISwitch` instance. Listing 6.6 shows the action method for the event `UIControlEventValueChanged`.

Listing 6.5   The creation and configuration of a `UISwitch` instance.

```
rect = CGRectMake(10,90, 100, 30);
mySwitch = [[UISwitch alloc] initWithFrame:rect];
[mySwitch addTarget:self
          action:@selector(switchValueChanged:)
          forControlEvents:UIControlEventValueChanged];
mySwitch.backgroundColor = [UIColor clearColor];
[theView addSubview: mySwitch];
```

Listing 6.6   The action method for the `UISwitch` instance example.

```
- (void)switchValueChanged:(id)sender{
  UISwitch  *aSwitch = sender;
  if(mySwitch == aSwitch){
    if([mySwitch isOn] == YES){
      printf("The switch is on\n");
    }
    else
      printf("The switch is off\n");
  }
}
```

6.5   Buttons

A `UIButton` class is a control that encapsulates the behavior of buttons. You create a button using the `UIButton` class method `buttonWithType:`. After that, you set up a target-action in order to handle the user taping on the button.

The following are some of the available button types:

- `UIButtonTypeRoundedRect`. This style is used to produce a rounded-rectangle button.
- `UIButtonTypeDetailDisclosure`. This style produces a detail-disclosure button.
- `UIButtonTypeInfoLight`. This style produces an information button that has a light background.
- `UIButtonTypeInfoDark`. This style produces an information button that has a dark background.
- `UIButtonTypeContactAdd`. This style produces a contact-add button.

Listing 6.7 shows the creation and configuration of a UIButton instance (see Figure 6.8).

Figure 6.8   A button-control example.

Listing 6.7   The creation and configuration of a UIButton instance.

```
myButton =
  [[UIButton buttonWithType:UIButtonTypeRoundedRect] retain];
myButton.frame = CGRectMake(40.0, 100.0, 100, 50);
[myButton setTitle:@"Click Me" forState:UIControlStateNormal];
[myButton addTarget:self
         action:@selector(buttonClicked:)
         forControlEvents:UIControlEventTouchUpInside];
[theView addSubview: myButton];
```

The listing above configures a target-action for the tapping event. Listing 6.8 shows the action method that handles the tapping on the button. As you notice, this is a basic mechanism inherited from UIControl and no new mechanism is introduced.

Listing 6.8   The action method for the UIButton instance example.

```
-(void)buttonClicked:(id)sender{
  UIButton *button = sender;
  if(myButton == sender){
    printf("The button was tapped\n");
  }
}
```

6.6   Segmented Controls

A *segmented control* is a horizontal control that manages a set of buttonlike items. Each item can be either a text string or an image. The user taps on an item within a segmented control and that item is selected by being highlighted.

To create a segmented control, you need to instantiate a UISegmentedControl object. After allocating an instance, you initialize the control with an array of items. The array of items can consist of objects of NSString or objects of UIImage. You can mix and match text and images in the same segmented control.

After the creation and initialization of the segmented control, you need to add a target-action for the control event `UIControlEventValueChanged:`. The action method will be invoked when the selected item has changed. To retrieve the index of the selected item, use the property `selectedSegmentIndex`, which is declared as

```
@property(nonatomic) NSInteger selectedSegmentIndex
```

The default value for this property is `UISegmentedControlNoSegment`, indicating that no item is selected. If you set the property to this value, no item is selected (i.e., highlighted).

After that, you need to specify the frame for the segmented control, which specifies the location and dimensions. Finally, the segmented control needs to be added to an existing view. Listing 6.9 shows the basic steps needed to display a functioning segmented control.

Listing 6.9   The creation and configuration of a `UISegmentedControl` instance.

```
NSArray  *textOptionsArray = [NSArray arrayWithObjects:
            @"Bart", @"Lisa", @"Maggie", nil];
segmentedCtrl = [[UISegmentedControl alloc]
                    initWithItems:textOptionsArray];
segmentedCtrl.frame = CGRectMake(20.0, 100.0, 280, 50);
[segmentedCtrl addTarget:self
            action:@selector(segmentChanged:)
            forControlEvents:UIControlEventValueChanged];
[theView addSubview:segmentedCtrl];
```

The control in the above listing has three items of text. The action invoked when the user taps on an item is `segmentChanged:` and this is shown in Listing 6.10.

Listing 6.10   The `segmentChanged:` action method invoked when the segmented control changes the selected item.

```
-(void)segmentChanged:(id)sender{
  if(segmentedCtrl == sender){
    printf("The segment was changed to %d\n",
            [segmentedCtrl selectedSegmentIndex]);
  }
}
```

Figure 6.9 shows the text-based segmented control and Figure 6.10 shows it with the middle item selected.

Figure 6.9   A segmented control of text items.

Figure 6.10   A segmented control of text items with a selected item.

To create an image-based segmented control, follow the same procedure except for the initialization phase. You can initialize the control by supplying an array of images as follows:

```
segmentedCtrl = [[UISegmentedControl alloc] initWithItems:
          [NSArray arrayWithObjects:
          [UIImage imageNamed:@"bart.png"],
          [UIImage imageNamed:@"lisa.png"],
          [UIImage imageNamed:@"maggie.png"],
          nil]];
```

Figures 6.11 shows the image-based segmented control, and Figure 6.12 shows it with the middle item selected.

Figure 6.11   A segmented control of image items.

Figure 6.12   A segmented control of image items with a selected item.

In the previous examples, we accepted the default appearance of the segmented control. The property `segmentedControlStyle` allows you to select the style of the control. The property is declared as

```
@property(nonatomic) UISegmentedControlStyle segmentedControlStyle
```

The available styles are

- `UISegmentedControlStylePlain`. This is the default style.
- `UISegmentedControlStyleBordered`. This is a bordered style. Figure 6.13 shows an example of this style.
- `UISegmentedControlStyleBar`. This is a toolbar style. Figure 6.14 shows an example of this style.

Figure 6.13   A segmented control of image items with a style `UISegmentedControlStyleBordered`.

Figure 6.14   A segmented control of image items with a style `UISegmentedControlStyleBar`.

You can also dynamically change the items in a given segmented control. You can use `setTitle:forSegmentAtIndex:` to change a text item or `setImage:forSegmentAtIndex:` to change an item's image.

You can also add a new item to the control. If you would like to add a string item, use `insertSegmentWithTitle:atIndex:animated:` declared as

```
- (void)insertSegmentWithTitle:(NSString *)title
        atIndex:(NSUInteger)segment animated:(BOOL)animated
```

If you want to add an image item, use `insertSegmentWithImage:atIndex:animated:` declared as

```
- (void)insertSegmentWithImage:(UIImage *)image
        atIndex:(NSUInteger)segment animated:(BOOL)animated
```

You can also remove an item using `removeSegmentAtIndex:animated:` declared as

```
- (void)removeSegmentAtIndex:(NSUInteger)segment
        animated:(BOOL)animated
```

To remove all items, invoke `removeAllSegments`.

6.7 Page Controls

A *page control* (see Figure 6.15) presents the user with a set of horizontal dots representing pages. The current page is presented as a white dot. The user can go from the current page to the next or to the previous page.

Figure 6.15   A page control with 15 pages.

To present a page control to the user, allocate a new instance of `UIPageControl` and initialize it with the frame. After that, set the number of pages (maximum 20). To respond to the changes in the current page, add a target-action for the control event `UIControlEventValueChanged`. Finally, you add the page control to a view. Listing 6.11 shows the basic steps needed to present a page control to the user.

Listing 6.11   The creation and configuration of a `UIPageControl` instance.

```
pageCtrl = [[UIPageControl alloc]
                    initWithFrame:CGRectMake(20.0, 100.0, 280, 50)];
[pageCtrl addTarget:self
            action:@selector(pageChanged:)
            forControlEvents:UIControlEventTouchUpInside];
pageCtrl.numberOfPages = 15;
[theView addSubview:pageCtrl];
```

The action method is shown below. To retrieve the current page, use the property `currentPage`.

```
-(void)pageChanged:(id)sender{
  if(pageCtrl == sender){
    printf("The page was changed to %d\n", [pageCtrl currentPage]);
  }
}
```

You can also change the current page programmatically and update the visual page indicator by invoking `updateCurrentPageDisplay`.

6.8   Date Pickers

The `UIDatePicker` is a control that allows the user to select a time and a date using rotating wheels. Figure 6.16 shows four examples of a `UIDatePicker` instance.

Here are several important properties and methods declared by this class:

- `calendar`. The calendar used in the `UIDatePicker` instance. The property is declared as

  `@property(nonatomic, copy) NSCalendar *calendar`

  If this value is `nil`, then the user's current calendar is used.

- `date`. This property represents the date used in the display of the date picker, as follows:

  `@property(nonatomic, copy) NSDate *date`

- `setDate:animated:`. This method is used to change the date. The method is declared as

  `- (void)setDate:(NSDate *)date animated:(BOOL)animated`

  If `animated` is `YES`, the change is animated.

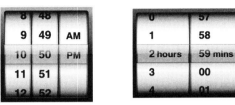

DatePickerModeTimeUI   UIDatePickerModeCountDownTimer

UIDatePickerModeDateAndTime   UIDatePickerModeDate

Figure 6.16   Four examples of `UIDatePicker`.

- `datePickerMode`. Using this property, you can select the date-picker mode. The property is defined as

```
@property(nonatomic) UIDatePickerMode datePickerMode
```

The `UIDatePicker` instance can be configured (see Figure 6.16 earlier in this chapter) to select a date, time, or time and date, or to act as a countdown timer.

Listing 6.12 shows how you can configure a date-picker instance and add it to a view as a subview.

Listing 6.12   Creating and configuring a `UIDatePicker` instance.

```
myDatePicker = [[UIDatePicker alloc] initWithFrame:CGRectZero];
myDatePicker.autoresizingMask = UIViewAutoresizingFlexibleWidth;
myDatePicker.datePickerMode = UIDatePickerModeDate;
CGSize pickerSize = [myDatePicker sizeThatFits:CGSizeZero];
rect = CGRectMake(0,150, pickerSize.width, pickerSize.height);
myDatePicker.frame = rect;
[myDatePicker addTarget:self
                action:@selector(datePickerChanged:)
                forControlEvents:UIControlEventValueChanged];
[theView addSubview: myDatePicker];
```

`UIDatePicker` instances differ from other controls in that they optimize their layout internally. You only need to specify the origin in the view; the size will be calculated automatically. The code above creates the instance and sets up an action method for receiving value changes for the control.

When the user rotates the wheel, the control will call the action method as soon as the wheel finishes rotating. Listing 6.13 shows the action method `datePickerChanged:` which is triggered when the value is changed.

Listing 6.13   Action method for date-picker value change.

```
-  (void)datePickerChanged:(id)sender{
  UIDatePicker  *datePicker = sender;
  if(myDatePicker == datePicker){
    printf("Value of picker is %s\n",
           [[[myDatePicker date] description] cString]);
  }
}
```

6.9   Summary

In this chapter, we covered the topic of controls in iOS. We started by presenting the base class of all controls, `UIControl`, and its main features. We then talked about the important target-action mechanisms used to communicate changes in the control to the clients. This chapter covered the text field, slider, switch, button, page control, segmented controls, and pickers.

Exercises

(1) Study the `UIControl.h` header file and the `UIControl` class in the documentation.

(2) How many different forms are available for an action selector? Name them.

7

View Controllers

The model-view-controller (MVC) is a popular design pattern that is used in software construction to isolate the business logic from the graphical user interface. In MVC, a controller is used for the purpose of coordination between the model (where the business logic resides) and the view (where the user's interactions occur).

In this chapter, you learn about the available view controllers that are provided in the iOS SDK. Although you can build iOS applications without the use of these view controllers, you shouldn't. As you will see in this chapter, view controllers greatly simplify your application.

Section 7.1 provides a gentle introduction to view controllers by presenting a simple application with a single view controller. This application demonstrates important view controller concepts. In Section 7.2, we talk about tab-bar controllers and how they can be used in the construction of radio interfaces. In Section 7.3, we talk about navigation controllers used primarily for presenting hierarchical information to the user. After that, Section 7.4 talks about modal view controllers and provides a detailed example showing their appropriate usage. Finally, we summarize the chapter in Section 7.5.

7.1   The Simplest View Controller

In this section, we demonstrate the simplest view controller. The application is composed of a view, a view controller, and a data model. The application simply displays a message that describes the orientation of the device. The view asks the controller for the message string, and the controller consults the device orientation and retrieves the appropriate text from the data model.

7.1.1   The view controller

Listing 7.1 shows the declaration of the view controller. The `UIViewController` is the base class for all view controllers. When creating a view controller, you either subclass this class or one of its subclasses. The data model is represented by three strings, each of which describes the orientation of the device. The method `message` is used by the view instance to retrieve the appropriate text describing the orientation of the device.

Listing 7.1 The declaration of a simple view controller `CDAViewController` in file `CDAViewController.h`.

```
#import <UIKit/UIKit.h>
@interface CDAViewController : UIViewController {
  NSString *strPortraitNormal, *strPortraitUpSideDown, *strLandscape;
}
-(NSString*)message;
@end
```

In Listing 7.2, we show the implementation of the view controller `CDAViewController`.

Listing 7.2 The implementation of a simple view controller `CDAViewController` in file `CDAViewController.m`.

```
#import "CDAViewController.h"
#import "CDAUIView.h"

@implementation CDAViewController
- (id)initWithNibName:(NSString *)nibNameOrNil
       bundle:(NSBundle *)nibBundleOrNil {
  if (self =[super initWithNibName:nibNameOrNil bundle:nibBundleOrNil]){
    strPortraitNormal = @"Portrait";
    strPortraitUpSideDown = @"Portrait UpSideDown";
    strLandscape = @"Landscape";
  }
  return self;
}
- (void)loadView {
  CGRect  rectFrame = [UIScreen mainScreen].applicationFrame;
  //Create the main view
  CDAUIView *theView  = [[CDAUIView alloc] initWithFrame:rectFrame];
  theView.backgroundColor = [UIColor whiteColor];
  theView.myController = self;
  theView.autoresizingMask = UIViewAutoresizingFlexibleHeight |
                             UIViewAutoresizingFlexibleWidth;
  self.view = theView;
  [theView autorelease];
}
- (BOOL)shouldAutorotateToInterfaceOrientation:
      (UIInterfaceOrientation)interfaceOrientation {
  return YES;
}
- (NSString*)message{
 switch (self.interfaceOrientation) {
   case UIInterfaceOrientationPortrait:
```

```
      return strPortraitNormal;
    case UIInterfaceOrientationPortraitUpsideDown:
      return strPortraitNormal;
    default:
      return strLandscape;
  }
}
@end
```

We override the initialization method `initWithNibName:bundle:` in order to initialize the data model. The three strings are set according to their purposes.

Because we are creating the view programmatically, we need to override the method `loadView`. Our method creates a view instance of the class `CDAUIView` (discussed in Section 7.1.2) and configures it to have flexible height and width. This is achieved by setting the `autoresizingMask` property with the appropriate value. Because the view needs a reference to the controller, we also set the property `myController` of our custom view with the view controller's instance.

The method `shouldAutorotateToInterfaceOrientation:` is also overridden. This method is called whenever the device's orientation changes. If you return `YES`, then the device orientation is changed; otherwise, no change in the device orientation occurs. Because our application requires that the orientation be changed, we return `YES`. The `message` method is the method used by the view to retrieve the text that needs to be displayed. The method simply queries the current orientation of the device and returns the appropriate string using the simple data model. The `UIViewController`'s property `interfaceOrientation` is used to retrieve the current orientation of the device. The property is declared as follows:

`@property(nonatomic, readonly) UIInterfaceOrientation interfaceOrientation`

There are four orientations of type `UIInterfaceOrientation`. These orientations are

- `UIInterfaceOrientationPortrait`. Indicates that the iPhone is in portrait orientation, where the Home button is on the bottom.

- `UIInterfaceOrientationPortraitUpsideDown`. Indicates that the iPhone is in portrait orientation, where the Home button is on the top.

- `UIInterfaceOrientationLandscapeLeft`. Indicates that the iPhone is in landscape orientation, where the Home button is on the left.

- `UIInterfaceOrientationLandscapeRight`. Indicates that the iPhone is in landscape orientation, where the Home button is on the right.

7.1.2   The view

The view managed by the view controller is an instance of the class `CDAUIView` declared in Listing 7.3. The view has a property used to assign the view controller that is managing the view.

Listing 7.3   The declaration of the view `CDAUIView` in `CDAUIView.h` used to demonstrate the simplest view controller.

```
#import <UIKit/UIKit.h>
@class CDAViewController;
@interface CDAUIView : UIView {
  CDAViewController *myController;
}
@property(nonatomic, assign) CDAViewController* myController;
@end
```

Listing 7.4 shows the implementation of the view class. The class overrides the `drawRect:` method. The method simply asks the controller for a text message and draws that message on the view.

Listing 7.4   The implementation of the view `CDAUIView` in `CDAUIView.m` used to demonstrate the simplest view controller.

```
#import "CDAUIView.h"
@implementation CDAUIView
@synthesize myController;
- (void)drawRect:(CGRect)rect {
  [[myController message]    drawAtPoint:CGPointMake(80, 30)
                             withFont:[UIFont systemFontOfSize:50]];
}
@end
```

7.1.3   The application delegate

Listing 7.5 shows the declaration of the application delegate. It holds two instance variables: a window instance and a view controller instance.

Listing 7.5   The declaration of the application delegate `CDAAppDelegate` in `CDAAppDelegate.h` demonstrating the simplest view controller.

```
@class CDAViewController;
@interface CDAAppDelegate : NSObject {
  UIWindow           *window;
  CDAViewController *viewController;
}
@end
```

In Listing 7.6, we show the implementation of the application delegate class. As usual, we initialize the user interface objects in the method `applicationDidFinishLaunching:`. First, we create the application window. Next, the view controller instance is created and initialized using `initWithNibName:bundle:`. Because we are creating the controller programmatically, we pass `nil` for both parameters. The controller's view is then added to the window as a subview, and the window is made key and visible.

Listing 7.6 The implementation of the application delegate `CDAAppDelegate` in `CDAAppDelegate.m` demonstrating the simplest view controller.

```
#import "CDAAppDelegate.h"
#import "CDAViewController.h"
@implementation CDAAppDelegate
- (void)applicationDidFinishLaunching:(UIApplication *)application {
  window =
      [[UIWindow alloc] initWithFrame:[[UIScreen  mainScreen] bounds]];
  viewController =
      [[CDAViewController alloc] initWithNibName:nil bundle:nil];
  [window addSubview:viewController.view];
  [window makeKeyAndVisible];
}
- (void)dealloc {
  [window release];
  [viewController release];
  [super dealloc];
}
@end
```

The `UIViewController` declares a `view` property as follows:

```
@property(nonatomic, retain) UIView *view
```

The `view` property is initially `nil`. When the property is accessed (as in the statement `viewController.view`), the controller checks to see if it is `nil`. If it is `nil`, it sends itself a `loadView` message. As we saw before, we create the view in the `loadView` method and set the property `view` with the instance created. Therefore, when the controller's view is eventually added to the window, our `CDAUIView` instance is actually added to the window as a subview.

Figures 7.1 and 7.2 show the application in portrait and landscape orientations, respectively.

7.1.4 A simple MVC application

Let's look at the major steps we have performed:

1. **Create a subclass of** `UIViewController`**.** Create the subclass and override the following methods:

   (a) `initWithNibName:bundle:`. This is the initializer of the view controller. You can perform initialization of the data model and the controller instance.

   (b) `loadView`. This method is used to load the view managed by the controller. You should create the view instance, configure it, and set its reference to the `view` property of the controller.

Figure 7.1   The application demonstrating the simplest view controller in portrait orientation.

Figure 7.2   The application demonstrating the simplest view controller in landscape orientation.

(c) `shouldAutorotateToInterfaceOrientation:`. If your application allows for the orientation to change, you should override this method and return `YES` for the acceptable orientations.

2. **Create a subclass of** `UIView`. If your application requires a specialized view, you should subclass the `UIView` class. Optionally, add a property for the controller so that the controller can set this property in order for the view to communicate with the controller concerning changes in the data model. Otherwise, the view can communicate with the application delegate.

3. **Create an application delegate class.** In the `applicationDidFinishLaunching:` method, you should create the main window and the view controller, and add the `view` property of the view controller to the main window as a subview.

The complete application can be found in the `CDA` project in the source downloads.

7.2 Tab-Bar Controllers

Often, you need to design an application that has several functionalities or operates in parallel modes. The interface of such an application is sometimes referred to as a *radio interface*. Each functionality or mode will be managed by a view controller, and the set of these controllers defines the application. You can use a tab-bar controller to manage several view controllers similar to the one you saw in the previous section. Each controller is represented by a button, and the set of buttons is available at the bottom of the screen on a tab bar managed by the tab-bar controller. When the user taps a button, the view of the corresponding controller becomes the visible view, and the button changes to indicate that it is the active mode. Adding a tab bar to your application is simple: You simply create a tab-bar controller, add the set of view controllers to it, and add its view to an existing view. In the next section, we present a simple application that demonstrates the basic steps needed in developing radio-based interface applications.

7.2.1 A detailed example of a tab-bar application

In this section, we create a simple application that utilizes a tab bar. The application screen shot is shown in Figure 7.3.

The application presents the user geometric shapes to choose among. Each item is represented by a view controller that, when its item is selected, displays the name of the shape in its view.

The first step is writing the classes for the view controllers of each item. In this example, we use a single view controller class to represent every item. Each controller instance will be configured to output a different message. Note that every item (or mode) usually has its own view controller class. The view controller class is `CDBViewController`, and it is declared in Listing 7.7.

Triangle

Figure 7.3   A screen shot of a simple tab-bar application.

Listing 7.7   The declaration of the view controller representing each item in the tab-bar application.

```
#import <UIKit/UIKit.h>
@interface CDBViewController : UIViewController {
  NSString *message;
}
@property (nonatomic, retain) NSString *message;
- (id)initWithMessage:(NSString *)theMessage andImage:(UIImage*) image;
@end
```

The view controller uses a custom initializer, `initWithMessage:andImage:`, which initializes the view controller with the custom message that will be displayed when it becomes active, and an image used to represent its item in the item list on the tab bar.

The implementation of the view controller class is shown in Listing 7.8.

Listing 7.8   The implementation of the view controller used in the tab-bar application.

```
#import "CDBViewController.h"
#import "CDBUIView.h"

@implementation CDBViewController
@synthesize message;
```

```
- (id)initWithMessage:(NSString *)theMessage andImage:(UIImage*) image {
  if (self = [super initWithNibName:nil bundle:nil]) {
    self.message = theMessage;
    self.tabBarItem.image  = image;
  }
  return self;
}
- (void)loadView {
  CGRect   rectFrame = [UIScreen mainScreen].applicationFrame;
  CDBUIView *theView = [[CDBUIView alloc] initWithFrame:rectFrame];
  theView.backgroundColor = [UIColor whiteColor];
  theView.myController = self;
  theView.autoresizingMask = UIViewAutoresizingFlexibleHeight |
                             UIViewAutoresizingFlexibleWidth;
  self.view = theView;
  [theView release];
}
@end
```

The initializer first calls the super's initializer, `initWithNibName:bundle:`. Because we are going to build our graphical interface programmatically, we pass a `nil` value for both parameters. The initializer then stores the custom message in the `message` property for later use by its managed view and stores the image representing this controller in the `image` property of the `tabBarItem` property of the view controller instance.

The `tabBarItem` property is declared in the `UIViewController` class as follows:

```
@property(nonatomic, readonly, retain) UITabBarItem *tabBarItem
```

The value for this property is an object (possibly `nil`) of the class `UITabBarItem` representing the view controller on the tab bar. The `UITabBarItem` class is a subclass of `UIBarItem`. It inherits from its superclass the `image` and `title` properties. The default value for the image is `nil`. However, the `title` value, if not set, is set to the value of the view controller's `title` property. The `UITabBarItem` class adds an additional property: `badgeValue`, which is an instance of `NSString`, and its value is shown inside a red oval to the right of the corresponding tab-bar item. We cover configuring badges in Section 7.2.2.

The controller, as usual, overrides the `loadView` method for setting up its managed view. This method is similar to what we saw in the previous section. The view class is a custom view class, `CDBUIView`, that we will see shortly. Because we plan to add the view controller to a tab-bar controller, the view managed by the view controller needs to be able to resize so that it fits above the tab bar. Therefore, it is important to set the `autoresizingMask` property of the managed view as shown in the method.

The `CDBUIView` view class is declared in Listing 7.9. It simply maintains a `myController` property to hold a reference to its controller. This reference is needed so that the view can retrieve the proper message to be drawn in the view.

Listing 7.9   The view class declaration used in the tab-bar application.

```
#import <UIKit/UIKit.h>
@class CDBViewController;
@interface CDBUIView : UIView {
  CDBViewController *myController;
}
@property(nonatomic, assign) CDBViewController* myController;
@end
```

The implementation of the `CDBUIView` class is shown in Listing 7.10. The class overrides the `drawRect:` method of its superclass to draw the message obtained from the controller.

Listing 7.10   The implementation of the view class used in the tab-bar application.

```
#import "CDBUIView.h"
@implementation CDBUIView
@synthesize myController;
- (void)drawRect:(CGRect)rect {
  [[myController message] drawAtPoint:CGPointMake(80, 30)
                            withFont:[UIFont systemFontOfSize:20]];
}
@end
```

Now that we have constructed the view controller and its required view class, we can use the application delegate to present the application window to the user. The application delegate class declaration is shown in Listing 7.11. In addition to maintaining a reference to the main window, it has six references to view controllers, all of type `CDBViewController`. These controllers will be added to a tab-bar controller of type `UITabBarController` whose reference is in the instance variable `tabBarController`.

Listing 7.11   The application delegate class declaration used to present the main window in the tab-bar application.

```
#import <UIKit/UIKit.h>
@class CDBViewController;
@interface CDBAppDelegate : NSObject {
  UIWindow            *window;
  CDBViewController   *viewController1, *viewController2,
                      *viewController3, *viewController4,
                      *viewController5, *viewController6;
  UITabBarController  *tabBarController;
}
@end
```

Listing 7.12 shows the implementation of the application delegate class.

Listing 7.12   The application delegate class implementation used to present the main window in the tab-bar application.

```objc
#import "CDBAppDelegate.h"
#import "CDBViewController.h"
@implementation CDBAppDelegate

- (void)applicationDidFinishLaunching:(UIApplication *)application {
  window =
    [[UIWindow alloc] initWithFrame:[[UIScreen  mainScreen] bounds]];
  viewController1 =
    [[CDBViewController alloc]
           initWithMessage:@"Triangle"
           andImage:[UIImage imageNamed:@"tri.png"]];
  viewController1.title =  @"Tri";
  viewController2 =
     [[CDBViewController alloc]
           initWithMessage:@"Rectangle"
           andImage:[UIImage imageNamed:@"rect.png"]];
  viewController2.title =  @"Rect";
  viewController3 =
     [[CDBViewController alloc]
           initWithMessage:@"Ellipse"
           andImage:[UIImage imageNamed:@"ellipse.png"]];
  viewController3.title =  @"Elli";
  viewController4 =
     [[CDBViewController alloc]
           initWithMessage:@"Rectangle+Ellipse"
           andImage:[UIImage imageNamed:@"rect-elli.png"]];
  viewController4.title =  @"R&E";
  viewController5 =
     [[CDBViewController alloc]
           initWithMessage:@"Rectangle+Triangle"
           andImage:[UIImage imageNamed:@"rect-tri.png"]];
  viewController5.title =  @"R&T";
  viewController6 =
     [[CDBViewController alloc]
           initWithMessage:@"Rectangle+Rectangle"
           andImage:[UIImage imageNamed:@"two-tri.png"]];
  viewController6.title =  @"R&R";
  tabBarController =  [[UITabBarController alloc] init];
  tabBarController.viewControllers =
                [NSArray arrayWithObjects:
                    viewController1, viewController2, viewController3,
                    viewController4, viewController5, viewController6,
                    nil];
  [window addSubview:tabBarController.view];
  [window makeKeyAndVisible];
```

```
}

- (void)dealloc {
  [window release];
  [viewController1 release];
  [viewController2 release];
  [viewController3 release];
  [viewController4 release];
  [viewController5 release];
  [viewController6 release];
  [tabBarController release];
  [super dealloc];
}
@end
```

The application delegate overrides the `applicationDidFinishLaunching:` method for setting up the main window. First, we create six instances of the `CDBViewController` view controller class. Each of these instances is initialized with the message that will be displayed in their view and the image that will be displayed as their representation on the tab bar. In addition, the view controller's title is set, which also has the side effect of setting the tab-bar item's title to the same value.

The image files are stored in the application's bundle. Using the class method `imageNamed:`, we retrieve the image encapsulated by a `UIImage` class. See Section 10.6 for more information on the application bundle.

After creating the view controllers, we create the tab-bar controller that will manage them. This class is of type `UITabBarController`. To add the view controllers, we set its `viewControllers` property. This property is declared as

```
@property(nonatomic, copy) NSArray *viewControllers
```

Therefore, all we have to do is create an instance of `NSArray` with the six view controller instances as its elements and use it as the value for the `viewControllers` property.

Finally, we have to add the tab bar's view to the main window as a subview. When the window appears, the tab bar's view appears, and it will consist of the tab bar (at the bottom) and the currently selected view controller's view above it. Initially, the first controller is selected.

The complete application can be found in the `CDB` project in the source downloads.

7.2.2   Some comments on tab-bar controllers

There are several additional aspects of the tab-bar controller that need to be highlighted:

- **The `More` list.** If there are more than five view controllers to be managed, the tab-bar will show the first four controllers and an additional `More` item is added as the fifth controller. Tapping on the `More` item will present a list of the rest of the view controllers. Figure 7.4 shows how the view changes when the `More` item is tapped.

Figure 7.4   Showing the additional items on the tab-bar by tapping on the `More` item.

Figure 7.5   Showing an item on the `More` list. Tapping on `More` shows the `More` list.

The user can then tap on any of the items to activate the corresponding view controller. Figure 7.5 shows what happens when the user taps on the `R&T` item. The user can tap on the `More` button to go back to the list of `More` items.

The `More` item is managed by a navigation controller that can be accessed using the tab-bar controller's property `moreNavigationController`, which is declared as

```
@property(nonatomic, readonly) UINavigationController
                              *moreNavigationController
```

We will talk more about navigational controllers in the next section. For now, note that a navigational controller allows the application developer to present the user with hierarchical information in a natural way.

- **Badge.** Every item on the tab bar can have an optional value displayed in its upper-right corner surrounded by a red oval. The property that controls this is `badgeValue`, which is declared as

```
@property(nonatomic, copy) NSString *badgeValue
```

The default value for this property is `nil`. You can assign any string value to it, but usually it is a short message (e.g., a number). For example, to add a badge value to the third controller, we can write

```
viewController3.tabBarItem.badgeValue = @"3";
```

Figure 7.6   Showing a badge value for a view controller on a tab bar.

Figure 7.6 shows the effect of this line on the appearance of the tab bar.

- **Selected controller.** You can retrieve or change the selected controller by manipulating the `selectedViewController` property. The property is declared as

```
@property(nonatomic,assign) UIViewController *selectedViewController
```

Note that if the `More` item is selected, the view controller for the `More` list is returned. Also note that you can change the selected view controller for the items that are displayed on the tab bar as well as the hidden view controllers. Starting with iOS 3.0, writing something like the following no longer results in an `NSRangeException` exception:

```
tabBarController.selectedViewController = viewController5;
```

You can also retrieve/change the selected view controller using the `selectedIndex`, property, which is declared as

```
@property(nonatomic) NSUInteger selectedIndex
```

where the index `0` (first controller selected) is the default value. The `selectedView-Controller` and `selectedIndex` properties are connected; changing one will result in a change to the other.

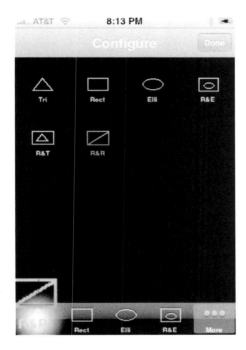

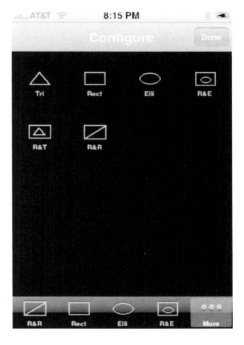

Figure 7.7   Rearranging the items on the tab bar by moving the R&R item to the first place.

Figure 7.8   The state of the tab bar after moving the R&R item to the beginning but while still being in editing mode.

- **Customization.** If you have more than five items managed by the tab-bar controller, you can give the user the ability to rearrange the position of these controllers. Because only the first four controllers will appear on the main screen, and the rest will be displayed in a table, the user may want to move some of the controllers in the table to the main window.

  You can specify that a view controller can be customized by putting its reference in the customizableViewControllers array, which is declared as follows:

  ```
  @property(nonatomic, copy) NSArray *customizableViewControllers
  ```

  To change the position of a specific controller, the user taps on the More list and then on the Edit button. Then he or she can tap the image of that controller and drag it to its new position. Figure 7.7 shows R&R while it is in the process of being moved to the first position. Figure 7.8 shows the state just after the move.

  A controller that has lost its position (in our example, the Tri controller), will be moved to the table display as shown in Figure 7.9.

  By default, when you set the viewControllers property, the same object references go to the customizableViewControllers property. That means that all view controllers are customizable. If you would like to pin down one or more view controllers, you need to change

Figure 7.9   The state of the tab bar after moving the R&R item to the beginning and exiting editing mode.

this property. For example, to make the only customizable view controllers the first, second, and fifth controllers, you can write something like the following:

```
tabBarController.customizableViewControllers =
        [NSArray arrayWithObjects:viewController1, viewController2,
                                    viewController5, nil];
```

7.3   Navigation Controllers

Often, you would like to present hierarchical information to the user. The user starts at the top level of the information hierarchy. Then he or she taps on a specific item, and the next level of the hierarchy is displayed. The process of drilling down continues until the user reaches the desired level.

The class UINavigationController is provided for managing hierarchical views to the user. As we saw in the previous section, the controller manages view controllers and each view controller manages the actual view for a given level. This class presents to the user a navigation bar and the view of the current level of hierarchy. In Section 9.8, you will see how table views are ideal for such data presentation. In that section, we will use a navigation controller with table views to present hierarchal information in a user-friendly manner. In this section, however, we would like to look at the basic mechanisms behind the UINavigationController class. We first present a detailed example showing the default behavior of this class and then discuss some of the customization options available to you.

7.3.1   A detailed example of a navigation controller

This section presents a detailed example that utilizes a navigation controller. The application has three levels of hierarchy: Level I, Level II, and Level III. To keep the example simple and to the point, the user moves to the next level of hierarchy by just tapping on the view of the previous level. Also, all view controllers managed by the navigation controller are instances of the same class; it's the message displayed inside each view that distinguishes these levels of hierarchy. Figure 7.10 shows the first level of hierarchy.

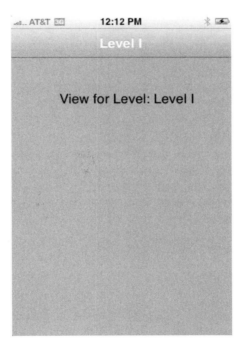

Figure 7.10   The navigation-controller application showing the first level of hierarchy.

The figure shows the navigation bar and the controller below it. The navigation bar has a title in the middle. By default, the title in the middle of the navigation bar is the same as the title property of the topmost view controller. Figure 7.11 shows the application screen shot when the user taps on the view of the first level.

A new view appears that shows the second level of hierarchy. The second view appears by *pushing* a new view controller on the stack of navigation managed by the navigation controller. Notice that

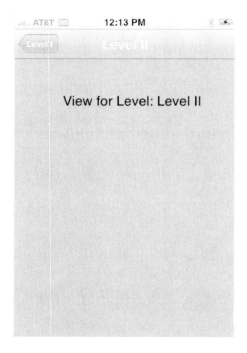

Figure 7.11   The navigation-controller application showing the second level of hierarchy.

by default, a back button appears on the left that has the title of the previous level. Tapping on the back button *pops* the current view controller from the stack, and the view of the previous view controller appears.

The view controller

Let's start by building the view controller classes whose instances will be pushed and popped on and off the navigation stack. To simplify things, we assume that all view controllers are instances of one view controller, CDCViewController. Listing 7.13 shows the declaration of this class. It declares the showNextLevel method used by the view to show the next level of the view hierarchy.

Listing 7.13   The declaration of the view controller used in the navigation-controller application.

```
#define  LEVELI    @"Level I"
#define  LEVELII   @"Level II"
#define  LEVELIII @"Level III"

@interface CDCViewController : UIViewController {
}
-(void)showNextLevel;
@end
```

Listing 7.14 shows the implementation of the view controller. `showNextLevel` uses the application delegate to push the view controller of the next level on the stack of the navigation controller (which itself is managed by the application delegate). To retrieve a reference to the single application delegate, use the class method `sharedApplication` of the `UIApplication` class. The `loadView` method is similar to what we saw before. It uses the `CDCUIView` class for the view.

Listing 7.14   The implementation of the view controller used in the navigation-controller application.

```
#import "CDCViewController.h"
#import "CDCUIView.h"

@implementation CDCViewController
-(void)showNextLevel{
  [[[UIApplication sharedApplication] delegate] showNextLevel:self.title];
}

- (void)loadView {
  CGRect  rectFrame = [UIScreen mainScreen].applicationFrame;
  CDCUIView *theView  = [[CDCUIView alloc] initWithFrame:rectFrame];
  theView.backgroundColor = [UIColor grayColor];
  theView.myController = self;
  theView.autoresizingMask = UIViewAutoresizingFlexibleHeight |
                             UIViewAutoresizingFlexibleWidth;
  self.view = theView;
  [theView release];
}
@end
```

The view

Listing 7.15 shows the declaration of the view class `CDCUIView` used by the view controller. The view has a reference to its controller in the property `myController`. We will see in Listing 7.16 how this reference is used in the method intercepting the user's tapping in order to navigate to the next level.

Listing 7.15   The declaration of the view class used in the navigation-controller application.

```
@class CDCViewController;

@interface CDCUIView : UIView {
  CDCViewController *myController;
}
@property(nonatomic, assign) CDCViewController*  myController;
@end
```

Listing 7.16 shows the implementation of the view class. As we mentioned before, to navigate to the next level, the user taps on the view. The method `touchesBegan:withEvent:` intercepts the tapping and invokes the controller's `showNextLevel` method, which in turn invokes the application delegate `showNextLevel:` method. The `drawRect:` method is used to display a unique message in the view area that is specific to each of the three navigation levels.

Listing 7.16   The implementation of the view class used in the navigation-controller application.

```
#import "CDCUIView.h"
#import "CDCViewController.h"

@implementation CDCUIView
@synthesize myController;

- (void)touchesBegan:(NSSet *)touches withEvent:(UIEvent *)event{
  [myController showNextLevel];
}
- (void)drawRect:(CGRect)rect {
  NSString *message;
  message =
     [NSString stringWithFormat:
                         @"View for Level: %@",[myController title]];
  [message
    drawAtPoint:CGPointMake(70, 50)
    withFont:[UIFont systemFontOfSize:20]];
}
@end
```

The application delegate

Listing 7.17 shows the declaration of the application delegate class. It keeps track of the window and the three view controllers. In addition, it maintains a reference to the navigation controller. The application delegate also declares the method `showNextLevel:` that will be invoked by the view controller to go to the next level.

Listing 7.17   The declaration of the application delegate class of the navigation-controller application.

```
@class CDCViewController;

@interface CDCAppDelegate : NSObject {
  UIWindow               *window;
  CDCViewController       *levelI, *levelII, *levelIII;
  UINavigationController  *navController;
}
- (void)showNextLevel:(NSString*) level;
@end
```

Listing 7.18 shows the implementation of the application delegate class. The `applicationDid-FinishLaunching:` method is used to initialize the application's graphical user interface (GUI). It starts by creating a window and then the view controller for the first level of hierarchy. After that, the navigation controller is created and initialized. A navigation controller is an instance of the class `UINavigationController`, which is a subclass of the `UIViewController` class. The instance of the navigation controller is initialized by the `initWithRootViewController:` method, which is declared as follows:

```
- (id)initWithRootViewController:(UIViewController *)rootViewController
```

The initializer has a single parameter: the view controller instance that will become the first level (root) of the hierarchy. This controller is pushed on the (empty) stack without animation. After creating and initializing the navigation controller, we add its view to the window as a subview. This will result in having the navigation bar added below the status bar and the view of the root controller below it.

The `showNextLevel:` method takes the current level's name as a parameter. It pushes the second-level controller if the current level is the root and the third-level controller if it is the second level. To push a new view controller on the stack, you need to first create it and then use the `pushViewController:animated:` method to put it on the stack. This method is declared as follows:

```
- (void)pushViewController:(UIViewController *)viewController
          animated:(BOOL)animated
```

If `animated` is `YES`, the transition to the next level is animated. By default, when a view controller is pushed on the stack, the title of the current view controller becomes the title of the left button. The title in the middle will be changed to reflect the title of the newly pushed view controller. When the user taps on the left button, the current view controller is popped from the stack, the view of the previous controller replaces the view below the navigation bar, the title in the middle of the navigation bar is replaced with the title of the previous view controller, and the back button's title is changed accordingly. The method for popping the top view controller is `popViewControllerAnimated:`, and it is declared as follows:

```
- (UIViewController *)popViewControllerAnimated:(BOOL)animated
```

If animated is `YES`, the popping is animated; otherwise, it is not. Notice that the method also returns a reference to the popped view controller. It is worth noting that if there is only one view controller on the stack (root), the method will not be able to pop it but will gracefully return without generating an exception.

Listing 7.18   The implementation of the application delegate class of the navigation-controller application.

```
#import "CDCAppDelegate.h"
#import "CDCViewController.h"

@implementation CDCAppDelegate

- (void)showNextLevel:(NSString*) level{
  if([level isEqualToString:LEVEL1]){
```

```
    levelII = [[CDCViewController alloc] initWithNibName:nil bundle:nil];
    levelII.title = LEVELII;
    [navController pushViewController:levelII animated:YES];
  }
  else if([level isEqualToString:LEVELII]){
    levelIII = [[CDCViewController alloc] initWithNibName:nil bundle:nil];
    levelIII.title = LEVELIII;
    [navController pushViewController:levelIII animated:YES];
  }
}

- (void)
applicationDidFinishLaunching:(UIApplication *)application {
  window =
    [[UIWindow alloc] initWithFrame:[[UIScreen  mainScreen] bounds]];
  levelI = [[CDCViewController alloc] initWithNibName:nil bundle:nil];
  levelI.title = LEVELI;
  navController =
    [[UINavigationController alloc] initWithRootViewController:levelI];
  [window addSubview:navController.view];
  [window makeKeyAndVisible];
}

- (void)dealloc {
  [window release];
  [levelI release];
  [levelII release];
  [levelIII release];
  [navController release];
  [super dealloc];
}
@end
```

The complete application can be found in the CDC project in the source downloads.

7.3.2 Customization

In the previous section, you learned the default behavior of navigation controllers. In this section, we look at ways to customize the appearance and behavior of navigation bars.

Every view controller is represented on the navigation bar by a navigation item. A navigation item is an instance of the UINavigationItem class. This class declares several properties that define the appearance of the view controller when it is pushed onto the stack or when another view controller is pushed on top of it (i.e., it becomes the immediate child controller). By default, when a view controller is pushed onto the stack, the title in the middle of the navigation bar becomes the same as the view controller's title. When another view controller is pushed onto the stack, the title of the back button becomes the title of the currently active view controller (the controller about to become a child). To change this behavior, you can access the navigation item of each view controller instance and set its various properties instead of allowing them to be taken from the default values. To obtain the instance of the navigation item, use the property `navigationItem`, which is declared in the `UIViewController` class as follows:

```
@property(nonatomic, readonly, retain) UINavigationItem *navigationItem
```

Following are some important properties of the navigation item:

- **The title.** To specify the title of the navigation bar when the view controller is topmost on the stack, set the `title` property of its navigation item. The `title` property is declared as

  ```
  @property(nonatomic, copy)    NSString    *title
  ```

  For example, to set the title of the navigation item for the view controller, `ctrl1`, change the `title` property as follows:

  ```
  ctrl1.navigationItem.title = @"Nav Title 1";
  ```

  Every time `ctrl1` is the topmost controller on the stack, the title of the navigation bar is `"Nav Title 1"`.

- **The prompt.** There is an optional text that can be displayed above the navigation bar buttons. To take advantage of this option, set the `prompt` property of the navigation item, which is declared as

  ```
  @property(nonatomic, copy)    NSString *prompt
  ```

  For example, the following code will result in the prompt in Figure 7.12:

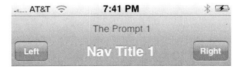

Figure 7.12   Customizing a navigation bar to show custom right/left buttons, prompt, and title.

```
ctrl1.navigationItem.prompt = @"The Prompt 1";
```

- **Right/left buttons.** You can add a right and/or a left button to the navigation bar. To add a right button that will appear when the view controller becomes the topmost on the stack, set the property `rightBarButtonItem`, which is declared as follows:

  ```
  @property(nonatomic, retain) UIBarButtonItem *rightBarButtonItem
  ```

  To add a left button to the navigation bar, set the `leftBarButtonItem` property, which is declared as

  ```
  @property(nonatomic, retain) UIBarButtonItem *leftBarButtonItem
  ```

Note that this custom left button will replace the regular back button on the bar if one exists.

For example, to create a right button, you can write something like the following in the view controller's initializer:

```
UIBarButtonItem * rightButton =
      [[UIBarButtonItem alloc]
                  initWithTitle:@"Right"
                  style:UIBarButtonItemStyleDone
                  target:self
                  action:@selector(rightButtonTapped:)];
self.navigationItem.rightBarButtonItem = rightButton;
[rightButton release];
```

In the above code, we are creating an instance of a `UIBarButtonItem` and initializing it with the title, the style, and the method that will be invoked when the button is tapped. You might want to review Section 6.1.2 and come back here for a better understanding of the target-action mechanism.

Figure 7.12 shows a navigation bar with right and left custom buttons. The right button is the one created by the code above, having a style of `UIBarButtonItemStyleDone`. The left button is created using the style `UIBarButtonItemStylePlain`. You can use another style: `UIBarButtonItemStyleBordered`.

- **Title view.** You have the option of displaying a view instead of the title of the navigation bar. To specify a view, set the `titleView` property, which is declared as follows:

```
@property(nonatomic, retain) UIView *titleView
```

To demonstrate this, let's consider the view class `MyBarView` shown in Listing 7.19. This class simply implements a view that has a white background and draws `Hello` text inside itself.

Listing 7.19   A custom view that will replace the title in a navigation bar.

```
@interface MyBarView : UIView {}
@end

@implementation MyBarView

- (id)initWithFrame:(CGRect)frame {
  if (self = [super initWithFrame:frame]) {
    self.backgroundColor = [UIColor whiteColor];
  }
  return self;
}


- (void)drawRect:(CGRect)rect {
  [@"Hello" drawAtPoint:CGPointMake(55, 5)
          withFont:[UIFont systemFontOfSize:20]];
}
@end
```

To replace the title text with a view (see Figure 7.13) for controller `ctrl1`, you write something like the following:

```
MyBarView *titleView = [[[MyBarView alloc]
  initWithFrame:CGRectMake(0, 0, 150, 30)] autorelease];
ctrl1.navigationItem.titleView = titleView;
```

Figure 7.13   A navigation bar with custom view title.

- **Editing support.** Some subclasses of `UIViewController`, such as `UITableView-Controller`, support editing a view. When the view managed by a controllers can be edited, it is customary to have an Edit button on the right-hand side. When this Edit button is tapped by the user, the view is supposed to enter editing mode and the button's title changes to Done. Once the user finishes editing, he or she taps on the Done button and the view controller is supposed to save the changes made.

It turns out that such a mechanism is already built in, and using it requires little effort. First, the `UIViewController` class has a method to communicate that change in its editing mode. This method is `setEditing:animated:`, which is declared as

```
- (void)setEditing:(BOOL)editing animated:(BOOL)animated
```

Subclasses of `UIViewController` override this method in order to respond appropriately.

Furthermore, the `UIViewController` declares a property called `editing` that can be set to change the editing mode of the view controller. This property is declared as

```
@property(nonatomic, getter=isEditing) BOOL editing
```

When you change the value of this property, `setEditing:animated:` is invoked with the corresponding change. Furthermore, when the user taps on the Edit/Done button, the property's value is changed accordingly.

To add an Edit/Done button to the right-hand side when `ctrl1` is the topmost view controller, you can write something like the following:

```
ctrl1.navigationItem.rightBarButtonItem = [ctrl1 editButtonItem];
ctrl1.editing = NO;
```

Notice how we have obtained the button using the view controller's instance method `editButtonItem`, which is declared as

```
- (UIBarButtonItem *)editButtonItem
```

Figures 7.14 and 7.15 show the Edit and Done buttons on a navigation bar, respectively.

Figure 7.14   An Edit button on a navigation bar.

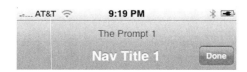

Figure 7.15   A Done button on a navigation bar.

7.4   Modal View Controllers

A *modal view controller* allows you to overlay another view controller on top of an existing one. When the modal view controller is presented to the user, it occupies the whole space below the status bar. Modal view controllers can appear animated from bottom to top (default behavior), flipped from right to left, or faded in.

Every view controller can present at most one modal view controller at a time. The `modalViewController` property holds the reference to the modal view controller. This property is declared as

```
@property(nonatomic, readonly) UIViewController *modalViewController;
```

Likewise, the view controller, if presented as a modal view controller by another view controller, has a reference to its parent view controller using the `parentViewController` property, which is declared as

```
@property(nonatomic,readonly) UIViewController *parentViewController
```

To display a modal view controller, the view controller invokes the instance method `presentModalViewController:animated:`, which is declared as

```
- (void)
  presentModalViewController:(UIViewController *)modalViewController
  animated:(BOOL)animated
```

Without any configuration, the previous statement presents the controller from bottom to top. If you want to show the controller differently, you can set its `modalTransitionStyle` property to either `UIModalTransitionStyleFlipHorizontal` or `UIModalTransitionStyleCrossDissolve`. The style for the default behavior is denoted by `UIModalTransitionStyleCoverVertical`, but you do not need to set it, as it is the default.

After the view of the modal view controller appears and the user finishes interacting with it, a mechanism (usually a button on the navigation bar) is used to dismiss the modal view controller. To dismiss the modal view controller, the parent view controller needs to invoke the method `dismissModalViewControllerAnimated:`, which is declared as

```
- (void)dismissModalViewControllerAnimated:(BOOL)animated
```

Let's illustrate modal view controllers using a detailed example. In the following, we build an application that first presents a view controller managed by a navigation controller. When the user taps on the view, another navigation controller is presented modally (Figure 7.16).

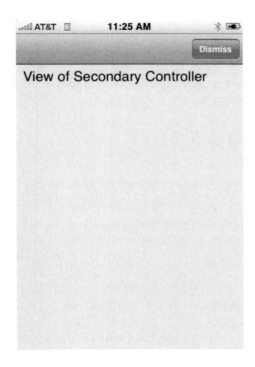

Figure 7.16   The view of the modal view controller and the navigation bar with the Dismiss button.

The modal controller has a Dismiss button on the navigation bar that, when tapped, will dismiss the modal controller and show the view of the hidden parent controller.

The parent view controller class is `MainViewController`, which is declared in Listing 7.20.

Listing 7.20   The declaration of `MainViewController` that presents a modal view controller.

```
@class SecondaryViewController;

@interface MainViewController : UIViewController {
    SecondaryViewController *secondaryCtrl1;
```

```
    UINavigationController   *secondaryNavigationCtrl;
}
-(void) showModalController;
-(void) dismissModalController;
@end
```

The controller has a reference to the modal view controller as it will create it when the user taps on its view. A reference to the navigation controller, which will also be created at that time, is also maintained. As we will see shortly, the showModalController method will be invoked from its view, and the dismissModalController is the action method of the Dismiss navigation bar button found on the modal controller. Listing 7.21 shows the implementation of the class.

Listing 7.21   The implementation of MainViewController that presents a modal view controller.

```
#import "MainViewController.h"
#import "SecondaryViewController.h"
#import "MainView.h"

@implementation MainViewController

- (void)loadView {
  CGRect   rectFrame = [UIScreen mainScreen].applicationFrame;
  MainView *theView   = [[MainView alloc] initWithFrame:rectFrame];
  theView.myController = self;
  theView.backgroundColor = [UIColor grayColor];
  theView.autoresizingMask = UIViewAutoresizingFlexibleHeight |
                             UIViewAutoresizingFlexibleWidth;
  self.view = theView;
  [theView release];
}

-(void) showModalController{
  secondaryCtrl1 = [[SecondaryViewController alloc]
                         initWithNibName:nil
                         bundle:nil parent:self];
  secondaryNavigationCtrl = [[UINavigationController alloc]
                         initWithRootViewController:secondaryCtrl1];
  [self presentModalViewController:secondaryNavigationCtrl animated:YES];
}

-(void) dismissModalController {
  [secondaryCtrl1 release];
  [secondaryNavigationCtrl release];
  [self dismissModalViewControllerAnimated:YES];
}
@end
```

The `loadView` method is very similar to the `loadView` methods we have seen so far. The view created is of type `MainView`, which we will see shortly. When the user taps on the view, the view invokes the `showModalController` method. This method creates the view controller of type `SecondaryViewController` and then makes it the root controller of a new navigation controller. It will then display the navigation controller on top of itself and the navigation bar by invoking the `presentModalViewController:animated:` method, animating the appearance from bottom to top. As we will see shortly, the `SecondaryViewController` adds a Dismiss button to the navigation bar and makes its target-action this controller instance and the `dismissModalController` method. The method simply deallocates the view and the navigation controllers, and invokes the `dismissModalViewControllerAnimated:` method, animating the dismissal of the navigation controller from top to bottom.

The view class for the parent view controller is declared in Listing 7.22. It is similar to what we have seen so far. The implementation of this class is shown in Listing 7.23. The view overrides the `touchesBegan:withEvent:` method to ask the view controller to show the modal view controller.

Listing 7.22   The declaration of the `MainView` class used as the view for the controller presenting a modal view controller.

```
@class MainViewController;
@interface MainView : UIView {
  MainViewController *myController;
}
@property(nonatomic, assign) MainViewController* myController;
@end
```

Listing 7.23   The implementation of the `MainView` class used as the view for the controller presenting a modal view controller.

```
#import "MainView.h"
#import "MainViewController.h"

@implementation MainView
@synthesize myController;
- (void)touchesBegan:(NSSet *)touches withEvent:(UIEvent *)event{
  [myController showModalController];
}
@end
```

Listing 7.24 shows the declaration of the `SecondaryViewController` class. The initializer has a reference parameter to the parent view controller, which will become the target of the Dismiss button.

Listing 7.24   The declaration of the `SecondaryViewController` class.

```
@class MainViewController;

@interface SecondaryViewController : UIViewController {
}
```

```
- (id)initWithNibName:(NSString *)nibNameOrNil
      bundle:(NSBundle *)nibBundleOrNil
      parent:(MainViewController*) myParent;
@end
```

Listing 7.25 shows the implementation of the `SecondaryViewController` class. The initializer
adds a right Dismiss button on the navigation bar.

Listing 7.25   The implementation of the `SecondaryViewController` class.

```
#import "SecondaryViewController.h"
#import "SecondaryView.h"
#import "MainViewController.h"

@implementation SecondaryViewController

- (id)initWithNibName:(NSString *)nibNameOrNil
      bundle:(NSBundle *)nibBundleOrNil
      parent:(MainViewController*) myParent{
  if (self = [super initWithNibName:nibNameOrNil
      bundle:nibBundleOrNil]) {
    UIBarButtonItem *rightButton = [[UIBarButtonItem alloc]
                          initWithTitle:@"Dismiss"
                          style:UIBarButtonItemStyleDone
                          target:myParent
                          action:@selector(dismissModalController)];
    self.navigationItem.rightBarButtonItem = rightButton;
    [rightButton release];
  }
  return self;
}


- (void)loadView {
  CGRect  rectFrame = [UIScreen mainScreen].applicationFrame;
  SecondaryView *theView =
        [[SecondaryView alloc] initWithFrame:rectFrame];
  theView.backgroundColor = [UIColor yellowColor];
  theView.autoresizingMask = UIViewAutoresizingFlexibleHeight |
                          UIViewAutoresizingFlexibleWidth;
  self.view = theView;
  [theView release];

}
@end
```

Listing 7.26 shows the `SecondaryView` class used by the `SecondaryViewController` view
controller.

Listing 7.26   The `SecondaryView` class.

```
@interface SecondaryView : UIView {
}
@end

@implementation SecondaryView
- (void)drawRect:(CGRect)rect {
  [@"View of Secondary Controller"
       drawAtPoint:CGPointMake(10, 5)
       withFont:[UIFont systemFontOfSize:20]];
}
@end
```

To put all the previous pieces together, the application delegate class is shown in Listings 7.27 and 7.28. The application delegate has a reference to the navigation controller and its lone view controller. It creates the navigation controller, initializes it with the view controller, and displays it to the user.

Listing 7.27   The declaration of the application delegate class for the modal view controller application.

```
@class MainViewController;

@interface CDEAppDelegate : NSObject <UIApplicationDelegate> {
  UIWindow              *window;
  MainViewController    *ctrl1;
  UINavigationController *navCtrl1;
}
@property (nonatomic, retain) UIWindow *window;
@end
```

Listing 7.28   The implementation of the application delegate class for the modal view controller application.

```
#import "CDEAppDelegate.h"
#import "MainViewController.h"

@implementation CDEAppDelegate
@synthesize window;

- (void)applicationDidFinishLaunching:(UIApplication *)application {
  window =
       [[UIWindow alloc] initWithFrame:[[UIScreen mainScreen] bounds]];
  ctrl1 = [[MainViewController alloc] initWithNibName:nil bundle:nil];
  navCtrl1 = [[UINavigationController alloc]
                       initWithRootViewController:ctrl1];
  [window addSubview:navCtrl1.view];
  [window makeKeyAndVisible];
}
```

```
- (void)dealloc {
    [window release];
    [ctrl1 release];
    [navCtrl1 release];
    [super dealloc];
}
@end
```

The complete application can be found in the CDE project in the source downloads.

7.5   Summary

In this chapter, we covered the topic of view controllers. In Section 7.1, we provided a gentle introduction to view controllers by presenting a simple application with a single view controller. This application demonstrated important view controller concepts. In Section 7.2, we talked about tab-bar controllers and how they can be used in the construction of radio interfaces. In Section 7.3, we talked about navigation controllers, used primarily for presenting hierarchical information to the user. After that, Section 7.4 talked about modal view controllers and provided a detailed example showing their appropriate usage.

Exercises

(1) Study the UIViewController.h header file and the documentation on UIViewController class.

(2) After reading the relevant chapters in this book, come back here and write an application that remembers the last tab before termination and selects that tab when it is launched the next time.

8

Special-Purpose Views

This chapter presents several important subclasses of the `UIView` class. In Section 8.1, we discuss picker views and show how they can be used for item selection. In Section 8.2, we discuss progress views and also talk about activity indicator views. Next, Section 8.3 shows how to use scroll views in order to display large (greater than 320×480) views. Section 8.4 presents text views used in displaying multiline text. In Section 8.5 we show how to use alert views for the display of alert messages to the user. Similar to alert views are action sheets, which are discussed in Section 8.6. In Section 8.7, we discuss several aspects of web views. Finally, we provide a summary in Section 8.8.

8.1 Picker View

The `UIPickerView` class can be used for giving the user a fancy way to select an item from a set of values. The class allows you to have multiple sets of values where each set is represented by a wheel (see Figure 8.1 for an example). The user spins the wheel in order to select a specific value from a given set. The values in a given set can be views (such as instances of `UILabel`, `UIImageView`, etc.) or strings.

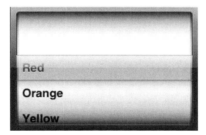

Figure 8.1 An example of a picker view.

Each wheel is a graphical representation of a *component*. Components are numbered starting from 0. Each component contains *rows* (i.e., the set of values). Rows are also numbered starting from 0.

You can dynamically change the contents of any component. To force a change in the contents of a specific component, change the underlying data model (e.g., the array) representing the values of the component and call the `UIPickerView`'s method `reloadComponent:` passing in the component index. If you would like to change all the components, call the method `reloadAllComponents`.

8.1.1   The delegate

To use an instance of a `UIPickerView`, you need to set up a delegate for it. This delegate must adopt the protocol `UIPickerViewDelegate` and implement specific methods defined by this protocol.

To actually construct the view contents, the `UIPickerView` instance needs the value for each (`component, row`) pair. The delegate has to implement either a method that returns an `NSString` instance or a `UIView` instance. The method that returns an `NSString` instance is declared as

```
- (NSString *)pickerView:(UIPickerView *)pickerView
            titleForRow:(NSInteger)row
            forComponent:(NSInteger)component
```

`pickerView` is the picker view requesting the title value, and `row` is the row number inside `component`.

The method that returns an instance of a `UIView` is declared as

```
- (UIView *)pickerView:(UIPickerView *)pickerView
            viewForRow:(NSInteger)row
            forComponent:(NSInteger)component
            reusingView:(UIView *)view
```

`view` is a previously used view for this (`component`, `row`) pair. If this is adequate, you can just return this value. Otherwise, return a new view instance.

In addition, the delegate must implement the following two methods:

```
- (NSInteger)numberOfComponentsInPickerView:(UIPickerView *)pickerView
```

This method provides the number of components (wheels) that the picker view instance should construct:

```
- (NSInteger)pickerView:(UIPickerView *)pickerView
            numberOfRowsInComponent:(NSInteger)component
```

This method provides the number of rows that the `component` contains.

In addition to these required methods, you can implement the following methods if you choose to:

- `pickerView:rowHeightForComponent:` is used to provide the view with the height (in points) of a given component. The method is declared as

    ```
    - (CGFloat)pickerView:(UIPickerView *)pickerView
                rowHeightForComponent:(NSInteger)component
    ```

- `pickerView:widthForComponent:` is used to provide the view with the width (in points) of a given component. The method is declared as

  - `(CGFloat)pickerView:(UIPickerView *)pickerView`
          `widthForComponent:(NSInteger)component`

- `pickerView:didSelectRow:inComponent:` is used by the picker view to inform the delegate that a given row in a specific component was selected. The method is called once the wheel settles on a specific row. The method is declared as

  - `(`**`void`**`)pickerView:(UIPickerView *)pickerView`
        `didSelectRow:(NSInteger)row`
        `inComponent:(NSInteger)component`

8.1.2   An example of picker view

Let's illustrate the concepts behind the `UIPickerView` class through a concrete example. We would like to construct a view in which the user chooses a street name and the direction on that street. The example utilizes two classes: the application delegate, `PVAppDelegate`, and the view controller, `PVViewController`.

Listings 8.1 and 8.2 show the declaration and definition of the application delegate class, respectively.

Listing 8.1   The file `PVAppDelegate.h` declaring the application delegate.

```
#import <UIKit/UIKit.h>
#import <Foundation/Foundation.h>

@class PVViewController;

@interface PVAppDelegate : NSObject {
  UIWindow          *window;
  PVViewController  *viewController;
}
@end
```

The application delegate creates the view controller and initializes it with the array of street names.

Listing 8.2   The file `PVAppDelegate.m` defining the application delegate.

```
#import "PVAppDelegate.h"
#import "PVViewController.h"

@implementation PVAppDelegate

- (void)applicationDidFinishLaunching:(UIApplication *)application {
```

```
    window=[[UIWindow alloc] initWithFrame:[[UIScreen mainScreen] bounds]];
    NSArray *arr = [NSArray arrayWithObjects:
                        @"Plano PKWY", @"Coit Road",
                        @"Preston Road", @"Legacy",
                        @"Independence", nil];
    viewController = [[PVViewController alloc] initWithStreetNames:arr];
    [window addSubview:viewController.view];
    [window makeKeyAndVisible];
}

- (void)dealloc {
    [window release];
    [viewController release];
    [super dealloc];
}
@end
```

Listings 8.3 and 8.4 show the view controller declaration and definition, respectively.

Listing 8.3   The file PVViewController.h declaring the view controller.

```
#import <UIKit/UIKit.h>
#import <Foundation/Foundation.h>

@interface PVViewController :UIViewController<UIPickerViewDelegate> {
    UIPickerView        *pickerView;
    NSArray             *streetNames;
    NSMutableArray      *directions;
}
-(id) initWithStreetNames:(NSArray*) streets;
@end
```

Listing 8.4   The file PVViewController.m defining the view controller.

```
#import "PVViewController.h"

@implementation PVViewController
-(id)initWithStreetNames:(NSArray*) streets{
    if (self = [super init]) {
        directions = [[NSMutableArray arrayWithObjects:@"East",@"West",nil]
                            retain];
        streetNames = [streets copy];
    }
    return self;
}
- (id)init{
    return [self initWithStreetNames:
                        [NSArray arrayWithObjects:@"Street Name", nil]];
```

```objc
}
- (void)loadView {
  //Create the main view
  UIView *theView    =
    [[UIView alloc] initWithFrame:[UIScreen mainScreen].applicationFrame];
  theView.autoresizingMask =
    UIViewAutoresizingFlexibleHeight | UIViewAutoresizingFlexibleWidth;
  // Create the picker view
  pickerView = [[UIPickerView alloc] initWithFrame:CGRectZero];
  CGSize pickerSize = [pickerView sizeThatFits:CGSizeZero];
  pickerView.frame= CGRectMake(0,0,pickerSize.width,pickerSize.height);
  pickerView.autoresizingMask = UIViewAutoresizingFlexibleWidth;
  pickerView.delegate = self;
  pickerView.showsSelectionIndicator = YES;
  [theView addSubview:pickerView];
  self.view = theView;
}
- (void)dealloc {
  [pickerView release];
  [directions release];
  [streetNames release];
  [super dealloc];
}
// Delegate methods
- (void)pickerView:(UIPickerView *)pickerView
        didSelectRow:(NSInteger)row
        inComponent:(NSInteger)component{
  NSString  *street, *direction;
  street =
    [streetNames objectAtIndex:[pickerView selectedRowInComponent:0]];
  direction  =
    [directions objectAtIndex:[pickerView selectedRowInComponent:1]];
  if(component ==0){
    if(  ([street isEqual:@"Coit Road"] == YES) ||
       ([street isEqual:@"Preston Road"] == YES) ||
       ([street isEqual:@"Independence"] == YES)){
      [directions removeAllObjects];
      [directions addObject:@"North"];
      [directions addObject:@"South"];
      [pickerView reloadComponent:1];
    }
    else{
      [directions removeAllObjects];
      [directions addObject:@"East"];
      [directions addObject:@"West"];
      [pickerView reloadComponent:1];
    }
    printf("Selected row in Component 0 is now %s.
```

```
                  Selected row in Component 1 remains %s\n",
            [street cStringUsingEncoding:NSUTF8StringEncoding],
            [direction cStringUsingEncoding:NSUTF8StringEncoding]);
  }
  else{
     printf("Selected row in Component 1 is now %s.
         Selected row in Component 0 remains %s\n",
            [direction cStringUsingEncoding:NSUTF8StringEncoding],
            [street cStringUsingEncoding:NSUTF8StringEncoding]);
  }
}
- (NSString *)pickerView:(UIPickerView *)pickerView
              titleForRow:(NSInteger)row
              forComponent:(NSInteger)component{
  if (component == 0){
    return [streetNames objectAtIndex:row];
  }
  else{
    return [directions objectAtIndex:row];
  }
}
- (CGFloat)pickerView:(UIPickerView *)pickerView
            widthForComponent:(NSInteger)component{
  if (component == 0)
    return 200.0;
  else
    return 100.0;
}
- (CGFloat)pickerView:(UIPickerView *)pickerView
            rowHeightForComponent:(NSInteger)component{
  return 40.0;
}
- (NSInteger)pickerView:(UIPickerView *)pickerView
               numberOfRowsInComponent:(NSInteger)component{
  if (component == 0){
    return [streetNames count];
  }
  else{
    return [directions count];
  }
}
- (NSInteger)numberOfComponentsInPickerView:(UIPickerView *)pickerView{
  return 2;
}
@end
```

The controller uses two arrays as the underlying data model for the picker view. The streetNames
array holds the names of the streets. The directions mutable array is a dynamic array that contains

the directions available on the currently selected street. Initialization of the data model is done in the method `initWithStreetNames:`.

The creation of the picker view is done in the controller's `loadView` method. The `UIPickerView` object is special in that it calculates the optimal size of itself internally. Therefore, you should use `CGRectZero` in the initialization. To fit the view using the internally calculated frame, use the `UIPickerView` instance method `sizeThatFits:` and pass a `CGRectZero`.

Once you have the optimal width and height of the view, you should update the picker view's frame. To finish the setup, set the property `showsSelectionIndicator` to `YES`, make the controller the delegate, and add the picker view to the main view.

Because the second component, the street directions, is a function of the selected street, we need to change its underlying data model when the currently selected street changes. The method `pickerView:didSelectRow:inComponent:` is a delegate method that is called whenever the selected row of a component changes. This is a good place to put the logic that will change the data model of the street-directions component.

The method starts by retrieving the two selected rows. To retrieve a selected value from a component, use the method `selectedRowInComponent:`. If the selected row is in the first component (the streets wheel), the method determines the street directions and updates the second wheel. To update a component, you should update the data model (the array `directions`) and call the picker view's method `reloadComponent:` passing in the component number.

Figure 8.2 shows the application main window. The complete application can be found in the `Picker View 1` project, available in the source downloads.

8.2   Progress View

Progress views (see Figures 8.3 and 8.4) are visual indicators to the user showing that a task is being executed. If you can quantify the progress of a task, an instance of `UIProgressView` is used. If, on the other hand, you do not know how long the task will take, an instance of `UIActivityIndicatorView` is more suitable.

There is only one main attribute of a `UIProgressView` instance: `progress`. The property declaration of `progress` is as follows:

```
@property(nonatomic) float progress
```

The value taken by `progress` ranges from `0.0` to `1.0`. Whenever the `progress` value is changed, the view updates itself.

To make an instance of `UIActivityIndicatorView` start spinning, invoke the method `startAnimating`. To make it stop, send the message `stopAnimating`. If the Boolean attribute `hidesWhenStopped` is `YES` (the default), the activity indicator view hides itself when you send the `stopAnimating` message. There are several `UIActivityIndicator-Style` values that you can use to set the `activityIndicatorViewStyle` property. Examples

Figure 8.2   A picker view allowing the user to choose a street name and a direction.

Figure 8.3   An example of a progress view.

Figure 8.4   An example of a activity indicator view.

include `UIActivityIndicatorViewStyleGray`, `UIActivityIndicatorViewStyleWhite`, and `UIActivityIndicatorViewStyleWhiteLarge`.

Let's illustrate the concepts behind the two classes through a concrete example. The example utilizes two classes: the application delegate, `PVAppDelegate`, and the view controller, `PVViewController`.

Listings 8.5 and 8.6 show the declaration and definition of the application delegate class, respectively.

Listing 8.5   The file `PVAppDelegate.h` declaring the application delegate.

```
#import <UIKit/UIKit.h>
#import <Foundation/Foundation.h>
@class PVViewController;
@interface PVAppDelegate : NSObject {
  UIWindow           *window;
  PVViewController   *viewController;
}
@end
```

Listing 8.6   The file `PVAppDelegate.m` defining the application delegate.

```
#import "PVAppDelegate.h"
#import "PVViewController.h"
@implementation PVAppDelegate
- (void)applicationDidFinishLaunching:(UIApplication *)application {
  window =
    [[UIWindow alloc] initWithFrame:[[UIScreen  mainScreen] bounds]];
  viewController = [[PVViewController alloc] init];
  [window addSubview:viewController.view];
  [window makeKeyAndVisible];
}
- (void)dealloc {
  [window release];
  [viewController release];
  [super dealloc];
}
@end
```

Listings 8.7 and 8.8 show the declaration and definition of the view controller class. The main view, `theView`, houses two subviews: an instance of a `UIProgressView` and an instance of a `UIActivityIndicatorView`.

We first create the progress bar and set the initial progress to `0`. After that, the activity indicator is created and the animation is started. Next, we create, for demonstration purposes, an instance of `NSTimer`. The timer is set up to invoke our method `updateProgress:` once every second.

Inside the `updateProgress:` method, we update the value for `progress`, thus advancing the indicator of the progress bar by 1/10. If the task is finished (i.e., 10 seconds have passed), we send a `stopAnimating` to the activity indicator and stop the timer.

Listing 8.7   The file `PVViewController.h` declaring the view controller.

```objc
#import <UIKit/UIKit.h>
#import <Foundation/Foundation.h>
@interface PVViewController : UIViewController {
  UIProgressView           *progressBar;
  UIActivityIndicatorView *activityIndicator;
}
@end
```

Listing 8.8   The file `PVViewController.m` defining the view controller.

```objc
#import "PVViewController.h"
@implementation PVViewController
- (void)loadView {
  //Create the main view
  UIView *theView   =
    [[UIView alloc] initWithFrame:[UIScreen mainScreen].applicationFrame];
  theView.autoresizingMask = UIViewAutoresizingFlexibleHeight |
                             UIViewAutoresizingFlexibleWidth;
  [theView setBackgroundColor:[UIColor grayColor]];
  //Create the progress bar
  CGRect frame = CGRectMake(50.0, 100.0, 200, 40);
  progressBar = [[UIProgressView alloc] initWithFrame:frame];
  progressBar.progressViewStyle = UIProgressViewStyleDefault;
  progressBar.progress = 0.0;
  [theView addSubview:progressBar];
  //Create the activity indicator
  frame = CGRectMake(150.0, 200.0, 40, 40);
  activityIndicator =
        [[UIActivityIndicatorView alloc] initWithFrame:frame];
  activityIndicator.activityIndicatorViewStyle =
     UIActivityIndicatorViewStyleWhite;
  [activityIndicator startAnimating];
  [theView addSubview:activityIndicator];
  //Create a timer for demo purposes
  [NSTimer scheduledTimerWithTimeInterval:1
          target:self
          selector:@selector(updateProgress:)
          userInfo:nil repeats:YES];
  self.view = theView;
}
- (void)updateProgress:(NSTimer*)theTimer{
  progressBar.progress += 0.1;
  if(progressBar.progress >= 1.0){
```

```
        [theTimer invalidate];
        [activityIndicator stopAnimating];
    }
}
-   (void)dealloc {
    [progressBar release];
    [activityIndicator release];
    [super dealloc];
}
@end
```

Figure 8.5 shows a screen shot of the application. The complete application can be found in the `ProgressView` project, available in the source downloads.

Figure 8.5   Providing visual clues to the user regarding the progress of a given task.

8.3   Scroll View

The `UIScrollView` class is used to display a view that is bigger than the screen dimensions. Usually, the scroll view takes the size of the full screen.

Let's illustrate the scroll view through an example. We would like to show a large picture on the screen. Because the size of this picture exceeds the screen dimensions, we need to use a scroll view to manage panning and zooming of the picture.

A `UIImageView` class is used to encapsulate an image in a view. We will create the image view and add it to a scroll view. The scroll view is used to set the `view` property of a view controller as shown below:

```
- (void)loadView {
UIImageView *imgView =
   [[[UIImageView alloc] initWithImage:
       [UIImage imageNamed:@"picture.jpg"]] autorelease];
 imgView.tag = 100;
 UIScrollView *scrollView = [[[UIScrollView alloc]
   initWithFrame:CGRectMake(0,0,320,480)] autorelease];
 scrollView.delegate = self;
 scrollView.minimumZoomScale = 0.25;
 scrollView.maximumZoomScale = 2;
 scrollView.bounces = NO;
 scrollView.showsHorizontalScrollIndicator = NO;
 scrollView.showsVerticalScrollIndicator = NO;
 scrollView.contentSize = imgView.frame.size;
 scrollView.contentOffset =
   CGPointMake((imgView.frame.size.width-320)/2,
                      (imgView.frame.size.height-480)/2);
 [scrollView addSubview:imgView];
 self.view = scrollView;
}
```

The code above shows the `loadView` method of the view controller. It starts by creating an image view initialized with an image. Next, the scroll view is created to fit the whole screen. The `minimum-ZoomScale` is used to control how small the image can be zoomed out relative to its size. The default is `1.0` and we choose `0.25`. The `maximumZoomScale` is used to specify how large the image can be zoomed in relative to its size. The default is `1.0` and we choose `2.0`.

The `contentSize` property is used to specify the size of the content the scroll view is supposed to manage. We set that value to the size of the image.

The `contentOffset` specifies the offset point of the origin of the image to the origin of the scroll view. We want to center the image when the view appears, so we offset the image origin relative to the scroll view origin.

To accommodate zooming in and out, we must implement the delegate method `viewForZooming-InScrollView:` as shown below:

```
- (UIView *)viewForZoomingInScrollView:(UIScrollView *)scrollView {
  return [self.view viewWithTag:100];
}
```

It suffices to return the image view. Because it was tagged with `100`, we retrieve that from its parent view, the scroll view. The complete source code of this application can be found in the `ScrollView` project in the source downloads.

8.4   Text View

The class `UITextView` is a subclass of `UIScrollView` (which extends `UIView`). You can use this class to display multiline text with a given color, font, and text alignment (see Figure 8.6).

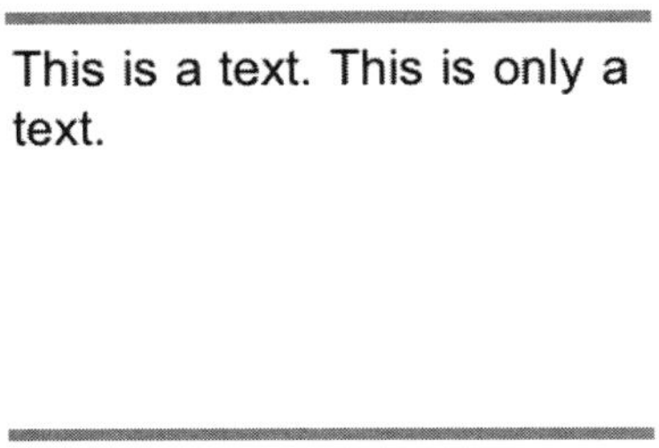

This is a text. This is only a
text.

Figure 8.6   An example of a text view.

The following are the main properties of this class:

- `text`. The value of this property is the text displayed inside this view. The property is declared as

  `@property(nonatomic, copy) NSString *text`

- `font`. This represents the font of the text. Note that you can have only one font for the whole text. The property is declared as

  `@property(nonatomic, retain) UIFont *font`

- `textColor`. This represents the color of the text. As in the font's case, only one color can be used. The property is declared as

  `@property(nonatomic, retain) UIColor *textColor`

- `textAlignment`. The value dictates the alignment of the text in the view. The property is declared as

  `@property(nonatomic) UITextAlignment textAlignment`

  The alignment can be left (`UITextAlignmentLeft`), right (`UITextAlignmentRight`), or center (`UITextAlignmentCenter`). The default is left alignment.

- `editable`. This value determines whether the text can be edited. The property is declared as

  `@property(nonatomic, getter=isEditable) BOOL editable`

8.4.1   *The delegate*

The delegate of this class should adopt the UITextViewDelegate protocol. All methods in this protocol are optional. The delegate will receive messages related to the editing of the text. These messages are the following:

- textViewShouldBeginEditing:. The delegate is queried whether the text view should begin editing. This is triggered by the user's touching inside the text area. You return YES if you want editing to begin and NO otherwise.

- textViewDidBeginEditing:. This is received immediately after editing starts but before the text is actually changed.

- textViewShouldEndEditing:. This is received when the text view resigns as the first responder. You return YES to end editing and NO otherwise.

- textViewDidEndEditing:. This is received to inform the delegate that the text view has ended the editing.

8.4.2   *An example of text view*

To illustrate the concepts behind the UITextView class, let's look at an example. We will create a multiline text area and allow the user to edit it. The user will be able to signal the end of the editing by pressing a Done button.

The example uses two classes: the application delegate, shown in Listings 8.9 and 8.10, and the view controller, shown in Listings 8.11 and 8.12.

Listing 8.9   The file TVAppDelegate.h declaring the application delegate.

```
#import <UIKit/UIKit.h>
#import <Foundation/Foundation.h>
@class TVViewController;
@interface TVAppDelegate : NSObject {
  UIWindow          *window;
  TVViewController  *viewController;
}
@end
```

Listing 8.10   The file TVAppDelegate.m defining the application delegate.

```
#import "TVAppDelegate.h"
#import "TVViewController.h"
@implementation TVAppDelegate
- (void)applicationDidFinishLaunching:(UIApplication *)application {
  window =
    [[UIWindow alloc] initWithFrame: [[UIScreen  mainScreen] bounds]];
```

```
    viewController = [[TVViewController alloc] init];
    [window addSubview:viewController.view];
    // make the window key and visible
    [window makeKeyAndVisible];
}
- (void)dealloc {
    [window release];
    [viewController release];
    [super dealloc];
}
@end
```

Inside the loadView method of the view controller, we allocate an instance of UITextView, initialize it with a size of (320, 200), and position it at (0, 50). The text color, font, and background color of the text area are then configured.

An initial text can be added to the view. Notice in Listing 8.12 how the \n is used to form a new line. The Return key type used is UIReturnKeyDefault. The keyboard type is assigned a value of UIKeyboardTypeDefault.

After creating the text view area and adding it to the view, theView, the method continues, and creates and configures a Done button. When pushed, the Done button will resign the text view instance as the first responder, thus hiding the keyboard.

Listing 8.11   The file TVViewController.h declaring the view controller.

```
#import <UIKit/UIKit.h>
#import <Foundation/Foundation.h>
@interface TVViewController : UIViewController <UITextViewDelegate>{
    UITextView *textView;
    UIButton   *doneButton;
}
@end
```

Listing 8.12   The file TVViewController.m defining the view controller.

```
#import "TVViewController.h"
@implementation TVViewController
- (void)loadView {
    //Create the main view
    UIView *theView   =
      [[UIView alloc] initWithFrame:[UIScreen mainScreen].applicationFrame];
    theView.autoresizingMask = UIViewAutoresizingFlexibleHeight |
                               UIViewAutoresizingFlexibleWidth;
    CGRect frame = CGRectMake(0.0, 50.0, 320, 200.0);
    textView = [[UITextView alloc] initWithFrame:frame];
    textView.textColor = [UIColor blackColor];
    textView.font = [UIFont fontWithName:@"Arial" size:20];
    textView.delegate = self;
```

```
textView.backgroundColor = [UIColor whiteColor];
textView.text = @"Dear Sir/Madam, \n I would like ";
textView.returnKeyType = UIReturnKeyDefault;
textView.keyboardType = UIKeyboardTypeDefault;
[theView addSubview: textView];

doneButton =
    [[UIButton buttonWithType:UIButtonTypeRoundedRect] retain];
doneButton.frame = CGRectMake(210.0, 5.0, 100, 40);
[doneButton setTitle:@"Done" forState:UIControlStateNormal];
[doneButton addTarget:self action:@selector(doneAction:)
            forControlEvents:UIControlEventTouchUpInside];
doneButton.enabled = NO;
[theView addSubview: doneButton];
self.view = theView;
}
- (void)doneAction:(id)sender{
  [textView resignFirstResponder];
  doneButton.enabled = NO;
}
//UITextView delegate methods
- (BOOL)textViewShouldBeginEditing:(UITextView *)textView{
  printf("textViewShouldBeginEditing\n");
  return YES;
}
- (void)textViewDidBeginEditing:(UITextView *)textView{
  printf("textViewDidBeginEditing\n");
  doneButton.enabled = YES;
}
- (BOOL)textViewShouldEndEditing:(UITextView *)textView{
  printf("textViewShouldEndEditing\n");
  return YES;
}
- (void)textViewDidEndEditing:(UITextView *)textView{
  printf("textViewDidEndEditing\n");

}
- (void)dealloc {
  [textView release];
  [doneButton release];
  [super dealloc];
}
@end
```

As we mentioned earlier, all the delegate methods are optional. Of those, we implement four methods. When the editing of the text view starts, the method textViewDidBeginEditing: is called. In this method, we enable the Done button, thus allowing the user to quit editing when finished. The other three methods are for demo purposes and achieve the default behavior. Figure 8.7 shows a screen shot of the application.

Figure 8.7   Editing a multiline text area.

8.5   Alert View

Alert views are used to display an alert message to the user. This alert message consists of a title, a brief message, and one or more buttons (see Figure 8.8).

Figure 8.8   An example of an alert view.

The class used for an alert view is `UIAlertView`, which is a subclass of `UIView`.

To initialize an alert view, you use the convenient initializer `initWithTitle:message:-delegate:cancelButtonTitle:otherButtonTitles:`, declared as

```
- (id)initWithTitle:(NSString *)title message:(NSString *)message
      delegate:(id<UIAlertViewDelegate>)delegate
      cancelButtonTitle:(NSString *)cancelButtonTitle
      otherButtonTitles:(NSString *)otherButtonTitles, ...
```

The `title` is a string used as the title for the alert view. The `message` is descriptive text providing more details about the purpose of the alert view. The `delegate` is an object that adopts the `UIAlertViewDelegate` that will receive messages from the `UIAlertView` instance. The `cancelButtonTitle` is the title of the cancel button used to dismiss the alert view. You need at least one button in order for the user to have the ability to dismiss the alert view. You can add one or more other buttons in `otherButtonTitles` by listing their titles in a comma-separated `nil`-terminated list. After initializing the alert view instance, you send it a show message to make it appear. The following shows the basic steps described above:

```
UIAlertView *alert = [[UIAlertView alloc]
              initWithTitle:@"Host Unreachable"
              message:@"Please check the host address"
              delegate:self cancelButtonTitle:@"OK"
              otherButtonTitles: nil];
[alert show];
```

The `UIAlertViewDelegate` has several declared methods. You mostly need the `alertView:-clickedButtonAtIndex:` method. This method will be invoked by the alert, informing the delegate of the index of the button used to dismiss the alert view. The method is declared as

```
- (void)alertView:(UIAlertView *)alertView
      clickedButtonAtIndex:(NSInteger)buttonIndex
```

`alertView` is the instance of the alert view that originated the call, and `buttonIndex` is the index of the button used to dismiss the alert view. The index of the first button is `0`. Our implementation for this example simply logs the index used to dismiss the alert view as shown below:

```
- (void)alertView:(UIAlertView *)alertView
      clickedButtonAtIndex:(NSInteger)buttonIndex{
  NSLog(@"The index of the alert button clicked is %d", buttonIndex);
}
```

In our example, the index logged will always be `0` as we have only one button. Figure 8.9 shows the alert view example.

As we mentioned above, you can have more than one button in an alert view. The following statement adds two buttons in addition to the cancel button:

```
UIAlertView *alert = [[UIAlertView alloc]
                      initWithTitle:@"Disk Error"
```

```
message:@"Error reading sector 18"
delegate:self cancelButtonTitle:@"Abort"
otherButtonTitles:@"Retry", @"Fail", nil];
```

The index of the Abort button remains 0. The indices of the Retry and Fail buttons are 1 and 2, respectively. Figure 8.10 shows the alert view with the three buttons.

The delegate defines the method `alertViewCancel:`. This method will be called when the user taps the Home button of the iPhone. If the delegate does not implement this method, tapping of the cancel button is simulated and the alert view is dismissed. If you decide not to implement this delegate method, make sure that the cancel button is used for *cancellation*. If you use it to, say, make a phone call, then receiving a phone call while the alert view is showing will result in the iPhone's rejecting the call and dialing the number!

Figure 8.9 An alert view with one button.

Figure 8.10 An alert view with three buttons.

8.6   Action Sheet

Action sheets are similar to alert views in that they present a message and one or more buttons to the user. Action sheets, however, differ in how they look and in how they are presented to the user (see Figure 8.11).

Figure 8.11   An example of an action sheet.

To present an action sheet to the user, allocate a new instance of the class UIActionSheet and initialize it using the initWithTitle:delegate:cancelButtonTitle:destructive-ButtonTitle:otherButtonTitles: initializer. The initializer is declared as

```
- (id)initWithTitle:(NSString *)title
      delegate:(id <UIActionSheetDelegate>)delegate
      cancelButtonTitle:(NSString *)cancelButtonTitle
      destructiveButtonTitle:(NSString *)destructiveButtonTitle
      otherButtonTitles:(NSString *)otherButtonTitles, ...
```

The title is used to specify the title of the action sheet. You specify a delegate using the delegate parameter. A cancel button title is specified in the cancelButtonTitle parameter. A destructive button (shown in red) title is specified in destructiveButtonTitle. Additional buttons can be specified in a comma-separated nil-terminated list using the otherButtonTitles parameter. After the creation and initialization of the action sheet, you show it in a view using the showInView: method, passing in the parent view instance. A simple action sheet is presented to the user as follows:

```
UIActionSheet *
actionSheet = [[UIActionSheet alloc]
      initWithTitle:@"Are you sure you want to erase all data?"
      delegate:self cancelButtonTitle:@"Cancel"
      destructiveButtonTitle:@"ERASE" otherButtonTitles:nil];
[actionSheet showInView:self.view];
```

Figure 8.12 shows the action sheet created by the above code.

Figure 8.12   An action sheet with two buttons.

The delegate `UIActionSheetDelegate` defines several optional methods. If you want to know which button was tapped by the user, you need to implement the method `actionSheet:clickedButtonAtIndex:`. The indices start at `0`. In the example above, Cancel has an index of `0` and ERASE has an index of `1`.

8.7   Web View

This section introduces the `UIWebView` class. `UIWebView` is a subclass of `UIView` that allows you to present rich content to the user. We begin by showing a simple web view application.

8.7.1   A simple web view application

Let's start by looking at a simple application that utilizes a web view. The application will present an array of personal records in the form of an HTML table (see Figure 8.13).

Records Found:

Database

Name	Address	Phone
John Doe	1234 Fake st	(555) 555-1234
Jane Doe	4321 Fake st	(555) 555-7898

Figure 8.13 A screen shot of the simple web view application showing the data in the form of an HTML table.

Listing 8.13 shows the declaration of the application delegate class.

Listing 8.13 The declaration of the application delegate class used in the simple web view application.

```
#import <UIKit/UIKit.h>

@interface DWebViewAppDelegate : NSObject <UIApplicationDelegate> {
  UIWindow *window;
  NSArray  *records;
}
@property (nonatomic, retain) UIWindow *window;
-(NSString*) allRecordsInHTML;
@end
```

The class keeps a reference to the records, to be presented in the form of a table, in the records NSArray instance. The allRecordsInHTML method is used by the application delegate to produce an HTML representation of the personal records found in the array, as we shall see later in this section.

Listing 8.14 shows the implementation of the application delegate class.

Listing 8.14 The implementation of the application delegate class used in the simple web view application.

```
#import "DWebViewAppDelegate.h"
#import "Person.h"

@implementation DWebViewAppDelegate
@synthesize window;

-(void)loadData{
  Person *a, *b;
  a = [[Person alloc] autorelease];
  a.name = @"John Doe";
  a.address = @"1234 Fake st";
  a.phone = @"(555) 555-1234";
  b = [[Person alloc] autorelease];
  b.name = @"Jane Doe";
```

```
    b.address = @"4321 Fake st";
    b.phone = @"(555) 555-7898";
    records = [NSArray arrayWithObjects:a, b, nil];
}

- (void)applicationDidFinishLaunching:(UIApplication *)application {
    [self loadData];
    CGRect  rectFrame = [UIScreen mainScreen].applicationFrame;
    window = [[UIWindow alloc] initWithFrame:rectFrame];
    UIWebView *webView =
      [[UIWebView alloc] initWithFrame:CGRectMake(0, 0, 320, 460)];
    webView.scalesPageToFit = YES;
    NSMutableString *html = [[NSMutableString alloc] initWithCapacity:200];
    [html appendString:
     @"<html>"
     " <meta name=\"viewport\" content=\"width=320\"/>"
     " <body>"
     " <h4>"
     " Records Found:"
     " </h4>"
     " <table border=\"6\">"
     " <caption>Database</caption>"
     " <tr>"
     " <td>Name</td>"
     " <td>Address</td>"
     " <td>Phone</td>"
     " </tr>"];
    [html appendString:[self allRecordsInHTML]];
    [html appendString:
     @"</table>"
     " </body>"
     " </html>"
     ];
    [webView loadHTMLString:html baseURL:nil];
    [window addSubview:webView];
    [webView release];
    [html release];
    [window makeKeyAndVisible];
}

-(NSString*) allRecordsInHTML{
    NSMutableString *myRecords =
        [[[NSMutableString alloc] initWithCapacity:200]autorelease];
    for (Person *p in records) {
      [myRecords appendString:[p html]];
    }
    return myRecords;
}
```

```
- (void)dealloc {
  [window release];
  [super dealloc];
}
@end
```

The `applicationDidFinishLaunching:` method builds the data model by invoking the method `loadData`. For demonstration purposes, two `Person` instances are initialized and added to the `records` array. After that, the `applicationDidFinishLaunching:` creates and initializes a `UIWebView` instance similar to other `UIView` subclasses. To make the content fit the screen and allow the user to zoom in and out, the `scalesPageToFit` property should be set to `YES`.

To load a web view instance with HTML content for display, the application uses the `loadHTMLString:baseURL:` method. This method is declared as follows:

```
- (void)loadHTMLString:(NSString *)string baseURL:(NSURL *)baseURL
```

The first parameter is the HTML to be displayed and the second parameter is the base URL for the content. Our application builds the HTML content (as we shall see later in this section) and uses `nil` as the base URL. The HTML content is composed of a static part and a dynamic part. The static part consists of the HTML tags and the formatting needed to display the HTML table. The dynamic part is the portion produced by concatenating the output of every personal record, as we shall see later in this section. Listing 8.15 shows the HTML page that is finally loaded and visualized by the web view.

If you would like the have the text of the page appear with reasonable size, you should use the meta tag `viewport` and specify `320` for the width of the page content as shown below:

```
<meta name="viewport" content="width=320"/>
```

The static part of the HTML also includes the table tag and the first row specifying the columns' headings.

Listing 8.15   The HTML page that is finally loaded and visualized by the web view for the simple web view application.

```
<html>
  <meta name="viewport" content="width=320"/>
  <body>
    <h4> Records Found: </h4>
    <table border="6">
      <caption>Database</caption>
      <tr>
        <td>Name</td> <td>Address</td> <td>Phone</td>
      </tr>
      <tr>
        <td>John Doe</td> <td>1234 Fake st</td>
         <td>(555) 555-1234</td>
      </tr>
      <tr>
```

```
      <td>Jane Doe</td> <td>4321 Fake st</td>
      <td>(555) 555-7898</td>
    </tr>
  </table>
 </body>
</html>
```

The dynamic part of the HTML page is produced in the `allRecordsInHTML` method. This method simply iterates over all the elements in the `records` array and appends each item's HTML content representation. Items in the `records` array are instances of the `Person` class shown in Listings 8.16 and 8.17.

Each `Person` instance contains references to the strings `name`, `address`, and `phone` of the individual represented. The `html` method is used to produce an HTML code for a row in the table with the values of these three strings as the columns.

Listing 8.16   The declaration of the `Person` class used in the simple web view application.

```
#import <Foundation/Foundation.h>

@interface Person : NSObject {
  NSString *name, *address, *phone;
}
@property(nonatomic, assign) NSString  *name;
@property(nonatomic, assign) NSString  *address;
@property(nonatomic, assign) NSString  *phone;
-(NSString*)html;
@end
```

Listing 8.17   The implementation of the `Person` class used in the simple web view application.

```
#import "Person.h"
@implementation Person
@synthesize name, address, phone;
-(NSString*)html{
  NSMutableString *output =
    [[[NSMutableString alloc] initWithCapacity:50] autorelease];
  [output appendString:@"<tr> <td>"];
  [output appendString:name];
  [output appendString:@"</td> <td>"];
  [output appendString:address];
  [output appendString:@"</td> <td>"];
  [output appendString:phone];
  [output appendString:@"</td> </tr>"];
  return output;
}
@end
```

The complete application can be found in the `DWebView` project in the source downloads.

8.7.2   *Viewing local files*

In this section, you learn how to embed images stored in your Home directory in a web page
and present the page to the user in a web view. Listings 8.18 and 8.19 show the application
delegate class declaration and implementation, respectively. The application delegate simply creates
a view controller of type MyWebViewController and adds its view to the main window as
a subview.

Listing 8.18   The declaration of the application delegate class used in viewing images in a web view.

```
#import <UIKit/UIKit.h>

@class MyWebViewController;
@interface BWebViewAppDelegate : NSObject <UIApplicationDelegate> {
  UIWindow            *window;
  MyWebViewController *ctrl;
}
@property (nonatomic, retain) UIWindow *window;
@end
```

Listing 8.19   The implementation of the application delegate class used in viewing images in a web view.

```
#import "BWebViewAppDelegate.h"
#import "MyWebViewController.h"

@implementation BWebViewAppDelegate
@synthesize window;

- (void)applicationDidFinishLaunching:(UIApplication *)application {
  window = [[UIWindow alloc]
            initWithFrame:[[UIScreen mainScreen] bounds]];
  ctrl = [[MyWebViewController alloc] initWithNibName:nil bundle:nil];
  [window addSubview:ctrl.view];
  [window makeKeyAndVisible];
}

- (void)dealloc {
  [ctrl release];
  [window release];
  [super dealloc];
}
@end
```

Listing 8.20 shows the declaration of the view controller used by the application delegate.
The view controller maintains a reference to a UIWebView instance. In addition, the
produceImageReference:withType: method, as we shall see later in this section, is used
internally to generate an IMG HTML tag for a given local image file.

Listing 8.20   The declaration of the view controller used by the application delegate of the application showing local image files in a web view.

```
#import <UIKit/UIKit.h>

@interface MyWebViewController : UIViewController {
  UIWebView  *webView;
}
-(NSString*)produceImageReference:(NSString*) imgFileName
          withType:(NSString*) imgType;
@end
```

Listing 8.21 shows the implementation of the view controller class.

Listing 8.21   The implementation of the view controller used by the application delegate of the application showing local image files in a web view.

```
#import "MyWebViewController.h"

@implementation MyWebViewController

- (void)loadView {
  CGRect  rectFrame = [UIScreen mainScreen].applicationFrame;
  UIView  *view = [[UIView alloc] initWithFrame:rectFrame];
  view.autoresizingMask = UIViewAutoresizingFlexibleHeight |
                    UIViewAutoresizingFlexibleWidth;
  webView =
    [[UIWebView alloc] initWithFrame:CGRectMake(0, 0, 320, 460)];
  webView.scalesPageToFit = YES;

  NSMutableString *htmlContents =
      [[NSMutableString alloc] initWithCapacity:100]; ;
  [htmlContents appendString:
   @"<meta name=\"viewport\" content=\"width=320\"/><html><body>"];
  [htmlContents appendString:@"<H2>Hurley</H2>"];
  [htmlContents
    appendString:[self produceImageReference:@"hurley" withType:@"jpg"]];
  [htmlContents appendString:@"<H1>Hugo</H1>"];
  [htmlContents
    appendString:[self produceImageReference:@"hurley" withType:@"jpg"]];
  [htmlContents appendString:@"<H3>Jorge Garcia</H3>"];
  [htmlContents
    appendString:[self produceImageReference:@"hurley" withType:@"jpg"]];
  [htmlContents appendString:@"</body></html>"];
  [webView loadHTMLString:htmlContents baseURL:nil];
  [view addSubview:webView];
  self.view = view;
  [view release];
  [htmlContents release];
```

```
}

-(NSString*)produceImageReference:(NSString*) imgFileName
           withType:(NSString*) imgType{
  NSMutableString *returnString =
    [[[NSMutableString alloc] initWithCapacity:100] autorelease];
  NSString *filePath =
    [[NSBundle mainBundle] pathForResource:imgFileName
                          ofType:imgType];
  if(filePath){
    [returnString appendString:@"<IMG SRC=\"file://"];
    [returnString appendString:filePath];
    [returnString appendString:@"\" ALT=\""];
    [returnString appendString:imgFileName];
    [returnString appendString:@"\">"];
    return returnString;
  }
  else return @"";
}
- (void)dealloc {
  [webView release];
  [super dealloc];
}
@end
```

The `loadView` method starts by creating the GUI objects (as we have seen in the previous section). It then proceeds to produce the web page containing image references.

To embed an image in a web page, you can use an IMG element. The IMG element has two required attributes: (1) the src, which is a URL specifying the location of the image and (2) the alt, defining a short description of the image.

In our example, the image is stored in the application bundle (see Figure 8.14 and Section 10.6).

To specify the URL of the local image, you simply use the file protocol with the full path of the image file. For example, the following HTML is dynamically generated on the device:

```
<IMG SRC="file:///var/mobile/Applications/
     8884F8E2-E466-4500-8FFF-6263C99016DB/web view 2.app/
     hurley.jpg" ALT="hurley"
>
```

You do not need to know how we obtained the path for the image as you will learn about that in Section 10.6. The `htmlContents` mutable string is incrementally constructed to contain the full web page source. For simplicity, we embed the same image three times with different headings. The full web page that is loaded on the device is shown in Listing 8.22.

Figure 8.14   The Groups & Files content showing the hurley.jpg image in the Resources group.

Listing 8.22   The HTML page that is finally loaded and visualized by the web view for the web view application with a page containing embedded local images.

```
<meta name="viewport" content="width=320"/>
<html>
  <body>
    <H2>Hurley</H2>
    <IMG SRC="file:///var/mobile/Applications/
      8884F8E2-E466-4500-8FFF-6263C99016DB/web view 2.app/
      hurley.jpg" ALT="hurley">
    <H1>Hugo</H1>
    <IMG SRC="file:///var/mobile/Applications/
      8884F8E2-E466-4500-8FFF-6263C99016DB/web view 2.app/
      hurley.jpg" ALT="hurley">
```

```
    <H3>Jorge Garcia</H3>
    <IMG SRC="file:///var/mobile/Applications/
       8884F8E2-E466-4500-8FFF-6263C99016DB/web view 2.app/
       hurley.jpg" ALT="hurley">
  </body>
</html>
```

Figure 8.15 shows a screen shot of the application showing local image files in a web view. The complete application can be found in the BWebView project in the source downloads.

Figure 8.15   A screen shot of the application showing local image files in a web view.

8.7.3   Evaluating JavaScript

In this section, we would like to build an application that presents the user with a web page with a form and one text field (Figure 8.16).

The user enters text in the field and taps on the Process button on the navigation bar. If the text entered is forbidden (we will define *forbidden* later in this section), the application presents an alert view informing the user that he or she needs to re-enter the text (Figure 8.17).

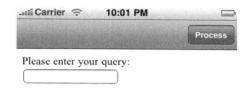

Figure 8.16 A screen shot of the application demonstrating the JavaScript–Objective-C interaction. An HTML form is provided to the user for inputting a search term.

Figure 8.17 A screen shot of the application that demonstrates JavaScript execution from within Objective-C code. The screen shot shows an alert view when a forbidden query is used.

The text field is cleared and the user is given the opportunity to re-enter the text. If the text entered is not forbidden, the application will retrieve the text value of the field and update the web page to have a link to a Google query of the word entered (Figure 8.18).

When the user taps on the generated link, the search result is displayed (Figure 8.19). That is what the application is supposed to do. Let's start constructing it.

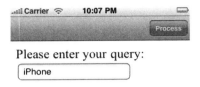

Figure 8.18   The application responding to a valid search term by updating the web page in the web view.

Figure 8.19   The search result of a valid search term viewed in the web view.

Listing 8.23 shows the declaration of the application delegate. It maintains both a navigation controller and a view controller.

Listing 8.23   The declaration of the application delegate class used to demonstrate the execution of JavaScript code in a web view.

```
#import <UIKit/UIKit.h>

@class MyViewController;
@interface AWebViewDelegate : NSObject <UIApplicationDelegate> {
  UIWindow                   *window;
  MyViewController           *ctrl;
  UINavigationController     *navCtrl;
}
@property (nonatomic, retain) UIWindow *window;
@end
```

Listing 8.24 shows the implementation of the application delegate class. The `applicationDid-FinishLaunching:` method creates a navigation controller, adds a `MyViewController` instance to it, and then adds the navigation controller's view to the main window as a subview.

Listing 8.24   The implementation of the application delegate class used to demonstrate the execution of JavaScript code in a web view.

```
#import "AWebViewDelegate.h"
#import "MyViewController.h"

@implementation AWebViewDelegate
@synthesize window;

- (void)applicationDidFinishLaunching:(UIApplication *)application {
  window =
     [[UIWindow alloc] initWithFrame:[[UIScreen  mainScreen] bounds]];
  ctrl = [[MyViewController alloc] initWithNibName:nil bundle:nil];
  navCtrl =
     [[UINavigationController alloc] initWithRootViewController:ctrl];
  [window addSubview:navCtrl.view];
  [window makeKeyAndVisible];
}

- (void)dealloc {
  [ctrl release];
  [navCtrl release];
  [window release];
  [super dealloc];
}
@end
```

Listing 8.25 shows the declaration of the view controller class.

Listing 8.25   The declaration of the view controller class used in demonstrating evaluation of JavaScript code in a web view.

```
#import <UIKit/UIKit.h>

@interface MyViewController : UIViewController {
  UIWebView        *webView;
  UIBarButtonItem *rightButton;
}
@end
```

The controller maintains a reference to the web view instance and a right button implementing the Process navigation-bar button.

Listing 8.26 shows the implementation of this class.

Listing 8.26   The implementation of the view controller class used in demonstrating evaluation of JavaScript code in a web view.

```
#import "MyViewController.h"
@implementation MyViewController
- (id)initWithNibName:(NSString *)nibNameOrNil
       bundle:(NSBundle *)nibBundleOrNil {
  if (self = [super initWithNibName:nibNameOrNil bundle:nibBundleOrNil]){
    rightButton = [[UIBarButtonItem alloc]
                                   initWithTitle:@"Process"
                                   style:UIBarButtonItemStyleDone
                                   target:self
                                   action:@selector(processJavaScript)];
    self.navigationItem.rightBarButtonItem = rightButton;
    [rightButton release];
  }
  return self;
}
-(void)processJavaScript{
  NSString* var =
     [webView stringByEvaluatingJavaScriptFromString:@"getQuery()"];
  if([var isEqualToString:@"dissent"] == YES){
    UIAlertView *alert = [[UIAlertView alloc]
                                   initWithTitle:@"Forbidden!"
                                   message:@"Please enter a valid query."
                                   delegate:nil
                                   cancelButtonTitle:@"OK"
                                   otherButtonTitles:nil];
    [alert show];
    [webView stringByEvaluatingJavaScriptFromString:@"clearQuery()"];
    return;
```

```
    }
    NSMutableString *query=[[NSMutableString alloc] initWithCapacity:200];
    [query appendString:@"document.getElementById('anchor').href"
                        "=\"http://www.google.com/search?q="];
    [query appendString:var];
    [query appendString:@"\";"];
    NSMutableString *innerHTML =
      [[NSMutableString alloc] initWithCapacity:200];
    [innerHTML appendString:
      @"document.getElementById('anchor').innerHTML=\"Google "];
    [innerHTML appendString:var];
    [innerHTML appendString:@"\";"];
    [webView
        stringByEvaluatingJavaScriptFromString:@"loseFocusOfField()"];
    [webView stringByEvaluatingJavaScriptFromString:innerHTML];
    [webView stringByEvaluatingJavaScriptFromString:query];
    rightButton.enabled = NO;
    [query release];
    [innerHTML release];
}
- (void)loadView {
    CGRect  rectFrame = [UIScreen mainScreen].applicationFrame;
    UIView  *view = [[UIView alloc] initWithFrame:rectFrame];
    view.autoresizingMask = UIViewAutoresizingFlexibleHeight |
                            UIViewAutoresizingFlexibleWidth;
    webView =
      [[UIWebView alloc] initWithFrame:CGRectMake(0, 0, 320, 460)];
    webView.scalesPageToFit = YES;
    [webView loadHTMLString:
      @"<html><head><title>Query Assistant</title>\n"
      "<meta name=\"viewport\" content=\"width=320\"/>"
      "<script>"
      "function getQuery(){"
      "return document.queryform.query.value;}"
      "function clearQuery(){"
      "return document.queryform.query.value=\"\";}"
      "function loseFocusOfField(){"
      "return document.queryform.query.blur();}"
      "</script>"
      "</head><body>Please enter your query: "
      "<form name=\"queryform\">"
      "<input name=\"Query\" type=\"text\" "
      "value=\"\" id=\"query\" />"
      "<br/>"
      "<br/>"
      "<br/>"
      "<a id=\"anchor\" href=\"\"></a>"
      "</form></body></html>" baseURL:nil];
```

```
    [view addSubview:webView];
    self.view = view;
    [view release];

}
- (void)dealloc {
    [webView release];
    [rightButton release];
    [super dealloc];
}
@end
```

The `initWithNibName:bundle:` initializes the view controller's instance and adds a Process navigation button. The action method for this button is `processJavaScript`, which we will cover later in this section.

The `loadView` method creates and initializes a `UIWebView` instance and adds it to the main window. The web view is loaded with the `loadHTMLString` string. The HTML in this string is all static and is shown in Listing 8.27. The HTML contains a form with one text field. It also declares the following three functions:

- `getQuery()`: retrieves the text value of the field in the form.

- `clearQuery()`: clears the contents of the text field.

- `loseFocusOfField()`: makes the text field lose focus so that the keyboard disappears.

Listing 8.27   A static HTML specifying the main page for the application and demonstrating the execution of JavaScript in a web view from within Objective-C code.

```
<html>
  <head>
    <title>Query Assistant</title>
    <meta name="viewport" content="width=320"/>
    <script>
      function getQuery(){
        return document.queryform.query.value;
      }
      function clearQuery(){
        return document.queryform.query.value="";
      }
      function loseFocusOfField(){
        return document.queryform.query.blur();
      }
    </script>
  </head>
  <body>Please enter your query:
    <form name="queryform">
```

```
        <input name="Query" type="text" value="" id="query" />
        <br/>
        <br/>
        <br/>
        <a id="anchor" href=""></a>
      </form>
  </body>
</html>
```

The UIWebView class allows you to evaluate JavaScript code on demand. To execute a JavaScript code, you use the stringByEvaluatingJavaScriptFromString: method. This method is declared as follows:

```
- (NSString *)stringByEvaluatingJavaScriptFromString:(NSString *)script;
```

The script parameter is an NSString instance containing the JavaScript code that you wish to execute. The result value of the executed JavaScript code, if any, is returned as an NSString object.

When the user taps on the Process navigation bar right button, the processJavaScript method is executed. In this method, we start by retrieving the text value of the field. The getQuery() JavaScript statement is executed and the result is returned to us. After retrieving the value, we check to see if it is equal to the text "dissent". If that is the case, we show an alert view to the user (see Figure 8.17) and clear the text field by invoking the clearQuery() JavaScript function.

If the text value is valid, we update the web page by changing the href of the element whose ID is anchor to the Google search query. Below, we show the code generated for the search term "iPhone":

```
document.getElementById('anchor').href=
    "http://www.google.com/search?q=iPhone";
```

We also update the innerHTML as shown in the example below:

```
document.getElementById('anchor').innerHTML="Google iPhone";
```

Both updates of the web page are then executed. In addition, we invoke the loseFocusOfField() JavaScript function in order to lose the keyboard.

The complete application can be found in the AWebView project in the source downloads.

8.7.4 The web view delegate

In this section, we build an application that intercepts the user's web navigation activity. If the user taps on a link for a PDF file, the user is asked whether he or she wants to download a copy for later use. We do not implement the actual downloading/storage management as this will be demonstrated in Section 17.7. What this section provides is an illustration of how you can intercept important changes to the web view instance due to the user's interaction.

The UIWebView class has an important property, delegate, that allows you to intercept important calls. The delegate property is declared as follows:

@property(nonatomic,assign) **id**<UIWebViewDelegate> delegate

The UIWebViewDelegate protocol declares the following four optional methods:

- webView:shouldStartLoadWithRequest:navigationType:. This method is invoked just before loading the content of the web page. The method is declared as follows:

  - (BOOL)webView:(UIWebView *)webView
          shouldStartLoadWithRequest:(NSURLRequest *)request
          navigationType:(UIWebViewNavigationType)navigationType

  You return YES if you want the web view to perform the loading of this request and NO otherwise. The first parameter is the web view instance. The second parameter is an instance of NSURLRequest representing the request, and the third is the navigation type that has led to loading the content.

  The NSURLRequest class defines the URL method for obtaining an instance of the NSURL class. The NSURL class defines the absoluteString for obtaining an NSString instance representing the URL of the request. As you will see later in this section, we will look into this string in order to decide whether to trigger actions.

  There are several predefined navigation type values. The values are as follows:

    - UIWebViewNavigationTypeLinkClicked indicates that the user tapped on a link on the page.
    - UIWebViewNavigationTypeFormSubmitted indicates that the user submitted a form.
    - UIWebViewNavigationTypeBackForward indicates that the user tapped on the forward/backward button.
    - UIWebViewNavigationTypeReload indicates that the user tapped on the reload button.
    - UIWebViewNavigationTypeFormResubmitted indicates that the user resubmitted the form.
    - UIWebViewNavigationTypeOther indicates some other navigation trigger.

  This method will be implemented in our application. If the URL is a request to a PDF file, we ask the user if he or she wants to download a copy of the file for later use.

- webViewDidStartLoad:. This method is used to communicate that the web view has started loading content. The method is declared as follows:

  - (**void**)webViewDidStartLoad:(UIWebView *)webView

- webViewDidFinishLoad:. This method is used to communicate that the web view has finished loading the content. The method is declared as follows:

    – (**void**)webViewDidFinishLoad:(UIWebView *)webView

- webView:didFailLoadWithError:. This method is used to communicate that the web view encountered an error in loading content. The method is declared as follows:

    – (**void**)webView:(UIWebView *)webView
        didFailLoadWithError:(NSError *)error

Listings 8.28 and 8.29 show the declaration and implementation, respectively, of the application delegate class. The delegate creates an instance of the MyViewController view controller and adds its view to the main window as a subview.

Listing 8.28   The declaration of the application delegate class of the application demonstrating interception of web view user interactions.

```
#import <UIKit/UIKit.h>
@class MyViewController;
@interface EWebViewAppDelegate : NSObject <UIApplicationDelegate> {
    UIWindow          *window;
    MyViewController *ctrl;
}
@property (nonatomic, retain) UIWindow *window;
@end
```

Listing 8.29   The implementation of the application delegate class of the application demonstrating interception of web view user interactions.

```
#import "EWebViewAppDelegate.h"
#import "MyViewController.h"

@implementation EWebViewAppDelegate
@synthesize window;
- (void)applicationDidFinishLaunching:(UIApplication *)application {
  window =
  [[UIWindow alloc] initWithFrame:[[UIScreen  mainScreen] bounds]];
  ctrl = [[MyViewController alloc] initWithNibName:nil bundle:nil];
  [window addSubview:ctrl.view];
  [window makeKeyAndVisible];
}
- (void)dealloc {
  [ctrl release];
  [window release];
  [super dealloc];
}
@end
```

Listings 8.30 and 8.31 show the declaration and implementation, respectively, of the view controller class. The class maintains a reference to the web view that is created in the loadView method. The web view is made to allow scaling and the delegate property is set to the view controller instance. The web view is made to start with the Google search page (Figure 8.20). The view controller only implements the `webView:shouldStartLoadWithRequest:navigationType:` method of the `UIWebViewDelegate` protocol.

The `webView:shouldStartLoadWithRequest:navigationType:` method first retrieves the URL string of the request. It checks to see if it is for a PDF file by using the `NSString`'s method `hasSuffix:`. If it is for a PDF file, an alert view is displayed to the user, asking for the opportunity to download it into a local directory (Figure 8.21). The PDF file is always downloaded into the web view (Figure 8.22).

Figure 8.20 A screen shot of the application allowing additional local caching of PDF files.

Figure 8.21 A screen shot of the application that allows additional downloading of PDF files.

Listing 8.30 The declaration of the view controller class used in the application demonstrating interception of web view user interactions.

```
#import <UIKit/UIKit.h>
@interface MyViewController : UIViewController<UIWebViewDelegate> {
    UIWebView       *webView;
    NSString        *url;
}
@end
```

Figure 8.22   Result of a search operation in the application allowing additional local caching of PDF files.

Listing 8.31   The implementation of the view controller class used in the application demonstrating interception of web view user interactions.

```
#import "MyViewController.h"
@implementation MyViewController
- (void)loadView {
  CGRect   rectFrame = [UIScreen mainScreen].applicationFrame;
  UIView  *view = [[UIView alloc] initWithFrame:rectFrame];
  view.autoresizingMask = UIViewAutoresizingFlexibleHeight |
                          UIViewAutoresizingFlexibleWidth;
  webView = [[UIWebView alloc] initWithFrame:CGRectMake(0, 0, 320, 460)];
  webView.scalesPageToFit = YES;
  webView.delegate = self;
  [webView  loadRequest:
          [NSURLRequest requestWithURL:
              [NSURL URLWithString:@"http://www.google.com"]]];
  [view addSubview:webView];
  self.view = view;
  [view release];
}
```

```
- (void)dealloc {
  [webView release];
  [super dealloc];
}
- (BOOL)webView:(UIWebView *)webView
        shouldStartLoadWithRequest:(NSURLRequest *)request
        navigationType:(UIWebViewNavigationType)navigationType{
  url = [[request URL] absoluteString];
  NSLog(url);
  if([url hasSuffix:@".pdf"] == YES){
    UIAlertView *alert =
    [[[UIAlertView alloc]
      initWithTitle:@"Do You Want To Also Save A Copy?"
      message:@"Download PDF file?"
      delegate:self
      cancelButtonTitle:@"No"
      otherButtonTitles:@"Download", nil] autorelease];
    [alert show];
  }
  return YES;
}
- (void)alertView:(UIAlertView *)alertView
        clickedButtonAtIndex:(NSInteger)buttonIndex{
  if(buttonIndex == 1){ //download?
    NSLog(@"Downloading %@ ...", url);
  }
}
@end
```

The complete application can be found in the EWebView project in the source downloads.

8.8   Summary

This chapter presented several important subclasses of the UIView class. In Section 8.1, we discussed picker views and showed how they can be used for item selection. In Section 8.2, we discussed progress views and also talked about activity indicator views. Next, Section 8.3 showed how to use scroll views in order to display large (greater than 320×480) views. Section 8.4 presented text views used in displaying multiline text. In Section 8.5 we showed how to use alert views for the display of alert messages to the user. Similar to alert views are action sheets, which were discussed in Section 8.6. Finally, in Section 8.7, we discussed several aspects of web views.

Exercises

(1) Study the `UIWebView` class, using its header file and the documentation.

(2) After reading Section 17.7, come back to this chapter and implement the downloading part discussed in Section 8.7. Use a table view to present the downloaded files.

(3) Construct a view that hosts a multiline text area and a label underneath it. The label shows the number of characters entered inside the text area out of 255. The text area should not accept more than 255 characters.

9

Table View

A table view is an important and widely used graphical user interface object in iOS. Understanding table views is essential to writing iOS applications. Fortunately, programming table views could not be any easier.

This chapter takes you on a step-by-step journey through the world of table views. We start by presenting an overview of the main concepts behind table views in Section 9.1. After that, we present a simple table view application in Section 9.2 and discuss the mandatory methods you need to implement in order to populate and respond to the user's interaction with the table view.

In Section 9.3, we show how easy it is to add images to table rows. Section 9.4 introduces the concept of sections and provides a table view application that has sections with section headers and footers.

In Section 9.5, we introduce the concept of editing a table view. An application that allows the user to delete rows is presented and the main ideas are clarified. In Section 9.6, we address the insertion of new rows in a table view. An application that presents a data entry view to the user and adds that new data to the table's rows is discussed. In Section 9.7, we continue our discussion of the editing mode and present an application for reordering table entries. The main concepts of reordering rows are presented.

Section 9.8 covers the mechanism for presenting hierarchical information to the user, and an application that uses table views to present three levels of hierarchy is discussed. In Section 9.9, we discuss grouped table views through an example. After that, we present the main concepts behind indexed table views in Section 9.10. In Section 9.11, we present a dynamic table view controller class. This class can be used to show cells with varying heights. In Section 9.12, we address the issue of turning the text color to white when a custom cell is selected. Finally, we summarize the chapter in Section 9.13.

9.1 Overview

To use a table view in your application, you need to create an instance of the class `UITableView`, configure it, and add it to another view as a subview. The `UITableView` class is a subclass of `UIScrollView`, which itself is a subclass of `UIView`. The table view allows for only one column and zero or more rows. Each row in the table is represented by a cell. A cell is an instance of the class `UITableViewCell`. The cell comes with four different styles to choose among. In addition, you can access its `contentView` property, which allows you to configure the cell any way you want.

The `UITableView` class relies on two external objects: one for providing the data that will be displayed and the other for controlling the appearance of the table. The object supplying the data model must adopt the `UITableViewDataSource` protocol, while the object supplying the visual aspects of the table must adopt the `UITableViewDelegate` protocol.

The following sections show you how to create and configure a table view, starting from a simple table and gradually adding more features.

9.2   The Simplest Table View Application

In this section, we present the simplest table view application. This application presents, in tabular form, a list of characters from the television series *The Simpsons*. The application accepts all the default values for the table view. It does not implement any of the table's delegate methods, as all of them are optional. It does, however, use the application delegate as the data source and implements the two required methods of the `UITableViewDataSource` protocol.

Listing 9.1 shows the declaration of the application delegate class `TVAppDelegate`. The application delegate manages the table view and acts as the data source. The complete source code can be found in the `TableView1` project in the source downloads.

As you have learned before, the class adopts the protocol by listing it after its superclass as follows: `NSObject<UITableViewDataSource>`. In addition to the `myTable` `UITableView` instance, we keep an array of strings representing the data model in `theSimpsons` instance of `NSArray`.

Listing 9.1   The application delegate declaration (`TVAppDelegate.h`) for a simple table view application.

```
#import <UIKit/UIKit.h>
#import <Foundation/Foundation.h>

@interface TVAppDelegate : NSObject<UITableViewDataSource> {
  UIWindow      *window;
  UITableView *myTable;
  NSArray       *theSimpsons;
}
@end
```

Listing 9.2 shows the implementation of the `TVAppDelegate` class. The application delegate manages the table view and acts as the data source.

Inside the `applicationDidFinishLaunching:` method, we perform all the initialization needed. After creating the main window, we create the table view instance. To initialize the table view, we use the method `initWithFrame:style:`. The frame used in the initialization is the area of the application frame, as we want the table to occupy the whole area available to the application. The style used is `UITableViewStylePlain`. The style of the table must be specified during the initialization phase and cannot be changed later. If you bypass this initialization method and use the `UIView`'s `initWithFrame:` initializer, the `UITableViewStylePlain` style will be used by default. To make your code readable, you should always explicitly specify the table's style even if it's the default.

The other table style that is available to you is `UITableViewStyleGrouped`. You learn about the other style in Section 9.9.

After that, we populate the array `theSimpsons` with the names that will be displayed inside the table.

Next, the data source of the table view is set to the application delegate instance. The `UITableView`'s property for the data source is `dataSource` and is declared as

`@property(nonatomic, assign)` **`id`** `<UITableViewDataSource> dataSource;`

Notice that this property uses `assign` rather than `retain`.

Finally, the table view is added to the main window, and the main window is made key and visible.

Listing 9.2   The application delegate definition (`TVAppDelegate.m`) for a simple table view application.

```
#import <Foundation/Foundation.h>
#import <UIKit/UIKit.h>
#import "TVAppDelegate.h"

@implementation TVAppDelegate

- (void)applicationDidFinishLaunching:(UIApplication *)application {
  window = [[UIWindow alloc]
                initWithFrame:[[UIScreen  mainScreen] bounds]] ;
  myTable = [[UITableView alloc]
                initWithFrame:[UIScreen mainScreen].applicationFrame
                style:UITableViewStylePlain];
  theSimpsons = [[NSArray arrayWithObjects:
        @"Homer Jay Simpson",
        @"Marjorie \"Marge\" Simpson",
        @"Bartholomew \"Bart\" J. Simpson",
        @"Lisa Marie Simpson",
        @"Margaret \"Maggie\" Simpson",
        @"Abraham J. Simpson",
        @"Santa's Little Helper",
        @"Ned Flanders",
        @"Apu Nahasapeemapetilon",
        @"Clancy Wiggum",
        @"Charles Montgomery Burns",
        nil] retain];
  myTable.dataSource = self;
  [window addSubview:myTable];
  [window makeKeyAndVisible];
```

```
}

- (NSInteger)tableView:(UITableView *)tableView
              numberOfRowsInSection:(NSInteger)section{
  return [theSimpsons count];
}

- (UITableViewCell *)
        tableView:(UITableView *)tableView
          cellForRowAtIndexPath:(NSIndexPath *)indexPath{
  UITableViewCell *cell =
        [tableViewdequeueReusableCellWithIdentifier:@"simpsons"];
  if (cell == nil) {
    cell = [[[UITableViewCell alloc]
                initWithStyle:UITableViewCellStyleDefault
                reuseIdentifier:@"simpsons"] autorelease];
  }
  cell.textLabel.text = [theSimpsons objectAtIndex:indexPath.row];
  return cell;
}

- (void)dealloc {
  [window release];
  [myTable release];
  [theSimpsons release];
  [super dealloc];
}
@end
```

The two required methods of the UITableViewDataSource protocol are

- tableView:numberOfRowsInSection:. By default, the table view will have one section. You still need to specify the number of rows in that section. This method of the data source is invoked asking for that number. The method is declared as

  ```
  - (NSInteger)tableView:(UITableView *)table
            numberOfRowsInSection:(NSInteger)section;
  ```

  You are given two values: the table view instance, which allows you to have the same data source method for multiple table view instances; and the section number, which in this example is always 0 (and is ignored) as we choose to take the default.

- tableView:cellForRowAtIndexPath:. The table view invokes this method asking the data source for a table cell representing a specific row. The method is declared as

  ```
  - (UITableViewCell *)
  ```

```
tableView:(UITableView *)tableView
cellForRowAtIndexPath:(NSIndexPath *)indexPath;
```

In addition to the table view instance, you are given an instance of `NSIndexPath`. `NSIndexPath` is used in Cocoa as a class representing a series of indices. For example, `1.5.8.33` represents an index path. This class is extended by `UITableView` by declaring a category on it as shown in Listing 9.3.

Listing 9.3   Extending the `NSIndexPath` for use in `UITableView`.

```
@interface NSIndexPath (UITableView)
+ (NSIndexPath *)indexPathForRow:(NSUInteger)row
                 inSection:(NSUInteger)section;
@property(nonatomic,readonly) NSUInteger section;
@property(nonatomic,readonly) NSUInteger row;
@end
```

The category adds two properties: `section` and `row`.

Given the `NSIndexPath` instance, you can determine the cell configuration you want to return. In returning a cell, you can either create one from scratch and return it autoreleased or return a cached cell that is already created. You are encouraged to reuse cells. After creating a cell, you should use the designated initializer `initWithStyle:reuseIdentifier:`, which is declared as

```
- (id)initWithStyle:(UITableViewCellStyle)style
        reuseIdentifier:(NSString *)reuseIdentifier
```

The value for `style` can be one the following constants:

- `UITableViewCellStyleDefault`. This is the default cell style prior to iOS 3.0. It gives you a cell with a text label that is left-aligned and an optional image view.
- `UITableViewCellStyleValue1`. This style will give you a cell with two labels; the one on the left uses black text and is left-aligned, while the one on the right holds blue text that is right-aligned.
- `UITableViewCellStyleValue2`. A cell configured with this style has two text labels: the one on the left is right-aligned with blue color, and the one on the right is left-aligned with black color. The font size of the label on the right is smaller than that of the label on the left side.
- `UITableViewCellStyleSubtitle`. A cell with this style has the two text labels stacked. The one on top is left-aligned with black color, while the one below it is also left-aligned but with gray color and a smaller font.

In all cases above, the larger text label is accessed via the property `textLabel` and the smaller text label is accessed via the `detailTextLabel` property. Figure 9.1 shows the four available styles.

Figure 9.1 Available cell styles. The row styles from top to bottom are as follows: `UITableView-CellStyleDefault`, `UITableViewCellStyleSubtitle`, `UITableViewCellStyleValue1`, and `UITableViewCellStyleValue2`.

The `reuseIdentifier` is a string used to tag the cell so that it can be easily identified for reuse in the future. Our method creates a new cell in the following statement:

```
cell = [[[UITableViewCell alloc]
              initWithStyle:UITableViewCellStyleDefault
              reuseIdentifier:@"simpsons"] autorelease];
```

We mentioned that you should always reuse a cached cell as much as possible. To obtain a reused cell, use the `UITableView` instance method `dequeueReusableCellWith-Identifier:`, which is declared as

```
- (UITableViewCell *)
      dequeueReusableCellWithIdentifier:(NSString *)identifier
```

The value for `identifier` is the same tag as used in creating the cell, which in our case is `@"simpsons"`. If there is an available cell, a pointer to it is returned. If, on the other hand, there are no available cells, a `nil` value is returned.

After having a `UITableViewCell` instance, we need to configure it with values appropriate to the section and row numbers. Because we are implementing a simple table view, we set

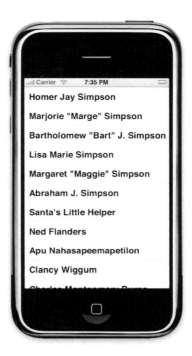

Figure 9.2   A screen shot of a simple text-only table view application.

the `text` property of `textLabel` with the corresponding value from the `theSimpsons` array (which represents the data model) as shown in the following statement:

```
cell.textLabel.text  = [theSimpsons objectAtIndex:indexPath.row];
```

Figure 9.2 shows a screen shot of the application.

9.3   A Table View with Both Images and Text

In the previous section, we showed you how to create a table view displaying text items. As we have mentioned before, each cell can have an image displayed to the left. In Listing 9.4, we show the updated `tableView:cellForRowAtIndexPath:` method that configures the cells to have images.

Listing 9.4   The updated method `tableView:cellForRowAtIndexPath:` for adding an image to the left side of each cell.

```
- (UITableViewCell *)
   tableView:(UITableView *)tableView
   cellForRowAtIndexPath:(NSIndexPath *)indexPath{
```

```
UITableViewCell *cell =
  [tableView dequeueReusableCellWithIdentifier:@"simpsons"];
if (cell == nil) {
    cell = [[[UITableViewCell alloc]
                    initWithStyle:UITableViewCellStyleDefault
                    reuseIdentifier:@"simpsons"] autorelease];
}
cell.textLabel.text  = [theSimpsons objectAtIndex:indexPath.row];
NSString *imageName =
  [NSString stringWithFormat:@"%d.png", indexPath.row];
cell.imageView.image = [UIImage imageNamed:imageName];
return cell;
}
```

To set up an image for the cell, set the `image` of the cell's `imageView` property to a `UIImage` instance. The property `imageView` is declared as

```
@property(nonatomic, readonly, retain) UIImageView  *imageView
```

Figure 9.3   A table view with both images and text. For copyright reasons, the actual images of the characters are replaced by geometric shapes.

The default value is `nil`. The image view is created on demand.

The image for each row is loaded from the application's bundle (see Section 10.6) using the `imageNamed:` class method of `UIImage`. The image files stored are named according to the row index. For example, the image for the first row is `0.png`. The `NSString` class method `stringWithFormat:` is used to obtain the name of the image to be used in the invocation of the `imageNamed:` method. Figure 9.3 shows a screen shot of the application.

9.4   A Table View with Section Headers and Footers

In the previous sections, we showed table views that had only one section. You can have a table with more than one section and have these sections presented with header and/or footer titles.

Let's modify our example so that it has a table with two sections. We need to have two arrays: one array, `theSimpsonsFamily`, holding the names of the family; and the `theSimpsonsOthers`, an array holding the names of the others. We need to do the following modifications in order to have two sections:

1. **Modify the** `numberOfSectionsInTableView:` **method to return** 2 **for the number of sections.**

2. **Modify** `tableView:numberOfRowsInSection:` **as follows:**

```
- (NSInteger)tableView:(UITableView *)tableView
              numberOfRowsInSection:(NSInteger)section{
  if(section == 0){
    return [theSimpsonsFamily count];
  }
  else{
    return [theSimpsonsOthers count];
  }
}
```

3. **If you would like a section header, add the following data source method:**

```
- (NSString *)
              tableView:(UITableView *)tableView
              titleForHeaderInSection:(NSInteger)section{
  if(section == 0){
    return @"The Simpsons Family";
  }
  else{
    return @"The Others";
  }
}
```

4. **If you would like a section footer, add the following data source method:**

```objc
- (NSString *)
            tableView:(UITableView *)tableView
            titleForFooterInSection:(NSInteger)section{
  if(section == 0){
    return @"End of Simpsons Family";
  }
  else{
    return @"End of The Others";
  }
}
```

5. **Modify the** `tableView:cellForRowAtIndexPath:` **to return the appropriate cell as follows:**

```objc
- (UITableViewCell *)
                tableView:(UITableView *)tableView
                cellForRowAtIndexPath:(NSIndexPath *)indexPath{
    UITableViewCell *cell =
        [tableView dequeueReusableCellWithIdentifier:@"simpsons"];
    if (cell == nil) {
        cell = [[[UITableViewCell alloc]
                initWithStyle:UITableViewCellStyleDefault
                reuseIdentifier:@"simpsons"] autorelease];
    }
    if(indexPath.section == 0){
        cell.textLabel.text  =
            [theSimpsonsFamily objectAtIndex:indexPath.row];
    }
    else{
        cell.textLabel.text  =
            [theSimpsonsOthers objectAtIndex:indexPath.row];
    }
    NSString *imageName =
        [NSString stringWithFormat:@"%d-%d.png",
            indexPath.row, indexPath.section];
    cell.imageView.image = [UIImage imageNamed:imageName];
    return cell;
}
```

Complete source code can be found in the `TableView2` project in the source downloads.

Figure 9.4 shows the table view with sections and section headers and footers. Notice how the headers and footers are always visible as you scroll through the table.

Figure 9.4   A table view with sections and section headers and footers.

9.5   A Table View with the Ability to Delete Rows

The table view can be manipulated at runtime to enter editing mode. In editing mode, you can delete, insert, and reorder rows. In this section, we will look at a table view application that allows the user to delete rows. The application uses a button that, when tapped, will make the table view instance enter the editing mode. The user will then tap on the delete button and confirm deletion. The data source of the table view will receive a message asking for confirmation of the deletion. If the data source approves such deletion, the data model, represented by a mutable array, will be updated by the removal of the corresponding element, and the table view instance is instructed to delete the row, optionally animating the deletion.

Listing 9.5 shows the declaration of the application delegate `TVAppDelegate`. The application delegate manages the table view and acts as its data source. The source code can be found in the `TableView3` project in the source downloads.

The application delegate will create and configure the table view and act as its data source. Notice that we have a mutable array, theSimpsons, that will capture our data mode. A button, editButton, is used in switching between editing and non-editing modes.

Listing 9.5   The declaration (TVAppDelegate.h) of the application delegate for a table view application with the ability to delete rows.

```
#import <UIKit/UIKit.h>
#import <Foundation/Foundation.h>
@interface TVAppDelegate : NSObject <UITableViewDataSource> {
    UIWindow        *window;
    UITableView     *myTable;
    NSMutableArray  *theSimpsons;
    UIButton        *editButton;
}
@end
```

In Listing 9.6 we show the definition of the application delegate.

Listing 9.6   Definition of the application delegate of an application with the ability to delete rows.

```
#import <Foundation/Foundation.h>
#import <UIKit/UIKit.h>
#import "TVAppDelegate.h"

@implementation TVAppDelegate

- (void)applicationDidFinishLaunching:(UIApplication *)application {
    window = [[UIWindow alloc]
                initWithFrame:[[UIScreen mainScreen] bounds]];
    editButton = [[UIButton
                buttonWithType:UIButtonTypeRoundedRect] retain];
    editButton.frame = CGRectMake(105.0, 25.0, 100, 40);
    [editButton setTitle:@"Edit" forState:UIControlStateNormal];
    [editButton addTarget:self action:@selector(editAction:)
                forControlEvents:UIControlEventTouchUpInside];
    [window addSubview:editButton];

    CGRect frame = CGRectMake(0, 70, 320, 420);
    myTable = [[UITableView alloc]
                initWithFrame:frame
                style:UITableViewStylePlain];
    theSimpsons = [[NSMutableArray
                arrayWithObjects:@"Homer Jay Simpson",
                @"Marjorie \"Marge\" Simpson",
                @"Bartholomew \"Bart\" J. Simpson",
                @"Lisa Marie Simpson",
                @"Margaret \"Maggie\" Simpson",
                @"Abraham J. Simpson",
```

```
                    @"Santa's Little Helper",
                    @"Ned Flanders",
                    @"Apu Nahasapeemapetilon",
                    @"Clancy Wiggum",
                    @"Charles Montgomery Burns",
                    nil] retain];
   myTable.dataSource = self;
   [window addSubview:myTable];
   [window makeKeyAndVisible];
}

-(void)editAction:(id)sender{
  if(sender == editButton){
    if([editButton.currentTitle isEqualToString:@"Edit"] == YES){
      [editButton setTitle:@"Done" forState:UIControlStateNormal];
      [myTable setEditing:YES animated:YES];
    }
    else {
      [editButton setTitle:@"Edit" forState:UIControlStateNormal];
      [myTable setEditing:NO animated:YES];
    }
  }
}

- (NSInteger)tableView:(UITableView *)tableView
            numberOfRowsInSection:(NSInteger)section{
  return [theSimpsons count];
}

- (void)
     tableView:(UITableView *)tableView
     commitEditingStyle:(UITableViewCellEditingStyle)editingStyle
     forRowAtIndexPath:(NSIndexPath *)indexPath{

  if(editingStyle == UITableViewCellEditingStyleDelete){
    [theSimpsons removeObjectAtIndex:indexPath.row];
    [myTable
        deleteRowsAtIndexPaths:[NSArray arrayWithObject:indexPath]
        withRowAnimation:UITableViewRowAnimationFade];
  }
}

- (UITableViewCell *)
      tableView:(UITableView *)tableView
      cellForRowAtIndexPath:(NSIndexPath *)indexPath{
  UITableViewCell *cell =
    [tableView dequeueReusableCellWithIdentifier:@"simpsons"];
  if (cell == nil) {
```

```
    cell = [[[UITableViewCell alloc]
                    initWithStyle:UITableViewCellStyleDefault
                reuseIdentifier:@"simpsons"] autorelease];
  }
  cell.textLabel.text  = [theSimpsons objectAtIndex:indexPath.row];
  return cell;
}

- (void)dealloc {
  [window release];
  [myTable release];
  [theSimpsons release];
  [editButton release];
  [super dealloc];
}
@end
```

We first create a button (see Section 6.5) that will trigger the switching between the two modes. The logic that will flip between editing and non-editing modes of the table view can be found in the action method `editAction:`. To make the table view enter editing mode, you invoke the method `setEditing:animated:`, which is declared as

- (**void**) setEditing: (BOOL) editing animated: (BOOL) animate

If `editing` is equal to YES, then the table view enters the editing mode. Set `animate` to YES to animate the change in mode. Once the table view instance receives this message, it sends it to every visible row (cell).

In editing mode, each row can allow either deletion or insertion. If a row is in delete editing mode, it will be marked by a circled red minus sign (–) icon to the left. If a row is in insert editing mode (addressed in Section 9.6), it will be marked by a circled green plus sign (+) icon to the left. The question remains: How does the table view know which mode to enter? The answer is simple: An optional method in the delegate, `tableView:editingStyleForRowAtIndexPath:` is used to provide the editing style for a specific cell. This method is declared as

- (UITableViewCellEditingStyle)
        tableView: (UITableView *) tableView
        editingStyleForRowAtIndexPath: (NSIndexPath *) indexPath

If the table view is in editing mode, it has a delegate, and if that delegate implements this method, then this method is called for every visible row, asking it for the editing style of that row. The value returned can be either `UITableViewCellEditingStyleDelete` or `UITableViewCell-EditingStyleInsert`. If there is no delegate assigned (as is the case in our example) or the delegate does not implement this method, the `UITableViewCellEditingStyleDelete` style is assumed.

Whenever the user taps on the button, the `editAction:` method is invoked. The method first checks the current mode by examining the button's title. If the title is Edit, the button title is changed to

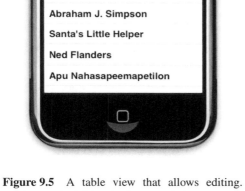
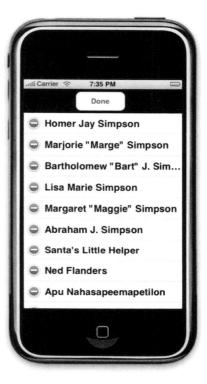

Figure 9.5 A table view that allows editing. Editing can be initiated using an Edit button.

Figure 9.6 A table view in editing mode. The default editing mode is deletion.

Done and the table view is asked to enter editing mode with animation. Otherwise, the button title is changed to Edit and the table view is asked to stop editing with animation. Figure 9.5 shows the application in non-editing mode and Figure 9.6 shows it in editing mode (deletion).

When the user taps on the – icon, a Delete confirmation button appears to the right. If the user taps on that button, the table view sends a `tableView:commitEditingStyle:forRowAtIndexPath:` message to the data source. This method is declared as

```
- (void)
    tableView:(UITableView *)tableView
    commitEditingStyle:(UITableViewCellEditingStyle)editingStyle
    forRowAtIndexPath:(NSIndexPath *)indexPath
```

The `tableView` is the table view instance asking for editing confirmation. The `editingStyle` is the style that the row is in (either deletion or insertion) and `indexPath` is the object holding the section and row numbers of the affected cell.

If the row should be deleted, the above method should update its data model by deleting the data for that row and invoke the table view's `deleteRowsAtIndexPaths:withRowAnimation:` method. The method is declared as

```
- (void)deleteRowsAtIndexPaths:(NSArray *)indexPaths
        withRowAnimation:(UITableViewRowAnimation)animation
```

`indexPaths` is an `NSArray` instance holding the instances of `NSIndexPath` for the rows that will be deleted. The `animation` value can be one of the following:

- `UITableViewRowAnimationFade` specifies that the deleted row should fade out of the table view.

- `UITableViewRowAnimationRight` specifies that the deleted row should slide out to the right.

- `UITableViewRowAnimationLeft` specifies that the deleted row should slide out to the left.

- `UITableViewRowAnimationTop` specifies that the deleted row should slide out toward the top.

- `UITableViewRowAnimationBottom` specifies that the deleted row should slide out toward the bottom.

Figure 9.7 A table view row with delete confirmation.

Figure 9.8 A table view after the deletion of a row while still in editing mode.

Figures 9.7 and 9.8 show the table view with the delete confirmation button and after a row has been deleted (while still in editing mode), respectively. Figure 9.9 shows the table view after exiting the editing mode and successfully deleting the `Lisa` row.

Figure 9.9   A table view after exiting the editing mode and successfully deleting a row.

9.6   A Table View with the Ability to Insert Rows

In the previous section, we saw how we can configure the table view to enter editing mode and manage deletion of rows. In this section, we will address insertion of new rows. Listing 9.7 shows the declaration of the application delegate of the demonstration application. The delegate allows for insertion of new table entries and acts as both the data source and the delegate of the table view. Complete source code can be found in the `TableView4` project in the source downloads.

The application delegate will create a new table view, an editing button, and a data entry view. It will also act as both the data source and the delegate of the table view.

Listing 9.7   The application delegate `TVAppDelegate` class declaration in file `TVAppDelegate.h`.

```
#import <UIKit/UIKit.h>
#import <Foundation/Foundation.h>

@interface TVAppDelegate :
```

```
        NSObject <UITableViewDelegate, UITableViewDataSource,
        UITextFieldDelegate> {
    UIWindow           *window;
    UITableView        *myTable;
    NSMutableArray     *theSimpsons;
    UIButton           *editButton;
    UIView             *inputACharacterView;
    UITextField        *characterTextField;
}
-(void)insertCharacter;
@end
```

Listing 9.8 shows the applicationDidFinishLaunching: method for our application delegate. First, the method creates and configures an edit button. After that, the table view is created and configured. As we saw in the previous section, when the user taps the edit button, the table view will enter the editing mode. The action method for the button is identical to the one you saw in the previous section. Figure 9.10 shows the starting window of the application.

Listing 9.8   The applicationDidFinishLaunching: method for the application delegate managing a table view with an insertion option.

```
- (void)applicationDidFinishLaunching:(UIApplication *)application {
  window = [[UIWindow alloc]
                          initWithFrame:[[UIScreen  mainScreen] bounds]];
  editButton = [[UIButton buttonWithType:
                      UIButtonTypeRoundedRect] retain];
  editButton.frame = CGRectMake(105.0, 25.0, 100, 40);
  [editButton setTitle:@"Edit" forState:UIControlStateNormal];
  [editButton addTarget:self action:@selector(editAction:)
                      forControlEvents:UIControlEventTouchUpInside];
  [window addSubview: editButton];

  CGRect frame = CGRectMake(0, 70, 320, 420);
  myTable = [[UITableView alloc]
              initWithFrame:frame
              style:UITableViewStylePlain];
  theSimpsons = [[NSMutableArray arrayWithObjects:
                  @"Homer Jay Simpson",
                  @"Marjorie \"Marge\" Simpson",
                  @"Bartholomew \"Bart\" J. Simpson",
                  @"Lisa Marie Simpson",
                  @"Margaret \"Maggie\" Simpson",
                  @"Abraham J. Simpson",
                  @"Santa's Little Helper",
                  @"Ned Flanders",
                  @"Apu Nahasapeemapetilon",
                  @"Clancy Wiggum",
                  @"Charles Montgomery Burns",
```

```
                            nil] retain];
    myTable.delegate = self;
    myTable.dataSource = self;
    [window addSubview:myTable];
    inputACharacterView  = nil;
    [window makeKeyAndVisible];
}
```

The application delegate defines the `tableView:editingStyleForRowAtIndexPath:` method needed to override the default (delete) editing style. The method simply returns `UITableView-CellEditingStyleInsert` as shown below:

```
- (UITableViewCellEditingStyle)
            tableView:(UITableView *)tableView
            editingStyleForRowAtIndexPath:(NSIndexPath *)indexPath{
    return UITableViewCellEditingStyleInsert;
}
```

Figure 9.11 shows a screen shot of the application after entering insert editing mode.

Figure 9.10   A table view that allows insertion of rows.

Figure 9.11   A table view after entering editing mode for insertion.

Listing 9.9 shows the `tableView:cellForRowAtIndexPath:` method. If the image cannot be found, a generic image is used. This will allow the newly added row to have an image.

Listing 9.9   The data source method producing cells with text and images.

```
- (UITableViewCell *)
             tableView:(UITableView *)tableView
             cellForRowAtIndexPath:(NSIndexPath *)indexPath{
  UITableViewCell *cell =
    [tableView dequeueReusableCellWithIdentifier:@"simpsons"];
  if (cell == nil) {
    cell = [[[UITableViewCell alloc]
                    initWithStyle:UITableViewCellStyleDefault
                    reuseIdentifier:@"simpsons"] autorelease];
  }

  cell.textLabel.text  = [theSimpsons objectAtIndex:indexPath.row];
  NSString *imageName =
    [NSString stringWithFormat:@"%d.png", indexPath.row];
  cell.imageView.image = [UIImage imageNamed:imageName];
  if(cell.imageView.image == nil){
    cell.imageView.image  = [UIImage imageNamed:@"unknown-person.gif"];
  }
  return cell;
}
```

The following listing shows the `tableView:commitEditingStyle:forRowAtIndexPath:` method. The method simply invokes the `insertCharacter` method that will actually present a data entry view to the user.

```
- (void)tableView:(UITableView *)tableView
        commitEditingStyle:(UITableViewCellEditingStyle)editingStyle
        forRowAtIndexPath:(NSIndexPath *)indexPath{
  if(editingStyle == UITableViewCellEditingStyleInsert){
    [self insertCharacter];
  }
}
```

Listing 9.10 shows the `insertCharacter` method.

Listing 9.10   The `insertCharacter` method that will present a data entry view to the user.

```
-(void)insertCharacter{
  inputACharacterView =
    [[[UIView alloc]
        initWithFrame:[UIScreen mainScreen].applicationFrame]
            autorelease];
  inputACharacterView.backgroundColor = [UIColor lightGrayColor];
  UIButton *cancelButton =
```

```
   [UIButton buttonWithType:UIButtonTypeRoundedRect];
cancelButton.frame = CGRectMake(105.0, 25.0, 100, 40);
[cancelButton setTitle:@"Cancel" forState:UIControlStateNormal];
[cancelButton addTarget:self action:@selector(cancelAction:)
           forControlEvents:UIControlEventTouchUpInside];
[inputACharacterView addSubview: cancelButton];
UILabel *label = [[[UILabel alloc]
   initWithFrame:CGRectMake(10,100, 70, 30)] autorelease];
label.backgroundColor = [UIColor clearColor];
label.text = @"Name:";
[inputACharacterView addSubview: label];
characterTextField =
   [[UITextField alloc] initWithFrame:CGRectMake(80,100, 220, 30)];
characterTextField.textColor = [UIColor blackColor];
characterTextField.font  = [UIFont systemFontOfSize:17.0];
characterTextField.placeholder = @"<enter a new character>";
characterTextField.backgroundColor = [UIColor clearColor];
characterTextField.borderStyle = UITextBorderStyleRoundedRect;
characterTextField.keyboardType = UIKeyboardTypeDefault;
characterTextField.returnKeyType = UIReturnKeyDone;
characterTextField.clearButtonMode = UITextFieldViewModeAlways;
characterTextField.enablesReturnKeyAutomatically = YES;
characterTextField.delegate = self;
[inputACharacterView addSubview: characterTextField];
[window addSubview:inputACharacterView];
}
```

The method creates a view and adds several controls to it. A Cancel button is added to the view for canceling the data entry. In addition, a `UILabel` instance is added with the value `Name:` as a label for a text field. The text field is where the user enters a new name to be added to the table view. Figures 9.12 and 9.13 show the data entry view.

The action for the cancel button is `cancelAction:`, which is defined as follows:

```
-(void)cancelAction:(id)sender{
  [inputACharacterView removeFromSuperview];
  inputACharacterView = nil;
}
```

It simply removes the data entry view `inputACharacterView` from its superview, `window`, and sets the `inputACharacterView` to `nil`. Notice that the `removeFromSuperview` method does `release` the receiver.

The text field delegate method `textFieldShouldReturn:` is invoked, as you have learned in previous chapters, when the user taps the Done button. Inside this method, we add the name entered in the text field to the data model (`theSimpsons` mutable array) and ask the table to reload its data by sending a `reloadData` to the table view instance. After that, we remove the data entry view as we did when we handled the data entry cancellation event.

Figure 9.12   The data entry view for adding a new entry to a table view before the appearance of the keyboard.

Figure 9.13   The data entry view for adding a new entry to a table view after the appearance of the keyboard.

```
- (BOOL)textFieldShouldReturn:(UITextField *)textField{
    [theSimpsons addObject:textField.text];
    [myTable reloadData];
    [inputACharacterView removeFromSuperview];
    inputACharacterView = nil;
    return YES;
}
```

Figure 9.14 shows the application after adding a new row.

9.7   Reordering Table Rows

A table view can be configured to allow reordering of its rows when it enters editing mode. By default, reordering is not enabled. To enable reordering, the data source needs to implement the method `tableView:moveRowAtIndexPath:toIndexPath:`. Once this method is defined,

Figure 9.14   A table view after the addition of a new row at the bottom.

a reordering icon appears on the right side of each row when the table view is in editing mode. To disable reordering of specific rows, the data source needs to implement the method `tableView:canMoveRowAtIndexPath:` and exclude specific rows.

In the following, we give a detailed example of a table view reordering application. Listing 9.11 shows the application delegate that also acts as the data source. The complete source code can be found in the `TableView5` project in the source downloads.

Notice that the data model, `theSimpsons`, is a mutable array because we need to change the order of the rows dynamically.

Listing 9.11   The file `TVAppDelegate.h` declaring the application delegate for the rows reordering application.

```
#import <UIKit/UIKit.h>
#import <Foundation/Foundation.h>
@interface TVAppDelegate : NSObject <UITableViewDataSource> {
  UIWindow        *window;
  UITableView     *myTable;
```

```
    NSMutableArray    *theSimpsons;
    UIButton          *editButton;
}
@end
```

In Listing 9.12, we show the implementation of the application delegate.

Listing 9.12   The file `TVAppDelegate.m` implementing the application delegate for the rows reordering application.

```
#import <Foundation/Foundation.h>
#import <UIKit/UIKit.h>
#import "TVAppDelegate.h"

@implementation TVAppDelegate

- (void)applicationDidFinishLaunching:(UIApplication *)application {
  window = [[UIWindow alloc]
                    initWithFrame:[[UIScreen  mainScreen] bounds]] ;
  editButton =
    [[UIButton buttonWithType:UIButtonTypeRoundedRect] retain];
  editButton.frame = CGRectMake(105.0, 25.0, 100, 40);
  [editButton setTitle:@"Edit" forState:UIControlStateNormal];
  [editButton addTarget:self action:@selector(editAction:)
            forControlEvents:UIControlEventTouchUpInside];
  [window addSubview: editButton];

  CGRect frame = CGRectMake(0, 70, 320, 420);
  myTable = [[UITableView alloc]
                    initWithFrame:frame style:UITableViewStylePlain];
  theSimpsons = [[NSMutableArray arrayWithObjects:
          @"Homer Jay Simpson",
          @"Marjorie \"Marge\" Simpson",
          @"Bartholomew \"Bart\" J. Simpson",
          @"Lisa Marie Simpson",
          @"Margaret \"Maggie\" Simpson",
          @"Abraham J. Simpson",
          @"Santa's Little Helper",
          @"Ned Flanders",
          @"Apu Nahasapeemapetilon",
          @"Clancy Wiggum",
          @"Charles Montgomery Burns",
          nil] retain];
  myTable.dataSource = self;
  [window addSubview:myTable];
  [window makeKeyAndVisible];
}
```

```objc
-(void)editAction:(id)sender{
  if(sender == editButton){
    if([editButton.currentTitle isEqualToString:@"Edit"] == YES){
      [editButton setTitle:@"Done" forState:UIControlStateNormal];
      [myTable setEditing:YES animated:YES];
    }
    else {
      [editButton setTitle:@"Edit" forState:UIControlStateNormal];
      [myTable setEditing:NO animated:YES];
    }
  }
}


- (NSInteger)
            tableView:(UITableView *)tableView
            numberOfRowsInSection:(NSInteger)section{
    return [theSimpsons count];
}


- (BOOL)
            tableView:(UITableView *)tableView
            canMoveRowAtIndexPath:(NSIndexPath *)indexPath{
  NSString  *string =
    [theSimpsons objectAtIndex:indexPath.row];
  if([string isEqualToString:@"Bartholomew \"Bart\" J. Simpson"]){
      return NO;
  }
  if([string  isEqualToString:@"Santa's Little Helper"]){
      return NO;
  }
  return YES;
}


- (void)
        tableView:(UITableView *)tableView
        moveRowAtIndexPath:(NSIndexPath *)fromIndexPath
        toIndexPath:(NSIndexPath *)toIndexPath{
  NSString *str= [[theSimpsons objectAtIndex:fromIndexPath.row] retain];
  [theSimpsons removeObjectAtIndex:fromIndexPath.row];
  [theSimpsons insertObject:str atIndex:toIndexPath.row];
  [str release];
}


- (UITableViewCell *)
        tableView:(UITableView *)tableView
        cellForRowAtIndexPath:(NSIndexPath *)indexPath{
  UITableViewCell *cell =
  [tableView dequeueReusableCellWithIdentifier:@"simpsons"];
```

```
  if (cell == nil) {
    cell = [[[UITableViewCell alloc]
                        initWithStyle:UITableViewCellStyleDefault
                reuseIdentifier:@"simpsons"] autorelease];
    }
  cell.textLabel.text = [theSimpsons objectAtIndex:indexPath.row];
  return cell;
}

- (void)dealloc {
  [window release];
  [myTable release];
  [theSimpsons release];
  [editButton release];
  [super dealloc];
}
@end
```

The method `applicationDidFinishLaunching:` is similar to what we have seen before. It creates the table view and an edit button. In addition, the data model is populated with the values.

The `tableView:canMoveRowAtIndexPath:` method is defined to allow the reordering of all rows except two: `Bart` and `Santa's Little Helper`. To disable reordering for a given row, the method needs to return `NO`.

If the user moves a row to a new position, the method `tableView:moveRowAtIndexPath:toIndexPath:` is called. This method is declared as

```
- (void)
            tableView:(UITableView *)tableView
            moveRowAtIndexPath:(NSIndexPath *)fromIndexPath
            toIndexPath:(NSIndexPath *)toIndexPath
```

The `fromIndexPath` is the current index path of the row and `toIndexPath` is the new index path. In our case, to move a name from one location in the array to a new location, we first retain the object at the current location in the statement

```
NSString *str =
 [[theSimpsons objectAtIndex:fromIndexPath.row] retain];
```

This is important as we are going to remove the object from the array, and this will result in releasing it. The statement that removes the object at the current row is as follows:

```
[theSimpsons removeObjectAtIndex:fromIndexPath.row];
```

After removing the object, we need to insert it at the new location as follows:

```
[theSimpsons insertObject:str atIndex:toIndexPath.row];
```

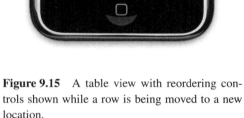

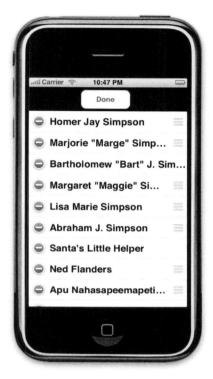

Figure 9.15   A table view with reordering controls shown while a row is being moved to a new location.

Figure 9.16   The table view after a row has been moved to a new location.

After that, we need to release the object `str`.

The method `tableView:canMoveRowAtIndexPath:` returns NO for the rows of `Bart` and `Santa's Little Helper`. It returns YES for all other rows. Figure 9.15 shows the table view while a row is being moved to a new location. Figure 9.16 shows the table view after a row has been moved to a new location.

9.8   Presenting Hierarchical Information

Table views are ideal for presenting hierarchical information. In interacting with hierarchical information, the user starts at the top level and drills down to the next level of the hierarchy. The user repeats this process until he or she reaches the desired level. For example, consider a user looking at a list of names of TV shows (Figure 9.17). Tapping on a show name, the user will be presented with another table view holding the names of the show characters (Figure 9.18). Tapping on a show character, the user will be presented with a simple view with information about that

Figure 9.17   A table view application for displaying information about TV shows. The figure shows the top level.

Figure 9.18   The second level of the table view hierarchy. The level shows the names of major characters of a specific TV show (*Lost*). Notice that the back button takes the user to the previous level of hierarchy.

character (Figure 9.19). The user can use the navigational buttons to go back to the previous levels of hierarchy or even edit the data of the current level. Figures 9.17, 9.18, and 9.19 show screen shots of the user drilling down to information about a specific character in a specific TV show.

There are two main classes that help you present hierarchical information to the user: (1) table view controller and (2) navigational controller. In previous chapters, we saw how to configure and use a navigational controller. A table view controller, UITableViewController is a subclass of UIViewController that creates and manages a UITableView instance. You allocate a table view controller and initialize it using the initWithStyle: method. The table view instance created by the controller can be accessed using its property tableView. In addition to creating the table view and initializing it, the controller acts as both the data source and the delegate of that table view. Therefore, you need to implement the table view's delegate and data source method in your subclass of that table view controller.

Figure 9.19 The last level of hierarchy in the TV-shows application. The back button takes the user to the show that this character is part of.

There are four major steps that you need to perform in order to create a working application that will present hierarchical information in the form of hierarchical table views:

1. **Create a subclass of** `UITableViewController` **for every level of the hierarchy.** Each subclass of these controllers should override the `initWithStyle:` method to configure its title and the back button title displayed in the navigation bar.

2. **Choose an object that will create the navigation controller.** Allocate and initialize the `UITableViewController` subclass that is the top of the hierarchy and push it onto the navigation controller as the root view controller. The object that will create these UI objects is usually the application delegate, and the work is done in its `applicationDidFinishLaunching:` method.

3. **Choose a global object that is accessible from each of the table view controllers.** Inside this object, provide methods to retrieve and set the data model. The application delegate is usually preferred to be such an object.

4. **Inside each table view controller, override the** `tableView:didSelectRowAtIndex-Path:` **method.** Inside this method, you should (1) store the selected row information with

a global object (usually the application delegate) and (2) create an instance of the controller for the next level and push it onto the navigation controller (obtained from the global object such as the application delegate). The object that will keep track of the selected row at each level should have a separate variable for each level — for example, level1IndexPath, level2IndexPath, etc. Required and optional methods for the table view data source and delegate should be implemented in each table view controller subclass.

9.8.1 Detailed example

Let's illustrate the creation of a hierarchical table view application using the TV Shows application shown in Figures 9.17, 9.18, and 9.19 earlier in this chapter. The TV Shows application has three levels of hierarchy. The first-level presents the user with a table containing the names of TV shows. The second level presents the user with a list of names of major characters for a given TV show. The third, and final, level of the hierarchy presents the user with a view showing the name and a picture of a given character.

Clearly, we need two UITableViewController subclasses for the first two levels and one UIViewController for the third and last level. The first table view controller subclass is called ShowTableViewController, and it manages the table view that lists the TV shows (i.e., the first level). The declaration of the controller is shown in Listing 9.13. The controller represents the first level of hierarchy showing the list of TV shows. Complete source code can be found in the TableView6 project in the source downloads.

Listing 9.13   The ShowTableViewController declared in ShowTableViewController.h.

```
#import <UIKit/UIKit.h>
@interface ShowTableViewController : UITableViewController {
}
@end
```

The implementation of the ShowTableViewController class is shown in Listing 9.14. The controller manages the first level of hierarchy in the TV Shows application.

Listing 9.14   The definition of the ShowTableViewController in the ShowTableView-Controller.m file.

```
#import "ShowTableViewController.h"
#import "ShowCharactersTableViewController.h"
#import "TVAppDelegate.h"
@implementation ShowTableViewController
- (id)initWithStyle:(UITableViewStyle)style {
  if (self = [super initWithStyle:style]) {
    self.title = @"TV Shows";
    self.navigationItem.backBarButtonItem.title = @"Shows";
  }
  return self;
}
- (NSInteger)tableView:(UITableView *)tableView
```

```
                 numberOfRowsInSection:(NSInteger)section{
    TVAppDelegate *delegate =
       [[UIApplication sharedApplication] delegate];
    return [delegate numberOfShows];
}
- (UITableViewCell *)tableView:(UITableView *)tableView
                   cellForRowAtIndexPath:(NSIndexPath *)indexPath {
    static NSString *MyIdentifier = @"Show";
    UITableViewCell *cell =
      [tableView dequeueReusableCellWithIdentifier:MyIdentifier];
    if (cell == nil) {
      cell = [[[UITableViewCell alloc]
                 initWithStyle:UITableViewCellStyleDefault
                 reuseIdentifier:MyIdentifier] autorelease];
    }
    TVAppDelegate *delegate =
        [[UIApplication sharedApplication] delegate];
    cell.textLabel.text =  [delegate showNameAtIndex:indexPath.row];
    cell.accessoryType = UITableViewCellAccessoryDisclosureIndicator;
    return cell;
}
- (void)tableView:(UITableView *)tableView
        didSelectRowAtIndexPath:(NSIndexPath *)indexPath{
    TVAppDelegate *delegate =
        [[UIApplication sharedApplication] delegate];
    delegate.selectedShow = indexPath;
    ShowCharactersTableViewController
      *showCharactersController =
        [[[ShowCharactersTableViewController alloc]
              initWithStyle:UITableViewStylePlain] autorelease];
    [[delegate navigationController]
         pushViewController:showCharactersController animated:YES];
}
@end
```

The `initWithStyle:` method sets the title of the controller to `"TV Shows"`. The navigation controller will display this title in the middle of the navigation bar when the first level of hierarchy is presented to the user. The back button title is also set in this method. The value used is `"Shows"`. When the user taps on a specific show, the next level of hierarchy, showing the list of characters of that show, will be presented, and the back-button title will be this value (i.e., `"Shows"`).

The data source methods needed are implemented in the controller. We have the `tableView:-numberOfRowsInSection:` method, which obtains a reference to the application delegate and asks it to retrieve the number of shows. We will talk more about the data model at the end of this section. The required data source method `tableView:cellForRowAtIndexPath:` is also implemented in the controller. To configure the cell, we ask the delegate for the show name using its method `showNameAtIndex:`. In addition, to indicate that the cell has children, the `accessoryType` property is set to `UITableViewCellAccessoryDisclosureIndicator`.

The `tableView:didSelectRowAtIndexPath:` method is where we move the user to the next level of hierarchy. First, we need to store the index path of the selected row in a location accessible by the next-level controller. We achieve this by setting the application delegate property `selectedShow` with the `indexPath` value passed to the method. Next, we create an instance of the next level controller and push it onto the stack of the navigation controller.

The second-level controller is an instance of the class `ShowCharactersTableViewController`. Listing 9.15 shows the declaration of the controller.

Listing 9.15   The `ShowCharactersTableViewController` declared in the `ShowCharacters-TableViewController.h` file. The class manages the second level of hierarchy in the TV Shows application.

```
#import <UIKit/UIKit.h>
@interface ShowCharactersTableViewController : UITableViewController {}
@end
```

The implementation of the controller is shown in Listing 9.16. As we did for the previous controller, we override the `initWithStyle:` method to update the controller's title and the title of the back button. The application delegate is asked for the show name using the method `showNameAtIndex:`. The index used in this method is the global value `selectedShow.row`, managed by the application delegate, which was stored in the `tableView:didSelectRowAtIndexPath:` method of the root table view controller.

Listing 9.16   The definition of the `ShowCharactersTableViewController` in the file Show-CharactersTableViewController.m.

```
#import "ShowCharactersTableViewController.h"
#import "TVAppDelegate.h"
#import "CharacterViewController.h"
@implementation ShowCharactersTableViewController
-(id)initWithStyle:(UITableViewStyle)style {
  if (self = [super initWithStyle:style]) {
    TVAppDelegate *delegate =
            [[UIApplication sharedApplication] delegate];
    self.title =
            [delegate showNameAtIndex:delegate.selectedShow.row];
    self.navigationItem.backBarButtonItem.title =
            [delegate showNameAtIndex:delegate.selectedShow.row];
  }
  return self;
}
- (NSInteger)tableView:(UITableView *)tableView
            numberOfRowsInSection:(NSInteger)section{
  TVAppDelegate *delegate =
            [[UIApplication sharedApplication] delegate];
  return [delegate
    numberOfCharactersForShowAtIndex:delegate.selectedShow.row];
}
```

```
- (void)tableView:(UITableView *)tableView
        didSelectRowAtIndexPath:(NSIndexPath *)indexPath{
  TVAppDelegate *delegate =
        [[UIApplication sharedApplication] delegate];
  delegate.selectedCharacter = indexPath;
  CharacterViewController *characterController =
        [[CharacterViewController alloc] init];
  [[delegate navigationController]
        pushViewController:characterController animated:YES];
  [characterController release];
}
- (UITableViewCell *)
        tableView:(UITableView *)tableView
        cellForRowAtIndexPath:(NSIndexPath *)indexPath {
  static NSString *MyIdentifier = @"Character";
  UITableViewCell *cell =
      [tableView dequeueReusableCellWithIdentifier:MyIdentifier];
  if (cell == nil) {
    cell = [[[UITableViewCell alloc]
              initWithStyle:UITableViewCellStyleDefault
            reuseIdentifier:MyIdentifier] autorelease];
  }
  TVAppDelegate *delegate =
        [[UIApplication sharedApplication] delegate];
  cell.textLabel.text =
   [delegate characterNameForShowIndex:delegate.selectedShow.row
              atIndex:indexPath.row];
  cell.accessoryType = UITableViewCellAccessoryDisclosureIndicator;
  return cell;
}
@end
```

The method `tableView:didSelectRowAtIndexPath:` is used to push a third controller onto the navigation controller. This view controller is the leaf controller `CharacterViewController`. Before pushing it onto the stack, we store the index path of the selected row in the delegate `selectedCharacter` property.

The `CharacterViewController` is declared in Listing 9.17 and is implemented in Listing 9.18.

Listing 9.17 The declaration of the `CharacterViewController` in file `CharacterView-Controller.h`. This controller manages the leaf view in the TV Shows application.

```
#import <UIKit/UIKit.h>
@interface CharacterViewController : UIViewController {
  UILabel      *nameLabel;
  UIView       *theView;
}
@end
```

The `init` method is overridden and the title is set to the character name. The character name is retrieved from the application delegate using the method `characterNameForShow-Index:atIndex:`. The index of the show is `selectedShow.row` and the index of the character is `selectedCharacter.row`.

The `loadView` method is where we present more information about the character. To simplify things, we use a `UILabel` instance for the name and a `UIImageView` for the picture of the character. You should be familiar with these UI objects from previous chapters.

Listing 9.18   The implementation of the `CharacterViewController` in file `CharacterView-Controller.m`.

```
#import "CharacterViewController.h"
#import "TVAppDelegate.h"
@implementation CharacterViewController
- (id)init{
  if (self = [super init]) {
    TVAppDelegate *delegate =
        [[UIApplication sharedApplication] delegate];
    self.title =
      [delegate characterNameForShowIndex:delegate.selectedShow.row
               atIndex:delegate.selectedCharacter.row];
  }
  return self;
}
- (void)loadView {
  TVAppDelegate *delegate =
        [[UIApplication sharedApplication] delegate];
  theView   = [[UIView alloc]
       initWithFrame:[UIScreen mainScreen].applicationFrame];
  theView.autoresizingMask =
       UIViewAutoresizingFlexibleHeight |
       UIViewAutoresizingFlexibleWidth;
  theView.backgroundColor = [UIColor  whiteColor];

  CGRect labelFrame =  CGRectMake(80, 10, 190, 50);
  nameLabel = [[UILabel alloc] initWithFrame:labelFrame];
    nameLabel.font = [UIFont systemFontOfSize:25.0];
  nameLabel.textColor = [UIColor  blackColor];
  nameLabel.backgroundColor = [UIColor clearColor];
  nameLabel.textAlignment = UITextAlignmentLeft;
  nameLabel.lineBreakMode = UILineBreakModeWordWrap;
  NSString  *theName =
      [delegate
          characterNameForShowIndex:delegate.selectedShow.row
           atIndex:delegate.selectedCharacter.row];
  nameLabel.text =
          [NSString stringWithFormat:@"%@:  %@", @"Name", theName];
```

```
  [theView addSubview: nameLabel];
  UIImageView    *imgView = [[UIImageView alloc]
               initWithImage:[UIImage imageNamed:
                  [NSString stringWithFormat:@"%@.png", theName]]];
  imgView.frame = CGRectMake(30, 70, 250, 300);
  [theView addSubview:imgView];
  [imgView release];
  self.view = theView;
}
- (void)dealloc {
  [nameLabel release];
  [theView release];
  [super dealloc];
}
@end
```

Listing 9.19 shows the declaration of the application delegate. The delegate maintains the two properties for storing the indices of the first and second levels in `selectedShow` and `selectedCharacter`, respectively. The three view controllers access the data model for the hierarchical information through the following four application delegate methods:

```
-(NSInteger)numberOfShows;
-(NSString*)showNameAtIndex:(NSInteger) index;
-(NSInteger)numberOfCharactersForShowAtIndex:(NSInteger) index;
-(NSString*)characterNameForShowIndex:(NSInteger) showIndex
          AtIndex:(NSInteger) index;
```

We have seen how these methods are used in the presentation.

Listing 9.19   The declaration of the application delegate for the TV Shows application.

```
#import <UIKit/UIKit.h>
#import <Foundation/Foundation.h>

@interface TVAppDelegate : NSObject {
  UIWindow               *window;
  UINavigationController  *navigationController;
  NSIndexPath            *selectedShow;
  NSIndexPath            *selectedCharacter;
  NSArray                *theShows;
}
@property(nonatomic, retain) NSIndexPath *selectedShow;
@property(nonatomic, retain) NSIndexPath *selectedCharacter;
@property(nonatomic, retain)
       UINavigationController *navigationController;

-(NSInteger)numberOfShows;
-(NSString*)showNameAtIndex:(NSInteger) index;
-(NSInteger)numberOfCharactersForShowAtIndex:(NSInteger) index;
```

```
-(NSString*)characterNameForShowIndex:(NSInteger)
          showIndex AtIndex:(NSInteger) index;
@end
```

The implementation of the application delegate is shown in Listing 9.20. The first thing we do in the `applicationDidFinishLaunching:` method is prepare the data mode. The data model is represented by an array of dictionaries. Each dictionary represents a TV show and has two entries. The first entry is name of that show and the second is an array of characters for that show. After initializing the data model, we create the navigation controller and push the first-level table view controller onto it. The methods called by the controllers to retrieve specific information about our data model are straightforward.

Listing 9.20   The implementation of the application delegate for the TV Shows application.

```
#import <Foundation/Foundation.h>
#import <UIKit/UIKit.h>
#import "TVAppDelegate.h"
#import "ShowTableViewController.h"
@implementation TVAppDelegate
@synthesize selectedShow;
@synthesize selectedCharacter;
@synthesize navigationController;
- (void)applicationDidFinishLaunching:(UIApplication *)application {
  [self prepareDataModel];
  window = [[UIWindow alloc]
        initWithFrame:[[UIScreen mainScreen] bounds]];
  ShowTableViewController *showViewController =
            [[ShowTableViewController alloc]
                initWithStyle:UITableViewStylePlain];
  navigationController = [[UINavigationController alloc]
        initWithRootViewController:showViewController];
  [showViewController release];
  [window addSubview:[navigationController view]];
  [window makeKeyAndVisible];
}
-(void)prepareDataModel{
  NSDictionary    *dic1 =
        [NSDictionary dictionaryWithObjectsAndKeys:
            @"Seinfeld",
            @"Name",
            [NSArray arrayWithObjects:
            @"Jerry", @"George", @"Elaine", @"Kramer",
            @"Newman", @"Frank",  @"Susan",
            @"Peterman",  @"Bania", nil],
            @"Characters",
             nil
            ];
  NSDictionary    *dic2 =
```

```
            [NSDictionary dictionaryWithObjectsAndKeys:
                    @"Lost",
                    @"Name",
                    [NSArray arrayWithObjects:
                     @"Kate", @"Sayid", @"Sun", @"Hurley",
                     @"Boone", @"Claire",  @"Jin",  @"Locke",
                     @"Charlie", @"Eko", @"Ben", nil],
                    @"Characters",
                    nil
                    ];
   theShows = [[NSArray arrayWithObjects:dic1, dic2, nil] retain];
}
-(NSInteger)numberOfShows{
  return [theShows count];
}
-(NSString*)showNameAtIndex:(NSInteger) index{
  return [[theShows objectAtIndex:index] valueForKey:@"Name"] ;
}
-(NSInteger)numberOfCharactersForShowAtIndex:(NSInteger) index{
    return [[[theShows objectAtIndex:index]
            valueForKey:@"Characters"] count];
}
-(NSString*)characterNameForShowIndex:(NSInteger)showIndex
                    atIndex:(NSInteger) index{
  return [[[theShows objectAtIndex:showIndex]
        valueForKey:@"Characters"] objectAtIndex:index];
}
- (void)dealloc {
  [window release];
  [navigationController release];
  [theShows release];
  [super dealloc];
}
@end
```

9.9   Grouped Table Views

Until now, we have been dealing with the plain table view style. There is another style, referred to as the *grouped* style, that you can use to configure the table view. A grouped table view is generally used as the final level of hierarchy for presenting information about a specific item selected in the penultimate level.

The configuration process of a grouped table view follows a similar approach to what we have seen so far. What you need to know is that the rows of each section are grouped together. An optional header title is used to name that group. Other than that, everything is pretty much the same.

Let's illustrate with an example. Consider an application that presents to the user a list of favorite TV shows sorted according to classification: comedy, political, and drama. Listing 9.21 shows the declaration of the application delegate of the demonstration application. The complete source code can be found in the `TableView7` project in the source downloads.

Listing 9.21   The declaration of the application delegate demonstrating the use of grouped table views.

```
#import <UIKit/UIKit.h>
#import <Foundation/Foundation.h>

@interface TVAppDelegate : NSObject <UITableViewDataSource> {
  UIWindow          *window;
  UITableView       *myTable;
  NSArray           *comedyShows, *politicalShows, *dramaShows;
}
@end
```

The data model is represented in the three `NSArray` instances: `comedyShows`, `politicalShows`, and `dramaShows`. Each array will hold the shows for the corresponding section.

The implementation of the application delegate is shown in Listing 9.22. In the `applicationDid-FinishLaunching:` method, we create the table view instance as we saw before. Instead of using the plain style, we use the `UITableViewStyleGrouped` style. The three arrays are then populated with the data.

We saw in Section 9.4 how to configure sections and headers. There are no differences between plain and grouped styles with respect to the implementation of the configuration methods.

Listing 9.22   The implementation of the application delegate for the grouped table view application.

```
#import <Foundation/Foundation.h>
#import <UIKit/UIKit.h>
#import "TVAppDelegate.h"

@implementation TVAppDelegate
- (void)applicationDidFinishLaunching:(UIApplication *)application {
  window = [[UIWindow alloc]
                  initWithFrame:[[UIScreen  mainScreen] bounds]];
  myTable = [[UITableView alloc]
                  initWithFrame:[UIScreen  mainScreen].applicationFrame
                     style:UITableViewStyleGrouped];
  comedyShows = [[NSArray arrayWithObjects:
          @"Seinfeld", @"Everybody Loves Raymond", nil] retain];
  politicalShows = [[NSArray arrayWithObjects:
          @"60 Minutes", @"Meet The Press", nil] retain];
  dramaShows  = [[NSArray arrayWithObjects:@"Lost", nil] retain];

  myTable.dataSource = self;
  [window addSubview:myTable];
```

```objc
    [window makeKeyAndVisible];
}

- (NSInteger) numberOfSectionsInTableView:(UITableView *)tableView {
    return 3;
}

- (NSInteger)
        tableView:(UITableView *)tableView
        numberOfRowsInSection:(NSInteger)section{
    switch (section) {
        case 0:
            return [comedyShows count];
            break;
        case 1:
            return [politicalShows count];
            break;
        case 2:
            return [dramaShows count];
            break;
    }
    return 0;
}

- (UITableViewCell *)
        tableView:(UITableView *)tableView
        cellForRowAtIndexPath:(NSIndexPath *)indexPath{
    UITableViewCell *cell =
        [tableView dequeueReusableCellWithIdentifier:@"shows"];
    if (cell == nil) {
        cell = [[[UITableViewCell alloc]
                    initWithStyle:UITableViewCellStyleDefault
                    reuseIdentifier:@"shows"] autorelease];
    }
    switch (indexPath.section) {
        case 0:
            cell.textLabel.text = [comedyShows objectAtIndex:indexPath.row];
            break;
        case 1:
            cell.textLabel.text =
                [politicalShows objectAtIndex:indexPath.row];
            break;
        case 2:
            cell.textLabel.text = [dramaShows objectAtIndex:indexPath.row];
            break;
    }
    return cell;
}
```

```
- (NSString *)
        tableView:(UITableView *)tableView
        titleForHeaderInSection:(NSInteger)section {
  NSString *title = nil;
  switch (section) {
    case 0:
      title = @"Comedy Shows";
      break;
    case 1:
      title = @"Political Shows";
      break;
    case 2:
      title = @"Drama Shows";
      break;
    default:
      break;
  }
  return title;
}

- (void)dealloc {
  [window release];
  [myTable release];
  [comedyShows release];
  [politicalShows release];
  [dramaShows release];
  [super dealloc];
}
@end
```

Figure 9.20 shows the grouped table view application.

9.10   Indexed Table Views

Sometimes you present a large amount of data to the user. To save the user's time when he or she is looking for a specific row, you can add an index to the table view. This index is displayed on the right-hand side of the table. When the user taps on a specific index value, the table view will scroll to the corresponding section.

In this section, we provide a demonstration application for indexed views. The application presents fives sections, each section corresponding to a U.S. political party. Inside each section, we list some of the candidates for the office of president. Each section has an index represented by the first letter of its name. Tapping on the letter makes the table view scroll (if necessary) to the corresponding party.

Figure 9.20   A grouped table view application.

Listing 9.23 shows the declaration of the application delegate demonstrating indexed table views. Five `NSArray` instances are used to represent the data model. The source code can be found in the `TableView8` project in the source downloads.

Listing 9.23   The declaration of the application delegate demonstrating the indexed table view.

```
#import <UIKit/UIKit.h>
#import <Foundation/Foundation.h>
@interface TVAppDelegate:NSObject<UITableViewDataSource> {
    UIWindow        *window;
    UITableView     *myTable;
    NSArray         *democratic, *republican, *independent,
                    *libertarian, *socialist;
}
@end
```

Listing 9.24 shows the implementation of the application delegate for the indexed table view application.

Listing 9.24 The implementation of the application delegate demonstrating the indexed table view.

```
#import <Foundation/Foundation.h>
#import <UIKit/UIKit.h>
#import "TVAppDelegate.h"
@implementation TVAppDelegate
- (void)applicationDidFinishLaunching:(UIApplication *)application {
  window = [[UIWindow alloc]
                initWithFrame:[[UIScreen  mainScreen] bounds]];
  myTable = [[UITableView alloc]
                initWithFrame:[UIScreen  mainScreen].applicationFrame
                   style:UITableViewStylePlain];
  democratic = [[NSArray arrayWithObjects:
            @"Barack Obama", @"Joe Biden",
            @"Hillary Clinton",
            @"Christopher Dodd", @"John Edwards",
            @"Maurice Robert \"Mike\" Gravel",
            @"Dennis Kucinich", nil] retain];
  republican = [[NSArray arrayWithObjects:
            @"Ron Paul", @"John McCain",
            @"Mike Huckabee", @"Mitt Romney", nil] retain];
  independent  = [[NSArray arrayWithObjects:
            @"Ralph Nader", nil] retain];
  libertarian = [[NSArray arrayWithObjects:@"Bob Barr", nil] retain];
  socialist   = [[NSArray arrayWithObjects:@"Brian Moore", nil] retain];
  myTable.dataSource = self;
  [window addSubview:myTable];
  [window makeKeyAndVisible];
}

- (NSInteger) numberOfSectionsInTableView:(UITableView *)tableView {
  return 5;
}

- (NSInteger)
        tableView:(UITableView *)tableView
        numberOfRowsInSection:(NSInteger)section{
  switch (section) {
    case 0:
      return [democratic count];
    case 1:
      return [independent count];
    case 2:
      return [libertarian count];
    case 3:
      return [republican count];
    case 4:
```

```objc
        return [socialist count];
    }
    return 0;
}

- (UITableViewCell *)
          tableView:(UITableView *)tableView
          cellForRowAtIndexPath:(NSIndexPath *)indexPath{
    UITableViewCell *cell =
    [tableView dequeueReusableCellWithIdentifier:@"shows"];
    if (cell == nil) {
      cell = [[[UITableViewCell alloc]
                              initWithStyle:UITableViewCellStyleDefault
                              reuseIdentifier:@"shows"] autorelease];
    }
    switch (indexPath.section) {
      case 0:
        cell.textLabel.text = [democratic objectAtIndex:indexPath.row];
        break;
      case 1:
        cell.textLabel.text = [independent objectAtIndex:indexPath.row];
        break;
      case 2:
        cell.textLabel.text = [libertarian objectAtIndex:indexPath.row];
        break;
      case 3:
        cell.textLabel.text = [republican objectAtIndex:indexPath.row];
        break;
      case 4:
        cell.textLabel.text = [socialist objectAtIndex:indexPath.row];
        break;
    }
    return cell;
}
- (NSString *)
          tableView:(UITableView *)tableView
          titleForHeaderInSection:(NSInteger)section {
    NSString *title = nil;
    switch (section) {
      case 0:
        title = @"Democratic";
        break;
      case 1:
        title = @"Independent";
        break;
      case 2:
```

```
        title = @"Libertarian";
        break;
     case 3:
        title = @"Republican";
        break;
     case 4:
        title = @"Socialist Party USA";
        break;
  }
  return title;
}


- (NSArray*)sectionIndexTitlesForTableView:(UITableView *)tableView {
  return[NSArray arrayWithObjects:@"D", @"I", @"L", @"R", @"S", nil];
}
- (NSInteger)
      tableView:(UITableView *)tableView
      sectionForSectionIndexTitle:(NSString *)title
      atIndex:(NSInteger)index {
  return index;
}


- (void)dealloc {
  [window release];
  [myTable release];
  [democratic release];
  [republican release];
  [independent release];
  [libertarian release];
  [socialist release];
  [super dealloc];
}
@end
```

As in the previous examples, the table view is created and configured, and the data model is populated with the candidates' names.

The method `tableView:titleForHeaderInSection:` was used in previous sections. It returns the headers for the table view's sections.

The method `sectionIndexTitlesForTableView:` is invoked by the table view, asking the data source for an array of `NSString` instances. This array of strings will form the index list on the right-hand side of the table view. The method is declared as follows:

`- (NSArray *)sectionIndexTitlesForTableView:(UITableView *)tableView`

Note that the number of elements in this array does not necessarily have to be equal to the number of sections in the table view. In our example, the index list is D, I, L, R, and S. Each letter represents one political party. Note, again, that we did not have to have an index letter for every section.

The method `tableView:sectionForSectionIndexTitle:atIndex:` is invoked, asking the data source for the section index corresponding to the section index title and section title index. The declaration of the method is given by

```
- (NSInteger)
            tableView:(UITableView *)tableView
            sectionForSectionIndexTitle:(NSString *)title
            atIndex:(NSInteger)index
```

This method is invoked when the user taps on a given index letter. Because the index of the index letter and the section index are the same, we simply return the index value passed to us. For example, if the user taps on the `S` index letter, the method is invoked with `title` equal to `S` and `index` equal to 4. Because `S` corresponds to the `Socialist Party USA` section, which has index 4, we simply return the `index` value passed to us. If you choose not to have a one-to-one correspondence between the index letters and the sections, you will have to do some extra work in order to return the section index.

Figure 9.21 shows the indexed table view application. Figure 9.22 shows the table view after the user taps on the `S` index letter. The table view scrolls up, making the corresponding section visible.

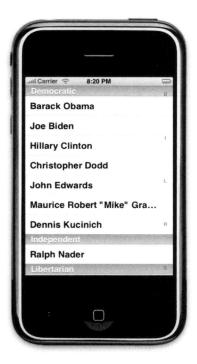

Figure 9.21   A indexed table view application.

Figure 9.22   A indexed table view application after tapping on an index.

9.11   Dynamic Table Views

Often, you want to present information with variable height depending on the data model (see Figure 9.23). One time, a cell has a height of 50 points because the underlying data model for this cell has two lines of text. Another time, its height is 150 points, to accommodate six lines of text.

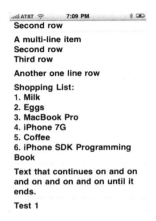

Figure 9.23   A screen shot of the dynamic table view application to be developed in this section.

In this section, we will extend the UITableViewController class with the new Dynamic-TableViewController class. This class will manage the sizing of table cells for us.

Listing 9.25 shows the interface of our class. The complete source code can be found in the DynamicTableView project in the source downloads.

Listing 9.25   The interface of the DynamicTableViewController class.

```
@interface DynamicTableViewController : UITableViewController {
  NSArray *data;
  UIFont  *textFont;
}
@property (nonatomic, retain) UIFont *textFont;
@property (nonatomic, retain) NSArray *data;
-(CGFloat) minHeightForText:(NSString*)_text;
-(id) initWithData:(NSArray*)_data;
@end
```

To use this class, you create a new object and initialize it using the initWithData: initializer. The parameter you pass in is an NSArray instance that holds the data you want to present. The Dynamic-TableViewController invokes the method description on the corresponding object in this array when it wants to show it in the cell. How this description method is defined is up to the user of this class. If the object is an NSString instance, then the description method (overridden by NSString class) simply returns the textual representation of the string instance.

The class also has a textFont property. This property can be set to be the font of the text of each cell. If not set, a default font will be used. This will keep our class simple. If you want, you can modify this class to provide variable fonts for cells.

The initWithData: method (shown below) simply invokes the initWithStyle: initializer of the UITableViewController class and retains the data:

```
-(id) initWithData:(NSArray*)_data{
  if(self = [super initWithStyle:UITableViewStylePlain]){
    self.data = _data;
  }
  return self;
}
```

At the heart of this class is the minHeightForText: method. This method computes the minimum height that a given text needs in order to be presented. It relies on the following method, declared in the category UIStringDrawing on NSString:

```
- (CGSize)sizeWithFont:(UIFont *)font
        constrainedToSize:(CGSize)size
        lineBreakMode:(UILineBreakMode)lineBreakMode;
```

This NSString method computes the minimum width and height that a text needs to render, given a specific font, line-break mode, and maximum size. The method finds the size by wrapping the text according to the parameter values and its content (e.g., \n). If the height of only one line exceeds that height specified in size, the method may return a height bigger than the one specified in size.

The trick that we use in the minHeightForText: method is to restrict the width of size to a value of 300 while having a very large value for height. This way, the NSString method will compute the height for all rows contained in the text. We also check for the font property in case the caller hasn't set it. We use a bold system font of size 16 as a default value.

```
-(CGFloat) minHeightForText:(NSString*)_text{
  if(!textFont){
    self.textFont = [UIFont boldSystemFontOfSize:16];
  }
  return [_text
            sizeWithFont:textFont
            constrainedToSize:CGSizeMake(LABEL_WIDTH, 999999)
            lineBreakMode:LABEL_LINE_BREAK_MODE].height;
}
```

To specify the height of a each cell, we implement the tableView:heightForRowAtIndexPath: delegate method as shown below:

```
- (CGFloat)tableView:(UITableView *)tableView
            heightForRowAtIndexPath:(NSIndexPath *)indexPath{
  return [self minHeightForText:
        [[data objectAtIndex:indexPath.row] description]] + 2*Y_ANCHOR;
}
```

The method simply uses the value from `minHeightForText:` and adds the values of the top and bottom margins.

Each of our cells will host a `UILabel`. The label will be added to the cell as a subview. To add a subview to a cell, you need to add that view using the `addSubView:` method of the cell's `content-View`. The `tableView:cellForRowAtIndexPath:` method is shown in Listing 9.26.

The method creates a new cell when a reusable cell cannot be found. It then configures and adds a `UILabel` to that cell. To make the label multiline, we assign 0 to the `numberOfLines` property. This in effect will make the label accept any number of lines. Because we want to access the label from a reused cell, we tag the label.

The cell is reconfigured each time (whether it has just been created or is dequeued). The configuration pertains only to the label. We retrieve the label view by sending the `viewWithTag:` message to the cell's `contentView`. Once it is retrieved, we adjust its frame to the proper computed value and set its text. Notice the use of the horizontal and vertical anchors of the label.

Listing 9.26   The `cellForRowAtIndexPath:` method for the dynamic table view controller.

```
- (UITableViewCell *)
        tableView:(UITableView *)tableView
        cellForRowAtIndexPath:(NSIndexPath *)indexPath {
  NSString  *textValue = [[data objectAtIndex:indexPath.row] description];
  static NSString *cellID = @"My Awesome Cell";
  UILabel *label;
  UITableViewCell *cell =
    [tableView dequeueReusableCellWithIdentifier:cellID];
  if (cell == nil) {
    cell = [[[UITableViewCell alloc]
                 initWithStyle:UITableViewCellStyleDefault
                 reuseIdentifier:cellID] autorelease];
    label =
        [[[UILabel alloc] initWithFrame:CGRectZero] autorelease];
    label.numberOfLines = 0;
    label.lineBreakMode = LABEL_LINE_BREAK_MODE;
    label.tag = 1234;
    label.font = textFont;
    [cell.contentView addSubview:label];
  }
  label = (UILabel*)[cell.contentView viewWithTag:1234];
  label.frame = CGRectMake(X_ANCHOR, Y_ANCHOR, LABEL_WIDTH,
                              [self minHeightForText:textValue]);
  label.text = textValue;
  return cell;
}
```

That's pretty much the `DynamicTableViewController` class. Listing 9.27 shows the use of this controller. As you can see, the controller takes care of almost everything. We just give it a list of items to display.

Listing 9.27 The use of the `DynamicTableViewController` class.

```
- (void)applicationDidFinishLaunching:(UIApplication *)application {
  window =
    [[UIWindow alloc] initWithFrame:[[UIScreen  mainScreen] bounds]];
  self.ctrl = [[[DynamicTableViewController alloc]
              initWithData:[NSArray arrayWithObjects:
              @"A single line item",
              @"A multi-line item \nSecond row",
              @"A multi-line item \nSecond row\nThird row",
              @"Another one line row",
              @"Shopping List:\n1. Milk\n2. Eggs\n3. MacBook Pro\n4."
               "iPhone 7G\n5. Coffee\n6. iPhone SDK Programming Book",
              @"Text that continues on and on and on and"
               "on and on until it ends.",
              @"Test 1\nTest 2\nTest 3\nTest 4\nTest 5\nTest 6",
              @"Line 1\nLine 2\nLine 3\nLine 4",
              nil]] autorelease];
  ctrl.textFont = [UIFont boldSystemFontOfSize:20];
  [window addSubview:ctrl.view];
  [window makeKeyAndVisible];
}
```

9.12 Whitening Text in Custom Cells

By now, you must have noticed that text in a cell turns white when that cell is selected. By turning the text's color to white, the user is able to see the text more clearly on the blue background. If the text remains black (or, worse, blue), the user will have a hard time reading the text.

You can rely on this behavior as long as you stick to using any of the four cell styles covered in Section 9.2. If you customize the cell by adding subviews to its `contentView`, you need to handle whitening any text yourself.

There are two methods that are involved in this process:

- `setSelected:animated:`. This method animates between regular and selected state and is declared as follows:

  - `(void)setSelected:(BOOL)selected animated:(BOOL)animated;`

- `setHighlighted:animated:`. This method animates between regular and highlighted state and is declared as follows:

  - `(void)setHighlighted:(BOOL)highlighted animated:(BOOL)animated;`

One approach to solving this problem is to subclass `UITableViewCell`, override these two methods, and change the text colors according to the highlighting/selection state. This approach requires subclassing of all cell types in the application. If you add a new cell, you'll need to add custom code that goes through all the subviews of that cell type, changing the color of the text.

In this section, we present one approach that solves this problem in a centralized fashion. The basic idea is to *patch* these two methods with custom code. When the cell is asked to highlight or enter selection state, our code records the colors of the text, turns all text to white, and forwards the call to the original highlighting/selecting code. When the cell is asked to stop being highlighted/selected, our code retrieves the original colors of the text and forwards the call to the original code.

At the start of the application, we make a call to `swapMethod:withMethod:`, which was developed in Section 2.13, to swap the two methods as shown below:

```
[UITableViewCell swapMethod:@selector(setHighlighted:animated:)
             withMethod:@selector(newSetHighlighted:animated:)];

[UITableViewCell swapMethod:@selector(setSelected:animated:)
             withMethod:@selector(newSetSelected:animated:)];
```

The `newSetHighlighted:animated:` is shown in Listing 9.28. The method uses a static mutable dictionary, `textColors`. This dictionary holds the text color of any subview of `contentView` that responds to the selector `text`.

At the start of this method, it checks to see if there is a need to process the text in the cell. If the method is asked to change to a state that it is already in, or the selection style of the cell is `UITableViewCellSelectionStyleNone`, the method simply calls itself (which results in calling the original method) and returns. Otherwise, the method continues and checks if the data structure holding the text colors has been created. If not, it creates it.

If the cell needs highlighting, the method calls the method `turnAllToWhite:`, passing the `contentView` as an argument. Otherwise, it calls the method `turnAllToOriginal:`, passing the `contentView` as an argument. In either case, it always forwards the message to the original method by calling itself.

Listing 9.28   A method used to patch the `setHighlighted:animated:` method in order to manage text color according to the highlighting state of the cell.

```
-(void)newSetHighlighted:(BOOL)highlighted animated:(BOOL)animated {
  if(highlighted == [self isHighlighted]  ||
   ([self selectionStyle] == UITableViewCellSelectionStyleNone)){
    [self newSetHighlighted:highlighted animated:animated];
    return;
  }
  if(!textColors) {
    textColors = [[NSMutableDictionary dictionary] retain];
  }
  if(highlighted == YES){
    [self turnAllToWhite:self.contentView];
  }
  else{
```

```
    [self turnAllToOriginal:self.contentView];
  }
  [self newSetHighlighted:highlighted animated:animated];
}
```

Listing 9.29 shows the `turnAllToWhite:` method. The method checks to see if the view responds to the `text` selector. If yes, it looks in the dictionary to see if the view has its color already stored. The key used to store the text color for a view is the view's `hash` value.

If the view is not in the dictionary, its text color is stored in the dictionary with the view's `hash` as a key. After that, the text color is set to white.

In all cases, the method calls itself for each subview of the view argument.

Listing 9.29   A method that turns the text colors of all subviews of a given view to white.

```
-(void)turnAllToWhite:(UIView*)theView{
  if([theView respondsToSelector:@selector(text)]){
    id existing =
        [textColors
            objectForKey:[NSString stringWithFormat:@"%x",theView.hash]];
    if(!existing){
      [textColors
        setObject:[((UILabel*)theView) textColor]
        forKey:[NSString stringWithFormat:@"%x", theView.hash]];
      [((UILabel*)theView) setTextColor:[UIColor whiteColor]];
    }
  }
  for(UIView *view in theView.subviews){
    [self turnAllToWhite:view];
  }
}
```

Listing 9.30 shows the `turnAllToOriginal:` method that turns all text to its original color. If the color is stored in the dictionary, the color is retrieved and used to set the text color of the view. After that, the color is removed from the dictionary. As in the previous method, all subviews are handled the same way through a recursive call.

Listing 9.30   A method that turns the text colors of all subviews of a given view to their original color.

```
-(void)turnAllToOriginal:(UIView*)theView{
  if([theView respondsToSelector:@selector(text)]){
    id color =
        [textColors
            objectForKey:[NSString stringWithFormat:@"%x",theView.hash]];
    if (color) {
      [((UILabel*)theView) setTextColor:color];
      [textColors removeObjectForKey:
        [NSString stringWithFormat:@"%x", theView.hash]];
```

```
    }
  }
  for(UIView *view in theView.subviews){
    [self turnAllToOriginal:view];
  }
}
```

Similar to what we have done to `setHighlighted:animated:`, the `setSelected:animated:` is patched with the method shown in Listing 9.31.

Listing 9.31   A method used to patch the `setSelected:animated:` method in order to manage text color according to the selection state of the cell.

```
- (void)newSetSelected:(BOOL)selected animated:(BOOL)animated {
  if(selected == [self isSelected] ||
   ([self selectionStyle] == UITableViewCellSelectionStyleNone)){
    [self newSetSelected:selected animated:animated];
    return;
  }
  if (!textColors) {
    textColors = [[NSMutableDictionary dictionary] retain];
  }
  if(selected == NO){
    [self turnAllToOriginal:self.contentView];
  }
  else{
    [self turnAllToWhite:self.contentView];
  }
  [self newSetSelected:selected animated:animated];
}
```

Listing 9.32 shows a data source method that builds a custom cell with three `UILabel` subviews, each with a different color.

Listing 9.32   A method that builds a custom cell with three `UILabel` subviews, each with a different color.

```
- (UITableViewCell *)
        tableView:(UITableView *)tableView
        cellForRowAtIndexPath:(NSIndexPath *)indexPath{
  UITableViewCell *cell =
    [tableView dequeueReusableCellWithIdentifier:@"cell"];
  UILabel *label1, *label2, *label3;
    if (cell == nil) {
      cell = [[[UITableViewCell alloc]
                  initWithStyle:UITableViewCellStyleDefault
                  reuseIdentifier:@"cell"] autorelease];
    label1 = [[[UILabel alloc]
            initWithFrame:CGRectMake(0, 0, 320, 60)] autorelease];
    label1.textColor = [UIColor redColor];
```

```
label1.font = [UIFont boldSystemFontOfSize:22];
label1.tag = 20;
label2 = [[[UILabel alloc]
        initWithFrame:CGRectMake(30, 25, 150, 40)] autorelease];
label2.textColor = [UIColor greenColor];
label2.font = [UIFont boldSystemFontOfSize:12];
label2.tag = 21;
label2.backgroundColor = [UIColor clearColor];
label3 = [[[UILabel alloc]
        initWithFrame:CGRectMake(10, 15, 100, 30)] autorelease];
label3.textColor = [UIColor orangeColor];
label3.font = [UIFont boldSystemFontOfSize:7];
label3.tag = 22;
label3.backgroundColor = [UIColor clearColor];
[label2 addSubview:label3];
[label1 addSubview:label2];
[cell.contentView addSubview:label1];
cell.selectionStyle = UITableViewCellSelectionStyleBlue;
}
label1 = (UILabel*)[cell.contentView viewWithTag:20];
label2 = (UILabel*)[cell.contentView viewWithTag:21];
label3 = (UILabel*)[cell.contentView viewWithTag:22];
label1.text = [NSString stringWithFormat:
  @"This is the grandfather #%d", indexPath.row+1];
label2.text = [NSString stringWithFormat:
  @"This is the father #%d", indexPath.row+1];
label3.text = [NSString stringWithFormat:
  @"This is the child #%d", indexPath.row+1];
return cell;
}
```

Figure 9.24 shows a screen shot of the application that uses the methods developed in this section. The complete source code that is presented in this section can be found in the `TableView-Whiten` project.

9.13 Summary

This chapter took you on a step-by-step journey through the world of table views. We started by presenting an overview of the main concepts behind table views in Section 9.1. After that, we presented, in Section 9.2, a simple table view application and discussed the mandatory methods you need to implement in order to populate and respond to users' interactions with the table view.

In Section 9.3, we showed how easy it is to add images to table rows. Section 9.4 introduced the concept of sections and provided a table view application that has sections with section headers and footers.

Figure 9.24   Turning the color of all text to white upon selection.

In Section 9.5, we introduced the concept of editing a table view. An application that allows the user to delete rows was presented, and the main ideas were clarified. In Section 9.6, we addressed the insertion of new rows in a table view. An application was discussed that presents a data entry view to the user and adds that new data to the table's rows. In Section 9.7, we continued our discussions of editing mode and presented an application for reordering table entries. The main concepts of reordering rows were presented.

In Section 9.8, we discussed the mechanism for presenting hierarchical information to the user. An application that uses table views to present three levels of hierarchy was discussed. In Section 9.9, we discussed grouped table views through an example. After that, we presented the main concepts behind indexed table views in Section 9.10. In Section 9.11, we presented a dynamic table view controller class. This class was used to adjust each cell's height depending on the number of lines of the corresponding item in the data model. Finally, in Section 9.12, we addressed the issue of turning the text color to white when a custom cell is selected.

Exercises

(1) Investigate the `UITableView` class further by reading the `UITableView.h` header file and the relevant documentation.

(2) Create a table view that has ten rows, where each row is a web view displaying the contents of a given URL. Each row's height is `50` points.

(3) Modify the whitening strategy described in Section 9.12 to bypass whitening if the default behavior suffices.

10

File Management

This chapter covers the topic of file management. Here, you learn how to use both high- and low-level techniques for storing and retrieving file data. To perform high-level operations on files and directories you use instances of the NSFileManager class. The NSFileHandle class is used in this chapter to demonstrate low-level file access.

Section 10.1 covers the Home directory of the application. Next, Section 10.2 shows how to enumerate the contents of a given directory using the high-level methods of NSFileManager. In that section, you learn more about the structure of the Home directory and where you can store files. After that, you learn in Section 10.3 how to create and delete directories. Next, Section 10.4 covers the creation of files. Section 10.5 deals with the topic of file and directory attributes, and you learn how to retrieve and set specific file and directory attributes. In Section 10.6, we demonstrate the use of application bundles and low-level file access. Finally, we summarize the chapter in Section 10.7.

10.1   The Home Directory

The application and its data are contained within a single directory called the Home directory. Your application can only access this directory and its contents. The absolute path of the Home directory on the simulator is different from that on the actual device. However, the organization and content are identical.

To access the absolute path of the Home directory, you can use the function NSHomeDirectory(), which is declared as follows:

```
NSString * NSHomeDirectory (void);
```

This function returns an NSString object holding the absolute path. As an example, the following is a Home directory on the simulator:

```
/Users/ali/Library/
Application Support/iPhone Simulator/User/Applications/
F9CC3A49-997D-4523-9AFA-B553B5AE41EA
```

On the device, it is

```
/var/mobile/Applications/F1C43BD0-1AB4-494B-B462-5A7315813D1A
```

In the next section, you will see the structure of the Home directory and where you can store files.

10.2   Enumerating a Directory

In this section, you learn how to enumerate (recursively) the contents of a given directory. Listing 10.1 shows the main() function for enumerating the contents of the Home directory.

Listing 10.1   A main() function listing the contents of the Home directory.

```
#import <Foundation/Foundation.h>

int main(int argc, char *argv[]) {
  NSAutoreleasePool * pool = [[NSAutoreleasePool alloc] init];
  NSLog(@"Absolute path for Home Directory: %@", NSHomeDirectory());
  NSFileManager *fileManager = [NSFileManager defaultManager];
  NSDirectoryEnumerator *dirEnumerator =
      [fileManager enumeratorAtPath:NSHomeDirectory()];
  NSString *currPath;
  while (currPath = [dirEnumerator nextObject]){
    NSLog(@"Found %@", currPath);
  }
  [pool release];
  return 0;
}
```

The function starts by logging the absolute path of the Home directory. The log output on the simulator is

```
Absolute path for Home Directory: /Users/ali/Library/
Application Support/iPhone Simulator/User/Applications/
F9CC3A49-997D-4523-9AFA-B553B5AE41EA
```

On the device, it is

```
Absolute path for Home Directory: /var/mobile/Applications/
F1C43BD0-1AB4-494B-B462-5A7315813D1A
```

After that, it obtains a default NSFileManager instance for the file system using the class method defaultManager. Using this instance, we can make our high-level calls manipulating files and directories inside the Home directory.

Finding all the files and directories inside a given directory is simple. You use the enumeratorAtPath: method, declared as follows:

```
- (NSDirectoryEnumerator *) enumeratorAtPath:(NSString *)path
```

You pass the path of the directory that you would like to enumerate the content of and receive an instance of the NSDirectoryEnumerator class. Each object in the directory enumerator is the full path of an item inside the directory used in obtaining the enumerator. The paths are all relative to this directory. You can iterate over this instance, skip subdirectories, and even access file and directory attributes.

Next, you use nextObject, a subclass of NSEnumerator, to retrieve objects. The main() function simply retrieves all objects and logs them. The log generated on the simulator is shown below. Note that the logging time stamps are removed to save space.

```
Found Documents
Found FileMgmt5.app
Found FileMgmt5.app/FileMgmt5
Found FileMgmt5.app/Info.plist
Found FileMgmt5.app/PkgInfo
Found Library
Found Library/Preferences
Found Library/Preferences/.GlobalPreferences.plist
Found Library/Preferences/com.apple.PeoplePicker.plist
Found tmp
```

The Documents directory is available to you for storing application data. The tmp directory is used for temporary files. The other two directories, AppName.app (e.g., FileMgmt5.app) and Library, should not be manipulated by file system calls. You can create directories inside Home, tmp, and Documents. You can assume that all the contents of the Home directory will be backed up by iTunes except for the tmp directory.

The NSDirectoryEnumerator does have several convenience methods that you can use:

- directoryAttributes. You use this method to return a dictionary of the attributes of the directory you are enumerating. We will talk about file and directory attributes in Section 10.5.

- fileAttributes. This method provides a dictionary of attributes for the current object of enumeration. This method works for both files and subdirectories. We will talk about file and directory attributes in Section 10.5.

- skipDescendents. During enumeration, if you are not interested in the contents of a given subdirectory, you can skip it altogether by calling this method.

10.3   Creating and Deleting a Directory

This section demonstrates creating and deleting subdirectories in the Home directory. Listing 10.2 shows the main() function.

Listing 10.2   A main() function demonstrating creation and deletion of directories.

```
#import <Foundation/Foundation.h>

int main(int argc, char *argv[]) {
  NSAutoreleasePool * pool = [[NSAutoreleasePool alloc] init];
  NSError *error;
  NSFileManager  *fileManager = [NSFileManager defaultManager];
  NSString *newDirPath =
      [NSHomeDirectory() stringByAppendingPathComponent:@"tmp/directory"];
  BOOL success =
      [fileManager createDirectoryAtPath:newDirPath attributes:nil];
  if(success == YES){
    NSLog(@"Directory %@ created successfully!", newDirPath);
    success = [fileManager removeItemAtPath:newDirPath error:&error];
    if(success == YES){
      NSLog(@"Directory %@ deleted successfully!", newDirPath);
    }
    else{
      NSLog(@"Error deleting directory  %@. %@",
            newDirPath, [error localizedDescription]);
      return -1;
    }
  }
  else{
    NSLog(@"Error creating directory %@.", newDirPath);
    return -1;
  }
  [pool release];
  return 0;
}
```

To create a directory, you use the createDirectoryAtPath:attributes: instance method of NSFileManager. This method is declared as follows:

```
- (BOOL)createDirectoryAtPath:(NSString *)path
        attributes:(NSDictionary *)attributes
```

The method takes as input parameters the path of the directory to be created and the attributes of that directory. We will tackle attributes in Section 10.5. To create a directory with default attributes, you need to pass a nil value for the second parameter. If the directory was created successfully, the method returns YES; otherwise, it returns NO.

Once the directory is successfully created, we remove it. The method for removing a file or a directory is `removeItemAtPath:error:`, which is declared as follows:

```
- (BOOL)removeItemAtPath:(NSString *)path error:(NSError **)error
```

It takes the path for the item (a directory, file, or link) to be removed and a reference to an `NSError` object. You can pass `NULL` in the second parameter if you are not interested in knowing what may have caused the failure (i.e., a return of `NO`).

The log output generated on the simulator is

```
Directory /Users/ali/Library/Application Support/
iPhone Simulator/User/Applications/
BCE1C2BE-FAF0-47C2-A689-C20F630604E2/
tmp/directory created successfully!
Directory /Users/ali/Library/Application Support/
iPhone Simulator/User/Applications/
BCE1C2BE-FAF0-47C2-A689-C20F630604E2/
tmp/directory deleted successfully!
```

The log output generated on the device is

```
Directory /var/mobile/Applications/
2E723F14-B89B-450B-81BF-6385EFF76D05/
tmp/directory created successfully!
Directory /var/mobile/Applications/
2E723F14-B89B-450B-81BF-6385EFF76D05/
tmp/directory deleted successfully!
```

10.4 Creating Files

In this section, we demonstrate the creation of files in the application's `Home` directory. To make things interesting, we load a web page from the Internet using the `http` protocol and store that `html` file in `tmp`. After that, we use a web view to load the `html` from the `tmp` directory and present it to the user. As you will see, these tasks can be easily achieved using the rich APIs available.

Listing 10.3 shows the declaration of the application delegate class used in our example. The class is similar to one that we use in Chapter 7.

Listing 10.3 The declaration of the application delegate class used in the file creation and local file viewing example.

```
#import <UIKit/UIKit.h>

@class MainViewController;
@interface FileAppDelegate : NSObject <UIApplicationDelegate> {
  UIWindow            *window;
```

```
  MainViewController    *mainCtrl;
}
@property (nonatomic, retain) UIWindow *window;
@end
```

The implementation of the application delegate is shown in Listing 10.4. The delegate simply uses the `MainViewController` as a subview of the main window.

Listing 10.4   The implementation of the application delegate class used in the file creation and local file viewing example.

```
#import "FileAppDelegate.h"
#import "MainViewController.h"

@implementation FileAppDelegate
@synthesize window;

- (void)applicationDidFinishLaunching:(UIApplication *)application {
  window =
    [[UIWindow alloc] initWithFrame:[[UIScreen  mainScreen] bounds]];
  mainCtrl = [[MainViewController alloc] initWithNibName:nil bundle:nil];
  [window addSubview:mainCtrl.view];
  [window makeKeyAndVisible];
}

- (void)dealloc {
  [window release];
  [mainCtrl release];
  [super dealloc];
}
@end
```

The `MainViewController` class is declared in Listing 10.5. It has a reference to the `UIWebView` instance, which will be used to visualize the contents of the local file in `tmp`. In addition, it declares two methods for the creation and visualization of the `html` file in `tmp`.

Listing 10.5   The declaration of the `MainViewController` class used in the file creation and local file viewing example.

```
#import <UIKit/UIKit.h>

@interface MainViewController : UIViewController {
  UIWebView   *webView;
}
-(void) createAFileInTMP;
-(void) loadWebViewWithFileInTMP;
@end
```

Listing 10.6 shows the implementation of the `MainViewController` class. The `loadView` method simply creates the web view object and makes it able to respond to zooming gestures. The web view object is made as the view managed by the controller; thus, it will be added to the main window as the subview.

The `viewDidLoad` method is invoked once the view has been loaded. It creates the file by invoking the `createAFileInTMP` method, and after that it loads the web view with the downloaded file by invoking the `loadWebViewWithFileInTMP` method.

Listing 10.6   The implementation of the `MainViewController` class used in the file creation and local file viewing example.

```
#import <Foundation/Foundation.h>
#import <UIKit/UIKit.h>
#import "MainViewController.h"

@implementation MainViewController

- (void)loadView {
  CGRect   rectFrame = [UIScreen mainScreen].applicationFrame;
  webView = [[UIWebView alloc] initWithFrame:rectFrame];
  webView.scalesPageToFit = YES;
  self.view = webView;
}

- (void)viewDidLoad {
  [self createAFileInTMP];
  [self loadWebViewWithFileInTMP];
}

-(void) loadWebViewWithFileInTMP{
  NSFileManager  *fileManager = [NSFileManager defaultManager];
  NSData *data;
  NSString *fileName =
    [NSHomeDirectory() stringByAppendingPathComponent:@"tmp/file.html"];
  data = [fileManager contentsAtPath:fileName];
  [webView loadData:data MIMEType:@"text/html" textEncodingName:@"UTF-8"
          baseURL:[NSURL URLWithString:@"http://csmonitor.com"]];
}


-(void) createAFileInTMP{
  // creating a file in tmp
  //http://www.csmonitor.com/textedition/index.html
  NSFileManager  *fileManager = [NSFileManager defaultManager];
  NSString *fileName =
    [NSHomeDirectory() stringByAppendingPathComponent:@"tmp/file.html"];
  NSURL *theURL = [[NSURL alloc] initWithScheme:@"http"
```

```
                                    host:@"www.csmonitor.com"
                                    path:@"/textedition/index.html"];
  NSData *data = [[NSData alloc] initWithContentsOfURL:theURL];
  BOOL fileCreationSuccess =
    [fileManager createFileAtPath:fileName contents:data attributes:nil];
  if(fileCreationSuccess == NO){
    NSLog(@"Failed to create the html file");
  }
  [theURL release];
  [data release];
}

- (void)dealloc {
  [webView release];
  [super dealloc];
}
@end
```

Figure 10.1   A screen shot of the file creation and web visualization example.

The `createAFileInTMP` method first builds an `NSURL` object pointing to the URL `http://www.csmonitor.com/textedition/index.html`. It then creates an `NSData` object having the contents of the `index.html` file downloaded from the server. To actually create the file on the local file system, we use the `createFileAtPath:contents:attributes:` method, which is declared as follows:

```
- (BOOL) createFileAtPath:(NSString *)path contents:(NSData *)data
        attributes:(NSDictionary *)attr
```

It takes the path of the file as the first parameter, the data as the second, and the attributes as the third. Here, we use the default attributes and pass a `nil`. The path used is the absolute path of the `Home` directory with the `tmp/file.html` appended at the end. If there was a problem in creating the file, the return value is `NO`; otherwise, it is `YES`.

The `loadWebViewWithFileInTMP` method loads the local `html` file and presents it using the web view. It starts by creating an `NSData` object and loading it with the contents of the local file using the `NSFileManager`'s instance method `contentsAtPath:`. After that, we simply load the web view object with the contents of the `NSData` object.

Figure 10.1 shows a screen shot of the file creation and web visualization example. The complete application can be found in the `FileMgmt` project in the source downloads.

10.5   Retrieving and Changing Attributes

Until now, we have been specifying `nil` for the dictionary attributes of files and directories. You can, however, specify a dictionary that provides attributes that are different from the default. Moreover, you can alter the attributes of a file system object after it has been created.

Following is an example showing how you can retrieve and set the attributes of a file. Listing 10.7 shows the `main()` function of the program.

Listing 10.7   An example showing how to retrieve and set the attributes of a file.

```
#import <Foundation/Foundation.h>

int main(int argc, char *argv[]) {
  NSAutoreleasePool * pool = [[NSAutoreleasePool alloc] init];
  BOOL success;
  NSFileManager  *fileManager = [NSFileManager defaultManager];
  NSString *filePath =
    [NSHomeDirectory() stringByAppendingPathComponent:@"tmp/file.txt"];
  NSData *data = [@"Hello! This is a line."
                    dataUsingEncoding:NSUTF8StringEncoding];
  success =
    [fileManager createFileAtPath:filePath contents:data attributes:nil];
  if(success == NO){
    NSLog(@"Error creating file");
```

```
      return -1;
   }
   NSDictionary *attributes =
         [fileManager fileAttributesAtPath:filePath traverseLink:NO];
   if(attributes){
      NSNumber *fSize = [attributes objectForKey:NSFileSize];
      NSLog(@"File size is %qi", [fSize longLongValue]);
   }
   NSDictionary *newAttributes;
   NSError *error;
   newAttributes =
         [NSDictionary dictionaryWithObject:[NSNumber numberWithBool:YES]
                        forKey:NSFileExtensionHidden];
   success = [fileManager setAttributes:newAttributes
                           ofItemAtPath:filePath error:&error];
   if(success == NO){
      NSLog(@"Error setting attributes of file. Error: %@",
               [error localizedDescription]);
      return -1;
   }
   attributes =
      [fileManager fileAttributesAtPath:filePath traverseLink:NO];
   [pool release];
   return 0;
}
```

It starts by creating file.txt file in tmp with one-line text stored in it. We first obtain an NSData object from a string by using the NSString's instance method dataUsingEncoding: with utf-8 encoding. After that, we create the file on the file system using the createFileAtPath:contents:attributes: method, which we have seen before. We use the default attributes in creating the file.

10.5.1   Retrieving attributes

After creating the file using the default attributes, we would like to retrieve the file's attributes to see what are the keys available and what are the values for these keys. To retrieve the attributes of a file, we use the NSFileManager's instance method fileAttributesAtPath:traverseLink:, which is declared as follows:

```
- (NSDictionary *)fileAttributesAtPath:(NSString *)path
                    traverseLink:(BOOL)flag
```

You pass the path of the file in the first parameter. If the path points to a symbolic link, you can then specify YES to traverse the link or NO to return the attributes of the link itself. The method returns an NSDictionary instance if successful or nil if not. The attributes variable is used to hold on to the returned value. If attributes is not nil, we log the value of one attribute: the file's size in bytes. The key in obtaining this value is `NSFileSize`. The log output and the (dumped) contents of the `attributes` object on the simulator just after retrieving the attributes of the file are shown in the following log:

```
2008-08-01 08:12:06.996 FileMgmt4[394:20b] File size is 22
(gdb) po attributes
{
    NSFileCreationDate = 2008-08-01 08:11:49 -0500;
    NSFileExtensionHidden = 0;
    NSFileGroupOwnerAccountID = 20;
    NSFileGroupOwnerAccountName = staff;
    NSFileHFSCreatorCode = 0;
    NSFileHFSTypeCode = 0;
    NSFileModificationDate = 2008-08-01 08:11:49 -0500;
    NSFileOwnerAccountID = 501;
    NSFileOwnerAccountName = ali;
    NSFilePosixPermissions = 420;
    NSFileReferenceCount = 1;
    NSFileSize = 22;
    NSFileSystemFileNumber = 2436813;
    NSFileSystemNumber = 234881026;
    NSFileType = NSFileTypeRegular;
}
```

10.5.2 Changing attributes

To change one or more attributes of a file or a directory, you can use the `setAttributes:ofItem-AtPath:error:` `NSFileManager`'s method, which is declared as follows:

```
- (BOOL)setAttributes:(NSDictionary *)attributes
        ofItemAtPath:(NSString *)path error:(NSError **)error;
```

In the first parameter, you pass a dictionary with one or more of the item's attributes that you wish to set. You pass the path of the item as the second parameter and a reference to an `NSError` object as the third.

The following are the attribute keys related to files and directories that are available to you:

- `NSFileBusy`. Use this key to specify whether the file is busy or not. The value is `NSNumber` with a Boolean value.
- `NSFileCreationDate`. Use this key to set the creation date of the file or directory. The value for this key is an `NSDate` object.
- `NSFileExtensionHidden`. Use this key to specify whether the file extension is hidden or not. The value is `NSNumber` with a Boolean value. The example below shows how to set this attribute.

- NSFileGroupOwnerAccountID. Use this key to specify the file's group ID. The value is specified in an NSNumber object containing an unsigned long value.

- NSFileGroupOwnerAccountName. Use this key to specify the name of the group that the file owner belongs to. The value of this key is an NSString object.

- NSFileHFSCreatorCode. Use this key to specify the file's Hierarchical File System (HFS) creator code. The value is specified in an NSNumber object containing an unsigned long value.

- NSFileHFSTypeCode. Use this key to specify the file's HFS type code. The value is specified in an NSNumber object containing an unsigned long value.

- NSFileImmutable. Use this key to specify whether the file is mutable or not. The value is NSNumber with a Boolean value.

- NSFileModificationDate. Use this key to specify the date of the last modification of the file. The value for this key is an NSDate object.

- NSFileOwnerAccountID. Use this key to specify the account ID of the file's owner. The value is specified in an NSNumber object containing an unsigned long value.

- NSFileOwnerAccountName. Use this key to specify the name of the file's owner. The value of this key is an NSString object.

- NSFilePosixPermissions. Use this key to specify the POSIX permissions of the file. The value is specified in an NSNumber object containing an unsigned long value.

After changing the NSFileExtensionHidden to YES, the attributes object on the simulator is as follows:

```
(gdb) po attributes
{
    NSFileCreationDate = 2008-08-01 08:11:49 -0500;
    NSFileExtensionHidden = 1;
    NSFileGroupOwnerAccountID = 20;
    NSFileGroupOwnerAccountName = staff;
    NSFileHFSCreatorCode = 0;
    NSFileHFSTypeCode = 0;
    NSFileModificationDate = 2008-08-01 08:11:49 -0500;
    NSFileOwnerAccountID = 501;
    NSFileOwnerAccountName = ali;
    NSFilePosixPermissions = 420;
    NSFileReferenceCount = 1;
    NSFileSize = 22;
    NSFileSystemFileNumber = 2436813;
    NSFileSystemNumber = 234881026;
    NSFileType = NSFileTypeRegular;
}
```

The `attributes` object on the device is a little bit different. We notice several changes such as the `NSFileGroupOwnerAccountName` and `NSFileOwnerAccountID`. Although the `NSFile-ExtensionHidden` was successfully changed by the API call, the `NSFileExtensionHidden` key does not appear at all in the `attributes` object. This serves as a reminder to always test your code on the actual device. The following are all the attributes of the file available to you on the device:

```
2008-08-01 08:17:39.982 FileMgmt4[164:20b] File size is 22
(gdb) po attributes
{
    NSFileGroupOwnerAccountID = 501;
    NSFileGroupOwnerAccountName = mobile;
    NSFileModificationDate = 2008-08-01 08:17:35 -0500;
    NSFileOwnerAccountID = 501;
    NSFileOwnerAccountName = mobile;
    NSFilePosixPermissions = 420;
    NSFileReferenceCount = 1;
    NSFileSize = 22;
    NSFileSystemFileNumber = 87161;
    NSFileSystemNumber = 234881026;
    NSFileType = NSFileTypeRegular;
}
```

10.6   Working with Resources and Low-Level File Access

This section demonstrates the use of bundles (accessing files stored at the time that the application was packaged) and low-level file access (seeking and updating a file).

Listing 10.8 shows the `main()` function demonstrating loading a file from a bundle and modifying it by inserting text.

Listing 10.8   The `main()` function demonstrating loading a file from a bundle and modifying it by writing text.

```
#import <Foundation/Foundation.h>

int main(int argc, char *argv[]) {
  NSAutoreleasePool * pool = [[NSAutoreleasePool alloc] init];
  BOOL success;
  NSFileManager *fileManager = [NSFileManager defaultManager];
  NSString *filePath = [[NSBundle mainBundle] pathForResource:@"file"
                                              ofType:@"txt"];
  NSData *fileData = [NSData dataWithContentsOfFile:filePath];
  if (fileData) {
    NSString *newFilePath = [NSHomeDirectory()
              stringByAppendingPathComponent:@"Documents/fileNew.txt"];
    success = [fileManager createFileAtPath:newFilePath
```

```
                            contents:fileData attributes:nil];
    if(success == NO){
      NSLog(@"Error creating file");
      return -1;
    }
    NSFileHandle   *fileHandle =
        [NSFileHandle fileHandleForUpdatingAtPath:newFilePath];
    if(fileHandle){
      [fileHandle seekToFileOffset:11];
      NSData *appendedData =
          [@" modified " dataUsingEncoding:NSUTF8StringEncoding];
      [fileHandle writeData:appendedData];
      [fileHandle closeFile];
    }
    else{
      NSLog(@"Error modifying the file");
      return -1;
    }
  }
  else{
    NSLog(@"Could not load file from the app bundle");
    return -1;
  }
  [pool release];
  return 0;
}
```

Our application stores a text file in the application bundle, as shown in the XCode's Groups & Files screen shot in Figure 10.2. You can store data files anywhere you want, but usually you store them in the Resources group as shown in Figure 10.2.

We have previously seen that inside the Home directory of every application, there is an XXX.app directory (where XXX stands for the name of the application). The data files go inside this directory.

To help in locating the data files inside the bundle, an instance method of the class NSBundle can be used to search for a specific file with a specific extension and return the absolute path of that resource. This method is declared as follows:

```
- (NSString *)pathForResource:(NSString *)name ofType:(NSString *)ext;
```

In the first parameter, you pass in the path of the resource file that you want to locate, and in the second, you pass its extension. You can pass an empty string or even nil for the extension if your file's name is unique in the bundle. The reason this works is because the search algorithm returns the first occurrence of a file with exactly the same name if the ext parameter is nil or empty. The location of file.txt in the bundle (value of filePath in the main() function) is

```
/var/mobile/Applications/5ABEB448-7634-4AE8-9833-FC846A81B418/
FileMgmt6.app/file.txt
```

Figure 10.2 XCode's Groups & Files screen shot.

Remember that you should not change items in the .app directory as it will affect code signing. Therefore, to modify a file in the bundle, you need to copy it to a different directory and change it there.

After locating the file in the bundle and storing its absolute path in filePath, we load its contents into an NSData object using the dataWithContentsOfFile: method. Next, the file Documents/fileNew.txt is created, containing the contents of the bundled file.

The original file contains a single line: This is the contents of a file. We would like to modify the copied file by replacing the text "contents" with the text "modified". We would like to perform this task by using low-level file operations involving seeking rather than loading the whole file into memory, changing it, and storing it back to disk.

To perform low-level file operations, you need to obtain an NSFileHandle instance. This class encapsulates the low-level mechanism for accessing files. The nature of operations that you would like to perform on the file determines the method you use to obtain the NSFileHandle instance. The following are the three NSFileHandle class methods available to you:

- **Reading.** To obtain the instance for read-only access, use the class method fileHandleFor-ReadingAtPath:, which is declared as follows:

  + (**id**) fileHandleForReadingAtPath: (NSString *)path

- **Writing.** To obtain the instance for write-only access, use the class method `fileHandle-ForWritingAtPath:`, which is declared as follows:

  + (**id**)fileHandleForWritingAtPath:(NSString *)path

- **Reading/writing.** To obtain the instance for update access, use the class method `fileHandleForUpdatingAtPath:`, which is declared as follows:

  + (**id**)fileHandleForUpdatingAtPath:(NSString *)path

When you obtain the instance using one of the three methods above, the file's pointer is set to the beginning of the file.

In our example, we open the file for updating. Because we know the location of the text that needs to be inserted, we use the seek operation on the `NSFileHandle` instance. To seek a file, use the `seekToFileOffset:` method, which is declared as follows:

- (**void**)seekToFileOffset:(**unsigned long long**)offset

The location to seek to in our example is 11. After seeking to that location, we write the "modified" text in the file by using the `writeData:` method. This method is declared as follows:

- (**void**)writeData:(NSData *)data

After finishing the update on the file, we close the `NSFileHandle` object by using the method `closeFile`.

10.7 Summary

This chapter covered the topic of file management. You learned how to use both high- and low-level techniques for storing and retrieving file data. To perform high-level operations on files and directories, you used instances of the `NSFileManager` class. The `NSFileHandle` class was used in this chapter to demonstrate low-level file access.

In Section 10.1, we talked about the `Home` directory of the application. Next, Section 10.2 showed how to enumerate the contents of a given directory using the high-level methods of `NSFileManager`. In that section, you learned more about the structure of the `Home` directory and where you can store files. After that, you learned in Section 10.3 how to create and delete directories. Next, Section 10.4 covered the creation of files. Section 10.5 covered the topic of file and directory attributes. You also learned how to retrieve and set specific file and directory attributes in that section. In Section 10.6 we demonstrated the use of application bundles and low-level file access.

Exercises

(1) Your app uses a database file to store data. You ship the app with a sample database file stored in the bundle. When your app first runs, it checks to see if the database file is available in a directory called `Database` in the `Home` directory. If it is not, the file is copied there and made available for modification. Write a method that implements the logic behind this.

(2) Read about the `NSFileManager` class in the documentation and in the `NSFileManager.h` header file.

11

Working with Databases

This chapter covers the basics of the SQLite database engine that is available to you using the iOS SDK. SQLite is different from the other databases that you may be familiar with. Databases such as Oracle and Sybase are server-based databases. In server-based databases, a server runs the database engine and serves the queries of clients running on other machines. SQLite is an embedded database in the sense that there is no server running, and the database engine is linked to your application. SQLite is 100 percent free to use.

This chapter is not an introduction to databases and it assumes that you know the basics of the Structured Query Language (SQL). You should know that a database is composed of a set of *tables* and each table has a name that uniquely identifies that table in the database. Each table consists of one or more *columns* and each column has a name that uniquely identifies it within that table. A *row* is a vector of values for each column in a given table. A row is often referred to as a *record*.

This chapter is organized as follows. Section 11.1 describes basic SQL statements and their implementation using SQLite function calls. In Section 11.2, we discuss the handling of result sets generated by SQL statements. In Section 11.3, we address the topic of prepared statements. In Section 11.4, we talk about extensions to the SQLite API through the use of user-defined functions. In Sections 11.5 and 11.6 we present, respectively, a detailed example for storing and retrieving BLOBs to and from the database. Finally, we summarize the chapter in Section 11.7.

11.1 Basic Database Operations

In this section, we talk about some of the basic SQL statements and how we can realize them in SQLite. We present a simple program that creates a database with one table. This table stores records of stock purchases. Each record stores the stock identifier (represented by the stock symbol), the purchase price, the number of shares bought, and the date of purchase.

To use SQLite in your application, you need to add the `libsqlite3.0.dylib` library to your target. See Section D.4 for general instructions on how to add libraries to your project. In addition, you need to add the following **#import** statement:

```
#import "/usr/include/sqlite3.h"
```

Listing 11.1 shows the `main()` function. The function creates a database (if one does not exist), adds a new table, and populates the table with some records.

Listing 11.1   The `main()` function demonstrating basic SQL statements using SQLite library function calls.

```
#import "/usr/include/sqlite3.h"
int main(int argc, char *argv[]) {
  char    *sqlStatement;
  sqlite3 *pDb;
  char    *errorMsg;
  int     returnCode;
  char    *databaseName;

  databaseName = "financial.db";
  returnCode = sqlite3_open(databaseName, &pDb);
  if(returnCode!=SQLITE_OK) {
    fprintf(stderr, "Error in opening the database. Error: %s",
            sqlite3_errmsg(pDb));
    sqlite3_close(pDb);
    return -1;
  }
  sqlStatement =  "DROP TABLE IF EXISTS  stocks";
  returnCode = sqlite3_exec(pDb, sqlStatement, NULL, NULL, &errorMsg);
  if(returnCode!=SQLITE_OK) {
    fprintf(stderr,
      "Error in dropping table stocks. Error: %s", errorMsg);
    sqlite3_free(errorMsg);
  }

  sqlStatement =  "CREATE TABLE stocks (symbol VARCHAR(5), "
                  "purchasePrice FLOAT(10,4), "
                  "unitsPurchased INTEGER, "
                  "purchase_date VARCHAR(10))";
  returnCode = sqlite3_exec(pDb, sqlStatement, NULL, NULL, &errorMsg);
  if(returnCode!=SQLITE_OK) {
    fprintf(stderr, "Error in creating the stocks table. Error: %s",
                      errorMsg);
    sqlite3_free(errorMsg);
  }

  insertStockPurchase(pDb, "ALU", 14.23, 100, "03-17-2012");
  insertStockPurchase(pDb, "GOOG", 600.77, 20, "01-09-2012");
  insertStockPurchase(pDb, "NT", 20.23,140, "02-05-2012");
  insertStockPurchase(pDb, "MSFT", 30.23, 5, "01-03-2012");
  sqlite3_close(pDb);
  return 0;
}
```

11.1.1   Opening, creating, and closing databases

The first thing that you do before working with a database is open it. The SQLite function for opening a database is `sqlite3_open()`. The function is declared as

```
int sqlite3_open(
    const char *filename,    /* Database filename (UTF-8) */
    sqlite3    **ppDb        /* OUT: SQLite db handle */
);
```

A database in SQLite is stored in a file. To open a database, you need to specify the filename of that database in the first parameter, `filename`. Upon successfully opening the database, the function will return a value of `SQLITE_OK`. For other SQLite functions to work with this database, a handle is needed. You specify a reference to a handle pointer in the second parameter. If the database was successfully opened, a handle is written in that address. The database connection handle is of type `sqlite3`. You pass the address of a variable of type `sqlite3*` in the second parameter. It is worth noting that if the database does not exist, it is created; thus, this function is used for both opening an existing database and creating a new one.

If the database was not opened successfully, you need to display an error message and close the database. The SQLite function `sqlite3_errmsg()` takes a pointer to a database handle and returns a meaningful string describing the error. The program shown in Listing 11.1 uses this function in displaying the error message for failed database opening. Once you are finished with a database, you should close it. The SQLite function `sqlite3_close()` is used for that purpose. It takes, as the sole parameter, a pointer to the opened database handle (`sqlite3*`) received when you opened the database.

11.1.2   Table operations

Once we have successfully opened a database, we would like to perform some table operations. SQLite provides a helper function that does a one-time evaluation of SQL statements. This function, `sqlite3_exec()`, is easy to use and works very well with many SQL statements. Later, we will talk about how this function is implemented using other SQLite functions. The `sqlite3_exec()` is declared as

```
int sqlite3_exec(
  sqlite3*,                /* An open database */
  const char *sql,     /* SQL to be evaluated */
  int (*callback)(void*,int,char**,char**),/*Callbk func*/
  void *,                  /* 1st argument to callback */
  char **errmsg     /* Error msg written here */
);
```

The first parameter is the pointer to the database handle we received from the `sqlite3_open()` function. The second parameter is the C string SQL statement. If an error occurs, an error message is written into memory obtained from `sqlite3_malloc()`, and `*errmsg` is made to point to that message. You are responsible for freeing that space using the SQLite function `sqlite3_free()`. The third and fourth parameters are used for callback functions operating on the result of the SQL statement. The callback function, if specified, will be called for every row in the result. We will cover callback functions in Section 11.2, but note that the first parameter passed to this callback function can be specified in the fourth parameter of the `sqlite3_exec()` function. A return value of `SQLITE_OK` indicates successful execution of the SQL statement.

The first thing that we do in the `main()` function is to delete the table `stocks`, if it exists. The SQL statement for that is

DROP TABLE IF EXISTS   stocks

This SQL statement does not return records. Therefore, in the invocation of the `sqlite3_exec()` function, we pass `NULL` for both the callback function and its first argument. The execution of this SQL statement is achieved by the following:

```
returnCode = sqlite3_exec(pDb, sqlStatement, NULL, NULL, &errorMsg);
```

Once we have deleted the `stocks` table, we can go ahead and create a new one. The SQL statement for creating the `stocks` table is as follows:

```
CREATE TABLE stocks (
                     symbol VARCHAR(5),
                     purchasePrice FLOAT(10,4),
                     unitsPurchased INTEGER,
                     purchase_date VARCHAR(10)
                   )
```

This SQL statement should be familiar to you. It states that the `stocks` table should have four columns. The first column is of variable (maximum five) characters. The second is of type float with ten digits in total and four of these digits are used after the decimal point. The third column is of type integer, and the fourth and final column is of variable characters with maximum size of ten characters.

Internally, SQLite has the following five classes for data storage:

- `INTEGER`. Used to store a signed integer value. The number of bytes actually used for storage depends on the magnitude of the value and ranges from 1 to 8 bytes.
- `REAL`. An 8-byte IEEE floating-point storage representing a floating-point number.
- `TEXT`. A storage area for text. The text can be in any of the following encodings: `UTF-8`, `UTF-16BE`, or `UTF-16-LE`.
- `BLOB`. Used to store data exactly as entered — for example, an image.
- `NULL`. Used to store the value `NULL`.

After creating the table `stocks`, we insert several records into it. The function `insertStock-Purchase()` shown in Listing 11.2 is used for that purpose.

Listing 11.2   The function `insertStockPurchase()` for adding records to the `stocks` table.

```
#import "/usr/include/sqlite3.h"
void insertStockPurchase(sqlite3 *pDb, const char*symbol,
           float price, int units, const char* theDate){
  char    *errorMsg;
  int     returnCode;
  char    *st;
  st = sqlite3_mprintf("INSERT INTO stocks VALUES"
           " ('%q', %f, %d, '%q')", symbol, price, units, theDate);
  returnCode = sqlite3_exec(pDb, st, NULL, NULL, &errorMsg);
  if(returnCode!=SQLITE_OK) {
    fprintf(stderr,
        "Error in inserting into the stocks table. Error: %s",
        errorMsg);
    sqlite3_free(errorMsg);
  }
  sqlite3_free(st);
}
```

As an example, the following SQL statement adds a record for purchasing 100 shares of Alcatel-Lucent's stock at $14.23 on 03-17-2012:

```
INSERT INTO stocks VALUES ('ALU', 14.23, 100, '03-17-2012')
```

We use the SQlite function `sqlite3_mprintf()` for formatted string printing. This function is similar to the standard C library function `printf()` except that it writes the result into memory obtained from the `sqlite3_malloc()` function, so you should release the string when you are finished with it using the `sqlite3_free()` function. In addition to the well-known formatting options, you have access to the options `%q` and `%Q`. You should use these options instead of the `%s` options when dealing with text. The option `%q` works like `%s` except that it doubles every ' character. For example, the string `"She said: 'Hey, y'all, what's up?'"` will be printed to the string as `"She said: "Hey, y"all, what"s up?""`. The `%Q` option works like the `%q` option except that it produces the string `NULL` when the value of the pointer being printed is equal to `NULL`. It also surrounds the whole string with a pair of '. The previous string will be printed as `"'She said: "Hey, y"all, what"s up?"'"` when `%Q` is used.

The complete application can be found in the `Database 1` project in the source downloads.

11.2   Processing Row Results

In the previous section, we saw how the function `sqlite3_exec()` can be used in executing SQL statements that do not produce results or in which the caller is not interested in processing the results.

If you are interested in the result set, however, you can pass a callback function pointer as the fourth parameter to the `sqlite3_exec()` function. This callback function will be invoked for every row in the result set.

The callback function should follow the following signature:

```
int (*callback)(void*,int,char**,char**)
```

The first parameter of this function is the same as the fourth parameter when the `sqlite3_exec()` function is invoked. The second parameter is the number of columns in the current row result. The third parameter is an array of pointers to strings holding the values for each column in the current result set row. The fourth parameter is an array of pointers to strings holding the names of result columns. If the callback function returns a value other than zero, the `sqlite3_exec()` function will stop executing and will return `SQLITE_ABORT`.

In the function `main()` shown in Listing 11.3, we demonstrate how a callback function can be used to process the result set. The database `financial.db` is opened as we have seen before and a `SELECT` query is executed. The query

```
SELECT * from stocks
```

retrieves all the records in the table `stocks`. The SQLite function call for executing the statement is as follows:

```
returnCode = sqlite3_exec(pDb,sqlStatement,processRow,NULL,&errorMsg);
```

The third parameter is not `NULL`, as we saw in the previous section. Instead, we pass in the function pointer `processRow`. The function `processRow()` is shown in Listing 11.4.

Listing 11.3   The function `main()` for retrieving records using the `sqlite3_exec()` function.

```
#import "/usr/include/sqlite3.h"
int main(int argc, char *argv[]) {
  char     *sqlStatement;
  sqlite3 *pDb;
  char     *errorMsg;
  int       returnCode;
  char     *databaseName;

  databaseName = "financial.db";
  returnCode = sqlite3_open(databaseName, &pDb);
  if(returnCode!=SQLITE_OK) {
    fprintf(stderr, "Error in opening the database. Error: %s",
          sqlite3_errmsg(pDb));
    sqlite3_close(pDb);
    return -1;
  }
  sqlStatement =  "SELECT * from stocks";
  returnCode = sqlite3_exec(pDb,sqlStatement,processRow,NULL,&errorMsg);
  if(returnCode!=SQLITE_OK) {
    fprintf(stderr, "Error in selecting from stocks table. Error: %s",
        errorMsg);
    sqlite3_free(errorMsg);
  }
```

```
    sqlite3_close(pDb);
    return 0;
}
```

This function follows the callback function signature. Inside the function, we have a `for` loop where we display the column name, and the row value for that column.

The result of executing the program is

```
Record Data:
The value for Column Name symbol is equal to ALU
The value for Column Name purchasePrice is equal to 14.23
The value for Column Name unitsPurchased is equal to 100
The value for Column Name purchase_date is equal to 03-17-2012

Record Data:
The value for Column Name symbol is equal to GOOG
The value for Column Name purchasePrice is equal to 600.77002
The value for Column Name unitsPurchased is equal to 20
The value for Column Name purchase_date is equal to 01-09-2012

Record Data:
The value for Column Name symbol is equal to NT
The value for Column Name purchasePrice is equal to 20.23
The value for Column Name unitsPurchased is equal to 140
The value for Column Name purchase_date is equal to 02-05-2012

Record Data:
The value for Column Name symbol is equal to MSFT
The value for Column Name purchasePrice is equal to 30.23
The value for Column Name unitsPurchased is equal to 5
The value for Column Name purchase_date is equal to 01-03-2012
```

Listing 11.4   The function `processRow()` for processing row results.

```
#import "/usr/include/sqlite3.h"

static int processRow(void *argument,
        int argc, char **argv, char **colName){
  printf("Record Data:\n");
  for(int i=0; i<argc; i++){
    printf("The value for Column Name %s is equal to %s\n",
          colName[i], argv[i] ? argv[i] : "NULL");
  }
  printf("\n");
  return 0;
}
```

The complete application can be found in the `Database 2` project in the source downloads.

11.3 Prepared Statements

In the previous two sections, we used the `sqlite3_exec()` function to execute SQL statements. This function is more appropriate for SQL statements that do not return data (such as `INSERT`, `DROP`, and `CREATE`). For SQL statements that return data, such as `SELECT`, prepared statements are usually used.

The use of prepared statements involves three phases:

- **Preparation.** In the preparation phase, you present a statement to the SQLite engine for compilation. The engine compiles this statement into byte code and reserves the resources needed for its actual execution.

- **Execution.** This phase is used to actually execute the byte code and obtain rows from the result of the statement. You repeat this phase for every row in the result set.

- **Finalization.** After obtaining all rows in the result set, you finalize the prepared statement so that resources reserved for it can be freed.

In the following sections, we discuss these three phases in detail.

11.3.1 Preparation

You prepare an SQL statement using the `sqlite3_prepare_v2()` function. The function is declared as follows:

```
int sqlite3_prepare_v2(
    sqlite3 *db,             /* Database handle */
    const char *zSql,    /* SQL statement, UTF-8 encoded */
    int nBytes,              /* Length of zSql in bytes. */
    sqlite3_stmt **ppStmt,   /* OUT: Statement handle */
    const char **pzTail  /*OUT: Ptr to unused portion of zSql*/
)
```

The first parameter, `db`, is the pointer to the database handle obtained from a prior `sqlite3_open()` call. The SQL statement (e.g., `SELECT` statement) is passed in the `zSql` parameter. You pass the length (in bytes) of that statement in the third parameter. The fourth parameter is used to obtain a statement handle. You pass a reference to a variable of type `sqlite3_stmt*`, and on successful preparation of the SQL statement, that variable will hold the statement handle. In the case that `*zSql` points to multiple SQL statements, the function will make `*pzTail` point to the first byte past the first SQL statement in `zSql`. If `*zSql` points to a single SQL statement, passing a `NULL` for the fifth parameter is appropriate.

11.3.2 Execution

Once you have compiled the SQL statement, you need to execute it and retrieve the first row result. The SQL statement is executed using the function `sqlite3_step()`. The declaration of the function is as follows:

```
int sqlite3_step(sqlite3_stmt*);
```

The function takes a pointer to the statement handle as its sole parameter. As long as there is a new row in the result set, the function returns `SQLITE_ROW`. When all rows have been exhausted, the function returns `SQLITE_DONE`.

11.3.3 Finalization

After retrieving the last row, the statement is finalized by calling `sqlite3_finalize()`. The function's declaration is as follows:

```
int sqlite3_finalize(sqlite3_stmt *pStmt);
```

It takes as the sole parameter a pointer to the statement handle. Finalization closes the statement and frees resources.

11.3.4 Putting it together

Let's demonstrate these concepts by showing a small working example. The function `main()` in Listing 11.5 is where we open a database, select some records from a table, and print them one by one.

Listing 11.5   The function `main()` demonstrating prepared statements.

```
#import "/usr/include/sqlite3.h"
int main(int argc, char *argv[]) {
  char    *sqlStatement;
  sqlite3 *database;
  int     returnCode;
  char    *databaseName;
  sqlite3_stmt *statement;

  databaseName = "financial.db";
  returnCode = sqlite3_open(databaseName, &database);
  if(returnCode!=SQLITE_OK) {
    fprintf(stderr, "Error in opening the database. Error: %s",
            sqlite3_errmsg(database));
    sqlite3_close(database);
    return -1;
  }
```

```
sqlStatement = sqlite3_mprintf(
            "SELECT S.symbol, S.unitsPurchased, "
            "S.purchasePrice FROM stocks AS S WHERE "
            "S.purchasePrice  >= %f", 30.0);
returnCode =
        sqlite3_prepare_v2(database,
        sqlStatement, strlen(sqlStatement),
        &statement, NULL);
if(returnCode != SQLITE_OK) {
  fprintf(stderr, "Error in preparation of query. Error: %s",
      sqlite3_errmsg(database));
  sqlite3_close(database);
  return -1;
}
returnCode = sqlite3_step(statement);
while(returnCode == SQLITE_ROW){
  char *symbol;
  int  units;
  double price;
  symbol = sqlite3_column_text(statement, 0);
  units  = sqlite3_column_int(statement, 1);
  price  = sqlite3_column_double(statement, 2);
  printf("We bought %d from %s at a price equal to %.4f\n",
          units, symbol, price);
  returnCode = sqlite3_step(statement);
}
sqlite3_finalize(statement);
sqlite3_free(sqlStatement);
return 0;
}
```

After opening the database, we invoke the `sqlite3_prepare_v2()` function on the following SQL statement:

SELECT
        S.symbol, S.unitsPurchased, S.purchasePrice
        FROM stocks **AS** S
        WHERE S.purchasePrice >= 30.0

The SQL statement will result in a set of records from the table `stocks` whose `purchasePrice` is greater than or equal to $30. The statement is compiled as follows:

```
returnCode = sqlite3_prepare_v2(database,
                                sqlStatement, strlen(sqlStatement),
                                &statement, NULL);
```

Notice that we pass `NULL` for the last parameter as we only have one SQL statement to compile. If the statement compilation is successful, the return code will be equal to `SQLITE_OK`. If there is an error, we display the error message and exit the `main()` function.

After compiling the statement, we execute the statement to retrieve the first result record. The function used in the execution of the statement is `sqlite3_step()`. If there is a successful retrieval of a row, the return code will be `SQLITE_ROW`. If we receive an `SQLITE_ROW` return code, we retrieve the values for the columns in that row. To retrieve a column value, you use an SQLite function of the form `sqlite3_column_XXX()`. The first parameter to this function is a pointer to the SQL statement (type `sqlite3_stmt`) that was returned by the `sqlite3_prepare_v2()` function. The second parameter is the column index, where the leftmost column has an index of 0. The return value depends on the version of the function.

We have the following three statements corresponding to the three columns:

```
symbol  = sqlite3_column_text(statement, 0);
units   = sqlite3_column_int(statement, 1);
price   = sqlite3_column_double(statement, 2);
```

The first statement corresponds to the `S.symbol` column. The column belongs to the `TEXT` storage class. The function `sqlite3_column_text()` will return a C string of the `symbol` column that is stored in that row. The other functions, `sqlite3_column_int()` and `sqlite3_column_double()`, work in the same way except that they return an integer and a double value, respectively.

After printing the values for the columns constituting the row, we move to the next row in the result by again invoking the `sqlite3_step()` function. When we are finished with the result, we exit the `while` loop and finalize the statement by invoking the `sqlite3_finalize()` function. The result of running this query, provided that the `stocks` table was populated as in the previous sections, is as follows:

```
We bought 20 from GOOG at a price equal to 600.7700
We bought 5 from MSFT at a price equal to 30.2300
```

The complete application can be found in the `Database 3` project in the source downloads.

11.4   User-Defined Functions

Often, you are faced with a situation requiring you to use a function that the SQL engine does not implement. SQLite provides a mechanism for extending the C API and allows for user-defined functions. The user can define new custom functions for use in SQL statements for a specific database connection. Such functions are transient in that they are available only during the life of a database connection. They are not stored in the database.

In this section, we demonstrate the use of user-defined functions by adding the function `Palindrome()` to a database connection. The function `Palindrome(t)` takes a text-based parameter, `t`, and checks to see if `t` is the same whether it is read from the right or from the left. Listing 11.6 shows the `main()` function demonstrating the installation of a user-defined function for an opened database connection.

Listing 11.6   The `main()` function demonstrating the installation of a user-defined function for an opened database connection.

```
int main(int argc, char *argv[]) {
  char    *sqlStatement;
  sqlite3 *database;
  int     returnCode;
  char    *databaseName;
  sqlite3_stmt *statement;

  databaseName = "financial.db";
  returnCode = sqlite3_open(databaseName, &database);
  if(returnCode!=SQLITE_OK) {
    fprintf(stderr, "Error in opening the database. Error: %s",
        sqlite3_errmsg(database));
    sqlite3_close(database);
    return -1;
  }
  sqlite3_create_function(database, "Palindrome", 1,
      SQLITE_UTF8, NULL, palindrome, NULL, NULL);
  sqlStatement = sqlite3_mprintf(
      "SELECT S.symbol, S.unitsPurchased, S.purchasePrice "
      "FROM stocks AS S WHERE "
      "Palindrome(S.symbol) = 1 AND S.purchasePrice  >= %f",
      30.0);

  returnCode = sqlite3_prepare_v2(
        database, sqlStatement, strlen(sqlStatement),
        &statement, NULL);
  if(returnCode!=SQLITE_OK) {
    fprintf(stderr, "Error in preparation of query. Error: %s",
        sqlite3_errmsg(database));
    sqlite3_close(database);
    return -1;
  }
  returnCode = sqlite3_step(statement);
  while(returnCode == SQLITE_ROW){
    char *symbol;
    int  units;
    double price;
    symbol = sqlite3_column_text(statement, 0);
    units  = sqlite3_column_int(statement, 1);
    price  = sqlite3_column_double(statement, 2);
    printf("We bought %d from %s at a price equal to %.4f\n",
        units, symbol, price);
    returnCode = sqlite3_step(statement);
  }
  sqlite3_finalize(statement);
```

```
    sqlite3_free(sqlStatement);
    return 0;
}
```

The user-defined function is installed for a given connection by calling `sqlite3_create_function()`. The function is declared as

```
int sqlite3_create_function(
    sqlite3 *connectionHandle,
    const char *zFunctionName,
    int nArg,
    int eTextRep,
    void*,
    void (*xFunc)(sqlite3_context*,int,sqlite3_value**),
    void (*xStep)(sqlite3_context*,int,sqlite3_value**),
    void (*xFinal)(sqlite3_context*)
)
```

The first parameter of this function is the connection (database) handle. The second parameter is the function name as it is used in SQL statements. This name can be different from the C function name that actually implements the function. The third parameter is used to specify the number of parameters for the custom function being created. The fourth parameter is used to specify the encoding of the parameters. You can install different versions of the same function that use different encodings. The SQLite engine will be able to route the calls to the appropriate function. The fifth parameter is an arbitrary pointer. Inside your user-defined function, you can access this pointer using `sqlite3_user_data()`. The seventh parameter is a pointer to the C function implementing the behavior whose logical name is the second parameter, `zFunctionName`. The eighth and ninth parameters are aggregate step and finalize functions, respectively. These two functions are used in executing aggregate SQL statements.

All user-defined functions have the same signature:

```
void (sqlite3_context *context, int nargs,sqlite3_value  **values)
```

The function returns `void` and all three of its parameters are input parameters. The first parameter is the SQL function context. Think of it as a channel ID for the function and the SQL engine to communicate on. The second parameter is the number of arguments used when the logical function was called from within the SQL statement. The third parameter is the array of parameter values passed to the function.

Since all user-defined functions are `void`, the results/errors are signaled back using SQLite3 routines. To signal back an error message to the caller, you use the function `sqlite3_result_error()`. The first parameter in this function is the context (so that the engine knows which SQL statement this error is related to). The second parameter is a C string providing the error message in text. Finally, the last parameter is the length of the error message.

The SELECT statement that we use here is similar to the one in the previous section, except that we require the stock transaction to have a palindrome symbol. The SELECT statement is as follows:

```
SELECT
  S.symbol, S.unitsPurchased, S.purchasePrice
  FROM stocks AS S
  WHERE Palindrome(S.symbol) = 1 AND S.purchasePrice  >=  30.0
```

For the SQLite engine to execute this query, Palindrome() needs to be defined for this connection. We define the function with the following statement:

```
sqlite3_create_function(database, "Palindrome", 1,SQLITE_UTF8, NULL,
                        palindrome, NULL, NULL);
```

Listing 11.7 shows the implementation of the palindrome() function.

Listing 11.7   The user-defined palindrome() function and its implementation.

```
#import "/usr/include/sqlite3.h"
int isPalindrome(char *text){
  unsigned char *p1, *p2;
  p1 = text;
  p2 = p1+strlen(text)-1;
  while (*p1==*p2 && (p1<=p2)){
    p1++;p2--;
  }
  if(p1>= p2)
    return 1;
  return 0;
}

void
palindrome(sqlite3_context *context,int nargs,sqlite3_value  **values){
  char  *errorMessage;
  if(nargs != 1){
    errorMessage = "Incorrect no of arguments. palindrome(string)";
    sqlite3_result_error(context, errorMessage, strlen(errorMessage));
    return;
  }
  if((sqlite3_value_type(values[0]) != SQLITE_TEXT)){
    errorMessage = "Argument must be of type text.";
    sqlite3_result_error(context, errorMessage, strlen(errorMessage));
    return;
  }
  unsigned char *text;
  text = sqlite3_value_text(values[0]);
  sqlite3_result_int(context, isPalindrome(text));
}
```

The `palindrome()` function first checks to see that the number of parameters is equal to `1`. If not, an error message is signaled back and the function returns. The function also checks the type of the parameter passed, as we are expecting a TEXT value. The function `sqlite3_value_type()` returns the type of the parameter. The function is declared as

int sqlite3_value_type(sqlite3_value*)

It takes a pointer to a value of type `sqlite3_value` and returns one of the following types: SQLITE_INTEGER, SQLITE_FLOAT, SQLITE_BLOB, SQLITE_NULL, or SQLITE3_TEXT.

After making sure that the type of the parameter is TEXT, we need to obtain the actual text value. The SQLite function `sqlite3_value_text()` is used for that purpose. There are similar functions (e.g., `sqlite3_value_int()`) for the other types. Once we have the string passed to us, we check if it is a palindrome using the function `isPalindrome()`. You should be familiar with this function from introductory computer science classes.

To send the result back to the SQLite engine, you use a function of the form `sqlite3_result_XXX()`, which takes the context as the first parameter and the result value as the second parameter. For example, we use the function `sqlite3_result_int()` to return an integer as follows:

sqlite3_result_int(context, isPalindrome(text))

The complete application can be found in the `Database 4` project in the source downloads.

11.5 Storing BLOBs

In the previous sections, we dealt primarily with simple data types (strings, integers, and floating points). In addition to scalar and text data types, the SQLite database engine supports the BLOB data type. A BLOB storage class allows you to store binary data (e.g., image files) as-is. We will demonstrate the mechanism for storing BLOBs in this section and the mechanism for retrieving them in the next section.

To explain the main concepts behind inserting BLOB values into a database, we consider a new table in the database that stores information about the companies we are investing in. In addition to the company's symbol and name, we add an image column of type BLOB that stores the logo of the company in PNG format.

Listing 11.8 shows the `main()` function. It creates a new `companies` table using the following SQL statement:

CREATE TABLE companies
  (symbol **VARCHAR**(5) **PRIMARY KEY**, name **VARCHAR**(128), image **BLOB**)

Listing 11.8   The `main()` function demonstrating storing BLOBs in a table.

```
#import "/usr/include/sqlite3.h"
int main(int argc, char *argv[]) {
```

```
char      *sqlStatement;
sqlite3   *pDb;
char      *errorMsg;
int       returnCode;
char      *databaseName;

NSAutoreleasePool * pool = [[NSAutoreleasePool alloc] init];
databaseName = "financial.db";
returnCode = sqlite3_open(databaseName, &pDb);
if(returnCode!=SQLITE_OK) {
  fprintf(stderr, "Error in opening the database. Error: %s",
    sqlite3_errmsg(pDb));
  sqlite3_close(pDb);
  return -1;
}
sqlStatement =  "DROP TABLE IF EXISTS  companies";
returnCode = sqlite3_exec(pDb, sqlStatement, NULL, NULL, &errorMsg);
if(returnCode!=SQLITE_OK) {
  fprintf(stderr, "Error in dropping table companies. Error: %s",
    errorMsg);
  sqlite3_free(errorMsg);
}

sqlStatement =
      "CREATE TABLE companies "
      "(symbol VARCHAR(5)  PRIMARY KEY, "
      " name VARCHAR(128), image BLOB)";
returnCode = sqlite3_exec(pDb, sqlStatement, NULL, NULL, &errorMsg);
if(returnCode!=SQLITE_OK) {
  fprintf(stderr, "Error in creating the companies table. Error: %s",
    errorMsg);
  sqlite3_free(errorMsg);
  return -1;
}
insertCompany(pDb, "ALU", "Alcatel-Lucent");
insertCompany(pDb, "GOOG", "Google");
insertCompany(pDb, "MSFT", "Microsoft");
insertCompany(pDb, "NT", "Nortel");
sqlite3_close(pDb);
[pool release];

return 0;
}
```

After creating the `companies` table, we add four records by invoking the `insertCompany()` function shown in Listing 11.9.

Listing 11.9   The `insertCompany()` function for inserting a company record that includes a BLOB image.

```
#import "/usr/include/sqlite3.h"

void insertCompany(sqlite3 *pDb, const char* symbol, const char* name){
  int              returnCode;
  sqlite3_stmt     *pStmt;
  unsigned char    *buffer;

  char   *st = "INSERT INTO companies VALUES (?, ?, ?)";
  returnCode = sqlite3_prepare_v2(pDb, st, -1, &pStmt, 0);
  if(returnCode != SQLITE_OK) {
    fprintf(stderr, "Error in inserting into companies table.");
    return;
  }

  NSMutableString *imageFileName =
      [NSMutableString stringWithCString:symbol];
  [imageFileName appendString:@".png"];
  NSData * pData = [NSData dataWithContentsOfFile:imageFileName];
  buffer = malloc([pData length]);
  [pData getBytes:buffer];

  sqlite3_bind_text(pStmt, 1, symbol, -1, SQLITE_STATIC);
  sqlite3_bind_text(pStmt, 2, name, -1, SQLITE_STATIC);
  sqlite3_bind_blob(pStmt, 3, buffer,[pData length], SQLITE_STATIC);
  returnCode = sqlite3_step(pStmt);
  if(returnCode != SQLITE_DONE) {
    fprintf(stderr, "Error in inserting into companies table.");
  }
  returnCode = sqlite3_finalize(pStmt);
  if(returnCode != SQLITE_OK) {
    fprintf(stderr, "Error in inserting into companies table. ");
  }
  free(buffer);
}
```

The `insertCompany()` function starts by compiling the following `INSERT` statement:

INSERT INTO companies **VALUES** (?, ?, ?)

This statement is a little bit different from what we have used before. This type of statement is called a `parametrized statement`. It uses ? to indicate that a value that will be bound later.

To actually bind a parameter to a specific value, you use one of several functions that have the form `sqlite3_bind_xxxx()`. For example, to bind an integer, you use `sqlite3_bind_int()`. The following are the important bind functions:

- **Binding BLOBs.** The bind function for BLOBs is declared as

```
int sqlite3_bind_blob(sqlite3_stmt*, int, const void*, int n,
                      void(*)(void*))
```

  The first parameter of this and all bind functions is a pointer to a statement handle received from the statement preparation function `sqlite3_prepare_v2()`. The second parameter is the index of the SQL statement's parameter that you want to bind. Note that the index starts at 1. The third parameter is the number of bytes in the BLOB. The fourth parameter is a pointer to a function that will be invoked when the SQLite engine finishes with the execution of the statement to release the BLOB's memory. There are two special values for this parameter:

  `SQLITE_STATIC`. This special value informs the SQLite engine that the BLOB is static and does not need to be freed.

  `SQLITE_TRANSIENT`. This special value informs the SQLite engine that the BLOB is transient and needs to be copied. The SQLite engine makes a copy of the BLOB before the bind function returns.

- **Binding text.** The bind function for text is very similar to the one for BLOBs:

```
int sqlite3_bind_text(sqlite3_stmt*, int, const char*,
                      int n, void(*)(void*))
```

  The first two parameters, as well as the last one, are the same as the BLOB's bind function. The third parameter is the zero-terminated text that you would like to bind. The fourth parameter is the length (in bytes) of the text, excluding the zero terminator. If the value is negative, then the number of bytes up to the first zero terminator is used.

- **Binding integers.** The bind function for integers is very simple:

```
int sqlite3_bind_int(sqlite3_stmt*, int, int)
```

  The first two parameters are the same as above. The last parameter is the integer value.

- **Binding reals.** The bind function for real numbers is also very simple and is similar to binding integers:

```
int sqlite3_bind_double(sqlite3_stmt*, int, double)
```

  The first two parameters are the same as above. The last parameter is the real number value.

- **Binding a NULL.** This is the simplest of them all:

```
int sqlite3_bind_null(sqlite3_stmt*, int)
```

  The first two parameters are the same as above and the value is, of course, implicit.

The `insertCompany()` (see Listing 11.9) function assumes that a PNG file for each company is available. The file names are assumed to have the same name as the symbol. For example, for Alcatel-Lucent, the logo is stored in the `ALU.png` file. To retrieve the bytes of an image file, we create an `NSData` object using `NSData`'s class method `dataWithContentsOfFile:`. This method retrieves the contents of a file and builds an `NSData` object around it. Once we have the bytes in the Objective-C object, we retrieve them into a C string using the following two statements:

```
buffer = malloc([pData length]);
[pData getBytes:buffer];
```

The first statement allocates a buffer of length equal to the `NSData` object length. To retrieve the bytes, we use the instance method `getBytes:` in the second statement.

Now that we have the three values for the three SQL parameters, we use the appropriate bind function in order to complete the SQL statement. Executing the `INSERT` statement is the same as executing any other prepared statement: Just use `sqlite3_step()`. Last, we finalize the statement and free the allocated buffer because we have specified `SQLITE_STATIC` in the BLOB bind function.

The complete application can be found in the `Database 5` project in the source downloads.

11.6   Retrieving BLOBs

In the previous section, we saw how we can populate a table with records containing BLOB columns. In this section, we will learn how we can retrieve these BLOB columns. The presentation will use the same `companies` table populated before.

Listing 11.10 shows the `main()` function used to demonstrate the retrieval of BLOBs. What we would like to do is to retrieve these images and write them to the file system with a different name. The `main()` function opens the database and retrieves the images by invoking the `retrieveCompany()` function shown in Listing 11.11.

Listing 11.10   The `main()` function demonstrating the retrieval of BLOB columns from a database.

```
int main(int argc, char *argv[]) {
  sqlite3    *pDb;
  int        returnCode;
  char       *databaseName;
  NSAutoreleasePool * pool = [[NSAutoreleasePool alloc] init];
  databaseName = "financial.db";
  returnCode = sqlite3_open(databaseName, &pDb);
  if(returnCode!=SQLITE_OK) {
    fprintf(stderr,"Error in opening the database. Error: %s",
      sqlite3_errmsg(pDb));
    sqlite3_close(pDb);
    return -1;
  }
  retrieveCompany(pDb, "ALU");
  retrieveCompany(pDb, "GOOG");
```

```
        retrieveCompany(pDb, "MSFT");
        retrieveCompany(pDb, "NT");
        sqlite3_close(pDb);
        [pool release];
        return 0;
}
```

We start by preparing the following parametrized SQL statement:

SELECT image **FROM** companies **WHERE** symbol = ?

After that, we bind the sole parameter with the `symbol` parameter of the function. Note that we could have just used `sqlite3_mprintf()` to do that job without using parametrized queries. We then execute the query and check for a row result. Because there should be at most one record (the symbol is a primary key), we retrieve the BLOB column value at most once. We use `NSData` as a wrapper of the image bytes as in the following statement:

```
NSData * pData =
            [NSData dataWithBytes:sqlite3_column_blob(pStmt, 0)
                    length:sqlite3_column_bytes(pStmt, 0)];
```

The class method `dataWithBytes:length:` is declared as follows:

```
+ (id)dataWithBytes:(const void *)bytes length:(NSUInteger)length
```

It takes the bytes and length as two parameters. To retrieve the BLOB bytes from the column result, we use the function `sqlite3_column_blob()`. This function takes a pointer to the statement handle we received when we invoked the `sqlite3_prepare_v2()` function and the column index (starting from 0). The length of the BLOB bytes can be retrieved by the function `sqlite3_column_bytes()`.

Once we have retrieved the image from the database and have used an `NSData` instance as a wrapper around it, we can use the `NSData`'s instance method `writeToFile:atomically:` to write the contents of this data to a file. The method is declared as

```
- (BOOL)writeToFile:(NSString *)path atomically:(BOOL)useAuxiliaryFile
```

In addition to the file path, the `useAuxiliaryFile` is used to specify whether a temporary file should be used. If the value is `YES`, the data will be written first to a temporary file and then that temporary file will be renamed to the new name. Once we have written the file, we finalize the statement and return from the function.

Listing 11.11   The `retrieveCompany()` function used to retrieve BLOB images from the database and write them back to the file system.

```
#import "/usr/include/sqlite3.h"
void retrieveCompany(sqlite3 *pDb, const char* symbol){
    int             returnCode;
    sqlite3_stmt    *pStmt;
```

```
char    *st = "SELECT image FROM companies WHERE symbol = ?";
returnCode = sqlite3_prepare_v2(pDb, st, -1, &pStmt, 0);
if(returnCode!=SQLITE_OK) {
  fprintf(stderr, "Error retrieving image from companies.");
  return;
}
sqlite3_bind_text(pStmt, 1, symbol, -1, SQLITE_STATIC);
returnCode = sqlite3_step(pStmt);
if(returnCode == SQLITE_ROW){
  NSData * pData =
        [NSData dataWithBytes:sqlite3_column_blob(pStmt, 0)
                length:sqlite3_column_bytes(pStmt, 0)];
  NSMutableString *imageFileName  =
      [NSMutableString stringWithCString:symbol];
  [imageFileName appendString:@"-2.png"];
  [pData writeToFile:imageFileName  atomically:YES];
}
returnCode = sqlite3_finalize(pStmt);
if(returnCode != SQLITE_OK) {
  fprintf(stderr, "Error inserting into companies.");
}
}
```

The complete application can be found in the `Database 6` project in the source downloads.

11.7   Summary

This chapter covered the main aspects of using the SQLite database engine from within an iOS application. We presented the main concepts through concrete examples. We started by talking about the basic SQL statements and their implementation using SQLite function calls in Section 11.1. Then we discussed the handling of result sets generated by SQL statements in Section 11.2. After that, we addressed the topic of prepared statements in Section 11.3. Next, in Section 11.4 we talked about extensions to the SQLite C API and demonstrated that through the use of a simple user-defined function. Finally, we presented a detailed treatment of BLOB handling through the storage and retrieval of image files in Sections 11.5 and 11.6, respectively.

Exercises

(1) After reading the related chapters in this text, write a proxy that intercepts the communication with a server and caches the response for every unique URL. The proxy should return cached responses when the device is offline.

(2) Visit the SQLite home page at `www.sqlite.org` and explore the API further.

12

XML Processing

In this chapter you learn how to effectively use XML in your iOS applications. The chapter follows the same theme used in other chapters and exposes the main concepts through a working iPhone application: an RSS feed reader.

The chapter is organized as follows. Section 12.1 explains the main concepts behind XML and RSS. Section 12.2 presents a detailed discussion of Document Object Model (DOM) parsing. Section 12.3 offers another, different XML parsing technique, Simple API for XML (SAX), and shows how you can write a SAX iPhone client. In Section 12.4 we look at a table-based RSS reader application. After that, Section 12.5 presents the final thoughts on this subject. Last, Section 12.6 provides a summary of the chapter.

12.1 XML and RSS

In this section we discuss XML and then talk about RSS as one of its applications.

12.1.1 XML

Extensible Markup Language (XML) is a meta language specification for exchanging information over the Internet. As a meta language, it can be used to define application-specific languages that are then used to instantiate XML documents that adhere to the semantics of these languages.

The power behind XML is due to

- Its extensibility, which allows anyone to define new XML elements.
- Its being based on text, thus opening your application data to being used on any computing system.

To create and use an XML language, you need to identify the elements used in that language. An XML element uses

- Begin tag
- Text content
- End tag

For example, the element `person` can appear in an XML document as

```
<person>
content ...
</person>
```

`<person>` is the begin tag and `</person>` is the end tag. The content can itself be composed of text and other elements. For example:

```
<person>
  <name>content of name...</name>
  <address>content of address...</address>
</person>
```

If the text content of a given element contains characters that are difficult to include (e.g., <, >, &, etc.), entities can be used for their representation. For example, < can be represented by the entity reference <.

The facts that an XML document must have exactly one root element and that any given element may contain other elements allow us to naturally represent the XML document as a tree. For example, the following XML document can be represented as a tree (see Figure 12.1):

```
<?xml version="1.0"?>
<person>
  <name>
      <first>Homer</first>
      <last>Simpson</last>
  </name>
  <address>
      <street>1094 Evergreen Terrace</street>
      <city>Springfield</city>
      <state>TA</state>
  </address>
</person>
```

To work with an XML document, you need to be able to parse it (e.g., construct a tree representation of the document in memory as shown in Figure 12.1). There are several techniques for parsing and we will cover those in this chapter. libxml2 is an XML parser written in C that is available on, and recommended for use with, iOS. As we will see in this chapter, working with this library is very easy.

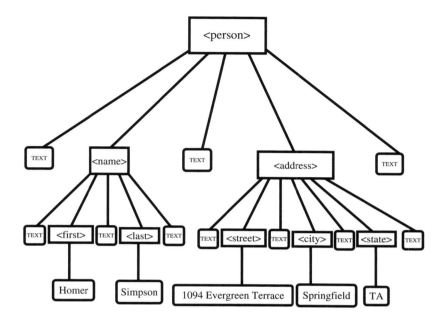

Figure 12.1   A tree representation of an XML document.

You will be able to use a few function calls to the library in order to construct a tree similar to the one shown in Figure 12.1.

We need to remember that white spaces are not ignored in XML. In Figure 12.1, we show the white spaces as TEXT nodes. In libxml2, text nodes are of type XML_TEXT_NODE, while element nodes are of type XML_ELEMENT_NODE.

Now that we have an understanding of what XML is, let's look at one of its applications: RSS.

12.1.2   RSS

Really Simple Syndication (RSS) is an XML language used for sharing web content. As a content publisher, RSS gives you the power to inform your readers about new content on your information channel. RSS allows you, as a content consumer, to target your web activities towards information that you are actually interested in. For example, if you are mainly interested in health news, you do not want to spend a lot of time on cnn.com or msnbc.com looking for health articles. What you want is a way for cnn.com or msnbc.com to tell you when new health articles become available on their web sites. The news channel can set up an XML instance file, based on the RSS language, advertising the newest health articles on its web site. You use RSS reader software to subscribe to this XML file. The reader can refresh the copy of this XML file and present it to you. This scheme provides you with efficiency and also privacy as the web site does not have to know your email address in order to inform you of new content. RSS can be thought of as both a *push* and a *pull* technology. The producer pushes filtered content that the consumer pulls.

Web sites advertise the existence of specific channels using several icons. Figure 12.2 shows some of these icons. The universal feed icon (bottom icon) is gaining wide acceptance.

Figure 12.2   Several RSS icons. The universal feed icon (bottom icon) is gaining wide acceptance.

Let's illustrate the basics of an RSS feed through an example. The Nebraska State Patrol provides an RSS feed about absconded offenders. Individuals can subscribe to this channel to stay informed. Like everything else on the Internet, an RSS feed has a URL. For example, the URL for absconded offenders in the state of Nebraska is `www.nsp.state.ne.us/SOR/Abscondedrss.xml`. Listing 12.1 shows a sample XML document of this feed.

Listing 12.1   An example of an RSS document.

```
<?xml version="1.0" encoding="UTF-8"?>
<rss version="2.0">
   <channel>
    <title>
        Nebraska State Patrol | Absconded Offenders
    </title>
    <link>
        http://www.nsp.state.ne.us/sor/
    </link>
    <description>
        The Nebraska State Patrol is currently
        seeking information on the location of the
     following individuals to determine if they are in
     compliance with the Nebraska Sex Offender
     Registration Act. This site is intended to
     generate information on these individuals
     and should not be used solely for the purpose
     of arrest. Anyone with information
```

```
   please call 402-471-8647.
</description>
<image>
   <title>Nebraska State Patrol | SOR</title>
   <url>http://www.nsp.state.ne.us/sor/rsslogo.jpg
   </url>
   <link>http://www.nsp.state.ne.us/sor/</link>
</image>

   <item>
    <title>Austen, Kate</title>
    <link>
    http://www.nsp.state.ne.us/sor/200403KA2
    </link>
    <description>
    Absconded - Jefe de una loca mujer
    </description>
   </item>

 </channel>
 </rss>
```

Every RSS feed document starts with the following :

```
<?xml version="1.0" encoding="UTF-8"?>
```

This line indicates that this is an XML document. The version attribute is mandatory, while the encoding attribute is not.

The root of the RSS feed is the rss element. This root element has only one child: the channel element. The channel element has three mandatory child elements: title, link, and description. In addition, it can hold several optional child elements, such as webMaster, image, and copyright.

The mandatory elements are required for an RSS feed to be valid. However, valid does not necessarily mean useful. To be useful, the channel element should have one or more item child elements. Each story in an RSS feed file is represented by an item element. An item element contains three child elements: (1) a title element, (2) a link element, and (3) an optional description element. The reader presents to you the title of the story, its link, and (optionally) its description. If you are interested in the story, you click the link (a URL) to visit the web page of that story.

Now that we know the structure of an RSS feed document, let's use the libxml2 library to extract information from an RSS feed. First, we present a reader using DOM; then we present another one using SAX.

But before getting into the use of the libxml2 library, we need to do some additional configurations to the XCode project.

12.1.3   Configuring the XCode project

Follow these steps to configure your project to use the `ibxml2` library:

1. **Add to Other Linker Flags of the project**. Double-click on your project node. Select the Build tab and search for `other`. Double-click on Other Linker Flags, and enter `-lxml2`. See Figure 12.3.

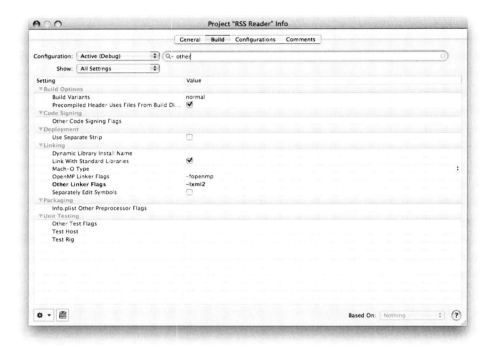

Figure 12.3   Adding OTHER_LDFLAGS = -lxml2 to the project.

2. **Add to Other Linker Flags of the target**. You also need to repeat the previous step, but instead of adding the flag to the project, you need to add it to the target. Choose `Project →
Edit Active Target` from the menu. Select the `Build` tab and search for `other`. Double-click on `Other Linker Flags` and enter `-lxml2`. See Figure 12.4.

3. **Add to the Header Search Path**. You need to add the following line to the project:

```
HEADER_SEARCH_PATHS = /usr/include/libxml2
```

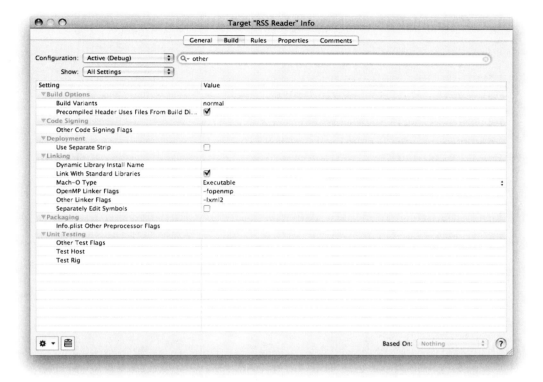

Figure 12.4 Adding OTHER_LDFLAGS = -lxml2 to the target.

Double-click on the project node, and select the Build tab. Search for header and enter the value as shown in Figure 12.5.

4. **Add the libxml2 library to the target**. Add the libxml2 library as explained in Section D.4. See Figure 12.6.

12.2   Document Object Model (DOM)

Using this model, the parser will load the whole XML document to memory and present it to the client as a tree. You can navigate the nodes of this tree and extract relevant information.

Listing 12.2 shows Objective-C code that fetches the RSS XML document from a URL, puts it into a string that the libxml2 library can work with, and then uses libxml2's functions to navigate the parsed tree and extract the relevant information.

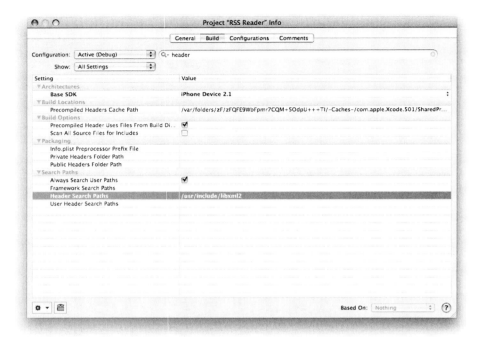

Figure 12.5   Adding `HEADER_SEARCH_PATHS` = `/usr/include/libxml2` to the project.

Figure 12.6   Adding the `libxml2` library to the target.

Listing 12.2   DOM XML parsing.

```
1  #include <libxml/xmlmemory.h>
2  #include <libxml/parser.h>
3
4  -(void)fetchAbsconders{
5    NSAutoreleasePool * pool = [[NSAutoreleasePool alloc] init];
6    NSError *err = nil;
7    NSURL * url = [NSURL URLWithString:feedURL];
```

```
8    NSString *URLContents = [NSString stringWithContentsOfURL:url
9                              encoding:NSUTF8StringEncoding error:&err];
10   if(!URLContents)
11     return;
12   const char *XMLChars =
13   [URLContents cStringUsingEncoding:NSUTF8StringEncoding];
14
15   if(parser == XML_PARSER_DOM){
16     xmlDocPtr doc = xmlParseMemory(XMLChars, strlen(XMLChars));
17     xmlNodePtr cur;
18     if (doc == NULL ) {
19       return;
20     }
21     cur = xmlDocGetRootElement(doc);
22     cur = findNextItem(cur);
23     while (cur){
24       XOAbsconder *absconder =  getitem(doc, cur);
25       if(absconder){
26         [absconders addObject:absconder];
27       }
28       cur = findNextItem(cur->next);
29     }
30     xmlFreeDoc(doc);
31   }
```

On line 7, we create an NSURL object from the URL address string representation, feedURL, of the RSS feed address. The statement on lines 8 and 9 uses the NSString's class method stringWithContentsOfURL:encoding:error: to create a string containing the contents of the URL. The method fetches the RSS feed file from the server and puts it in the NSString instance, URLContents.

On line 10, we check to see if the string was successfully created. If it was not, the fetchAbsconders method returns without changing the absconders array. Of course, in a production code, you will use the error object to propagate the error to the client.

Once we have an NSString object with the contents of the RSS feed file, we need to convert it to a C string (**char***), the format that libxml2 works with. The statement on lines 12 and 13 does just that. We use the NSString instance method cStringUsingEncoding: with the encoding NSUTF8StringEncoding.

The fetchAbsconders method demonstrates the use of two XML parsing schemes. Listing 12.2 shows the first half of this method and covers the DOM parsing.

To work with any XML document using DOM, you first need to load it into memory in the form of a tree. The function to achieve that is xmlParseMemory(). The function is declared in parser.h as

xmlDocPtr xmlParseMemory (**const char** * buffer, **int** size)

It takes the XML document, represented by a C string, and the size of this string as input. It returns a pointer to the tree representation of the parsed document in the form of `xmlDocPtr` (a pointer to `xmlDoc`).

The `xmlDoc` is a structure defined in `tree.h`. The following shows the first few lines of this structure:

```
struct _xmlDoc {
    void            *_private; /* application data */
    xmlElementType  type;       /* XML_DOCUMENT_NODE */
    char    *name;  /* name/filename/URI of the document */
    struct _xmlNode *children;  /* the document tree */
    struct _xmlNode *last;  /* last child link */
    struct _xmlNode *parent;  /* child->parent link */
...
};
```

Now that we have a tree representation of the XML document, we can start traversing it. To begin traversing, line 21 obtains the root node using the function `xmlDocGetRootElement()`. The function returns `xmlNodePtr`, which is a pointer to the root node, `xmlNode`.

Every node is represented by the `xmlNode` structure defined in `tree.h` as follows:

```
typedef struct _xmlNode xmlNode;
typedef xmlNode *xmlNodePtr;

struct _xmlNode {
    void            *_private; /* application data */
    xmlElementType   type;/* type number*/
    const xmlChar   *name; /* name of the node, or entity */
    struct _xmlNode *children;/* parent->children link */
    struct _xmlNode *last;   /* last child link */
    struct _xmlNode *parent;/* child->parent link */
    struct _xmlNode *next;/* next sibling link  */
    struct _xmlNode *prev;  /* previous sibling link  */
    struct _xmlDoc  *doc; /* the containing document */

    /* End of common part */
    xmlNs   *ns; /* pointer to the associated namespace */
    xmlChar *content;   /* the content */
    struct _xmlAttr *properties;/* properties list */
    xmlNs   *nsDef; /* namespace definitions on this node */
    void    *psvi; /* for type/PSVI informations */
    unsigned short  line;   /* line number */
    unsigned short  extra; /* extra data for XPath/XSLT */
};
```

Most of these fields are self-explanatory. You will be dealing mostly with the fields that link to other nodes. If you are at a given node, you can go to its parent using the `parent` field. If you want its children, use `children`. If you want the siblings (i.e., those nodes with same parent as your parent), use the `next` field.

Figure 12.7 shows a graphical representation of the navigational links available for various nodes in the document tree.

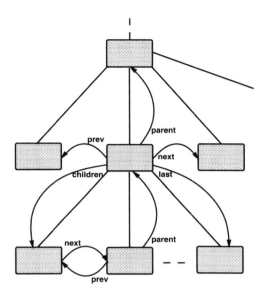

Figure 12.7   Representation of the navigational links available for various nodes in the document tree.

Now that we have a pointer to the root of the document, we search for the first `item` in the RSS feed. This is shown in the statement on line 22: `cur = findNextItem(cur)`. The function `findNextItem()` is defined in Listing 12.3.

Listing 12.3   Searching for an `item` element in the RSS feed.

```
xmlNodePtr findNextItem(xmlNodePtr curr){
  if(!curr)
    return curr;
  if ((!xmlStrcmp(curr->name, (const xmlChar *)"item")) &&
        (curr->type == XML_ELEMENT_NODE)) {
    return curr;
  }
  if(curr->type == XML_TEXT_NODE){
    return findNextItem(curr->next);
  }
  if(curr->type == XML_ELEMENT_NODE){
    if ((!xmlStrcmp(curr->name, (const xmlChar *)"channel"))
        || (!xmlStrcmp(curr->name, (const xmlChar *)"rss"))){
```

```
            return  findNextItem(curr->xmlChildrenNode);
    }
  }
  if(curr->type == XML_ELEMENT_NODE){
    if((!xmlStrcmp(curr->name, (const xmlChar *)"title"))
        || (!xmlStrcmp(curr->name, (const xmlChar *)"link"))
        || (!xmlStrcmp(curr->name,(const xmlChar *)"description"))
        || (!xmlStrcmp(curr->name, (const xmlChar *)"image")))){
          return  findNextItem(curr->next);
    }
  }
  return NULL;
}
```

The function makes recursive calls to itself as long as the item tag has not been found. At the beginning, we check for the termination condition. We use the xmlStrcmp() function to see if the node's name is "item". If yes, we return the pointer to that node. The rest of the code has similar logic. The only difference is that when we are interested in a given subtree, we use the xmlChildrenNode link to traverse that subtree. If we are not interested in the node, we skip the subtree altogether and go to the next sibling using the next link.

Now that we have a pointer to an item element node, we retrieve the three element children and build an Objective-C object from the data. The function getitem() is where such logic is found. The function is called as follows:

```
XOAbsconder *absconder =  getitem(doc, cur);
```

getitem() takes the document and node pointers and returns either the XOAbsconder object or nil. Listing 12.4 presents the implementation of the getitem() function.

Listing 12.4   Building an XOAbsconder object from an item element.

```
XOAbsconder* getitem (xmlDocPtr doc, xmlNodePtr curr){
  xmlChar *name, *link, *description;
  curr = curr->xmlChildrenNode;
  if(!curr)
    return nil;
  while (curr && (curr->type == XML_TEXT_NODE))
    curr = curr->next;
  if(!curr)
    return nil;
  if ((!xmlStrcmp(curr->name,(const xmlChar *)"title")) &&
      (curr->type == XML_ELEMENT_NODE)) {
    name = xmlNodeListGetString(doc, curr->xmlChildrenNode, 1);
    curr = curr->next;
    while (curr && (curr->type == XML_TEXT_NODE))
      curr = curr->next;
    if(!curr){
```

```
        xmlFree(name);
        return nil;
    }
}
else
    return nil;
if ((!xmlStrcmp(curr->name, (const xmlChar *)"link")) &&
(curr->type == XML_ELEMENT_NODE)) {
    link = xmlNodeListGetString(doc, curr->xmlChildrenNode, 1);
    curr = curr->next;
    while (curr && (curr->type == XML_TEXT_NODE))
        curr = curr->next;
    if(!curr){
        xmlFree(name);
        xmlFree(link);
        return nil;
    }
}
else
    return nil;
if ((!xmlStrcmp(curr->name, (const xmlChar *)"description")) &&
        (curr->type == XML_ELEMENT_NODE)) {
    description = xmlNodeListGetString(doc, curr->xmlChildrenNode, 1);
}
else{
    xmlFree(name);
    xmlFree(link);
    xmlFree(description);
    return nil;
}
XOAbsconder *abscender = [[XOAbsconder alloc]
    initWithName:[NSString stringWithCString:name]
    andURL:[NSString stringWithCString:link]
    andDescription:[NSString stringWithCString:description]];
[abscender autorelease];
xmlFree(name);
xmlFree(link);
xmlFree(description);
return abscender;
}
```

We traverse all the children of the node. Because in XML white space is recognized as a valid child node, we skip those at the beginning:

```
while (curr && (curr->type == XML_TEXT_NODE))
    curr = curr->next;
```

Once we have skipped the text nodes, we check for the three elements: title, link, and description. The function requires that they appear in that order.

To retrieve the text value for each of these three elements, we can use the xmlNodeListGet-String function. The function is declared in tree.h as

```
xmlChar *xmlNodeListGetString  (xmlDocPtr doc,xmlNodePtr list,int inLine)
```

It constructs a string from the node list. If inLine is 1, the entity contents are replaced. The function returns the string and the caller is responsible for freeing the memory of the string using the xmlFree() function.

After retrieving the text of the three elements, we create the XOAbsconder, autorelease it, free the memory of the three strings, and return the XOAbsconder object.

Back to Listing 12.2, the fetchAbsconders method keeps calling the getitem() function and adding the objects to the absconders array in the statement

```
[absconders addObject:absconder];
```

When the fetchAbsconders method is finished, the absconders array contains the absconder objects created and populated from the RSS feed document.

12.3   Simple API for XML (SAX)

We have seen in Section 12.2 how DOM loads the entire XML document to memory and allows you to navigate the nodes. In some applications, the size of the XML document may prevent loading the whole document due to limited device memory. *Simple API for XML* (SAX) is another XML parsing model that is different from DOM. In SAX, you configure the parser with callback functions. The SAX parser will use these function pointers to call your functions, informing you of important events. For example, if you are interested in the event Start of Document, you set up a function for this event and give the parser a pointer to it.

Listing 12.5 shows the remainder of the fetchAbsconders method pertaining to SAX parsing.

Listing 12.5   SAX XML parsing. Remainder of fetchAbsconders method.

```
  else if(parser == XML_PARSER_SAX){
    xmlParserCtxtPtr ctxt = xmlCreateDocParserCtxt(XMLChars);
    int parseResult =
      xmlSAXUserParseMemory(&rssSAXHandler, self, XMLChars,
                            strlen(XMLChars));
    xmlFreeParserCtxt(ctxt);
    xmlCleanupParser();
  }
  [pool release];
}
```

To use SAX in `libxml2`, you first set up a parser context using the function `xmlCreateDocParserCtxt()`, which takes a single parameter: the XML document represented as a C string. After that, you start the SAX parser by calling the `xmlSAXUserParse-Memory()` function. The function is declared in `parser.h` as

```
int xmlSAXUserParseMemory (xmlSAXHandlerPtr sax, void * user_data,
                           const char * buffer, int size)
```

This function parses an in-memory buffer and calls your registered functions as necessary. The first parameter to this function is a pointer to the SAX handler. The SAX handler is a structure holding the pointers to your callback functions. The second parameter is an optional pointer that is application-specific. The value specified will be used as the context when the SAX parser calls your callback functions. The third and fourth parameters are used for the C string XML document in memory and its length, respectively.

The SAX handler is where you store the pointers to your callback functions. If you are not interested in an event type, just store a `NULL` value in its field. The following is the definition of the structure in `tree.h`:

```
struct _xmlSAXHandler {
    internalSubsetSAXFunc internalSubset;
    isStandaloneSAXFunc isStandalone;
    hasInternalSubsetSAXFunc  hasInternalSubset;
    hasExternalSubsetSAXFunc  hasExternalSubset;
    resolveEntitySAXFunc  resolveEntity;
    getEntitySAXFunc  getEntity;
    entityDeclSAXFunc entityDecl;
    notationDeclSAXFunc notationDecl;
    attributeDeclSAXFunc  attributeDecl;
    elementDeclSAXFunc  elementDecl;
    unparsedEntityDeclSAXFunc unparsedEntityDecl;
    setDocumentLocatorSAXFunc setDocumentLocator;
    startDocumentSAXFunc  startDocument;
    endDocumentSAXFunc  endDocument;
    startElementSAXFunc startElement;
    endElementSAXFunc endElement;
    referenceSAXFunc  reference;
    charactersSAXFunc characters;
    ignorableWhitespaceSAXFunc  ignorableWhitespace;
    processingInstructionSAXFunc  processingInstruction;
    commentSAXFunc  comment;
    warningSAXFunc  warning;
    errorSAXFunc  error;
    fatalErrorSAXFunc fatalError;
    getParameterEntitySAXFunc getParameterEntity;
    cdataBlockSAXFunc  cdataBlock;
    externalSubsetSAXFunc  externalSubset;
    unsigned int  initialized;
```

```
    // The following fields are extensions
    void * _private;
    startElementNsSAX2Func  startElementNs;
    endElementNsSAX2Func  endElementNs;
    xmlStructuredErrorFunc  serror;
};
```

Listing 12.6 shows our SAX handler.

Listing 12.6 SAX handler.

```
static xmlSAXHandler rssSAXHandler ={
NULL,                          /* internalSubset */
NULL,                          /* isStandalone   */
NULL,                          /* hasInternalSubset */
NULL,                          /* hasExternalSubset */
NULL,                          /* resolveEntity */
NULL,                          /* getEntity */
NULL,                          /* entityDecl */
NULL,                          /* notationDecl */
NULL,                          /* attributeDecl */
NULL,                          /* elementDecl */
NULL,                          /* unparsedEntityDecl */
NULL,                          /* setDocumentLocator */
NULL,                          /* startDocument */
NULL,                          /* endDocument */
NULL,                          /* startElement*/
NULL,                          /* endElement */
NULL,                          /* reference */
charactersFoundSAX,            /* characters */
NULL,                          /* ignorableWhitespace */
NULL,                          /* processingInstruction */
NULL,                          /* comment */
NULL,                          /* warning */
errorEncounteredSAX,           /* error */
fatalErrorEncounteredSAX,      /* fatalError */
NULL,                          /* getParameterEntity */
NULL,                          /* cdataBlock */
NULL,                          /* externalSubset */
XML_SAX2_MAGIC,                //
NULL,
startElementSAX,               /* startElementNs */
endElementSAX,                 /* endElementNs */
NULL,                          /* serror */
};
```

Aside from the function pointers, the initialized field should be set to the value XML_SAX2_MAGIC in order to indicate that the handler is used for a SAX2 parser. Once you call the xmlSAXUserParseMemory(), the SAX parser starts the parsing of the document and calling your registered callback functions.

We are mainly interested in three functions: `startElementNsSAX2Func()`, `endElement-NsSAX2Func()`, and `charactersSAXFunc()`.

`startElementNsSAX2Func()` is called when the parser encounters the start of a new element. `startElementNsSAX2Func()` is defined in `tree.h` as

```
void  startElementNsSAX2Func (void * ctx, const xmlChar * localname,
                              const xmlChar * prefix, const xmlChar *URI,
                              int nb_namespaces,
                              const xmlChar ** namespaces,
                              int nb_attributes, int nb_defaulted,
                              const xmlChar ** attributes)
```

`ctx` is the user data, and it is the second value you used when you called the function `xmlSAXUserParseMemory()`. In our case, it is a pointer to the class `XORSSFeedNebraska`. Then `localname` is the local name of the element. `prefix` is the element namespace prefix (if available). `URI` is the element namespace name (if available). `nb_namespaces` is the number of namespace definitions on that node. `namespaces` is a pointer to the array of prefix/URI pair namespace definitions. `nb_attributes` is the number of attributes on that node. `nb_defaulted` is the number of defaulted attributes. The defaulted ones are at the end of the array. `attributes` is a pointer to the array of (local name/prefix/URI/value/end) attribute values.

Listing 12.7 shows the definition of our `startElementNsSAX2Func()` function.

Listing 12.7   The `startElementSAX()` callback function.

```
static void
startElementSAX(void *ctx,
                const xmlChar *localname,
                const xmlChar *prefix,
                const xmlChar *URI,
                int nb_namespaces,
                const xmlChar **namespaces,
                int nb_attributes,
                int nb_defaulted,
                const xmlChar **attributes)
{
  NSAutoreleasePool *pool = [[NSAutoreleasePool alloc] init];
  XORSSFeedNebraska  *feedNebraska = (XORSSFeedNebraska*) ctx;
  if (feedNebraska.currentElementContent) {
    [feedNebraska.currentElementContent release];
    feedNebraska.currentElementContent = nil;
  }
  if ((!xmlStrcmp(localname, (const xmlChar *)"item"))) {
    feedNebraska.currAbsconder = [[XOAbsconder alloc] init];
  }
  [pool release];
}
```

It's good practice to have an autorelease pool per function. We start by casting the `ctx` to a pointer to our class `XORSSFeedNebraska`. The class and its parent are declared in Listings 12.8 and 12.9.

Listing 12.8   The `XORSSFeedNebraska` class declaration.

```
#import "XORSSFeed.h"
@interface XORSSFeedNebraska : XORSSFeed {
}
@end
```

Listing 12.9   The `XORSSFeed` class declaration.

```
@class XOAbsconder;
typedef enum {
  XML_PARSER_DOM,
  XML_PARSER_SAX
} XMLParser;

@interface XORSSFeed : NSObject {
  NSString            *feedURL;
  NSMutableArray      *absconders;
  XMLParser           parser;
  NSMutableString     *currentElementContent;
  XOAbsconder         *currAbsconder;
}
@property(nonatomic, copy)   NSString            *feedURL;
@property(nonatomic, assign) XMLParser           parser;
@property(nonatomic, assign) NSMutableString     *currentElementContent;
@property(nonatomic, assign) XOAbsconder *currAbsconder;
-(id)init;
-(id)initWithURL:(NSString*) feedURL;
-(void)fetchAbsconders;
-(NSUInteger)numberOfAbsconders;
-(XOAbsconder*)absconderAtIndex:(NSUInteger) index;
-(void)addAbsconder:(XOAbsconder*)absconder;
@end
```

The `XORSSFeedNebraska` object has an instance variable of type `NSMutableString` called `currentElementContent`. This variable holds the text value inside an element. It's constructed in our `charactersFoundSAX()` function and used in the `endElementSAX()` function. The function `startElementSAX()` always `releases` and so we set this instance variable to `nil` (if it is not already `nil`). This will ensure that we start with an empty string for holding the text. If the element name is `item`, we create a new object of the `XOAbsconder` class. This is a simple class holding the three pieces of information about an individual absconder. Listing 12.10 shows the declaration of the `XOAbsconder` and Listing 12.11 shows its definition.

Listing 12.10   The XOAbsconder class declaration.

```objc
#import <UIKit/UIKit.h>
@interface XOAbsconder : NSObject {
NSString *name;
NSString *furtherInfoURL;
NSString *desc;
}

@property(copy) NSString *name;
@property(copy) NSString *furtherInfoURL;
@property(copy) NSString *desc;
-(id)init;
-(id)initWithName:(NSString*)name
     andURL:(NSString*)url
     andDescription:(NSString*)desc;
-(NSString*)description;
@end
```

Listing 12.11   The XOAbsconder class definition.

```objc
#import "XOAbsconder.h"

@implementation XOAbsconder
@synthesize name;
@synthesize furtherInfoURL;
@synthesize desc;

-(id)initWithName:(NSString*)name
     andURL:(NSString*)url
     andDescription:(NSString*)description{
  self = [super init];
  if(self){
    self.name = name;
    self.furtherInfoURL = url;
    self.desc = description;
  }
  return self;
}

-(id)init{
  return [self initWithName:@"" andURL:@"" andDescription:@""];
}

-(NSString*)description{
  return [NSString stringWithString:name];
}

-(void)dealloc{
```

```
    [name release];
    [furtherInfoURL release];
    [desc release];
    [super dealloc];
}
@end
```

Our endElementNsSAX2Func() function is called endElementSAX() and is shown in
Listing 12.12.

Listing 12.12   The endElementSAX() function definition.

```
static void
endElementSAX (void *ctx,
                const xmlChar *localname,
                const xmlChar *prefix,
                const xmlChar *URI)
{
  NSAutoreleasePool *pool = [[NSAutoreleasePool alloc] init];
  XORSSFeedNebraska  *feedNebraska = (XORSSFeedNebraska*) ctx;
  if ((!xmlStrcmp(localname, (const xmlChar *)"item"))) {
    if(feedNebraska.currAbsconder){
      [feedNebraska    addAbsconder:feedNebraska.currAbsconder];
    }
    [feedNebraska.currAbsconder release];
    feedNebraska.currAbsconder = nil;
  }
  else if ((!xmlStrcmp(localname,(const xmlChar *)"title"))) {
    if(feedNebraska.currAbsconder){
      feedNebraska.currAbsconder.name =
          feedNebraska.currentElementContent;
    }
  }
  else if ((!xmlStrcmp(localname, (const xmlChar *)"link"))) {
    if(feedNebraska.currAbsconder){
      feedNebraska.currAbsconder.furtherInfoURL =
          feedNebraska.currentElementContent;
    }
  }
  else if ((!xmlStrcmp(localname,(const xmlChar *)"description"))) {
    if(feedNebraska.currAbsconder){
      feedNebraska.currAbsconder.desc =
                            feedNebraska.currentElementContent;
    }
  }

  if (feedNebraska.currentElementContent) {
    [feedNebraska.currentElementContent release];
```

```
            feedNebraska.currentElementContent = nil;
    }
    [pool release];
}
```

The function first checks to see if the element's name is item. If it is, then we add the XOAbsconder object, which was constructed by the other callback functions. Otherwise, we check for the three element names: title, link, and description. For each of these elements, we set its respective text value gathered by the charactersSAXFunc() function. For example, the following sets the desc instance variable with the current text value:

```
feedNebraska.currAbsconder.desc = feedNebraska.currentElementContent;
```

The text of the element is stored in charactersSAXFunc(). The function is declared in parser.h as

```
void charactersSAXFunc (void * ctx, const xmlChar * ch, int len)
```

This function is called by the parser, informing you of newfound characters. In addition to the context, you receive the string of characters and its length. Between the start of an element and the end of that element, this function might be called several times. Your function should take this into account and append the new text to the current string.

Our charactersFoundSAX() function is shown in Listing 12.13.

Listing 12.13   The charactersFoundSAX() function definition.

```
static void charactersFoundSAX(void * ctx, const xmlChar * ch, int len){
    NSAutoreleasePool *pool = [[NSAutoreleasePool alloc] init];
    XORSSFeedNebraska  *feedNebraska =(XORSSFeedNebraska*) ctx;
    CFStringRef str =
          CFStringCreateWithBytes(kCFAllocatorSystemDefault,
                ch, len, kCFStringEncodingUTF8, false)
    if (!feedNebraska.currentElementContent) {
      feedNebraska.currentElementContent = [[NSMutableString alloc] init];
    }
    [feedNebraska.currentElementContent appendString:(NSString *)str];
    CFRelease(str);
    [pool release];
}
```

The function starts by casting the ctx into a XORSSFeedNebraska instance. Using this pointer, we can call our Objective-C class. After that, we create a string from received characters by using the function CFStringCreateWithBytes(), which is declared as follows:

```
CFStringRef CFStringCreateWithBytes (
    CFAllocatorRef alloc,
    const UInt8 *bytes,
    CFIndex numBytes,
```

```
    CFStringEncoding encoding,
    Boolean isExternalRepresentation
);
```

The first parameter is used to specify the memory allocator. kCFAllocatorDefault is used for the current default allocator. The second parameter is the buffer that contains the characters. The third parameter specifies the number of bytes. The fourth parameter is the encoding. We use kCFStringEncodingUTF8 for UTF8 encoding. The fifth parameter is used to specify if the characters in the buffer are in an external representation format. Because they are not, we use false.

Once we have the string representation of the characters, we check to see if this is the first time charactersFoundSAX has been called for the current element. Recall that the parser can call this function multiple times, supplying the content of a single element. If it is the first time, we allocate our mutable string. After that, we append the string that we created from the character buffer to the mutable string. When the endElementSAX() function is called, we retrieve this string to build our Objective-C object, currAbsconder. When we are finished with the string str, we use the CFRelease() function to deallocate it.

Finally, the error handling functions are shown in Listings 12.14 and 12.15. As in all other event functions, what you do for error handling depends on your application. In our example, we release the currAbsconder object that we are constructing and log the problem.

Listing 12.14 The errorEncounteredSAX() function definition.

```
static void errorEncounteredSAX (void * ctx, const char * msg, ...){
  XORSSFeedNebraska  *feedNebraska = (XORSSFeedNebraska*) ctx;
  if(feedNebraska.currAbsconder){
    [feedNebraska.currAbsconder release];
    feedNebraska.currAbsconder = nil;
  }
  NSLog(@"errorEncountered: %s", msg);
}
```

Listing 12.15 The fatalErrorEncounteredSAX() function definition.

```
static void fatalErrorEncounteredSAX (void * ctx, const char * msg, ...){
  XORSSFeedNebraska  *feedNebraska = (XORSSFeedNebraska*) ctx;
  if(feedNebraska.currAbsconder){
    [feedNebraska.currAbsconder release];
    feedNebraska.currAbsconder = nil;
  }
  NSLog(@"fatalErrorEncountered: %s", msg);
}
```

12.4 An RSS Reader Application

In this section, we present a working iPhone application based on the code developed so far. The application will present the contents of an RSS feed to the user in a scrollable table view. The complete application can be found in the RSS Reader project in the source downloads.

Listing 12.16 shows the application delegate declaration and definition. The application delegate uses an instance of the class XORSSFeedNebraska to retrieve the XML document and parse it to generate the items.

Listing 12.16   The RSS reader application delegate declaration and definition.

```
#import <UIKit/UIKit.h>
#import "XORSSFeedNebraska.h"
@interface XORSSFeedAppDelegate : NSObject {
 UIWindow *window;
 UINavigationController *navigationController;
 XORSSFeedNebraska *rssFeed;
}
@property (nonatomic, retain)
   UINavigationController *navigationController;
@end


#import "XORSSFeedAppDelegate.h"
#import "XORSSFeedNebraska.h"
#import "RootViewController.h"


@implementation XORSSFeedAppDelegate
@synthesize navigationController;
- (void)applicationDidFinishLaunching:(UIApplication *)application {
    window =
        [[UIWindow alloc] initWithFrame:[[UIScreen  mainScreen] bounds]];
   // Create the navigation and view controllers
   RootViewController *rootViewController =
       [[RootViewController alloc] init];
   UINavigationController *aNavigationController =
       [[UINavigationController alloc]
            initWithRootViewController:rootViewController];
   self.navigationController = aNavigationController;
   [aNavigationController release];
   [rootViewController release];
   // Configure and show the window
   [window addSubview:[navigationController view]];
   rssFeed = [[XORSSFeedNebraska alloc] init];
   [rssFeed fetchAbsconders];
   [window makeKeyAndVisible];
}
-(NSString*)xoTitle{
```

```
    return @"Nebraska Absconders";
}
- (NSInteger)countOfList {
    return [rssFeed numberOfAbsconders];
}
- (id)objectInListAtIndex:(NSUInteger)theIndex {
    return [rssFeed absconderAtIndex:theIndex];
}
- (void)dealloc {
    [window release];
    [navigationController release];
    [rssFeed release];
    [super dealloc];
}
@end
```

The delegate's `applicationDidFinishLaunching:` method creates a window and the table view
controller. It then asks the instance of `XORSSFeedNebraska` to fetch the XML and parse it by calling
the `fetchAbsconders` method. The table view controller's declaration and definition are shown in
Listing 12.17.

Listing 12.17   The RSS reader table controller declaration and definition.

```
#import <UIKit/UIKit.h>
@interface RootViewController : UITableViewController {
}
@end


#import "RootViewController.h"
#import "XOAbsconder.h"
#import "XORSSFeedAppDelegate.h"
@implementation RootViewController
- init {
  if (self = [super init]) {
    XORSSFeedAppDelegate *appDelegate =
      (XORSSFeedAppDelegate*)[[UIApplication sharedApplication] delegate];
    self.title = [appDelegate xoTitle];
  }
  return self;
}
- (NSInteger)numberOfSectionsInTableView:(UITableView *)tableView {
  return 1;
}
- (NSInteger)tableView:(UITableView *)tableView
    numberOfRowsInSection:(NSInteger)section {
  XORSSFeedAppDelegate *appDelegate =
   (XORSSFeedAppDelegate*)[[UIApplication sharedApplication] delegate];
  return [appDelegate countOfList];
```

```
}
- (UITableViewCell *)tableView:(UITableView *)tableView
  cellForRowAtIndexPath:(NSIndexPath *)indexPath{
  UITableViewCell *cell =
     [tableView dequeueReusableCellWithIdentifier:@"XO"];
  if (cell == nil) {
    cell = [[[UITableViewCell alloc]
                      initWithStyle:UITableViewCellStyleDefault
                      reuseIdentifier:@"XO"] autorelease];
  }
  XORSSFeedAppDelegate *appDelegate =
     (XORSSFeedAppDelegate*)[[UIApplication sharedApplication] delegate];
  XOAbsconder *absconder =
     [appDelegate objectInListAtIndex:indexPath.row];
  cell.textLabel.text = [absconder description];
  return cell;
}
@end
```

As you have learned from previous chapters, the table view controller is the data source and delegate of the table view. It uses the application delegate to respond to the queries about the table's data model (e.g., number of rows, etc.).

Figure 12.8 shows a screen shot of the application main window.

Figure 12.8 The Nebraska Absconders RSS reader application.

12.5   Putting It Together

There are two approaches to XML parsing: DOM and SAX. DOM builds a tree representation of the XML document and allows you to navigate the nodes. SAX sequentially parses the document, calling your registered functions appropriately. If you like to write the least amount of code, use DOM. If the XML document is large, use SAX. If you are interested in a couple of nodes in the XML document, use SAX. If you will process most of the document, use DOM. If you would like to write the XML document back to a file, use DOM. If the application accesses the XML document sequentially, use SAX. If you want to make a lot of modifications to the XML document, use DOM. If the XML document is central to your application and you have many methods or objects working on it, use DOM.

To use DOM parsing in your application, follow these steps:

1. **Create an** `NSURL` **object from the XML document URL address.**

2. **Create an** `NSString` **instance to hold the actual XML document by calling** `NSString`**'s class method** `stringWithContentsOfURL:encoding:error:`. This method will fetch the XML document from the Internet and store it in a Cocoa string.

3. **Convert the Cocoa string to a C-based string using the** `NSString` **instance method** `cStringUsingEncoding:`**, and use** `NSUTF8StringEncoding`**.**

4. **Use the** `libxml2` **function** `xmlParseMemory()` **to load the C string XML document into memory in the form of a tree.**

5. **Obtain a pointer to the root element and start traversing the tree according to your application's requirements.**

6. **To obtain the text value of an element, use the function** `xmlNodeListGetString()`**.**

7. **Any time you retrieve a string value from** `libxml2`**, know that it is your responsibility to deallocate it.** Use the `xmlFree()` function to do just that. Call `xmlFreeDoc()` when you are finished.

To use SAX parsing in your application, follow these steps:

1. **Create a structure of type** `xmlSAXHandler`**.** Fill the entries representing the events that you are interested in receiving with pointers to your event functions. Make sure that the `initialized` entry is set to `XML_SAX2_MAGIC`.

   Different events have different function signatures. For example, `charactersFoundSAX()` is declared as

   ```
   charactersFoundSAX(void *ctx, const xmlChar *ch, int len)
   ```

2. **Locate the appropriate function signature in** `libxml2`**'s** `tree.h` **file.**

3. **For meaningful XML parsing, create at least three functions:**

- `startElementNsSAX2Func`. This function is called when the parser encounters a begin tag.
- `charactersSAXFunc`. This function is called (potentially more than once for a given element) to provide you with characters found inside the element.
- `endElementNsSAX2Func`. This function is called when the parser encounters an end tag.

4. **Before you start parsing the document, create a document parser context by calling** `xmlCreateDocParserCtxt()` **and passing the C string XML document as the sole argument.**

5. **After setting up the event functions and the SAX handler, call** `libxml2`**'s function** `xmlSAXUserParseMemory()`**, passing in**

   - A pointer to the handler.
   - A pointer to a context. The context can point to any object (e.g., a Cocoa object).
   - The C string representing the XML document and its length in bytes.

   The parser will start parsing the document and firing the events. If you have registered in the handler a function for a given event, that function will be called.

6. **Following the call to** `xmlSAXUserParseMemory()`**, free the context by calling** `xmlFreeParserCtxt()`**, and clear the parser by calling** `xmlCleanupParser()`**.**

12.6   Summary

This chapter addressed the techniques used to natively process XML on iOS devices. Section 12.1 explained the main concepts behind XML and one of its languages, RSS. Section 12.2 presented a detailed discussion of DOM parsing. Section 12.3 offered a different XML parsing technique, SAX, and showed how you can write a SAX iPhone client. In Section 12.4 we looked at a table-based RSS reader application. Finally, Section 12.5 presented the final thoughts on this subject.

Exercises

(1) There are several web services available at `http://ws.geonames.org/`. The Wikipedia Full-Text Search returns the Wikipedia entries found for a given query. The returned result of executing this web service is an XML document. There are several parameters for this web service. The parameter `q` is where you specify the query, and `maxRows` is the maximum number of records that can be returned. The full description of the web service can be found at

   `www.geonames.org/export/wikipedia-webservice.html#wikipediaSearch`.

   As an example, the URL request

   `http://ws.geonames.org/wikipediaSearch?q=plano,texas&maxRows=10`

will return an XML document with result entries. Here is a partial listing of the XML document:

```
<?xml version="1.0" encoding="UTF-8" standalone="no"?>
<geonames>
<entry>
<lang>en</lang>
<title>Plano, Texas</title>
<summary>
Plano is a city in Collin and Denton Counties in
the US state of Texas. Located mainly within
Collin County, it is a wealthy northern suburb
of Dallas. The population was 222,030 at the
2000 census, making it the ninth largest city in
Texas. According to a 2005 census estimate,
Plano had grown to 250,096 making
Plano the sixty-ninth most populous city in the
United States (...)
</summary>
<feature>city</feature>
<countryCode>US</countryCode>
<population>245411</population>
<elevation>0</elevation>
<lat>33.0193</lat>
<lng>-96.7008</lng>
<wikipediaUrl>
http://en.wikipedia.org/wiki/Plano%2C_Texas
</wikipediaUrl>
<thumbnailImg/>
</entry>
.
.
.
</geonames>
```

Write an iPhone application that presents this information in tabular form.

(2) XPath (XML Path Language) is a language for selecting nodes from an XML document. Read more about it at www.w3.org/TR/xpath and investigate how you can use the libxml2 library to perform XPath operations.

13

Location Awareness

This chapter addresses the topic of location awareness. First, Section 13.1 covers the Core Location framework and how to use it to build location-aware applications. After that, Section 13.2 discusses a simple location-aware application. Next, Section 13.3 covers the topic of geocoding. In that section, you learn how to translate postal addresses into geographical locations. In Section 13.4, you learn how to sample movement of the device and display that information on maps. After that, Section 13.5 discusses how to relate zip codes to geographical information. In that section, you also learn the actual formula that implements the distance between two locations. Next, Section 13.6 shows you how to utilize the Map Kit API to add an interactive map to your view hierarchy. Finally, we summarize the chapter in Section 13.7.

13.1   The Core Location Framework

The second generation of the iPhone (iPhone 3G) and later models are equipped with a Global Positioning System (GPS) chip. GPS utilizes three or four satellites to triangulate the position of a point on Earth. The accuracy of the point's position using this technique ranges from 5 to 40 meters.

The first generation of the iPhone uses non-GPS techniques for identifying the location of the device. Non-GPS techniques such as cell identification, time of arrival (TOA), and Enhanced Observed Time Difference (E-OTD) can be used in conjunction with Wi-Fi and Bluetooth to provide a reasonable substitute for the lack of a GPS chip [1]. Of course, the locational accuracy of these methods is much lower than GPS and ranges from 100 to 500 meters.

Regardless of the technique used, iOS provides the Core Location framework [2] as a software interface with whatever technique(s) are used to find the location. The framework provides classes and protocols that you can use to get the current location within a specified accuracy as well as to schedule future updates of the current location.

The main class of the Core Location framework is `CLLocationManager`. `CLLocationManager` is the entry point that the developer uses to gain current and future location information. You use an instance of `CLLocationManager` to schedule future updates of the current location of the device.

To gain access to the current location's information, follow these steps:

1. **Create an instance of** `CLLocationManager` **if one does not exist.**

2. **Configure the** `CLLocationManager` **instance.** You need to configure the instance of the manager with the following parameters:

   - `desiredAccuracy`. Using this property, you tell the framework about your needs with respect to the accuracy of the location (in terms of meters). The `desiredAccuracy` property is declared as follows:

     `@property(assign, nonatomic) CLLocationAccuracy desiredAccuracy`

     Different applications require different accuracies. The framework tries to deliver location accuracies according to the value of this property, but it cannot guarantee that. There are several values you can choose among:

     `kCLLocationAccuracyBest`. This specifies the best accuracy available and is the default.
     `kCLLocationAccuracyNearestTenMeters`. This represents accuracy within 10 meters.
     `kCLLocationAccuracyHundredMeter`. This represents accuracy within 100 meters.
     `kCLLocationAccuracyKilometer`. This value represents accuracy within 1,000 meters.
     `kCLLocationAccuracyThreeKilometers`. This value represents accuracy within 3,000 meters.

   - `distanceFilter`. The value of this property determines how often you will receive location updates. You will receive a new update only when the device moves a distance greater than or equal to this distance. If a more accurate reading is available, this value is ignored and you will receive a new location update. This property is declared as

     `@property(assign, nonatomic) CLLocationDistance distanceFilter`

     `CLLocationDistance` is declared as

     `typedef double` `CLLocationDistance`

     All values are in meters. If you specify `kCLDistanceFilterNone`, you will get updates for all device movements.

   - `delegate`. This property specifies the delegate object receiving the updates. The property is declared as

     `@property(assign,nonatomic)`**`id`**`<CLLocationManagerDelegate> delegate`

     The delegate implements the `CLLocationManagerDelegate` protocol. This protocol has two optional methods:

(a) `locationManager:didUpdateToLocation:fromLocation:.`
This method is invoked whenever the location manager wants to update you with a location. The method is declared as follows:

```
- (void)locationManager:(CLLocationManager *)manager
        didUpdateToLocation:(CLLocation *)newLocation
        fromLocation:(CLLocation *)oldLocation
```

You receive a reference to the location manager in the first parameter. The second parameter is an instance of the `CLLocation` class encapsulating the new location. The third parameter is another, possibly `nil`, `CLLocation` object holding the previous location.

(b) `locationManager:didFailWithError:.` This method of the delegate gets called whenever the manager fails to compute the current location. The method is declared as follows:

```
- (void)locationManager:(CLLocationManager *)manager
        didFailWithError:(NSError *)error
```

You should implement a class that adopts the `CLLocationManagerDelegate` protocol and assign the instance of this class to the delegate property of the `CLLocationManager` instance.

3. **Invoke** `startUpdatingLocation.` Call the `startUpdatingLocation` method of the `CLLocationManager` instance to start receiving location updates.

4. **Invoke** `stopUpdatingLocation.` You should call `stopUpdatingLocation` as soon as you are satisfied with the current location information.

The previous steps represent the basic usage of the location services.

13.1.1   The CLLocation class

Latitude and longitude define a logical grid system of the world. They are developed and implemented to locate places on Earth. Latitude lines are parallel and equally distant from one another. The Equator is 0 degrees; the North and South poles are 90 degrees. A degree is approximately 69 miles. Longitude lines run from north to south. The range for longitudes is 0 to 180 degrees east and 0 to 180 degrees west.

To locate a point on Earth, you can describe it with a `(latitude, longitude)` pair, such as `(33°1′12″, -96°44′19.67″)`. This degree-minute-second format can be converted to decimal format. The previous location can be written in decimal form as `(33.02, -96.7388)`.

The location of the device is encapsulated by the class `CLLocation`, which contains the geographical position of the device represented by the latitude and longitude. In addition, it holds the altitude of the device and various values describing the location measurement. You typically receive objects of this kind from the location manager.

The following are some of the important properties of this class:

- coordinate. This property is the latitude and longitude of the device in degrees. This property is declared as follows:

  ```
  @property(readonly, nonatomic) CLLocationCoordinate2D coordinate
  ```

  CLLocationCoordinate2D is a structure declared as follows:

  ```
  typedef struct {
    CLLocationDegrees latitude;
    CLLocationDegrees longitude;
  } CLLocationCoordinate2D;
  ```

  CLLocationDegrees is of type **double**.

- altitude. This returns the altitude of the device in meters. Positive values indicate above sea level, while negative ones indicate below sea level. The property is declared as follows:

  ```
  @property(readonly, nonatomic) CLLocationDistance altitude
  ```

- horizontalAccuracy. If you imagine that the latitude and longitude are the coordinates of the center of a circle, and the horizontalAccuracy is the radius of that circle, then the device can be within any point inside that circle. The property is declared as

  ```
  @property(readonly, nonatomic) CLLocationAccuracy horizontalAccuracy
  ```

  The property is of type CLLocationAccuracy, which is defined as **double**. A negative value indicates an invalid lateral location.

- verticalAccuracy. This property provides the vertical accuracy of the location. The altitude is within $+/-$ of this value. The property is declared as follows:

  ```
  @property(readonly, nonatomic) CLLocationAccuracy verticalAccuracy
  ```

  Negative values indicate an invalid altitude reading.

- timestamp. This provides the time when the location was determined. The property is declared as follows:

  ```
  @property(readonly, nonatomic) NSDate *timestamp
  ```

Most of the time, you receive CLLocation objects from the location manager. If you would like to cache objects of this type, you need to allocate and initialize a new location object. You can use one of the following two initialization methods, depending on your situation:

- initWithLatitude:longitude:. This method is declared as follows:

  ```
  - (id)initWithLatitude:(CLLocationDegrees)latitude
       longitude:(CLLocationDegrees)longitude
  ```

- initWithCoordinate:altitude:horizontalAccuracy:
  verticalAccuracy:timestamp:. This method is declared as follows:

  - (**id**)initWithCoordinate:(CLLocationCoordinate2D)coordinate
          altitude:(CLLocationDistance)altitude
          horizontalAccuracy:(CLLocationAccuracy)hAccuracy
          verticalAccuracy:(CLLocationAccuracy)vAccuracy
          timestamp:(NSDate *)timestamp;

There is one last method that can be useful in finding the distance (in meters) from one given location to another. This method is getDistanceFrom:, and it returns the lateral distance from the location provided in the first parameter to the location encapsulated by the receiver. The method is declared as follows:

- (CLLocationDistance) getDistanceFrom:(**const** CLLocation *)location

In Section 13.5, we will show how such a method can be implemented and used within a database engine.

13.2   A Simple Location-Aware Application

This section starts by providing a simple location-aware application. The application will configure a location manager and display the updates in a text view. To keep things simple, we implement the functionality of the application in one class: the application delegate.

Listing 13.1 shows the declaration of the application delegate class. The class maintains references to the text view and the location manager. The noUpdates instance variable is used to count the number of location updates received by the application delegate so far. We stop the location updates when we reach ten updates. Notice that we have added a new **#import** statement for the Core Location framework.

Listing 13.1   The declaration of the application delegate class used in the simple location-aware example.

```
#import <UIKit/UIKit.h>
#import <CoreLocation/CoreLocation.h>

@interface Location1AppDelegate : NSObject
<UIApplicationDelegate, CLLocationManagerDelegate> {
  UIWindow            *window;
  UITextView          *textView ;
  CLLocationManager   *locationMgr;
  NSUInteger          noUpdates;
}
@property (nonatomic, retain) UIWindow *window;
@end
```

Listing 13.2 shows the implementation of the application delegate class. The `applicationDid-FinishLaunching:` method configures a text view and adds it to the main window as a subview. An instance of the location manager is created, and its `delegate` property is set to the application delegate instance. The location manager is made to start updating, and the window is made visible.

Location updates are received by the `CLLocationManagerDelegate`'s method `location-Manager:didUpdateToLocation:fromLocation:`. In our implementation of this method, we simply concatenate the text in the text view with the description of the new location object. The text view's `text` property is then set to this value. When ten updates have been received, the location manager is made to stop updating us by invoking its `stopUpdatingLocation` method.

Listing 13.2   The implementation of the application delegate class used in the simple location-aware example.

```
#import "Location1AppDelegate.h"

@implementation Location1AppDelegate
@synthesize window;

- (void)locationManager:(CLLocationManager *)manager
        didUpdateToLocation:(CLLocation *)newLocation
        fromLocation:(CLLocation *)oldLocation{
  noUpdates++;
  if(noUpdates >= 10){
    [locationMgr stopUpdatingLocation];
  }
  [self updateLocation:[newLocation description]];
}

-(void) updateLocation:(NSString*) update{
  NSMutableString *newMessage =
      [[NSMutableString alloc] initWithCapacity:100];
  [newMessage appendString:
      [NSString stringWithFormat:@"Update #:%i\n", noUpdates]];
  [newMessage appendString:update];
  [newMessage appendString:@"\n"];
  [newMessage appendString:[textView text]];
  textView.text = newMessage;
  [newMessage release];
}

- (void)applicationDidFinishLaunching:(UIApplication *)application {
  window =
      [[UIWindow alloc] initWithFrame:[[UIScreen  mainScreen] bounds]];
  CGRect  rectFrame = [UIScreen mainScreen].applicationFrame;
  textView  = [[UITextView alloc] initWithFrame:rectFrame];
  textView.editable = NO;
  locationMgr = [[CLLocationManager alloc] init];
  locationMgr.delegate = self;
```

```
    noUpdates = 0;
    [locationMgr startUpdatingLocation];
    [window addSubview:textView];
    [window makeKeyAndVisible];
}

- (void)dealloc {
    [textView release];
    [locationMgr release];
    [window release];
    [super dealloc];
}
@end
```

For this code to build successfully, you need to add a reference to the `Core Location` library (see Section D.4). The complete application can be found in the `Location1` project available in the source downloads.

Figure 13.1 shows a screen shot of the application after receiving ten location updates.

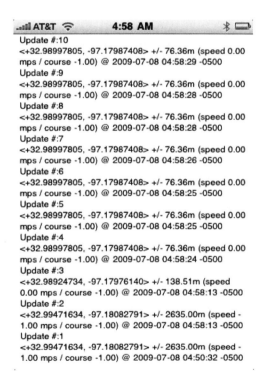

Figure 13.1   A screen shot of the application after receiving ten location updates.

13.3   Google Maps API

Google provides an HTTP interface for geocoding. *Geocoding* is a translation process where addresses such as `3400 W Plano Pkwy, Plano, TX 75075` can be converted to actual geographic coordinates in latitude and longitude. To access this service, the client sends an HTTP request to `http://maps.google.com/maps/geo?` with the following parameters:

- `q`. This parameter represents the address for which you want to find its geo data.

- `output`. This parameter represents the format of the result to be sent back to you. Several formats exist, such as `xml` and `csv`. The comma-separated-values (`csv`) format is the easiest to deal with.

- `key`. To access the service, you need an API key from Google. At this writing, the usage is free for public web sites. Google does, however, police the service.

For example, sending the following HTTP request

```
http://maps.google.com/maps/geo?q=3400+W+Plano+Pkwy+Plano,
+TX+75075&output=csv&
key=ABQIAAAAERNgBiSqUogvAN3O7LdVDxSkQMtcTv75TNsQ97PejimT5pm-
BxST0Gma_YCBaUccn3pRis8XjkxM8w
```

will return the following (provided that you used your Google-supplied key):

```
200,8,33.010003,-96.757923
```

There are four comma-separated values received from Google when you use `csv` format. The first value is the HTTP protocol status code. `200` is `OK` (see RFC 2616[1] for more information). The second value is the `accuracy`. A value of 8 means `Address Level Accuracy`. For a complete list, see `GGeoAddressAccuracy` in the Google Maps API reference. The last two pieces of the result, which is what we are really interested in, are the `latitude` and the `longitude`, respectively.

In this section, we build an application that finds the distance between two addresses. First, we build the `GoogleMapsWrapper` helper class, a class that encapsulates the geocoding service. After that, we show an application delegate that uses this helper class to display the distance between two addresses using a text view.

Listing 13.3 shows the declaration of the `GoogleMapsWrapper` class. The main method declared by this class is the `findGeoInfoForAddress:andReturnLatitude:andLongitude:` method. This method takes the address as an input parameter and returns the latitude and longitude as output parameters. The return code for success is `0`.

The `GoogleMapsWrapper` also maintains a set of Google Maps keys. These keys can be used to load-balance the HTTP requests, as Google puts a limit on the number of queries used per key. The method `addKey:` is used to store a key, and the method `getKey` is used to retrieve one.

---

[1] `www.ietf.org/rfc/rfc2616.txt`

Listing 13.3   The declaration of the `GoogleMapsWrapper` class used in the geocoding application.

```objc
#import <UIKit/UIKit.h>

@interface GoogleMapsWrapper : NSObject {
  NSMutableArray *keys;
}
-(id)init;
-(void)addKey:(NSString*) key;
-(NSString*)getKey;
-(int)findGeoInfoForAddress:(NSString*)address
      andReturnLatitude:(float*) latitude
      andLongitude:(float*) longitude;
@end
```

Listing 13.4 shows the implementation of the `GoogleMapsWrapper` class.

Listing 13.4   The implementation of the `GoogleMapsWrapper` class used in the geocoding application.

```objc
#import "GoogleMapsWrapper.h"

#define GEO_QUERY      @"http://maps.google.com/maps/geo?q="
#define GEO_CSV_KEY    @"&output=csv&key="
@implementation GoogleMapsWrapper

-(int)findGeoInfoForAddress:(NSString*)address
      andReturnLatitude:(float*) latitude
      andLongitude:(float*) longitude{
  if(!address || !latitude || !longitude){
    return -1;
  }
  NSMutableString *query =
        [[NSMutableString alloc] initWithString:GEO_QUERY];
  [query appendString:address];
  [query appendString:GEO_CSV_KEY];
  [query appendString:[self getKey]];
  [query replaceOccurrencesOfString:@" "
        withString:@"%20" options:NSLiteralSearch
        range:NSMakeRange(0, [query length])];
  NSURL *url= [[NSURL alloc] initWithString:query];
  if(!url){
    [query release];
    return -1;
  }
  NSData *data = [[NSData alloc] initWithContentsOfURL:url];
  if(!data){
    [query release];
    [url release];
```

```objc
    *latitude = *longitude = 404;
    return -1;
}
NSString *contents = [[NSString alloc] initWithData:data
                                  encoding:NSUTF8StringEncoding];
if(!contents){
  [query release];
  [url release];
  [data release];
  return -1;
}
/*
 A reply returned in the csv format consists of four numbers,
 separated by commas:
 HTTP status code
 accuracy (See accuracy constants)
 latitude
 longitude
 example: 200,6,42.730070,-73.690570
 */
NSScanner *theScanner;
NSCharacterSet *comma  =
    [NSCharacterSet characterSetWithCharactersInString:@","];
NSString  *statusCode;
theScanner = [NSScanner scannerWithString:contents];
if([theScanner scanUpToCharactersFromSet:comma
              intoString:&statusCode]){
  if([statusCode intValue] != 200){
    *latitude = *longitude = 404;
    [query release];
    [url release];
    [data release];
    [contents release];
    return -1;
  }
}
if(
   [theScanner scanCharactersFromSet:comma intoString:NULL] &&
   [theScanner scanUpToCharactersFromSet:comma intoString:NULL] &&
   [theScanner scanCharactersFromSet:comma intoString:NULL] &&
   [theScanner scanFloat:latitude] &&
   [theScanner scanCharactersFromSet:comma  intoString:NULL] &&
   [theScanner scanFloat:longitude]
   ){
  [query release];
  [url release];
  [data release];
  [contents release];
```

```
        return 0;
    }
    [query release];
    [url release];
    [data release];
    [contents release];
    return -1;
}

-(NSString*)getKey{
    if([keys count] < 1){
        return @"NULL_KEY";
    }
    return [keys objectAtIndex:0];
}

-(void)addKey:(NSString*) key{
    [keys addObject:key];
}

- (id)init{
    self = [super init];
    keys = [[NSMutableArray arrayWithCapacity:1] retain];
    return self;
}

- (void)dealloc {
    [keys release];
    [super dealloc];
}
@end
```

The findGeoInfoForAddress:andReturnLatitude:andLongitude: method first builds the query to be used in the HTTP request. After creating an NSURL object for the request, it contacts Google by invoking the initWithContentsOfURL: of NSData.

The response of the query is in comma-separated format (csv) that needs to be parsed. To retrieve the four values in the response, we utilize the Cocoa class NSScanner. An NSScanner class is used to scan an NSString object for strings and numbers by progressing through the string. In addition, you can use it to skip characters in a given set. The response of the query is first converted to an NSString object, contents. After that, an NSScanner object is created by invoking the scannerWithString: class method of NSScanner, passing in that string.

First, we need to check the status-code value of the response. To retrieve the status code, we ask the scanner to extract all characters starting from the current position (beginning of string) up to the first comma. The method scanUpToCharactersFromSet:intoString: is used for that purpose.

Once we have the status code in the string `statusCode`, we check to see if it is equal to the value `200`. If it is not, we return `-1`, indicating an error. If the status code is equal to `200`, we retrieve the latitude and the longitude values using the `scanFloat:` method.

The `GoogleMapsWrapper` class does not implement load balancing (e.g., a simple randomization algorithm). We use only one key in our application.

Listing 13.5 shows the declaration of the application delegate class.

Listing 13.5   The declaration of the application delegate class used in the geocoding example.

```
#import <UIKit/UIKit.h>
#import <CoreLocation/CoreLocation.h>
#import "GoogleMapsWrapper.h"

@interface Location2AppDelegate : NSObject <UIApplicationDelegate> {
  UIWindow            *window;
  UITextView          *textView ;
  GoogleMapsWrapper   *gWrapper;
}
@property (nonatomic, retain) UIWindow *window;
@end
```

As we have mentioned before, the application delegate will create the main window and attach a text view to it. It will then use the `GoogleMapsWrapper` class to find the distance between two addresses and display that information to the user in a text view as shown in Figure 13.2. The class maintains references to the `UITextView` and the `GoogleMapsWrapper` classes.

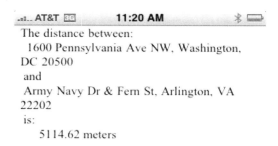

Figure 13.2   A screen shot of the geocoding application showing the distance between two addresses.

Listing 13.6 shows the implementation of the application delegate class. The `applicationDid-FinishLaunching:` method configures the GUI and invokes the method `findDistanceFrom-Address:toAddress:` to find the distance between the White House and the Pentagon. The result is then formatted and assigned to the `text` property of the text view object.

Listing 13.6   The implementation of the application delegate class used in the geocoding example.

```objc
#import "Location2AppDelegate.h"
#import "GoogleMapsWrapper.h"

#define FROM_ADDRESS @"1600 Pennsylvania Ave NW, Washington, DC 20500"
#define TO_ADDRESS   @"Army Navy Dr & Fern St, Arlington, VA 22202"

@implementation Location2AppDelegate

@synthesize window;

-(double) findDistanceFromAddress:(NSString*) from
          toAddress:(NSString *) to{
  float lat, lon;
  CLLocation *fromLocation;
  CLLocation *toLocation;
  if([gWrapper findGeoInfoForAddress:from
             andReturnLatitude:&lat andLongitude:&lon] == 0){
    fromLocation =
       [[[CLLocation alloc] initWithLatitude:lat longitude:lon]
               autorelease];
    if([gWrapper findGeoInfoForAddress:to andReturnLatitude:&lat
               andLongitude:&lon] == 0){
     toLocation =[[[CLLocation alloc]
                   initWithLatitude:lat longitude:lon] autorelease];
      return [toLocation getDistanceFrom:fromLocation];
    }
    return -1;
  }
  return -1;
}

- (void)applicationDidFinishLaunching:(UIApplication *)application {
   window =
    [[UIWindow alloc] initWithFrame:[[UIScreen  mainScreen] bounds]];
  CGRect  rectFrame = [UIScreen mainScreen].applicationFrame;
  textView  = [[UITextView alloc] initWithFrame:rectFrame];
  textView.editable = NO;
  gWrapper = [[GoogleMapsWrapper alloc] init];
  [gWrapper addKey:@"ABQIAAAAERNgBiSqUogvAN307LdVDx"
                   "SkQMtcTv75TNsQ97PejimT5pm-MAxST0Gma_Y"
                   "CBaUccn3pRis8XjkxM8w"];
  NSMutableString *outStr = [[NSMutableString alloc]
      initWithFormat:@"The distance between: \n  %@ \n and"
                   "\n %@ \n is:\n \t \t  %.2f meters\n",
                   FROM_ADDRESS, TO_ADDRESS,
                   [self findDistanceFromAddress:FROM_ADDRESS
                   toAddress:TO_ADDRESS]];
```

```
    textView.text = outStr;
    [window addSubview:textView];
    [window makeKeyAndVisible];
}

- (void)dealloc {
    [gWrapper release];
    [textView release];
    [window release];
    [super dealloc];
}
@end
```

The complete application can be found in the `Location2` project, available in the source downloads.

13.4   A Tracking Application with Maps

Many iOS applications require the display of a map. If you are faced with the task of developing one of these applications, you can use Google Maps API and the `UIWebView` class for that purpose.

In this section we develop a tracking application. The application will first track and store the movement of the device for a configurable number of movements. The user can interrupt the tracking or wait until a specified number of movements has been recorded. In either case, the user is able to go through these movements and visualize (on a map) the geographic location and the time of the recording of each movement.

Listing 13.7 shows the declaration of the application delegate class. The application delegate will have a navigation controller for the GUI; thus, it maintains references to a view and a navigation controller.

Listing 13.7   The declaration of the application delegate class used in the tracking application.

```
#import <UIKit/UIKit.h>
#import "LocationsViewController.h"

@interface Location3AppDelegate : NSObject <UIApplicationDelegate> {
    UIWindow                  *window;
    LocationsViewController   *ctrl;
    UINavigationController    *navCtrl;
}
@property (nonatomic, retain) UIWindow *window;
@end
```

Listing 13.8 shows the implementation of the application delegate class. The `application-DidFinishLaunching:` method simply creates a view controller of type `LocationsViewController` and uses it as the root controller for a navigation controller. The view of the navigation controller is then added to the main window as a subview and the main window is made visible.

Listing 13.8   The implementation of the application delegate class used in the tracking application.

```
#import "Location3AppDelegate.h"
@implementation Location3AppDelegate
@synthesize window;

- (void)applicationDidFinishLaunching:(UIApplication *)application {
  window = [[UIWindow alloc]
                    initWithFrame:[[UIScreen  mainScreen] bounds]];
  ctrl = [[LocationsViewController alloc]
                    initWithNibName:nil bundle:nil];
  navCtrl = [[UINavigationController alloc]
                    initWithRootViewController:ctrl];
  [window addSubview:navCtrl.view];
  [window makeKeyAndVisible];
}

- (void)dealloc {
  [ctrl release];
  [navCtrl release];
  [window release];
  [super dealloc];
}
@end
```

Our view controller is declared in Listing 13.9. The view controller adopts the CLLocation-ManagerDelegate as it will be the delegate of the location manager that it will create. It declares two bar buttons for stopping the sampling of movements, navigating to the next recording, and navigating to the previous recording. The right bar button will be used for both stopping the sampling of movements and as a Next button. In addition, the view controller maintains a reference to a web view for visualizing the locations sampled.

Listing 13.9   The declaration of the LocationsViewController view controller class used in the tracking application.

```
#import <UIKit/UIKit.h>
#import <CoreLocation/CoreLocation.h>

@interface LocationsViewController :
    UIViewController <CLLocationManagerDelegate>{
  CLLocationManager   *locationMgr;
  NSUInteger          noUpdates;
  NSMutableArray      *locations;
  UIWebView           *webView;
  UIBarButtonItem     *rightButton, *leftButton;
  NSUInteger          current;
}
@end
```

Listing 13.10 shows the implementation of the view controller. In the initialization method, initWithNibName:bundle:, we create two bar buttons. The right button is labeled Stop and the left is labeled Previous and disabled.

Listing 13.10   The implementation of the LocationsViewController view controller class used in the tracking application.

```
#import "LocationsViewController.h"

#define NO_OF_LOCATIONS 100
#define MIN_DISTANCE   100

@implementation LocationsViewController

- (void)locationManager:(CLLocationManager *)manager
        didUpdateToLocation:(CLLocation *)newLocation
        fromLocation:(CLLocation *)oldLocation{
  noUpdates++;
  [locations addObject:newLocation];
  self.title = [NSString stringWithFormat:@"Locations: %i", noUpdates];
  if(noUpdates == 1){
    [self centerMap:0];
  }
  if(noUpdates >= NO_OF_LOCATIONS){
    [locationMgr stopUpdatingLocation];
    leftButton.enabled = YES;
    rightButton.title = @"Next";
    current = 0;
    [self centerMap:current];
  }
}

-(void) centerMap:(NSUInteger) index{
  CLLocation *loc = [locations objectAtIndex:index];
  NSString *js = [NSString stringWithFormat:
   @"var map = "
   "new GMap2(document.getElementById(\"map_canvas\"));"
   "map.setMapType(G_HYBRID_MAP);"
   "map.setCenter(new GLatLng(%lf, %lf), 18);"
   "map.panTo(map.getCenter());"
   "map.openInfoWindow(map.getCenter(),"
   "document.createTextNode(\"Loc: (%i/%i), Time: %@\"));",
   [loc coordinate].latitude, [loc coordinate].longitude,
   index+1, [locations count], [loc timestamp]];
  [webView stringByEvaluatingJavaScriptFromString:js];
}

- (id)initWithNibName:(NSString *)nibNameOrNil
     bundle:(NSBundle *)nibBundleOrNil {
```

```
  if (self=[super initWithNibName:nibNameOrNil bundle:nibBundleOrNil]){
    rightButton = [[UIBarButtonItem alloc]
                                initWithTitle:@"Stop"
                                style:UIBarButtonItemStyleDone
                                target:self action:@selector(stopOrNext)];
    self.navigationItem.rightBarButtonItem = rightButton;
    leftButton = [[UIBarButtonItem alloc]
                                initWithTitle:@"Previous"
                                style:UIBarButtonItemStyleDone
                                target:self action:@selector(prev)];
    self.navigationItem.leftBarButtonItem = leftButton;
    leftButton.enabled = NO;
  }
  return self;
}

-(void)stopOrNext{
  if([rightButton.title isEqualToString:@"Stop"] == YES){
    [locationMgr stopUpdatingLocation];
    leftButton.enabled = YES;
    rightButton.title = @"Next";
    current = 0;
    [self centerMap:current];
  }
  else
  if(current < ([locations count]-1)){
    [self centerMap:++current];
  }
}

-(void)prev{
  if(current > 0 && (current < [locations  count])){
    current = current -1;
    [self centerMap:current];
  }
}

- (void)loadView {
  locations = [[NSMutableArray arrayWithCapacity:10] retain];
  locationMgr = [[CLLocationManager alloc] init];
  locationMgr.distanceFilter  = MIN_DISTANCE;
  locationMgr.delegate = self;
  noUpdates = 0;

  CGRect  rectFrame = [UIScreen mainScreen].applicationFrame;
  webView = [[UIWebView alloc] initWithFrame:rectFrame];
  NSString *htmlFilePath =
    [[NSBundle mainBundle] pathForResource:@"map3" ofType:@"html"];
```

```
    NSData   *data = [NSData dataWithContentsOfFile:htmlFilePath];
    [webView loadData:data MIMEType:@"text/html"
            textEncodingName:@"utf-8" baseURL:[NSURL
            URLWithString:@"http://maps.google.com/"]];
    [locationMgr startUpdatingLocation];
    self.view = webView;
}

- (void)dealloc {
    [rightButton release];
    [leftButton release];
    [locationMgr release];
    [locations release];
    [super dealloc];
}
@end
```

The `loadView` method creates and configures a location manager. The distance needed to receive an update is made to be equal to MIN_DISTANCE. In addition, a web view is created and initialized with the contents of an HTML file stored in the bundle. The file `map3.html` is shown in Listing 13.11. This file is one of many sample files demonstrating the use of the Google Maps API provided by Google. As you will see in this section, we will use JavaScript to modify the appearance of the map dynamically.

Listing 13.11   The HTML page used for displaying a Google map for the geo tracking application.

```
<!DOCTYPE html PUBLIC "-//W3C//DTD XHTML 1.0 Strict//EN"
    "http://www.w3.org/TR/xhtml1/DTD/xhtml1-strict.dtd">
<html xmlns="http://www.w3.org/1999/xhtml"
       xmlns:v="urn:schemas-microsoft-com:vml">
  <head>
  <meta http-equiv="content-type" content="text/html;
        charset=utf-8"/>
  <title>Geotracking Example</title>
  <script
  src="http://maps.google.com/maps?file=api&amp;v=2&amp;key=K"
          type="text/javascript">
  </script>
  <script type="text/javascript">
  function initialize() {
  }
    </script>
  </head>
  <body onload="initialize()" onunload="GUnload()">
    <div id="map_canvas" style="width: 500px; height: 500px">
    </div>
  </body>
</html>
```

On receiving location updates, we store these locations in an array. When we have sampled NO_OF_LOCATIONS locations, we enable the left bar button, change the title of the right button to Next and point out the first location on the map.

The centerMap: method is used to display the location on the map. The method takes as an input parameter the index of the location in the array of sampled locations. It extracts the latitude and longitude information from the location, sets the center of the map to that location, and pans to the center. In addition, it opens an information window with the time of the sampling of the location. All of this is done in JavaScript, as in the following example. Finally, we execute the JavaScript code using the web view's method stringByEvaluatingJavaScriptFromString:.

```
var map = new GMap2(document.getElementById("map_canvas"));
map.setMapType(G_HYBRID_MAP);
map.setCenter(new GLatLng(37.331689, -122.030731), 18);
map.panTo(map.getCenter());
map.openInfoWindow(map.getCenter(),document.createTextNode("Loc: (1/1),
Time: 2008-08-06 19:51:27 -0500")));
```

Figure 13.3 shows a screen shot of the tracking application while sampling movements, and Figure 13.4 shows a screen shot of the tracking application while viewing one of those sampled locations.

Figure 13.3   A screen shot of the tracking application while sampling movements.

The application poses some ethical (and maybe legal) issues. If you find a need to launch this application and hide it in someone's car or bag, you should think again! Spying is not nice, and it may land you in jail. Moms, of course, are an exception! One may want to modify the application and add real-time reporting of movements to interested parties. This is left to the reader as an exercise.

13.5   Working with Zip Codes

The United States Postal Service (USPS) uses a coding system to help in the efficient distribution of mail in the United State. Each potential recipient of mail is thought to live in a specific zone represented by a Zone Improvement Plan (Zip) code. Zip codes are, in theory, tied to geographical locations.

There are various databases available on Zip codes. These databases differ in their accuracy and pricing. Databases referring to the latitude and longitude of a given Zip code can be thought to describe the center of the Zip code servicing area. There are several places where you can buy U.S. Zip code databases. You can even download a recent database for free from the site http://geocoder.ibegin.com/downloads.php.

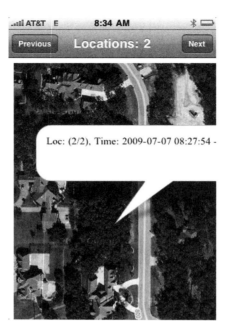

Figure 13.4 A screen shot of the tracking application while viewing a sampled location.

The contents of the U.S. Zip codes file are comma-separated. For example, the last few entries in the file are as follows:

```
89508,Reno,NV,39.5296329,-119.8138027,Washoe
91008,Duarte,CA,34.1394513,-117.9772873,Los Angeles
92058,Oceanside,CA,33.1958696,-117.3794834,San Diego
94505,Discovery Bay,CA,37.9085357,-121.6002291,Contra Costa
95811,Sacramento,CA,38.5815719,-121.4943996,Sacramento
```

In the following, we present the major steps that you can take in order to fulfill requests like the following: Give me all Zip codes that are within 10 miles of 68508.

1. **Create an SQLite** `zipcodes` **table.** To efficiently search, it is advisable to represent your data in a database. The following table can be used to store the Zip code data:

   ```
   CREATE TABLE zipcodes (
      zipcode int NOT NULL PRIMARY KEY,
      latitude float(10,8), longitude float(10,8),
      state varchar(2), city varchar(128),
      county varchar(128))
   ```

   `zipcode` will be our primary key, and for each Zip code, we have the `latitude`, `longitude`, `state`, `city`, and `county`.

2. **Populate the** `zipcodes` **table.** Populate the table with the Zip code geographical data obtained from the text file. The data is stored in a comma-separated ASCII file. Use an `NSScanner` object for value extraction. The extracted tokens of each line are used as input to an **INSERT** SQL statement.

3. **Construct an Objective-C class for answering questions.** After you have produced the database for online use, you need to develop a new class that will answer geographical queries. A major query that one would like to ask is: Give me all Zip codes that are within `10` miles of `20007`. This query might be implemented with a method having the following signature:

```
-(NSArray*)zipcodesNearLatitude:(float)lat andLongitude:(float) lon
         withinDistance:(float)distance;
```

Let's take a look at a possible implementation of the above method. The method's main focus is the execution and the manipulation of results of the following SQL statement:

```
SELECT Z.zipcode FROM zipcodes AS Z WHERE
Distance(latitude1, latitude2, Z.latitude, Z.longitude) <= distance
```

This **SELECT** statement finds all Zip codes such that the distance between a Zip code's `(latitude, longitude)` and a given point `(latitude1, longitude1)` is within the value `distance` (in kilometers).

You have learned how to write code for these SQL statements. You have also learned how to create C functions and use them in SQL queries. The `Distance()` function in the above SQL statement must be implemented by you. Listing 13.12 presents a C implementation.

Listing 13.12   The C implementation of the `Distance` user-defined function.

```
void distance(sqlite3_context *context, int nargs,
              sqlite3_value **values){
  char  *errorMessage;
  double  pi = 3.14159265358979323846;
  if(nargs != 4){
    errorMessage="Wrong # of args. Distance(lat1,lon1,lat2,lon2)";
    sqlite3_result_error(context,errorMessage,strlen(errorMessage));
    return;
  }
  if((sqlite3_value_type(values[0]) != SQLITE_FLOAT)  ||
     (sqlite3_value_type(values[1]) != SQLITE_FLOAT)  ||
     (sqlite3_value_type(values[2]) != SQLITE_FLOAT)  ||
     (sqlite3_value_type(values[3]) != SQLITE_FLOAT)){
    errorMessage ="All four arguments must be of type float.";
    sqlite3_result_error(context, errorMessage,strlen(errorMessage));
    return;
  }
  double latitude1, longitude1, latitude2, longitude2;
  latitude1 = sqlite3_value_double(values[0]);
  longitude1 = sqlite3_value_double(values[1]);
  latitude2 = sqlite3_value_double(values[2]);
```

```
    longitude2 = sqlite3_value_double(values[3]);
    double x = sin( latitude1 * pi/180 ) *
    sin( latitude2 * pi/180  ) + cos(latitude1 *pi/180 ) *
    cos( latitude2 * pi/180 ) *
    cos( abs( (longitude2 * pi/180) -
    (longitude1 *pi/180) ) );
    x = atan( ( sqrt( 1- pow( x, 2 ) ) ) ) / x );
    x = ( 1.852 * 60.0 * ((x/pi)*180) ) / 1.609344;
    sqlite3_result_double(context, x);
}
```

The complete application can be found in the `Location3` project, available in the source downloads.

13.6   Working with the Map Kit API

The Map Kit framework provides the ability to embed an interactive map in an application as a subview. The map behaves similarly to the one used by the `Maps.app` application that ships with iOS devices.

You can specify the center of this map and annotate it with any number of items. The map has a delegate that allows it to communicate touch events on the annotated objects that you provide.

13.6.1   The MKMapView class

The `MKMapView` class is the center of the Map Kit API. It is a subclass of `UIView`, which means that you can create an instance of it as you do with any `UIView` class.

To use this class, you need to add the `MapKit.framework` to your application and **#import** <Map­Kit/MapKit.h>. Adding a framework to your project is explained in Section D.4 of Appendix D.

The following shows a code fragment that creates an instance of this class and adds it as a subview:

```
MKMapView  *mapView =
    [[[MKMapView alloc] initWithFrame:
        [UIScreen mainScreen].applicationFrame] autorelease];
 [self.view addSubview:mapView];
```

The above code specifies the size of the map to be full-screen. You can specify any dimension you want.

13.6.2   The MKCoordinateRegion structure

When you present a map, you need to specify the area that this map should display and the zoom-level of that area. The `MKCoordinateRegion` structure encapsulates this as shown below:

```
typedef struct {
    CLLocationCoordinate2D center;
    MKCoordinateSpan span;
} MKCoordinateRegion;
```

From the above declaration, we see that the center of the region is a latitude/longitude pair. The zoom level is specified by an MKCoordinateSpan value, which is basically a pair of two **double** values as shown below:

```
typedef struct {
    CLLocationDegrees latitudeDelta;
    CLLocationDegrees longitudeDelta;
} MKCoordinateSpan;
```

Both the latitudeDelta and longitudeDelta are specified in degrees. One degree of latitudeDelta corresponds to approximately 111 kilometers (69 miles). One degree of longitudeDelta varies depending on the center value. The value ranges from 111 kilometers (69 miles) at the Equator to 0 kilometers at the poles.

The MKMapView class declares the following property for use as its region:

```
@property (nonatomic) MKCoordinateRegion region
```

The following shows an example of setting up the region of a map:

```
MKCoordinateRegion region;
region.center.latitude = 33.5;
region.center.longitude = -97;
region.span.latitudeDelta = 1;
region.span.longitudeDelta = 1;
mapView.region = region;
```

You can change the map's region at any time, with the option of animating the change, by using the following method:

```
- (void) setRegion:(MKCoordinateRegion) region animated:(BOOL) animated
```

13.6.3   The MKAnnotation protocol

Locations that you wish to show on the map can be specified as annotations. An *annotation* is composed of a data model and a view. The data model specifies the title, subtitle, and latitude/longitude of the location. The view is a visual representation of the data model.

The MKAnnotation protocol describes the data model of the annotation. This protocol is declared as follows:

```
@protocol MKAnnotation <NSObject>
@property (nonatomic, readonly) CLLocationCoordinate2D coordinate;
@optional
```

```
-  (NSString *)title;
-  (NSString *)subtitle;
@end
```

The above protocol basically says that any annotation must be able to specify its coordinate and optionally specify its title and subtitle. You usually adapt your data model to adopt this protocol and use instances of your data model as annotation objects.

For example, the following shows the declaration of a data model `Person` that adopts the `MK-Annotation` protocol:

```
@interface Person : NSObject <MKAnnotation>{
  NSString  *_title, *_subTitle;
  CLLocationCoordinate2D _coordinate;
}
@property (nonatomic, readonly) CLLocationCoordinate2D coordinate;
@property (nonatomic, readonly) NSString *title;
@property (nonatomic, readonly) NSString *subtitle;
@end
```

The following shows the implementation of the `Person` class:

```
@implementation Person
@synthesize coordinate=_coordinate, title=_title, subtitle=_subTitle;

-(id)initWithTitle:(NSString*)theTitle subTitle:(NSString*)theSubTitle
    andCoordinate:(CLLocationCoordinate2D) theCoordinate{
  if(self = [super init]){
    _title = [theTitle copy];
    _subTitle = [theSubTitle copy];
    _coordinate = theCoordinate;
  }
  return self;
}
-(void)dealloc{
  [_title release];
  [_subTitle release];
  [super dealloc];
}
@end
```

To add an annotation to a map, you simply use the `addAnnotation:` method as shown in the example below:

```
  CLLocationCoordinate2D coordinate = {33, -97};
  [mapView addAnnotation:
              [[[Person alloc]
                    initWithTitle:@"Homer" subTitle:@"Father"
                    andCoordinate:coordinate] autorelease]];
```

13.6.4   *The MKAnnotationView class*

To show the annotation to the user on the screen, you need to set a delegate object to the map view instance and implement a specific method that returns a view for a given annotation.

The `delegate` property of the `MKMapView` class is declared as follows:

```
@property (nonatomic, assign) id <MKMapViewDelegate> delegate
```

The delegate method that is called to retrieve a visual representation of an annotation is declared as follows:

```
- (MKAnnotationView *)mapView:(MKMapView *)mapView
                viewForAnnotation:(id <MKAnnotation>)annotation;
```

The `MKAnnotationView` class is a subclass of `UIView`. To create a new instance of this class and return it from the delegate method above so that it is used to represent the `annotation` object, you are encouraged to reuse existing views whose annotation objects are outside the current viewing area of the map.

The `MKMapView` method `dequeueReusableAnnotationViewWithIdentifier:` should be called before attempting to create a new view. This method is declared as follows:

```
- (MKAnnotationView *)
  dequeueReusableAnnotationViewWithIdentifier:(NSString *)identifier;
```

If this method returns a `nil` value, you can create the view and initialize it with the `initWith-Annotation:reuseIdentifier:` method. This initializer is declared as follows:

```
- (id)initWithAnnotation:(id <MKAnnotation>)annotation
        reuseIdentifier:(NSString *)reuseIdentifier;
```

The following shows an example of how you should obtain a view for a given annotation:

```
MKAnnotationView *view =
      [mapView dequeueReusableAnnotationViewWithIdentifier:@"ID1"];
if(!view){
   view = [[[MKAnnotationView alloc]
      initWithAnnotation:annotation reuseIdentifier:@"ID1"] autorelease];
}
```

You can, if you choose to, give the view an image. This can be achieved by setting the `image` property of the annotation view.

An annotation view can display a standard callout bubble when tapped. To enable this feature, you need to set the `canShowCallout` property of the `MKAnnotationView` instance to `YES`.

If the callout bubble is enabled, the title and the subtitle of the corresponding annotation are displayed when the user taps on the view.

You can also configure a right and a left accessory view if you want to. The right callout accessory view property is declared as follows:

```
@property (retain, nonatomic) UIView *rightCalloutAccessoryView
```

As you can see, it can be just a simple view. Normally, however, this property is set to an accessory button (e.g., `UIButtonTypeDetailDisclosure`) used by the user to get more information about the annotation. The left callout view is declared similarly.

There is a default behavior that the API provides for you if you make the right/left callout view an instance of `UIControl` or one of its subclasses. This default behavior is to invoke a specific method in the delegate when the user taps on the accessory view. You can, however, bypass this default behavior and handle the touch events yourself.

The following code fragment creates and dequeues an annotation view, and configures both its right and left callout accessory views. The right callout accessory view is configured to be a button, while the left callout accessory view is configured to be a simple yellow view.

```
MKAnnotationView *view =
    [mapView dequeueReusableAnnotationViewWithIdentifier:Reuse_ID1];
if(!view){
    view = [[[MKAnnotationView alloc]
        initWithAnnotation:annotation reuseIdentifier:Reuse_ID1]
            autorelease];
}
view.canShowCallout = YES;
view.image = [UIImage imageNamed:@"7.png"];
view.rightCalloutAccessoryView =
    [UIButton buttonWithType:UIButtonTypeDetailDisclosure];
UIView *aView =
    [[[UIView alloc] initWithFrame:CGRectMake(0, 0, 50, 20)]
            autorelease];
aView.backgroundColor = [UIColor yellowColor];
view.leftCalloutAccessoryView =  aView;
```

Figure 13.5 shows the annotation view created by the above code.

Figure 13.5 An example of an annotation view.

When the user taps on any of the right/left accessory views (provided that the view is a `UIControl`), the delegate method `mapView:annotationView:calloutAccessoryControlTapped:` gets called.

You can provide your own logic in this method. For example, the following code fragment displays an alert view only if the title of the annotation that is tapped is equal to `Marge`:

```
- (void)mapView:(MKMapView *)mapView
        annotationView:(MKAnnotationView *)view
        calloutAccessoryControlTapped:(UIControl *)control{
  if([view.annotation.title isEqualToString:@"Marge"]){
    [[[[UIAlertView alloc] initWithTitle:view.annotation.title
                          message:view.annotation.subtitle
                          delegate:nil cancelButtonTitle:@"OK"
                          otherButtonTitles:nil] autorelease] show];
  }
}
```

13.6.5 The MKUserLocation class

The map view provides an annotation for the user's location. This annotation is an instance of the `MKUserLocation` class.

To access the user's location annotation object, you can use the `userLocation` property, which is declared as follows:

```
@property (nonatomic, readonly) MKUserLocation *userLocation
```

If you want to use the built-in view for the user's location annotation, you need to return `nil` in the `mapView:viewForAnnotation:` delegate method. For example:

```
- (MKAnnotationView *)mapView:(MKMapView *)mapView
                     viewForAnnotation:(id <MKAnnotation>)annotation {
  if(NSClassFromString(@"MKUserLocation") == [annotation class]){
    return nil;
  }
  //process regular annotations ...
}
```

The above code fragment first checks to see if the annotation is an instance of the `MKUserLocation` class. If that is the case, a `nil` value is returned, which will result in the default visual element's being displayed (see Figure 13.6).

If you do not want the user's location to show up on the map, you can set the map's view `showsUserLocation` property to `NO`.

13.6.6 The MKPinAnnotationView class

The `MKPinAnnotationView` is a subclass of the `MKAnnotationView` class that you can use as a visual representation of your annotations. This view represents a pin icon. You can specify the color of this pin as well as whether the pin should be animated when it is dropped on the map.

Figure 13.6   The default annotation view for the user's current location.

For example, the following code fragment creates a new pin view, if one is not available; configures the pin to animate when it's dropped; and gives it a green color:

```
//... Code continues in the delegate method
   MKPinAnnotationView *pin =
     (MKPinAnnotationView*)
        [mapView dequeueReusableAnnotationViewWithIdentifier:Reuse_ID2];
   if(!pin){
     pin = [[[MKPinAnnotationView alloc]
        initWithAnnotation:annotation reuseIdentifier:Reuse_ID2]
          autorelease];
   }
   pin.animatesDrop = YES;
   pin.pinColor = MKPinAnnotationColorGreen;
   return pin; // return a pin for an annotation object
```

Figure 13.7 shows the pin annotation view.

Refer to the `MapView` project in the code downloads for a complete application that utilizes the Map Kit API.

Figure 13.7   The pin annotation view.

13.7   Summary

In this chapter, we addressed the topic of location awareness. First, we talked in Section 13.1 about the Core Location framework and how to use it to build location-aware applications. After that, Section 13.2 discussed a simple location-aware application. Next, Section 13.3 covered the topic of geocoding. In that section, you learned how to translate postal addresses into geographical locations. In Section 13.4, you learned how to sample movement of the device and display that information on maps. After that, Section 13.5 discussed how to relate Zip codes to geographical information. In that section, you also learned the actual formula that implements the distance between two locations. Finally, Section 13.6 showed you how to utilize the Map Kit API to add an interactive map to your view hierarchy.

Exercises

(1) Study the `MKMapView` class in the `MKMapView.h` header file and the documentation. If this class references other Map Kit classes, study those too.

(2) Write a view controller that takes as input a set of points (latitude and longitude pairs) and displays these points on an interactive map. When the right accessory view of the annotation view of any of these points is tapped, a new table view controller is pushed, showing a table view. Each cell of this table view shows the distance between the point represented by the tapped annotation view and another point in the set. Order the table rows such that closer points are shown first.

14

Working with Devices

In this chapter, we demonstrate the use of several of the devices available on an iOS device. Section 14.1 discusses the usage of the accelerometer. In Section 14.2, you learn how to play short and long audio files, how to record audio files, and how to utilize the iPod Library. Next, Section 14.3 shows how to play video files. After that, Section 14.4 shows how to obtain iPhone/iPod touch device information. Using the camera and the photo library is described in Section 14.5. After that, Section 14.6 shows you how to obtain state information regarding the battery of the device. Next, we discuss the proximity sensor in Section 14.7. Finally, we summarize the chapter in Section 14.8.

14.1 Working with the Accelerometer

The iPhone is equipped with an easy-to-use accelerometer. The accelerometer provides you with the current orientation of the device in 3D space. You subscribe to these updates with a given frequency (10 updates/s to 100 updates/s) and you receive three floating-point values in each update. These values represent the acceleration of x, y, and z in space. The acceleration on each axis is measured in gs, where g is the acceleration due to gravity on Earth at sea level ($1g$ is equal to 9.80 m s^{-2}).

14.1.1 Basic accelerometer values

If you hold the iPhone in front of you and imagine an axis that goes through the Home button and the earpiece that is orthogonal to the floor, then that axis is the y axis. Positive values of y indicate that the phone is accelerating up and negative values indicate that it is accelerating down towards the floor. The x axis goes from right to left perpendicular to the y axis. Positive values indicate that the force is towards your right side and negative values indicate that the force is towards the left. The z axis passes through the device. Negative values indicate that the device is moving away from you and positive values indicate that the force is moving the device towards you.

Due to the force of gravity, the device will report nonzero values on some or all of the axes even if the device is stationary. For example, if you hold the device in front of you in portrait mode as shown in Figure 14.1, the x and z axes will report $0g$ while the y axis will report $-1g$. This basically says that there is no force moving the device to the right/left or forward/backward, but there is a $1g$ force on the device downwards. This force, of course, is gravity.

Figure 14.1   Stationary iPhone reporting an accelerometer vector of (0, -1, 0).

If you hold the device in landscape mode as shown in Figure 14.2, the x axis becomes the axis affected by the force of gravity. The value of the *x* component of the vector reported by the accelerometer will be 1*g*. If you hold the device as in Figure 14.3, the value will be −1*g*. If you rest the iPhone face up on the table, the z reading will be −1*g*, and if you put it face down, it will report 1*g*.

If you hold the iPhone facing you as shown in Figure 14.1 and tilt it to the right, the y value will start increasing and the x value increasing. If you tilt it to the left, the y value will start increasing and the x value decreasing.

14.1.2 Accelerometer example

In this section, we present a simple application that demonstrates the use of the accelerometer. The example will show you how to configure the accelerometer and how to intercept a shake, a hug, and a punch. In addition, the application will report when the iPhone is in portrait mode with the Home button up or down while being perpendicular to the floor.

Figure 14.2   Stationary iPhone reporting an accelerometer vector of (1, 0, 0).

Figure 14.3   Stationary iPhone reporting an accelerometer vector of (-1, 0, 0).

To use the accelerometer, follow these steps:

1. **Obtain the shared accelerometer object.** The application has one accelerometer object. Use the `sharedAccelerometer` method to obtain that object. The method is declared as follows:

   ```
   + (UIAccelerometer *)    sharedAccelerometer
   ```

2. **Configure the accelerometer.** Configure the frequency of updates using the `update-Interval` property. This property is declared as follows:

   ```
   @property(nonatomic) NSTimeInterval updateInterval;
   ```

NSTimeInterval is declared as **double**. The value you specify for this property ranges from 0.1 (a frequency of 10 Hz) to 0.01 (a frequency of 100 Hz) seconds.

You also need to configure the delegate property delegate, which is declared as follows:

```
@property(nonatomic, assign) id<UIAccelerometerDelegate> delegate
```

The protocol UIAccelerometerDelegate has a single optional method accelerometer:didAccelerate:, which is declared as follows:

```
- (void) accelerometer:(UIAccelerometer *)accelerometer
         didAccelerate:(UIAcceleration *)acceleration;
```

The method receives the accelerometer object and a UIAcceleration instance. The UIAcceleration object holds the values for the 3D vector (x, y, and z) and a time stamp (timestamp).

Listing 14.1 shows the application delegate class declaration for the accelerometer example. The application delegate adopts both UIApplicationDelegate and UIAccelerometerDelegate protocols. In addition, it maintains the previous accelerometer reading in the accelerationValues instance variable.

Listing 14.1   The application delegate class declaration for the accelerometer example.

```
#import <UIKit/UIKit.h>

@interface AccelAppDelegate :
  NSObject <UIApplicationDelegate,UIAccelerometerDelegate> {
  UIWindow *window;
  UIAccelerationValue accelerationValues[3];
}
@end
```

Listing 14.2 shows the implementation of the application delegate class.

Listing 14.2   The implementation of the application delegate class used in the accelerometer example.

```
#import "AccelAppDelegate.h"

#define BETWEEN(arg, v1, v2) ((arg >= v1) && (arg <= v2 ))

@implementation AccelAppDelegate

- (void)accelerometer:(UIAccelerometer *)accelerometer
        didAccelerate:(UIAcceleration *)acceleration{
  UIAccelerationValue x, y, z;
  x = acceleration.x;
  y = acceleration.y;
  z = acceleration.z;
  NSLog(@"X: %4.2f, Y:%4.2f, Z:%4.2f", x, y, z);
```

```
  // shake
  BOOL x_big_difference = (fabs(x - accelerationValues[0]) >3);
  BOOL y_big_difference = (fabs(y - accelerationValues[1]) >3);
  BOOL z_big_difference = (fabs(z - accelerationValues[2]) >3);
  int axes = x_big_difference + y_big_difference + z_big_difference;
  if(axes>= 2){
    NSLog(@"iPhone Shaken!");
  }
// orientation
  if(BETWEEN(x, -0.05, 0.05) && BETWEEN(y, -1, -0.95) &&
      BETWEEN(z, -0.05, 0.05)){
    NSLog(@"iPhone perpendicular to ground, Home button down");
  }
  if(BETWEEN(x, -0.05, 0.05) && BETWEEN(y,  0.95, 1) &&
      BETWEEN(z, -0.05, 0.05)){
    NSLog(@"iPhone perpendicular to ground, Home button up");
  }
// hug/punch
  BOOL x_change = (fabs(x - accelerationValues[0]) < 1);
  BOOL y_change = (fabs(y - accelerationValues[1]) < 1);
  BOOL z_change = (fabs(z - accelerationValues[2]) >= 3);
  if(x_change && y_change && z_change){
    if(z > accelerationValues[2])
      NSLog(@"hug");
    else
      NSLog(@"punch");
  }
  accelerationValues[0] = x;
  accelerationValues[1] = y;
  accelerationValues[2] = z;
}

- (void)applicationDidFinishLaunching:(UIApplication *)application {
  CGRect fullScreen = [[UIScreen  mainScreen] bounds];
  window = [[UIWindow alloc] initWithFrame:fullScreen];
  UIAccelerometer *accelerometer =
        [UIAccelerometer sharedAccelerometer];
  accelerometer.updateInterval = 0.1; // 10Hz
  accelerometer.delegate = self;
  [window makeKeyAndVisible];
}

- (void)dealloc {
  [window release];
  [super dealloc];
}
@end
```

The `applicationDidFinishLaunching:` method starts by configuring the accelerometer to a 10 Hz frequency of updates and setting the delegate to the application delegate.

The `accelerometer:didAccelerate:` method is where we have the recognition logic for the movements described above. To recognize a shake, it suffices to observe an alteration of acceleration on at least two axes. We use a $3g$ value difference for each axis. For example, the statement

```
BOOL x_big_difference = (fabs(x - accelerationValues[0]) >3);
```

will result in the value `YES` (1) if the difference between the previous and the current acceleration on the x axis is larger than $3g$.

To recognize that the iPhone is in portrait mode with the axis of the Home button and earpiece orthogonal to the floor while the Home button is at the bottom, we make sure that the x and z values are 0 with some tolerance interval and the y value is about -1. Similarly, to recognize that the iPhone is upside down, the value of y must be around $1g$.

To check for an iPhone hug or punch, the method checks to see a major acceleration on the z axis with a negligible change on the x and y axes. If the z value has changed towards a negative acceleration, we interpret that as a *punch*. If, on the other hand, the value has changed to a positive acceleration, we interpret that as a *hug*.

14.2　Working with Audio

In this section, you learn how to play short and long audio files, how to record audio files, and how to utilize the iPod Library.

14.2.1　*Playing short audio files*

In this section, we demonstrate the playing of short audio files (less than 30 seconds in length). To play a short sound file, you first register the file as a system sound and obtain a handle. After that, you can play the sound using this handle. When you are finished and do not want to play this sound again, you deallocate that system sound.

To register a sound file as a system sound, use the function `AudioServicesCreateSystem-SoundID()`, which is declared as follows:

```
OSStatus
AudioServicesCreateSystemSoundID(
        CFURLRef            inFileURL,
        SystemSoundID       *outSystemSoundID)
```

The first parameter is `CFURLRef` (or its counterpart `NSURL` instance). This parameter specifies the URL of the sound file. The second parameter is a reference to a `SystemSoundID`. In it, a 32-bit unsigned integer, representing the ID of the system sound, will be stored. The return value must be 0 to indicate successful registration of the system sound.

To play the system sound, use the `AudioServicesPlaySystemSound()` function, which is declared as

void AudioServicesPlaySystemSound(SystemSoundID inSystemSoundID)

You pass in the system sound handle you obtained from the previous function. The predefined identifier `kSystemSoundID_Vibrate` can be used to trigger vibration.

To deallocate the system sound, use the function `AudioServicesDisposeSystemSoundID()`, which is declared as follows:

OSStatus AudioServicesDisposeSystemSoundID(SystemSoundID inSystemSoundID)

You pass in the system sound handle, which you obtained from the registration function.

Here, we build an application that plays a sound file every minute. Listing 14.3 shows the declaration of the application delegate class. Notice the `include` for the `<AudioToolbox/AudioToolbox.h>` header file. Also, you need to add the `AudioToolbox.framework` linked library to the project in XCode, as explained in Section D.4 of Appendix D.

Listing 14.3   The declaration of the application delegate class demonstrating the playing of small audio files.

```
#import <UIKit/UIKit.h>
#include <AudioToolbox/AudioToolbox.h>

@interface AudioAppDelegate : NSObject <UIApplicationDelegate> {
  UIWindow        *window;
  SystemSoundID   audioSID;
}
@end
```

Listing 14.4 shows the implementation of the application delegate class. The sound file is stored in the application bundle. In the `applicationDidFinishLaunching:` method, we first obtain the absolute file path of the `sound.caf` file. Then an `NSURL` object is created from this file path using the method `fileURLWithPath:isDirectory:`. The system sound is then registered. The types `CFURL` and `NSURL` are interchangeable or, in Cocoa's terminology, toll-free bridged. Therefore, we pass in the `NSURL` object in place of the reference to `CFURL`, `CFURLRef`. If there is no error, the sound is played.

The `play:` method plays the sound and then schedules a timer to invoke the `play:` method in one minute.

Listing 14.4   The implementation of the application delegate class demonstrating the playing of small audio files.

```
#import "AudioAppDelegate.h"
@implementation AudioAppDelegate
- (void)applicationDidFinishLaunching:(UIApplication *)application {
  CGRect screenFrame = [[UIScreen  mainScreen] bounds];
  window = [[UIWindow alloc] initWithFrame:screenFrame];
```

```
   NSString *filePath = [[NSBundle mainBundle]
                                   pathForResource:@"sound" ofType:@"caf"];
   NSURL *aFileURL = [NSURL fileURLWithPath:filePath isDirectory:NO];
   OSStatus error =
    AudioServicesCreateSystemSoundID((CFURLRef)aFileURL, &audioSID);
   if(error == 0)
     [self play:nil];
   [window makeKeyAndVisible];
}
- (void)play:(NSTimer*)theTimer{
   AudioServicesPlaySystemSound(audioSID);
   // schedule a 1 minute play
   [NSTimer scheduledTimerWithTimeInterval:60.0
            target:self selector:@selector(play:) userInfo:nil repeats:NO];
}
- (void)dealloc {
   AudioServicesDisposeSystemSoundID (audioSID);
   [window release];
   [super dealloc];
}
@end
```

14.2.2   Recording audio files

To record and play long audio files, you need to utilize the AVFoundation framework. Just add this framework, as explained in Section D.4 of Appendix D, and include the following header files:

```
#import <AVFoundation/AVFoundation.h>
#import <CoreAudio/CoreAudioTypes.h>
```

The AVAudioRecorder adds audio recording features to your application. To use it, you first need to allocate it and then initialize it using the initWithURL:settings:error: method, which is declared as follows:

```
- (id)initWithURL:(NSURL *)url settings:(NSDictionary *)settings
        error:(NSError **)outError;
```

You pass in an NSURL instance that represents a file in the first argument. In the second argument you pass in a dictionary holding the key/value pair of the recording session. The third argument is a reference to an NSError pointer.

After initializing the recorder instance, you can send it a record message to start recording. To pause recording, send it a pause message. To resume from a pause, send it a record message. To stop recording and close the audio file, send it a stop message.

The following method demonstrates the basic use of this class. It assumes that it is the action of a UIButton instance. If we are currently recording (the recorder instance is not nil), the method simply stops the recording and changes the button's title to Record.

```
-(void)recordStop{
  if(self.recorder){
    [recorder stop];
    self.recorder = nil;
    UIButton  *button = (UIButton*)[self.view viewWithTag:1000];
    [button setTitle:@"Record" forState:UIControlStateNormal];
    return;
  }

  NSString *filePath =
    [NSHomeDirectory() stringByAppendingPathComponent:@"tmp/rec.aif"];
  NSMutableDictionary *dic = [NSMutableDictionary dictionary];
  [dic setObject:[NSNumber numberWithInt:kAudioFormatLinearPCM]
      forKey:AVFormatIDKey];
  [dic setObject:[NSNumber numberWithFloat:16000]
      forKey:AVSampleRateKey];
  [dic setObject:[NSNumber numberWithInt:2]
      forKey:AVNumberOfChannelsKey];
  self.recorder = [[[AVAudioRecorder alloc]
                          initWithURL:[NSURL URLWithString:filePath]
                          settings:dic error:NULL] autorelease];
  [recorder record];
  UIButton  *button = (UIButton*)[self.view viewWithTag:1000];
  [button setTitle:@"Stop" forState:UIControlStateNormal];
}
```

If we are not currently recording, the method creates an instance of the recorder and initializes it with a URL pointing to the rec.aif audio file in the tmp directory of the Home directory of the application.

We use minimal settings for the recording session. We specify 16 kHz for the sample rate, two audio channels, and Linear PCM audio format.

Once the recorder has been initialized, we send it a record message and change the button's title to Stop.

14.2.3 *Playing audio files*

The counterpart of the AVAudioRecorder class is the AVAudioPlayer class. Using AVAudio-Player, you can play audio files of any size.

You allocate an instance of the audio player and then initialize it using the initWithContentsOf-URL:error: method passing in the URL of the file you want to play and a pointer (possibly nil) to an NSError instance. After that, you send it a play message to start playing the audio file.

The following code fragment shows an example:

```
-(void)play{
  NSString *filePath = [NSHomeDirectory()
                stringByAppendingPathComponent:@"tmp/recording.aif"];
  self.player = [[[AVAudioPlayer alloc]
                initWithContentsOfURL:[NSURL URLWithString:filePath]
                error:NULL] autorelease];
  [player play];
}
```

For a complete application that demonstrates recording and playing of audio files, consult the
RecordAudio project, available in the source downloads.

14.2.4   Using the media picker controller

The MediaPlayer framework provides a view controller that can be used to pick media items from
the iPod Library. Media items include music, podcasts, audiobooks, etc.

You present this controller modally and ask the user to select the media items from the iPod Library.
Once the user taps on the Done button, you receive a collection of these items (no deletion, of
course). You can then do whatever you intend to do with these items. For example, you could put
them in a queue and play them all.

The MPMediaPickerController class

The media picker is represented by the MPMediaPickerController class. There are two
initializers for this class:

- init. This method initializes the media picker to be able to pick any media type.
- initWithMediaTypes:. This method initializes the media picker to pick specific media
  types. The method is declared as follows:

  - (id)initWithMediaTypes:(MPMediaType)mediaTypes

MPMediaType is declared as integer and can be set to any combination of the following flags:

- MPMediaTypeMusic. This flag is used to denote music type.
- MPMediaTypePodcast. This flag is used to denote podcast type.
- MPMediaTypeAudioBook. This flag is used to denote audiobook type.
- MPMediaTypeAnyAudio. This flag is used to denote general audio type.
- MPMediaTypeAny. This flag is used to denote any media type.

After creating and initializing the controller, you can specify nondefault behavior by setting its properties. For example, to allow the user to select more than one media item, you can set the `allowsPickingMultipleItems` property to `YES` (the default is `NO`).

You can also specify some text that can be shown above the navigation bar by setting the `prompt` property to any `NSString` instance.

The following code fragment creates, initializes, configures, and presents a media picker:

```
MPMediaPickerController *mp =
  [[[MPMediaPickerController alloc] initWithMediaTypes:MPMediaTypeAny]
          autorelease];
mp.delegate = self;
mp.allowsPickingMultipleItems = YES;
[self presentModalViewController:mp animated:YES];
```

The media controller delegate

The media controller has a `delegate` property that you can set. This property is declared as follows:

`@property(nonatomic, assign) id<MPMediaPickerControllerDelegate> delegate`

The `MPMediaPickerControllerDelegate` protocol declares two optional methods. The first method gives you the selected items and is invoked when the user taps on the Done button. This method is declared as follows:

```
- (void)mediaPicker:(MPMediaPickerController *)mediaPicker
      didPickMediaItems:(MPMediaItemCollection *)mediaItemCollection;
```

The `MPMediaItemCollection` class represents a sorted set of media items from the iPod Library. You can obtain an `NSArray` of the items by accessing the `items` property.

If the user chooses to cancel the media picker, the `mediaPickerDidCancel:` method is called. This method is declared as follows:

`- (void)mediaPickerDidCancel:(MPMediaPickerController *)mediaPicker`

You should implement both of these methods and dismiss the controller in each of them.

The MPMediaItem class

Media items are represented by the `MPMediaItem` class. Every media item has a unique identifier. In addition, a number of metadata key/value pairs are associated with the item.

You can access the unique identifier or any of the metadata values using the `valueForProperty:` method, which is declared as follows:

`- (id)valueForProperty:(NSString *)property`

The following shows some of the predefined properties:

- MPMediaItemPropertyPersistentID. The value for this property is an NSNumber object encapsulating a 64-bit integer (**unsigned long long**). This number is the unique identifier of the item in the iPod Library.
- MPMediaItemPropertyTitle. The value for this property is an NSString object storing the title of the media item.
- MPMediaItemPropertyArtist. The value for this property is an NSString object storing the artist's name of the media item.
- MPMediaItemPropertyPlaybackDuration. The value for this property is an NSNumber object storing the duration (in seconds) of the media item. The duration is stored as a **double**.

Refer to the MPMediaItem.h header file for a complete list of available keys.

Putting it together

Assuming that we presented the media picker, and the user selected the items and tapped on the Done button, the following delegate method would be invoked:

```
- (void)mediaPicker:(MPMediaPickerController *)mediaPicker
        didPickMediaItems:(MPMediaItemCollection *)mediaItemCollection{
  for (MPMediaItem *item in mediaItemCollection.items){
    NSLog(@"\nTitle: %@\nAlbum title: %@\nDuration: %.2f sec",
          [item valueForProperty:MPMediaItemPropertyTitle],
          [item valueForProperty:MPMediaItemPropertyAlbumTitle],
          [[item valueForProperty:MPMediaItemPropertyPlaybackDuration]
                                            doubleValue]
    );
  }
  [self dismissModalViewControllerAnimated:YES];
}
```

As you can see, the method simply iterates over the items in the collection. For each item, the method logs the values of some of its associated metadata. As always, you need to dismiss the controller.

You can see a complete application demonstrating the media picker in the MediaPicker project, available in the source downloads.

14.2.5   Searching the iPod Library

If you want to search the iPod Library, you need to create and configure a media query. A *media query* is an instance of the MPMediaQuery class and can be configured with the following two important pieces of information:

- **Zero or one grouping scheme.** You can group the media items that are returned from executing the query according to a specific grouping scheme. For example, you can ask the MPMediaQuery object to group the result set according to the artist.

- **A query filter.** A query filter consists of zero or more media property predicates. For a media item to be returned as a result of executing this query, it has to pass through all the media property predicates that make up the filter provided. If you specify no predicates, all media items will be returned from the query.

Grouping method

The groupingType property of the MPMediaQuery class specifies the grouping method of the query. This property is declared as follows:

@property (nonatomic) MPMediaGrouping groupingType

The MPMediaGrouping type is an integer that can hold one of the following values declared in an **enum**:

- MPMediaGroupingTitle. This value is used to specify grouping based on the media item title. This is the default.

- MPMediaGroupingAlbum. This value is used to specify grouping based on the media item album.

- MPMediaGroupingArtist. This value is used to specify grouping based on the media item artist.

- MPMediaGroupingAlbumArtist. This value is used to specify grouping based on the media item album artist.

- MPMediaGroupingComposer. This value is used to specify grouping based on the media item composer.

- MPMediaGroupingGenre. This value is used to specify grouping based on the media item genre.

- MPMediaGroupingPlaylist. This value is used to specify grouping based on the media item playlist.

- MPMediaGroupingPodcastTitle. This value is used to specify grouping based on the media item podcast title.

There are several class methods declared in the MPMediaQuery class that give you media queries with different groupings. For example, to create a media query that groups and sorts media items according to the album's name, you can use the following class method:

+ (MPMediaQuery *)albumsQuery

Other class methods include artistsQuery, genresQuery, and playlistsQuery.

Once you have configured the media query object, you can retrieve the result media items using the MPMediaQuery instance variable items. This instance variable is declared as follows:

```
@property(nonatomic, readonly) NSArray *items
```

The items array holds instances of MPMediaItem class that match the query. If the result of the query is empty, the array will contain no elements. If, on the other hand, an error occurred during the execution of the query, the value of this property will be nil.

The following code fragment retrieves all songs in the iPod Library, grouping them based on artist name. It then logs specific values of each media item.

```
MPMediaQuery *query = [MPMediaQuery songsQuery];
[query setGroupingType:MPMediaGroupingArtist];
for(MPMediaItem *item in query.items){
  NSLog(@"\nTitle: %@\nAlbum title: %@\nArtist: %@",
        [item valueForProperty:MPMediaItemPropertyTitle],
        [item valueForProperty:MPMediaItemPropertyAlbumTitle],
        [item valueForProperty:MPMediaItemPropertyArtist]);
}
```

To actually retrieve the query result grouped, you need to access the collections property. This property is declared as follows:

```
@property(nonatomic, readonly) NSArray *collections
```

Each element of this array is an instance of the MPMediaItemCollection class. An instance of this class represents a set of media items that are sorted and grouped according to some criterion. To retrieve the items in a collection, you need to access the items property, which is declared as follows:

```
@property (nonatomic, readonly) NSArray *items
```

The following code fragment shows the retrieval of the query results in grouped form:

```
for(MPMediaItemCollection *mc in query.collections){
    NSLog(@"-------------------------------------------");
    for(MPMediaItem *item in mc.items){
      NSLog(@"\nTitle: %@\nAlbum title: %@\nArtist: %@",
            [item valueForProperty:MPMediaItemPropertyTitle],
            [item valueForProperty:MPMediaItemPropertyAlbumTitle],
            [item valueForProperty:MPMediaItemPropertyArtist]);
    }
  }
```

Media property predicate

To specify conditions for the query, you need to add property predicates. A property predicate is an instance of the MPMediaPropertyPredicate class.

To create a predicate instance, you can use one of the following two class methods:

- `predicateWithValue:forProperty:comparisonType:`. This method is declared as follows:

```
+ (MPMediaPropertyPredicate *)
    predicateWithValue:(id)value
    forProperty:(NSString *)property
    comparisonType:(MPMediaPredicateComparison)comparisonType
```

  You specify the value of the property you are matching on in the first argument. In the second argument, you specify the property name. The third argument is used to specify the comparison type. You can specify either `MPMediaPredicateComparisonEqualTo` or `MPMediaPredicateComparisonContains`.

- `predicateWithValue:forProperty:`. This is a convenience method that behaves similarly to the above factory method, except that it uses a `MPMediaPredicateComparisonEqualTo` comparison type.

The following code fragment shows the creation of a predicate and the addition of that predicate to a media query:

```
MPMediaPropertyPredicate *mPredicate =
    [MPMediaPropertyPredicate predicateWithValue:artist
                            forProperty:MPMediaItemPropertyArtist];
    [query addFilterPredicate:mPredicate];
```

To add a predicate filter to the query, use the `addFilterPredicate:` method.

A predicate can be created only for filterable properties. You can check if a property is filterable or not by looking it up in the header file or the documentation, or by using the `canFilterByProperty:` `MPMediaItem` class method, which is declared as follows:

```
+ (BOOL)canFilterByProperty:(NSString *)property
```

14.3   Playing Video

To play video from within your application, you can use the `MPMoviePlayerController` class. You create and initialize an instance of this class and ask it to play. This controller plays the video file in full-screen mode. When playback is finished, the applications screen will become visible.

The following code fragment plays the movie `MyMovie.m4v` stored in the application's bundle:

```
NSString *filePath =
        [[NSBundle mainBundle] pathForResource:@"MyMovie" ofType:@"m4v"];
  NSURL    *fileUrl = [NSURL fileURLWithPath:filePath];
  MPMoviePlayerController *movieController =
        [[MPMoviePlayerController alloc] initWithContentURL:fileUrl];
```

```
movieController.backgroundColor = [UIColor grayColor];
movieController.movieControlMode = MPMovieControlModeDefault;
[movieController play];
```

The above code first finds the full path of the movie in the bundle and uses it to create an NSURL instance. The MPMoviePlayerController is created afterwards and initialized using the initializer initWithContentURL:, passing in the NSURL instance. Optionally, you can set the background color and the control mode. For the movieControlMode property, you can specify (or accept the default of) MPMovieControlModeDefault to allow for the standard controls (e.g., play, pause, timeline, etc.) to appear. To hide all controls, use MPMovieControlModeHidden. The MPMovie-ControlModeVolumeOnly is used to show only the volume control.

After the initialization phase, the controller is asked to play the movie using the method play.

To use the MPMoviePlayerController class, you need to add the Media Player framework as explained in Section D.4 of Appendix D.

You can see a complete application that streams a movie from the Internet by looking at the Video1 project, available in the source downloads. Figure 14.4 shows the view just after sending the play message to the controller.

Figure 14.4   Streaming a movie from the Internet.

14.4   Accessing Device Information

The UIDevice class is used to provide information about the iPhone, iPod touch, and iPad. There is a single instance of this class that can be obtained using the class method currentDevice. The following are some of the pieces of information you can obtain using this instance:

- **Unique identifier.** You can obtain a string that uniquely identifies the iPhone device using the property uniqueIdentifier. This property is declared as follows:

  ```
  @property(nonatomic,readonly,retain) NSString    *uniqueIdentifier
  ```

- **Operating system.** You can obtain the name of the operating system using the `systemName` property. This property is declared as follows:

```
@property(nonatomic,readonly,retain) NSString    *systemName
```

- **Operating-system version.** You can obtain the OS version using the `systemVersion` property. This property is declared as follows:

```
@property(nonatomic,readonly,retain) NSString    *systemVersion
```

- **The model.** You can distinguish among an iPhone, an iPod touch, and an iPad using the `model` property. This property is declared as follows:

```
@property(nonatomic, readonly, retain) NSString *model
```

- **Device orientation.** The orientation of the device can be obtained using the `orientation` property. This property is declared as follows:

```
@property(nonatomic,readonly) UIDeviceOrientation orientation
```

Possible values are

```
UIDeviceOrientationUnknown.
UIDeviceOrientationPortrait.
UIDeviceOrientationPortraitUpsideDown.
UIDeviceOrientationLandscapeLeft.
UIDeviceOrientationLandscapeRight.
UIDeviceOrientationFaceUp.
UIDeviceOrientationFaceDown.
```

14.5   Taking and Selecting Pictures

In this section, you learn how to use the camera for taking pictures. You learn that you do not have direct access to the camera or the photo library, but you use a supplied controller that handles the user's interaction for taking and editing the picture. The controller provides you with the final image when the user finishes. The same controller can be used to pick photos stored in the user's library. This section is organized as follows. In Section 14.5.1, we outline the major steps needed to access the camera and the photo library. Then, in Section 14.5.2, we provide a detailed example of taking and picking pictures.

14.5.1   Overall approach to taking and selecting pictures

To access the camera or to select pictures from the user's library, you have to use a system-supplied interface that is provided to you. The main class used for either taking new pictures or selecting existing ones is `UIImagePickerController`. The major steps for taking and selecting pictures are as follows:

1. **Check the availability of the action.** Whether you would like to take a new picture or select an existing one, you need to check if this function is available to you. The `UIImagePicker-Controller`'s class method used for this purpose is `isSourceTypeAvailable:`.

2. **Create the controller instance.** If the specified action is available, you need to create an instance of `UIImagePickerController`, initialize it, and configure it with the specified function. If no source type is available, the controller should not be allocated.

3. **Set the delegate.** The `UIImagePickerController` will be responsible for the user's interaction while picking or taking a new picture. You need to set the delegate to an object and implement specific methods in order to receive the result. The delegate follows the `UIImagePickerControllerDelegate` protocol.

4. **Present the controller.** You modally present the controller to the user by calling `present-ModalViewController:animated:` on an existing view controller, passing the `UIImage-PickerController` instance as the first parameter.

5. **Handle picture selection.** When the user picks a photo, the delegate's method `image-PickerController:didFinishPickingMediaWithInfo:` is called. You should retrieve the image from the dictionary and dismiss the picker controller that was presented modally.

6. **Handle cancellation.** If the user cancels the operation, the method `imagePicker-ControllerDidCancel:` of the delegate is called. You should dismiss the picker controller that was presented modally.

14.5.2   Detailed example of taking and selecting pictures

In this section, we present a detailed application demonstrating the use of the `UIImagePicker-Controller` class. This application can be found in the `Camera` project, available in the source downloads.

The application uses a navigation-bar button item with the camera icon to take a picture. When this button is tapped, the application checks the availability of the camera. If there is a camera available, the image picker is configured to take a new picture. Otherwise, the image picker is configured to pick a photo from the photo library. Once an image is retrieved, either way, that image is put in a scroll view so that the user can play with it.

Presenting the image picker

When the user taps on the camera icon, the `takePic` method gets executed. This method starts by creating a picker controller. After that, it checks to see if the camera is available. If it is, the picker's source is configured to be the camera. Otherwise, the source is configured to be the photo library.

You can also allow editing of the image by the user by setting the `allowsImageEditing` property to YES. You will see in this section how you can obtain both the original and the edited photos. The `takePic` method is shown below:

```
-(void)takePic{
  UIImagePickerController *picker =
      [[[UIImagePickerController alloc] init] autorelease];
  if([UIImagePickerController
     isSourceTypeAvailable:UIImagePickerControllerSourceTypeCamera]){
    picker.sourceType = UIImagePickerControllerSourceTypeCamera;
  }
  else{
    picker.sourceType = UIImagePickerControllerSourceTypePhotoLibrary;
  }
  picker.allowsImageEditing = YES;
  picker.delegate = self;
  [self presentModalViewController:picker animated:YES];
}
```

Handling successful picking of the photo

When the user selects a photo, the `imagePickerController:didFinishPickingMediaWith-Info:` delegate method is invoked. This method is declared as follows:

```
- (void)imagePickerController:(UIImagePickerController *)picker
        didFinishPickingMediaWithInfo:(NSDictionary *)info;
```

You get, in the second argument, a dictionary with several key/value pairs. Some of these keys are as follows:

* `UIImagePickerControllerOriginalImage`. Using this key, you retrieve the original uncropped image selected by the user. For example, the following retrieves the original photo:

  ```
  UIImage *image =
      [info valueForKey:UIImagePickerControllerOriginalImage];
  ```

* `UIImagePickerControllerEditedImage`. Using this key, you retrieve the edited image manipulated by the user. For example, the following retrieves the edited image:

  ```
  UIImage *editedImage =
      [info valueForKey:UIImagePickerControllerEditedImage];
  ```

* `UIImagePickerControllerCropRect`. Using this key, you retrieve the original cropping rectangle applied by the user to the original image. Because `CGRect` is a structure and not an object, an `NSValue` instance is used to encapsulate the value. For example, the following retrieves the cropping rectangle:

  ```
  CGRect cropRect;
  [[info valueForKey:UIImagePickerControllerCropRect]
              getValue:&cropRect];
  ```

The following shows a possible implementation of the delegate method:

```
- (void)imagePickerController:(UIImagePickerController *)picker
        didFinishPickingMediaWithInfo:(NSDictionary *)info{
  UIImage *image =
    [info valueForKey:UIImagePickerControllerOriginalImage];
  UIImageView *imgView = (UIImageView*)[self.view viewWithTag:100];
  imgView.frame = CGRectMake(0, 0, image.size.width, image.size.height);
  imgView.image = image;
  [(UIScrollView*)self.view setContentSize:image.size];
  NSData *theData = UIImagePNGRepresentation(image);
  NSLog(@"Image size is %d", theData.length);
  [self dismissModalViewControllerAnimated:YES];
}
```

The method obtains the original image and uses it to set the image property of the image view. After that, it dismisses the image picker controller.

Should you need to obtain the data of the image — for example, to upload it to a server — you can use the UIImagePNGRepresentation() function.

You also need to handle the cancellation of the image picking by implementing the following delegate method and dismissing the image picker controller:

```
- (void)imagePickerControllerDidCancel:(UIImagePickerController *)picker{
    [self dismissModalViewControllerAnimated:YES];
}
```

Figure 14.5 shows a screen shot of the application.

14.6   Monitoring the Device Battery

The UIDevice class provides access to the current battery charge level and the state of battery power.

14.6.1   Battery level

You can retrieve the current battery level using the batteryLevel property, which is declared as follows:

```
@property(nonatomic,readonly) float batteryLevel
```

The value retrieved can range from 0.0 (fully discharged) to 1.0 (fully charged). If the battery level cannot be determined, the value is equal to -1.0.

Figure 14.5   A screen shot of the application that demonstrates the image picker.

14.6.2 *Battery state*

You can retrieve the state of the battery using the batteryState property. This property is declared as follows:

@property(nonatomic,readonly) UIDeviceBatteryState batteryState

The returned value can be one of the following:

- UIDeviceBatteryStateUnknown. This value indicates that the battery state cannot be determined. This is the value you get when you use the simulator.

- UIDeviceBatteryStateUnplugged. This value indicates that the battery is discharging due to the device's being unplugged.

- UIDeviceBatteryStateCharging. This value indicates that the battery is charging and the device is plugged into power.

- UIDeviceBatteryStateFull. This value indicates that the battery is fully charged and the device is plugged into power.

14.6.3   Battery state and level notifications

Any object can be added as an observer to the following two notifications:

- `UIDeviceBatteryLevelDidChangeNotification`. This notification is sent when the battery level has changed. The rate of this notification is less than once a minute.
- `UIDeviceBatteryStateDidChangeNotification`. This notification is sent when the battery state has changed, such as when the device is plugged into power.

In order to receive notifications about the battery, you need to enable battery monitoring by setting the value of the `batteryMonitoringEnabled` property to `YES`.

14.6.4   Putting it together

The application `BatteryMonitor`, which is available from the source downloads, is used to monitor and show the state and level of the battery in real time. Figure 14.6 shows a screen shot of that application.

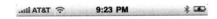

Battery Level: 0.85

Battery State: Charging

Figure 14.6   A screen shot of the application that monitors and displays the battery level and state.

The application enables battery monitoring and adds its controller as an observer in the `loadView` method as shown below:

```
[UIDevice currentDevice].batteryMonitoringEnabled = YES;
[[NSNotificationCenter defaultCenter] addObserver:self
        selector:@selector(handleBatteryLevelChangeNotification:)
        name:UIDeviceBatteryLevelDidChangeNotification object:nil];
[[NSNotificationCenter defaultCenter] addObserver:self
        selector:@selector(handleBatteryStateChangeNotification:)
        name:UIDeviceBatteryStateDidChangeNotification object:nil];
[self updateState];
```

The methods that get called when a notification is received are shown below:

```
-(void)
handleBatteryLevelChangeNotification:(NSNotification*)notification {
  [self updateState];
}

-(void)
handleBatteryStateChangeNotification:(NSNotification*)notification {
  [self updateState];
}
```

These methods simply update the display by calling the method `updateState`, which is shown below:

```
-(void)updateState{
  message.text =
    [NSString stringWithFormat:
        @"  %@\n\n  %@",
        [NSString stringWithFormat:@"Battery Level: %.2f",
          [UIDevice currentDevice].batteryLevel],
          [NSString stringWithFormat:
          @"Battery State: %@",
        [UIDevice currentDevice].batteryState==
            UIDeviceBatteryStateUnplugged?@"Unplugged":
        [UIDevice currentDevice].batteryState==
            UIDeviceBatteryStateCharging?@"Charging":
        [UIDevice currentDevice].batteryState==
            UIDeviceBatteryStateFull?@"Full":@"Unknown"]];
}
```

Refer to the `BatteryMonitor` project, available from the source downloads, for the complete listing of the application. Make sure you run it on the device in order to see the results.

14.7 Accessing the Proximity Sensor

Some of the devices running iOS are equipped with a proximity sensor. The proximity sensor monitors whether the device is held close to the user's face or not.

On the devices that are equipped with a proximity sensor, you can subscribe to notifications about the change in the proximity value. Before subscribing to these notifications, however, you need to successfully enable proximity monitoring.

14.7.1 Enabling proximity monitoring

To check whether a proximity sensor exists or not, you can enable monitoring of the proximity state and then check to see if the proximity monitoring is enabled.

To enable proximity monitoring, you can use the following `UIDevice` property:

```
@property(nonatomic, getter=isProximityMonitoringEnabled)
                        BOOL proximityMonitoringEnabled
```

The following method enables proximity monitoring and returns `YES` if and only if monitoring is enabled:

```
-(BOOL) proximitySensoredIsEnabled{
  [UIDevice currentDevice].proximityMonitoringEnabled = YES;
  return [UIDevice currentDevice].isProximityMonitoringEnabled;
}
```

14.7.2   Subscribing to proximity change notification

After successfully enabling the proximity monitoring, you can subscribe to notifications regarding the change in the state of the proximity.

To subscribe to the proximity state notifications, you register an object (usually a view controller) as an observer to the `UIDeviceProximityStateDidChangeNotification` notification name.

The following shows an example:

```
if([self proximitySensoredIsEnabled]){
   [[NSNotificationCenter defaultCenter] addObserver:self
       selector:@selector(handleProximityChangeNotification:)
       name:UIDeviceProximityStateDidChangeNotification object:nil];
}
```

14.7.3   Retrieving the proximity state

To check whether the device is close to the user's face or not, you can use the `UIDevice` property `proximityState`, which is declared as follows:

```
@property(nonatomic,readonly)    BOOL proximityState
```

The getter returns `YES` if and only if the device is close to the user's face.

You can use the above property in the method that receives the proximity-state updates. For example, the following method logs a message relative to the closeness of the device to the user's face:

```
-(void)handleProximityChangeNotification:(NSNotification*)notification {
  if([UIDevice currentDevice].proximityState){
    NSLog(@"Whisper: I Love You!");
  }
  else{
    NSLog(@"Whisper: I Hate You!");
  }
}
```

You can see a fully functioning application that monitors the proximity sensor in the `Whisper` project, available in the source downloads.

14.8 Summary

In this chapter, we demonstrated the use of several of the devices available on an iOS device. Section 14.1 discussed the usage of the accelerometer. In Section 14.2, you learned how to play short and long audio files, how to record audio files, and how to utilize the iPod Library. Next, Section 14.3 showed how to play video files. After that, Section 14.4 showed how to obtain iPhone/iPod touch device information. Using the camera and the photo library was described in Section 14.5. After that, Section 14.6 showed you how to obtain state information regarding the battery of the device. Finally, we discussed the proximity sensor in Section 14.7.

Exercises

(1) Read the documentation about `UIDevice` class and study the `UIDevice.h` header file.

(2) Make the iPhone scream when it's dropped.

(3) Detect a shake of the user's head.

15

Internationalization

Internationalization (abbreviated i18n for 18 characters separating the *i* and the *n*), *globalization* (g11n), and *localization* (l10n) are terms used to describe equipping software with the ability to adapt to different regions, languages, and customs without modifying the binary code.

Building adaptable software is a major undertaking. It involves having localized text for every supported language, culture-sensitive images and colors, appropriate date and currency formats, and much more.

Once the business decision for globalizing the software has been made and the supported languages and regions have been chosen, developers can use the i18n support built into the iPhone SDK to provide localized behavior of the software.

At the heart of localization in the iOS SDK is the NSLocale class. An NSLocale instance is an object that encapsulates parameters for language, country, currency, dates, etc. A locale can be identified by a string consisting of the language and the region. For example, U.S. English is represented by en_US, while Saudi Arabian Arabic is represented by ar_SA.

You use the NSLocale class and create instances (using, for example, a locale identifier) from it to accomplish various tasks. For example, to obtain an array of the available locales on your system, use the following:

```
[NSLocale availableLocaleIdentifiers];
```

The above statement returns an NSArray instance of locale identifiers (NSString objects) whose content is similar to the following: ti_ER, ar_LY, kok_IN, mk_MK,..., vi_VN, nl_BE, and or_IN.

In this chapter, we start in Section 15.1 by looking at a step-by-step procedure for localizing strings for a set of supported languages. Next, we look in Section 15.2 at date formatting. After that, Section 15.3 covers formatting currencies and numbers. Next, we discuss in Section 15.4 how to generate a sorted list of countries. Finally, we summarize the chapter in Section 15.5.

15.1 String Localization

There are several languages available on the iPhone. The user can switch to a specific language by launching the Settings app, navigating to General → International → Language, and selecting a language. Once a new language is selected, Apple's applications such as Phone, Calendar, and

Voice Memos begin to interact with the user in that language. In addition, Apple and third-party apps will show their names on the home screen in the new language.

As a developer, you can programmatically query the available languages on the device. The list of available languages can be retrieved from the user's defaults database by first obtaining the standard user-defaults object and then retrieving that list (an NSArray instance) using the key AppleLanguages. The following code fragment shows how to do that:

```
NSUserDefaults *defaults = [NSUserDefaults standardUserDefaults];
NSArray *languages = [defaults objectForKey:@"AppleLanguages"];
NSLog(@"%@", languages);
```

The value for the key is an array of language codes in the International Organization for Standardization (ISO) 639 style[1]. Here is a partial list of what you might get: ar, en, fr, de, ja, nl, it, ..., es, pt, sk, th, id, and ms. The preferred language is always number 1 (i.e., index 0). When the user switches languages, the order of the codes in this array changes.

Another method for querying the supported languages on the device is through the use of the NSLocale class as shown in the following statement:

```
[NSLocale preferredLanguages]
```

The contents of the NSArray instance returned are identical to the one obtained using the first method.

Let's assume that our application consists of a single view with a button in the middle of that view. We would like to support, in addition to English, Arabic and Spanish. Once the user switches to one of these languages, our application should show the title of the button in the chosen language. In addition, we would like to change the name of our application and display a localized name on the home screen in the currently chosen language.

Listing 15.1 shows the loadView method of the MainViewController of the LocalizedString project, which is available in the source downloads.

The method simply creates a view and adds a button with the title Validate.

Listing 15.1   The loadView method in our LocalizedString project.

```
- (void)loadView {
  self.view = [[[UIView alloc] initWithFrame:CGRectMake(0, 0, 320, 480)]
                                          autorelease];
  self.view.backgroundColor = [UIColor grayColor];
  UIButton  *button = [UIButton buttonWithType:UIButtonTypeRoundedRect];
  [button setTitle:@"Validate"  forState:UIControlStateNormal];
  [button addTarget:self action:@selector(buttonPushed)
          forControlEvents:UIControlEventTouchUpInside];
  button.frame = CGRectMake(100, 200, 95, 40);
  [self.view addSubview:button];
}
```

[1]http://en.wikipedia.org/wiki/ISO_639

Let's look at the steps needed to support the additional two languages:

1. **Apply the** `NSLocalizedString` **macro.** For every string that needs localization, you need to retrieve its value by calling the `NSLocalizedString` macro. In the code above, only the `Validate` string will be localized. Therefore, the line for setting the title of the button should be changed to

```
[button setTitle:
   NSLocalizedString(@"Validate",
                      @"A button's title asking the user to validate")
         forState:UIControlStateNormal];
```

2. **Generate the** `.strings` **files for every supported language.** In the root directory of your XCode project, create the following three directories: `ar.lproj`, `en.lproj`, and `es.lproj`.

3. **Generate the three** `Localizable.strings` **files.** Each directory needs to have a file named `Localizable.strings` that contains a value for every localized string. You can create this file manually, or you can use the `genstrings` command from the `Terminal` application. While in the root of your project, issue the following commands:

```
genstrings -o ar.lproj ./Classes/*.m
genstrings -o en.lproj ./Classes/*.m
genstrings -o es.lproj ./Classes/*.m
```

What these commands do is generate a `Localizable.strings` file in each of the three directories. Each line in the `Localizable.strings` file consists of a key and a value for a given localized string. In addition, each line will be preceded by the comment passed on from the `NSLocalizedString` macro. This is supposed to help the translator, who need not be the same as the developer.

4. **Update the** `Localizable.strings` **files with the localized strings for each language.** Figures 15.1, 15.2, and 15.3 show the contents of the `Localizable.strings` for the English, Arabic, and Spanish languages, respectively.

```
/* A button's title asking the user to validate */
"Validate" = "Validate";
```

Figure 15.1   The `Localizable.strings` file for the English language.

```
/* A button's title asking the user to validate */
"Validate" = "ابعرش هلعج";
```

Figure 15.2   The `Localizable.strings` file for the Arabic language. As a Semitic language, Arabic script goes from right to left and appears in reverse order in XCode. However, it shows in the right order on the button.

```
/* A button's title asking the user to validate */
"Validate" = "Validar";
```

Figure 15.3   The `Localizable.strings` file for the Spanish language.

5. **Add references to the three files in XCode.** Drag each of these `Localizable.strings` files to the `Resources` group in your project. When prompted, choose not to copy and select UTF-16 encoding as shown in Figure 15.4.

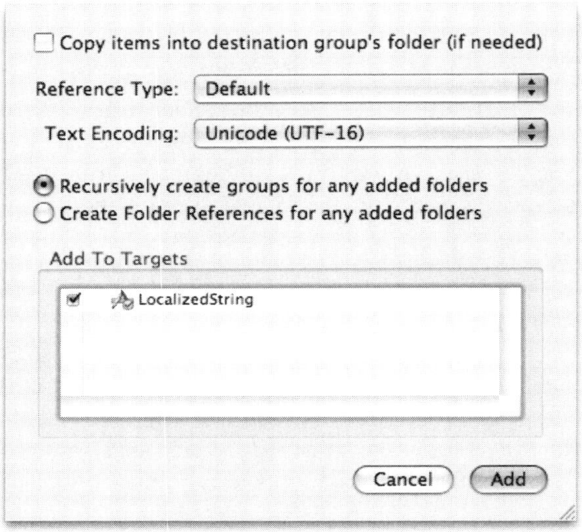

Figure 15.4   The options used in adding references to the three `Localizable.strings` files.

You'll notice (as shown in Figure 15.5) that XCode shows only one `Localizable.strings` group with three languages underneath it.

Figures 15.6, 15.7, and 15.8 show the button after the user selects each of the three languages.

In addition to localization of UI elements, you need to localize the name of the app on the user's home screen. For that, you need to add two additional `.strings` files for the Arabic and Spanish languages. Each file will be used to specify the app name in a given language.

Create one `InfoPlist.strings` file for each of the two languages (in the corresponding directory) and add references to them in XCode. The English version of the app will use the main `plist` of the app, shown in Figure 15.9.

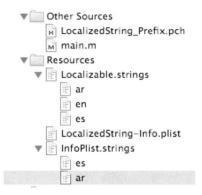

Figure 15.5 The three `Localizable.strings` files after being added to the project's `Groups &` `Files` in XCode.

Figure 15.6 The look of the button when the user selects English as the main language.

Figure 15.7 The look of the button when the user selects Arabic as the main language.

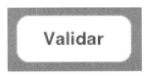

Figure 15.8 The look of the button when the user selects Spanish as the main language.

To specify a display name of the app, enter one line in each file as shown in Figures 15.10 and 15.11. Figures 15.12, 15.13, and 15.14 show the application as shown on the home screen.

Key	Value
▼ Information Property List	(12 items)
Localization native development	English
Bundle display name	Hello
Executable file	${EXECUTABLE_NAME}
Icon file	
Bundle identifier	com.yourcompany.${PRODUCT_NAME:rfc1034identifier}
InfoDictionary version	6.0
Bundle name	${PRODUCT_NAME}
Bundle OS Type code	APPL
Bundle creator OS Type code	????
Bundle version	1.0
Application requires iPhone env	☑
Main nib file base name	MainWindow

Figure 15.9   The main `LocalizedString-Info.plist` of the project. The value for the `Bundle Display Name` key has, as its value, the name of the app in English.

CFBundleDisplayName = "مرحبا";

Figure 15.10   Specifying the bundle display name for the Arabic language.

CFBundleDisplayName = "Hola";

Figure 15.11   Specifying the bundle display name for the Spanish language.

Figure 15.12   The application as shown on the user's home screen when Arabic is the default language.

Figure 15.13   The application as shown on the user's home screen when Spanish is the default language.

Figure 15.14   The application as shown on the user's home screen when English is the default language.

15.2   Date Formatting

The `NSFormatter` class defines an interface for two subclasses: `NSDateFormatter` and `NSNumberFormatter`. These classes are used to manipulate textual representations of dates and numbers, respectively.

The `NSDateFormatter` class is used to convert a date to a string representation and vice versa. It performs these conversions relative to a specific locale. Before using this class, you need to set the default formatter behavior to a formatting behavior equivalent to that of Mac OS X 10.4. The following statement does just that:

```
[NSDateFormatter setDefaultFormatterBehavior:
                              NSDateFormatterBehavior10_4];
```

After that, you can create instances of this class and use them. The function shown in Listing 15.2, for example, prints out a formatted date in every available locale on the system.

Listing 15.2   A function that prints out today's date in every available locale.

```
void showTodayInAllAvailableLocales(){
  NSDateFormatter *formatter =
    [[[NSDateFormatter alloc] init] autorelease];
  [formatter setDateStyle:NSDateFormatterFullStyle];
  [formatter setTimeStyle:NSDateFormatterFullStyle];
  NSArray *locales = [NSLocale availableLocaleIdentifiers];
  for(NSString  *locale in locales){
    [formatter setLocale:[[[NSLocale alloc]
                                    initWithLocaleIdentifier:locale]
                                           autorelease]];
    NSLog(@"Today is %@ in Locale %@",
              [formatter stringFromDate:[NSDate date]], locale);
  }
}
```

The function starts by creating an `NSDateFormatter` instance. After that, it sets the date and the time style of that instance to full style. The following styles are available:

- `NSDateFormatterNoStyle`. This style forces the use of no style. For example, setting the date component's style to this value results in removing the date component from the log generated by the function above.

- `NSDateFormatterShortStyle`. This style, applied to both date and time components, results in a string representation of the current date as `3/26/12 7:13 PM`.

- `NSDateFormatterMediumStyle`. This style, applied to both date and time components, results in a string representation of the current date as `Mar 26, 2012 7:19:39 PM`.

- `NSDateFormatterLongStyle`. This style, applied to both date and time components, results in a string representation of the current date as `March 26, 2012 7:20:58 PM CDT`.

- `NSDateFormatterFullStyle`. This style, applied to both date and time components, results in a string representation of the current date as `Thursday, March 26, 2012 7:22:12 PM CT`.

Next, the function obtains a list of identifiers of available locales and logs the current date for each of these locales. To do that, it creates an `NSLocale` instance for every locale identifier and simply logs today's date in the chosen style. The method `stringFromDate:` takes as a parameter an `NSDate` instance and produces a textual representation of that instance using the currently selected styles. For example, for the locale `ar_KW`, we have a textual representation of an `NSDate` instance as shown in Figure 15.15.

الخميس، ٢٦ مارس، ٢٠٠٩ الولايات المتحدة الأمريكية (شيكاغو) ١٢:٢٢:٧ م

Figure 15.15   The textual representation of an `NSDate` instance using `NSDateFormatterFullStyle` for both date and time in the `ar_KW` locale.

Let's look at another example. Suppose we want to show the days of the week in a given locale. This can be easily achieved using the following function:

```
void showWeekDaySymbols(NSString* locale){
  NSDateFormatter *formatter =
    [[[NSDateFormatter alloc] init] autorelease];
  [formatter setLocale:[[[NSLocale alloc]
                     initWithLocaleIdentifier:locale] autorelease]];
  NSArray *wkDays = [formatter weekdaySymbols];
  NSLog(@"%@", wkDays);
}
```

The function above takes as input the locale identifier and uses the `weekdaySymbols` method to obtain the array of localized weekdays. For example, if we pass in the value `fr_FR`, the contents of the array will be as follows: `dimanche`, `lundi`, `mardi`, `mercredi`, `jeudi`, `vendredi`, and `samedi`.

In addition to using `NSDateFormatter` with predefined styles, you can define flexible patterns and use them to generate textual representations of dates. You can also obtain `NSDate` instances from custom-format strings. To configure an `NSDateFormatter` with a custom format, use the `setDateFormat:` method. It takes an `NSString` object whose value is the custom pattern. The pattern should adhere to the Unicode Standard version tr35-4. For example, to generate the era of the date, add the letter `G` to your custom format.

In the discussion that follows, we will use the date `03/26/2012 6:15:09 PM` in Plano, Texas local time. The following are the main date format patterns:

- **Year.** If the `NSDate` object represents the year 2012, then `yy` will produce `12`, and everything else such as `y`, `yyy`, and `yyyyyy` will produce `2012`.

- **Month.** `M` or `MM` will produce `03`. `MMM` will produce `Mar`, while `MMMM` will produce `March`. `MMMMM` will produce `M` (the short name).

- **Day.** `d` or `dd` will produce `26`. `D` will produce `86` (day of year).

- **Period.** `a` will produce `PM`. The period of the day can be `AM`, `PM`, or the overridden symbol(s) as we shall see shortly in this section.

- **Hour.** `h` will produce `6`, while `hh` will produce `06`. Use `H` for 24-hour presentation.

- **Minute.** `m` will produce `15`, and so will `mm` (zero padding is used if necessary).

- **Second.** `s` will produce `9`, while `ss` will produce `09`.

- **Zone.** `z` will produce `CDT`, while `zzzz` will produce `Central Daylight Time`.

Using the above symbols, you can build the date format in the manner suitable for your application. Listing 15.3 shows a function that logs the custom representation of a given date. After creating the formatter and setting its behavior to 10.4, we set the custom date format. We also use the `setAMSymbol:` and `setPMSymbol:` methods to set a custom symbol for the output of the `a` pattern. The textual representation using this format is obtained, as before, using the `stringFromDate:` method. The output is something like this: `Friday 27/03/2012 at 08:50:16 before midday CDT`. The `EEEE` pattern is used to generate a full name of the weekday.

Listing 15.3   A function that generates a custom format for a given `NSDate` instance.

```
void stringFromDate(NSDate *_date) {
    NSDateFormatter *formatter =
        [[[NSDateFormatter alloc] init]  autorelease];
    [formatter setFormatterBehavior:NSDateFormatterBehavior10_4];
    [formatter setDateFormat:@"EEEE dd/MM/yyyy 'at' hh:mm:ss a zz"];
    [formatter setAMSymbol:@"before midday"];
    [formatter setPMSymbol:@"after midday"];
    NSLog([formatter stringFromDate:_date]);
}
```

As we mentioned above, you can use a formatter in the other direction: obtaining an `NSDate` instance from a string. To obtain the `NSDate` object, use the `dateFromString:` method as shown in Listing 15.4.

Listing 15.4   A function that generates an NSDate instance from a parsed NSString object.

```
void dateFromString(NSString *_stringDate) {
    NSDateFormatter *formatter =
        [[[NSDateFormatter alloc] init]  autorelease];
    [formatter setFormatterBehavior:NSDateFormatterBehavior10_4];
    [formatter setDateFormat:@"EEEE dd/MM/yyyy 'at' hh:mm:ss a zz"];
    [formatter setAMSymbol:@"before midday"];
    [formatter setPMSymbol:@"after midday"];
    NSLog(@"%@", [formatter dateFromString:_stringDate]);
}
```

15.3   Number Formatting

The other concrete subclass of NSFormatter is NSNumberFormatter. This class can be used in the formatting of NSNumber objects. NSNumber is used to provide an object-oriented representation of C scalar (numeric) types such as **int** and **float**.

Let's start by looking at the decimalNumbers() function shown in Listing. 15.5.

Listing 15.5   A function that displays a number in decimal format using a given locale.

```
void decimalNumbers(NSNumber* number, NSString *locale){
    NSNumberFormatter *numberFormatter =
        [[[NSNumberFormatter alloc] init] autorelease];
    [numberFormatter    setFormatterBehavior:NSNumberFormatterBehavior10_4];
    [numberFormatter    setNumberStyle:NSNumberFormatterDecimalStyle];
    NSLocale *theLocale =
        [[[NSLocale alloc] initWithLocaleIdentifier:locale] autorelease];
    [numberFormatter setLocale:theLocale];
    NSLog(@"The value in Locale %@ is: %@",
        [theLocale displayNameForKey:NSLocaleIdentifier value:locale],
        [numberFormatter stringFromNumber:number]);
}
```

This function takes as a parameter an NSNumber object and a locale identifier in an NSString object. It outputs the number in the specified locale in decimal style.

It starts by creating an NSNumberFormatter instance and setting its behavior to that of Mac OS X 10.4. After that, its sets the number style to NSNumberFormatterDecimalStyle in order to specify a decimal style. Next, it creates an NSLocale instance representing the locale identifier argument. The textual representation of the number in the given locale and style is then obtained and logged using the method stringFromNumber:. Notice the use of the method displayNameForKey:value:. The first parameter is a constant representing the key and the second parameter is the value for that key. The key used here is NSLocaleIdentifier, which has a non-nil display name. Another valid key is NSLocaleCurrencySymbol, which is used to represent the currency symbol. The display name for it is a nil value, though. Not all keys have a display name. To obtain that symbol, you need to send an `objectForKey:` message to an `NSLocale` instance with `NSLocaleCurrencySymbol` as the argument.

Figure 15.16 shows the decimal textual representation of the floating-point value `33.45` in the `en_US`, `fr_FR`, and `ar_SA` locales.

The value in Locale English (United States) is: 33.45
The value in Locale français (France) is: 33,45
The value in Locale العربية (المملكة العربية السعودية) is: ٣٣.٤٥

Figure 15.16   The decimal textual representation of the floating-point value `33.45` in the `en_US`, `fr_FR`, and `ar_SA` locales.

You can use the `NSNumberFormatter` class to generate a spelled-out representation of a number. Listing 15.6 shows a function that does just that. The formatter's style is set to `NSNumberFormatterSpellOutStyle` and the representation of the number argument is generated, as before, using the `stringFromNumber:` method.

Listing 15.6   A function that displays a number in spelled-out format using a given locale.

```
void spellOutNumbers(NSNumber* number, NSString *locale){
  NSNumberFormatter *numberFormatter =
        [[[NSNumberFormatter alloc] init] autorelease];
  [numberFormatter    setFormatterBehavior:NSNumberFormatterBehavior10_4];
  [numberFormatter    setNumberStyle:NSNumberFormatterSpellOutStyle];
  NSLocale *theLocale =
        [[[NSLocale alloc] initWithLocaleIdentifier:locale] autorelease];
  [numberFormatter setLocale:theLocale];
  NSLog(@"The spelled-out value in Locale %@ is: %@",
        [theLocale displayNameForKey:NSLocaleIdentifier value:locale],
        [numberFormatter stringFromNumber:number]);
}
```

Figure 15.17 shows the spelled-out representation of the integer `10239` in the `en_US`, `fr_FR`, and `ar_SA` locales.

The spelled-out value in Locale English (United States) is: ten thousand two hundred and thirty-nine
The spelled-out value in Locale français (France) is: dix mille deux cents trente-neuf
The spelled-out value in Locale العربية (المملكة العربية السعودية) is: ten thousand two hundred and thirty-nine

Figure 15.17   The spelled-out representation of the integer `10239` in the `en_US`, `fr_FR`, and `ar_SA` locales.

You can also use the `NSNumberFormatter` to generate a currency textual representation of a value. Listing 15.7 shows a function that does just that.

Listing 15.7   A function that generates a currency textual representation of a value.

```
void money(NSNumber* number, NSString *locale){
  NSNumberFormatter *numberFormatter =
        [[[NSNumberFormatter alloc] init] autorelease];
  [numberFormatter   setFormatterBehavior:NSNumberFormatterBehavior10_4];
  [numberFormatter setNumberStyle:NSNumberFormatterCurrencyStyle];
  NSLocale *theLocale =
        [[[NSLocale alloc] initWithLocaleIdentifier:locale] autorelease];
  [numberFormatter setLocale:theLocale];
  NSLog(@"I owe you %@ in Locale %@",
        [numberFormatter stringFromNumber:number],
        [theLocale displayNameForKey:NSLocaleIdentifier value:locale]);
}
```

Figure 15.18 shows the value 99 represented as currency in three different locales.

> *I owe you $99.00 in Locale English (United States)*
> *I owe you 99,00 € in Locale français (France)*
> *I owe you* ٩٩.٠٠٠.ر.س *in Locale* (العربية (المملكة العربية السعودية

Figure 15.18   The currency representation of 99 in the en_US, fr_FR, and ar_SA locales.

15.4   Sorted List of Countries

Before closing this chapter, let's look at the task of generating a sorted list of countries. Listing 15.8 shows such a function. First, the function obtains the list of ISO country codes using the ISOCountryCodes class method of NSLocale. After that, the display name for that country code is obtained. Both the code and the display name are put in an array and that array is added to another array. After generating the list of code/display name pairs, we sort that list in alphabetical order by display names using the function countrySort shown below.

```
NSInteger countrySort(id number1, id number2, void *context) {
  return [[number1 objectAtIndex:1] compare:[number2 objectAtIndex:1]];
}
```

Listing 15.8   A function that logs a sorted list of countries.

```
void sortedListOfCountries(){
  NSMutableArray  *sortedCountryArray = [NSMutableArray array];
  for (NSString *countryCode in [NSLocale ISOCountryCodes]) {
    NSString *displayNameString =
        [[NSLocale currentLocale] displayNameForKey:NSLocaleCountryCode
                value:countryCode];
    [sortedCountryArray addObject:
        [NSArray arrayWithObjects:countryCode, displayNameString, nil]];
  }
```

```
    [sortedCountryArray sortUsingFunction:countrySort context:nil];
    NSLog(@"%@", sortedCountryArray);
}
```

15.5 Summary

In this chapter, we started in Section 15.1 by looking at a step-by-step procedure for localizing strings for a set of supported languages. Next, we looked in Section 15.2 at date formatting. After that, Section 15.3 covered formatting currencies and numbers. Finally, we discussed in Section 15.4 how to generate a sorted list of the countries.

Exercises

(1) Study the NSLocale class in the documentation and the NSLocale.h header file.

(2) Write a view controller that displays, in a table, all known countries. Each cell representing a country should display the name of that country and two subtitles: (1) the population and (2) the current local time. The two subtitles should be localized for the country represented by that cell. You can use reasonable random numbers for the population size and the current time.

16

Custom User Interface Components

The iOS SDK provides basic UI components for everyday use. Sometimes during the development of your projects, you need a UI component that is not provided by the iOS SDK. In this chapter, we show you how to marry various UI components and build custom reusable ones.

First, we show how to build an alert view with a text field in it, in Section 16.1. Next, Section 16.2 presents a table view inside an alert view. After that, Section 16.3 shows how to build a progress alert view. Finally, we summarize the chapter in Section 16.4.

16.1 Text Field Alert View

Often, you want to get a small piece of text from the user. You do not want to build a dedicated page for it, but you want a dialog box with a text field and OK and Cancel buttons. An example of this feature is the iTunes Store password prompt.

In this section, we will build such a custom UI component whose usage is shown in Figure 16.1.

The component can be configured for inputting telephone, password, or normal text. The trick is to add a `UITextField` to a `UIAlertView` instance as a subview.

Listing 16.1 shows the interface for our UI component, `InputAlertView`, a subclass of `UIAlertView`. Each instance of this class maintains a reference to the text field and its caller. The caller should implement the `InputAlertViewDelegate` protocol declared as follows:

```
@protocol InputAlertViewDelegate
-(void)handleEnteredValue:(NSString*)_value;
-(void)handleCancellation;
@end
```

The object using this class will be notified when the user taps the OK button using `handleEnteredValue:` method, passing the text entered. In the case of tapping the Cancel button, `handleCancellation` gets called.

Listing 16.1 The interface for the `InputAlertView` class.

```
@interface InputAlertView : UIAlertView <UIAlertViewDelegate> {
  UITextField *textField;
```

```
  id<InputAlertViewDelegate> caller;
}
@property(nonatomic, retain) UITextField *textField;
@property(nonatomic, retain) id<InputAlertViewDelegate> caller;
-(NSString*)  theText;
-(void) prepare;
-(void) makePassword;
-(void) makeTelephone;
+(InputAlertView*) inputAlertViewWithTitle:(NSString*)_title
                 initialFieldText:(NSString*)_text
                 caller:(id<InputAlertViewDelegate>)_caller;
@end
```

Figure 16.1 A text field alert view.

To obtain an instance of this class, you call the factory method `inputAlertViewWithTitle:-initialFieldText:caller:`. The `_title` parameter is the `UIAlertView` title, the `_text` is the initial text in the text field, and `_caller` is the object implementing the `InputAlertView-Delegate` protocol.

Listing 16.2 shows the implementation of the factory method. It starts by creating an instance of `InputAlertView` and uses the `UIAlertView` initializer. Notice the use of **self** as a substitute for `InputAlertView`. This works the same as spelling out the class name because this method is a class method and **self** refers to the class object. The delegate of the alert view is set to be itself. After that, the `prepare` method that creates the text field is called.

Listing 16.2   Implementation of the `inputAlertViewWithTitle:initialFieldText:caller:` factory method.

```
+(InputAlertView*) inputAlertViewWithTitle:(NSString*)_title
                     initialFieldText:(NSString*)_text
                     caller:(id<InputAlertViewDelegate>)_caller{
  InputAlertView   *_alert =
                  [[[self alloc]
                      initWithTitle:_title
                      message:@"\n" delegate:nil
                      cancelButtonTitle:@"Cancel"
                      otherButtonTitles:@"OK", nil] autorelease];
  _alert.delegate = _alert;
  _alert.caller = _caller;
  [_alert prepare];
  _alert.textField.text = _text;
  return _alert;
}
```

Listing 16.3 shows the `prepare` method. This method is used in setting up the text field and moving the alert view up in order to make space for the keyboard. A `UITextField` instance is created with rounded corners to match the rounded corners of the parent and then added to the alert view as a subview. The frame of the text field is such that it lies between the title and the OK and Cancel buttons. Because the alert view always shows up in the middle of the screen, you will be faced with the situation shown in Figure 16.2, where the OK and Cancel buttons sit behind the keyboard.

To fix this problem, we need to shift the alert view up `130` points. We can easily achieve that with two lines. First, make a transform that translates the y axis by `130` and then apply it to the view by setting its `transform` property.

Listing 16.3   The `prepare` method of `InputAlertView` class used in setting up the text field and moving the alert view up in order to make space for the keyboard.

```
-(void)prepare{
  self.textField = [[[UITextField alloc]
                  initWithFrame:CGRectMake(12.0, 45, 260.0, 30.0)]
                              autorelease];
  [textField setBackgroundColor:[UIColor clearColor]];
  textField.borderStyle = UITextBorderStyleRoundedRect;
  textField.autocapitalizationType = UITextAutocapitalizationTypeWords;
  [self addSubview:textField];
  CGAffineTransform myTransform =
       CGAffineTransformMakeTranslation(0.0, 130.0);
  [self setTransform:myTransform];
}
```

Figure 16.2   An `InputAlertView` with the OK and Cancel buttons sitting behind the keyboard.

After obtaining an instance of `InputAlertView`, you send it a `show` message. The method simply brings up the keyboard and asks the alert view to show itself, as follows:

```
-(void) show{
  [textField  becomeFirstResponder];
  [super show];
}
```

Because the object hosting the alert view is the alert view's delegate, the delegate method `alert-View:clickedButtonAtIndex:` is overridden as follows:

```
- (void)alertView:(UIAlertView *)alertView
       clickedButtonAtIndex:(NSInteger)buttonIndex{
  if(buttonIndex == 1){
    [self.caller handleCancellation];
  }
  else{
    [self.caller  handleEnteredValue:[self theText]];
  }
}
```

If the user taps the OK button, the value of the text field is obtained and passed on to the caller. If, on the other hand, the Cancel button is tapped, the caller is informed using the `handleCancellation` method. The `InputAlertView` project, in the source downloads, demonstrates the use of this component, and the source code can be found there.

16.2   Table Alert View

Imagine that you are faced with the situation where you need to disambiguate some information. For example, the user enters a city name and there are multiple cities in the country with the same name. Instead of taking the user to a totally new page, for example, by pushing a new view controller or presenting it modally, you want some modal window to appear with a small table with the list of cities (with states) inside.

In this section, we will build such a UI component and make it available for reuse. Figure 16.3 shows an example of our component being utilized to disambiguate the city of Springfield. Notice that the table has rounded corners (courtesy of the grouped style) matching the alert view's rounded-edges style. The table can be cancelled any time with the alert dismissed and the object using this component getting notified. Selecting any of the rows in the table will result in dismissal of the alert view and notification of the calling object.

Figure 16.3   A table alert view with scrollable content.

Figure 16.4 shows a table alert view with just two options. Notice that the table and alert views adjust their heights accordingly.

Listing 16.4 shows the interface for our `TableAlertView` UI component.

Listing 16.4   The interface for our `TableAlertView` UI component.

```
@protocol TableAlertViewDelegate
-(void)didSelectRowAtIndex:(NSInteger)row withContext:(id)context;
@end
```

```
@interface TableAlertView : UIAlertView
            <UITableViewDelegate, UITableViewDataSource>{
  UITableView              *myTableView;
  id<TableAlertViewDelegate> caller;
  id                       context;
  NSArray                  *data;
  NSUInteger               tableHeight;
}
-(id)initWithCaller:(id<TableAlertViewDelegate>)_caller
      data:(NSArray*)_data
      title:(NSString*)_title andContext:(id)_context;
@property(nonatomic, retain) id<TableAlertViewDelegate> caller;
@property(nonatomic, retain) id context;
@property(nonatomic, retain) NSArray *data;
@end

@interface TableAlertView(HIDDEN)
-(void)prepare;
@end
```

Figure 16.4 A table alert view with two items. Notice that the views adjust their heights.

The caller of this component uses the `initWithCaller:data:title:andContext:` initializer. The first parameter is a reference to the calling object. The caller needs to implement the `didSelectRowAtIndex:withContext:` method declared in the `TableAlertViewDelegate` protocol. The second parameter is the array of items that need to be shown as options to the user. Each item in this array needs to override the `description` method to provide a textual representation of itself to the user. The third parameter is the title of the alert view. Finally, the last parameter is a context. This argument is used as a token by the caller to route the user selection in case of multiple usage of the component. It can be `nil`.

The `prepare` method is used internally by the component for the layout of the table view inside the alert view. It is not part of the public interface (defined in a category). As you may know from previous chapters, this does not prevent other objects from using it because there are *no* private methods in Objective-C.

Listing 16.5 shows the implementation of the `initWithCaller:data:title:andContext:` initializer method.

Listing 16.5 The `initWithCaller:data:title:andContext:` initializer for the table alert view component.

```
-(id)initWithCaller:(id<TableAlertViewDelegate>)_caller
      data:(NSArray*)_data
      title:(NSString*)_title andContext:(id)_context{
  tableHeight = 0;
  NSMutableString *msgString = [NSMutableString string];
  if([_data count] >= MAX_VISIBLE_ROWS){
    tableHeight = 225;
    msgString = @"\n\n\n\n\n\n\n\n\n\n";
  }
  else{
    tableHeight = [_data count]*50;
    for(id value in _data){
      [msgString appendString:@"\n\n"];
    }
    if([_data count] == 1){
      tableHeight +=5;
    }
    if([_data count] == MAX_VISIBLE_ROWS-1){
      tableHeight -=15;
    }
  }
  if(self = [super initWithTitle:_title message:msgString
                    delegate:self cancelButtonTitle:@"Cancel"
                    otherButtonTitles:nil]){
    self.caller  = _caller;
    self.context = _context;
    self.data    = _data;
    [self prepare];
  }
  return self;
}
```

The method performs three tasks. First, it calculates the height of the window by adjusting the dummy alert view message based on the size of the elements to be selected. The details of the adjustment are not that important as it is a hack. Next, the `UIAlertView` initializer is called to create the container view. Finally, a call to the `prepare` method is issued in order to create and lay out the table view with the items.

The `prepare` method is shown in Listing 16.6. It creates a table view with dimensions to fit an alert view container, enables scrolling only if we have scrollable content, and sets the table view's delegate and data source to be the `TableAlertView` instance.

Listing 16.6   The `prepare` method for layout of the table view inside an alert view.

```
-(void)prepare{
  myTableView =
    [[UITableView alloc]
                  initWithFrame:CGRectMake(15, 35, 255, tableHeight)
                  style:UITableViewStyleGrouped];
  myTableView.backgroundColor = [UIColor clearColor];
  if([data count] < MAX_VISIBLE_ROWS){
    myTableView.scrollEnabled = NO;
  }
  myTableView.delegate   = self;
  myTableView.dataSource = self;
  [self addSubview:myTableView];
}
```

A caller performs two steps in initiating the table alert view, similar to the following:

```
TableAlertView  *alert =
            [[[TableAlertView alloc] initWithCaller:self data:data
            title:@"Did you mean..." andContext:nil] autorelease];
[alert show];
```

The `show` method of the component is shown below. It hides itself, schedules a timer, and cascades the `show` call to the `UIAlertView` `show` method. The first two steps are not necessary; they just accomplish better user experience vis-à-vis the rendering of the table view.

```
-(void)show{
  self.hidden = YES;
  [NSTimer scheduledTimerWithTimeInterval:.5 target:self
          selector:@selector(myTimer:) userInfo:nil repeats:NO];
  [super show];
}
```

The timer is scheduled to fire in `0.5` seconds, and when it does, it sets the alert view's `hidden` property to `NO` and flashes the table view scroll indicators, but only when we have enough scrollable content. The method is shown below:

```
-(void)myTimer:(NSTimer*)_timer{
  self.hidden = NO;
```

```
  if([data count] > MAX_VISIBLE_ROWS){
    [myTableView flashScrollIndicators];
  }
}
```

Because the `TableAlertView` is the delegate of the `UIAlertView`, we define the `alertView:-clickedButtonAtIndex:` method. The method simply informs the user that the action has been cancelled. Instead of requiring another method in the protocol, we use a negative index of the selected item to signal cancellation of the process, as follows:

```
- (void)alertView:(UIAlertView *)alertView
      clickedButtonAtIndex:(NSInteger)buttonIndex{
  [self.caller didSelectRowAtIndex:-1 withContext:self.context];
}
```

In addition to being a delegate of the alert view, the component is the data source and delegate for the table view. The component defines the `tableView:cellForRowAtIndexPath:` shown in Listing 16.7. You have already seen plenty of this method! The cell text is retrieved from the `description` of the corresponding data item provided to the component by the user.

Listing 16.7 The `tableView:cellForRowAtIndexPath:` method for the `TableAlertView` component.

```
- (UITableViewCell *)tableView:(UITableView *)tableView
                    cellForRowAtIndexPath:(NSIndexPath *)indexPath{
  static NSString *cellID = @"ABC";
  UITableViewCell *cell =
    (UITableViewCell*)
          [tableView dequeueReusableCellWithIdentifier:cellID];
    if (cell == nil) {
        cell = [[[UITableViewCell alloc]
                          initWithStyle:UITableViewCellStyleDefault
                          reuseIdentifier:cellID] autorelease];
        cell.selectionStyle = UITableViewCellSelectionStyleBlue;
  }
  cell.textLabel.text =
    [[data objectAtIndex:indexPath.row] description];
  return cell;
}
```

The `tableView:didSelectRowAtIndexPath:` delegate method simply dismisses the alert view and calls back the caller, passing in the index of the selected row and the token (context). This method is shown below:

```
- (void)tableView:(UITableView *)tableView
        didSelectRowAtIndexPath:(NSIndexPath *)indexPath{
  [self dismissWithClickedButtonIndex:0 animated:YES];
  [self.caller didSelectRowAtIndex:indexPath.row
                withContext:self.context];
}
```

For more information, consult the `TableAlertView` project in the source downloads; this is a complete application utilizing this component.

16.3 Progress Alert View

Often, you would like to perform a task and show the user the progress of this task while giving the user the option of canceling this task. Examples include uploading a file for processing or performing image analysis. In this section, we will develop a UI component that does just that. Figure 16.5 shows how this UI component looks.

Figure 16.5   The progress alert view UI component.

Let's start with the interface. Listing 16.8 shows the interface for the `ProgressAlertView` UI component.

Listing 16.8   The interface for the `ProgressAlertView` UI component.

```
@interface ProgressAlertView : NSObject {
  UIProgressView   *progressView;
  UILabel          *statusLabel;
  NSThread         *thread;
  UIAlertView      *alertView;
  SEL              task;
  id               delegate;
}
```

```
@property                      SEL                task;
@property(nonatomic, retain) id                  delegate;

-(void)start;
-(BOOL)isCancelled;
-(void)updateProgress:(NSDictionary*)_progressData;
@end
```

The interface is simple. You create an instance of ProgressAlertView and set its task property to the task you would like to perform, set the delegate to your reference, and send a start message to the component.

Immediately, the progress alert view appears and your task method is invoked. At any time, you can update the progress bar and the message beneath it using the updateProgress: method, passing a dictionary with two values: an NSNumber encapsulating a float and a NSString object encapsulating the message.

Because your task is running on its own thread, the user can interact with the progress alert view. If the user taps Cancel, the progress alert view object becomes tainted. You can, at any time, check for this state using the isCancelled method. Just returning from the task method you've supplied removes the progress alert view.

Listing 16.9 shows the implementation of the start method. It creates the UIAlertView, UIProgressView, and UILabel instances; adds the progress and label views to the alert view; shows the alert view, and starts a new thread.

Listing 16.9   The start method for the ProgressAlertView UI component.

```
-(void)start{
  if(thread){
    return;
  }
  alertView = [[UIAlertView alloc]
                  initWithTitle:nil message:@"\n"
                  delegate:self cancelButtonTitle:@"Cancel"
                  otherButtonTitles:nil];
  progressView =
    [[UIProgressView alloc]
          initWithProgressViewStyle:UIProgressViewStyleDefault];
  [progressView setBackgroundColor:[UIColor clearColor]];
  progressView.frame = CGRectMake(12.0, 20, 260.0, 20.0);
  [alertView addSubview:progressView];
  statusLabel = [[UILabel alloc]
    initWithFrame:CGRectMake(12.0, 30, 260.0, 20.0)];
  statusLabel.backgroundColor = [UIColor clearColor];
  statusLabel.textColor = [UIColor whiteColor];
  statusLabel.textAlignment = UITextAlignmentCenter;
  [alertView addSubview:statusLabel];
  [alertView show];
```

```
thread = [[NSThread alloc]
        initWithTarget:self selector:@selector(performTask)
     object:nil];
[thread start];
}
```

The `performTask` method is the new thread body. It creates a new autorelease pool and performs the task method, as follows:

```
-(void)performTask{
  NSAutoreleasePool *pool = [[NSAutoreleasePool alloc] init];
  [delegate performSelector:task];
  [self stop];
  [pool release];
}
```

The `stop` method simply dismisses the alert view, as follows:

```
-(void)stop{
  [alertView dismissWithClickedButtonIndex:0 animated:YES];
}
```

The `updateProgress:` method updates the UI. You should always perform UI updates from the main thread. The method simply routes the call to an internal method that updates the progress bar and the message label. It achieves that by sending a `performSelectorOnMainThread:with-Object:waitUntilDone:` message to **self**. The two methods are shown below:

```
-(void)safeUpdate:(NSDictionary*)_progressData{
  progressView.progress +=
    [[_progressData objectForKey:PROGRESS_PERCENTAGE_KEY] floatValue];
  statusLabel.text =
    [_progressData objectForKey:PROGRESS_MESSAGE_KEY];
}
```

```
-(void)updateProgress:(NSDictionary*)_progressData{
  [self performSelectorOnMainThread:@selector(safeUpdate:)
      withObject:_progressData waitUntilDone:NO];
}
```

Because the UI component instance is the delegate of the alert view, it defines the `alertView:clickedButtonAtIndex:`. We simply cancel the thread by sending a `cancel` message to it:

```
- (void)alertView:(UIAlertView *)alertView
      clickedButtonAtIndex:(NSInteger)buttonIndex{
  [thread cancel];
}
```

The `isCancelled` simply returns the cancellation status of the thread:

```
-(BOOL)isCancelled{
  return [thread isCancelled];
}
```

Using this UI component is simple. The following code fragment creates the `ProgressAlert-`
`View` instance, sets its `delegate` to self, sets its `task` to the method `compute`, and sends it a
`start` message:

```
self.progress = [[[ProgressAlertView alloc] init] autorelease];
progress.delegate = self;
progress.task = @selector(compute);
[progress start];
```

Our demo `compute` method (shown in Listing 16.10) doesn't do anything useful. It simply fakes
several computation phases and updates the view at the end of each phase. The delay is achieved
using the `sleepForTimeInterval:` `NSThread` class method. When this method returns, the
progress alert view disappears.

Listing 16.10   The `compute` method used in demonstrating the usage of the `ProgressAlertView`
component.

```
-(void)compute{
  [self updateUIWithProgress:0.0 andMessage:@"Initializing..."];
  [NSThread sleepForTimeInterval:1];
  if([progress isCancelled]){
    self.progress = nil;
    return;
  }
  [self updateUIWithProgress:0.2 andMessage:@"Preparing data..."];
  [NSThread sleepForTimeInterval:2];
  if([progress isCancelled]){
    self.progress = nil;
    return;
  }
  [self updateUIWithProgress:0.4 andMessage:@"Crunching numbers..."];
  [NSThread sleepForTimeInterval:1];
  if([progress isCancelled]){
    self.progress = nil;
    return;
  }
  [self updateUIWithProgress:0.8 andMessage:@"Almost done!"];
  [NSThread sleepForTimeInterval:2];
  if([progress isCancelled]){
    self.progress = nil;
    return;
  }
  [self updateUIWithProgress:1.0 andMessage:@"Done!"];
}
```

The following is a convenience method for updating the UI:

```
-(void)updateUIWithProgress:(float)_progress
       andMessage:(NSString*)_message{
   NSMutableDictionary  *_progressData =
       [NSMutableDictionary dictionary];
   [_progressData setObject:[NSNumber numberWithFloat:_progress]
               forKey:PROGRESS_PERCENTAGE_KEY];
   [_progressData setObject:_message
               forKey:PROGRESS_MESSAGE_KEY];
   [progress updateProgress:_progressData];
}
```

See the `ProgressAlertView` project in the source downloads for a complete application utilizing this component.

Figure 16.6   The tabbed-control UI component.

16.4   Summary

The iOS SDK provides basic UI components for everyday use. Sometimes during the development of your projects, you need a UI component that is not provided by the iOS SDK. In this chapter, we showed you how to marry various UI components and build custom reusable ones.

First, we showed how to build an alert view with a text field in it, in Section 16.1. Next, Section 16.2 presented a table view inside an alert view. Finally, Section 16.3 showed how to build a progress alert view.

Exercises

(1) Build a tabbed-control UI component. For each tab, the user should be able to provide just the title and the view. In addition, an optional title for the control should be accommodated. The UI component manages the switching from one view to the other. The UI component should support a variable number of tabs and variable title lengths. The UI component should support scrolling if a given view has a height that exceeds the available space for it. See Figure 16.6 for an example.

(2) Build a scrolled-menu UI component as shown in Figure 16.7.

Figure 16.7   A scrolled-menu UI component.

17

Advanced Networking

This chapter addresses several advanced networking topics. We start by looking in Section 17.1 at how we can determine the network connectivity of the device. This is important for several reasons. First, your application needs to determine the status of network connectivity and alert the user connectivity problems instead of presenting an empty view to the user. In addition, some applications require Wi-Fi connection for specific services (e.g., downloading large files). You should be able to enable such services dynamically, based on the connectivity of the device.

In Section 17.2, we tackle the issue of uploading multimedia content (e.g., photos) to remote servers. Next, in Section 17.3, we present a category on `NSString` that allows you to easily compute the MD5 digest of a string. This is important as some services, such as Flickr, require posting parameters with the appropriate signature. Section 17.4 then shows you how to present a responsive table view whose data rows are fed from the Internet without sacrificing the user experience. Next, Sections 17.5 and 17.6 address the topics of remote and local push notification, respectively. Section 17.7 shows how to utilize the multitasking API in downloading large amounts of data even after the app is suspended. Section 17.8 discusses sending email from within your iOS application. Finally, Section 17.9 summarizes the chapter.

17.1 Determining Network Connectivity

In this section, we look at a mechanism that allows you to determine the network connectivity of the device. We develop the following three methods in a category on `UIDevice` class:

- `cellularConnected`. This method is used to determine whether the device is connected to the network via Enhanced Data Rate for Global Evolution (EDGE) or General Packet Radio Service (GPRS).

- `wiFiConnected`. This method is used to determine whether the device is connected to the network via Wi-Fi.

- `networkConnected`. This method is used to determine network connectivity in general.

Listing 17.1 shows the declaration of the category.

Listing 17.1   A category on `UIDevice` for network connectivity.

```
@interface UIDevice (DeviceConnectivity)

+(BOOL)cellularConnected;
+(BOOL)wiFiConnected;
+(BOOL)networkConnected;

@end
```

In order to use the methods in this section, you need to add the `SystemConfiguration` framework as explained in Section D.4 of Appendix D. In addition, you need to add the following import statement to your code:

```
#import <SystemConfiguration/SCNetworkReachability.h>
```

17.1.1   Determining network connectivity via EDGE or GPRS

Listing 17.2 shows the `cellularConnected` method, which determines whether the device is connected via EDGE or GPRS.

Listing 17.2   The `cellularConnected` method for determining connectivity to the network via EDGE or GPRS.

```
+(BOOL)cellularConnected{// EDGE or GPRS
  SCNetworkReachabilityFlags     flags = 0;
  SCNetworkReachabilityRef       netReachability;
  netReachability      = SCNetworkReachabilityCreateWithName
    (CFAllocatorGetDefault(), [EXTERNAL_HOST UTF8String]);
  if(netReachability){
    SCNetworkReachabilityGetFlags(netReachability, &flags);
    CFRelease(netReachability);
  }
  if(flags & kSCNetworkReachabilityFlagsIsWWAN){
    return YES;
  }
  return NO;
}
```

The method first creates a network reachability object using the function `SCNetwork-ReachabilityCreateWithName()`. This function is declared as follows:

```
SCNetworkReachabilityRef SCNetworkReachabilityCreateWithName (
  CFAllocatorRef allocator,
  const char *nodename
);
```

You pass in the allocator in the first argument. An allocator is used throughout Cocoa for allocating and deallocating objects. In our case, we just use the default allocator by obtaining it using the `CFAllocatorGetDefault()` function. The second parameter is the node name (e.g., `google.com`) that you want to test for reachability.

After obtaining the reachability reference, the method determines network connectivity to the host by calling the `SCNetworkReachabilityGetFlags()` function. You pass in the network reference and a reference to the `flags` local variable (a 32-bit number). The method checks the `flags` by looking for a 1 in bit 18. If it is 1, that means the device is reachable via a cellular connection, such as EDGE or GPRS.

17.1.2 Determining network connectivity in general

Listing 17.3 shows a method that determines network connectivity in general.

> **Listing 17.3**   The method `networkConnected` that determines network connectivity.

```
+(BOOL)networkConnected{
  SCNetworkReachabilityFlags       flags = 0;
  SCNetworkReachabilityRef         netReachability;
  BOOL                             retrievedFlags = NO;
  netReachability     = SCNetworkReachabilityCreateWithName(
    CFAllocatorGetDefault(), [EXTERNAL_HOST UTF8String]);
  if(netReachability){
    retrievedFlags       =
        SCNetworkReachabilityGetFlags(netReachability, &flags);
    CFRelease(netReachability);
  }
  if (!retrievedFlags || !flags){
    return NO;
  }
  return YES;
}
```

It uses the same procedure as in Section 17.1.1, except that we simply check that the return value is YES and `flags` is not 0. If that is the case, we report network connectivity by returning YES; otherwise, we return NO.

17.1.3 Determining network connectivity via Wi-Fi

Finally, the following method determines Wi-Fi connectivity by checking for network connectivity via a transport mechanism other than EDGE or GPRS:

```
+(BOOL)wiFiConnected{
  if([self cellularConnected]){
```

```
    return NO;
  }
  return [self networkConnected];
}
```

17.2   Uploading Multimedia Content

In this section, we will see how we can use the NSURLConnection class to upload multimedia content to a remote server. For demonstration purposes, we will use the example of uploading a photo and several other parameters to a remote server. The procedure presented here also applies to uploading other types of multimedia content (e.g., audio).

To communicate with a server, you follow these steps:

1. **Create a request (instance of** NSURLRequest **class or its subclasses).**

2. **Configure that request with the** url **property (an instance of the** NSURL **class).**

3. **Specify the** HTTP **method (**Post, Get**, etc.).**

4. **Set the values of some of the request headers.**

5. **Build the request body (instance of** NSData **class) and assign it to the request.**

6. **Use either a synchronous or asynchronous version of the** NSURLConnection **to send the request to the server.**

7. **Obtain the response from the server and act according to the HTTP status code and/or application-level return values.**

Listing 17.4 shows a method that posts a photo to a server.

Listing 17.4   A method that posts a photo to a server.

```
-(void)postPhoto:(UIImage *)_photo withLat:(float)_lat
        withLng:(float)_lng andCaption:(NSString*)_caption{
NSMutableURLRequest *req =
  [NSMutableURLRequest requestWithURL:
        [NSURL URLWithString:@"http://192.168.1.100:3000/photos"]];
[req setHTTPMethod:@"POST"];
NSString *contentType = [NSString stringWithFormat:
      @"multipart/form-data; boundary=%@", boundary];
[req setValue:contentType forHTTPHeaderField:@"Content-type"];
NSMutableData *postBody = [NSMutableData data];
[postBody appendData:[[NSString stringWithFormat:
  @"--%@\r\n", boundary] dataUsingEncoding:NSUTF8StringEncoding]];
[self appendPhoto:_photo
      withParamName:@"photo[uploaded_data]"
      toData:postBody];
[self appendParamValue:_caption
```

```
        withParamName:@"photo[caption]"
            toData:postBody];
  [self appendParamValue:[NSNumber numberWithFloat:_lat]
        withParamName:@"photo[lat]" toData:postBody];
  [self appendParamValue:[NSNumber numberWithFloat:_lng]
        withParamName:@"photo[lng]" toData:postBody];
  [postBody appendData:[[NSString stringWithFormat:
  @"\r\n--%@--\r\n", boundary] dataUsingEncoding:NSUTF8StringEncoding]];
  [req setHTTPBody:postBody];
  NSHTTPURLResponse * returnResponse = nil;
  NSError * returnError = nil;
  NSData *returnData =
    [NSURLConnection sendSynchronousRequest:req
                          returningResponse:&returnResponse
                          error:&returnError];
  int statusCode = returnResponse.statusCode;
  NSString    *str = [[[NSString alloc]
                        initWithData:returnData
                          encoding:NSUTF8StringEncoding] autorelease];
  if([str isEqualToString:@"OK"] &&(statusCode == 200) && !returnError){
    NSLog(@"Photo uploaded successfully! Status code: 200");
  }
  else{
    NSLog(@"Failed to upload photo error: %@. Status code: %d. Error:%@",
        str, statusCode, [returnError localizedDescription]);
  }
}
```

The first argument is the photo in a UIImage instance. The second and third arguments are the latitude and longitude, respectively. The fourth and last argument is the caption for this photo.

First, the method creates a mutable request and initializes it with an NSURL instance representing the post address. In this example, we are posting to a Rails server, available in the source downloads. Nevertheless, this method should work with any other service (such as Flickr) with minimal changes to accommodate the service.

Next, we set the HTTP method type to Post and the Content-type to

```
multipart/form-data; boundary=--------75023658052007
```

The value for the boundary should be a unique pattern that does not occur within the post data.[1]

After that, we add the parts of this post to a mutable NSData object one after the other. The separators are needed between these parameters and should be used literally; otherwise, the post will be invalid.

Listing 17.5 shows the method used to add the caption and the geo data to a post body with the postPhoto:withLat:withLng:andCaption: method.

---

[1] RFC 1867 Form-based File Upload in HTML, www.faqs.org/rfcs/rfc1867.html.

Listing 17.5   A method that adds a parameter to a post body.

```
-(void)appendParamValue:(id)_value withParamName:(NSString*)_param
      toData:(NSMutableData*)_data{
  NSString  *_tmp = [NSString stringWithFormat:
   @"Content-Disposition: form-data; name=\"%@\"\r\n\r\n", _param];
  [_data appendData:[[NSString stringWithFormat:
   @"\r\n--%@\r\n", boundary] dataUsingEncoding:NSUTF8StringEncoding]];
  [_data appendData:[_tmp dataUsingEncoding:NSUTF8StringEncoding]];
  [_data appendData:[[[_value description] urlEncodedVersion]
    dataUsingEncoding:NSUTF8StringEncoding]];
}
```

Again, the separator is defined by the RFC and should be used as is. The NSNumber and NSString classes define the description method in a way suitable for our purpose. If you would like to use this method to add a parameter of a different type, make sure that its description method is defined in the correct way.

Listing 17.6 shows the method for adding a photo parameter to the post body.

Listing 17.6   Appending a photo to a post body after compression.

```
-(void)appendPhoto:(UIImage*)_photo withParamName:(NSString*)_param
      toData:(NSMutableData*)_data{
  NSData *_photoData =  UIImageJPEGRepresentation(_photo, 0.6);
  NSString  *_tmp = [NSString stringWithFormat:
  @"Content-Disposition: form-data; name=\"%@\"; filename=\"p.jpg\"\r\n",
    _param];
  [_data appendData:[_tmp dataUsingEncoding:NSUTF8StringEncoding]];
  [_data appendData:[@"Content-Type: image/jpeg\r\n\r\n"
    dataUsingEncoding:NSUTF8StringEncoding]];
  [_data appendData:_photoData];
}
```

The method first compresses the image to a reasonable size; the post of an iPhone 320×320 photo should take around 10 seconds over EDGE. The compressed data is then appended to the post body (after the headers, of course).

One last comment about communicating with a server: You need to encode the data. Listing 17.7 shows a category on NSString to allow strings to produce encoded versions of their content. The method urlEncodedVersion simply replaces all occurrences of an encodable character with the encoded version of that character.

Listing 17.7   A category on NSString to extend strings with the ability to produce encoded versions of themselves.

```
@interface NSString(URL_ENCODE)
-(NSString *)urlEncodedVersion;
@end
```

```
@implementation NSString(URL_ENCODE)

-(NSString *)urlEncodedVersion{
  NSArray *escapeChars = [NSArray arrayWithObjects:
              @" ",@";",@"/",@"?",@":",@"@",
              @"&",@"=",@"+",@"$",@",",
              @"[",@"]",@"#",@"!",@"'",@"(",
              @")",@"*", nil];
  NSArray *replaceChars = [NSArray arrayWithObjects:
              @"%20",@"%3B",@"%2F",@"%3F",@"%3A",
              @"%40",@"%26",@"%3D",
              @"%2B",@"%24",@"%2C",@"%5B",@"%5D",
              @"%23",@"%21",@"%27",
              @"%28",@"%29",@"%2A",nil];
  NSMutableString *tempStr = [[self mutableCopy] autorelease];
  for(int i = 0; i < [escapeChars count]; i++) {
    [tempStr replaceOccurrencesOfString:[escapeChars objectAtIndex:i]
            withString:[replaceChars objectAtIndex:i]
            options:NSLiteralSearch
            range:NSMakeRange(0,[tempStr length])];
  }
  return [[tempStr copy] autorelease];
}
@end
```

You can simply post a photo as follows:

```
[self postPhoto:[UIImage imageNamed:@"clouds.jpg"]
     withLat:38.44 withLng:-97.76
     andCaption:@"This is a nice photo!"];
```

Consult the upload_image project files for a complete iPhone client and Rails server source code. These projects are available in the source downloads.

17.3   Computing MD5 Hash Value

MD5 is an algorithm that generates a 128-bit hash value for a given string. MD5 is often used to check the integrity of files downloaded from the Internet. MD5 is also used by web services such as Flickr. This section presents a category on NSString to allow a string to produce an MD5 digest of its content.

Listing 17.8 shows a category on NSString defining the md5 method, which generates a 128-bit digest on the value stored in the instance. The md5 method uses the CC_MD5 function to compute the digest, and it then outputs the hexadecimal representation of the result.

Listing 17.8   A category on `NSString` defining the md5 method, which generates a 128-bit digest.

```
#import <CommonCrypto/CommonDigest.h>

@interface NSString(MD5)
-(NSString*) md5;
@end

@implementation NSString(MD5)
-(NSString*) md5{
    const char *cStrValue = [self UTF8String];
    unsigned char theResult[CC_MD5_DIGEST_LENGTH];
    CC_MD5(cStrValue, strlen(cStrValue), theResult);
    return [NSString stringWithFormat:
            @"%02X%02X%02X%02X%02X%02X%02X%02X"
            @"%02X%02X%02X%02X%02X%02X%02X%02X",
            theResult[0], theResult[1], theResult[2],
            theResult[3], theResult[4], theResult[5],
            theResult[6], theResult[7], theResult[8],
            theResult[9], theResult[10], theResult[11],
            theResult[12], theResult[13], theResult[14],
            theResult[15]
            ];
}
@end
```

The following code fragment demonstrates the use of this category:

```
NSString   *value1 = @"The quick brown fox jumps over the lazy dog";
NSString   *value2 = @"The quick brown fox jumps over the lazy dog.";
NSLog(@"MD5 of zero-length string is %@", [@"" md5]);
NSLog(@"MD5(%@) = %@", value1, [value1 md5]);
NSLog(@"MD5(%@) = %@", value2, [value2 md5]);
```

The output (after removing extra logging information) is as follows:

```
MD5 of zero-length string is D41D8CD98F00B204E9800998ECF8427E
MD5(The quick brown fox jumps over the lazy dog) = \
    9E107D9D372BB6826BD81D3542A419D6
MD5(The quick brown fox jumps over the lazy dog.) = \
    E4D909C290D0FB1CA068FFADDF22CBD0
```

Notice how just adding a period (`.`) to the end of the text completely changes the digest. MD5 has its weaknesses, but if a service requires it, then you need to use it.

Please see the MD5 project in the source downloads for a complete application.

17.4   Multithreaded Downloads

In this section, we develop an application that presents a table view with downloadable resources. The download of a resource will not start until the corresponding cell hosting that resource becomes visible. If the resource has been successfully downloaded, that resource is used to decorate the cell. If, on the other hand, that resource has not been downloaded yet, we ask the resource to download itself in the background. If the resource cannot be downloaded, due to network or application failure, we signal failure to the user by using a bundled image (a red X) instead.

17.4.1   The Multithreaded Downloads application

In the following sections, we develop the Multithreaded Downloads application. The source code of the complete application can be found in the MThreadedDownloads project, available in the source downloads.

Figure 17.1 shows a screen shot of the application.

Figure 17.1   Screen shot of the Multithreaded Downloads application.

At the heart of our application is the InternetResource class, which encapsulates the download of the resource in a new thread. We start by developing this class and then write a table view controller that uses it.

The `InternetResource` class encapsulates an Internet resource that is downloaded, on demand, in a separate thread (i.e., without locking the UI of the user). Listing 17.9 shows the interface for this class.

Listing 17.9   The interface for the `InternetResource` class.

```
#define FinishedLoading @"FinishedLoading"

typedef enum   {
  NEW,
  FETCHING,
  FAILED,
  COMPLETE
} STATUS;

@interface InternetResource : NSObject {
  NSString                *url, *title;
  UIImage                 *image;
  STATUS                  status;
  NSMutableData           *receivedData;
}
-(void)start;
-(id)initWithTitle:(NSString*)_title andURL:(NSString*)_url;
@property(nonatomic, retain) NSString    *url;
@property(nonatomic, retain) NSString    *title;
@property(nonatomic, retain) UIImage     *image;
@property(nonatomic, assign) STATUS      status;
@end
```

An object of this class is initialized with the title of the resource and its URL. An `InternetResource` object can be in one of the following four states:

- NEW. It has just been created.
- FETCHING. It has received a `start` message and is currently fetching the resource from the Internet.
- COMPLETE. It has successfully downloaded the resource.
- FAILED. A network or application-level failure has occurred.

To access the state of the resource, objects should use the `status` property. If the object is in COMPLETE state, the picture can be retrieved from the `image` property.

The following shows the implementation of the initializer:

```
-(id)initWithTitle:(NSString*)_title andURL:(NSString*)_url{
  if(self = [super init]){
    self.title = _title;
    self.url = _url;
```

```
    self.status = NEW;
  }
  return self;
}
```

The `start` method simply sets the `status` to `FETCHING` and initializes the `receivedData` instance variable. `receivedData` will hold the downloaded image data as we get chunks of it over time. After that, the method starts a new thread to proceed with the download. It uses the `NSThread` class method `detachNewThreadSelector:toTarget:withObject:`, which is declared as follows:

```
+ (void)detachNewThreadSelector:(SEL)selector
        toTarget:(id)target withObject:(id)argument;
```

The method to host the thread is `fetchURL`, the `target` is **self**, and `nil` is passed for the argument:

```
-(void)start{
  self.status = FETCHING;
  receivedData = [[NSMutableData data] retain];
  [NSThread detachNewThreadSelector:@selector(fetchURL)
          toTarget:self withObject:nil];
}
```

The `fetchURL` method starts by creating an `autorelease` pool.[2] After that, an `NSURLRequest` object is created and initialized with the `url` property (which was set by the user of the object).

The following is the implementation of the `fetchURL` method:

```
-(void)fetchURL {
  NSAutoreleasePool *pool = [[NSAutoreleasePool alloc] init];
  NSMutableURLRequest *theRequest =
    [NSMutableURLRequest requestWithURL:[NSURL URLWithString:self.url]];
  [[NSURLConnection alloc] initWithRequest:theRequest delegate:self];
  [[NSRunLoop currentRunLoop ]
    runUntilDate:[NSDate dateWithTimeIntervalSinceNow:60]];
  [pool release];
}
```

17.4.2 Asynchronous networking

We have been discussing synchronous `NSURLConnection` networking up to now. In this example, however, we will use the other kind of `NSURLConnection` networking: *asynchronous* networking. To download asynchronously, the instance of `NSURLConnection` is created and initialized with the `NSURLRequest` object and the delegate as **self**. Download starts immediately after that. Because the download is asynchronous, we need to keep the thread running. To achieve that, we tell the run loop to keep running for `60` seconds. The `runUntilDate:` method of `NSRunLoop` keeps

---

[2]Remember, every thread needs its own `autorelease` pool.

checking for input sources for 60 seconds. Whenever 60 seconds have passed or no input sources are scheduled on this run loop, it quits, freeing the pool and ending the download process. Because NSURLConnection instance is considered an input source, we achieve what we want.

The delegate of NSURLConnection will receive calls during the lifetime of the download. The methods that are interesting to this discussion are implemented. The rest are left to you to explore.

The first method we implement is connection:didFailWithError: This is the last message the delegate will receive regarding this connection. It informs the delegate that the connection has failed. You should release the connection and any opened resource. The following shows our implementation of this method. In addition to freeing resources, we set the status of this resource to FAILED. Because other objects might access this property, we synchronize to prevent corrupted data. It's always a good idea to synchronize.

```
- (void)connection:(NSURLConnection *)connection
        didFailWithError:(NSError *)error {
  [connection release];
  if(receivedData){
      [receivedData release];
      receivedData = nil;
  }
  @synchronized(self){
    self.status = FAILED;
  }
}
```

The second method we implement is connection:didReceiveResponse:. This method is declared as follows:

```
- (void)connection:(NSURLConnection *)connection
        didReceiveResponse:(NSURLResponse *)response;
```

This method is called when the system has enough information to construct a response. You usually check for connection success and initialize your buffer. You can also check for the HTTP status code and flag the resource as FAILED if it is different from 200. It all depends on your application.

The following is the implementation of the connection:didReceiveResponse: method:

```
- (void)connection:(NSURLConnection *)connection
        didReceiveResponse:(NSURLResponse *)response {
  int statusCode = ((NSHTTPURLResponse*) response).statusCode;
  if(statusCode != 200){
    @synchronized(self){
      self.status = FAILED;
    }
  }
  [receivedData setLength:0];
}
```

In asynchronous networking, you receive chunks of data over time. The method `connection:did-ReceiveData:` is called multiple times with these chunks. You need to append each chunk to the end of the accumulated data. The following shows our implementation of this delegate method:

```
- (void)connection:(NSURLConnection *)connection
       didReceiveData:(NSData *)data {
          [receivedData appendData:data];
}
```

When the download is complete, `connectionDidFinishLoading:` is called. This method sets the `status` instance variable to `COMPLETE`, frees resources, and builds the image from the data. The method used is `imageWithData:` of the `UIImage` class method. We also need to inform the object using this resource that the image is ready. We do that by posting a notification with the name `FinishedLoading`. In our case, our table view controller listens to this event and reloads its data. If the cell corresponding to this resource is visible, the user sees it immediately. The following shows our implementation of the method:

```
- (void)connectionDidFinishLoading:(NSURLConnection *)connection {
  @synchronized(self){
    if(self.status != FAILED){
      self.status = COMPLETE;
      self.image = [UIImage imageWithData:receivedData];
      [receivedData release];
      receivedData = nil;
    }
  }
  [[NSNotificationCenter defaultCenter]
                  postNotificationName:FinishedLoading object:self];
  [connection release];
}
```

Now that we have multithreaded downloads, we can build a simple table view controller, populate it with Internet resources, and show it to the user.

Listing 17.10 shows the initializer of the table view controller.

Listing 17.10 The initializer of the table view controller used in the Multithreaded Downloads application.

```
- (id)initWithStyle:(UITableViewStyle)style {
  if (self = [super initWithStyle:style]) {
    [[NSNotificationCenter defaultCenter]
                  addObserver:self
                  selector:@selector(handleFinishedLoading:)
                  name:FinishedLoading object:nil];
    self.iResources = [NSArray  arrayWithObjects:
              [[[InternetResource alloc] initWithTitle:@"First pic"
                          andURL:BAD_RESOURCE_URL2] autorelease],
              [[[InternetResource alloc] initWithTitle:@"Second pic"
                          andURL:SOME_RESOURCE_URL] autorelease],
```

```
                [[[InternetResource alloc] initWithTitle:@"Third pic"
                               andURL:SOME_RESOURCE_URL] autorelease],
                [[[InternetResource alloc] initWithTitle:@"Fourth pic"
                               andURL:SOME_RESOURCE_URL] autorelease],
                [[[InternetResource alloc] initWithTitle:@"Fifth pic"
                               andURL:SOME_RESOURCE_URL] autorelease],
                [[[InternetResource alloc] initWithTitle:@"Sixth pic"
                               andURL:SOME_RESOURCE_URL] autorelease],
                   nil];
  }
  return self;
}
```

We first add the controller as an observer for the notification `FinishedLoading`. After that, a number of `InternetResource` objects are created and put in an array.

The table view controller adds a delegate and a data source to the table view. Listing 17.11 shows the `tableView:cellForRowAtIndexPath:` for the table view controller. The method obtains the `InternetResource` object corresponding to the cell. After that, it displays the appropriate image depending on the state of the resource.

Listing 17.11   The `tableView:cellForRowAtIndexPath:` for the table view controller demonstrating multithreaded downloading.

```
- (UITableViewCell *)
        tableView:(UITableView *)tableView
        cellForRowAtIndexPath:(NSIndexPath *)indexPath {
  static NSString *CellIdentifier = @"Cell";
  UITableViewCell *cell =
    [tableView dequeueReusableCellWithIdentifier:CellIdentifier];
  if (cell == nil) {
    cell = [[[UITableViewCell alloc]
                     initWithStyle:UITableViewCellStyleDefault
                     reuseIdentifier:CellIdentifier] autorelease];
  }
  InternetResource  *iResource =
          [self.iResources objectAtIndex:indexPath.row];
  cell.textLabel.text = iResource.title;
  cell.imageView.image = nil;
  @synchronized(iResource){
    switch (iResource.status) {
      case NEW:
        cell.imageView.image = [UIImage imageNamed:@"loading.png"];
        [iResource start];
        break;
      case COMPLETE:
        cell.imageView.image = iResource.image;
        break;
```

```
      case FAILED:
        cell.imageView.image = [UIImage imageNamed:@"failed.png"];
        break;
      case FETCHING:
        cell.imageView.image = [UIImage imageNamed:@"loading.png"];
        break;
      default:
        cell.imageView.image = nil;
        break;
    }
  }
  return cell;
}
```

When a resource posts a notification, the method `handleFinishedLoading:` gets called immediately. The following method simply invokes the method `reloadTheData:` on the main thread. It is *always* a good idea to change the UI from the *main* thread.

```
-(void)handleFinishedLoading:(NSNotification*)notification{
  [self performSelectorOnMainThread:@selector(reloadTheData:)
      withObject:notification.object waitUntilDone:NO];
}
```

The `reloadTheData:` is shown below. It simply asks the table view to reload its data, thus calling the `tableView:cellForRowAtIndexPath:` method.

```
-(void)reloadTheData:(InternetResource*)_resource{
  [self.tableView reloadData];
}
```

It's worth noting that in the `handleFinishedLoading:` method we did not need to pass in NO for the `waitUntilDone` parameter. The table view's `reloadData` method does not block until the table refreshes; it simply sets the table as requiring refresh. When the run loop of the main thread takes control, it refreshes the table view.

Finally, the `dealloc` method of the controller frees the resources and removes itself from being an observer of all notifications:

```
- (void)dealloc {
  [[NSNotificationCenter defaultCenter] removeObserver:self];
  self.iResources = nil;
  [super dealloc];
}
```

17.5   Push Notification

Push notification is a mechanism that allows a machine (server) on the Internet to notify a specific iOS application installed on an iOS device about an event.

The server prepares a small message and communicates this message to an Apple server, using a Secure Sockets Layer (SSL) certificate for authentication. The iOS device, in turn, registers itself with an Apple server every time it boots up.

The message sent by the server to Apple to be delivered to a specific application is tagged with a device token. This device token is computed by the iOS application and communicated to the server. This token is usually communicated to the server once and saved on the server thereafter.

When a push notification message is received by the device, the operating system checks to see if the targeted application is running. If that is the case, the application's delegate of the application is sent the message. If the application is not running, an alert is shown to the user with the option to launch the target application.

Development of a push notification involves coding for the server and the client. In addition, an SSL certificate must be generated for each application provisioned for push notification. This SSL certificate must be installed on the server. The client does use SSL authentication, but you do not have to manage that.

17.5.1   Configuring push notification on the server

In this section, we outline the major steps needed to set up a server application that can send push notifications to our iOS application. Some of the steps here are needed for the client side as well.

Configuring the App ID

Click on the iPhone Developer Program Portal in the iPhone Dev Center. Select App IDs from the menu as shown in Figure 17.2.

Click on the Add ID button as shown in Figure 17.3.

An App ID is needed so that the notification server and the iOS know how to deliver the message that your server sends to a given application. An App ID consists of two parts:

- **Bundle seed ID.** This is a 10-digit number that Apple automatically generates for you during the App ID creation process.

- **Bundle identifier.** This part is determined by you the developer. Usually, it is a string in reverse-DNS format, such as `com.mycompany.appname`.

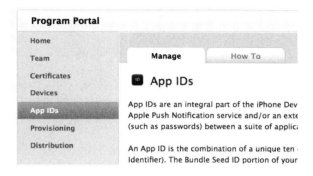

Figure 17.2   Selecting App IDs from the menu.

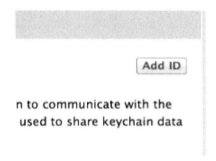

Figure 17.3   The Add ID button.

Under the Manage tab, you will see two text boxes that you need to fill in. In the first field, you enter a distinguishable name for this App ID. This is used for display purposes only and does not affect the App ID.

In the second text field, you enter the bundle identifier. Figure 17.4 shows an example.

Figure 17.4   Creating App ID in the program portal.

After filling in the two required fields, you hit Submit. The App ID will be generated and you will be returned to the page where all your App IDs are listed. You should see your App ID as one of the items listed as shown in Figure 17.5.

Figure 17.5   The newly created App ID.

In the ID column, you will see the App ID, which is composed of the 10-digit random number and your bundle identifier. The Apple Push Notification column says that the service is available, and the icon is orange.

Configuring the App ID for notification

We need to configure the App ID for notification. Click on the Configure button. The Configure App ID page will appear. You will need to enable push by checking Enable Push Notification Services as shown in Figure 17.6.

Figure 17.6   The Enable Push Notification Services check box.

Once you have checked the box, the Configure button (see Figure 17.7) becomes enabled, so click it.

Figure 17.7   The Configure button.

Once you have clicked the Configure button, a pop-up window appears with a new workflow. This wizard will guide you through the process of generating an SSL certificate to be used by the server. Figure 17.8 shows that window.

Generating the SSL certificate

The first step in this process is the generation of the certificate signing request (CSR) using the Keychain Access application. Launch the Keychain Access application and choose `Keychain Access` → `Certificate Assistant` → `Request a Certificate from a Certificate Authority`. Fill in the request similar to the one shown in Figure 17.9 and hit Continue.

Figure 17.8   The first window in the wizard for generating the SSL certificate for push notification.

Figure 17.9   Filling in the certificate information.

A dialog box appears, asking you for the location of the CSR file. Choose a location such as the Desktop and hit Save as shown in Figure 17.10.

After saving the file, hit Done. Now go back to the wizard and hit Continue.

Save As: CertificateSigningRequest.certSigningR ▾

Where: ▣ Desktop ⇕

Cancel   Save

Figure 17.10   Saving the CSR file.

You need to upload this CSR file to Apple's server. Click Browse and locate the file on the Desktop.
Click on Generate. See Figure 17.11.

Select the Certificate Signing request (CSR) file that you saved to your disk.

/Users/ali/Desktop/Certific (Browse...)

Figure 17.11   Locating the CSR file.

After a few seconds, the Apple Push Service (APS) certificate will be generated. See Figure 17.12.

Certificate Name: **Maher Ali**   ◔

Your APS Certificate has been generated.
Please continue to the next step.

Figure 17.12   Successfully generating the SSL certificate.

Now we need to download it so that we install the certificate on our server. Click on Download Now
as shown in Figure 17.13.

Download & Install Your Development Certificate

Step 1: Download

Download your APS SSL Certificate to your
Notification Server. Your private key should also
be installed on this server.

Maher Ali's Cert...

Download Now ▾

Figure 17.13   Downloading the SSL certificate.

Click Done. You'll see that the Apple Push Notification service for the App ID says Enabled and it is green. See Figure 17.14.

Figure 17.14   An App ID enabled for APS.

Installing the SSL certificate on the server

Now that we have the SSL certificate, we need to install it on the server. In addition, we need to configure the server application so that it uses this certificate when talking with Apple's notification servers.

Double-click on the SSL certificate and install it on the server as shown in Figure 17.15.

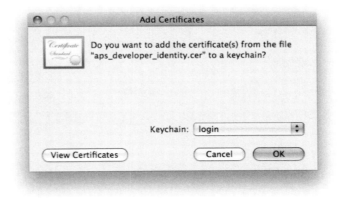

Figure 17.15   Installing the SSL certificate on the server.

Now that the SSL certificate is installed on the server, we need to tell the server about this certificate.

How you configure the server to use the certificate depends on the environment in which you wrote the server. Here, we are using a simple server written in Objective-C that runs on a Mac. You will find this server in the PushMeBaby project, available in the source downloads.

Rename the SSL .cer file to apns.cer and drag and drop it in the bundle of the PushMeBaby project as shown in Figure 17.16.

This completes the server configuration. Now you need to take care of one more thing. The first time you launch the PushMeBaby server application, the Mac OS asks you for permission to sign using your key. You should choose Always Allow as shown in Figure 17.17.

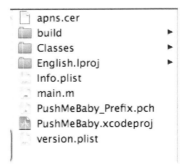

Figure 17.16   The `apns.cer` file referenced in the bundle of the server application.

Figure 17.17   Giving permission to the server to use the key.

17.5.2   Configuring the client

Now that we have configured the server, we need to configure the client.

Creating a provisioning profile

We need to create a provisioning profile for our application. Go back to the program portal and choose the Provisioning menu as shown in Figure 17.18.

Click on Add Profile as shown in Figure 17.19.

Now you need to fill in a form so that the provisioning profile can be created. Choose a name for this profile, select the certificate, choose the push notification App ID you created and the devices you want to install this profile on, and click Submit (see Figure 17.20).

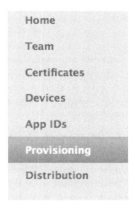

Figure 17.18   The Provisioning menu in the program portal.

Figure 17.19   The Add Profile button.

Create iPhone Development Provisioning Profile

Generate provisioning profiles here. To learn more, visit the How To section.

Profile Name	Third Push Profile
Certificates	☑ Maher Ali
App ID	My ID Name ⬍
Devices	Select All

Devices:
- ☑ Ali iPhone
- ☑ First iPhone
- ☐ Josh Taylor
- ☐ Burin Asavesna
- ☐ Johnathan Conley

Figure 17.20   Creation of the iPhone development provisioning profile.

After creating the profile, you will see it available for download and listed with development provisioning profiles as shown in Figure 17.21.

Figure 17.21   A ready-to-download iPhone development profile.

Installing the provisioning profile on the device and XCode

Now we need to install the provisioning profile to the device(s) and make XCode aware of it. Click on Download and save the profile on your computer. In XCode, choose `Windows → Organizer`. Select the device you want to install the profile on as shown in Figure 17.22.

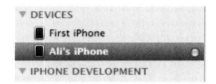

Figure 17.22   Selecting the device in the organizer.

Drag and drop the provisioning profile to the Provisioning section of the organizer, as shown in Figure 17.23.

Figure 17.23   The Provisioning section of the device info in Organizer.

Double-click the provisioning profile file in Finder and choose XCode to open it. This will make XCode aware of this profile.

Configuring the XCode application

In XCode, change the bundle identifier of the application (in the `.plist` file) to the one you used in generating the App ID as shown in Figure 17.24.

Figure 17.24   Specifying the bundle ID of the application in the `.plist` file.

Now we need to configure the target so that XCode builds the application with the correct profile. Double-click on the target as shown in Figure 17.25.

Figure 17.25   Specifying the provisioning profile in the target.

Select the Build tab and choose the provisioning profile in the Code Signing section as shown in Figure 17.26.

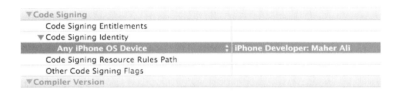

Figure 17.26   Specifying the provisioning profile in the target.

Now you should be able to build and install the application on the device. Make sure that you are targeting the device as shown in Figure 17.27.

17.5.3   Coding the client

Coding the client involves registering for push notification, sending the device token to the server, and responding to notification messages.

Registering for push notification

The push-enabled application is required to register for remote notification on startup. You usually do that in the `applicationDidFinishLaunching:` method as shown below:

```
- (void)applicationDidFinishLaunching:(UIApplication *)application {
  [[UIApplication sharedApplication] registerForRemoteNotificationTypes:
            UIRemoteNotificationTypeBadge |
            UIRemoteNotificationTypeSound |
            UIRemoteNotificationTypeAlert];
}
```

Figure 17.27   Targeting the device from XCode.

The `registerForRemoteNotificationTypes:` method takes an integer whose bits specify the request for accepting a given notification type. This method is declared as follows:

```
-(void)registerForRemoteNotificationTypes:(UIRemoteNotificationType)types
```

The `UIRemoteNotificationType` is declared as follows:

```
typedef enum {
    UIRemoteNotificationTypeNone    = 0,
    UIRemoteNotificationTypeBadge   = 1 << 0,
    UIRemoteNotificationTypeSound   = 1 << 1,
    UIRemoteNotificationTypeAlert   = 1 << 2
} UIRemoteNotificationType;
```

When your application registers for receiving notifications, the user sees an alert as shown in Figure 17.28.

If the user approves the action and the registration is successful, the method `application:did-RegisterForRemoteNotificationsWithDeviceToken:` gets called.

You get the device token in the second parameter. The following shows a sample implementation that just logs the token:

```
- (void)application:(UIApplication *)application
        didRegisterForRemoteNotificationsWithDeviceToken:(NSData *)token{
  NSLog(@"Inform the server of this device token: %@", token);
}
```

Figure 17.28   An alert asking the user to approve notifications for a given application.

The device token remains constant for a given application. Your application should send the token to the server so that the device can be targeted for future notifications.

If the registration fails, the method `application:didFailToRegisterForRemoteNotificationsWithError:` gets called with the error. The method is declared as follows:

```
- (void)application:(UIApplication *)application
        didFailToRegisterForRemoteNotificationsWithError:(NSError *)error
```

Receiving notifications

If the device receives a notification for an application, and that application is running, the `application:didReceiveRemoteNotification:` method of the application delegate is called. The following shows an example implementation:

```
- (void)application:(UIApplication *)application
        didReceiveRemoteNotification:(NSDictionary *)userInfo{
  NSLog(@"The user info: %@", userInfo);
}
```

For example, if the server sends the message

```
{"aps":{"alert":"This is message.","badge":1,"sound":"beep.aif"}}
```

the contents of the `userInfo` dictionary will be as follows:

```
2009-04-12 21:02:29.870 TestingAPNS[92:107] The user info: {
    aps =       {
        alert = "This is message.";
        badge = 1;
        sound = "beep.aif";
    };
}
```

If, on the other hand, the application is not running, an alert is shown to the user with a message similar to Figure 17.29.

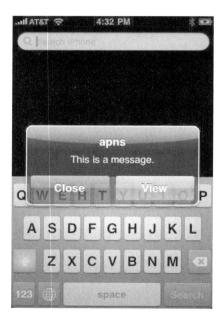

Figure 17.29   An alert displaying a notification message.

17.5.4   Coding the server

The server is required to generate a JavaScript Object Notation (JSON) dictionary with information about what message to be sent, what number to store as a badge on the application icon, and the name of the sound that needs to play should the application happen to be inactive.

Coding for the server is beyond the scope of this book. You can look at an example in the `PushMe-Baby` project, available in the source downloads.

17.6   Local Notification

In the previous section, we introduced remote push notification. Starting with iOS 4, you are given access to an API allowing you to schedule local push notifications. This API gives your app the ability to add events in the future notifying the user of important information.

To schedule a local notification, your app needs to create and initialize an instance of `UILocal-Notification` class. After that, you schedule the notification by calling the `scheduleLocal-Notification:` method of the `UIApplication` instance.

The following shows a code fragment that illustrates this concept:

```
UIApplication* app = [UIApplication sharedApplication];
UILocalNotification* notif;
notif  = [[[UILocalNotification alloc] init] autorelease];
if (notif){
    notif.fireDate = [NSDate dateWithTimeIntervalSinceNow:60];
    notif.timeZone = [NSTimeZone defaultTimeZone];
    notif.repeatInterval = 0;
    notif.soundName = @"default";
    notif.alertBody = @"Local notification has been received";
    [app scheduleLocalNotification:notif];
}
```

`fireDate` is the date/time that you want this notification to be raised. In `timeZone`, you specify `defaultTimeZone` to interpret the date as local to the device or `nil` to indicate that the date is absolute (GMT). You can specify how many times you want this notification to be repeated by setting the value of the `repeatInterval` property. `soundName` is the name of a bundled sound file that you want to be played when the notification is fired. Finally, `alertBody` is used to specify the text that the user sees when the notification is fired.

Figure 17.30 shows the alert that the user sees when the local notification is fired.

When the user taps the View button, the app is launched and the method `application:did-ReceiveLocalNotification:` of the application delegate is called.

The complete application can be found in the `LocalNotifications` project in the source downloads.

17.7   Large Downloads and Uploads

Some applications require downloading large amounts of data from the Internet. Users are not expected to wait for the download to complete. Even if you perform this networking function in the background, as you should, the user cannot be expected to keep the application in the foreground while doing so.

Starting with iOS 4, you have access to APIs that allow you to perform a long-running task in the background. When the user quits the app, this task continues to run even after the app is suspended.

Figure 17.30   The firing of a local notification.

To start a background task, you should call the beginBackgroundTaskWithExpiration-Handler: method of the UIApplication instance. And when you're done with the task, you need to call the endBackgroundTask: method.

Let's illustrate this concept with a concrete example. We would like to keep a copy of a PDF file up-to-date. When the app is first launched, we check to see if the time stamp of the PDF file is within the acceptable threshold. If not, we start a background process that updates the PDF file from the Internet.

To signal the start of the background process, we can do the following:

```
UIApplication *app = [UIApplication sharedApplication];
self.assetUpdateTaskID = [app beginBackgroundTaskWithExpirationHandler:^{
    dispatch_async(dispatch_get_main_queue(), ^{
        [self endTask];
    });
}];
```

The beginBackgroundTaskWithExpirationHandler: method takes a block that is executed when the task is running out of time and is about to be terminated by the system. Here, we simply end the task as we shall see in this section. Notice how we schedule the ending of the task on the main queue as this will guarantee synchronization with the other call in ending the task (as we shall see in this section). The `beginBackgroundTaskWithExpirationHandler:` method returns a task ID that must be used in ending the task.

After that, we need to schedule a task in the background. Here, we can use Grand Central Dispatch (GCD) (see Section 2.12) or any other API to accomplish this. The following code fragment shows how to do that using GCD:

```
dispatch_async(dispatch_get_global_queue(0, 0), ^{
        //update the assets from the internet
        NSData *data =
          [NSData dataWithContentsOfURL:
            [NSURL URLWithString:
                @"http://www.nwcg.gov/pms/pubs/GSTOP7.pdf"]];
        //4. TODO: Save assets to disk
        dispatch_async(dispatch_get_main_queue(), ^{
            [self endTask];
            //5. update UI
            [webView loadData:data MIMEType:@"application/pdf"
                    textEncodingName:@"UTF-8"
                    baseURL:[NSURL URLWithString:@""]];
        });
});
```

You've seen background scheduling of tasks using GCD before. The PDF downloading is performed and the ending of the task and display of the PDF file are scheduled on the main queue for synchronization purposes.

To end the task, you simply make a simple call to the `UIApplication` instance as follows:

```
- (void) endTask{
    if(self.assetUpdateTaskID != UIInvalidBackgroundTask){
        [[UIApplication sharedApplication]
            endBackgroundTask:self.assetUpdateTaskID];
        self.assetUpdateTaskID = UIInvalidBackgroundTask;
    }
}
```

The complete application can be found in the `Multitasking1` project in the source downloads.

17.8   Sending Email

To send email from within your iOS application, you can choose one of the following four approaches:

- **Use the standard email interface.** This approach allows you to set up the initial configuration of a new email message. You can prefill the recipients, the subject, and any attachments you want. After that, you present the standard email interface to the user. The user can edit the email fields and possibly change your initial values. The user can then send or cancel the email altogether.

- **Use a back-end service.** Using this approach, you send the email fields to the server and the server then sends the email.

- **Use the** UIApplication openURL: **method.** You can set up a URL with the encoded email message and invoke the openURL: static method of the UIApplication class. Using this approach will result in your application quitting and the Mail.app application being launched with a new message. This approach does not allow for file attachment.

- **Use an SMTP library.** Simple Mail Transfer Protocol (SMTP) is a protocol used to send email over the Internet. Using this approach you utilize SMTP to send the email from the iPhone without the user's intervention.

In this section, we discuss the first approach.

The class MFMailComposeViewController is used to show an email interface that the user can interact with. You create an instance of this controller, initialize it, configure the different email fields, and present it to the user modally.

Before you do all that, you need to check whether your application can send the email. You check that by using the following static method:

```
+ (BOOL)canSendMail
```

If you can send the email, you can proceed to create the mail controller as shown below:

```
MFMailComposeViewController *mailCtrl =
   [[[MFMailComposeViewController alloc] init] autorelease];
```

Once it is created, you can add a subject line using the setSubject: method, which is declared as follows:

```
- (void)setSubject:(NSString *)subject
```

This method takes a string as an argument and uses that string to set the Subject header of the email message. The user can later modify this value.

To set the recipients of the message, you use the setToRecipients: method, which is declared as follows:

```
- (void)setToRecipients:(NSArray *)toRecipients
```

You pass in an array of string values where each value is a valid email address. The method uses this array to set the To message header.

To add a Cc header, you can use a similar method called setCcRecipients:. To set the Bcc header, use the setBccRecipients: method. Both methods take an array of strings.

To set the message body, you can use the following method:

```
- (void)setMessageBody:(NSString *)body isHTML:(BOOL)isHTML
```

You pass in the email body as a string in the first argument and YES in the second argument if and only if the message is in HTML format.

If you want to attach any files, you can use the following method:

```
- (void)addAttachmentData:(NSData *)attachment
        mimeType:(NSString *)mimeType
        fileName:(NSString *)filename
```

You pass in the attachment data in the first argument and its MIME type in the second argument. The filename is passed in the last argument. For example, to attach an image from the bundle called Flower1.jpg, you can write something like the following:

```
[mailCtrl addAttachmentData:
    UIImageJPEGRepresentation([UIImage imageNamed:@"Flower1.jpg"], 0.6)
    mimeType:@"image/jpeg" fileName:@"Flower1.jpg"];
```

Here, we obtain a compressed data representation of the image with a 60 percent compression rate. The compressed data is then used to add the attachment of MIME type image/jpeg.

After setting up the email message, you need to assign the delegate of the mail view controller using the mailComposeDelegate property. Finally, you can present the mail message controller as you present any other controller.

The delegate object should (and is expected to) implement the following method:

```
- (void)mailComposeController:(MFMailComposeViewController *)controller
        didFinishWithResult:(MFMailComposeResult)result
        error:(NSError *)error
```

You receive the result of the user's decision and any queuing error. The following are potential result values:

- MFMailComposeResultCancelled. This value indicates that the email message composition was cancelled by the user.
- MFMailComposeResultSaved. This value indicates that the email message composition was saved by the user.
- MFMailComposeResultSent. This value indicates that the email message was queued in the Mail.app program.
- MFMailComposeResultFailed. This value indicates that there was an error in the user's action. The message is neither queued nor saved.

In all cases, you should dismiss the mail composition controller.

Figure 17.31   A screen shot showing email composition.

The project Email (available in the source downloads) contains a complete application for email composition demonstrating the concepts in this section. A screen shot of the application is shown in Figure 17.31.

17.9   Summary

In this chapter, we addressed several advanced networking topics. We started by looking in Section 17.1 at how we can determine network connectivity of the device. After that, we tackled the issue of uploading multimedia content to remote servers in Section 17.2. In Section 17.3, we presented a category on NSString that allows us to easily compute the MD5 digest of a string. After that, Section 17.4 showed you how to present a responsive table view whose data rows are fed from the Internet without sacrificing the user experience. Next, Sections 17.5 and 17.6 addressed the topics of remote and local push notification, respectively. Section 17.7 showed how to utilize the multitasking API in downloading large amounts of data even after the app is suspended. Finally, Section 17.8 discussed sending email from your iOS application.

Exercises

(1) The application presented in Section 17.4 will start downloading the Internet resource as soon as the corresponding cell becomes visible. Improve on this behavior so that downloading starts only when the user stops the scrolling. This is a more efficient behavior and is used by the App Store application.

(2) Write an application that uploads images to Flickr.

18

Working with the Address Book Database

In this chapter, we discuss the foundation of the Address Book API and several UI elements that can be used to modify the contacts database.

In Section 18.1, we provide a brief introduction to the subject. Next, Section 18.2 discusses property types. After that, Sections 18.3 and 18.4 show how to access single value and multi value properties, respectively. Next, Sections 18.5 and 18.6 go into the details of the person record and the Address Book, respectively. Issues related to multithreading and identifiers are addressed in Section 18.7.

After covering the foundation of the Address Book API, we provide several sample applications. Section 18.8 shows how to use a query to retrieve the photo of a given record. Next, Section 18.9 shows how to use the `ABUnknownPersonViewController` class. After that, Section 18.10 covers the `ABPeoplePickerNavigationController` class. The `ABPersonViewController` class is covered in Section 18.11. Section 18.12 covers the `ABNewPersonViewController` class. Finally, we summarize the chapter in Section 18.13.

18.1 Introduction

The iOS SDK supports full access to the user's Address Book. The Address Book API provides a simple interface to query the Address Book, create new records, modify records, and delete records. To use this API, you need to add the following import statement:

```
#import <AddressBook/AddressBook.h>
```

You also need to add the `AddressBook` framework to your project as explained in Section D.4 of Appendix D.

The Address Book consists of a set of records. A record can be either a person record or a group record. A group is a container with a name and zero or more references to group and/or person records.

Every record has properties. A property can be a single-value property or a multivalue property. An example of a single-value property is the last name of a person. An example of a multivalue property is the person's address; which consists of street, city, Zip code, country, etc.

You can determine the type of a record using the `ABRecordGetRecordType` function. The properties (whether single-value or multivalue) of person and group records are accessed using the same functions but with different property identifiers. You can set the value of a property using the `ABRecordSetValue` function. You can retrieve the value of a property using the `ABRecordCopyValue` function. You can remove a property altogether using the `ABRecordRemoveValue` function.

To access the Address Book database, you create an Address Book object. This will result in creating a reference to the Address Book database in memory. The Address Book reference is valid only within the thread that created it.

You can modify the Address Book by adding, removing, and updating records. These modifications remain in memory until you save the Address Book. You can also revert changes that you've made.

18.2   Property Types

There are ten record property types available to you. Five of those are for single-value properties and the other five are for multivalue properties.

- **String.** The single-value property type is defined as `kABStringPropertyType`, while the multivalue property type is defined as `kABMultiStringPropertyType`. The value retrieved from a single-value property is of type `CFStringRef`, which is equivalent to `NSString*`. The values retrieved from the multivalue property are all of type `CFStringRef`.

- **Integer.** The single-value is referred to using `kABIntegerPropertyType`, while the multivalue is referred to using `kABMultiIntegerPropertyType`. The value retrieved from a single-value property is of type `CFNumberRef`, which is equivalent to `NSNumber*`. The values retrieved from the multivalue property are all of type `NSNumber*`.

- **Date.** `kABDateTimePropertyType` is used for single value and `kABMultiDateTimePropertyType` is used for multivalue. The values are of type `CFDateRef` or `NSDate*`.

- **Real.** `kABRealPropertyType` is used for single-value and `kABMultiRealPropertyType` for multivalue properties. The values are of type `CFNumberRef` or `NSNumber*`.

- **Dictionary.** `kABDictionaryPropertyType` is used for single-value and `kABMultiDictionaryPropertyType` for multivalue properties. The values are of type `CFDictionaryRef` or `NSDictionary*`.

18.3   Accessing Single-Value Properties

In this section, we discuss the functions used to manipulate single-value properties for person and group records.

18.3.1   Retrieving single-value properties

To retrieve the value for a single-value property, you need to copy that value from a record. The function `ABRecordCopyValue` is used for this purpose. The function is declared as follows:

```
CFTypeRef ABRecordCopyValue(ABRecordRef record, ABPropertyID property);
```

The first parameter of this function is the record you want to retrieve the specific property value from, and the second parameter is the property identifier. In the documentation, you can find out what predefined constant identifiers exist for a given property. For example, the first name of a person has the property identifier `kABPersonFirstNameProperty`. The return value depends on the property being retrieved. The core foundation (hence the `CF` prefix) framework uses the `CFType-Ref` generic reference as a pointer to any core foundation object. As you might have guessed, it's declared as follows:

```
typedef const void * CFTypeRef;
```

The value retrieved is copied, which means that you are responsible for its release. You release this value using the `CFRelease` function. You can also release it by assigning the value to a Cocoa variable with an equivalent type and sending a `release` message to it. If you would rather work with the Foundation Framework (classes prefixed by `NS`), you can cast the retrieved object to the Cocoa type to disable warnings.

Enough talk. Let's see how we can retrieve the first name of a person. The following retrieves that value and stores it in the `firstName` variable:

```
NSString *firstName  =
    (NSString*)ABRecordCopyValue(person,  kABPersonFirstNameProperty);
```

To see a list of property identifiers for a person record, Command-double-click in XCode the `kAB-PersonFirstNameProperty` token.

Let's see another example. Suppose we have a group object and we want to retrieve the name of the representative group. The following shows how we can do that:

```
NSString *groupName  =
    (NSString*)ABRecordCopyValue(group,  kABGroupNameProperty);
```

Again, Command-double-click the `kABGroupNameProperty` to see other property identifiers for a group record. You will find none. The `kABGroupNameProperty` is the only predefined property for a group.

The following are some of the single-value property identifiers defined for a person record:

- `kABPersonLastNameProperty`. Returns a string value representing the last name of the person.

- `kABPersonMiddleNameProperty`. Returns a string value representing the middle name of the person.

- kABPersonNicknameProperty. Returns a string value representing the nickname of the person.

- kABPersonBirthdayProperty. Returns a date value representing the birthday of the person.

- kABPersonNoteProperty. Returns a string value for the note associated with the person.

18.3.2   Setting single-value properties

To change the value for a given property, you use the ABRecordSetValue function. The function is declared as follows:

```
bool ABRecordSetValue(ABRecordRef record, ABPropertyID property,
                      CFTypeRef value, CFErrorRef* error
                     );
```

You pass in the record object, the property identifier you want to change, the value you want to set, and a reference to an NSError object. The function returns YES if successful and NO otherwise.

For example, to change the first name of the record in person to Barack, use

```
ABRecordSetValue(person, kABPersonFirstNameProperty, @"Barack", NULL);
```

Here, we are passing NULL for the NSError reference as we are not interested in dealing with errors. Of course, you should always write code that does deal with potential errors.

To set the group name for a group record, you can write something like the following:

```
ABRecordSetValue(group, kABGroupNameProperty, @"Presidents", NULL);
```

Again, notice that we are using the same function in dealing with group and person records.

18.4   Accessing Multivalue Properties

In this section, we talk about the manipulation of multivalue properties.

18.4.1   Retrieving multivalue properties

To retrieve the value of a multivalue property, you use the same function you used to retrieve a single-value property, ABRecordCopyValue. The value returned is of type ABMultiValueRef, which is declared as an alias to the generic CFTypeRef type.

The following shows how to retrieve the person's emails:

```
ABMultiValueRef emailsProperty =
                ABRecordCopyValue(person, kABPersonEmailProperty);
```

Once we have the multivalue object, we can retrieve its values (in this case, the strings of emails) using the function ABMultiValueCopyArrayOfAllValues, which is declared as follows:

```
CFArrayRef ABMultiValueCopyArrayOfAllValues(ABMultiValueRef multiValue);
```

The function returns the values in an NSArray object. You can then iterate through this array and access the values.

Each value stored for a multivalue property has a label identifying this value and a unique identifier. The label can be any string value, and several values can have the same label. Some of the generic labels defined are kABWorkLabel, kABHomeLabel, and kABOtherLabel.

To retrieve the label for a given value, you can use the ABMultiValueCopyLabelAtIndex function. It returns an NSString object with the label of a given value. The function is declared as follows:

```
CFStringRef ABMultiValueCopyLabelAtIndex(
            ABMultiValueRef multiValue, CFIndex index);
```

The first parameter is the multivalue object and the second is the index of the value whose label you want to retrieve. For example, the following retrieves the label value for the email at index:

```
NSString  *emailLabel =
        (NSString*)ABMultiValueCopyLabelAtIndex(emailsProperty, index);
```

As usual, because the function has a copy in it, you are responsible for the object's memory.

The following are some of the multivalue property identifiers defined for the person record:

- kABPersonAddressProperty. This identifier is used to access the person's address multivalue property. The property type is kABMultiDictionaryPropertyType, which means that each value of this property is an NSDictionary instance.
- kABPersonDateProperty. This identifier is used to access all the dates associated with this person. Each value is an NSDate instance.
- kABPersonPhoneProperty. This identifier is used to retrieve all phone numbers associated with the person. Each value is an NSString instance.
- kABPersonURLProperty. This identifies all the URLs associated with this person. Each value is an NSString object.

Listing 18.1 shows a code fragment that retrieves all the emails of a given person and logs them labeled.

Listing 18.1   Logging all the emails associated with a given person record.

```
//Access emails
ABMultiValueRef emailsProperty =
    ABRecordCopyValue(person, kABPersonEmailProperty);
NSArray* emailsArray =
```

```
     (NSArray*)ABMultiValueCopyArrayOfAllValues(emailsProperty);
NSLog(@"Emails:");
for(int index = 0; index< [emailsArray count]; index++){
  NSString  *email = [emailsArray objectAtIndex:index];
  NSString  *emailLabel =
    (NSString*)ABMultiValueCopyLabelAtIndex(emailsProperty, index);
  NSLog(@"%@: %@",
    [emailLabel isEqualToString:(NSString*)kABWorkLabel]?@"Work":
    [emailLabel isEqualToString:(NSString*)kABHomeLabel]?
        @"Home":@"Other", email);
  [emailLabel release];
}
CFRelease(emailsProperty);
[emailsArray release];
```

Listing 18.2 shows a code fragment that retrieves all the phone numbers of a given person and logs them labeled.

Listing 18.2   Logging all the phone numbers associated with a given person record.

```
// Access   phones
  ABMultiValueRef phonesProperty =
      ABRecordCopyValue(person, kABPersonPhoneProperty);
  NSArray* phonesArray =
      (NSArray*)ABMultiValueCopyArrayOfAllValues(phonesProperty);
  NSLog(@"Phones:");
  for(int index = 0; index< [phonesArray count]; index++){
    NSString *aPhone = [phonesArray objectAtIndex:index];
    NSString  *phoneLabel =
      (NSString*)ABMultiValueCopyLabelAtIndex(phonesProperty, index);
    NSLog(@"%@: %@",
     [phoneLabel isEqualToString:(NSString*)kABPersonPhoneMobileLabel]?
                 @"Mobile":@"Phone", aPhone);
    [phoneLabel release];
  }
  CFRelease(phonesProperty);
  [phonesArray release];
}
```

18.4.2   Setting multivalue properties

To modify a multivalue property, you need a mutable version of that property. If you want to create a brand-new value, you use `ABMultiValueCreateMutable` function, add the values and labels to it, and set the corresponding property with the new value. If, on the other hand, you want to modify an existing multivalue, you retrieve this value, create a mutable copy of it using the function `ABMultiValueCreateMutableCopy`, add to or delete from it, and set the value in the record.

Let's make these steps concrete through some examples. First, let's look at creating a brand-new multivalue.

We want to set a person's record with one work address. First, we create a mutable multivalue as follows:

```
ABMutableMultiValueRef multiValueAddress =
    ABMultiValueCreateMutable(kABMultiDictionaryPropertyType);
```

Here, we are asking the Address Book framework to create a new multivalue object of `kABMulti-DictionaryPropertyType` type. As we mentioned before, this is the type of the street address property (a person can have multiple addresses and each address is a dictionary).

After that, we create one address and store its parts in a dictionary as follows:

```
NSMutableDictionary *theAddress =
    [[[NSMutableDictionary alloc] init] autorelease];
 [theAddress setValue:@"1600 Pennsylvania Avenue NW"
    forKey:(NSString *)kABPersonAddressStreetKey];
 [theAddress setValue:@"Washington"
    forKey:(NSString *)kABPersonAddressCityKey];
 [theAddress setValue:@"DC"
    forKey:(NSString *)kABPersonAddressStateKey];
 [theAddress setValue:@"20500"
    forKey:(NSString *)kABPersonAddressZIPKey];
 [theAddress setValue:@"us"
    forKey:(NSString *)kABPersonAddressCountryCodeKey];
```

This is pretty straightforward dictionary creation. The keys used are defined by the framework. You can set any or all of them as they are all optional.

Now that we have a new value, we need to add it to the multivalue and give it a label. The function to use is `ABMultiValueAddValueAndLabel`. The first parameter of this function is the multivalue object, the second is the value to add, and the third is the label. You can pass a reference to an `NS-Error` object in the fourth parameter if you want to. The following shows the addition of the new address to the multivalue object:

```
ABMultiValueAddValueAndLabel(multiValueAddress, theAddress,
                        kABWorkLabel, NULL);
```

You can repeat these steps for each additional address. Once you have what you want, you set the multivalue property with the new value using our old friend `ABRecordSetValue` as follows:

```
ABRecordSetValue(person,kABPersonAddressProperty,multiValueAddress,NULL);
```

If, on the other hand, you want to modify an existing multivalue, you need to retrieve it, create a mutable copy of it, add to the mutable copy, and set it back to the record. The following code fragment shows exactly that:

```
ABMultiValueRef streetAddressProperty =
   ABRecordCopyValue(person, kABPersonAddressProperty);
ABMutableMultiValueRef mutableStreetAddressProperty =
   ABMultiValueCreateMutableCopy(streetAddressProperty);
CFRelease(streetAddressProperty);
NSMutableDictionary *theAddress =
   [[[NSMutableDictionary alloc] init] autorelease];
[theAddress setValue:@"1600 Pennsylvania Avenue NW"
   forKey:(NSString *)kABPersonAddressStreetKey];
[theAddress setValue:@"Washington"
   forKey:(NSString *)kABPersonAddressCityKey];
[theAddress setValue:@"DC"
   forKey:(NSString *)kABPersonAddressStateKey];
[theAddress setValue:@"20500"
   forKey:(NSString *)kABPersonAddressZIPKey];
[theAddress setValue:@"us"
   forKey:(NSString *)kABPersonAddressCountryCodeKey];
ABMultiValueAddValueAndLabel(mutableStreetAddressProperty,
   theAddress, kABHomeLabel, NULL);
ABRecordSetValue(person, kABPersonAddressProperty,
   mutableStreetAddressProperty, NULL);
CFRelease(mutableStreetAddressProperty);
```

18.5   Person and Group Records

Creating a new person record is simple. You use the function `ABPersonCreate` to create a new `ABRecordRef`. After that, you set its properties and add it to the Address Book object using the `ABAddressBookAddRecord` function, which we will discuss later in this chapter.

To create a group, you use the `ABGroupCreate` function. You set its properties (only one is defined) and add it to the Address Book object as you would add any record using the `ABAddressBookAdd-Record` function. You can add a person as a member to this group by using the `ABGroupAddMember` function. This function is declared as follows:

```
bool
 ABGroupAddMember(ABRecordRef group,ABRecordRef person,CFErrorRef* error)
```

You can retrieve all members of a given group using the function `ABGroupCopyArrayOfAll-Members`, which is declared as follows:

```
CFArrayRef ABGroupCopyArrayOfAllMembers(ABRecordRef group)
```

Each person has an image. You can retrieve that image using the function `ABPersonCopyImage-Data`, which is declared as follows:

```
CFDataRef ABPersonCopyImageData(ABRecordRef person);
```

The previous function returns an `NSData` object containing the image data. You can then use the `UIImage imageWithData:` method to build a `UIImage` object from it.

To set the photo of a person, use the `ABPersonSetImageData` function, which is declared as follows:

```
bool ABPersonSetImageData(ABRecordRef person, CFDataRef imageData,
                          CFErrorRef* error);
```

18.6   Address Book

In the previous sections, we mostly covered records. In order to modify the actual database, however, you need to use the Address Book.

You usually start by creating an Address Book and initializing it with references to existing records. You modify, add, and delete records. After that, you save the Address Book.

To create an Address Book object, you use the function `ABAddressBookCreate`. This code will return a reference to an Address Book, `ABAddressBookRef`, which we will discuss in this section.

```
ABAddressBookRef addressBook = ABAddressBookCreate();
```

To save an Address Book back to the database, you use the `ABAddressBookSave` function as shown below:

```
ABAddressBookSave(addressBook, NULL);
```

After finishing with an Address Book, you need to release it as follows:

```
CFRelease(addressBook);
```

Remember that all your changes to the records are in memory. To persist these changes, you'll need to save the Address Book object.

The following are some of the useful functions that operate on an Address Book object:

- `ABAddressBookGetPersonCount`. This function returns the number of person records in the Address Book. The function is declared as follows:

  ```
  CFIndex ABAddressBookGetPersonCount(ABAddressBookRef addressBook);
  ```

  `CFIndex` is basically a **signed long**.

- `ABAddressBookGetGroupCount`. This function returns the number of groups in the Address Book and is declared as follows:

```
CFIndex ABAddressBookGetGroupCount(ABAddressBookRef addressBook);
```

- `ABAddressBookCopyArrayOfAllPeople`. This function returns an array of all person records. The function is declared as follows:

```
CFArrayRef
    ABAddressBookCopyArrayOfAllPeople(ABAddressBookRef addressBook);
```

Again, you need to release this array when you are finished with it.

- `ABAddressBookCopyArrayOfAllGroups`. This function returns an array of all groups in the Address Book and is declared as follows:

```
CFArrayRef
    ABAddressBookCopyArrayOfAllGroups(ABAddressBookRef addressBook);
```

- `ABAddressBookCopyPeopleWithName`. This function is actually pretty useful. You specify a query string and it will return all person records matching this query. The function is declared as follows:

```
CFArrayRef
    ABAddressBookCopyPeopleWithName(ABAddressBookRef addressBook,
                                    CFStringRef name);
```

We will use this function in Section 18.8.

- `ABAddressBookHasUnsavedChanges`. This function will return YES if and only if there are changes to the Address Book that need saving. The function is declared as follows:

```
bool ABAddressBookHasUnsavedChanges(ABAddressBookRef addressBook);
```

- `ABAddressBookAddRecord`. This function is used to add a record (either person or group record) to the Address Book. The function is declared as follows:

```
bool ABAddressBookAddRecord(ABAddressBookRef addressBook,
                            ABRecordRef record, CFErrorRef* error);
```

- `ABAddressBookRemoveRecord`. This function is used to remove a record from the Address Book database. The function is declared as follows:

```
bool ABAddressBookRemoveRecord(ABAddressBookRef addressBook,
                               ABRecordRef record,CFErrorRef *error)
```

- `ABAddressBookRevert`. Using this function will discard all your modifications to the Address Book. After calling this function, the Address Book will be refreshed from the database. Also, after calling this function, you can see the changes that other threads have committed after your last save. The function is declared as follows:

```
ABAddressBookRevert(ABAddressBookRef addressBook);
```

If a record has been removed from the database before reverting, all properties of this record will return NULL.

18.7   Multithreading and Identifiers

Every record has a unique identifier. This identifier should be used to communicate records between threads. To retrieve the identifier of a person or a group record, use the function `ABRecordGet-RecordID`, which is declared as follows:

```
ABRecordID ABRecordGetRecordID(ABRecordRef record);
```

We mentioned before that in multivalue properties, each value has a unique identifier. You retrieve these values using an index. Moreover, if you need to store references to specific entries, you need to store the unique identifier of that value rather than its index. The function `ABMultiValueGet-IndexForIdentifier` is used to retrieve the index for the value using its unique identifier. This function is declared as follows:

```
CFIndex ABMultiValueGetIndexForIdentifier(ABMultiValueRef multiValue,
    ABMultiValueIdentifier identifier);
```

To retrieve the unique identifier of a value using its index, use the function `ABMultiValueGet-IdentifierAtIndex`, which is declared as follows:

```
ABMultiValueIdentifier
 ABMultiValueGetIdentifierAtIndex(ABMultiValueRef multiValue,
                                  CFIndex index)
```

You will see the use of identifiers when we discuss some of the applications (for example, see Section 18.11).

18.8   Person Photo Retriever Application

In this section, we present a sample application that prompts the user to enter a query for a person. This query is used to retrieve a person with a photo and display it on the screen as shown in Figure 18.1

The source code for this application can be found in the `PersonPhotoRetriever` project, available in the source downloads.

Listing 18.3 shows a category on `UIImage` to return the photo of the first person in the Address Book whose name matches a given query.

Listing 18.3   A category on `UIImage` to return the photo of the first person in the Address Book whose name matches a given query.

```
@interface UIImage (AddressBook)
+(UIImage*)photoForAperson:(NSString*)_name;
@end

@implementation UIImage (AddressBook)
// returns the image of the first person give a query
```

```
+(UIImage*)photoForAperson:(NSString*)_name{
  UIImage *_image = nil;
  ABAddressBookRef addressBook = ABAddressBookCreate();
  NSArray    *people = (NSArray*)
    ABAddressBookCopyPeopleWithName(addressBook, (CFStringRef)_name);
  int index = 0;
  while (index < [people count]){
    ABRecordRef person = (ABRecordRef)[people objectAtIndex:index++];
    NSData *photoData = (NSData*) ABPersonCopyImageData(person);
    if(photoData){
      _image = [UIImage imageWithData:photoData];
      [photoData release];
      break;
    }
  }
  [people release];
  CFRelease(addressBook);
  return _image;
}
@end
```

Figure 18.1   The photo retriever application.

The `photoForAperson:` method takes the query text as an argument and returns the photo. It starts by creating an Address Book object. After that, the method `ABAddressBookCopyPeople-WithName` is used to perform a prefix search using the given query. The function returns an array of person records that match this query. The method then iterates through this array, retrieving the image data of each person record using `ABPersonCopyImageData` function. If the photo data is not `nil`, a `UIImage` instance is created from this data and the image is returned.

Listing 18.4 shows the method triggered when the user taps the Retrieve Photo button. It simply retrieves the image view and sets it to the image if an image with the query exists. Otherwise, it displays an alert view.

Listing 18.4   The method triggered when the user taps the Retrieve Photo button.

```
-(void)buttonPushed{
  NSString  *name = [(UITextField*)[self.view viewWithTag:999] text];
  UIImageView *imageView = (UIImageView*)[self.view viewWithTag:1234];
  UIImage *image = [UIImage photoForAperson:name];
  if(image){
    imageView.image = image;
    [[self.view viewWithTag:999] resignFirstResponder];
  }
  else{
    [[[UIAlertView alloc] initWithTitle:@"No Records!"
      message:[NSString stringWithFormat:@"%@ photo not found", name]
      delegate:self
      cancelButtonTitle:nil
      otherButtonTitles:@"OK", nil] show];
  }
}
```

18.9   Using the ABUnknownPersonViewController Class

Often, you want to present to the user a partial record and allow him or her to use this partial information to create a new record or add this information to an existing record. The `ABUnknown-PersonViewController` is used for this purpose. In addition to the `AddressBook` framework, you will need to add the `AddressBookUI` framework as explained in Section D.4 of Appendix D. Also, don't forget to add the following import statement:

`#import <AddressBookUI/AddressBookUI.h>`

To use this controller, you first allocate it and initialize it. Next, you set its `displayedPerson` property to a person record with its relevant properties filled in. After that, you set the delegate property `unknownPersonViewDelegate` to an object that implements the `ABUnknownPerson-ViewControllerDelegate` protocol. If you want the user to change the Address Book database, you set the `allowsAddingToAddressBook` property to `YES`. Finally, you push the controller on the stack.

The delegate needs to implement the method `unknownPersonViewController:didResolve-ToPerson:`, which is declared as follows:

```
- (void)unknownPersonViewController:(ABUnknownPersonViewController *)
  unknownCardViewController didResolveToPerson:(ABRecordRef)person;
```

If the user cancelled the controller, `person` will have the value `NULL`. Otherwise, you receive the `person` object with the user's modifications. The `person` record would have been added to the database by this time. You will need to pop the controller in this method.

Listing 18.5 shows the method that pushes an `ABUnknownPersonViewController` instance and the delegate method that pops it. The delegate method does not inspect the person returned. Depending on your application, you may want to use this object. The complete application can be found in the `VisuallyAddingContact` project, available in the source downloads.

Listing 18.5   Utilizing an `ABUnknownPersonViewController` class to add or modify a person record visually.

```
- (void)buttonPushed{
  ABUnknownPersonViewController *unknownPersonViewController =
  [[[ABUnknownPersonViewController alloc] init] autorelease];
  ABRecordRef person = ABPersonCreate();
  ABRecordSetValue(person, kABPersonFirstNameProperty, @"Barack", NULL);
  ABRecordSetValue(person, kABPersonLastNameProperty, @"Obama", NULL);
  unknownPersonViewController.displayedPerson = person;
  CFRelease(person);
  unknownPersonViewController.allowsAddingToAddressBook = YES;
  unknownPersonViewController.unknownPersonViewDelegate = self;
  [self.navigationController
    pushViewController:unknownPersonViewController animated:YES];
}

- (void)unknownPersonViewController:(ABUnknownPersonViewController *)
    unknownCardViewController didResolveToPerson:(ABRecordRef)person{
  [self.navigationController popViewControllerAnimated:YES];
}
```

18.10   Using the ABPeoplePickerNavigationController Class

If you want to ask the user to choose a person record or, say, a phone number from the Address Book, then the `ABPeoplePickerNavigationController` class is your friend.

To use this class, you allocate it, initialize it, set its delegate to an object implementing its delegate, optionally specifying the properties (emails, phone numbers, etc.) that should be displayed when the user peeks into a specific record, and finally present it modally. The following code fragment shows a people picker that shows only the phone numbers of records:

```
ABPeoplePickerNavigationController *peoplePickerViewController =
  [[[ABPeoplePickerNavigationController alloc] init] autorelease];
  peoplePickerViewController.peoplePickerDelegate = self;
```

```
peoplePickerViewController.displayedProperties =
    [NSArray arrayWithObject:
        [NSNumber numberWithInt:kABPersonPhoneProperty]];
[self presentModalViewController:peoplePickerViewController
            animated:YES];
```

The `displayedProperties` property uses an array of `ABPropertyID`s of the properties you want to show. Notice that we did not push the controller but presented it.

The delegate should implement three methods, starting with

```
- (void)peoplePickerNavigationControllerDidCancel:
    (ABPeoplePickerNavigationController *)peoplePicker;
```

This method is called when the user cancels the operation. You should dismiss the controller as follows:

```
[self dismissModalViewControllerAnimated:YES];
```

The second method is the following:

```
- (BOOL)
 peoplePickerNavigationController:(ABPeoplePickerNavigationController *)
 peoplePicker shouldContinueAfterSelectingPerson:(ABRecordRef)person;
```

This method is called when the user selects a person record wanting to see its details or confirming that this is the record he or she is interested in. Depending on the purpose of the people picker, you should either return YES to allow showing of the selected properties or return NO and dismiss the controller as shown above.

Finally, the following method is called when the user selects a specific property (see Figure 18.2):

```
- (BOOL)
        peoplePickerNavigationController:
            (ABPeoplePickerNavigationController *)peoplePicker
        shouldContinueAfterSelectingPerson:(ABRecordRef)person
        property:(ABPropertyID)property
        identifier:(ABMultiValueIdentifier)identifier;
```

If you want the default action to be performed (e.g., dialing a phone number), you should return YES and possibly dismiss the controller. If, on the other hand, you're just interested in the value the user has selected, you should return NO and dismiss the controller.

The method is passed the `person` record and the value `identifier` in a multivalue `property` that was selected. For example, if you show phone numbers, and the `person` record contains three phone numbers, you get to know which of these phone numbers was selected (by its unique identifier).

The following shows a possible implementation:

```
ABMultiValueRef phoneProperty = ABRecordCopyValue(person, property);
NSInteger phoneIndex =
```

```
    ABMultiValueGetIndexForIdentifier(phoneProperty, identifier);
NSString *phone =
    (NSString *)ABMultiValueCopyValueAtIndex(phoneProperty, phoneIndex);
NSLog(@"The phone number selected is %@:", phone);
CFRelease(phoneProperty);
[phone release];
[self dismissModalViewControllerAnimated:YES];
return NO;
```

Figure 18.2   People-picker controller showing a record details.

In the above method, we retrieve the value of the property. Because this property is multivalue, we retrieve its index. After that, we retrieve the value chosen by the user using this index. We release memory and dismiss the controller.

The project `PersonPicker`, available in the source downloads, contains a complete application using the people picker.

18.11   Using the ABPersonViewController Class

The `ABPersonViewController` class allows you to present the details of a specific record to the user. As with its other sisters, you need to create it and initialize it. Next, you set its delegate (one method to implement). After that, you configure some of its options. The `allowsEditing` property is set to `YES` if you want the user to edit the record. `NO` is the default. The `displayedPerson` must be set to the person record you want to show. The `displayedProperties` is an array of all properties you want to show. If you allow editing, then the other properties will show as well while editing.

If you want to highlight a given property, use the `setHighlightedItemForProperty:with-Identifier:` method, which is declared as follows:

```
- (void)setHighlightedItemForProperty:(ABPropertyID)property
         withIdentifier:(ABMultiValueIdentifier)identifier;
```

The `property` parameter specifies the property identifier you want to highlight. If the property is single-value, the second parameter is ignored. If, on the other hand, the property is multivalue (e.g., phone), the `identifier` specifies which value to highlight. You can highlight as many values as you want.

Listing 18.6 shows how one can set-up and invoke a person-view controller. In this example, we retrieve the first person record and show it. The displayed properties are the phone and email properties. The method also highlights the phone value with identifier `0`.

Listing 18.6   Showing a person record using the `ABPersonViewController` class.

```
- (void)buttonPushed{
  ABAddressBookRef addressBook = ABAddressBookCreate();
  NSArray    *allPeople =
    (NSArray*) ABAddressBookCopyArrayOfAllPeople(addressBook);
  if(allPeople.count){
    ABRecordRef person = (ABRecordRef)[allPeople objectAtIndex:0];
    ABPersonViewController *personViewController =
       [[[ABPersonViewController alloc] init] autorelease];
    personViewController.personViewDelegate = self;
    personViewController.displayedPerson = person;
    personViewController.displayedProperties =
    [NSArray arrayWithObjects:
     [NSNumber numberWithInt:kABPersonEmailProperty],
     [NSNumber numberWithInt:kABPersonPhoneProperty], nil];
    [personViewController
        setHighlightedItemForProperty:kABPersonPhoneProperty
        withIdentifier:0];
    [self presentModalViewController:personViewController animated:YES];
  }
  [allPeople release];
  CFRelease(addressBook);
}
```

Listing 18.7 shows the delegate method of the person-view controller. If the property selected by the user is an email property, we log it, disallow default action, and dismiss the controller. Otherwise, we dismiss the controller and allow default action to occur.

Listing 18.7   The delegate method of a person-view controller.

```
- (BOOL)
    personViewController:(ABPersonViewController *)personViewController
    shouldPerformDefaultActionForPerson:(ABRecordRef)person
    property:(ABPropertyID)property
    identifier:(ABMultiValueIdentifier)identifierForValue{
  if(property == kABPersonEmailProperty){
    ABMultiValueRef emailProperty = ABRecordCopyValue(person, property);
    NSInteger emailndex =
     ABMultiValueGetIndexForIdentifier(emailProperty, identifierForValue);
    NSString *email =
      (NSString *)ABMultiValueCopyValueAtIndex(emailProperty, emailndex);
    NSLog(@"The email  selected is %@:", email);
    CFRelease(emailProperty);
    [email release];
    [self dismissModalViewControllerAnimated:YES];
    return NO;
  }
  else{
    [self dismissModalViewControllerAnimated:YES];
    return YES;
  }
}
```

Figure 18.3 shows a view from the person-view controller.

18.12   Using the ABNewPersonViewController Class

If you want the user to create a new person record, you can use the `ABNewPersonViewController` controller. You create and initialize the controller and set the delegate. The controller is then pushed on the stack. The following shows a typical invocation:

```
ABNewPersonViewController *newPersonViewController =
  [[[ABNewPersonViewController alloc] init] autorelease];
  newPersonViewController.newPersonViewDelegate = self;
  [self.navigationController
    pushViewController:newPersonViewController animated:YES];
```

The only delegate method is `newPersonViewController:didCompleteWithNewPerson:`. You should dismiss the controller and inspect the new `person` record. Note that the person will be added to the Address Book by the time this method is called. If the user cancelled, the `person` parameter is `NULL`. The following is the implementation of the `newPersonViewController:didComplete-WithNewPerson:` method:

```
- (void)
newPersonViewController:(ABNewPersonViewController *)newPersonView
    didCompleteWithNewPerson:(ABRecordRef)person{
  [self.navigationController popViewControllerAnimated:YES];
}
```

Figure 18.3   A view from a person-view controller.

Figure 18.4 shows a view of the ABNewPersonViewController controller.

18.13   Summary

In this chapter, we discussed the foundation of the Address Book API and several UI elements that can be used to modify the contacts database.

In Section 18.1, we provided a brief introduction to the subject. Next, Section 18.2 discussed property types. After that, Sections 18.3 and 18.4 showed how to access single- and multivalue properties, respectively. Next, Sections 18.5 and 18.6 went into the details of the person record and the Address Book, respectively. Issues related to multithreading and identifiers were addressed in Section 18.7.

After covering the foundation of the Address Book API, we provided several sample applications. Section 18.8 showed how to use a query to retrieve the photo of a given record. Next, Section 18.9 showed how to use the ABUnknownPersonViewController class. After that, Section 18.10 covered the ABPeoplePickerNavigationController class. The ABPersonViewController class was covered in Section 18.11. Finally, Section 18.12 covered the ABNewPersonViewController class.

Figure 18.4   Adding a new contact using the `ABNewPersonViewController` class.

Exercises

(1) Study the `ABRecordRef` type in the `ABRecordRef.h` header file and the documentation.

(2) Write a view controller that lists the contacts in the Address Book and allows the user to perform multiple selections of person records.

(3) Enhance the view controller by adding search capability.

19

Core Data

In this chapter, you learn how to use the Core Data framework in your application. In Section 19.1, you learn about the main components of the Core Data application. Next, in Section 19.2, we talk about the major classes in the Core Data framework. In Section 19.3, you learn how to use the graphical modeling tool to build a data model. After that, Section 19.4 addresses the basic operations in persistence storage using Core Data. Next, Section 19.5 shows how to use relationships in the Core Data model. After that, Section 19.6 presents a search application that utilizes Core Data for storage. Finally, we summarize the chapter in Section 19.7.

19.1 Core Data Application Components

Data models in a Core Data application are represented by entities. *Entities* are composed of *attributes* (such as `salary`) and *relationships* (such as `manager`). Attributes and relationships are called *properties*.

For entities to come to life, they need to be represented by a managed object. In the relational database world, an entity can be thought of as a table and a managed object as a specific row in that table. In the object world, an entity can be thought of as a class and a managed object as an instance of that class.

A collection of entities with their attributes and relationships represents a *schema* in a Core Data application. This schema is represented by a managed object model. You can create the model using Objective-C code (not recommended) or using the more convenient graphical modeling tool within XCode.

In addition to an entity, a managed object needs a managed object context. Object contexts manage the life cycle of a collection of managed objects. A managed object context needs a persistence store coordinator to manage the persistence of managed objects as well as their retrieval from the store. A store can be a SQLite database, in-memory, or binary file storage.

19.2 Key Players

In this section, we talk about the major classes in the Core Data framework. In essence, we present the Core Data stack.

19.2.1   Entity

Entities are represented by an instance of the NSEntityDescription class. As a minimum, this instance needs a name. The following code fragment shows how to create an instance of this class:

```
NSEntityDescription *userEntity =
    [[[NSEntityDescription alloc] init] autorelease];
[userEntity setName:@"User"];
```

Attributes are represented by the NSAttributeDescription class. To add an attribute, such as name, to an entity, you first create it as follows:

```
NSAttributeDescription *nameAttribute;
nameAttribute = [[[NSAttributeDescription alloc] init] autorelease];
[nameAttribute setName:@"name"];
[nameAttribute setAttributeType:NSStringAttributeType];
[nameAttribute setOptional:NO];
```

In the above code fragment, we set the name of this attribute, provide its type (a string), and specify that it is mandatory. After creating the attribute(s), add the properties as follows:

```
[userEntity setProperties:
    [NSArray arrayWithObjects: dobAttribute, nameAttribute, nil]];
```

In the above code, we set the properties of the User entity to two attributes.

19.2.2   Managed object model

A managed object model is an instance of the NSManagedObjectModel class. There are two options available to create an instance of this class:

- **Objective-C code.** You start by creating entities and then adding these entities to an instance of NSManagedObjectModel using the setEntities: method.

- **Data modeling.** You use a data modeling tool in XCode to graphically build your data model, save it to a file, and load it at runtime into an instance of the NSManagedObjectModel class. The easiest initializer is the mergedModelFromBundles: method. If you pass in nil as the argument, all models in the main bundle are loaded and used to initialize the instance as shown below:

```
NSManagedObjectModel  *managedObjectModel =
    [[NSManagedObjectModel mergedModelFromBundles:nil] retain];
```

19.2.3   *Persistent store coordinator*

A persistence store coordinator is an instance of the NSPersistentStoreCoordinator class. You first create an instance of this class and then initialize it with the managed object model instance. After that, you add a persistence store to it. The following code shows a typical setup:

```
NSURL *storeUrl = [NSURL fileURLWithPath:[NSHomeDirectory()
    stringByAppendingPathComponent:@"Documents/database.sqlite"]];
NSError *error;
NSPersistentStoreCoordinator  *persistentStoreCoordinator =
    [[NSPersistentStoreCoordinator alloc]
        initWithManagedObjectModel:self.managedObjectModel];
if (![persistentStoreCoordinator
    addPersistentStoreWithType:NSSQLiteStoreType
    configuration:nil URL:storeUrl options:nil error:&error]) {
    NSLog(@"error");
}
```

In the above code, we specify the SQLite store type and the location of the database file in the home directory of the application.

19.2.4   *Managed object context*

Managed object contexts are instances of the NSManagedObjectContext class. The following code fragment shows the setup of an instance of this class:

```
managedObjectContext = [[NSManagedObjectContext alloc] init];
[managedObjectContext
        setPersistentStoreCoordinator:persistentStoreCoordinator];
```

Notice how a managed object context needs a persistence store coordinator in order to retrieve and persist the managed objects it manages.

19.2.5   *Managed object*

In a model-view-controller (MVC) Core Data application, the model is captured by the managed object; an instance of NSManagedObject. To create a managed object, you can use the following class method of NSEntityDescription:

```
+ (id)insertNewObjectForEntityForName:(NSString *)entityName
        inManagedObjectContext:(NSManagedObjectContext *)context;
```

Here, you attach a managed object instance configured to work with a specific entity to a managed object context. The method returns the managed object autoreleased.

The following shows a typical example:

```
User *user = (User *)[NSEntityDescription
                      insertNewObjectForEntityForName:@"User"
                      inManagedObjectContext:self.managedObjectContext];
user.dob    = [NSDate date];
user.name   = @"Kate";
user.social = @"555-12-9898";
```

To save this object in the persistence store (e.g., a database table), you must send its context a `save:` message passing a reference to an `NSError` object or `NULL` if you are not interested in receiving potential error messages.

19.2.6   The Core Data wrapper class

If the previous description seems somewhat abstract, this section will make things concrete by giving a complete Core Data wrapper class that you can find in the `CoreDataBasic1` project, which can be found in the source downloads. The class interface is shown in Listing 19.1.

An application needs one instance of this class. It provides a basic Core Data stack that can be used. The three needed main objects (context, coordinator, and model) are created and initialized for you as we shall see later in this section. In addition, it provides a `save` method for saving all managed objects to the store.

Listing 19.1   Interface for the Core Data wrapper.

```
#import <CoreData/CoreData.h>
#import "User.h"
@interface CoreDataWrapper : NSObject {
  NSPersistentStoreCoordinator   *persistentStoreCoordinator;
  NSManagedObjectModel           *managedObjectModel;
  NSManagedObjectContext         *managedObjectContext;
}
@property(nonatomic, readonly, retain)
    NSPersistentStoreCoordinator   *persistentStoreCoordinator;
@property(nonatomic, readonly, retain)
    NSManagedObjectModel           *managedObjectModel;
@property(nonatomic, readonly, retain)
    NSManagedObjectContext         *managedObjectContext;
-(id)init;
-(BOOL)save;
@end
```

Listing 19.2 shows some of the implementation of the wrapper class. We've talked about most of these methods. The `init` method simply starts the stack build process by retrieving the value of the context. The method `managedObjectContext` gets called and checks to see if the object was initialized before. Because all instance variables are initialized to `nil`, the method proceeds by retrieving the persistence coordinator and attaching this coordinator to the context.

The `persistentStoreCoordinator` method checks to see if the coordinator was created before. If not, it creates it and initializes it as you saw in Section 19.2.3. The initialization uses a managed object model instance.

The `managedObjectModel` checks to see if the model was created before. If not, it creates the model from code (shown in Listing 19.3) or loads it from file.

Listing 19.2   Some of the implementation of the wrapper class.

```
#import "CoreDataWrapper.h"
@implementation CoreDataWrapper
-(id)init{
  if(self = [super init]){
    self.managedObjectContext;
  }
  return self;
}
-(BOOL)save{
  NSError *error;
  if ([self.managedObjectContext save:&error]) {
      return YES;
  }
  return NO;
}
- (NSManagedObjectContext *) managedObjectContext {
  if (managedObjectContext) {
    return managedObjectContext;
  }
  NSPersistentStoreCoordinator *coordinator =
    self.persistentStoreCoordinator;
  if (coordinator) {
    managedObjectContext = [[NSManagedObjectContext alloc] init];
    [managedObjectContext setPersistentStoreCoordinator:coordinator];
  }
  return managedObjectContext;
}
-(NSManagedObjectModel*) managedObjectModel{
#if FALSE
  return [self managedObjectModelFromCode];
#else
  if(managedObjectModel){
    return managedObjectModel;
  }
  managedObjectModel =
    [[NSManagedObjectModel mergedModelFromBundles:nil] retain];
  return managedObjectModel;
#endif
}
-(NSPersistentStoreCoordinator*) persistentStoreCoordinator{
```

```objc
  if (persistentStoreCoordinator) {
    return persistentStoreCoordinator;
  }
  NSURL *storeUrl =
    [NSURL fileURLWithPath:[NSHomeDirectory()
        stringByAppendingPathComponent:@"Documents/database.sqlite"]];
    NSError *error;
  persistentStoreCoordinator =
    [[NSPersistentStoreCoordinator alloc]
        initWithManagedObjectModel:self.managedObjectModel];
  if (![persistentStoreCoordinator
    addPersistentStoreWithType:NSSQLiteStoreType configuration:nil
      URL:storeUrl options:nil error:&error]){
    NSLog(@"error");
  }
  return persistentStoreCoordinator;
}
-(void)dealloc{
  [persistentStoreCoordinator release];
  [managedObjectModel release];
  [managedObjectContext release];
  [super dealloc];
}
@end
```

Listing 19.3   Creating a managed object model with a User entity from code.

```objc
-(NSManagedObjectModel*) managedObjectModelFromCode{
  if(managedObjectModel){
    return managedObjectModel;
  }
  managedObjectModel = [[NSManagedObjectModel alloc] init];
  NSEntityDescription *userEntity = [[[NSEntityDescription alloc] init]
                                                    autorelease];
  [userEntity setName:@"User"];
  [userEntity setManagedObjectClassName:@"User"];
  [managedObjectModel setEntities:[NSArray arrayWithObject:userEntity]];
  NSAttributeDescription *dobAttribute;
  dobAttribute = [[[NSAttributeDescription alloc] init] autorelease];
  [dobAttribute setName:@"dob"];
  [dobAttribute setAttributeType:NSDateAttributeType];
  [dobAttribute setOptional:NO];
  NSAttributeDescription *nameAttribute;
  nameAttribute = [[[NSAttributeDescription alloc] init] autorelease];
  [nameAttribute setName:@"name"];
  [nameAttribute setAttributeType:NSStringAttributeType];
  [nameAttribute setOptional:NO];
  NSAttributeDescription *socialAttribute;
```

```
    socialAttribute = [[[NSAttributeDescription alloc] init] autorelease];
    [socialAttribute setName:@"social"];
    [socialAttribute setAttributeType:NSStringAttributeType];
    [socialAttribute setOptional:NO];
    [userEntity setProperties:
     [NSArray arrayWithObjects:dobAttribute, nameAttribute,
                                socialAttribute, nil]];
    return managedObjectModel;
}
```

In Listing 19.3, we associated the `User` entity with the Objective-C class `User` using the following statement:

```
[userEntity setManagedObjectClassName:@"User"];
```

The `User` class is shown in Listing 19.4. It simply inherits all the behavior from `NSManaged-Object` class and declares three attributes. Because the Core Data framework will generate the accessor methods, you are encouraged to use the `@dynamic` directive. This directive will simply stop compiler warnings.

Listing 19.4   The `User` managed object class.

```
#import <CoreData/CoreData.h>
@interface User : NSManagedObject {
}
@property (retain) NSString *social;
@property (retain) NSString *name;
@property (retain) NSDate   *dob;
@end

@implementation User
@dynamic dob, social, name;
@end
```

19.3   Using the Modeling Tool

In this section, we show you how to build a simple model using the graphical modeling tool. The model will consist of two entities: `User` and `Comment`. A user can have many comments, and every comment belongs to a specific user.

The model resides in a file in the bundle. To create the model, start by creating this file:

1. **Right-click on the** `Resources` **group, choose** `Add`, **and then choose** `New File`.
2. **Select** `Resource`, **choose** `Data Model`, **and hit** `Next` **(see Figure 19.1).**
3. **Choose the model name, click** `Next` **(see Figure 19.2), and then click** `Finish`.
4. **Right-click the diagram window and choose** `Add Entity` **(Figure 19.3).**

Figure 19.1   Selecting a data model resource.

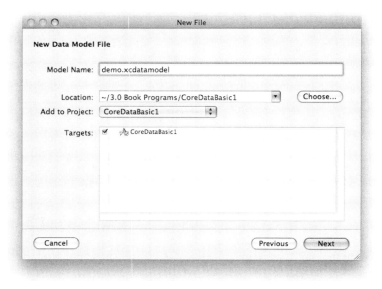

Figure 19.2   Naming the data model.

Figure 19.3   Adding a new entity to the model.

5. **Enter the name of the entity and the name of its class as shown in Figure 19.4.**

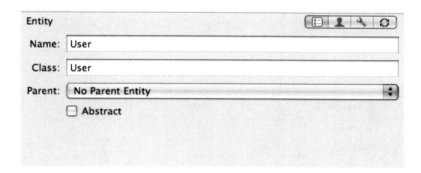

Figure 19.4   Configuring the new User entity.

6. **Select the User entity and click on the + icon to add an attribute as shown in Figure 19.5.**

7. **Name the attribute name and choose the type to be String as shown in Figure 19.6.**

8. **Repeat the process, and add a dob attribute of type Date and a social attribute of type String.**

   The state of the User entity at this stage is shown in Figure 19.7.

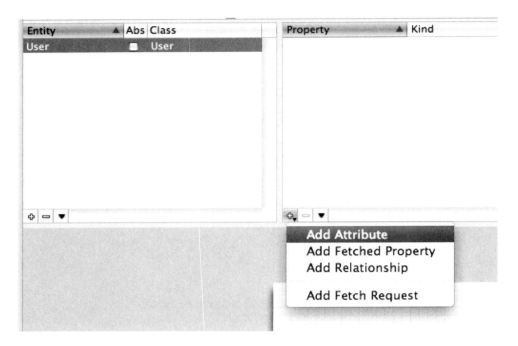

Figure 19.5   Adding a new attribute to the User entity.

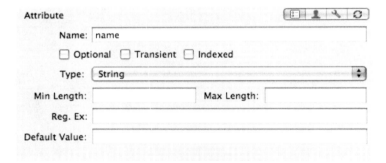

Figure 19.6   Specifying the parameters for the name attribute of the User entity.

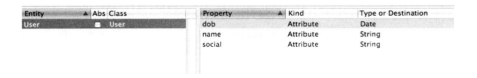

Figure 19.7   The User entity with three attributes.

9. **Now, go ahead and add another model,** Comment. Comment has a lat attribute of type Double, a lon attribute of type Double, and a text attribute of type String. All are mandatory.

Our data model declares that a user has many comments and each comment belongs to one user. Let's declare these relationships using the tool.

10. **Select the** User **entity and choose** Add Relationship **as shown in Figure 19.8.**

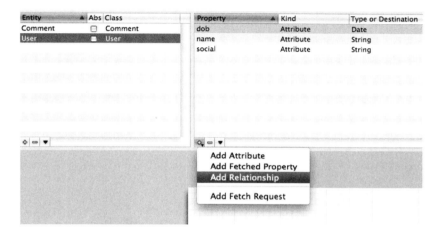

Figure 19.8   Adding a relationship in the User model.

11. **Name the relationship** comments **and pick the destination to be the** Comment **entity.**

12. **Choose a** To-Many **relationship (meaning that the user will have many comments) and make the delete rule** Cascade. This way, all comments that belong to a user will be deleted when that user is deleted. See Figure 19.9.

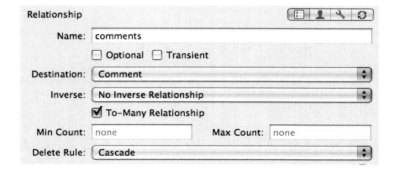

Figure 19.9   The comments relationship in the User model.

13. **Select the** `Comment` **entity and add a relationship as shown in Figure 19.10.**

    Notice that we choose the inverse to be `comments` and the delete rule to be `No Action`.

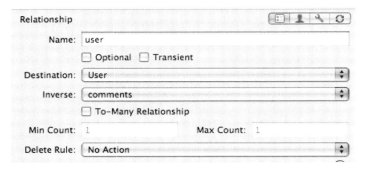

Figure 19.10   The `user` relationship in the `Comment` model.

The resulting model diagram is shown in Figure 19.11.

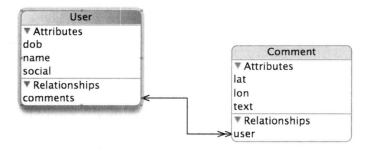

Figure 19.11   The data model consisting of `User` and `Comment` entities with relationships. Double arrows indicate a `To-Many` relationship.

19.4   Create, Read, Update, and Delete (CRUD)

In this section, we address the basic operations in persistence storage using Core Data.

19.4.1   Create

Creating a new managed object and saving it to the store is pretty straightforward. You use `NSEntityDescription`'s class method `insertNewObjectForEntityForName:inManaged-ObjectContext:` to obtain a fresh managed object for a given entity in a given context. After that, you simply assign values to its attributes and send a `save:` message to its context.

The following method creates a new record in the persistence store for a user with name, date of birth, and Social Security number:

```
-(BOOL)addUser:(NSString*) _userName dateOfBirth:(NSDate*)_dob
        andSocial:(NSString*)_social{
  User *user = (User *)[NSEntityDescription
        insertNewObjectForEntityForName:@"User"
        inManagedObjectContext:self.managedObjectContext];
  user.dob = _dob;
  user.name = _userName;
  user.social = _social;
  return [self.managedObjectContext save:NULL];
}
```

19.4.2   Delete

Deleting a record is simple. Given a managed object, you send a `deleteObject:` message to the context with that object as an argument. After that, you send the context a `save:` message to persist the change. The following shows a code fragment that accomplishes that:

```
[self.managedObjectContext deleteObject:user];
[self.managedObjectContext save:NULL];
```

19.4.3   Read and update

To update a record, you retrieve it (read), change its attributes, and save its context.

Let's turn our attention to retrieval in Core Data. To retrieve managed objects from the persistence store, you execute fetch requests. A *fetch request* is an instance of the `NSFetchRequest` class. An instance of this class can be configured with three pieces of information:

- **The name of the entity.** The fetch request must be associated with an entity. To set the entity of a fetch request instance, you use the method `setEntity:`, which takes an instance of the `NSEntityDescription` class as an argument.
- **The conditions of the search.** You specify the conditions using a predicate. A *predicate* is an instance of the class `NSPredicate`. This is optional.
- **The sort criteria.** You specify the sort criteria by using the method `setSortDescriptors:`, passing in an array of `NSSortDescriptor` instances. Sort descriptors with lower indices in this array are given higher precedence in the sorting algorithm. Sorting is optional.

Once you have configured the fetch request object, you use the following instance method of the `NSManagedObjectContext` class to retrieve the managed objects:

```
- (NSArray *)
executeFetchRequest:(NSFetchRequest *)request error:(NSError **)error
```

Unconditional fetch

The following method shows how to retrieve all of `User`'s managed objects:

```
-(NSArray*)allUsers{
  NSFetchRequest *request =
    [[[NSFetchRequest alloc] init] autorelease];
  NSEntityDescription *entity =
    [NSEntityDescription entityForName:@"User"
        inManagedObjectContext:self.managedObjectContext];
    [request setEntity:entity];
  return [self.managedObjectContext
                    executeFetchRequest:request error:NULL];
}
```

The method simply specifies the name of the entity whose managed objects are being retrieved and executes the fetch. No sorting or conditions are specified (i.e., in the case of a SQL table, all rows are retrieved with no ordering).

Conditional fetch

As an example of specifying fetch conditions, the following method searches for all `User` records where the `name` attribute matches a query:

```
-(NSArray*)usersWithNameQuery:(NSString*)_query{
  NSFetchRequest *request = [[[NSFetchRequest alloc] init] autorelease];
  NSEntityDescription *entity =
    [NSEntityDescription
          entityForName:@"User"
          inManagedObjectContext:self.managedObjectContext];
    [request setEntity:entity];
  NSPredicate *predicate =
    [NSPredicate predicateWithFormat:
    @"name like[cd] %@", [NSString stringWithFormat:@"*%@*", _query]];
  [request setPredicate:predicate];
  return [self.managedObjectContext
                          executeFetchRequest:request error:NULL];
}
```

To specify the condition, a new `NSPredicate` object is generated using the `predicateWith-Format:` class method. Here, we are saying that the `name` attribute must contain the query string. `[cd]` means case- and diacritic-insensitive and `*` is used to denote zero or more characters. The `predicateWithFormat:` method does add quotes to the query. After setting the predicate, the context is asked to execute the fetch.

Another example of using a predicate is retrieval of older users. If you set the predicate to something like `dob < some_date`, you can retrieve all users older than that given date. The following method does just that:

```
-(NSArray*)olderUsers:(NSDate*)_date{
  NSFetchRequest *request = [[[NSFetchRequest alloc] init] autorelease];
  NSEntityDescription *entity =
     [NSEntityDescription entityForName:@"User"
             inManagedObjectContext:self.managedObjectContext];
  [request setEntity:entity];
  NSPredicate *predicate =
     [NSPredicate predicateWithFormat:@"dob < %@", _date];
  [request setPredicate:predicate];
  return [self.managedObjectContext
          executeFetchRequest:request error:NULL];
}
```

Sorted fetch

To generate a sorted result set, you use the NSSortDescriptor class. You create a new NSSort-Descriptor instance and initialize it with the initWithKey:ascending: initializer. After that, you set the sort descriptors array of the fetch request object using the setSortDescriptors: method. The following example shows how you can retrieve all users, sorted according to their date of birth (descending):

```
-(NSArray*)allUsersSorted{
  NSFetchRequest *request = [[[NSFetchRequest alloc] init] autorelease];
  NSEntityDescription *entity =
    [NSEntityDescription entityForName:@"User"
      inManagedObjectContext:self.managedObjectContext];
  [request setEntity:entity];
  NSSortDescriptor *sortDescriptor =
   [[[NSSortDescriptor alloc] initWithKey:@"dob" ascending:NO]
                autorelease];
  [request setSortDescriptors:
    [NSArray arrayWithObject:sortDescriptor]];
  return [self.managedObjectContext
                executeFetchRequest:request error:NULL];
}
```

19.5   Working with Relationships

Relationships in Core Data are easy. In the class representing a To-Many relationship, you declare a property of type reference to an NSSet class. For example, in the User class, you can declare the relationship with Comment as follows:

```
@property (retain) NSSet *comments;
```

In the Comment class, you declare the Belongs-To relationship with User as follows:

```
@property (retain) User *user;
```

In an inverse relationship, you can change one side of the relationship, and the other side will change automatically. For example, if you want to create a new comment for a given user, you can simply create the comment managed object; configure it with the text, latitude, and longitude; set its user property to the user managed object; and save the context. Now the user's comments property (represented by an instance of NSSet in the User class) has a new member.

The following method adds a new comment to an existing user:

```
-(BOOL)addCommentByUser:(User*)user withText:(NSString*)text
        lat:(float)lat andLon:(float)lon{
  Comment *comment = (Comment *)[NSEntityDescription
        insertNewObjectForEntityForName:@"Comment"
        inManagedObjectContext:self.managedObjectContext];
  comment.user = user;
  comment.text = text;
  comment.lat = [NSNumber numberWithDouble:lat];
  comment.lon = [NSNumber numberWithDouble:lon];
  return [self.managedObjectContext save:NULL];
}
```

19.6   A Search Application

In this section, we present a search application that uses a search-display controller to search for stars of TV series. The data store is an SQLite database managed by Core Data. The records (instances of Star managed object class) are presented in a table view.

In order to use the Core Data framework, you need to add the CoreData.framework to your project as explained in Section D.4 of Appendix D. In addition, you need to add the following import statement to your code:

```
#import <CoreData/CoreData.h>
```

First, we discuss the UISearchDisplayController class and how it is used for managing a search bar and displaying the results of the search. Next, we present the main pieces of the application.

19.6.1   The UISearchDisplayController class

The UISearchDisplayController class is used to manage a search-bar as well as provide an overlay table view for search results. When the user starts entering text in the search-bar text field, the search-display controller displays an overlay table view. The table view, whose data source and delegate are configured using properties of the search-display controller, is then populated with records corresponding to the search. As the user changes the search text, the contents of the overlay table view is conditionally updated. If the user taps on one of the search-results rows, the delegate of the overlay table view gets notified, which can result in, for example, the details of this record to be shown by pushing a new view controller. Figure 19.12 shows the search display controller in action.

Figure 19.12 A search-display controller overlaying a table view with results from a text query in a search bar.

When the user taps the Cancel button, the overlay table view is removed from the display. In addition, the navigation bar reappears and the search bar is brought down.

To use the search-display view controller, you need to do the following:

1. Create and initialize it. The controller is initialized by the following method:

```
- (id)initWithSearchBar:(UISearchBar *)searchBar
        contentsController:(UIViewController *)viewController;
```

The initializer takes as the first argument the search bar (an instance of the `UISearchBar` class). The second argument should be the view controller that manages the display of the original content.

A search bar is a view that displays a text field, and cancel and bookmark buttons. In addition, you can add different scope buttons beneath it.

2. **Specify the data source for the search results.** You need to specify a value for the data source of the search results using the `searchResultsDataSource` property. This property is declared as follows:

```
@property(nonatomic,assign)
    id<UITableViewDataSource>    searchResultsDataSource;
```

The object should adopt the `UITableViewDataSource` protocol, and usually this object is the same as the view controller used in the initialization of the search-display controller.

3. **Specify the delegate of the search results.** The delegate of the overlay table view is specified using the `searchResultsDelegate` property. The object should implement the `UITableViewDelegate` protocol. As in the case of the data source, the view controller used to initialize the search-display controller is usually used as the delegate of the search-results table view.

4. **Specify the search-display view controller delegate.** You also need to specify a delegate for the search-display view controller. All methods are optional. The following two delegate methods are used to specify if the search results in the overlay table view should be reloaded when the user changes the text in the search-bar text field or changes the scope of the search:

- `searchDisplayController:shouldReloadTableForSearchString:`.
  This method is called when the user changes the text in the text field of the search bar. The method is declared as follows:

  ```
  - (BOOL)
  searchDisplayController:(UISearchDisplayController *)controller
  shouldReloadTableForSearchString:(NSString *)searchString;
  ```

  If you return `YES`, the results table view is reloaded. If you determine that the search will take a long time, you may want to fire up a thread to do the actual search and return `NO`. When the search is finished, you can reload the table. You can access the table view of the results via the `searchResultsTableView` property, which is declared as follows:

  ```
  @property(nonatomic,readonly)UITableView *searchResultsTableView
  ```

- `searchDisplayController:shouldReloadTableForSearchScope:`.
  This method is called when the search scope of the search bar is changed. The method is declared as follows:

  ```
  - (BOOL)
  searchDisplayController:(UISearchDisplayController *)controller
  shouldReloadTableForSearchScope:(NSInteger)searchOption;
  ```

  The `searchOption` is used to pass in the index of the scope. The same logic used in the previous callback also applies here.

19.6.2   *Main pieces*

In this section, we present the main pieces of the application. We use a single table view controller as the data source and delegate for the main table view, the search-results overlay table view, and the search-display controller.

The application uses an instance of the table view controller `SearchTableViewController`. This instance is used as a root of the navigation controller of the application. The following code fragment shows the setup of the main display in the application delegate (see the `CoreDataBasic3` project in the source downloads for a complete listing):

```
navCtrl = [[UINavigationController alloc] initWithRootViewController:
  [[[SearchTableViewController alloc]
                       initWithStyle:UITableViewStylePlain] autorelease]];
[window addSubview:navCtrl.view];
```

The initializer of the table view controller is shown below. It creates and initializes a `CoreData-Wrapper` instance and uses it to retrieve all the stars' records:

```
- (id)initWithStyle:(UITableViewStyle)style{
  if(self = [super initWithStyle:style]){
    self.cdw = [[[CoreDataWrapper alloc] init] autorelease];
    self.allStars = [cdw allStars];
    self.title = @"Stars Info";
  }
  return self;
}
```

Listing 19.5 shows the `viewDidLoad` method of the table view controller.

Listing 19.5   The `viewDidLoad` method in the Core Data search application.

```
- (void)viewDidLoad {
  [super viewDidLoad];
  self.filteredListContent = [NSMutableArray array];
  self.searchBar =
    [[[UISearchBar alloc] initWithFrame:CGRectMake(0, 0, 320, 44)]
               autorelease];
  searchBar.scopeButtonTitles =
    [NSArray arrayWithObjects:@"All", @"Lost", @"Simpsons", nil];
  searchBar.autocorrectionType = UITextAutocorrectionTypeNo;
    searchBar.autocapitalizationType = UITextAutocapitalizationTypeNone;
  self.tableView.tableHeaderView = searchBar;
  self.searchDisplayController =
    [[[UISearchDisplayController alloc]
    initWithSearchBar:searchBar contentsController:self] autorelease];
  searchDisplayController.searchResultsDataSource = self;
  searchDisplayController.searchResultsDelegate = self;
  searchDisplayController.delegate = self;
}
```

The controller uses `filteredListContent` to store the search result records. The method creates a search bar and initializes its scope buttons with three titles. Here, we want the user to search for all stars, stars only in the *Lost* series, or stars only in the *Simpsons* series. The header view of the table view is set to be the search bar.

The search-display controller is created and initialized with the search-bar instance and **self** (the table view controller itself). The delegates and data source are set to be the table view controller instance. Figure 19.13 shows the main view of the search application.

Figure 19.13   The main view in the Search app. The search bar is the table view's header.

The table view controller instance acts as a data source for two table views: (1) the main table view displaying all the records and (2) the search-results table view. The table view controller instance provides the following for the two table views:

- **The number of rows in a table.** The data source method shown below checks the `table-View` argument. If it is the search-results table, it returns the number of records obtained from executing the query. Otherwise, it returns the number of all records.

```
- (NSInteger) tableView:(UITableView *)tableView
            numberOfRowsInSection:(NSInteger)section {
  if (tableView == searchDisplayController.searchResultsTableView) {
```

```
  return filteredListContent.count;
  }
  else{
    return allStars.count;
  }
}
```

- **The cell.** If the table view is the search results table view, the cell is obtained from `filtered-ListContent` array. Otherwise, the `allStars` array is used. The method is shown below:

```
- (UITableViewCell *) tableView:(UITableView *)tableView
                      cellForRowAtIndexPath:(NSIndexPath *)indexPath{
  static NSString *CellIdentifier = @"Cell";
  UITableViewCell *cell =
   [tableView dequeueReusableCellWithIdentifier:CellIdentifier];
  if (cell == nil) {
    cell = [[[UITableViewCell alloc]
             initWithStyle:UITableViewCellStyleDefault
             reuseIdentifier:CellIdentifier] autorelease];
  }
  if (tableView == searchDisplayController.searchResultsTableView){
    cell.textLabel.text =
        [[filteredListContent objectAtIndex:indexPath.row] name];
  }
  else {
    cell.textLabel.text =
        [[allStars objectAtIndex:indexPath.row] name];
  }
  return cell;
}
```

As we mentioned before, you can change the results table view's contents dynamically as the user types in the search bar (see Figures 19.14 and 19.15).

The following two methods are called by the search display controller. Both modify the `filtered-ListContent` array based on the new search and return YES (for reload).

```
- (BOOL)
    searchDisplayController:(UISearchDisplayController *)controller
    shouldReloadTableForSearchString:(NSString *)searchString {
  [self filterContentForSearchText:searchString
       scope:[[searchBar scopeButtonTitles]
              objectAtIndex:[searchBar selectedScopeButtonIndex]]];
  return YES;
}
```

Figure 19.14 Searching in the Lost scope.

Figure 19.15 Searching in the Simpsons scope.

```
- (BOOL)
    searchDisplayController:(UISearchDisplayController *)controller
    shouldReloadTableForSearchScope:(NSInteger)searchOption {
  [self filterContentForSearchText:[searchBar text]
      scope:[[searchBar scopeButtonTitles] objectAtIndex:searchOption]];
  return YES;
}
```

Both methods use the following custom method in the table view controller that does the actual search:

```
- (void)filterContentForSearchText:(NSString*)searchText
        scope:(NSString*)scope{
  [filteredListContent removeAllObjects];
  if([scope isEqualToString:@"All"]){
    [filteredListContent addObjectsFromArray:
      [self.cdw starsWithNameQuery:searchText]];
  }
  else{
```

```
    [filteredListContent addObjectsFromArray:
        [self.cdw starsWithNameQuery:searchText andSeries:scope]];
    }
}
```

The `starsWithNameQuery:` method retrieves all stars that have `searchText` in their names. This method is shown below:

```
-(NSArray*)starsWithNameQuery:(NSString*)_query{
    NSFetchRequest *request = [[[NSFetchRequest alloc] init] autorelease];
    NSEntityDescription *entity =
        [NSEntityDescription entityForName:@"Star"
                inManagedObjectContext:self.managedObjectContext];
    [request setEntity:entity];
    NSPredicate *predicate =
        [NSPredicate predicateWithFormat:@"name like[cd] %@",
            [NSString stringWithFormat:@"*%@*", _query]];
    [request setPredicate:predicate];
    return
        [self.managedObjectContext executeFetchRequest:request error:NULL];
}
```

The `starsWithNameQuery:andSeries:` method adds an equality condition to the above search condition and is shown below:

```
-(NSArray*)
starsWithNameQuery:(NSString*)_query andSeries:(NSString*)_series{
    NSFetchRequest *request = [[[NSFetchRequest alloc] init] autorelease];
    NSEntityDescription *entity =
        [NSEntityDescription entityForName:@"Star"
            inManagedObjectContext:self.managedObjectContext];
    [request setEntity:entity];
    NSPredicate *predicate =
            [NSPredicate predicateWithFormat:
                    @"name like[cd] %@ AND series = %@",
                    [NSString stringWithFormat:@"*%@*", _query], _series];
    [request setPredicate:predicate];
    return
        [self.managedObjectContext executeFetchRequest:request error:NULL];
}
```

19.7 Summary

In this chapter, you learned how to use the Core Data framework in your applications. In Section 19.1, you learned the main components of the Core Data application. Next, in Section 19.2, we talked about the major classes in the Core Data framework. In Section 19.3, you learned how to use the graphical modeling tool to build a data model. After that, Section 19.4 addressed the basic operations in persistence storage using Core Data. Next, Section 19.5 showed how to use relationships in the Core Data model. Finally, Section 19.6 presented a search application that utilized Core Data for storage.

Exercises

(1) Read about the `NSManagedObjectModel` class in the `NSManagedObjectModel.h` header file and the documentation.

(2) Write an application that manages users using Core Data. The application lists the users in a table view and allows the basic CRUD operations on the records. A user has a name, photo, and address. Use SQLite for persistence.

20

Undo Management

In this chapter, you learn about undo management support in iOS. In Section 20.1, we discuss the basic steps needed to utilize undo management. After that, in Section 20.2, we present a detailed example that shows how to use undo management. Next, we summarize the main rules in using the undo capabilities in an application. Finally, we summarize the chapter in Section 20.4.

20.1 Understanding Undo Management

In this section, you learn the basic steps needed to add undo capabilities to your application. First, we discuss the basic idea in Section 20.1.1. After that, we talk about the undo manager in Section 20.1.2. Next, you learn in Section 20.1.3 how to register undo and redo operations. After that, you learn in Section 20.1.4 about the role that the first responder plays in the undo management. Finally, Section 20.1.5 shows what you need to do to enable shake-to-undo behavior.

20.1.1 Basic idea

Undo support provides a simple interface for managing undo and redo of user actions. Whenever the user requests an operation that he or she expects to have the option of undoing, you ask an undo manager to record an action that reverts this operation.

Recording undo actions is performed on a stack. The user can shake the device to see the most recent action that can be reverted. If the user selects that action, the undo operation is executed. In addition, that undo operation can itself record its counterpart operation so that the user can redo the original operation. In essence, two stacks are maintained: one for undo and the other for redo.

You can invoke undo and redo operations from code if you choose to. In addition, you can disable the ability of the user to undo and redo operations by shaking the device.

If you want to utilize the undo capability in a text view, you can rely on the built-in support defined in that UI element. If, however, you want to implement this capability in, say, a view controller, you need to follow some basic rules.

20.1.2   Creating an undo manager

The undo/redo operations are managed by the NSUndoManager class. Any object that inherits from UIResponder (e.g., a UIView, a UIViewController, etc.) can create its own NSUndoManager instance.

Once created, the responder object can use it to store callback operations that undo other operations. When the NSUndoManager is asked to undo, it pops the topmost operation from the stack and calls the callback registered to undo it.

When the undo callback is executed, it can register yet another undo operation that will redo the original operation. The registration process is similar to the one that registered the undo action. The undo manager is smart enough to register an operation as a redo when it is currently undoing that operation.

20.1.3   Registering an undo operation

There are two types of undo operations that can be registered:

- Simple undo
- Invocation-based undo

In simple undo, the undo operation is a selector that takes one argument. To register a simple undo operation, you send the undo manager instance a registerUndoWithTarget:selector:-object: message. This method is declared as follows:

```
- (void)registerUndoWithTarget:(id)target selector:(SEL)selector
        object:(id)anObject;
```

The target argument is the object that will receive the undo/redo message when the undo/redo operation is invoked. That message is basically the second and third argument. For example, an undo manager that is sent the message

```
[undoManager registerUndoWithTarget:aTarget
                selector:@selector(addValue:)
                object:@"Original"];
```

will send a addValue:@"Original" message to aTarget when an undo operation is requested.

If, however, your undo operation takes more than one argument, you need to use invocation-based undo. This is a two-step process. First, you need to prepare the undo manager by sending it a prepareWithInvocationTarget: message, passing in the object that should receive the undo message. After that, you send the undo manager a message that the target object you passed in the first step should receive when the undo operation is requested. For example, the statement

```
[[undoManager prepareWithInvocationTarget:anObject]
    setFather:@"Homer" mother:@"Marge" spouse:nil];
```

will result in the undo manager's sending `anObject` the following message when undo is requested:

```
setFather:@"Homer" mother:@"Marge" spouse:nil
```

The `NSUndoManager` object implements this behavior using the concepts behind the `forward-Invocation:` method and the `NSInvocation` class. Refer to Section 2.13 for more information.

Note that after an undo operation is registered, the redo stack is cleared.

20.1.4 Hooking into the undo management mechanism

Whenever the user shakes the device, a call to retrieve the value of the property `undoManager` is sent to the first responder. This property is defined in the `UIResponder` class as follows:

```
@property(readonly) NSUndoManager *undoManager
```

If the first responder object has its own undo manager, that undo manager object is returned to the system and the appropriate options are displayed to the user (see Figure 20.1).

Figure 20.1   Undo menu appearing in the middle of an undo/redo session after a device shake.

When the user makes a selection, that selection, whether undo or redo, is sent to the undo manager of the first responder in the form of an `undo` or `redo` message. The corresponding operation is executed on the target of the registered undo message that is on top of the stack. If the first-responder object is the target of the undo/redo message, it can reflect that change in its data as well as in the UI. If, on the other hand, the target is different, and the object responsible for maintaining the UI has previously registered to receive undo/redo notifications, then it will receive such notifications and can update the UI accordingly. Examples of notifications include

- `NSUndoManagerWillUndoChangeNotification`. Posted just before an `NSUndoManager` object performs an undo operation.

- `NSUndoManagerDidUndoChangeNotification`. Posted just after an `NSUndoManager` object performs an undo operation.

- `NSUndoManagerWillRedoChangeNotification`. Posted just before an `NSUndoManager` object performs a redo operation.

- NSUndoManagerDidRedoChangeNotification. Posted just after an NSUndoManager object performs a redo operation.

View controllers are subclasses of the UIResponder class. To be able to interact with the user using the Undo menu, a view controller needs to follow simple rules:

- **Become first responder while its view is showing.** The view controller needs to be the first responder so that it receives actions from the Undo menu. To achieve that, the view controller needs to do two things:

  (a) Override the canBecomeFirstResponder method and return YES.

  (b) Override viewDidAppear: and send itself a becomeFirstResponder message.

- **Resign first responder when the view it is managing disappears.** The controller needs to override the viewDidDisappear: method and send itself a resignFirstResponder message.

- **Define an** NSUndoManager **property.** To be hooked into the undo mechanism, the view controller needs to declare a property similar to the following:

  @property(nonatomic, retain) NSUndoManager *undoManager;

  The undoManager name must be used exactly as shown. It is not enough to declare a property of type NSUndoManager*; it has to be called undoManager.

- **Create an instance of** NSUndoManager **when the user requests editing.** Once the user hits Done, the NSUndoManager instance should be deleted.

20.1.5   Enabling shake-to-edit behavior

To enable the Undo menu, the UIApplication instance must be configured so that shaking the device displays that menu. This can be done in the delegate method applicationDidFinish-Launching: as follows:

application.applicationSupportsShakeToEdit = YES;

20.2   Detailed Example

In this section, we present an application that supports undo management. The application uses a table view to show a list of items. If the user chooses to edit the table by tapping on the Edit button, the table view enters editing mode, where the user can delete specific rows. When the user asks for a row to be deleted, the table view controller registers the value stored in this row to be added as an undo operation. After that, the row is deleted and the UI is updated.

When the user shakes the device and selects to undo the topmost operation, the method for adding a row is called with the old value of that row passed in as an argument. The method adds a new row with the value passed as its content, registers an undo event with the old value, and updates the UI. Because the undo manager is undoing while the undo registration is requested, it interprets that operation as a redo operation.

20.2.1 The view controller class

The view controller is declared in Listing 20.1.

Listing 20.1   The view controller used in demonstrating undo management.

```
@interface MyTableViewController : UITableViewController {
  NSUndoManager    *undoManager;
  NSMutableArray   *data;
}
@property(nonatomic, retain)  NSUndoManager   *undoManager;
@property(nonatomic, retain)  NSMutableArray  *data;
@end
```

The view controller maintains its own instance of the NSUndoManager class. In addition, its data model is captured by a mutable array.

20.2.2 First-responder status

The view controller maintains its responsibility as a first responder using the following method overrides:

```
- (BOOL)canBecomeFirstResponder {
    return YES;
}

- (void)viewDidAppear:(BOOL)animated {
    [super viewDidAppear:animated];
    [self becomeFirstResponder];
}

- (void)viewDidDisappear:(BOOL)animated{
    [super viewDidDisappear:animated];
    [self resignFirstResponder];
}
```

20.2.3 Editing mode and the NSUndoManager instance

To support editing, the view controller adds an Edit button in its viewDidLoad method as follows:

```
- (void)viewDidLoad {
  [super viewDidLoad];
  self.navigationItem.rightBarButtonItem = self.editButtonItem;
}
```

To respond to changes in editing mode, the controller overrides the `setEditing:animated:` method as follows:

```
- (void)setEditing:(BOOL)editing animated:(BOOL)animated {
  [super setEditing:editing animated:animated];
  if(editing){
    self.undoManager = [[[NSUndoManager alloc] init] autorelease];
    [undoManager setLevelsOfUndo:10];
  }
  else{
    self.undoManager = nil;
  }
}
```

The undo manager is created and configured if the view controller is entering editing mode. Because the undo stack capacity is defaulted to unlimited, the view controller sets appropriate stack capacity according to its needs and memory constraints. Here, it sets it to a maximum of 10 undo operations. If this limit is exceeded, the oldest undo operation is deleted first to make space. Note that the `setLevelsOfUndo:0` message will result in unlimited stack capacity.

If the view controller is leaving editing mode, the undo manager is released. This event occurs when the user taps the Done button, which means that the user is expecting the changes to be permanent.

20.2.4   Registering undo actions

When the user requests the deletion of a row, the view controller deletes the row by calling the method `deleteRowAtIndex:` This method is defined as follows:

```
-(void)deleteRowAtIndex:(NSInteger)index{
  NSString  *item = [data objectAtIndex:index];
  [undoManager registerUndoWithTarget:self
              selector:@selector(addValue:)
              object:[data objectAtIndex:index]];
  [data removeObjectAtIndex:index];
  if (![undoManager isUndoing]) {
    [undoManager
        setActionName:[NSString stringWithFormat:@"Delete %@", item]];
  }
  [self.tableView reloadData];
}
```

The method starts by retrieving the value of the item to be deleted. It then registers a simple undo action having a selector equal to `addValue:` and an object value equal to the item to be deleted. After that, it deletes the item from the data model. Next, the name of the undo/redo operation is set using the `setActionName:` method. Finally, the table view is reloaded to reflect the change in the data model. It's worth noting that the deleted item is retained by the `NSUndoManager` but the target (i.e., the view controller object) is not. Also, notice that the action name is set only if the `deleteRowAtIndex:` is invoked while the undo manager is not in the process of undoing an operation.

When an undo operation is requested from the view controller, the method `addValue:` is invoked, passing in the original value of the item that was deleted. The method is defined as follows:

```
-(void)addValue:(NSString*)value{
  [undoManager registerUndoWithTarget:self
             selector:@selector(delete:)
             object:value];
  [data addObject:value];
  [self.tableView reloadData];
}
```

The method above starts by registering a redo operation but this time passing in the `delete:` selector and the object value that is about to be added to the data model. After adding the new item, the UI is refreshed by reloading the table view. Notice that the just-registered operation is considered a redo as it was invoked while the undo manager is performing an undo.

The `delete:` method simply iterates over the elements in the mutable array, looking for the item whose value is passed in. When the item is found, the `deleteRowAtIndex:` method is called, passing in the index of that item. The method is shown below:

```
-(void)delete:(NSString*)value{
  for(int i=0; i< data.count; i++){
    if([[data objectAtIndex:i] isEqualToString:value]){
      [self deleteRowAtIndex:i];
      break;
    }
  }
}
```

The complete application can be found in the `UndoMgmt` project, available in the source downloads.

20.3 Wrapping Up

To employ undo management in your application, you need to observe some simple rules:

- If you use, as is mostly the case, a view controller to manage undo/redo operations, that view controller needs to become the first responder when its view appears, and resign as first responder when its view disappears.

- The view controller needs to create a new instance of `NSUndoManager` when it enters editing mode. It also needs to delete that undo manager instance when it quits editing mode.

- The view controller needs to register undo callback operations as well as the action names. When the user requests an undo operation, the view controller should undo the operation and register a redo operation so that the user can redo the operation.

20.4   Summary

In this chapter, you learned about undo management support in iOS. In Section 20.1, we discussed the basic steps needed to utilize undo management. After that, we presented a detailed example that showed how to use undo management. Finally, we summarized the main rules governing the use of the undo capabilities in an application in Section 20.3.

Exercises

(1) Study the NSUndoManager class in the NSUndoManager.h header file and the documentation.

(2) Update the sample application described in this chapter to accommodate insertion of new rows.

(3) In the example we presented in Section 20.2, we did not need the receipt of notifications from the NSUndoManager instance. In the documentation, read about what kind of notifications you can receive.

21

Copy and Paste

This chapter examines the copy and paste capabilities of iOS and the supporting APIs. We start in Section 21.1 by discussing pasteboards. In Section 21.2, you learn about pasteboard items and the various methods you can use to manipulate them. In Section 21.3, we address the subject of the editing menu, which the user employs to issue editing commands. Section 21.4 puts all the ideas behind copy and paste together and presents a simple image editing application. Finally, we summarize the chapter in Section 21.5.

21.1 Pasteboards

Pasteboards are regions in memory that are shared among applications. The system can have an unlimited number of pasteboards, each pasteboard being identified by a name. A pasteboard can be configured to be persistent across application and device restarts.

21.1.1 System pasteboards

Two persistent system pasteboards are defined for you:

- **General pasteboard.** The General pasteboard, identified by the unique name `UIPasteboardNameGeneral`, can be used to store any type of information.
- **Find pasteboard.** The Find pasteboard, identified by the name `UIPasteboardNameFind`, is used to store the search text that the user enters in the search bar.

21.1.2 Creating pasteboards

A pasteboard is represented by the class `UIPasteboard`. You can obtain a reference to a system pasteboard using one of the methods of this class. For example, to obtain the shared instance of the General pasteboard, you can use the `generalPasteboard` class method. To obtain a reference to the Find pasteboard, use `pasteboardWithName:create:`, which is declared as follows:

```
+ (UIPasteboard *)pasteboardWithName:(NSString *)pasteboardName
                    create:(BOOL)create;
```

You pass in `UIPasteboardNameFind` for the first argument and `NO` for the second.

To create a new pasteboard, you can use the method above by passing in a unique name for the first argument and `YES` for the second argument.

If, on the other hand, you want the system to create a pasteboard with a unique name, you can use the method `pasteboardWithUniqueName`, which is declared as follows:

```
+ (UIPasteboard *)pasteboardWithUniqueName
```

21.1.3   Properties of a pasteboard

To access the name of a pasteboard, you can use the read-only `name` property, which is declared as follows:

```
@property(readonly, nonatomic) NSString *name
```

To free the resources of a pasteboard, you can invalidate it by calling the method `removePasteboardWithName:`, passing in the name of the pasteboard. Any messages sent to a pasteboard after the previous message will be ignored.

The persistent status of a pasteboard is determined by the following property:

```
@property(getter=isPersistent, nonatomic) BOOL persistent
```

A persistent application pasteboard remains persistent until the application that created it is uninstalled.

21.2   Pasteboard Items

A pasteboard is a collection of items. Each pasteboard item is a dictionary containing key/value pairs. The key is a string that identifies the type of the representation of the value. For example, the key `public.png` (`kUTTypePNG`) identifies a value as a `.png` image.

A pasteboard item can, and usually does, store more than one value. For example, an application might store three images as an item, where each image represents the same picture in a specific format (e.g., `.png`, `.tiff`, `.jpeg`). Other applications can query this item for a format that they can use.

21.2.1   Pasteboard items

To find out how many items are stored in a given pasteboard, you can use the `numberOfItems` property, which is declared as follows:

```
@property(readonly, nonatomic) NSInteger numberOfItems
```

To obtain an array of the items stored, you can use the `items` property, declared as follows:

```
@property(nonatomic, copy) NSArray *items
```

You can use this property to set the items of a pasteboard by providing an array of dictionaries where each dictionary represents an item.

21.2.2 *Manipulating pasteboard items*

To overwrite a pasteboard with a given value for a specific type, you can use the `setValue:for-PasteboardType:` method, which is declared as follows:

```
- (void)setValue:(id)value forPasteboardType:(NSString *)pasteboardType
```

For example, to store a UTF8[1] string in the General pasteboard, you can write something like the following:

```
[[UIPasteboard generalPasteboard]
              setValue:@"This is a text."
              forPasteboardType:@"public.utf8-plain-text"];
```

After this statement executes, all items on the General pasteboard will be removed and the pasteboard will hold a single item.

Most of the time, a uniform type identifier (UTI) is used as the representation type of a pasteboard item's value. Applications can define their own UTI types, but for values to be communicated across applications, the type must be known to these applications.

The following shows some of the predefined UTI types:

- `public.jpeg` (kUTTypeJPEG). This UTI type represents a JPEG image.
- `public.mpeg` (kUTTypeMPEG). This UTI type represents an MPEG movie.
- `public.rtf` (kUTTypeRTF). This UTI type represents a rich-text document.
- `public.html` (kUTTypeHTML). This UTI type represents HTML content.

You use the `valueForPasteboardType:` method to retrieve the value of a given type from the first item in the pasteboard. All other items are ignored by this method. The method is declared as follows:

```
- (id)valueForPasteboardType:(NSString *)pasteboardType
```

The class of the returned object depends on the `pasteboardType` argument. If the value is not identified to be an instance of `NSString`, `NSArray`, `NSDictionary`, `NSDate`, `NSNumber`, or `NSURL`, an `NSData` instance representing the raw value is returned.

---

[1]http://en.wikipedia.org/wiki/UTF-8.

To retrieve the raw data, you use the `dataForPasteboardType:`. This method returns an `NSData` instance representing the value having the passed-in type. This method, too, works only on the first item in the pasteboard.

You use the `setValue:forPasteboardType:` method to store `NSString`, `NSArray`, `NSDictionary`, `NSDate`, `NSNumber`, or `NSURL` values. If you want to store the value of some other type, you use the `setData:forPasteboardType:` method, which is declared as follows:

```
- (void)
  setData:(NSData *)data forPasteboardType:(NSString *)pasteboardType
```

You pass in the data in the first argument and the type in the second.

The following are convenient properties that can be used to retrieve and set values of common types:

- **String(s).** To store or retrieve a string value, use the following property:

  ```
  @property(nonatomic, copy) NSString *string
  ```

  To store or retrieve an array of strings, use the `strings` property:

  ```
  @property(nonatomic, copy) NSArray *strings
  ```

- **Image(s).** To store or retrieve an image value, use the following property:

  ```
  @property(nonatomic, copy) UIImage *image
  ```

  To store or retrieve an array of images, use the `images` property:

  ```
  @property(nonatomic, copy) NSArray *images
  ```

- **URL(s).** To store or retrieve an `NSURL` value, use the following property:

  ```
  @property(nonatomic, copy) NSURL *URL
  ```

  To store or retrieve an array of `NSURL` values, use the `URLs` property:

  ```
  @property(nonatomic, copy) NSArray *URLs
  ```

- **Color(s).** To store or retrieve a `UIColor` value, use the following property:

  ```
  @property(nonatomic, copy) UIColor *color
  ```

  To store or retrieve an array of `UIColor` values, use the `colors` property:

  ```
  @property(nonatomic, copy) NSArray *colors
  ```

21.3   The Editing Menu

The editing menu is used to provide basic Copy, Cut, Paste, Select, and Select All commands. When you present the menu to the user, he or she can select the appropriate command. When your responder object (e.g., a view controller) receives that command, it needs to update the affected view and, if required by the command, update the pasteboard.

21.3.1   *The standard editing actions*

The UIResponder.h header file declares a category on NSObject that any responder that wishes to receive commands from the editing menu is expected to implement. This category is UIResponder-StandardEditActions and is shown below:

```
@interface NSObject(UIResponderStandardEditActions)
- (void)cut:(id)sender;
- (void)copy:(id)sender;
- (void)paste:(id)sender;
- (void)select:(id)sender;
- (void)selectAll:(id)sender;
@end
```

The sender in the above methods is usually the singleton editing menu instance.

When the user taps on a command in the editing menu, the first responder is checked for the corresponding method. If that method is implemented, it will be invoked. Otherwise, the search continues along the responder chain.

The first responder can enable a subset of the editing commands, if it wishes to, by overriding the UIResponder method canPerformAction:withSender:, which is declared as follows:

```
- (BOOL)canPerformAction:(SEL)action withSender:(id)sender
```

The above method allows you to provide meaningful commands that are appropriate for the current situation. For example, if there are no images in the pasteboard and the user can paste only images, the above method should return NO if action is equal to @selector(paste:). Once there are images in the pasteboard, that method should return YES. You can force the editing menu to update itself (which will result in the above method's getting called for each possible editing menu item) should you deem that necessary. All you have to do to force an update is send an update message to the singleton editing menu instance.

21.3.2   *The UIMenuController class*

The editing menu is a singleton of the class UIMenuController. You can obtain this singleton by invoking the sharedMenuController class method. Once you have obtained this menu, you need to set its target rectangle. The *target rectangle* conceptually defines the bounding box of the user's selection. However, it can be anything.

Once you have set up the menu, you can make it visible by sending the instance a setMenu-Visible:YES animated:YES message. The menu will try to position itself above the target rectangle. If there is not enough space, the menu is positioned under the target rectangle. The menu has a pointer, and that pointer is positioned at the center of the top or bottom of the target rectangle depending on the menu placement decision.

21.3.3   The role of the view controller

The view controller is usually the one responsible for displaying the editing menu and responding to its commands. In order for a view controller to work with the editing menu, a few rules must be observed:

- The view controller must override the `canBecomeFirstResponder` method and return YES as follows:

```
- (BOOL) canBecomeFirstResponder {
  return YES;
}
```

- The view controller must become the first responder when its view appears. This is usually done as follows:

```
-(void)viewDidAppear:(BOOL)animated{
  [super viewDidAppear:animated];
  [self becomeFirstResponder];
}
```

- The view controller must resign as the first responder when its view disappears. This is usually done as follows:

```
-(void)viewDidDisappear:(BOOL)animated{
  [super viewDidDisappear:animated];
  [self resignFirstResponder];
}
```

- The view controller should implement the appropriate action method declared in the UI-ResponderStandardEditActions category. In addition, it should implement the canPerformAction:withSender: method and return the appropriate value depending on the current state of the editing process.

- The view controller should show the menu at the appropriate time so that the user can perform editing actions.

21.4   Putting It Together

In this section, we present a complete editing application. The application presents the user a number of small images. The user can select or unselect an image by tapping on it or by tapping on the area near it and choosing Select from the editing menu. In addition, the user can copy, cut, and paste some or all of the images. The complete application can be found in the CopyPaste2 project, available in the source downloads.

21.4.1   *The image view*

Each image is represented by the `MyImageView` class. This class is declared as follows:

```
@interface MyImageView : UIView {
  BOOL    selected;
  UIImage *image;
}
@property(assign)          BOOL selected;
@property(nonatomic, retain) UIImage *image;
@end
```

Each instance of this class maintains a reference to its image. In addition, the selected state of the image view is maintained by the `selected` instance variable.

The designated initializer `initWithImage:` is shown below:

```
- (id)initWithImage:(UIImage *)_image{
  if(self = [super init]){
    self.image = _image;
  }
  return self;
}
```

The method simply stores a reference to the image in its instance variable.

To enable selection when the image view is tapped, the following `UIResponder` method is overridden:

```
- (void)touchesEnded:(NSSet *)touches withEvent:(UIEvent *)event{
  self.selected = !selected;
}
```

The method simply toggles the selection state. The setter of the selected property is custom and is shown below:

```
-(void)setSelected:(BOOL)_selected{
  selected = _selected;
  [self setNeedsDisplay];
}
```

The method updates the instance variable with the new value and sends a message to its instance so that the view redraws itself. As a result, `drawRect:` is invoked. The `drawRect:` method is shown below:

```
- (void)drawRect:(CGRect)rect{
  [super drawRect:rect];
  [self.image drawInRect:rect];
  if(selected){
    CGContextRef  context = UIGraphicsGetCurrentContext();
```

```
    [[UIColor redColor] set];
    CGContextSetLineWidth(context, 7.0);
    CGContextMoveToPoint(context, 0, 0);
    CGContextAddLineToPoint(context, self.bounds.size.width, 0);
    CGContextAddLineToPoint(context, self.bounds.size.width,
                            self.bounds.size.height);
    CGContextAddLineToPoint(context, 0, self.bounds.size.height);
    CGContextAddLineToPoint(context, 0, 0);
    CGContextStrokePath(context);
  }
}
```

The `drawRect:` method simply draws the image in the view. After that, it draws a red rectangle around that image if the image view is selected.

21.4.2   The view controller

The view controller is responsible for the editing of its view. The `loadView` method is shown below:

```
- (void)loadView {
  MyView *theView =
    [[[MyView alloc] initWithFrame:CGRectMake(0, 0, 320, 480)]
      autorelease];
  theView.delegate = self;
  self.view = theView;
  self.view.backgroundColor = [UIColor grayColor];
  MyImageView *imgView =
  [[[MyImageView alloc]
        initWithImage:[UIImage imageNamed:@"Flower1.jpg"]] autorelease];
  imgView.frame = CGRectMake(50, 50, 70, 70);
  [self.view addSubview:imgView];

  imgView =
    [[[MyImageView alloc]
        initWithImage:[UIImage imageNamed:@"Flower2.jpg"]] autorelease];
  imgView.frame = CGRectMake(50, 150, 70, 70);
  [self.view addSubview:imgView];
}
```

The method simply creates the container view (an instance of `MyView` class) and adds two image views (instances of `MyImageView` class) as subviews.

The `MyView` class declaration is shown below:

```
@interface MyView : UIView {
  UIResponder *delegate;
}
```

```
@property(nonatomic, assign) UIResponder *delegate;
@end
```

It declares a `delegate` property that is required to be a responder.

The implementation of the class simply overrides one of the `UIResponder` methods and proxies that call to the delegate as shown below:

```
- (void)touchesEnded:(NSSet *)touches withEvent:(UIEvent *)event{
  [self.delegate touchesEnded:touches withEvent:event];
}
```

The view controller, acting as the delegate of its view, overrides that `UIResponder` method as shown below:

```
- (void)touchesEnded:(NSSet *)touches withEvent:(UIEvent *)event{
  UIMenuController *menu = [UIMenuController sharedMenuController];
  self.lastTouchRect =
    (CGRect){[[touches anyObject] locationInView:self.view], CGSizeZero};
  [menu setTargetRect:lastTouchRect inView:self.view];
  [menu setMenuVisible:YES animated:YES];
}
```

The method above shows the editing menu near where the touch occurred.

All editing actions are implemented. However, not all actions are enabled all the time. Therefore, `canPerformAction:` must be implemented. The method is shown below:

```
- (BOOL)canPerformAction:(SEL)action withSender:(id)sender{
  BOOL somethingSelected = [self selectedObjects].count;
  if((action == @selector(copy:)) && somethingSelected){
    return YES;
  }
  if((action == @selector(cut:)) && somethingSelected){
    return YES;
  }
  if(action == @selector(selectAll:)){
    return YES;
  }
  if(action == @selector(select:)){
    return YES;
  }
  if( (action == @selector(paste:)) && [self pasteableItem]){
    return YES;
  }
  return NO;
}
```

Copying and cutting are enabled only if at least one image is selected. Pasting is enabled if there is at least one image in the pasteboard. Selection is always enabled.

To determine if there is at least one image selected, the method selectedObjects is invoked to obtain all selected images. The method simply iterates over the subviews of the main view, checking for the selection state as shown below:

```
-(NSArray*)selectedObjects{
  NSMutableArray   *arr = [NSMutableArray array];
  for(MyImageView *imgView in [self.view subviews]){
    if([imgView  isKindOfClass:[MyImageView class]]){
      if(imgView.selected){
        [arr addObject:imgView];
      }
    }
  }
  return [[arr copy] autorelease];
}
```

Notice how the method uses the isKindOfClass: method to check if each subview is an instance of MyImageView before sending the selected message to that view. Of course, in our case, all subviews of the main view are instances of MyImageView class and this check is not needed. If in the future, not all subviews are instances of MyImageView class, this check becomes essential.

To enable pasting, the following method is used:

```
-(id)pasteableItem{
  return (id)(
    [[UIPasteboard generalPasteboard]
            valueForPasteboardType:@"public.png"] ||
      [[UIPasteboard generalPasteboard]
         valueForPasteboardType:@"public.jpeg"]);
}
```

The method simply checks to see if there is an image in the pasteboard that is of type PNG or JPEG. It returns the UIImage instance if one is found. Otherwise, it returns nil. Notice that the method checks only the first pasteboard item. It's worth noting that images are treated as a special case and you do not need to convert them to NSData. An image is stored as a UIImage instance in the pasteboard.

The cut: and copy: methods are shown below:

```
- (void)cut:(id)sender {
  [self saveImagesInPasteboardAndDelete:YES];
}

- (void)copy:(id)sender{
  [self saveImagesInPasteboardAndDelete:NO];
}
```

These two methods invoke the same method, each passing a different value for its argument. The saveImagesInPasteboardAndDelete: method is shown below:

```objc
-(void)saveImagesInPasteboardAndDelete:(BOOL)alsoDelete{
  NSMutableArray *images = [NSMutableArray array];
  NSArray *selectedObjects = [self selectedObjects];
  for(MyImageView *imgView in selectedObjects){
    [images addObject:
      [NSDictionary dictionaryWithObject:imgView.image
                                  forKey:@"public.png"]];
    if(alsoDelete){
      [imgView removeFromSuperview];
    }
  }
  [UIPasteboard generalPasteboard].items = images;
}
```

The method first obtains all the image views that are selected. After that, it iterates over these objects and creates a pasteboard item for each image. If the alsoDelete argument is equal to YES, the corresponding image view is removed from the main view. After all selected views are iterated over, the pasteboard items are used to set the items property of the General pasteboard. This in effect overwrites all items in the pasteboard with the selected images.

The paste: method is shown below:

```objc
- (void)paste:(id)sender {
  float xOffset = 0.0;
  float yOffset = 0.0;
  for(UIImage *image in [UIPasteboard generalPasteboard].images){
    MyImageView *imgView =
      [[[MyImageView alloc] initWithImage:image] autorelease];
    imgView.frame =
      CGRectMake(lastTouchRect.origin.x + xOffset,
                 lastTouchRect.origin.y + yOffset, 70, 70);
    [self.view addSubview:imgView];
    xOffset += 15;
    yOffset += 15;
  }
}
```

The method simply obtains all the images in the pasteboard, creates a MyImageView instance for each image, and adds that instance to the main view as a subview. To keep these images from overwriting one another in the case of multiple images, the frame of each view is adjusted.

The selectAll: method is shown below:

```objc
- (void)selectAll:(id)sender {
  for(MyImageView *imgView in [self.view subviews]){
    if([imgView  isKindOfClass:[MyImageView class]]){
```

```
        imgView.selected = YES;
    }
  }
}
```

The method simply sets the `selected` property of every image view to `YES`;

The `select:` method is shown below:

```
- (void)select:(id)sender {
  for(MyImageView *imgView in [self.view subviews]){
    if([imgView  isKindOfClass:[MyImageView class]]){
      if(CGRectContainsPoint(
            CGRectMake(0, imgView.frame.origin.y, 320,
                        imgView.frame.size.height),
            lastTouchRect.origin)){
        imgView.selected = YES;
      }
    }
  }
}
```

The method above simply iterates over all image views, creating a virtual rectangle whose height is the height of the current image view and whose width is the width of the display (`320`). The y coordinate of the origin of the imaginary rectangle is assumed to be the origin of the current image view.

After that imaginary rectangle is created, the last touch on the main view is checked to see if it lies inside this rectangle. If that is the case, that image view is selected. This algorithm is arbitrary. You can devise your own algorithm according to your needs.

Figure 21.1 shows a screen shot of the editing application. Refer to the `CopyPaste2` project, available in the source downloads, for a complete listing.

21.5   Summary

This chapter examined the copy and paste capabilities of iOS and the supporting APIs. We started in Section 21.1 by discussing pasteboards. In Section 21.2, you learned about pasteboard items and the various methods available to you to manipulate them. In Section 21.3, we addressed the subject of the editing menu, which the user employs to issue editing commands. Section 21.4 put all the ideas behind copy and paste together and presented a simple image editing application.

Figure 21.1   A screen shot of the editing application.

Exercises

(1) Add undo capabilities to the application presented in Section 21.4.

(2) Study the UIMenuController class in the documentation and in the UIMenuController.h header file.

(3) Study the UIPasteboard class in the documentation and in the UIPasteboard.h header file.

22

Offline Mode

Mobile applications that rely on the Internet for providing useful information to the user should provide some, albeit limited, functionality even when the user's phone is not connected to the Internet.

For example, a Twitter client should immediately show old tweets to the user when he or she launches the app. While the user is scrolling through these tweets, the application launches a separate thread that attempts to retrieve new tweets from the Internet. This behavior has become expected of mobile applications.

To realize this behavior, your application needs to implement a caching strategy. This chapter will walk you through the development of a Really Simple Syndication (RSS) reader that caches data and provides fast and responsive UI to the user.

The RSS reader retrieves an RSS-feed XML document from a server describing the current parking availability at the University of Baltimore. This document is always cached on disk and retrieved immediately when the application is launched the next time. When the application is launched, it always checks the cache before making a call to the server. The caching strategy provides (1) the ability to immediately serve the user data and (2) the ability to use the application even when the device has no network connectivity.

This chapter is organized as follows. In Section 22.1, we discuss the setup of the project and the installation of the `TouchXML` Objective-C wrapper. `TouchXML` makes working with XML much easier than dealing directly with the `libxml` library, as you saw in Chapter 12. In Section 22.2, we address the problem of parsing the XML document representing the RSS feed. Next, Section 22.3 deals with the issue of taking a screen shot of the application when it's about to exit and presenting that image immediately after launching it the next time. After that, Section 22.4 discusses the display of available parking in a table view. Finally, we summarize the chapter in Section 22.5.

22.1 Setting Up the Project

Let's start by creating a new window-based project in XCode and naming it `OfflineMode`. After that, we want to configure the project to use the `libxml` library encapsulated by the `TouchXML` Objective-C wrapper.

22.1.1 Adding support for libxml2

Right-click on the `OfflineMode` project node and select Get Info. Select the Build tab and the All Configurations item. Type `OTHER_LDFLAGS` in the search field as shown in Figure 22.1.

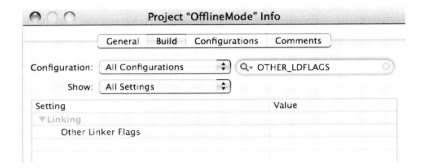

Figure 22.1 The `Other Linker Flags` linking option.

Double-click on the Value column of this entry, click the + button, enter `-lxml2` as the value (as shown in Figure 22.2), and click OK.

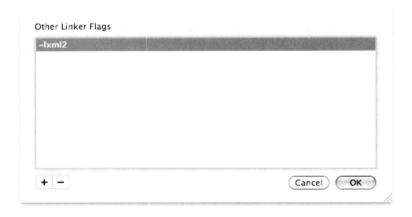

Figure 22.2 Specifying the value for the `OTHER_LDFLAGS` linker flag.

Next, we need to specify a value for the `HEADER_SEARCH_PATHS` setting. Search for it as shown in Figure 22.3.

Double-click on the Value column of this entry, click the + button, and make your window similar to the one shown in Figure 22.4.

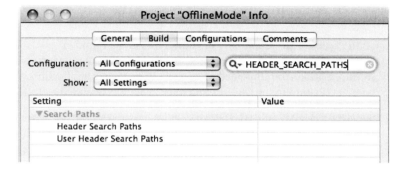

Figure 22.3   The HEADER_SEARCH_PATHS setting option.

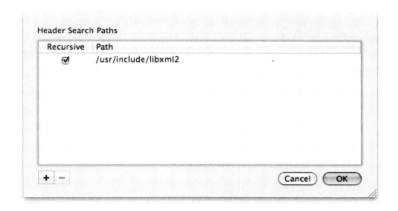

Figure 22.4   Entering a value for the HEADER_SEARCH_PATHS setting option.

Now we need to add the libxml library to our project. Follow the procedure outlined in Section D.4 of Appendix D to add the libxml2.2.7.3.dylib (or a later version) library.

22.1.2   *Adding the TouchXML Objective-C wrapper*

TouchXML can be downloaded from http://code.google.com/p/touchcode/. Click on the Downloads link on that page and download the code. Unzip the file and drag the Common directory to the root of your project (the node called OfflineMode with the blue icon).

Add the following lines to OfflineMode_Prefix.pch:

```
#import "CXMLDocument.h"
#import "CXMLElement.h"
#import "CXMLNode.h"
#import "CXMLNode_XPathExtensions.h"
```

22.2   Parsing XML Using the TouchXML Wrapper

The parking-availability feed for the University of Baltimore can be found at
`https://www.pmi-parking.com/ub/rss.aspx`. In this section, we develop several methods
that extract relevant information from this feed to be used later by our application. We encapsulate
the data model for our application in the `UBParking` class, which is declared as follows:

```
#define PARKING_UPDATE @"PARKING_UPDATE"

@interface UBParking : NSObject {
}
+ (void) startMonitor;
+ (void) stopMonitor;
@end
```

The `UBParking` class refreshes parking-availability data every 60 seconds. New parking data is
posted using the notification system. All you have to do is register for the `PARKING_UPDATE`
notification and send the class object a `startMonitor` message. You can stop the refreshment of
the feed by sending a `stopMonitor` to the class object.

Before delving into the implementation details of this class, you need to be aware of the following
three global variables declared in the `UBParking.m` file:

```
static NSThread *monitor    = NULL;
static NSArray  *spots      = NULL;
static NSString *fileName    = NULL;
```

22.2.1   The structure of the RSS feed

The following shows a sample snapshot of the University of Baltimore Lot RSS feed:

```
<?xml version="1.0" encoding="utf-8" ?>
<rss version="2.0">
  <channel>
    <title>University of Baltimore Lot Availability</title>
    <item>
        <title>Cathedral</title>
        <description>Spaces Available: 38</description>
        <pubDate>Thu, 11 Nov 2010 9:15:00 EDT</pubDate>
        <category>Parking Counts</category>
    </item>

    <item>
        <title>Fritzgerald Garage</title>
        <description>Spaces Available: 1115</description>
        <pubDate>Thu, 11 Nov 2010 9:15:00 EDT</pubDate>
        <category>Parking Counts</category>
```

```
    </item>
.
.
.
    </channel>
</rss>
```

The feed complies with RSS version 2.0 and is self-explanatory.

22.2.2   Obtaining the XML document

Before we start working on the document, we need to obtain it from the Internet. Listing 22.1 shows the getParking method, which is the main driver for obtaining this feed.

Listing 22.1   The main method for obtaining the RSS feed for parking availability.

```
+ (NSArray*) getParking{
    UIApplication *app = [UIApplication sharedApplication];
    app.networkActivityIndicatorVisible = true;
    NSData *data =
        [NSData dataWithContentsOfURL:
            [NSURL URLWithString:
                        @"https://www.pmi-parking.com/ub/rss.aspx"]];
    NSString *feedXML =
        [[[NSString alloc]
            initWithData:data
            encoding:NSStringEncodingConversionAllowLossy] autorelease];
    if(feedXML != nil){
        [feedXML writeToFile:fileName  atomically:YES
                encoding:NSStringEncodingConversionAllowLossy error:nil];
        return [self parseXML:feedXML];
    }
    return nil;
}
```

The method starts by showing the network activity indicator in the status bar. Next, it proceeds by retrieving the data from the URL of the feed and then creating an NSString instance from that data. After that, it saves the RSS document to disk for offline/fast loading support. Finally, the method extracts the parking availability (in the form of an array) by utilizing the parseXML: method.

22.2.3   Extracting parking availability

Each <item> element in the feed represents a parking lot. We would like to construct an array of objects where each object is a dictionary whose keys and values represent relevant information related to that particular parking lot.

Let's start by implementing the main driver for this. The method parseXML: shown in Listing 22.2 takes the RSS feed in the form of a string and returns an array of dictionaries.

Listing 22.2   The main XML parsing method.

```
+ (NSArray*) parseXML:(NSString*)feedXML{
    CXMLDocument *feed =
        [[[CXMLDocument alloc] initWithXMLString:feedXML
                    options:0 error:nil] autorelease];
    UIApplication *app = [UIApplication sharedApplication];
    app.networkActivityIndicatorVisible = false;
    NSArray *parkingSptsNodes = [feed nodesForXPath:@"//item" error:nil];
    NSMutableArray *parkingSpotsArr = [[NSMutableArray new] autorelease];
    for (CXMLElement *aSpot in parkingSptsNodes) {
            [parkingSpotsArr addObject:[self parseTerminal:aSpot]];
    }
    return parkingSpotsArr;
}
```

The method starts by creating a CXMLDocument object from the string representation of the RSS feed XML. This document object is then used to extract all nodes whose tag is <item>. We achieve that through the use of an XPath expression. The prefix // in the expression simply says: Give me all nodes described by the rest of the expression regardless of their positions in the document tree. The rest of the expression specifies the actual path, which in this case is the tag <item>.

The objects extracted from the XPath expression are of type CXMLElement. We loop through these objects and parse them one at a time. Parsing each results in a dictionary that we add to our array. Finally, we return the array of the dictionaries.

The information describing each parking lot is extracted using the parseTerminal: method, which is shown in Listing 22.3.

Listing 22.3   The parseTerminal: method.

```
+ (NSDictionary*) parseTerminal:(CXMLElement*)parkingSpot{
    NSMutableDictionary *parkingDict =
            [[NSMutableDictionary new] autorelease];
    for(int j=0; j< [parkingSpot childCount]; j++) {
        if([[parkingSpot childAtIndex:j] kind] == XML_ELEMENT_NODE){
            CXMLElement *child =
                (CXMLElement*)[parkingSpot childAtIndex:j];
            if([[child name] isEqualToString:@"title"]){
                [parkingDict setValue:[child stringValue]
                            forKey:@"title"];
            }
            if([[child name] isEqualToString:@"description"]){
                [parkingDict setValue:[child stringValue]
```

```
                                    forKey:@"status"];
                }
            }
        }
    return parkingDict;
}
```

The method looks for two child elements in the item: (1) title and (2) description. To achieve that, the method simply goes through all children of the `<item>` element and checks to see if each node is an ELEMENT child as opposed to a TEXT child. If that's the case, the element name of that node is checked. To check for a node name, send the `name` message to the `CXMLElement` object. To extract the actual value for this element, use the `stringValue` method. The `title` and `status` keys are used to store the respective values in the dictionary.

Now that we have an array of dictionaries where each dictionary describes parking-lot availability, we are ready to use it in our application.

22.2.4 *Monitoring the feed and disseminating the updates*

The application we are developing needs to continue monitoring the feed and provide updates to the actual view that consumes the feed information. To achieve that, we fire up a background thread. Any part of the application that is interested in receiving updates from the feed will need to register a `PARKING_UPDATE` notification and issue a `startMonitor` message (shown below) to the `UBParking` class object:

```
+ (void) startMonitor{
    fileName = [[NSHomeDirectory() stringByAppendingPathComponent:
            @"Documents/feed.xml"] retain];
    if(monitor == NULL){
        monitor = [[NSThread  alloc] initWithTarget:self
                selector:@selector(keepMonitoring) object:nil];
        [monitor start];
    }
}
```

The `startMonitor` method checks to see if the thread is running. If not, it creates a thread and starts it. This background thread is initialized with the `UBParking` class object as the target and `keepMonitoring` as the selector.

The `keepMonitoring` method is shown in Listing 22.4.

Listing 22.4 The `keepMonitoring` method.

```
+ (void) keepMonitoring{
    NSAutoreleasePool * pool = [[NSAutoreleasePool alloc] init];
    while(![[NSThread currentThread]  isCancelled]){
        if(!spots){
```

```
            spots = [self getCachedCopy];
            NSFileManager *mgr = [NSFileManager defaultManager];
            NSDictionary  *dict = [mgr attributesOfItemAtPath:fileName
                                    error:nil];
            NSDate *modiDate = [dict objectForKey:NSFileModificationDate];
            if(spots){
                NSDictionary *dict =
                    [NSDictionary dictionaryWithObjectsAndKeys:
                            spots, @"spots", modiDate, @"date", nil];
                [[NSNotificationCenter defaultCenter]
                    postNotificationName:PARKING_UPDATE object:dict];
            }
        }
        NSArray *arr = [self getParking];
        if(arr!= nil){
            spots = arr;
            NSDictionary *dict =
                [NSDictionary dictionaryWithObjectsAndKeys:
                    spots, @"spots", [NSDate date], @"date", nil];
            [[NSNotificationCenter defaultCenter]
                postNotificationName:PARKING_UPDATE object:dict];
        }
        [NSThread  sleepForTimeInterval:60];
    }
    [pool release];
}
```

As you already know, every thread needs its own autorelease pool, so the keepMonitoring method creates one at the beginning and releases it at the end. The method then enters a while loop, executing its body as long as the thread has not been canceled.

Inside the body of this while loop, we check for the existence of a valid parsed feed. This valid parsed feed is stored in the spots NSArray static instance. If there is no valid parking availability, we look into the cached data using the getCachedCopy method which is declared as follows:

```
+ (NSArray*) getCachedCopy{
    NSData *data = [NSData dataWithContentsOfFile:fileName];
    NSString *feedXML =
      [[[NSString alloc] initWithData:data
        encoding:NSStringEncodingConversionAllowLossy] autorelease];
    if(feedXML){
        return [self parseXML:feedXML];
    }
    return nil;
}
```

The getCachedCopy method reads the contents of the file given in fileName, converts it to a string, and parses the string as XML.

If, on the other hand, there is a valid cache, we broadcast this parking availability via a notification. The object of this notification is a dictionary with two entries: (1) the parking-lot availability array and (2) the time that this data was recorded by the application.

After that, we go ahead and retrieve a fresh copy of the feed and broadcast it, similar to what we did for the cached data. The thread sleeps for a minute and starts all over again. This loop is repeated until the thread is canceled.

To stop the process, the method `stopMonitor` (shown below) needs to be called:

```
+ (void) stopMonitor{
    if(monitor != NULL){
        [monitor cancel];
        [monitor release];
        monitor = NULL;
        [fileName release];
    }
}
```

This method cancels the thread and releases the relevant retained objects. Our application does not need such a method, as the user expects the feed to remain in sync with the actual data all the time. However, your specific application may have different requirements. Also, the time the thread sleeps between requests is arbitrary. You should be considerate and balance how often you hit the Internet with the device's battery life and the user's expectation.

22.3   Showing a Screen Shot of the Last Session

When the user launches the app for the first time, we want him or her to immediately see some useful information. One way to achieve that is to take a screen shot of the last thing that the user saw when he or she closed the app.

We store this screen shot in a `.jpg` file in the `Documents` directory. The `applicationDidFinish-Launching:` method, which is declared in the `OfflineModeAppDelegate` app delegate class, is shown in Listing 22.5. This method illustrates how you can retrieve this screen shot and show it to the user.

Listing 22.5   The `applicationDidFinishLaunching:` method.

```
- (void) applicationDidFinishLaunching:(UIApplication *)application {
    [window addSubview:navCtrl.view];
    NSData *data = [NSData dataWithContentsOfFile:[NSHomeDirectory()
            stringByAppendingPathComponent:@"Documents/screenshot.jpg"]];
    if(data){
        UIImage *image = [UIImage imageWithData:data];
        UIImageView *imgView =
            [[[UIImageView alloc] initWithImage:image] autorelease];
        imgView.tag = 12345;
```

```
        [window addSubview:imgView];
    }
    [window makeKeyAndVisible];
}
```

A .jpg file is like any other file. You retrieve its data using the NSData dataWithContentsOf-File: class method. If there is an actual screen-shot file, we construct an image out of its content using the imageWithData: UIImage class method. The image is then used to build a UIImage-View instance and that image view is added to the window. Whatever the user saw the last time he or she closed the app will be shown when the user launches it the next time.

To actually take a screen shot, we put the logic behind this functionality in the applicationWill-Terminate:, method, which is shown below:

```
- (void) applicationWillTerminate:(UIApplication *)application{
    UIGraphicsBeginImageContext(window.bounds.size);
    [window.layer renderInContext:UIGraphicsGetCurrentContext()];
    UIImage *viewImage = UIGraphicsGetImageFromCurrentImageContext();
    UIGraphicsEndImageContext();
    NSData *data = UIImageJPEGRepresentation(viewImage, 1.0);
    [data writeToFile:[NSHomeDirectory()
            stringByAppendingPathComponent:@"Documents/screenshot.jpg"]
    atomically:YES];
}
```

We create an image context by calling the UIGraphicsBeginImageContext() function, passing in the dimensions of the image we are constructing. After that, we ask the layer of the main window to render itself in that image context. Next, we get an image out of that image context using the function UIGraphicsGetImageFromCurrentImageContext(). This image is then translated into an NSData object — using the UIImageJPEGRepresentation() function — that is then written to the file system.

Because we tag the image view showing the screen shot, it is easy to remove it once we have actual data. The removeScreenshot method shown below does just that:

```
- (void) removeScreenshot{
    [[window viewWithTag:12345] removeFromSuperview];
}
```

22.4 The TableView Controller

The actual parking availability is shown to the user in a table view that is managed by the TerminalsViewController class. You've seen a lot of these controllers throughout this book. In this section, however, we show you how to create one using Interface Builder. (You may want to review Appendix F before reading on.)

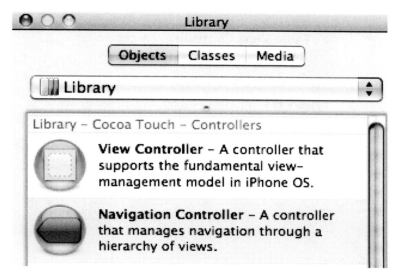

Figure 22.5   The navigation controller UI element.

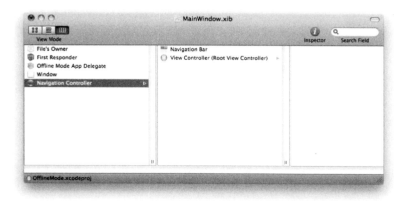

Figure 22.6   The document after adding a navigation controller UI element.

To add a table view controller to the project, double-click the `MainWindow.xib` file under `Resources-iPhone` group. This will open the Interface Builder. Drag and drop a navigation controller (see Figure 22.5) on the document as shown in Figure 22.6.

Drag and drop a table view controller (see Figure 22.7) on the navigation controller.

Click on the `Offline Mode App Delegate` node and link the `navCtrl` outlet to the navigation controller as shown in Figure 22.8.

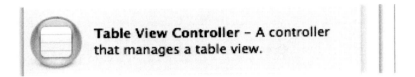

Figure 22.7   A table view controller UI element.

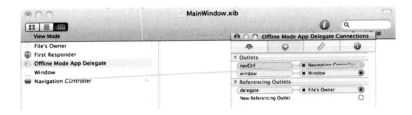

Figure 22.8   Connecting the `navCtrl` outlet to the navigation controller.

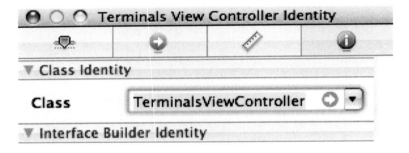

Figure 22.9   Changing the identity of the table view controller.

Click on the `TableView Controller` inside the navigation controller and change its identify to `TerminalsViewController` as shown in Figure 22.9.

The controller starts by registering itself to parking-updates notification and starts the parking-availability monitoring as shown below:

```
[[NSNotificationCenter defaultCenter]
 addObserver:self selector:@selector(parkingUpdate:)
 name:PARKING_UPDATE object:nil];
[UBParking startMonitor];
```

In the `dealloc` method of this controller, don't forget to deregister it; otherwise, the system will send notification to an invalid object and the app will crash!

```
- (void) dealloc {
    [[NSNotificationCenter defaultCenter] removeObserver:self];
```

```
    self.data = nil;
    [super dealloc];
}
```

The `parkingUpdate:` method receives the parking updates as follows:

```
- (void) parkingUpdate:(NSNotification*)notification{
    NSDictionary *dict = notification.object;
    NSArray *arr = [dict objectForKey:@"spots"];
    NSDate *date = [dict objectForKey:@"date"];
    if(arr!=nil){
        self.data = arr;
        [self performSelectorOnMainThread:@selector(reload:)
            withObject:date waitUntilDone:NO];
    }
}
```

The notification object is a dictionary with two entries: (1) the actual array of parking availabilities and (2) the time this data was recorded by our app. These two pieces of information are retrieved. In addition, the data model for the table's rows are reset with the new data. Finally, we ask the table view to reload itself. However, because we receive the notification from a different thread from the main thread, we must reload the table view from the main thread; otherwise, we will have crashes in our app. We fix that by creating a simple method and executing that method on the main thread using the `performSelectorOnMainThread:withObject:waitUntilDone:` `NSObject` instance method.

The reload method simply reloads the table view to reflect the new data and shows the "time ago" of the parking-availability statistics. The method is defined as follows:

```
- (void) reload:(NSDate*)date{
    [self.tableView reloadData];
    NSTimeInterval secondsOld = -[date timeIntervalSinceNow];
    NSString *displayUpdated;
    if(secondsOld < 60){
        displayUpdated = @"moments ago";
    }
    else if (secondsOld < 60*60){
        displayUpdated = @"minutes ago";
    }
    else if (secondsOld < 60*60*24){
        displayUpdated = @"hours ago";
    }else{
        displayUpdated = [NSString stringWithFormat:
                @"%.0f days ago", secondsOld/(24*60*60)];
    }
    self.navigationItem.prompt =
        [NSString stringWithFormat:@"Updated: %@",  displayUpdated];
}
```

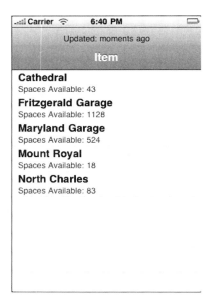

Figure 22.10   A screen shot of the finished app.

Figure 22.10 shows a screen shot of the finished app.

The complete application can be found in the `OfflineMode` project in the source downloads.

22.5   Summary

Developing applications that are graceful under bad network connectivity conditions is very important. In this chapter, we provided a simple application that caches its data and presents this data on startup regardless of network connectivity.

First, in Section 22.1, we provided a detailed setup of the project, focusing on XML support. Instead of using the raw `libxml` function calls as we did back in Chapter 12, we used an Objective-C wrapper called `TouchXML` and showed how to set up the project to use it. After that, Section 22.2 showed how to parse the XML to extract the parking-availability information. To further enhance the experience of the user, we showed in Section 22.3 how to take a screen shot of the application on exit and present it on startup. Finally, Section 22.4 showed how to create the UI in Interface Builder.

Exercises

(1) The notification for parking-status updates is generated on a background thread. Change it so that it's sent on the main thread and the receiver of these notifications updates its UI without worrying about possible app crashes.

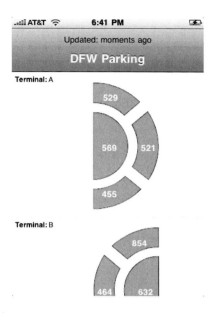

Figure 22.11   A screen shot of the DFW parking status app.

(2) The Dallas Fort Worth (DFW) International Airport has a parking-availability feed at `www.dfwairport.com/apps/parkstatusfeed/`. Implement an application with caching capabilities for this feed. Use graphics to present the status information as shown in Figure 22.11.

23

Peer-to-Peer Communication

The GameKit framework facilitates constructing ad hoc networks among devices running iOS 3.1 or later. In this chapter, we show how easy it is to connect two iPhone devices and send data back and forth between them.

In Section 23.1, we show an application that transmits text between two iPhones. Next, Section 23.2 shows how to exchange pictures between devices. Finally, Section 23.3 summarizes this chapter.

23.1 Basic Chat Application

In this section, we will develop a simple chat application. The application running on one iPhone device uses Bluetooth technology to communicate with another application running on another iPhone device.

To simplify things, we assume that each application sends the same token to the other application. Each application shows the name of the other device and the token received. Each user is able to send a token at any time by tapping on a Send button. Moreover, any device can initiate the connection establishment.

23.1.1 Peer discovery and connection establishment

The simplest mechanism for discovering new peers and establishing a connection to a specific peer is through the use of the GKPeerPickerController class. To use this class, you allocate an instance of it, set its delegate to an object implementing the GKPeerPickerControllerDelegate protocol, and show it. Figure 23.1 shows the initial view presented to the user. At this time, the controller is using Bluetooth technology to search for other iPhone devices to peer with.

The following code fragment shows how to allocate and configure a GKPeerPickerController instance:

```
self.mPeerPicker = [[[GKPeerPickerController alloc] init] autorelease];
mPeerPicker.delegate = self;
mPeerPicker.connectionTypesMask = GKPeerPickerConnectionTypeNearby;
[mPeerPicker show];
```

Figure 23.1 Discovering other iPhone devices using a `GKPeerPickerController` instance.

The `connectionTypesMask` property is set to `GKPeerPickerConnectionTypeNearby`, meaning that we are interested in nearby devices (i.e., using Bluetooth). To present the controller, just send a `show` message to the instance.

23.1.2 Creating the session

The `GKPeerPickerControllerDelegate` declares several methods. When you show the peer picker, the following delegate method is called:

```
- (GKSession *)peerPickerController:(GKPeerPickerController *)picker
    sessionForConnectionType:(GKPeerPickerConnectionType)type
```

The peer-picker controller asks for a session (instance of the `GKSession` class) to be used for the connection. Your implementation should create the session, configure it, and return it to be used by the peer picker. The following shows a possible implementation of this callback method:

```
- (GKSession *)peerPickerController:(GKPeerPickerController *)picker
          sessionForConnectionType:(GKPeerPickerConnectionType)type{
    self.mSession = [[[GKSession alloc] initWithSessionID:@"MySession"
                        displayName:nil sessionMode:GKSessionModePeer]
                                        autorelease];
    mSession.delegate = self;
    return mSession;
}
```

There are several session modes that can be used in configuring the session. You can use a GK-SessionModeServer value to represent a server session that advertises itself to nearby devices, use the GKSessionModeClient to represent a client session that searches for nearby devices, or act as both a server and a client using the GKSessionModePeer value. Because our application allows either device to initiate the connection, we use the GKSessionModePeer mode.

If there are other devices nearby, the peer picker will show them in a list (see Figure 23.2).

Figure 23.2   Discovered nearby devices.

When the user selects a device by tapping on it, the peer picker waits for the other device to accept the connection, as shown in Figure 23.3.

The other device, upon receiving a connection request, presents to the user a dialog box asking for permission to accept the connection request. See Figure 23.4.

23.1.3   Setting up a data-receive handler

If the user accepts the connection, the following delegate method is called on both apps:

```
- (void)peerPickerController:(GKPeerPickerController *)picker
        didConnectPeer:(NSString *)peerID
        toSession:(GKSession *)session
```

Figure 23.3   Waiting for a device to accept connection.

Figure 23.4   Asking for permission to accept the connection request.

Inside this method, you usually dismiss the peer picker and assign a data handler to the session. The following shows a possible implementation:

```
- (void)peerPickerController:(GKPeerPickerController *)picker
        didConnectPeer:(NSString *)peerID
        toSession:(GKSession *)session{
    [mSession setDataReceiveHandler:self withContext:NULL];
    [mPeerPicker dismiss];
    self.mPeerPicker = nil;
    [cmdButton setTitle:@"Send" forState:UIControlStateNormal];
}
```

The object used as a data-receive handler to the session must implement the receiveData:from-Peer:inSession:context: method. A possible implementation of this method is shown below:

```
- (void) receiveData:(NSData *)data fromPeer:(NSString *)peer
        inSession: (GKSession *)session context:(void *)context{
    textArea.text = [NSString stringWithFormat:@"%@\n%@> %@",
        textArea.text , [mSession displayNameForPeer:peer],
        [NSString stringWithUTF8String:[data bytes]]];
}
```

In this method, we simply append the text received to the transcript of the chat as shown in Figure 23.5.

Figure 23.5 The chat transcript.

23.1.4 Sending data

To send data to the other device, you can use the sendDataToAllPeers:withDataMode:error: method. Here is an example:

```
[self.mSession sendDataToAllPeers:[@"Hi!"
        dataUsingEncoding:NSStringEncodingConversionAllowLossy]
        withDataMode:GKSendDataReliable error:nil];
```

You can either use the reliable data mode specified using the `GKSendDataReliable` value or the best-effort data mode specified by the `GKSendDataUnreliable` value. The former data type requires fragmentation and reassembly for large messages and may stall if network congestion occurs, while the latter provides immediate delivery of messages without guarantee of delivery or order.

These are the basic steps needed to communicate between two iPhone apps. The complete source code of the `Gaming` project is available in the source downloads.

23.2   Exchanging Pictures

Text is not the only thing you can send from a device to another. You can send any type of data you want as long as the two applications agree on the data protocol.

In the `Gaming2` project, we develop an application that transmits small images between two iPhone devices. The app's structure is very similar to the one developed in the previous section. The main differences are in the sending and receiving of images.

23.2.1   Sending an image

Once we have established a session between the two devices, we send an image by first obtaining the data representation of an image and then sending it using Bluetooth. The following code fragment shows an example:

```
NSData *imageData = UIImageJPEGRepresentation(
  [UIImage imageNamed:
        [NSString stringWithFormat:@"%d.png", rand()%13]], .7);
[self.mSession sendDataToAllPeers:imageData
                      withDataMode:GKSendDataReliable error:nil];
```

The example above randomly selects 1 of 13 images bundled in the app as the image to be sent to the other device.

23.2.2   Receiving an image

Showing a received image is straightforward. All we need to do is obtain an image from the data and set the `image` property of an image view to the constructed image. The following code fragment shows an example:

```
- (void) receiveData:(NSData *)data fromPeer:(NSString *)peer
      inSession: (GKSession *)session context:(void *)context{
    imageView.image = [UIImage imageWithData:data];
}
```

The complete source code of the `Gaming2` project is available in the source downloads.

23.3 Summary

The GameKit framework can be used to transfer data between two iPhones. You use the GKPeer-PickerController class to allow the user to establish the connection. The delegate of this picker responds by creating a GKSession instance representing the session between the two devices. Transferring information involves converting the data to an NSData instance and sending it through the channel. To receive data, the session's data-receive handler is called back, with an NSData instance representing the received data.

Exercises

(1) The GameKit framework is suitable for communicating small messages between users of different iPhone devices. To transfer large amounts of data, you may want to look into using Internet technologies such as FTP. In this exercise, let's consider sending a large image using the GameKit framework. In order to do that, we need to divide the image into chunks of, say, 1024 bytes. Each packet transmitted needs to hold the number of bytes in the chunk and the chunk itself. The receiver needs to reassemble the image data and construct the image when the last chunk is received. Show how the transmission component can be constructed.

(2) Show how you can build the receiver part in the preceding exercise. Do not assume that the data-receive handler method is called with a complete chunk.

24

Developing for the iPad

Like the iPhone and iPod touch, the iPad device runs iOS. This means that all you have learned so far can be applied to the iPad. In addition, the iOS SDK provides you with some view controllers that are more appropriate to a larger screen.

In this chapter, we will investigate the different view controllers available on the iPad. In Sections 24.1 and 24.2, we investigate popover controllers. Next, Section 24.3 shows you how to use split view controllers. After that, Section 24.4 discusses several presentation styles for modal view controllers. Finally, we summarize the chapter in Section 24.5.

24.1   The Cities App: Iteration 1

In this section, we will develop a simple iPad application. This application shows a toolbar with two buttons. Each button represents a U.S. state. When the user taps on a button, a popover appears, showing a table listing the cities in that state. When the user selects a city, the flag of that city is shown in an image view and the popover controller is dismissed. Tapping anywhere outside the popover controller will dismiss the popover controller.

24.1.1   The application delegate class

Let's start by writing the `CitiesAppDelegate` class, as declared in Listing 24.1.

Listing 24.1   The declaration of the `CitiesAppDelegate` class.

```
#import "StatesViewController.h"

@interface CitiesAppDelegate : NSObject <UIApplicationDelegate> {
    UIWindow                *window;
    StatesViewController    *viewController;
}
@property (nonatomic, retain) IBOutlet UIWindow     *window;
@property (nonatomic, retain)
          IBOutlet StatesViewController     *viewController;
@end
```

The class declares an instance of `StatesViewController` class. This class, which we will develop in Section 24.1.3, is used to manage the toolbar along with the two buttons. In addition, it uses an image view that shows the flag of a selected city.

The implementation of the app delegate class is straightforward. It adds the view controller to the window and then shows it. It also cleans after itself when it gets deallocated. Listing 24.2 shows the implementation code.

Listing 24.2   The implementation of the `CitiesAppDelegate` class.

```
#import "CitiesAppDelegate.h"

@implementation CitiesAppDelegate

@synthesize window, viewController;

- (BOOL)application:(UIApplication *)application
        didFinishLaunchingWithOptions:(NSDictionary *)launchOptions {
  [window addSubview:viewController.view];
  [window makeKeyAndVisible];
  return YES;
}

- (void)dealloc {
    self.window = nil;
    self.viewController = nil;
    [super dealloc];
}
@end
```

24.1.2   The CitiesViewController class

The `CitiesViewController` is a table view controller that is used to show the list of the cities in a given state. Its declaration is shown in Listing 24.3.

Listing 24.3   The declaration of the `CitiesViewController` class.

```
@interface CitiesViewController : UITableViewController {
    NSArray                              *data;
    id<CitiesViewControllerDelegate>     caller;
}

@property (nonatomic, retain)  NSArray                              *data;
@property (nonatomic, assign)  id <CitiesViewControllerDelegate> caller;

@end
```

The `data` property holds the array of cities represented by this controller. The `caller` property holds a reference to an object implementing the `CitiesViewControllerDelegate` protocol. The object using this controller will set this property with a reference to an object implementing this protocol. When the user selects a city, the `didSelectCity:` method, defined by this protocol, is called on the object referenced by the `caller` property.

The actual implementation of the `CitiesViewController` class is shown in Listing 24.4.

Listing 24.4   The implementation of the `CitiesViewController` class.

```
#import "CitiesViewController.h"

@implementation CitiesViewController

@synthesize data, caller;

- (BOOL)shouldAutorotateToInterfaceOrientation:
            (UIInterfaceOrientation)interfaceOrientation {
    return YES;
}

- (void) viewWillAppear:(BOOL)animated{
    [super viewWillAppear:animated];
    [self.tableView reloadData];
}

- (NSInteger)numberOfSectionsInTableView:(UITableView *)tableView {
    return 1;
}

- (NSInteger)tableView:(UITableView *)tableView
                numberOfRowsInSection:(NSInteger)section {
    return data.count;
}

- (UITableViewCell *)tableView:(UITableView *)tableView
            cellForRowAtIndexPath:(NSIndexPath *)indexPath {

    static NSString *CellIdentifier = @"Cell";
    UITableViewCell *cell =
        [tableView dequeueReusableCellWithIdentifier:CellIdentifier];
    if (cell == nil) {
        cell = [[[UITableViewCell alloc]
            initWithStyle:UITableViewCellStyleDefault
            reuseIdentifier:CellIdentifier] autorelease];
    }
    cell.textLabel.text = [data objectAtIndex:indexPath.row];
```

```
      return cell;
}

- (void)tableView:(UITableView *)tableView
        didSelectRowAtIndexPath:(NSIndexPath *)indexPath {
    [self.caller didSelectCity:[data objectAtIndex:indexPath.row]];
}

- (CGSize)contentSizeForViewInPopoverView {
    return CGSizeMake(300.0, 200.0);
}

- (void)dealloc {
    self.data = nil;
    [super dealloc];
}
@end
```

You have certainly seen many forms of this controller throughout this book. What you need to notice here is first the fact that we are overriding the shouldAutorotateToInterface-Orientation: method and returning YES. Providing support for different device orientations is highly-recommended for the iPad.

The other method that you need to observe is the contentSizeForViewInPopoverView method. The contentSizeForViewInPopoverView property is a read/write property declared as a category on the UIViewController class. You can use this property to set the size of the content of the view controller hosted by the popover controller.

24.1.3   The StatesViewController class

The StatesViewController class is the main view controller of the application. This view controller manages a toolbar with two buttons representing two states, a popover controller, and an image view showing the flag of the selected city. Listing 24.5 shows the declaration of this class.

Listing 24.5   The declaration of the StatesViewController class.

```
#import "CitiesViewController.h"

@interface StatesViewController : UIViewController
            <UIPopoverControllerDelegate, CitiesViewControllerDelegate>{
    UIToolbar              *toolbar;
    UIPopoverController     *citiesPopoverController;
    CitiesViewController    *citiesViewController;
    UIImageView             *imageView;
}

@property (nonatomic, retain) IBOutlet UIToolbar *toolbar;
```

```
@property (nonatomic, retain) UIPopoverController
                                   *citiesPopoverController;
@property (nonatomic, retain) CitiesViewController
                                   *citiesViewController;
@property (nonatomic, retain) IBOutlet UIImageView *imageView;
- (IBAction) texas;
- (IBAction) california;
@end
```

The `UIPopoverController` instance is used to present the content of the `CitiesView-Controller` instance. The `viewDidLoad` method of the `StatesViewController` class is shown below:

```
- (void) viewDidLoad{
    [super viewDidLoad];
    self.citiesViewController =
        [[[CitiesViewController alloc]
            initWithStyle:UITableViewStylePlain] autorelease];
    citiesViewController.caller = self;
    self.citiesPopoverController =
        [[[UIPopoverController alloc]
            initWithContentViewController:citiesViewController] autorelease];
}
```

As you can see, we create the `CitiesViewController` instance and use it in the initialization of the popover controller.

Showing the `CitiesViewController` inside the popover controller is simple. For example, if the button representing the state of Texas is tapped, we configure the `CitiesViewController` instance with some cities in Texas and use the `presentPopoverFromRect:inView:permittedArrow-Directions:animated:` instance method of the `UIPopoverController` class to present it to the user as shown below:

```
- (IBAction) texas{
    citiesViewController.data =
        [NSArray arrayWithObjects:@"Plano", @"Austin", @"Dallas", nil];
    [citiesPopoverController
            presentPopoverFromRect:[toolbar bounds]
            inView:self.toolbar
            permittedArrowDirections:UIPopoverArrowDirectionAny
            animated:YES];
}
```

Whenever the user selects a city in the table, the method `didSelectCity:` will be called. Inside this method we show the flag of the selected city and dismiss the popover controller as shown below:

```
- (void) didSelectCity:(NSString*) city{
    imageView.image = [UIImage imageNamed:
```

```
                          [NSString stringWithFormat:@"%@.png", city]];
        [citiesPopoverController dismissPopoverAnimated:YES];
}
```

Because we support all orientations of the device, we override the `willAnimateRotationTo-`
`InterfaceOrientation:toInterfaceOrientation:duration:` method, and in it we adjust
the image view so that it remains centered. See the implementation below:

```
- (void)willAnimateRotationToInterfaceOrientation:
        (UIInterfaceOrientation)toInterfaceOrientation
        duration:(NSTimeInterval)duration {
    if (toInterfaceOrientation == UIDeviceOrientationPortrait ||
        toInterfaceOrientation == UIDeviceOrientationPortraitUpsideDown){
        imageView.center = CGPointMake(384, 512);
    }else{
        imageView.center = CGPointMake(512, 384);
    }
}
```

24.1.4   Creating the UI

In this section, we will create the user interface of the application. We will be using Interface Builder
instead of the programmatic approach used throughout most of the book. (Make sure you refresh
your Interface Builder skills by reviewing Chapter 1 and Appendix F.)

Start by creating a new iPad project as shown in Figure 24.1.

Figure 24.1   Creating an iPad project.

Make sure you select iPad for the product type. Next, we will need to create the interface document for the `StatesViewController`. Right-click on the Resources group and select Add → New File. Select Empty XIB under User Interface and make sure the product type is iPad. See Figure 24.2. Name the interface document file `StatesViewController.xib`.

Figure 24.2   Creating a new interface document.

Now we want to add the UI elements to this empty interface document. Locate a view UI element from the library as shown in Figure 24.3.

Drag and drop the view on the document as shown in Figure 24.4.

Drag and drop a toolbar UI element on the view as shown in Figure 24.5.

Drag and drop a bar button item and a flexible space bar button item on the toolbar as shown in Figure 24.6.

Rename the two buttons Texas and California.

Add a `UIImageView` UI element as shown in Figure 24.7.

Click on the file's owner node in the document window and change the class identity of the file's owner to `StatesViewController`. See Figure 24.8.

Connect the outlets as shown in Figure 24.9.

Now open the `MainWindow.xib` file by double-clicking on it. Drag and drop a view controller UI element on the document. Change the class identity of this controller to `StatesViewController`.

Figure 24.3   A `UIView` UI element.

Figure 24.4   Adding a `UIView` UI element to the document.

Figure 24.5   Adding a toolbar UI element to the view.

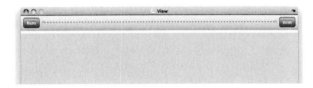

Figure 24.6   Adding a bar button item and a flexible space bar button item on the toolbar.

Figure 24.7   Adding an image view UI element to the view.

Specify the NIB name as shown in Figure 24.10.

Control-click the Cities App Delegate node in the document and connect the `viewController` to the States View Controller as shown in Figure 24.11.

Figure 24.8   Changing the class identity of the file's owner.

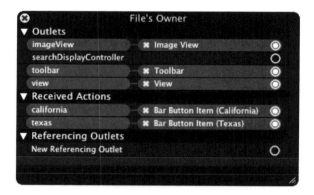

Figure 24.9   Connecting the outlets of the controller.

24.1.5   Wrapping it up

Figure 24.12 shows a screen shot of the Cities application.

The complete application can be found in the `Cities` project in the source downloads.

24.2   The Cities App: Iteration 2

Let's improve on the application developed in the previous section. We would like to have one bar button called States that shows a list of states in a table view inside a popover view controller. When

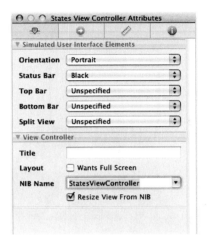

Figure 24.10   Specifying the NIB name of the controller.

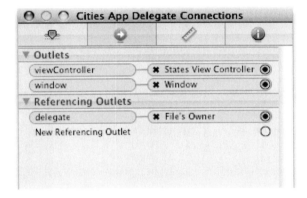

Figure 24.11   Connecting the `viewController` outlet to the states view controller.

a state is tapped inside this table, the cities inside this state are shown in another view controller and inside the same popover view controller.

24.2.1   Initializing the popover view controller with a navigation controller

We can place the state and city table view controllers inside the same popover view controller by initializing the popover view controller with a navigation controller.

The `viewDidLoad` method starts by creating an instance of the `StatesViewController`. This instance is then used as the root view controller of a navigation controller. The navigation controller

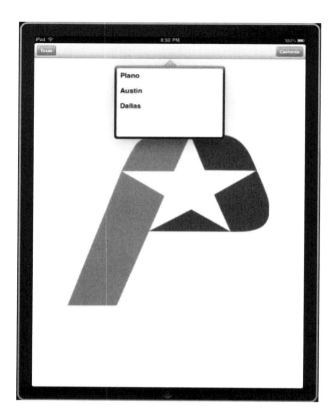

Figure 24.12   A screen shot of the Cities application.

is set as the content view controller of an instance of a popover view controller. The following shows
the viewDidLoad method:

```
- (void) viewDidLoad{
    [super viewDidLoad];
    self.statesViewController =
        [[[StatesViewController alloc] initWithStyle:UITableViewStylePlain]
                                                            autorelease];
    statesViewController.caller = self;
    UINavigationController *navCtrl =
        [[[UINavigationController alloc] initWithRootViewController:
                statesViewController] autorelease];
    self.citiesPopoverController =
        [[[UIPopoverController alloc]
                initWithContentViewController:navCtrl] autorelease];
}
```

24.2.2   *Showing the popover*

When the user taps on the button, we show the popover controller as follows:

```
- (IBAction) states{
    [citiesPopoverController presentPopoverFromRect:[toolbar bounds]
        inView:self.toolbar
        permittedArrowDirections:UIPopoverArrowDirectionAny
        animated:YES];
}
```

24.2.3   *Wrapping it up*

Figures 24.13 and 24.14 show the navigation process to a given state.

The complete application can be found in the `Cities2` project in the source downloads.

Figure 24.13   The view showing the available states.

Figure 24.14   The view after selecting a state.

24.3   Split View Controller

The large screen of the iPad requires intelligent presentation of information. `UISplitView-Controller` gives you the capability to manage two view controllers: one used to present a list of items (e.g., list of emails) and the other used to show the details of a selected item (e.g., the contents of an email).

When the iPad is held in landscape mode, both the list of items and the details of a given item are shown side by side. This makes sense as this mode provides the largest width for data presentation. When the user changes the orientation to portrait mode, the `UISplitViewController` hides the list of items and adjusts the detail view controller so that it takes the whole width of the device. To show the list of items when in portrait mode, the view controller provides a button that shows the list of items in a popover controller. All of this is built in, and you only need to provide the two controllers and adjust the display within each depending on the current orientation of the device.

24.3.1   An example of the split view controller

Creating an app that utilizes the split view controller functionality is quite simple. Start by creating a new iPad project called `SplitView` and choose the Split View-Based Application template, as shown in Figure 24.15.

Figure 24.15   Creating a new split view-based controller app.

The template provides a fully functional app. Click the Build and Go toolbar button to see it. Figure 24.16 shows the app in portrait mode.

Notice that the detail view occupies the whole area. Tap the button called Root List to see the list of items (see Figure 24.17).

Figure 24.16   The split view application in portrait mode.

Figure 24.17   The list of items in a popover view controller.

Notice how selecting an item in the list results in displaying information about that item in the detail view and dismissing the popover controller.

Let's change the orientation of the iPad. In the simulator, choose Hardware → Rotate Left (see Figure 24.18).

Figure 24.18   The split view application in landscape mode.

24.3.2   Dissecting the split view controller

We mentioned before that the split view controller manages exactly two view controllers: (1) the list of items which is represented by default by the `RootViewController` class and (2) the detail view controller represented by default by the `DetailViewController` class.

The RootViewController class

The `RootViewController` class is usually a subclass of the `UITableViewController` class. You need to notice the following:

- **Popover awareness.** Because the `RootViewController` will be hosted in a popover controller while the iPad is in portrait mode, we need to specify the content size as follows:

  ```
  self.contentSizeForViewInPopover = CGSizeMake(320.0, 600.0);
  ```

- **Item selection.** We need a way to inform the detail view controller about the selected item when it is selected by the user. The template provides a reference to the detail view controller and provides the basic mechanism of updating the detail view through a custom setter. Here is the statement that informs the detail view controller to update itself:

  ```
  detailViewController.detailItem =
      [NSString stringWithFormat:@"Row %d", indexPath.row];
  ```

Of course, this is the basic structure. You are supposed to modify it to fit your needs.

The DetailViewController class

If you open the `MainWindow.xib` file and inspect the `delegate` property of the split view controller, you'll notice that `delegate` is set to the `DetailViewController` instance.

The delegate is supposed to implement the `UISplitViewControllerDelegate` protocol. This protocol declares the following three optional methods to handle different events of the split view controller:

- **Adding a button to the toolbar.** When the split view controller hides `RootView-Controller`, it invokes the following method on the delegate if it is declared:

  - (**void**) splitViewController: (UISplitViewController*) svc
    willHideViewController: (UIViewController *) aViewController
    withBarButtonItem: (UIBarButtonItem*) barButtonItem
    forPopoverController: (UIPopoverController*) pc;

  The standard implementation of this method is to take the button given to you and add it to the toolbar. In addition, you need to retain a reference to the popover controller so that you can dismiss it when the user selects an item from `RootViewController` while in portrait mode.

  The following is the standard implementation provided by the template:

  ```
  barButtonItem.title = @"Root List";
  NSMutableArray *items = [[toolbar items] mutableCopy];
  [items insertObject:barButtonItem atIndex:0];
  [toolbar setItems:items animated:YES];
  [items release];
  self.popoverController = pc;
  ```

  The implementation is straightforward. We set the title of the button, add the button to the toolbar, and retain a reference to the popover hosting the `RootViewController` instance.

- **Removing the button from the toolbar.** When the user moves the iPad into landscape mode, the button on the toolbar should be removed as the `RootViewController` instance will be shown to the left alongside the detail view controller. To facilitate this, the following delegate method is called if it is defined:

  - (**void**) splitViewController: (UISplitViewController*) svc
    willShowViewController: (UIViewController *) aViewController
    invalidatingBarButtonItem: (UIBarButtonItem *) barButtonItem;

  The standard implementation of this method is to remove the bar button and lose the reference to the popover controller. Here is the standard implementation:

  ```
  NSMutableArray *items = [[toolbar items] mutableCopy];
  [items removeObjectAtIndex:0];
  [toolbar setItems:items animated:YES];
  [items release];
  self.popoverController = nil;
  ```

- **Handling popover presentation.** When `RootViewController` is about to be presented in a popover controller while in portrait mode, the following method is called:

```
- (void)splitViewController:(UISplitViewController*)svc
    popoverController:(UIPopoverController*)pc
    willPresentViewController:(UIViewController *)aViewController;
```

Inside this method, you usually perform actions that clear the view from, for example, other popover controllers.

24.4   Modal View Controller Presentation Styles

Controllers presented modally on the iPad can be configured with a specific presentation stye. The presentation style is one of the types declared by the `UIModalPresentationStyle` type.

To configure a view controller with a presentation style, you need to set the `modalPresentation-Style` to one of several defined values. For example, the following code configures a view controller to be shown as a form sheet and then presents it modally:

```
SimpleController *ctrl = [[[SimpleController alloc] init] autorelease];
ctrl.modalPresentationStyle = UIModalPresentationFormSheet;
[self presentModalViewController:ctrl animated:YES];
```

Figure 24.19 shows the modal view controller presented in portrait mode, and Figure 24.20 shows it in landscape mode.

Notice that we need to specify a mechanism to dismiss the view controller as the grayed areas are not responsive to touch events. Here we use a button, but you are free to use other mechanisms.

Another style that you can use is `UIModalPresentationPageSheet`. This style will present the view controller with a height equal to the height of the screen regardless of the device orientation. The width is always the width of the screen in portrait orientation.

Take a look at a simple application demonstrating this style. The application can be found in the `PresentationStyles` project in the source downloads.

24.5   Summary

In this chapter, we investigated the different view controllers available on the iPad. In Sections 24.1 and 24.2, we investigated popover controllers. Next, Section 24.3 showed you how to use split view controllers. Finally, Section 24.4 discussed several presentation styles for modal view controllers.

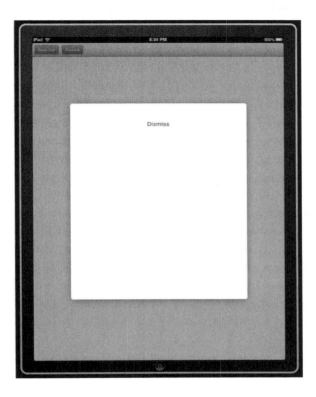

Figure 24.19   A view controller presented modally in portrait mode, using the form sheet presentation style.

Figure 24.20   A view controller presented modally in landscape mode, using the form sheet presentation style.

Exercises

(1) Write an iPad app that presents the flags of the 50 states in a split view. The root view consists of the names of the states in a table view and the detail view consists of the flag of the selected state shown in an image view. See the ipad1 project for an example.

(2) You should know by now that the Default.png file is used to show a splash screen when the app is first launched. On the iPad, you can specify different splash screens for different orientations. These files include Default-Portrait.png (768 × 1004) and Default--Landscape.png (1004 × 768). In addition, you can be more specific and specify files such as Default-PortraitUpsideDown.png, Default-LandscapeLeft.png, and Default--LandscapeRight.png.

Investigate splash screens by first specifying images for the generic portrait and landscape orientations and then adding more images for specific orientations.

Appendix A
Saving and Restoring App State

Because one application at most can run at a given time, your application should give the user the illusion of being active all the time even if the user presses the Home button. To achieve that, your application should save its current state (e.g., which level of hierarchy it is currently displaying, the current search term, etc.) when the application is terminated and restore that state when it is relaunched.

There are several ways in which you can maintain this state information. You can, for example, use the SQLite database or flat files. A property list, however, is ideal for this situation and is the subject of this appendix.

To use property lists for capturing/restoring the state of an application, you need to follow the following guidelines:

- Represent the state in a dictionary or in an array. The state elements can be instances of NSDictionary, NSArray, NSData, NSDate, NSNumber, and NSString.
- Add the state elements to the dictionary or the array.
- Serialize the dictionary or the array into an NSData object using the NSPropertyList-Serialization class method. The NSData object represents the state information in either XML or a binary format. For efficiency, use binary format.
- Write the NSData object into a local file in the Documents directory.
- To restore the state, load the written file into an NSData object and use the NSPropertyListSerialization class method to obtain the dictionary or the array.

In the following, we give an example of saving and restoring an application state using property lists. The state of the application is assumed to be captured by a dictionary. This dictionary has five elements: two NSStrings, one NSNumber, one NSArray, and one NSDate value.

Listing A.1 shows the application delegate method that demonstrates the property list concept. The method builds the state of the application (a dictionary), invokes saveAppState to save the state, and then invokes restoreState to restore it.

Listing A.1   The delegate method used in building the app state, saving it, and then restoring it using property lists.

```
- (void) applicationDidFinishLaunching:(UIApplication *)application {
  // build app state
  state = [[NSMutableDictionary alloc] initWithCapacity:5];
  [state setObject:@"http://www.thegoogle.com" forKey:@"URL"];
  [state setObject:@"smartphones" forKey:@"SEARCH_TERM"];
  [state setObject:[NSNumber numberWithFloat:3.14] forKey:@"PI"];
  [state setObject:
              [NSMutableArray arrayWithObjects:@"Apple iPhone 3G",
                                               @"Apple iPhone",
                                               @"HTC Touch Diamond",
                                               nil]
                              forKey:@"RESULT"];
  [state setObject:[NSDate date]  forKey:@"DATE"];
  // save state of app
  [self saveAppState];
  // restore state of app
  [self restoreState];
}
```

Of course, in a real app, you will restore the state of the app in the applicationDidFinish-Launching: method and save it in the applicationWillTerminate: method. The above example does both in the same method to keep things simple.

Listing A.2 shows the saveAppState method. The method uses the class method dataFrom-PropertyList:format:errorDescription: of the class NSPropertyListSerialization to obtain an NSData object of the serialized dictionary. There are two formats you can use: binary format specified using NSPropertyListBinaryFormat_v1_0 or XML format specified using NSPropertyListXMLFormat_v1_0. You can also give a reference to an NSString object that can be used to signal back an error message. It is your responsibility to release that object if an error should occur. Once you have obtained the NSData object, you can write it to a local file.

Listing A.2   Saving the state of the application in a property list.

```
-(void) saveAppState{
  NSString *theError;
  NSData *theData = [NSPropertyListSerialization
                        dataFromPropertyList:state
                        format:NSPropertyListXMLFormat_v1_0
                        errorDescription:&theError];
  if(theData){
    NSString *fileName = [NSHomeDirectory()
      stringByAppendingPathComponent:@"Documents/state.plist"];
    [theData writeToFile:fileName atomically:YES];
  }
  else{
```

```
        NSLog(@"Error saving app state: %@", theError);
        [theError   release]; // need to release
    }
}
```

Listing A.3 shows the contents of the XML file `state.plist` used to store the application's state. The number of bytes used to store the state in XML format is 543; it is 204 when the binary format is used.

Listing A.3   The property list in XML format.

```
<?xml version="1.0" encoding="UTF-8"?>
<!DOCTYPE plist PUBLIC "-//Apple//DTD PLIST 1.0//EN"
"http://www.apple.com/DTDs/PropertyList-1.0.dtd">
<plist version="1.0">
<dict>
  <key>DATE</key>
  <date>2008-09-04T17:47:28Z</date>
  <key>PI</key>
  <real>3.1400001049041748</real>
  <key>RESULT</key>
  <array>
    <string>Apple iPhone 3G</string>
    <string>Apple iPhone</string>
    <string>HTC Touch Diamond</string>
  </array>
  <key>SEARCH_TERM</key>
  <string>smartphones</string>
  <key>URL</key>
  <string>http://www.thegoogle.com</string>
</dict>
</plist>
```

Listing A.4 shows the method used to restore the application's state. First, the file is read into an NSData object using the techniques in Chapter 10. After that, the class method `propertyList-FromData:mutabilityOption:format:errorDescription:` is used to obtain the dictionary object. The parameter `mutabilityOption` is used to specify the mutability of the objects returned. If you specify `NSPropertyListImmutable`, then the dictionary, as well as all of its entries, will be returned as immutable. If you specify `NSPropertyListMutableContainersAndLeaves`, then the dictionary and all of its entries will be created as mutable objects. The option `NSPropertyList-MutableContainers`, which we use here, generates mutable objects for arrays and dictionaries only.

Listing A.4   Restoring the state of the application in a property list.

```
-(void) restoreState{
  NSString            *theError;
  NSPropertyListFormat  format;
```

```
NSString *fileName = [NSHomeDirectory()
            stringByAppendingPathComponent:@"Documents/state.plist"];
NSData   *theData = [[NSData alloc] initWithContentsOfFile:fileName];
if(theData){
  [state release];
  state = [NSPropertyListSerialization
                      propertyListFromData:theData
                      mutabilityOption:NSPropertyListMutableContainers
                      format:&format  errorDescription:&theError];
  if(state){
    [state retain];
  }
  else{
    NSLog(@"Error retrieving app state: %@", theError);
    [theError   release]; // need to release
  }
  [theData release];
}
}
```

Appendix B

Invoking External Applications

Your iOS application can programmatically invoke other iOS applications. Moreover, you can open your iOS application to be invoked by other iOS applications. To accomplish that, you specify a new URL scheme in the application's bundle, and the system will register that new scheme once the application is installed.

To invoke another iOS application, you use the `UIApplication` instance method `openURL:` and pass in the URL of that application. The following code fragment will open the Maps application and display a specific address:

```
NSString  *address = @"http://maps.google.com/maps?q=plano,tx";
NSURL *myURL = [NSURL URLWithString:address];
[[UIApplication sharedApplication] openURL:myURL];
```

To register a new URL scheme, you need to add it to the `Info.plist` file. In Figure B.1, we show what needs to be added to register the new URL scheme `lookup`. The URL identifier can be any unique string.

▼ URL types		(1 item)
▼ Item 1		(2 items)
URL identifier		com.mycompany.lookup
▼ URL Schemes		(1 item)
Item 1		lookup

Figure B.1 Adding a new URL scheme in the `Info.plist` file.

To actually service the invocation, you need to implement the application delegate's method `application:handleOpenURL:`, which is declared as follows:

```
- (BOOL)
      application:(UIApplication *)application handleOpenURL:(NSURL *)url
```

You receive an instance of NSURL encapsulating the URL used in the invocation. You can use the many methods of NSURL in order to retrieve queries, parameters, and fragments according to your needs. For example, our `lookup` scheme can be invoked by using either the Zip code or the city. To look up based on the Zip code, you invoke it as follows: `lookup://www?zip#68508`. To invoke it using the city, you use `lookup://www?city#Lincoln`.

Listing B.1 shows an implementation of the `lookup` URL scheme handling. To retrieve the query, we use the `query` method of NSURL. This can be either `"city"` or `"zip"`. To retrieve the fragment, we use the `fragment` method. The implementation below simply displays the important parts of the invocation URL. If you cannot process the request, you return NO. Otherwise, you service it and return YES.

Listing B.1   An implementation of the `lookup` URL scheme handling.

```
- (BOOL)
    application:(UIApplication *)application handleOpenURL:(NSURL *)url{
  NSString  *query =     [url query];
  NSString  *fragment = [url fragment];
  NSMutableString *output;
  if([query isEqualToString:@"zip"]){
    output = [NSMutableString
                stringWithFormat:@"Looking up by zip code %@", fragment];
  }
  else  if([query isEqualToString:@"city"]){
    output = [NSMutableString
                stringWithFormat:@"Looking up by city  %@", fragment];
  }
  else return NO;
  textView.text = output;
  return YES;
}
```

Appendix C

App Store Distribution

The App Store submission process consists of the following phases:

1. The development team uses XCode to build a binary of the application with appropriate code signing. You use the iPhone Developer Program portal to obtain the required certificates and profiles in order to prepare the application for distribution. Consult the program portal user guide for step-by-step instructions.

2. Once the application has been successfully built and code signed, it needs to be compressed and uploaded to Apple's iTunes Connect site. In addition to the compressed binary, a 512×512 image representing the app in the App Store must be uploaded. A scaled-down (57×57) icon of the same image must be used by the application as an icon on the customer's springboard screen. An additional five snapshots of the app can be uploaded. These images will be used by users browsing the store to get a feeling for the application. Your app can choose to show a splash screen that is displayed for a second or so when the user launches the app. It's preferable to make the splash screen identical (scaled up to 320×480, of course) to the icon of the app. To add a splash screen, just name the image `Default.png` and put it in the main bundle of the app before code signing.

3. Description of the app (for every localization) is also required in this process. Ideally, it needs to be limited to `700` characters, but you can go up to `3,000` characters. Marketing should work hard on producing the best app description. You may want initially to limit your claims, though. The reviewers do go over your claims while reviewing the app. Once the app has been approved, you can modify the description. But remember to always be truthful.

4. The price and geographic distribution (only U.S., global, etc.) is also required. This determines the App Stores where your application can be purchased.

After providing this information, the app can be submitted for review. Apple's review team usually responds within a week. If you're lucky, you don't hear from the review team at all. Instead, you will receive a wonderful message saying, "Dear John Doe: The status of the following application has changed to Ready for Sale." It takes several hours from the receipt of this email for the app to show up in the App Store.

If, on the other hand, the review team is not happy with some aspect of your app, you will receive a description of the problem (with possible screen shots of the offending feature) and a possible reference to a section in the iPhone's Human Interface Guidelines (HIG) document. For example, you might receive something like the following:

```
"Please review the Handling Common Tasks section of the
iPhone's Human Interface Guideline (HIG) here:
https://developer.apple.com/iphone/library/documentation/
UserExperience/Conceptual/MobileHIG>"
```

You fix the problem and submit a new binary. You do not need to change other aspects of the submission if the problem is in the application itself. If the review team finds another problem, it responds (within a week or so) with another screen shot and another section of the HIG to read.

This process repeats until you give up, have a heart attack, or receive a "ready for sale" email. Sorry, but you don't receive a list of issues in one go. One issue at a time!

One of the first things that a reviewer will do is to check your handling of network connectivity. Your application needs to detect network failure and display meaningful text explaining to the user the problem and how he or she can fix it (e.g., disable Airplane Mode). You cannot just display a white screen and a loading activity indicator that does not stop! Check out Section 17.1 for information on how you can detect network connectivity.

You can change the price of the app, its description, geographic distribution market, etc., any time after the app appears in the store. A new binary, however, requires that you go through the process again. Once a revision is approved, the old version is removed and is replaced by the new one. This swap is not instantaneous, though. This might result in lost sales for a few hours. Note that if you exclude a given market, which the previous version used to be distributed in, the customers in that market will not receive your app updates.

There are thousands and thousands of apps in 20 categories available for download. Marketing your app cannot be overemphasized.

Appendix D

Using XCode

XCode is a powerful integrated development environment (IDE) for Mac/iOS development. In this appendix, we cover several topics related to using XCode. First, we show some useful shortcuts. Next, we talk about writing custom templates for your classes, and after that we cover build configuration. Finally, we show you how to add references to other libraries (also known as *frameworks*).

D.1 XCode Shortcuts

The following are some of the common shortcuts in XCode:

- **Quick open.** To open a file quickly, use Command-Shift-D.
- **Build project.** To build your project, use Command-B.
- **Global search.** To search for something in your project, use Shift-Command-F.
- **Spelling and grammar.** To show spelling and grammar, use Command-:.
- **Shift text.** To shift text to the right, use Command-]. To shift to the left, use Command-[. Select a block to shift it. No selection is needed for a single line.
- **Message bubbles.** To show message bubbles, use Shift-Command-H. To hide message bubbles, use Option-Shift-Command-H.
- **Documentation.** To open documentation on something (e.g., a class), Option-double-click it. To show its declaration, Command-double-click it.

D.2 Creating Custom Templates

File templates are widely used in XCode. For example, to create a `TableViewController`, you choose File → New and select the `TableViewController` under the `Cocoa Touch Class` category. This is very helpful as you do not want to write all the necessary delegate and data source method signatures, etc.

In this section, you learn how easy it is to create your own templates. All templates live in the `/Developer/Platforms/iPhone-OS.platform/Developer/Library/Xcode/File Templates` directory. To create a template (`XYZ`) for a class, you create a directory with the name `XYZ.pbfiletemplate` and place `class.h`, `class.m`, and `TemplateInfo.plist` files in it. See Figure D.1 for an example of the directory structure of a template.

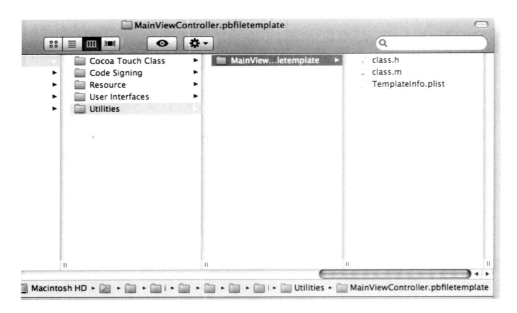

Figure D.1   The directory structure for a new class template. The template is for the class `MainView-Controller` in a new category, `Utilities`.

Inside the `class.h` file, you put the interface template for this class. The implementation of the class goes into `class.m`. The `.pbfiletemplate` file has three key/value pairs. The `MainTemplate-File` key has the value `class.m`. The `CounterpartTemplateFile` key has the value `class.h`. The `Description` key has as its value the description of this template. Figure D.2 shows the contents of an example `.pbfiletemplate` file.

Key	Value
▼ Information Property List	(3 items)
MainTemplateFile	class.m
CounterpartTemplateFile	class.h
Description	An Objective-C class which is a subclass of UIViewController, with an optional header file which

Figure D.2   The `.pbfiletemplate` file describing the file template.

Inside the `class.h` and `class.m` files, you write the template as if you are trying to write a class from scratch. Of course, you want to use tags in the template in order for it to be reusable. There are several tags you can put in the two files. These tags are all caps and enclosed between « and »[1]. The following are some of the tags you can use:

- «FILEBASENAMEASIDENTIFIER». This is the filename (without extension) that the user enters when he or she creates a class based on your template. The filename will be fixed if it is not a valid C identifier. For example, if the user enters `Hello World` for the filename, you get `Hello_World` out of this tag.

  You use this tag in your class interface and implementation. For example:
  `@interface «FILEBASENAMEASIDENTIFIER»: UIViewController{`

- «FULLUSERNAME». This tag provides the full name of the user. You can use it in the copyright header, etc.

- «TIME». This tag provides the current time.

- «PROJECTNAME». This tag provides the project's name.

Once you have these three files written inside the directory, you can start using them from XCode.

You can change the default values of most of the tags mentioned above by setting their values in the `PBXCustomTemplateMacroDefinitions` dictionary.

The easiest way to change these default values is to use the `defaults` command from the Terminal application. For example, the following command changes the organization to `Alcatel-Lucent`:

```
defaults write com.apple.Xcode PBXCustomTemplateMacroDefinitions \
'{ORGANIZATIONNAME = "Alcatel-Lucent";}'
```

You will need to restart XCode for the above command to take effect. From this point on, any file you create in XCode will have a comment block at the top, the copyright of which is similar to the following:

```
//
//  UntitledAppDelegate.m
//  CrossLight
//
//  Created by Maher Ali on 9/19/10.
//  Copyright Alcatel-Lucent 2010. All rights reserved.
//
```

---

[1]To get «, use Option-\. To get », use Shift-Option-\.

D.3   Build-Based Configurations

You are building an iOS app that uses an application server. During testing in the simulator, you want the application to hit the server running on your local machine. During testing on the device, you want to hit a beta external server. When you build for the App Store, you want to hit a secured production server. You do not want to change your code based on the build. You would rather have the server name as part of the build.

In this section, we show how easy it is to accomplish this task. Let's build a project in XCode with the following simple `main` function:

```
int main(int argc, char *argv[]) {
  NSAutoreleasePool * pool = [[NSAutoreleasePool alloc] init];
  NSLog([[NSBundle mainBundle]  objectForInfoDictionaryKey:@"Server"]);
  [pool release];
}
```

In `main`, we retrieve from the `.plist` file of the app the value for the key `Server`. The value can be retrieved using the method `objectForInfoDictionaryKey:` of the main bundle instance.

In XCode, locate your `.plist` file in the Resources group and click on it. Right-click to add a new row as shown in Figure D.3.

Figure D.3   Adding a new row in the `.plist` file.

Add the `Server/$AppServer` key/value pair in the `.plist` file as shown in Figure D.4. This line will add a new key with the value of the variable `$AppServer`.

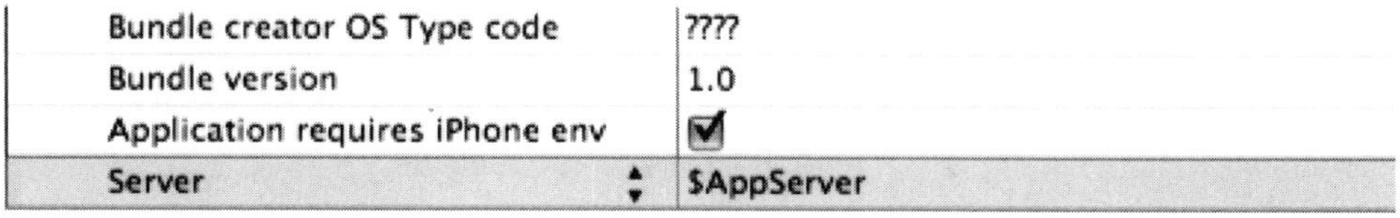

Bundle creator OS Type code	????
Bundle version	1.0
Application requires iPhone env	☑
Server	$AppServer

Figure D.4   Adding the `Server/$AppServer` key/value in the `.plist` file.

Now we will specify the value for $AppServer in the Debug and Release builds. Double-click on the target in the Targets group as shown in Figure D.5.

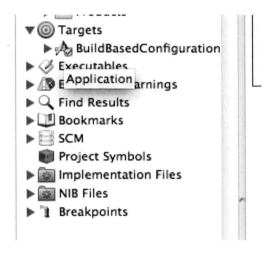

Figure D.5   Locating the target in the Targets group.

Select the Debug configuration as shown in Figure D.6.

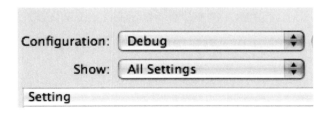

Figure D.6   Selecting the configuration (here, either Debug or Release).

Add a user-defined setting as shown in Figure D.7.

GCC_OPTIMIZATION_LEVEL
GCC_PRECOMPILE_PREFIX_HEADER
GCC_PREFIX_HEADER
GCC_WARN_ABOUT_RETURN_TYPE
GCC_WARN_UNUSED_VARIABLE
Edit Definition at This Level
Delete Definition at This Level
Add Build Setting Condition
Add User-Defined Setting

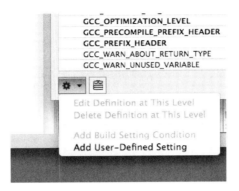

Figure D.7 Adding a user-defined setting for a specific configuration in a given target.

Figure D.8 shows the highlighted key/value pair to enter for the Debug configuration.

Show Warnings
User-Defined
AppServer
http://localhost:3000
GCC_C_LANGUAGE_STANDARD
c99
GCC_DYNAMIC_NO_PIC
NO
GCC_OPTIMIZATION_LEVEL
0

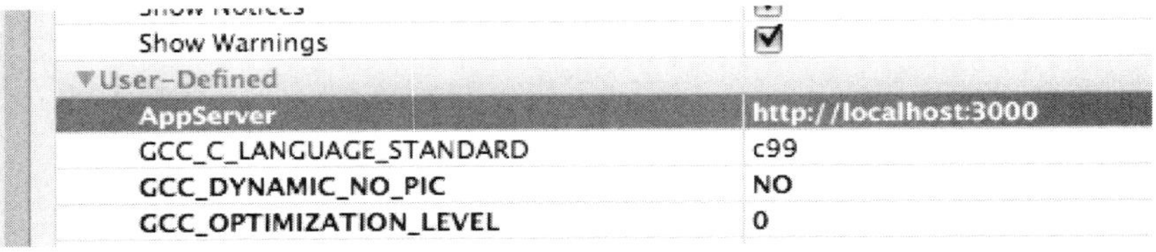

Figure D.8 The key/value pair for the Debug configuration.

Repeat this process and enter the key/value pair for the Release configuration as shown in Figure D.9.

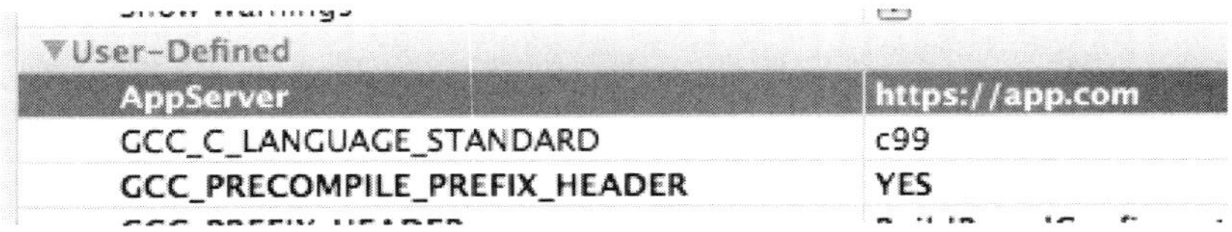

User-Defined
AppServer
https://app.com
GCC_C_LANGUAGE_STANDARD
c99
GCC_PRECOMPILE_PREFIX_HEADER
YES

Figure D.9 The key/value pair for the Release configuration.

Now when you change the configuration, the output of the `main()` function will change.

D.4   Using Frameworks

The iOS SDK comes with a variety of frameworks that you can use. To use a framework, you need to **#import** its main header file and include a reference to that framework in the target.

When you create a new project, three frameworks are automatically added for you. These three frameworks are Foundation, UIKit, and CoreGraphics. In addition, two import statements are added to the xxx_prefix.pch file, where xxx stands for the project's name entered by you. These two statements are

```
#import <Foundation/Foundation.h>
#import <UIKit/UIKit.h>
```

In this section, we show how you can add other frameworks to your target. The Core Location framework is used here as an example.

First, you need to add a reference to the main header file by adding the following statement so that any code that references the Core Location classes is able to find it.

#import <CoreLocation/CoreLocation.h>

You can simply add this statement to the xxx_prefix.pch file. This way, all other files can benefit from this import.

In addition, you need to add the framework to the target. In XCode, choose Project → Edit Active Target as shown in Figure D.10.

Figure D.10   Choose Project → Edit Active Target.

Figure D.11   Target Info window.

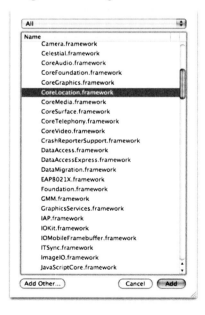

Figure D.12   The CoreLocation.framework library.

Figure D.13   The added Core Location library in the Linked Libraries section.

The `Target Info` window will appear as shown in Figure D.11. Click on the + button located at the bottom left-hand side. A list of libraries will be shown. Scroll down and locate the `CoreLocation.framework` as shown in Figure D.12. Select it and click Add. Figure D.13 shows the added Core Location library in the Linked Libraries section.

Appendix E

Unit Testing

In this appendix, we show you how to add unit tests to your project. By adding unit testing support, you'll be able to write tests for your methods. These tests will be added as a dependency on the building of your application. This will result in the tests being run before you build your application.

In the following, we walk you through a step-by-step process for adding unit testing. We use a simple `Employee` class for demonstration purposes.

E.1 Adding a Unit Test Target

In this section, we show you how to create a unit test target in your project. Later, we will make our main target dependent on this unit test target, thus making sure that the unit tests are executed before building our target.

Right-click on the Targets node in Groups & Files. Select Add → New Target as shown in Figure E.1.

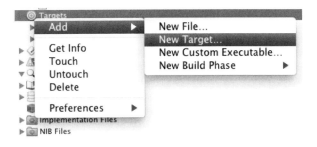

Figure E.1   Selecting Add New Target from the context menu.

Select Cocoa under the Mac OS X category. Scroll down and double-click on Unit Test Bundle as shown in Figure E.2.

Enter the name of the target, such as `MyUnitTestBundle`, as shown in Figure E.3.

Figure E.2   Choosing Unit Test Bundle for the new target.

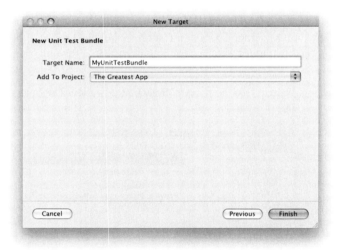

Figure E.3   Naming the unit test bundle.

E.2   Adapting to Foundation

The target you added in the previous section needs to be configured for use with the iOS SDK instead of Mac OS X.

Double-click on the unit test target. Choose All Configurations as shown in Figure E.4.

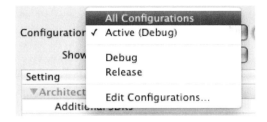

Figure E.4   Choosing All Configurations in the Build tab of the Target Info window.

Search for Other Linker Flags by entering **other linker** in the search box as shown in Figure E.5.

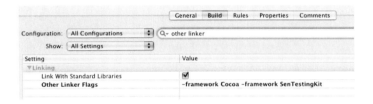

Figure E.5   Searching for the other linker flags.

Double-click on the value and change Cocoa to Foundation as shown in Figure E.6.

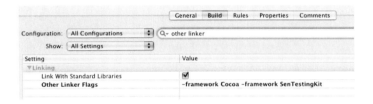

Figure E.6   Changing from Cocoa configuration to Foundation.

Search for GCC_PREFIX_HEADER as shown in Figure E.7.

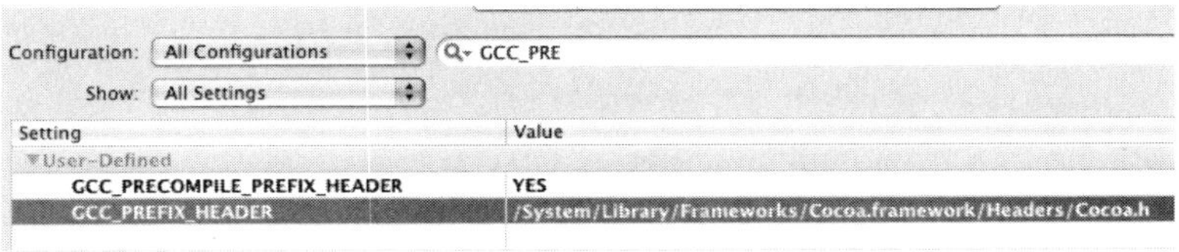

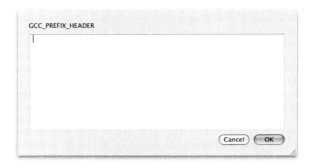

Figure E.7   Searching for the GCC_PREFIX_HEADER setting.

Double-click on the value field and clear the content as shown in Figure E.8.

Figure E.8   Removing the GCC_PREFIX_HEADER setting.

Hit OK. Close the target Info window.

E.3   The Model

For demonstration purposes, we will use the Employee class as an example. Let's first add it to our targets.

Right-click on the Classes group. Select Add → New File. Select the NSObject subclass. Name the class Employee as shown in Figure E.9. Make sure that you select both targets.

Replace the Employee.h header file with the contents shown in Listing E.1.

Listing E.1   The Employee.h header file.

```
#import <Foundation/Foundation.h>
#import <UIKit/UIKit.h>
```

```
@interface Employee : NSObject {
    NSString    *firstName, *lastName;
    NSInteger   salary;
    Employee    *manager;

}

@property(nonatomic, retain) NSString   *firstName;
@property(nonatomic, retain) NSString   *lastName;
@property(assign)            NSInteger  salary;
@property(nonatomic, retain) Employee   *manager;
@end
```

Figure E.9   Creating a new class and adding it to the two targets.

Replace the Employee.m implementation file with the contents shown in Listing E.2.

Listing E.2   The Employee.m implementation file.

```
#import "Employee.h"

@implementation Employee

@synthesize firstName, lastName, salary, manager;
-(void)setSalary:(NSInteger)theSalary{
```

```
    if(theSalary > 0){
        salary = theSalary;
    }
}

-(void)dealloc{
    self.manager = nil;
    self.firstName = nil;
    self.lastName = nil;
    [super dealloc];
}
@end
```

E.4   Writing Unit Tests for the Employee Class

In this section, we show you how to write a unit test for the Employee class.

Create a new group in your project and call it something like Unit Testing. Right-click on the new group and select Add → New File. Select Cocoa and double-click on the Objective-C test case class as shown in Figure E.10.

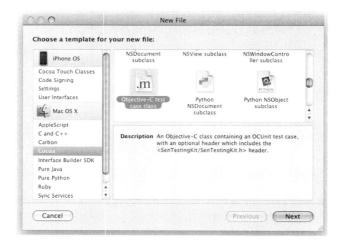

Figure E.10   Creating a new Objective-C test case class.

Type the name of the new test case. The name should end with TestCase. See Figure E.11.

Edit the SampleTestCase.h file and make it look like the following:

```
#import <SenTestingKit/SenTestingKit.h>
#import "Employee.h"
```

```
@interface SampleTestCase : SenTestCase {
}
@end
```

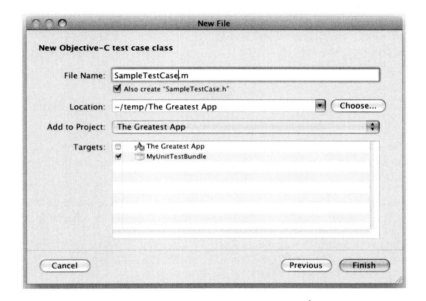

Figure E.11   Naming the test case. The name must end with `TestCase`.

E.4.1   The setUp and tearDown methods

Every unit test case has a `setUp` and a `tearDown` method. In the `setUp` method, you put any initialization code you would like to be executed before executing the tests. In the `tearDown` method, you provide any cleaning code that needs to be executed before finishing the tests. This code is executed after all tests have been executed.

In the example shown below, we have these methods as empty, but you are free to customize them as you see fit:

```
-(void)setUp{
    //do any initialization here
}
- (void) tearDown{
    // do any cleaning up here
}
```

E.4.2   Testing for equality

To create a test, add a method in the test case class. The method's name needs to start with `test`.

The following method tests the `Employee` class initialization:

```
-(void)testSalaryShouldBeInitializedToZero{
    Employee *emp = [[[Employee alloc] init] autorelease];
    STAssertEquals(emp.salary, 0,
        @"Salary should be initialized to zero");
}
```

The method starts by creating an `Employee` instance. After that it asserts that the employee's salary is initialized to `0`.

The test uses the `STAssertEquals` macro. This macro takes C scalars, structs, or unions for the first two arguments and an `NSString` instance for the third argument. If the first two arguments are not equal, the test fails.

The following test tries to assign a negative value for the salary. Because the `Employee` class rejects negative values, the existing value for salary remains unchanged. The test checks for that.

```
-(void)testSalaryCannotBeNegative{
    Employee *emp = [[[Employee alloc] init] autorelease];
    NSInteger salary = emp.salary;
    [emp setSalary:-100];
    STAssertEquals(emp.salary, salary,
        @"Setting salary to a negative value should be ignored");
}
```

E.4.3   Testing for nullity

You can use the `STAssertNil` macro to test for expected `nil` values.

The following test asserts that the manager property is set to `nil`:

```
-(void)testNullifyingManager{
    Employee *emp = [[[Employee alloc] init] autorelease];
    Employee *manager = [[[Employee alloc] init] autorelease];
    emp.manager = manager;
    emp.manager = nil;
    STAssertNil(emp.manager, @"Should be able to nullify manager");
}
```

E.5   Adding a Build Dependency

If you would like the unit tests to be executed and the success of the unit testing to be a condition of the successful building of your application, you can add a build dependency.

Edit the info of the main target of your application. Click on the + icon to add a dependency, and add the unit test target as that dependency as shown in Figure E.12.

Figure E.12   Adding a build dependency for the main target on the unit test target.

E.6   Running the Tests

When you add the test target as a dependency for the main target of your application, running the test becomes an automatic task. Every time you build your application, the tests are run.

Suppose someone, for some reason, removed the `setSalary:` method of the `Employee` class, thinking that the `@synthesize` directive would generate one for us and there is no need for a custom setter.

Now the `testSalaryCannotBeNegative` test will fail with errors shown in the build console as shown in Figure E.13.

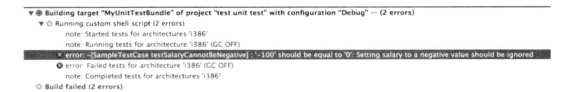

Figure E.13   Build failure due to test failure.

Seeing that the test `testSalaryCannotBeNegative` has failed, you can inspect it as well as inspect the `Employee` class and quickly come to the conclusion that the `setSalary:` method was removed by someone. You can then go to the version control software and pinpoint that person. What happens next is beyond the scope of this text!

Appendix F

Working with Interface Builder

In this appendix, we use Interface Builder (IB) to build a couple of iPhone applications. The techniques you learn from building these applications should prove to be useful in building similar iPhone applications.

F.1   National Debt Clock Application

In this section, we develop the National Debt Clock application. The application's UI is developed using Interface Builder. A screen shot of the completed product is shown in Figure F.1.

F.1.1   Creating the project

Launch XCode. Choose File → New Project. Click on the Application category under iOS. Choose Window-Based Application and click on Choose. Name the project `NationalDebt` and click Save.

F.1.2   Creating the view controller class

Right-click on the Classes group and select Add → New File as shown in Figure F.2.

Select `UIViewController subclass` under the Cocoa Touch Class as shown in Figure F.3 and click on Next.

Name the file `DebtViewController.m`, make sure that the check box for generating the header file is checked, and click Finish.

As the screen shot of the application in Figure F.1 shows, there are four main UI elements:

- **A label.** An instance of `UILabel` is used to show the text `National Debt Clock`. This is a static text that our application need not change. No code in our controller needs to know about this UI element.

Figure F.1   A screen shot of the National Debt Clock application.

Figure F.2   Adding a new class.

- **An activity indicator**. An instance of the UIActivityIndicatorView class is used to indicate that we are busy fetching the image representing the national debt figure from the Internet. Our controller code needs to know about this UI element.

To connect an object in our controller's code with this UI element, we need to add an Interface Builder outlet property of type UIActivityIndicatorView. In addition, we need to add a link between the UI element and the outlet in Interface Builder.

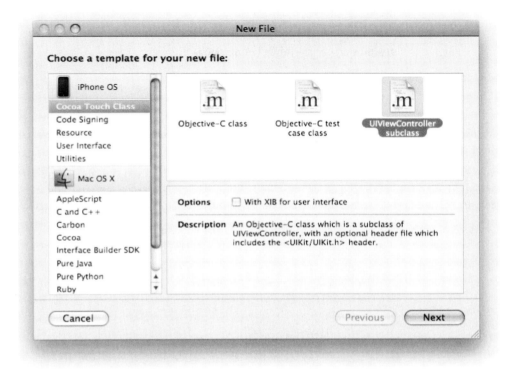

Figure F.3   Adding a subclass of the `UIViewController` class.

- **An image view.** The national debt clock is retrieved as an image from the Internet. We need to add an instance of `UIImageView` to the view of the view controller. In addition, we need to add an outlet in our view controller header file and connect it to the image view UI element. Whenever we retrieve the image from the Internet, we need to set the `image` property of the `UIImageView` object to the fetched image.

- **A refresh navigation item.** Whenever the user taps on the Refresh button, we need to bring a fresh image from the Internet. We need to add a method that is tagged with `IBAction` and connect it to the button.

The following shows the updated header file for the `DebtViewController` class:

```
@interface DebtViewController : UIViewController {
  UIImageView              *imageView;
  UIActivityIndicatorView   *busy;
}
@property(nonatomic, retain) IBOutlet UIImageView             *imageView;
@property(nonatomic, retain) IBOutlet UIActivityIndicatorView *busy;
```

```
-(IBAction)refresh;
@end
```

The IBOutlet tag is defined as empty as shown below:

```
#ifndef IBOutlet
#define IBOutlet
#endif
```

It is just used to facilitate the communication between XCode and Interface Builder. The IBAction is defined as **void**.

Now our controller has an imageView instance variable holding a reference to the image view UI element. Also, we have a busy instance variable holding a reference to the activity indicator view UI element. We still need to create these UI elements in Interface Builder and make the connections.

We also need to update the .m file of the view controller and add the following statement:

```
@synthesize  imageView, busy;
```

Also, we need to deallocate the objects in the dealloc method as shown below:

```
- (void)dealloc {
  self.busy = nil;
  self.imageView = nil;
  [super dealloc];
}
```

The refresh method is declared in the view controller class using the IBAction tag. This will help in connecting the button's action with our refresh method.

F.1.3 The application delegate class

Now we turn our attention to the application delegate class. As you can see from the screen shot of our application in Figure F.1, we are using a navigation controller. The navigation controller will be created in Interface Builder. We still need a reference to it in the application delegate so that we can add its view (which is basically the view of its root view controller) to the main window as a subview when the application is launched.

Modify the NationalDebtClockAppDelegate.h header file by adding a new instance variable as shown below:

```
UINavigationController *navCtrl;
```

Add the property for this instance variable with an outlet tag as shown below:

```
@property (nonatomic, retain) IBOutlet  UINavigationController *navCtrl;
```

We also need to synthesize the `navCtrl` property and release it in the `dealloc` method of the application delegate.

In the `applicationDidFinishLaunching:` method, we need to add the view property of the navigation controller to the main window as a subview.

The following shows the updated method:

```
- (void)applicationDidFinishLaunching:(UIApplication *)application {
    [window addSubview:navCtrl.view];
    [window makeKeyAndVisible];
}
```

Notice that we did not create an instance of `UINavigationController`. This instance will be created by deserializing a file that we will populate in Interface Builder in the next section.

F.1.4   Building the UI

Now we need to use Interface Builder to build the UI and connect it to our code through `IBOutlets` and `IBActions`.

Double-click on `MainWindow.xib` under the Resources group as shown in Figure F.4.

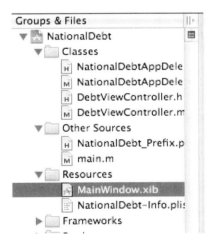

Figure F.4   Opening the `MainWindow.xib` file.

Interface Builder will be launched, and the `MainWindow.xib` document will be opened.

Choose the Browser mode to display the document's objects in a browser control while showing the parent–child relationships (see Figure F.5).

Figure F.5 The Browser display mode for objects in an XIB document.

Adding a navigation controller

Now we would like to add a navigation controller. This navigation controller will manage the navigation between several views that can be represented hierarchically.

Although our application does not need to present views hierarchically, it does utilize a navigation controller for the placement of a refresh button on its navigation bar.

When you open the XIB document, several windows open in Interface Builder. One of these windows is the Library window. Inside the Library window, you are given a list of several categories of elements. You select an element in the list and drag and drop it onto the XIB document or another element.

Click on the Controllers category in the Library window and locate the Navigation Controller element in the list as shown in Figure F.6.

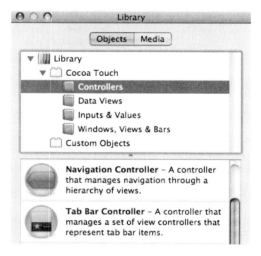

Figure F.6 The Controllers category in the Library window.

Click on the Navigation Controller object and drag and drop it onto the document as shown in Figure F.7.

Figure F.7   Adding a navigation controller to our XIB document.

The document should look as shown in Figure F.8.

Figure F.8   The XIB document after adding a navigation controller.

Now we would like to connect the navigation controller we've just added to the `navCtrl` property in the application delegate class. Control-click the application delegate object to show the Connections panel as shown in Figure F.9.

Click on the `navCtrl` connector and link this outlet to the navigation controller object as shown in Figure F.10.

The status of the application delegate outlets should look like the one in Figure F.11.

Adding a root view controller

A navigation controller must have at least one view controller. This view controller is referred to as the root view controller.

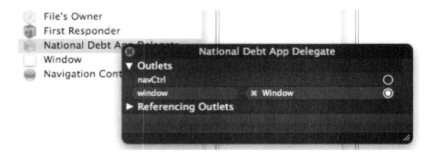

Figure F.9   The Connections panel of the application delegate.

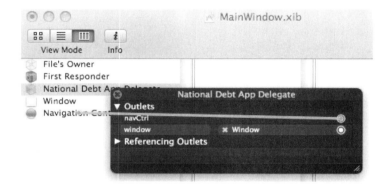

Figure F.10   Connecting the `navCtrl` property to the navigation controller component.

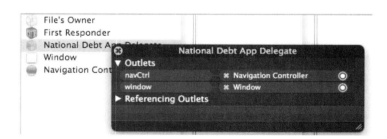

Figure F.11   The status of the application delegate connections after adding a connection to the navigation controller.

Figure F.12   The navigation controller window before adding the root view controller.

Figure F.13   Adding a root view controller to the navigation controller.

To add a root view controller, all we need to do is to drag and drop a view controller on the open navigation controller element.

Make sure that the navigation controller is open (if it is not, double-click on it). It should look like the one in Figure F.12.

Drag and drop a view controller object from the Library on the navigation controller as shown in Figure F.13.

Once the view controller is dropped onto the navigation controller, you will be able to see this controller as a child element in the Browser view of the XIB document as shown in Figure F.14.

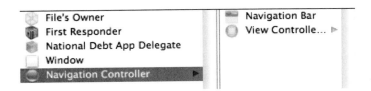

Figure F.14   A view controller added as a root controller of a navigation controller.

Building the main view of the root controller

Now we want to build a view for the view controller. Select Windows, Views, & Bars from the Library and drag and drop a View object onto the view controller window as shown in Figure F.15.

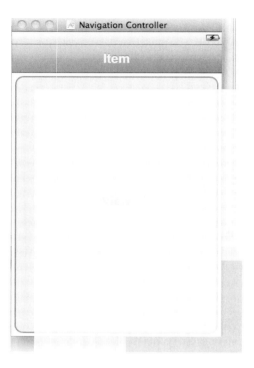

Figure F.15   Adding a View UI element to the root view controller.

Now the view controller has a View object and a Navigation Item object as shown in Figure F.16.

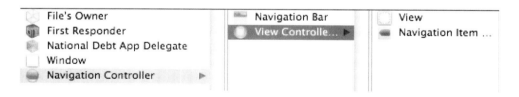

Figure F.16   The Browser view for the view controller after adding a View UI element.

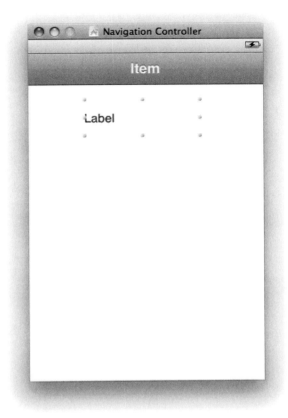

Figure F.17   Adding a Label UI element.

Drag and drop a Label object (from the Inputs & Values category) onto the view as shown in Figure F.17.

Double-click on the Label object and change the label text as shown in Figure F.18. You also need to resize the label's frame.

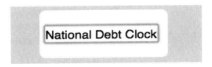

Figure F.18   Changing the text and dimensions of the Label UI element.

Change the color and font size attributes of the label to red and 24 points as shown in Figure F.19.

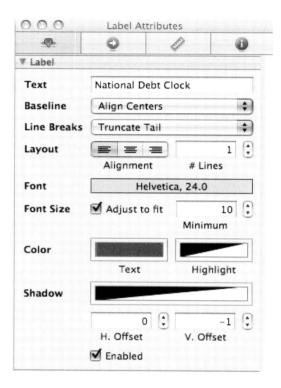

Figure F.19   Changing the color and font size of the Label UI element.

Drag and drop an image view object (found under the Data Views category) as shown in Figure F.20.

Resize the image view as shown in Figure F.21.

Select Aspect Fit mode as shown in Figure F.22.

Drag and drop an activity indicator view as shown in Figure F.23.

Click on it and configure it to Hide When Stopped as shown in Figure F.24.

Double-click on the Navigation Item title and enter National Debt Clock as shown in Figure F.25.

Linking the UI elements with the code

Now we would like to link the view controller object with our code.

Figure F.20   Adding an Image View UI element to the view.

Figure F.21   Resizing the Image View UI element.

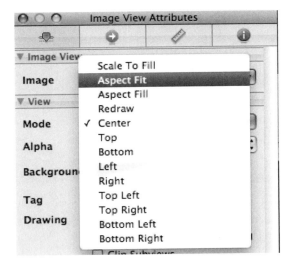

Figure F.22   Changing the view mode to Aspect Fit.

Figure F.23   Adding an activity indicator view.

Figure F.24   Configuring the activity indicator view to Hide When Stopped.

Figure F.25   Changing the navigation item title.

Make sure that the view controller object is selected and click on the Identity tab in the Inspector window as shown in Figure F.26.

Select `DebtViewController` for the Class attribute.

Control-click the view controller and connect the `busy` property to the activity indicator view as shown in Figure F.27.

Figure F.26   The Identity tab in the Inspector window of the view controller.

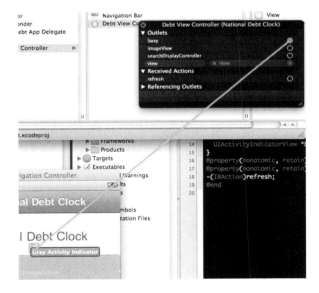

Figure F.27   Connecting the busy property to the activity indicator view.

Connect the `imageView` property to the image view as shown in Figure F.28.

Now we would like to add a Refresh button on the navigation bar so that the user can refresh the National Debt Clock.

In the Windows, Views, & Bars window, select the Bar Button Item object and drop it on the navigation bar as shown in Figure F.29.

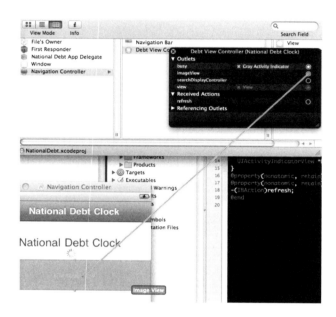

Figure F.28   Connecting the `imageView` property to the image view.

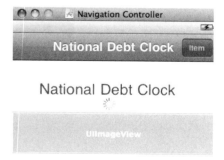

Figure F.29   Adding a bar button item to the navigation bar.

Click on it and choose Refresh from the Identifier drop-down menu, as shown in Figure F.30.

Now Control-click on the view controller and connect the `refresh` action to the button as shown in Figure F.31.

The connectivity of the outlets and actions of the view controller should look like Figure F.32.

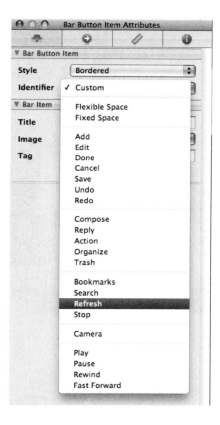

Figure F.30   Choosing a Refresh style for the bar button item.

Finishing the view controller class

We would like to show the National Debt Clock on startup. Override the `viewDidLoad` of the view controller as shown below:

```
- (void)viewDidLoad {
    [super viewDidLoad];
    [self refresh];
}
```

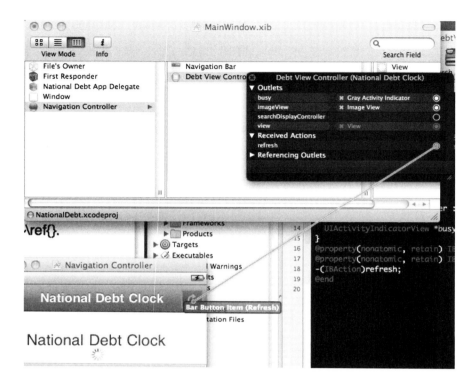

Figure F.31   Connecting the `refresh` action method to the button.

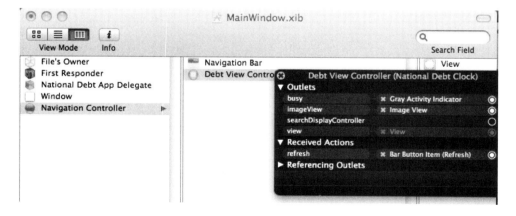

Figure F.32   The connectivity of the outlets and actions of the view controller.

The `refresh` action method shows the activity indicator view while fetching the image from the Internet and is shown below:

```
-(IBAction)refresh{
  [self performSelectorInBackground:@selector(showActivityIndicator:)
        withObject:[NSNumber numberWithBool:YES]];
  self.imageView.image = [UIImage imageWithData:
        [NSData dataWithContentsOfURL:[NSURL URLWithString:DEBT_IMAGE]]];
  [self performSelectorInBackground:@selector(showActivityIndicator:)
        withObject:[NSNumber numberWithBool:NO]];
}
```

The `DEBT_IMAGE` is defined as follows:

```
#define DEBT_IMAGE @"http://www.brillig.com/debt_clock/debtiv.gif"
```

The `showActivityIndicator:` method, which is shown below, shows and hides the activity view in its own thread:

```
- (void)showActivityIndicator:(NSNumber*)show{
  NSAutoreleasePool *pool = [[NSAutoreleasePool alloc] init];
  [show boolValue]? [busy startAnimating] :[busy stopAnimating];
  [pool release];
}
```

The complete application can be found in the `NationalDebtClock` project, available in the source downloads.

F.2   Toolbar Application

In this section, you learn how to create a view controller whose view is loaded from an XIB file. The view will consist of a toolbar with four buttons and a label. When the user taps on a button, the label's text changes to reflect the tapped button. Figure F.33 shows a screen shot of the application.

F.2.1   Writing code

Create a new project and call it `ToolBarDemo`. Create a new view controller subclass and call it `ToolBarController`.

The `ToolBarController` class has a reference to the label UI element and four action outlets. The following shows the declaration of this view controller:

```
@interface ToolBarController : UIViewController {
  UILabel *message;
}
@property(nonatomic, retain)  IBOutlet UILabel *message;
```

```
-(IBAction)bart;
-(IBAction)lisa;
-(IBAction)homer;
-(IBAction)marge;
@end
```

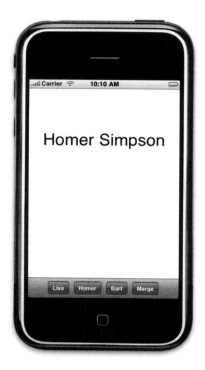

Figure F.33   A screen shot of a toolbar-based application.

The view controller has a message IBOutlet referring to a UILabel instance that will be loaded from the XIB file. In addition, four actions are declared, each corresponding to a button on the toolbar.

The implementation of this view controller class is shown below:

```
#import "ToolBarController.h"
@implementation ToolBarController
@synthesize message;
-(IBAction)bart{
  [self.message  setText:@"Bart Simpson"];
}
-(IBAction)lisa{
  [self.message  setText:@"Lisa Simpson"];
}
```

```
-(IBAction)homer{
  [self.message setText:@"Homer Simpson"];
}
-(IBAction)marge{
  [self.message setText:@"Marge Simpson"];
}
-(void)dealloc{
  self.message = nil;
  [super dealloc];
}
@end
```

Each action method simply changes the label's text.

F.2.2 Building the UI

Let's go ahead and create the view of this controller using Interface Builder.

Right-click on the Resources group and select Add → New File as shown in Figure F.34.

Figure F.34   Adding a new file to the Resources group.

Select the User Interface category and the Empty XIB template as shown in Figure F.35.

Click on Next, name the file `ToolBarView.xib`, and hit Finish. Now open the `ToolBarView.xib` file by double-clicking on it. Interface Builder will be launched and the file will be opened as shown in Figure F.36.

Select the File's Owner node and click on the Identity tab. Choose the class to be `ToolBar-Controller` as shown in Figure F.37.

Select the View UI element under Windows, Views & Bars shown in Figure F.38.

Drag and drop a view on the `ToolBarView.xib` document. The document should look like the one shown in Figure F.39.

Change the height of the view to `480` as shown in Figure F.40.

Drag and drop a Label UI element on the view. Change the layout of the label to center and its font's size to 36 as shown in Figure F.41.

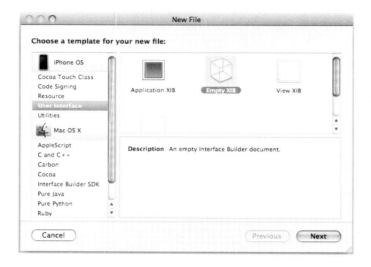

Figure F.35   Selecting the Empty XIB template.

Figure F.36   An empty XIB file.

Figure F.37   Changing the identity of the file's owner to the `ToolBarController` class.

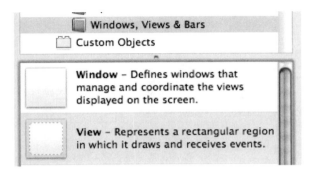

Figure F.38   The View UI element in the Library.

Figure F.39   The XIB document after adding a view to it.

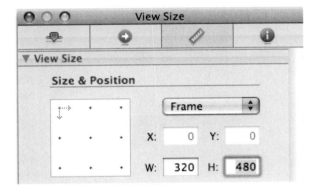

Figure F.40   Changing the height of the view.

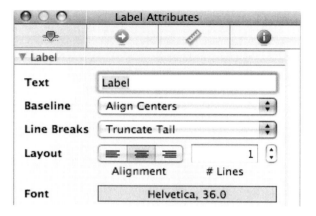

Figure F.41   Changing the label's layout and font size.

Drag and drop a Toolbar UI element on the view as shown in Figure F.42.

Figure F.42   The state of the view after adding a label and a toolbar.

Add three bar button items (Figure F.43) to the toolbar as shown in Figure F.44.

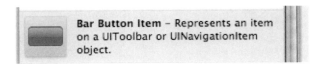

Figure F.43   A Bar Button Item UI element.

Figure F.44   Adding three bar button items to the toolbar.

Locate the Fixed Space Bar Button Item UI element shown in Figure F.45.

Figure F.45   Fixed Space Bar Button Item.

Drag and drop it on the left-hand side of the toolbar as shown in Figure F.46.

Figure F.46   A fixed space bar button item added to the toolbar.

You can resize this element to make the right and left margins of the toolbar equal.

Control-click File's Owner and link the `message` outlet to the label as shown in Figure F.47.

Connect the `view` property to the View UI element as shown in Figure F.48.

Connect the `marge` action method to the Marge bar button item as shown in Figure F.49.

Figure F.47   Connecting the `message` outlet to the Label UI element.

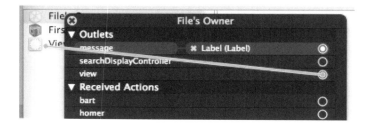

Figure F.48   Connecting the `view` property to the View UI element.

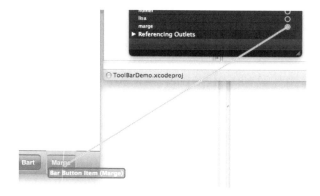

Figure F.49   Connecting the `marge` action method to the Marge bar button item.

Repeat the process for the other three bar button items. The connectivity state of the `ToolBar-Controller` is shown in Figure F.50.

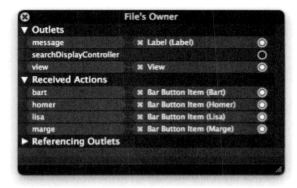

Figure F.50   The state of connectivity of `ToolBarController`.

F.2.3   *Putting it together*

Now that the view controller is complete, we can create a new instance of it and add its view as a subview of the main window as shown below:

```
- (void)applicationDidFinishLaunching:(UIApplication *)application {
  self.ctrl = [[[ToolBarController alloc]
                initWithNibName:@"ToolBarView" bundle:nil] autorelease];
  [window addSubview:ctrl.view];
  [window makeKeyAndVisible];
}
```

The complete application can be found in the `ToolBarDemo` project, available in the source downloads.

REFERENCES AND BIBLIOGRAPHY

[1] B'Far, R., *Mobile Computing Principles: Designing and Developing Mobile Applications with UML and XML*, Cambridge University Press, 2004.

[2] Core Location Framework Reference, Apple documentation.

Bibliography

[3] Apple Push Notification Service Programming Guide.

[4] Core Data Programming Guide, Apple documentation.

[5] The XML standard: www.w3.org/TR/REC-xml.

[6] Locale Data Markup Language (LDML), Unicode Technical Standard #35. http://unicode.org/reports/tr35/tr35-4.html#Date_Format_Patterns.

[7] Davidson, JD., *Learning Cocoa with Objective C*, 2nd edition, O'Reilly, 2002.

[8] Duncan, A., *Objective-C Pocket Reference*, 1st edition, O'Reilly, 2002.

[9] Garfinkel, S. and Mahoney, MK., *Building Cocoa Applications: A Step-by-Step Guide*, O'Reilly, 2002.

[10] Hillegass, A., *Cocoa Programming for Mac OS X*, Addison-Wesley Professional, 2008.

[11] Kochan, S., *Programming in Objective-C*, Sams, 2003.

[12] Mott, T., *Learning Cocoa*, O'Reilly, 2001.

[13] Owens, M., *The Definitive Guide to SQLite*, A press, Inc., 2006.

[14] Tejkowski, E., *Cocoa Programming For Dummies*, Wiley Publishing, Inc., 2003.

[15] Introduction to the Objective-C 2.0 Programming Language, Apple documentation.

[16] Beam, M. and Davidson, JD., *Cocoa in a Nutshell: A Desktop Quick Reference*, O'Reilly, 2003.

[17] Brownell, D., *SAX2*, O'Reilly, 2002.

[18] Williams, E., Aviation Formulary V1.43: http://williams.best.vwh.net/avform.htm.

[19] Collections Programming Topics for Cocoa, Apple Reference Library.

[20] Document Object Model (DOM): www.w3.org/TR/DOM-Level-2-Core/.

[21] Exception Programming Topics for Cocoa, Apple documentation.

[22] Key-Value Coding Programming Guide, Apple documentation.

[23] libxml2: The XML C parser and toolkit: http://xmlsoft.org/.

[24] Threading Programming Guide, Apple Reference Library.

Index